PHR® and SPHR®
Complete Deluxe Study Guide
Second Edition

PHR® and SPHR®
Complete Deluxe Study Guide
Professional in Human Resources Certification 2018 Exams
Second Edition

Sandra M. Reed

SYBEX®
A Wiley Brand

Senior Acquisitions Editor: Kenyon Brown
Development Editor: Kelly Talbot
Technical Editor: Pantelis Markou
Senior Production Editor: Christine O'Connor
Copy Editor: Elizabeth Welch
Editorial Manager: Pete Gaughan
Production Manager: Kathleen Wisor
Associate Publisher: Jim Minatel
Book Designers: Judy Fung and Bill Gibson
Proofreader: Nancy Carrasco
Indexer: Johnna VanHoose Dinse
Project Coordinator, Cover: Brent Savage
Cover Designer: Wiley
Cover Image: Getty Images Inc. / Jeremy Woodhouse

Copyright © 2019 by John Wiley & Sons, Inc., Indianapolis, Indiana

Published simultaneously in Canada

ISBN: 978-1-119-42673-8
ISBN: 978-1-119-47994-9 (ebk.)
ISBN: 978-1-119-47993-2 (ebk.)
ISBN: 978-1-119-47990-1 (ebk.)

Manufactured in the United States of America

For general information on our other products and services or to obtain technical support, please contact our Customer Care Department within the U.S. at (877) 762-2974, outside the U.S. at (317) 572-3993 or fax (317) 572-4002.

Wiley publishes in a variety of print and electronic formats and by print-on-demand. Some material included with standard print versions of this book may not be included in e-books or in print-on-demand. If this book refers to media such as a CD or DVD that is not included in the version you purchased, you may download this material at http://booksupport.wiley.com. For more information about Wiley products, visit www.wiley.com.

Library of Congress Control Number: 2019938093

V10009381_041519

To my husband Chris, whose three little words never fail to inspire me: "Go for it." To my children, Calvin and Clara, because the best part of me will eternally be each of you. I am filled with love and gratitude for having the three of you in my life.

Acknowledgments

Any acknowledgment in the updating of this book must begin by recognizing the professionalism and intellect of Anne Bogardus. Her thoroughness and attention to detail represented in the previous editions of this work made writing these updates an absolute career highlight.

To the editors Kenyon Brown, Kelly Talbot, Elizabeth Welch, Pete Gaughan, and Christine O'Connor, thank you for your professionalism, encouragement, superior organizational skills, insightful additions, and most importantly your patience as we updated the book not once but twice—it absolutely made for a better final product. To Pantelis Markou, I cannot describe the comfort level of having your expertise and conscientiousness as my technical editor. If I missed a critical element, I knew you would find it!

A book like this requires a great deal of time and thought, and the contributions from experts Dr. Erin Richard, Reut Schwartz-Hebron, Hector Alvarez, and Joanne Walters added different voices and critical perspectives to the exam content. I am in awe of and grateful for their contribution.

Finally, to the students, a brief mention of my own testing experience: I remember sitting in my hotel room the night before my SPHR exam, trying to cram in a few more details, desperate to figure out what I didn't already know. It was around Christmas time, and my youngest child was just two years old. Feeling guilty for being away from my family and with my confidence at an all-time low, I wondered if I was really up for the challenge. Then, surrounded by my books and flashcards, I suddenly "got" it. The pieces starting fitting together, the processes had rationale, and the big picture came into clear focus. The next morning, I took a four-hour exam in just two hours and passed it on the first go-round. My excitement about being a part of this project is a reflection of that one "a-ha" moment, representing for me when HR crosses over from just being a job to an intelligent, strategic career choice. My hope is that with each pass through this material, you will get closer to your own enlightened moment when you suddenly just get it. Many thanks, and good luck in your career—this absolutely can happen for you!

About the Author

Sandra M. Reed, SPHR, has more than 20 years of experience in human resources, the last 15 of which have been spent in training and instruction. Her undergraduate degree is in industrial-organizational psychology, and she is a lifelong student of organizational leadership. Sandra is a certified practitioner of the MBTI personality assessment and is qualified to instruct the Leadership Training for Managers and Foundation for Success programs through Dale Carnegie. She obtained her PHR and her SPHR designations through the Human Resource Certification Institute and received her teaching credential in adult vocational education from California State University, San Bernardino. Sandra is the author of The Official Guide to the Human Resource Body of Knowledge (HRBoK) and The PHR and SPHR Professional in Human Resources Certification Complete Practice Tests: 2018 Exams, both available through John Wiley & Sons. She has authored learning modules and case studies for the Society for Human Resource Management, focusing on educating the emerging workforce and future human resource professionals. She currently is the owner of Epoch Resources, a consulting firm located in the Central Valley of California that specializes in the unique HR needs of small businesses. Find her on the web at http://epochresources.com.

About the Technical Editor

Pantelis Markou is the senior vice president of human resources and administration for Mikimoto America and an adjunct professor of business psychology. With over 18 years of corporate experience in the fashion and jewelry industries, some of his specialties include business strategy, executive selection and coaching, leadership development, change management, organizational design and restructuring, and cultural integration for mergers and acquisitions. In addition to his responsibilities in human resources, he oversees information technology, real estate, legal, and commercial insurance. Pantelis holds a BS in psychology from Brooklyn College, an MA in organizational psychology from Columbia University, and a PhD in business psychology from the Chicago School of Professional Psychology.

Contents at a Glance

Contents

Introduction

Congratulations on taking the first step toward achieving your Professional in Human Resources (PHR) or Senior Professional in Human Resources (SPHR) certification! The process you're embarking on is rewarding and challenging, and as more than 500,000 of your fellow human resource colleagues in more than 100 countries have already discovered, it's an excellent opportunity to explore areas of HR management with which you may not work every day. In the next few pages, you'll find some general information about HR certification, some suggestions for using this book, information about what to expect in the following chapters, and a discussion of the organizations involved in certification.

Before we begin, a word about what you should already know. This study guide was designed to serve as a refresher for experienced professionals who have practiced for several years or have been educated in human resources. We assume that those who are pursuing certification have the basic HR knowledge that comes not only from education in human resources but also, more importantly, from exempt-level experience. If your daily work is truly generalist in nature, you likely have touched on many of the topics I cover, but you may not have in-depth knowledge in all of them. Conversely, if you specialize in one or two areas of HR, you probably have extensive experience in those areas but may need to refresh your knowledge in other areas.

Additionally, for SPHR candidates, there is an assumption that you have the benchmark knowledge that PHR candidates are learning. This means that there is likely opportunity within the PHR chapters for SPHR candidates to refresh their knowledge. These are referenced throughout the SPHR chapters where appropriate.

The goal of this study guide is to provide enough information about each of the functional areas of HR management to enable candidates in either situation to find what they need to prepare themselves for successfully completing the exam. More than 50,000 books related to human resources are listed on Amazon.com alone, and there is obviously no way we can cover all the aspects of HR in a single book. So, we've organized the information around the exam content outline (ECO) established by the Human Resource Certification Institute (HRCI), the certifying body for our profession. We'll talk more about the content outline in Chapter 1, "Certifying Human Resource Professionals," but for now, suffice it to say that the key to success on the exam is a thorough understanding of and ability to apply the test specs when answering questions on the exams.

About Human Resource Certification

What exactly *is* human resource certification? Briefly, certification is a way of acknowledging individuals who have met the standard of competency established by HR practitioners as that which is necessary to be considered a fully competent HR professional. To understand whether this book is for you, you'll want to know why you should become certified and how the certification process works.

Who Certifies HR Professionals?

Two organizations are involved in the certification of HR professionals: the Human Resource Certification Institute (HRCI) and Pearson VUE.

The Human Resource Certification Institute

HRCI is the certifying body for the HR profession. It was formed by the American Society of Personnel Administrators (ASPA) in 1972, when it was known as the ASPA Accreditation Institute (AAI). In its early stages, HRCI was financially dependent on the Society for Human Resource Management (SHRM), but it's now financially independent. Both HRCI and SHRM have individual boards of directors that govern their operations. Although HRCI and SHRM have a long history of affiliation and mutual support, the certification process is a separate and distinct function of HRCI.

 You can find HRCI's organizational mission statement at www.hrci.org/about-hrci/overview/mission.

Pearson VUE

Pearson VUE is a computer-based testing administrator headquartered in the United States with locations in the United Kingdom, Japan, Australia, India, Dubai, and China. More than 400 credential owners use their services to administer exams, including HRCI. Pearsonvue.com is where certification seekers will register for their exam date and location.

We'll refer to these organizations frequently in Chapter 1 as we discuss the body of knowledge and the certification process.

Why Become Certified?

Over time, the certification offered by HRCI has become the industry standard for determining competence in the field of human resources. There are many reasons that individuals may decide to seek professional certification. Let's talk about just a few of them.

First, certification is an acknowledgment that you have met the standards of excellence determined by other HR professionals to be those that are necessary to be fully competent in the field. Because the standards are developed by working professionals, not just by those who teach and consult in the field, this credential demonstrates that you're a fully competent HR practitioner based on a standard set by your peers.

Second, certification is a way to increase your marketability. In difficult economic times, when there is tough competition for jobs, certification provides an edge that can be advantageous in your job search. With an abundance of job seekers for a limited number of jobs, whatever you can do to set yourself apart from the crowd can give you the edge when potential employers are making the final hiring decision. Additionally, a 2018 Payscale survey found that certified HR professionals rank the HRCI exams as #1 of all professional exams and that they are the most valuable. The survey also noted that "We found that for the most part, having an HR certification is beneficial from a pay perspective and a career advancement perspective." See the full survey results at www.payscale.com/data/hr-certifications-pay.

Third, those who spend the time to advance their own knowledge and achieve certification have demonstrated their ability to continue learning and growing as times and business needs change. A person who is willing and able to set a significant goal and do what is necessary to achieve it demonstrates characteristics that are in great demand in business today: results orientation, technical competence, commitment, and excellence.

Finally, certification enhances your credibility with co-workers and customers by demonstrating to the people you encounter during your workday that you have proven competence in the field.

Whether your reason for seeking certification falls into one of these categories or you're motivated to do so for some other reason, it can be a great opportunity to validate how much you already know about the practice of human resources as a profession.

How to Become Certified

To become a certified HR professional, you must pass either the PHR or SPHR exam, both of which have been developed by HRCI in a comprehensive process described in Chapter 1.

Each exam, PHR and SPHR, consists of 175 questions. Of these questions, 150 are scored to determine whether you pass the exam. The additional 25 questions are being "pretested" in order to determine their reliability and validity for inclusion in future test cycles. You can find a detailed discussion of how the questions are developed and scored in the *HR Certification Institute's 2019 Certification Policies and Procedures Handbook*, which can be viewed and/or downloaded at the HRCI website (www.hrci.org). The handbook is an essential guide to all aspects of the exams and includes test dates, application deadlines, fee information, and answers to frequently asked questions about the certification process, as well as the full list of test specifications.

Chapter 1 explains in greater detail how much and what kinds of experience are required for each exam level and how the questions differ on each level.

How This Book Is Organized

We've talked a little about Chapter 1, which provides information about requirements for certification and the testing process. Chapter 1 also provides some suggestions on the best ways to study for the exam.

Chapters 2–6 get down to the specifics of each functional area of the PHR exam. Chapters 7–11 dive into SPHR exam content. Each of these chapters consists of a list of responsibilities and knowledge requirements for its functional area. We have also provided appendices to facilitate your study. Appendix A, "Answers to Review Questions," provides all of the answers to the questions at the end of every chapter.

Appendix B, "PHR and SPHR Case Studies," gives you an opportunity to pull information from multiple functional areas to solve typical HR challenges in a fictitious company.

Appendix C, "Federal Employment Legislation and Case Law," is a listing of the federal legislation as well as significant court decisions with implications for human resources.

Appendix D, "Resources," is just that: a list of additional sources of information about each of the functional areas of human resources.

Appendix E, "Summarizing the Summaries: What Meta-Analyses Tell Us About Work Engagement," and Appendix F, "Neuroscience Principles and Applications for HR Leaders," provide further insights from leading experts in the field.

Finally, we've provided additional study tools, including sample tests, electronic flash-cards, and a glossary of terms (an alphabetical listing of key HR terms with their corresponding definitions).

The Elements of a Study Guide

You'll see many recurring elements as you read this study guide. Here's a description of some of those elements:

Assessment Test   At the end of this introduction is an assessment test that you can use to check your readiness for the exam. Take this test before you start reading the book; it will help you determine the areas on which you may need to brush up. The answers to the assessment test questions appear separately after the last question of the test. Each answer includes an explanation and a note telling you the chapter in which the material appears.

Summary   The summary is a brief review of the chapter to sum up what was covered.

Exam Essentials   The "Exam Essentials" section at the end of each chapter highlights topics that could appear on one or both of the exams in some form. Although we obviously don't know exactly what will be included in a particular exam, these sections reinforce significant concepts that are key to understanding the functional area and the test specs HRCI has developed.

Review Questions   Each chapter includes 20 practice questions designed to measure your knowledge of key ideas discussed in the chapter. After you finish each chapter, answer the questions; if some of your answers are incorrect, it's an indication that you need to spend more time studying that topic. The answers to the practice questions can be found in Appendix A. The chapter review questions are designed to help you measure how much information you retained from your reading and are different from the kinds of questions you'll see on the exam.

Interactive Online Learning Environment and Test Bank

The interactive online learning environment that accompanies *Complete Deluxe Study Guide* provides a test bank with study tools to help you prepare for the certification exam—and increase your chances of passing it the first time! The test bank includes the following:

Sample Tests   All the questions in this book are provided, including the chapter tests that include the review questions at the end of each chapter. In addition, there are two practice exams (one each for the PHR® and SPHR®) that have a variety of question formats that match the newly structured exams as of the fall of 2018. Use these questions to test your knowledge of the review guide material. The online test bank runs on multiple devices.

Flashcards   Two sets of questions are provided in digital flashcard format (a question followed by a single correct answer); one set is for the PHR® and the other set is for the SPHR®. You can use the flashcards to reinforce your learning and provide last-minute test prep before the exam.

Other Study Tools   eBooks in multiple formats enable you to read this Deluxe Study Guide on your favorite device. Also a glossary of key terms from this book and their definitions is available as a fully searchable PDF.

> **NOTE**   Go to www.wiley.com/go/sybextestprep to register and gain access to this interactive online learning environment and test bank with study tools.

How to Use This Book and the Additional Study Tools

This book has a number of features designed to guide your study efforts for either the PHR or the SPHR certification exam. All of these features are intended to assist you in doing the most important thing you can do to pass the exam: understand and apply the test specs in answering questions. This book helps you do that by listing the current responsibilities and knowledge requirements at the beginning of each chapter and by ensuring that each of them is fully discussed in the chapter.

The practice questions at the end of each chapter and the practice exams (which can be found in the online test bank at www.wiley.com/go/sybextestprep) are designed to assist you in testing your retention of the material you've read to make you aware of areas on which you should spend additional study time. We've provided web links and other resources to assist you in mastering areas where you may require additional study materials. Here are some suggestions for using this book and study tools:

- Take the assessment test before you start reading the material. These questions are designed to measure your knowledge and will look different from the questions you'll see on the exam. They will give you an idea of the areas on which you need to spend additional study time, as well as those areas for which you may just need a brief refresher.

- Review the exam content outline at the beginning of each chapter before you start reading. Make sure you read the associated knowledge requirements in the *HR Certification Institute's 2019 Certification Policies and Procedures Handbook* because they may help you in your study process. After you've read the chapter, review the requirements again to be sure you understand and are able to apply them.

- Answer the review questions after you've read each chapter. If you miss any of them, go back over the chapter and review the topic, or use one of the additional resources if you need more information. If in true learning mode, answer the questions open-book first.

- Download the flashcards, and review them when you have a few minutes during the day.

- Take every opportunity to test yourself. In addition to the assessment test and review questions, there are bonus practice exams. Take these exams without referring to the chapters, and see how well you've done—go back and review any topics you've missed until you fully understand and can apply the concepts.

Finally, find a study partner if possible. Studying for, and taking, the exam with someone else will make the process more enjoyable, and you'll have someone to help you understand topics that are difficult for you. You'll also be able to reinforce your own knowledge by helping your study partner in areas where they are weak.

PHR Assessment Test

1. According to the WARN Act, an employer with 200 employees is required to provide 60 days' notice of a mass layoff when which of the following is true?

   A. The employer is seeking additional funding and will lay off 70 employees if the funding falls through.

   B. A major client unexpectedly selects a new vendor for the company's products, and the company lays off 75 employees.

   C. The employer lays off 5 employees a week for 3 months.

   D. A flood requires that one of the plants be shut down for repairs, and 55 employees are laid off.

2. An employee has come forward with an allegation of quid pro quo harassment by her supervisor. As the HR manager, you are responsible for investigating the complaint. The supervisor in question is someone with whom you have become quite friendly. In this case, who is the best person to conduct the investigation?

   A. You

   B. The corporate attorney

   C. The direct manager of the accused supervisor

   D. A third-party investigator

3. As of 2009, the federal minimum wage is set at which of the following?

   A. $5.15 per hour

   B. $7.25 per hour

   C. $5.75 per hour

   D. $6.55 per hour

4. During the union-organizing process, how is the bargaining unit determined?

   A. By the union organizers

   B. Jointly, by the union and the employer

   C. By the National Labor Relations Board

   D. By the employees during the election

5. The motivation theory that suggests people are motivated by the reward they will receive when they succeed and that they weigh the value of the anticipated reward against the effort required to achieve it is known as what?

   A. Vroom's expectancy theory

   B. Adams' equity theory

   C. McClelland's acquired needs theory

   D. McGregor's Theory X and Theory Y

6. What is the most effective method of performance evaluation?
    A. A field-review process
    B. A continuous-feedback process
    C. A forced-ranking process
    D. A behaviorally anchored rating-scale process

7. Which of the following is an example of a nonqualified deferred-compensation plan?
    A. An excess-deferral plan
    B. A target-benefit plan
    C. A money-purchase plan
    D. A cash-balance plan

8. Which of the following is an example of a passive training method?
    A. Vestibule training
    B. Demonstration
    C. Distance learning
    D. Self-study

9. What is the purpose of the OSHA consulting service?
    A. Helps employers identify the OSHA standards that apply to their workplace
    B. Fines employers for violating OSHA safety standards
    C. Does not require compliance with OSHA standards
    D. Acts as a one-time service

10. Measuring staffing needs against sales volume could be done most effectively by using which of the following techniques?
    A. A multiple linear regression
    B. A ratio
    C. A simulation model
    D. A simple linear regression

11. What is an employer's responsibility when workplace conditions pose a threat to an unborn child?
    A. Do nothing. It is up to employees to protect their unborn children.
    B. Move the employee into a different job that does not pose a threat to the unborn child.
    C. Advise the employee of the potential threat, and allow the employee to make the decision.
    D. Allow only sterile employees to work in jobs that pose a threat to unborn children.

12. What does the Health Insurance Portability and Accountability Act do?

    A. Prevents HR from investigating claims issues

    B. Requires continuation of health benefits

    C. Establishes EPO networks

    D. Limits preexisting condition restrictions

13. The concept that recognizes that businesses are social organizations as well as economic systems and that productivity is related to employee job satisfaction is known as what?

    A. Human resource management

    B. Strategic management

    C. Human relations

    D. Human resource development

14. Total quality management focuses all employees on producing products that meet customer needs. This is achieved by doing what?

    A. Eliminating processes that waste time and materials

    B. Developing a high level of expertise in all employees

    C. Sharing information with all levels in the organization

    D. Balancing the needs of all stakeholders in the organization

15. The correlation coefficient is a statistical measurement that is useful for which of the following?

    A. Determining whether one variable affects another

    B. Compensating for data that may be out-of-date

    C. Determining which variables are outside acceptable ranges

    D. Describing standards of quality

16. The process of identifying risks and taking steps to minimize them is referred to as what?

    A. Liability management

    B. Risk management

    C. Qualitative analysis

    D. Risk assessment

17. What is the most effective method to use when an employer wants to obtain insight into employee goals and job satisfaction and provide career counseling to those in the work group?

    A. An employee survey

    B. A skip-level interview

    C. An employee focus group

    D. A brown-bag lunch

18. Which of the following is an example of workplace ethics issues?

    A. Workplace privacy

    B. Conflicts of interest

    C. Whistle-blowing

    D. All of the above

19. Which of the following statements about substance abuse policies is *not* true?

    A. Substance abuse policies identify who will be tested.

    B. Federal law requires all employers to implement substance abuse policies.

    C. An effective policy describes when tests will occur and what drugs will be tested.

    D. An effective policy describes what happens to employees who test positive.

20. Which one of the following statements is true of a hostile work environment?

    A. When a single incident of unwanted touching occurs, a hostile work environment has been created.

    B. A hostile work environment may be created when an individual witnesses the ongoing harassment of a co-worker.

    C. Only a supervisor can create a hostile work environment.

    D. A grievance procedure/policy against discrimination protects employers from hostile work environment claims.

21. An HR audit is designed to help management do what?

    A. Improve employee morale.

    B. Analyze HR policies, programs, and procedures against applicable legal requirements.

    C. Improve HR effectiveness.

    D. All of the above

22. A high-involvement organization is an example of what type of OD intervention?

    A. Human process

    B. Human resource management

    C. Techno-structural

    D. Strategic

23. Claims of disparate treatment for employees caring for elders, children, or disabled family members increased 450 percent between 1990 and 2005. Which of the following provides one of the bases for filing these claims?

    A. Sarbanes-Oxley

    B. Davis-Bacon Act

    C. Family Medical Leave Act

    D. None of the above

24. Which of the following would be considered an extrinsic reward?

   A. Challenging work on a new project

   B. A 10 percent salary increase

   C. A feeling of accomplishment after completing a tough assignment

   D. Recognition by the CEO at a company meeting

25. According to the Copyright Act of 1976, which of the following is most likely to be considered a fair use of copyrighted material?

   A. Distributing 30 copies of a chapter in a book to a study group

   B. Copying a book for 10 staff members of a nonprofit organization

   C. Distributing 30 copies of a paragraph in a book to a study group

   D. None of the above

SPHR Assessment Test

1. Which of the following negative outcomes best reflects the failure to align the human resource strategic plan with the organization's strategic plan?
   A. Lack of plan management
   B. Misdirection of the organization's human talent
   C. Failure to respond to external market conditions
   D. Out-of-compliance HR policies, procedures, and rules

2. Before selecting an HRIS system, which of the following questions should be answered?
   A. What information will be converted to the HRIS?
   B. Who will have access to the information stored in the HRIS?
   C. How will the HRIS be accessed?
   D. All of the above

3. Which of the following is not a breach of a human resource professional's fiduciary responsibility?
   A. Profiting from the HR role
   B. Paying someone less based solely on their race
   C. Conflicting duties
   D. Acting in their own self-interest

4. Which of the following is not a component of a SWOT analysis?
   A. Strengths
   B. Weaknesses
   C. Outsourcing
   D. Threats

5. Adverse impact determines whether there is statistical evidence of unlawful discrimination by calculating selection ratios for a protected class group by using what percentage?
   A. 10%
   B. 50%
   C. 80%
   D. It varies by group.

6. Succession planning is best described by which of the following?
   A. A systematic approach to identify, assess, and develop talent for leadership roles in an organization
   B. Predetermining employees within the company to fill management roles
   C. Planning the career path of entry level employees to fill different roles in the company
   D. None of the above

7. Which of the following describes deep-level diversity?

  A. Biological variables that may or may not correlate to job attitudes or overall performance

  B. Various people working together, often with differences in culture, race, generation, gender or religion

  C. Individual differences in values or beliefs

  D. A program for training employees in diversity awareness

8. Which of the following describes the difference between a STEP analysis and a PEST analysis?

  A. A STEP analysis identifies opportunities, whereas a PEST analysis identifies threats.

  B. A STEP analysis is part of a SWOT analysis, whereas a PEST analysis is independent.

  C. There is no such thing as a PEST analysis.

  D. There is no difference. They are the same thing.

9. A critical aspect of retaining quality employees in an organization is _____.

  A. Rigid management that is focused on achieving business results

  B. Limiting training to increase productivity of the workforce

  C. A strong socialization and onboarding of new employees

  D. Providing higher compensation or a raise in salary

10. Measuring how much a job is worth is known as _____.

  A. Job analysis

  B. Job evaluation

  C. Job grading

  D. Job ranking

11. Which of the following is not one of the four key questions of a strategic HR plan?

  A. Where have we been?

  B. Where are we now?

  C. Where do we want to be?

  D. How will we know when we arrive?

12. Which of the following collective-bargaining positions is a type of principled bargaining?

  A. Positional bargaining

  B. Interest-based bargaining

  C. Concession bargaining

  D. Distributed bargaining

13. A recent round of turnover has your executive team questioning the existing salary structure. What should be your first strategic approach?

    A. Recommend pay increases for critical staff positions.

    B. Implement exit interviews to find out if inadequate pay is the reason for leaving.

    C. Conduct a wage survey to compare your pay rates to those of similar employers in the area.

    D. Meet with employees to determine if they are satisfied with their pay.

14. The executive committee has asked HR to provide them with copies of all employee personnel files, EEO reports, collective-bargaining agreements, and the employee handbook. They are most likely engaged in the practice of executing which activity?

    A. Exercising due diligence

    B. Responding to a labor dispute

    C. Union busting

    D. A wage review

15. Strategic OD interventions would include making changes to which of the following business practices?

    A. Mission, vision, and values

    B. Tactical measures

    C. Organizational policies, procedures, and rules

    D. Management development

16. A strategic workforce plan allows an employer to accomplish which of the following?

    A. Determine what skill sets are needed to meet future training or staffing needs.

    B. Comply with affirmative action requirements.

    C. Identify recruitment sources based on skill sets required.

    D. Provide a framework to ensure that the right people are doing the right jobs when the employer needs them.

17. Which of the following provides the framework for collecting information to be used in strategic planning?

    A. Environmental scan

    B. SWOT audit

    C. Statistical model

    D. Force analysis

18. When privately held companies provide the benefits of employee ownership without actually granting stock, it is known as which of the following?

   A. Restricted stock

   B. Phantom stock

   C. Incentive stock options

   D. Nonqualified stock options

19. Computing the cost per hire is a way to determine which of the following?

   A. HR's internal budget

   B. The time needed to onboard a new employee

   C. Staffing effectiveness

   D. None of the above

20. Which of the following is the main type of strategic analysis?

   A. Gap analysis

   B. Supply analysis

   C. Demand analysis

   D. All of the above

21. Many companies have fiscal years that begin on July 1 and end on June 30 of the following calendar year. This function is guided by what?

   A. SMART

   B. LMS

   C. ZBB

   D. GAAP

22. A company located in Seattle, Washington, as part of the post-employment activities for a new employee residing in Boston, Massachusetts, may engage in which of the following?

   A. Contact references to verify employment history.

   B. Assist the employee with relocation.

   C. Use online teleconferencing technology to facilitate the interviews.

   D. Offer a signing bonus.

23. A statement of cash flows is a financial report that tells you which of the following?

   A. The financial condition of the business at a specific point in time

   B. Where the money used to operate the business came from

   C. The financial results of operations over a period of time

   D. How much money is owed to the company by its customers

24. One purpose of a diversity initiative is to do what?

   A. Increase workplace creativity.

   B. Increase the effectiveness of the workforce.

   C. Increase the organization's ability to attract customers.

   D. All of the above

25. Billingsworth Entertainment recently joined forces with its largest competitor, WWE, combining assets into one functioning entity. This is an example of which of the following?

   A. Hostile takeover

   B. Corporate restructuring

   C. Merger

   D. Workforce expansion

Answers to PHR Assessment Test

1. **C.** The WARN Act requires employers to provide 60 days' notice when 500 employees or 50 employees making up 33 percent of the workforce are laid off, and it requires the number to be counted over a period of 90 days. Five employees a week for 3 months is a total of 65 employees (5 employees times 13 weeks), which is 33 percent of the workforce. The three exceptions are the "faltering company exception" (A) when knowledge of a layoff will negatively impact the company's ability to obtain additional funding, the "unforeseeable business circumstance" (B) when unexpected circumstances occur, and the "natural disaster" (D) exception. See Appendix C for more information.

2. **D.** In this case, the organization will be best served by a third-party investigator. The most important consideration in an investigation of sexual harassment is that the investigator is seen as credible and impartial. Because you have become friendly with the accused, it will be difficult to maintain impartiality during an investigation. While the corporate attorney (B) may be selected to conduct investigations, this solution can lead to conflict-of-interest issues. The direct manager of the accused supervisor (C) may not be viewed as impartial by the accuser or by regulatory agencies. See Chapter 6 for more information.

3. **B.** As of 2009, the federal minimum wage was raised to $7.25 per hour. For workers on or affiliated with federal contracts, the minimum wage may be $10.35 in 2019 and beyond. The minimum wage in some states and other localities may be different. See Appendix C for more information.

4. **C.** The National Labor Relations Board (NLRB) determines which jobs will be included in the bargaining unit based on the "community of interest" shared by the requirements of the jobs. See Chapter 6 for more information.

5. **A.** Vroom explains his theory with three terms: expectancy (the individual's assessment of their ability to achieve the goal), instrumentality (whether the individual believes they are capable of achieving the goal), and valence (whether the anticipated goal is worth the effort required to achieve it). Adams's equity theory (B) states that people are constantly comparing what they put into work to what they get from it. McClelland's acquired needs theory (C) states that people are motivated by one of three factors: achievement, affiliation, or power. McGregor's Theory X and Theory Y (D) explain how managers relate to employees. Theory X managers are autocratic, believing that employees do not want to take responsibility. Theory Y managers encourage employees to participate in the decision-making process, believing that they respond to challenges. See Chapter 6 for more information.

6. **B.** A continuous-feedback review process is most effective because it provides immediate feedback to employees, enabling them to correct performance issues before they become major problems. In a field review (A), reviews are conducted by someone other than the direct supervisor. Forced ranking (C) is an evaluation method in which all employees are listed in order of their value to the work group. The BARS process (D) identifies the most important job requirements and creates statements that describe varying levels of performance. See Chapter 6 for more information.

7.   A. An excess-deferral plan makes up the difference between what an executive could have contributed to a qualified plan if there had not been a limit on contributions and how much was actually contributed because of the discrimination test required by ERISA. These plans are nonqualified because they are not protected by ERISA; they are limited to a small group of executives or highly compensated employees. A target-benefit plan (B) is a hybrid with elements of defined-benefit and money-purchase plans. A money-purchase plan (C) defers a fixed percentage of employee earnings. A cash-balance plan (D) combines elements of defined-benefit and defined-contribution plans. See Chapter 5 for more information.

8.   C. In a lecture, a presenter provides information to a group of participants and does not require active participation. Vestibule training (A) is a form of simulation training. Demonstration (B) is an experiential training method. Self-study (D) is an active training method. See Chapter 4 for more information.

9.   A. OSHA consultants provide free services to assist employers in identifying workplace hazards and the standards that apply in their workplaces. The consulting service requires employers to abate any hazards that are identified during the consultation but does not fine them for violations. To receive a free consultation, employers must agree to advise OSHA of changes in operating processes that may require additional consultations. See Chapter 6 for more information.

10. D. A simple linear regression measures one variable against another. Multiple linear regression (A) measures more than one variable against others. A ratio (B) compares one number to another. A simulation model uses a computer program (C) to predict the possible outcomes of different business scenarios. See Chapter 2 for more information.

11. C. The Supreme Court determined in *Automobile Workers vs. Johnson Controls, Inc.* that it is the responsibility of prospective parents to protect their unborn children. Although employers must provide information about potential hazards, the employer may not decide for the employee whether they can work in a job that poses a risk to an unborn child. See Appendix C for more information.

12. D. HIPAA prohibits health insurance providers from discriminating on the basis of health status and limits restrictions for preexisting conditions. HIPAA does not prevent HR from investigating claims issues (A) as long as the employee provides written permission. COBRA requires continuation of health benefits (B). EPO networks (C) are established by physicians connected to a hospital. See Appendix C for more information.

13. C. The concept of human relations was first introduced in the 1920s and challenged previous assumptions that people work only for economic reasons and could be motivated to increase productivity simply by increasing monetary incentives. Human resource management (A) is the business function responsible for activities related to attracting and retaining employees, including workforce planning, training and development, compensation, employee and labor relations, and safety and security. Strategic management (B) is the process by which organizations look for competitive advantages, create value for customers, and execute plans to achieve goals. Human resource development (D) is the functional area of human resources focused on upgrading and maintaining employee skills and developing employees for additional responsibilities. See Chapter 6 for more information.

14. A. The TQM concept reviews processes to eliminate waste, relies on teamwork, and involves all members of the organization in meeting customer needs. Personal mastery, a high level of employee expertise (B), is one of the five disciplines of a learning organization. Information sharing is one characteristic of a high-involvement organization (C). The ability to balance stakeholder needs is a requirement of a change agent (D). See Chapter 4 for more information.

15. A. The correlation coefficient is useful in determining whether two factors are connected. For example, the correlation coefficient will tell you whether an increase in resignations is related to a change in location of the worksite and, if so, whether the change had a strong impact on resignations. See Chapter 2 for more information.

16. B. Risk management identifies areas of possible legal exposure for the organization and reduces those risks with preventive actions. Liability management (A) occurs after a liability is incurred, while risk management seeks to prevent liability. Qualitative analysis (C) covers several subjective tools for analysis. A risk assessment (D) is used to determine how likely it is that an identified risk will actually occur. See Chapter 6 for more information.

17. B. A skip-level interview provides an opportunity for a manager's manager to obtain insight into the goals and satisfaction of employees in the work group. An employee survey (A) is best used to gather information about various issues that can be collated and summarized. A focus group (B) can be used to involve employees in the decision-making process. A brown-bag lunch (D) is an effective way for senior managers to meet with small groups of employees to answer questions about the company goals and mission and to obtain feedback about operations. See Chapter 6 for more information.

18. D. Workplace privacy, conflicts of interest, and whistle-blowing are all examples of workplace ethics issues. Ethics are considered a standard of conduct and moral judgment defined by the processes that occur and the consequences of these processes. See Chapter 2 for more information.

19. B. The Drug-Free Workplace Act of 1988 requires only federal contractors and subcontractors to establish substance abuse policies. A fair and effective policy will describe which employees will be tested (A) and whether it is all or specific job groups. The policy should describe (C) when tests will be done (preemployment, randomly, on reasonable suspicion, or according to a predetermined schedule), what drugs are included in the process, and the consequences for employees who test positive (D). See Chapter 6 for more information.

20. B. A co-worker who witnesses the ongoing harassment of another individual may have an actionable claim of a hostile work environment. A single incident of unwanted touching (A), unless it is particularly offensive or intimidating, will not reach the threshold of a hostile work environment established by the courts. A hostile work environment may be created by any individual in the workplace, including customers, vendors, or visitors, in addition to supervisors or co-workers (C). In the case of *Meritor Savings Bank vs. Vinson*, the Supreme Court held that the mere existence of a grievance procedure and antiharassment policy (D) does not necessarily protect an employer from hostile work environment claims. See Chapter 6 for more information.

21. **D.** An HR audit is an organized process designed to identify key aspects of HR in the organization such as employee morale, HR policies, programs and procedures, and HR effectiveness. See Chapter 2 for more information.

22. **C.** Techno-structural interventions address issues of how work gets done in an organization. A high-involvement organization is one in which employees at all levels are involved in making decisions about how work is accomplished. Human-process interventions (A) are designed to build competencies at the individual level of the organization. HRM interventions (B) focus on HR processes and programs such as selection procedures or performance management that address individual employee needs. Strategic interventions (D) are used to execute changes to an organization's vision, mission, or values. See Chapter 4 for more information.

23. **C.** According to guidance published by the EEOC, caregivers are not a protected class, but there are circumstances in which disparate treatment becomes unlawful based on violations of FMLA caregiving requirements. This can also be true of stereotyping prohibited by Title VII and association with disabled individuals prohibited by the ADA. Sarbanes-Oxley deals with financial reporting (A), and the Davis-Bacon Act established minimum wages (B). See Appendix C for more information.

24. **D.** Extrinsic rewards are nonmonetary rewards where self-esteem comes from others, such as formal recognition for a job well done. Challenging work on a new project (A) is an intrinsic reward. Salary increases (B) are monetary rewards. A feeling of accomplishment after completing a tough assignment (C) is another type of intrinsic reward. See Chapter 5 for more information.

25. **C.** Four factors are considered in determining whether the use of published material is a fair use: the purpose of the use, the nature of the work being copied, how much of the work is copied, and what economic effect copying the material will have on the market value of the work. See Appendix C for more information.

Answers to SPHR Assessment Test

1. B. A primary responsibility of human resource business partners is to align a workforce plan with the business strategic plan. Failure to do so may result in the misapplication of a company's employees, both from a skill perspective in the employees' current roles and in their identification and development for future staffing needs as well. See Chapter 8 for more information.

2. D. A needs analysis will provide answers to these questions, as well as whether the HRIS will be integrated with payroll or other systems and what kinds of reports will be produced. See Chapter 7 for more information.

3. B. The three breaches of a human resource professional's fiduciary responsibility include acting in their own self-interest, having conflicting duties, and profiting from their role. Paying someone less based solely on their race is not specifically a breach of the human resource professional's fiduciary responsibilities, although it is unethical and illegal. See Chapter 10 for more information.

4. C. The four components of a SWOT analysis include strengths, weaknesses, opportunities, and threats. See Chapter 7 for more information.

5. C. Adverse impact is also known as the 4/5ths rule, which is also 80%. It is used to calculate the selection ratio for all protected class groups. For more information, see Chapter 8.

6. A. Succession planning is a process to identify talent in the organization, assess their potential, and develop them over time. It does not preselect people for positions but ideally creates a pool that can be drawn from to fill roles that are vacated by senior employees who transition or separate from the company. See Chapter 9 for more information.

7. C. Deep-level diversity refers to individual differences in values or beliefs. It is valuable in employee relations and behavior management because when employee values and attitudes are aligned with organizational culture and outcomes, job performance is enhanced. By contrast, more general diversity is a combination of various people working together, often with differences in culture, race, generation, gender or religion (B), which is a form of surface-level diversity, the biological variables that may or may not correlate to job attitudes or overall performance (A). See Chapter 11 for more information.

8. D. A STEP analysis (also known as a PEST analysis) scans the external environment to identify opportunities and threats as part of the SWOT analysis. STEP is an acronym for social, technological, economic, and political factors. See Chapter 7 for more information.

9. C. Companies that socialize and successfully onboard new employees integrate them into the culture of the organization. This builds brand loyalty and a shared sense of belonging and purpose, which strengthens an employee's commitment to the company based on values. These employees are more likely to be retained by a company in the future. See Chapter 8 for more information.

10. B. Measuring how much a job is worth is known as job evaluation. Job analysis is a study of the major tasks and responsibilities of jobs to determine their importance and relation to other jobs in a company (A). Job grading is a means of determining different job levels and pay scales based on the required knowledge, skills, and abilities (C). Job ranking compares jobs to each other based on their importance to the organization (D). See Chapter 10 for more information.

11. A. The four key questions of a strategic HR plan are "Where are we now?", "Where do we want to be?", "How do we get there?" and "How will we know when we arrive?" These follow a natural order and are answered in the strategic-planning process. See Chapter 8 for more information.

12. B. Interest-based bargaining (IBB) is when both sides in the negotiation have harmonious interests, which is a form of principled bargaining where both parties are more concerned with solving a problem than winning a position. Concession bargaining (D) is when a union gives something up in return for job security. Positional bargaining (A) and distributive bargaining (C) are synonymous and refer to when each side's primary concern is winning their own position. See Chapter 11 for more information.

13. C. Conducting equity surveys both internally and externally is necessary to determine if your pay structure is positively or negatively influencing turnover. Exit interviews are important, but they usually come too late to have an immediate effect on retention. See Chapter 10 for more information.

14. A. Due diligence is described by HRCI as "the gathering and analysis of important information related to a business acquisition or merger, such as assets and liabilities, contracts, and benefit plans." Due diligence is a type of investigation that will take place as part of a merger or an acquisition. See Chapter 8 for more information.

15. A. Mission, vision, and values statements are at the heart of strategic HRM. Implementing changes to these areas will result in the tactical and operational changes required to achieve the desired results. See Chapter 7 for more information.

16. D. A strategic workforce plan will ensure that qualified employees are available when the organization needs them by forecasting business needs, assessing employee skill, bridging gaps between them, and embedding ways to engage to retain employees. See Chapter 8 for more information.

17. A. An environmental scan includes activities related to both internal and external data collection. This data is used to determine the course of action for businesses once the goals and objectives have been developed. Although a SWOT audit might be part of the process, it is not the complete framework in itself. See Chapter 7 for more information.

18. B. Phantom stock is used in privately held companies to provide the benefits of employee ownership without actually granting stock. Restricted stock is common stock offered to employees, typically executives or employees who demonstrate outstanding performance (A). Nonqualified stock options can be used for consultants and external members of the BOD as well as for employees (D). Incentive stock options are stock options that can be offered only to employees. See Chapter 10 for more information.

19. C. Staffing effectiveness can be measured in a variety of ways to ensure that the cost of human capital is not excessive for what duties and tasks are to be performed. Turnover ratios, cost per hire, and number of applicants to number of qualified applicants are metrics that can be used. See Chapter 7 for more information.

20. D. Together, supply analysis, demand analysis, and gap analysis make up the three main types of strategic analysis. See Chapter 8 for more information.

21. D. Generally Accepted Accounting Principles (GAAP) guide the use of a fiscal year that begins on July 1 and ends on June 30 of the following calendar year. SMART (specific, measurable, action-oriented, realistic, time-based) is a system used in establishing effective corporate goals (A). A learning management system (LMS) streamlines the administration of employee training programs (B). Zero-based budgeting (ZBB) is an approach to creating budgets (C). For more information, see Chapter 7.

22. B. Among the myriad of tasks that HR might perform with new employees is to provide information on relocation or coordinate relocation services. This is done in the post-employment phase after an offer of employment has been made and accepted by the employee. See Chapter 8 for more information.

23. B. A statement of cash flows provides information about the money that flowed through the business. It identifies whether the cash was received from customers, loans, or other sources; how much cash was spent to operate the business; and how much was reinvested in the business. A balance sheet describes the financial condition of the business at a specific point in time (A). The income statement, or profit and loss statement, tells you the financial results of operations over a period of time (C). An accounts-receivable ledger describes how much money is owed to the company by each customer (D). See Chapter 7 for more information.

24. B. The purpose of a diversity initiative is to increase the effectiveness of an already diverse workforce by educating the employee population about the benefits of a diverse workforce, which include increased creativity (A) and an enhanced ability to attract customers (C). See Chapter 11 for more information.

25. C. A merger is similar to an acquisition as both result in a new, single business entity. A merger, however, is usually a mutual effort to leverage assets, whereas an acquisition is often completed by the strategic purchase of the target's stock, allowing the purchaser to assume (or take over) control. See Chapter 8 for more information.

Chapter

1

Certifying Human Resource Professionals

Human resources. Ask ten different people what human resources (HR) is or does, and you'll get at least eight different answers. Business partner, engagement officer, change agents, management adviser, recruiter, talent manager, employee advocate, paper pusher, union negotiator, counselor, policy police, coach, mediator, administrative expert, corporate conscience, and even "chief happiness officers"—these are just a few of the roles that those both inside and outside the profession think we play. Some of these descriptions are based on misperceptions from nonpractitioners, others describe the roles we aspire to attain within our organizations, and some describe what we do each day. The HR Certification Institute (HRCI) provides the *HRBoK™ (A Guide to the Human Resource Body of Knowledge)*, which is the means by which we define ourselves to the larger business community and that communicates to them what roles are appropriate for the human resource function in an organization. The *HRBoK™* was updated in 2017 to reflect the most current competencies of an HR professional.

The book *Victory Through Organization* (McGraw-Hill Education), also published in 2017, sheds new light on the correlation of emerging HR competencies to general business principles. Based on the findings of over 30 years of research, author Dave Ulrich succinctly declares that "HR is not about HR. HR begins and ends with the business" (Ulrich, 2017, p. 3). Ulrich and his team identified nine major competencies for a 21st-century HR professional, which include Strategic Positioner, Credible Activist, Paradox Navigator, Culture and Change Champion, Human Capital Curator, Total Rewards Steward, Technology and Media Integrator, Analytics Designer and Interpreter, and Compliance Manager. The identification of these competencies also means that certifying HR professionals will evolve to include the measurement of these nine competencies.

The benefits of professional human resource certification are many. An independent report conducted in 2015 by the Human Resources Research Organization (HumRRO) found that HRCI certification holders report better employment prospects, higher annual salaries, faster income growth, and higher levels of career satisfaction. Additionally, businesses benefit from hiring certification holders, a point made clear by the fact that 98 percent of Fortune 500 companies have HRCI-certified professionals among their leadership ranks (https://www.hrci.org/docs/default-source/web-files/humrroreporthrci-vocwhitepaper.pdf?sfvrsn=2).

This chapter provides you with an overview of HR certification: the growth of human resources as a profession, a little history about the certification process, and a discussion of the types of professional HR certification. (There are seven—PHR, SPHR, GPHR, PHRca, PHRi, SPHRi, and the most recent, aPHR.) This chapter will also review the required eligibility standards for the PHR and SPHR, updated in July 2018 for the first time since 2012. Additionally, you'll learn about the HR body of knowledge and get a few tips to assist you in preparing for the PHR and SPHR exams.

The Human Resource Profession

By the end of the 19th century, the Industrial Revolution had changed the nature of work—businesses were no longer small organizations that could be managed by a single owner with a few trusted supervisors. As a result, many support functions were delegated to individuals who began to specialize in certain areas. One of these functions became known as *industrial relations* or *personnel* and evolved into what we know today as *human resources.*

As businesses continued to become even larger entities, standards began to develop as practitioners met and shared information about the ways they performed their jobs. The need for more formal training standards in various aspects of this new function became apparent, and colleges began to develop courses of study in the field. By the middle of the 20th century, the personnel function was part of almost every business, and numerous individuals worked in the field. A small group of these individuals got together in 1948 and determined that the personnel function was developing into a profession and was in need of a national organization to define it, represent practitioners, and promote its interests in the larger business community. Thus, the American Society for Personnel Administration (ASPA) was born.

For the first 16 years of its existence, ASPA was strictly a volunteer organization. By 1964, membership had grown from the small group of charter members in 1948 to more than 3,100—enough to support a small staff to serve the members. With membership growing, the discussion quite naturally turned to the topic of defining the practice of personnel as a profession. Although established professions have similar characteristics, such as a code of ethics, a specific and unique body of knowledge, and an education specific to the profession, there are aspects of most professions that set them apart from each other—and personnel was no different. To solicit the contribution of practitioners in this process, ASPA cosponsored a conference with Cornell University's School of Industrial Relations to determine how best to define the characteristics that made personnel a profession. This conference spawned a year of consideration and debate among ASPA members.

The culmination of this process was an agreement on five characteristics that would set personnel/HR apart as a profession:

- HR would need to require full-time practice.
- The HR profession must be defined by a common body of knowledge that defines a course of study at educational institutions.
- There must be a national professional association that represents the views of practitioners in the larger business community and in the legislative process.
- There must be a certification program for HR professionals.
- There must be a code of ethics for the HR profession.

Once ASPA had a clear definition of what was required for the practice of personnel to be considered a profession, the members knew what needed to be done to make this a reality: Develop a body of knowledge and a certification program to evaluate the competence of practitioners.

Development of the Human Resource Body of Knowledge

With its goal clearly set, ASPA went about the process of developing a body of knowledge for the profession. ASPA created a task force to study and report on the issues involved and recommend a course of action. The ASPA Accreditation Institute (AAI) was formed in 1975 with a mandate to define a national body of knowledge for the profession and develop a program to measure the knowledge of its practitioners.

As a first step in the process, AAI created six functional areas for the Human Resource Body of Knowledge (HRBOK):

- Employment, Placement, and Personnel Planning
- Training and Development
- Compensation and Benefits
- Health, Safety, and Security
- Employee and Labor Relations
- Personnel Research (later replaced by Management Practices)

Over time, as personnel evolved into human resources, ASPA changed its name to the Society for Human Resource Management (SHRM) to reflect changes in the profession. At that point, AAI became the Human Resources Certification Institute (HRCI) for the same reason. These associations exist today to represent and certify the profession.

HRCI ensures the continued relevance of the *BOK* to actual practice with periodic codification studies. The first of these occurred in 1979; subsequent studies were conducted in 1988, 1993, 1997, 2000, 2005, 2012, and 2017. These reviews enlisted the participation of thousands of human resource experts in ongoing assessments of what a human resource generalist needs to know to be fully competent.

As with all previous codification studies, HRCI began the most current review with the question, "What should a human resource practitioner know and be able to apply to be considered a competent HR generalist?" HRCI commissioned the Professional Examination Service (PES) to conduct a *practice analysis study* to obtain information from a variety of sources on the existing state of human resource practices as well as trends predicted for future needs of the profession. Under the guidance of PES, additional information was collected through the use of critical-incident interviews, subject-matter experts, validation surveys, and focus groups. The culmination of this data collection was a comprehensive look at how HR is being practiced in the field and a relevant picture of what the business climate needs from its HR representatives. From this, the exam content was developed.

Clearly, the nomenclature has changed over the past 30 years, yet the basic functional areas of HR have remained fairly stable. Significant changes have occurred, however, within the original six functional areas, ensuring the relevance of human resource practice to the changing needs of business in the 21st century.

In early 2018, HRCI announced a revision to the PHR/SPHR Exam Content Outline based on the results of the regularly scheduled practice-analysis study. The structure of the exam content outline (ECO) changed fairly significantly, with the highlights as follows:

- HRCI split content into two separate outlines: one for the PHR exam and one for the SPHR exam.
- HRCI eliminated a separate "Core Knowledge" section, instead choosing to embed the knowledge elements into the relevant functional areas for each exam. Note that these *knowledge of* components are listed in numeric order through all functional areas—the ordering does not begin anew as do the responsibilities.
- The original sixth functional area—Risk Management—was eliminated in the new ECOs, with many objectives re-homed where appropriate.
- HRCI updated the exam content weights to be more reflective of a current HR practitioner.
- The changes reflect current HR practices and terminology.

In HRCI's press release, they noted specifically that PHR exam hopefuls will need to prepare for a greater emphasis on their role in the employee experience. This includes updating their business decision-making skills and analytics skills to help build a positive employee-employer relationship. The new PHR ECO has been compressed into just five content areas:

- Functional area 1—Business Management
- Functional area 2—Talent Planning & Acquisition
- Functional area 3—Learning & Development
- Functional area 4—Total Rewards
- Functional area 5—Employee & Labor Relations

SPHR exam preparers will need to focus their preparation activities on workforce strategies that are aligned to clear business outcomes. The five functional areas for this exam are:

- Functional area 1—Leadership & Strategy
- Functional area 2—Talent Planning & Acquisition
- Functional area 3—Learning & Development
- Functional area 4—Total Rewards
- Functional area 5—Employee Relations & Engagement

It is very important that you use the appropriate exam content outline to prepare for your exam. It should be the primary tool you use to identify where to focus your preparation resources. You can find the updated ECOs at https://www.hrci.org/how-to-get-certified/preparation-overview/exam-content-outlines.

Although compressed, many of the exam essentials remained the same. However there were a few changes worth noting. For example, many of the global and international exam objectives were removed. This may be an indication that HR practitioners of today need more specialized knowledge and competencies to serve their multinational corporations.

With the rapid rise of responsibilities in this area, a generalist's knowledge is no longer sufficient. For this reason, HR practitioners based in the United States with global responsibilities (in two or more countries) should consider the Global Professional in Human Resources (GPHR) certification. HR practitioners located outside of the United States should consider the Professional in Human Resources International (PHRi) or the Senior Professional in Human Resources International (SPHRi). Both are separate exams administered by HRCI.

In 2007, HRCI implemented the first state certification examination for California. As of January 2016, more than 1,200 California practitioners have earned the "ca" certification.

The seventh exam to be administered by HRCI is the aPHR certification, designed for professionals who are just beginning their HR career. This exam is designed to measure foundational HR concepts.

Currently, and with more and more employers recognizing the value of this exam and the preparation process, more than 100,000 HR professionals in over 100 countries have earned a certification as a mark of high professional distinction.

Defining the Functional Areas of the *BOK*

Once HRCI collated the information from the practice-analysis study, test specifications were developed to define each functional area. The test specifications have two parts: responsibilities and knowledge requirements. The *responsibilities* describe areas of practice with which a fully qualified generalist must be competent. The *knowledge of* section identifies what knowledge is necessary to perform the work of HR.

Professional in Human Resources (PHR)

The PHR certification measures a candidate's ability to apply HR knowledge at an operational or technical level, according to the HRCI website. This exam tests a candidate's ability to apply HR knowledge to situations occurring on a day-to-day basis. PHR candidates are skilled in implementing processes and procedures and are knowledgeable in the requirements of employment legislation for problems or situations with a narrow organizational impact. They're able to develop solutions by drawing on a variety of sources and knowledge that apply to a particular situation.

The functional areas in the PHR exam are weighted to reflect its emphasis on the operational, administrative, and tactical application of the elements of the body of knowledge. Table 1.1 shows the functional area weightings for the PHR exam. Here is a brief overview of the five functional areas of the PHR:

Business Management—20% of Exam Content   This content area asks candidates to apply their knowledge and skill to help reinforce employee expectations; make quality, data-driven decisions; and help avoid or manage organizational risk. It is here you will find content related to a company's mission, vision, and values; ideas about corporate governance and ethical behaviors; and how to harness the tools of Human Resource Information (and other systems) to effectively report and analyze data.

Talent Planning & Acquisition—16% of Exam Content   Formerly known as Workforce Planning & Employment, this functional area focuses on the talent management systems of the organizations of today. Prepare for content related to all types of workforce plans; the availability, recruitment, and selection of qualified talent; and assessing/managing the talent once onboard.

Learning & Development—10% of Exam Content   Similar to the former functional area of Human Resource Development, the functional area of Learning & Development focuses on employee professional growth. Prepare to apply your skills toward questions related to learning and development theories, organizational development concepts and practices, coaching and mentoring techniques, and of course, employee retention concepts. New to this area is the exam knowledge related to creativity and innovation, a nod to the many digital and virtual choices in 21st century training and development practices.

Total Rewards—15% of Exam Content   Total Rewards continues to combine compensation and employee benefits as one functional area. This means that you can expect to find questions related to compensation and benefits, labor laws, employee payroll processing, job analysis, and the application of non-cash compensation initiatives.

Employee & Labor Relations—39% of Exam Content   As you can see from the exam weighting, here is where PHR candidates can expect the most number of questions. In fact, on a 175-question exam, you can expect to see more than 65 questions related to Employee and Labor Relations, so you must prepare accordingly on topics such as the employee life cycle, safety, employee engagement data analysis, components of organizational culture, and the support of performance management systems.

TABLE 1.1   PHR functional area weighting

Functional area	Exam weight
Business Management	20%
Talent Planning & Acquisition	16%
Learning & Development	10%
Total Rewards	15%
Employee & Labor Relations	39%

Senior Professional in Human Resources (SPHR)

The SPHR certification measures a candidate's strategic perspective and ability to pull information from a variety of sources to address issues with organization-wide impact. This exam measures the candidate's ability to apply HR knowledge and experience in developing policies that will meet the organization's long-term strategic objectives and impact the entire organization.

The SPHR exam measures a senior-level candidate's strategic ability to integrate HR processes into the big picture of an organization's needs and to develop policies to support the achievement of business goals. Table 1.2 demonstrates how the weightings for the functional areas reflect this. Here is a brief overview of the 2018 updates to the five functional areas of the SPHR exam:

Leadership & Strategy—40% of Exam Content   For SPHR candidates, this should be the primary focus for exam preparation. Expect about 70 questions related to this functional area on the SPHR exam. Content will include heavy emphasis on strategy, such as strategic planning, risk-management strategies, change management strategies, and efficacy measurements. This area also includes knowledge of management functions, corporate governance procedures, project management, and the use of technology to influence company and employee performance.

Talent Planning & Acquisition—16% of Exam Content   This functional area shares about the same amount of content weight of the PHR exam, but with a slightly different focus. Talent management strategies, including addressing talent shortages and surpluses, will most likely be found in this area, as will content related to engaging employees for maximum retention as well as the design of separation systems that address downsizing, mergers and acquisitions, divestitures, and global expansion. It's important to note that this is one of the only remaining functional areas that contains an element of international practices. Exam responsibility 03 references strategies for global expansion, and the knowledge area references offshoring, so pay particular attention to these concepts as you study.

TABLE 1.2   SPHR functional area weighting

Functional area	Exam weight
Leadership % Strategy	40%
Talent Planning & Acquisition	16%
Learning & Development	12%
Total Rewards	12%
Employee Relations & Engagement	20%

Learning & Development—12% of Exam Content   Formerly Human Resource Development, the title change suggests a narrower focus to this functional area. The "Learning" portion of this functional area points you in the direction of content related to training programs and design, including practical training strategies such as delivery and timing. It will also include being well-versed in adult learning theories, instructional design principles, and metrics to assess training effectiveness. The "Development" portion of the exam will focus on three elements: employee development, leadership development, and organizational development. All of the above will require effective communication skills.

Total Rewards—12% of Exam Content   There are two primary exam objectives in this functional area, and the title gives them away. SPHR candidates must be able to analyze and evaluate strategies related to compensation and benefits programs—a total rewards system. In the context of study plans, it may be helpful to use the term "analyze" to address activities such as identifying the company compensation philosophy and conducting job evaluation to properly price jobs. The term "evaluate" in the exam objectives relates to identifying how well a company's total rewards program is attracting, rewarding, and retaining talent. Both compensation and benefits strategies at the SPHR level will involve making decisions and managing risks associated with this practice.

Employee Relations & Engagement—20% of Exam Content   The fifth and final functional area on the SPHR exam contributes to quite a bit of total exam content. To put it in perspective, Leadership & Strategy and Employee Relations & Engagement will make up 60% of the 175 exam questions. So it is important that SPHR candidates are prepared to tackle content related to employee satisfaction and performance. Study content related to diversity and inclusion, as well as information related to safety and security. Be sure to understand human relations concepts and the ethical standards of the HR profession.

The *HR Certification Institute Certification Policies and Procedures Handbook (aPHR, PHR, PHRca, SPHR, GPHR, PHRi and SPHRi)* contains the most current listing of the HRCI test specs. Because both the PHR and SPHR exams are built around them, we strongly urge those preparing for the test to review the handbook and familiarize themselves with the test specs for each functional area prior to reading the related chapter. The HRCI website (www.hrci.org) provides information on downloading or ordering this free publication.

HRCI's functional areas, test specifications, and functional-area weightings are subject to change at any time and at the Human Resource Certification Institute's sole discretion. Please visit HRCI's website (www.hrci.org) for the most current information on the exams' content. On the HRCI website, you'll find the 2018 *HR Certification Institute Certification Policies and Procedures Handbook (aPHR, PHR, PHRca, SPHR, GPHR, PHRi and SPHRi)*, HRCI's authoritative publication for PHR/SPHR/GPHR certification and requirements, containing the most current version of the test specifications.

Eligibility Requirements

As we've mentioned, complete information on eligibility requirements for the exams is available in the *HR Certification Institute Certification Policies and Procedures Handbook (aPHR, PHR, PHRca, SPHR, GPHR, PHRi and SPHRi)*, and HRCI, of course, makes the final decision as to whether or not a candidate meets them. In this section, we'll provide a broad overview of the requirements, along with some suggestions based on the experience of successful candidates.

The current eligibility requirements reflect a candidate's education and experience. According to HRCI, "professional-level experience" means that candidates have the following:

- The ability to use independent judgment and discretion in performing work duties
- Some authority for decision-making
- In-depth work requirements, such as data gathering, analysis, and interpretation
- Interaction with people at multiple levels, including decision makers
- Individual accountability for results

It's important to note that almost all supervisors and managers perform some HR functions as part of their daily requirements, but because these activities aren't usually the major function of the position and constitute less than 51 percent of their time at work, this experience most likely would not meet the requirements established by HRCI. See Table 1.3 for the exam eligibility requirements.

TABLE 1.3   PHR and SPHR eligibility

	Professional-level experience	Education
PHR	1 year	Master's degree or higher
	2 years	Bachelor's degree
	4 years	Less than a bachelor's degree
SPHR	4 years	Master's degree or higher
	5 years	Bachelor's degree
	7 years	Less than a bachelor's degree

So, the minimum requirements are pretty simple. Let's be realistic for a moment, though. The PHR and SPHR exams don't measure just book knowledge. They measure your ability to apply that knowledge in work situations. The more experience you have in applying knowledge at work, the greater your chances of passing the test. To give candidates an idea of what is needed to be successful (as opposed to what is minimally required), HRCI recommends PHR candidates have two–four years of experience prior to taking the exam; for SPHR candidates, they recommend six–eight years. HRCI provides profiles of the ideal candidate for each of the exams, which can be found in the *HR Certification Institute Certification Policies and Procedures Handbook (aPHR, PHR, PHRca, SPHR, GPHR, PHRi and SPHRi)* on the HRCI website, www.hrci.org. If you are still unsure about which exam to take, HRCI has an online tool that can help: https://www.hrci.org/our-programs/which-certification-is-right-for-you.

Recommendations for PHR Candidates   To summarize the ideal PHR profile, HRCI suggests that candidates have two–four years of professional-level, generalist HR experience before they sit for the exam. PHR candidates generally report to a more senior HR professional within the organization and during the course of their daily work focus on implementation of programs and processes that have already been developed. PHR experience focuses on providing direct services to HR customers within the organization.

Recommendations for SPHR Candidates   The ideal SPHR candidate has six–eight years of increasingly responsible HR experience. An SPHR needs to be able to see the big picture for the entire organization, not just what works best for the human resource department. This requires the ability to anticipate the impact of policies and decisions on the achievement of organizational goals. SPHR candidates are business-focused and understand that HR policies and processes must integrate with and serve the needs of the larger organization. Whereas a PHR's decisions and activities have a more limited effect within narrow segments of the organization, decisions made by SPHR candidates will have organization-wide impact.

Student or Recent Graduate Requirements   As of 2011, students are no longer eligible to take the exams. However, students who took the exam under the former eligibility requirements may apply for conversion once the two-year exempt-level experience has been satisfied. HRCI has responded to the need for entry-level HR certification with their aPHR testing option. Candidates with a high school diploma or global equivalent are eligible to sit for the aPHR.

Recertification

Until 1996, HRCI awarded lifetime certification to individuals who successfully recertified twice. At that time, the policy was changed to reflect the need for professionals to remain current with developments in the field. As a result, the lifetime certification program ended, and with the exception of those who were awarded lifetime certification prior to 1996, all PHRs and SPHRs are now required to recertify every three years by:

- Earning 45 hours of HR-related professional activities for the aPHR
- Earning 60 hours of HR-related professional development activities for all other exams, including the PHR and SPHR

There are a number of ways to be recertified; they fall into two basic categories:

Recertification by Exam   HR professionals may retake either exam to maintain certification at that level. Information on recertifying by exam is available in the *HR Certification Institute Certification Policies and Procedures Handbook (aPHR, PHR, PHRca, SPHR, GPHR, PHRi and SPHRi)*.

Professional Development   To recertify on this basis, PHRs and SPHRs must complete 60 credit hours of professional development during the three-year period. These 60 hours may be accomplished in a variety of ways. One of the most common is by attending continuing education courses, including workshops and seminars related to HR functions. However, not all activities are preapproved for certification credits. Be sure to visit HRCI's website for the most up-to-date recertification information:

https://www.hrci.org/recertification/what-is-recertification/
recertification-resources.

Another way to earn recertification credit is by developing and/or presenting HR-related courses, seminars, or workshops. Recertification credit for teaching a specific course is awarded only for the first time it's taught.

On-the-job experience can also be the basis for recertification credit: The first time you perform a new task or project that adds to your mastery of the *HRBoK*™ , you may earn credits for the work if it meets the criteria established by HRCI.

Professionals who take on leadership roles in HR organizations or on government boards or commissions may earn certification for those activities if they meet the criteria established by HRCI.

Finally, certified professionals receive credit for membership in SHRM and other national professional associations or societies, as well as for publishing HR-related articles or blogs. HRCI publishes the *HR Certification Institute Certification Policies, and Procedures Handbook (aPHR, PHR, PHRca, SPHR, GPHR, PHRi and SPHRi)* to provide detailed information on the various methods of recertifying and the amount of credit that can be earned for the different activities. You can download this guide at www.hrci.org, or you can request a copy by calling HRCI at (866) 898-4724.

The Test

Now, a little information about the test.

One question frequently asked by candidates preparing for the exam is, "What are the questions like?" The HRCI website provides a detailed explanation of testing theory and question development. In this section, we've summarized what we think is the most practical information for those preparing to take the exams. If you're interested in the details, you'll find more than you ever wanted to know about it on the HRCI website. Click the HR Certification tab, and then click How Exams Are Developed in the menu on the left; you'll see several sections explaining how HRCI builds the tests.

The questions in these tests are designed to measure whether candidates meet the objectives established by HRCI as the standard required for a minimally qualified human resource professional to achieve certification. The exam questions are designed to assess the depth and breadth of candidates' knowledge and their ability to apply it in practice. Questions at the basic level examine a candidate's ability to not only recall information but comprehend it as well. Questions designed to measure knowledge and comprehension constitute the smallest percentage of questions on both the exams, but there are slightly more of them on the PHR exam. Questions at the next level, application, are more complex and require candidates to apply their knowledge in practical situations that require the ability to differentiate which information is most relevant to the situation and will solve the problem. Questions of this type are most prevalent on both the exams. Questions at the highest level of complexity, synthesis, require candidates to use their knowledge in multifaceted situations by drawing on information from different areas of the body of knowledge to create the best possible result. They require the ability to review actions taken in a variety of situations and evaluate whether the best solution was implemented. This type of question appears on both the exams but is more prevalent on the SPHR.

The exam questions, which HRCI refers to as *items*, are developed by two panels of volunteers, all of whom are SPHR-certified professionals trained to write test items for the exams. These panels meet twice a year to review items that each member has written between meetings. Each volunteer generates about 50 questions annually that are then reviewed by the entire panel. Questions that make it through the item-writing panel process move to an item-review panel for additional consideration. As a question travels through either panel, one of three things can happen to it:

- The item can be rejected as not meeting the criteria for the exam.

- The item can be returned to the writer for additional work.

- The item can be forwarded to the next step in the process.

When an item is accepted by the review panel, it moves on to the pretest process for inclusion as an unscored pretest question.

Each item consists of the *stem*, or premise, and four possible answers: One of these is the correct or best possible answer, and three others are known as *distractors*. There may be two answers that could be technically correct, but one of them is the best possible answer. As part of the item-development process, HRCI requires that the correct answers are documented and takes great care to ensure that the best possible answer is one that is legally defensible.

Both the PHR and SPHR exams have 175 questions, consisting of 150 multiple-choice test questions (which are used to determine your score) and 25 pretest items (which aren't scored). The exams are three hours long. This means you'll have just over a minute to answer each question. You'll be surprised how much time this gives you to consider your answers if you're well prepared by your experience and have taken sufficient time to study the test specifications. As you answer practice questions in preparation for the exam, be sure to time yourself so you can get a feel for how much time it takes you to answer each question.

Test candidates often ask why the pretest questions are included on the exam, and the answer is simple: These items are included to validate them prior to inclusion on future exams as scored questions. Although the 25 pretest items aren't scored, you won't know which questions are the pretest questions while taking the exam, so it's important to treat every question as though it will be scored.

The more you know about how the questions are designed, the better able you will be to focus your study—which leads us to the next section: some tips on preparing for the exam and what to expect on test day.

If you're anything like the tens of thousands of HR professionals who have taken the certification exam since 1976, you're probably a little nervous about how you will do and the best way to prepare. In this section, we'll provide you with some hints and tips gathered from our experiences as well as from others who have generously shared their experiences in taking these exams.

It's Experiential and Federal

The most important thing to keep in mind—and this can't be stressed enough—is that these exams are *experiential*. That means they test your ability to *apply* knowledge, not just that you *have* knowledge. For this reason, memorizing facts isn't all that helpful. With a few exceptions, it's far more important to understand the *concepts* behind laws and practices and how they're best applied in real-life situations.

Another crucial factor to keep in mind is that these exams test your ability to apply knowledge of *federal* requirements, so you should be aware of legislation and significant case law that has developed since the 1960s. As experienced professionals are aware, federal law is very often different from the requirements of a particular state. This brings us to our first bit of advice from previous test candidates:

> Do not rely on your past experiences too heavily. Just because you have done it that way at one company doesn't mean it is the right (or legal!) way.
>
> —*Becky Rasmussen, PHR*

> Don't necessarily think of how you would do it at work. It is possible the way your company is doing it is wrong, so you will answer the question wrong. Look for the most correct answer, and take plenty of practice tests. The more you take, the more familiar you will become with test taking.
>
> —*Susan K. Craft, MS, PHR*

These tips apply to several situations: Your state requirements may be different from the federal requirements that are the subject of the test, your company practice may not be up-to-date with current requirements, and in some cases, you may be operating on the basis of a common myth about legal requirements or HR practices that is not, in fact, accurate. One way that HRCI tests candidates' depth of knowledge is to provide one of those commonly held myths as a distractor for a question. It's not really a trick question, but a candidate with minimal experience may not know the difference. As you study, think about why you do things in a particular way, how you got that information, and how sure you are that it's the most current and up-to-date approach. If it is current, great! You're a step ahead of the study game. If you aren't sure it's the most current, do a little research to find out whether it will apply on the exam, whether it's a state requirement, or whether it's possibly misinformation you picked up somewhere along the way.

What the Questions Look Like

As mentioned earlier, the HRCI website goes into a fair amount of detail about the technical aspects of test development. Much of that technical information won't help you in developing a study plan. However, you may find it useful to know the types of questions that the item-writing panels are trained to develop.

In the previous section, we discussed the different parts that make up a test item. Each item begins with a stem, which presents a statement or a question requiring a response. The stems will either ask a question or present an unfinished statement to be completed. Within that context, the stem can be categorized in one of the following ways:

Additionally, the item (question) structure has been updated to include all of the following:

- **Traditional Multiple Choice** These items contain a stem (or premise) and four (4) answer choices, including only one (1) correct answer.
- **Multiple Choice, Multiple Response** These are like multiple-choice items except there are two or more correct answers. The item will tell you how many correct options there are.
- **Fill in the Blank** You will be asked to provide a numeral, word, or phrase to complete the sentence.
- **Drag and Drop** You will be asked to click on certain pieces of information and drag them with your cursor to place them in the correct position.
- **Scenarios** Scenario questions present typical HR situations, followed by a series of exam items based on the scenario. These scenarios require you to integrate facts from different subject areas.

> My experience was that the actual test differed from any of the prep materials or sample tests that I had seen. The exam questions were differentiated by nuance rather than clear distinctions. Studying from multiple sources helped me be better prepared for this unexpected approach.
>
> —*Lyman Black, SPHR*

Preparing for the Exam

A number of options are available to assist candidates in preparing for the exams. One option is a self-study program that you put together for yourself based on the test specifications. Another option, depending on your location, is to attend a formal preparation course. In the past few years, informal online study groups have become popular and effective ways to prepare for the exam. Regardless of the option you choose, the most important step is to know what you already know. Then figure out what you need to learn, and develop a study plan to help you learn it.

Study Options

Several study options are available for exam candidates: study partners, self-study, and formal preparation courses are the most common. Whichever option you choose, be sure to review the *HR Certification Institute Certification Policies and Procedures Handbook (aPHR, PHR, PHRca, SPHR, GPHR, PHRi and SPHRi)*, specifically Appendix 1, to ensure that you cover all areas of the test specifications:

Study Partners   No matter which study option works best for you, many have found that partnering with someone else is a critical part of the process. Find one or two others who are studying, develop a group study plan, and meet each week to review the material for that week. Working with a reliable study partner makes the process more enjoyable and helps you stay focused. The ideal study partner is one whose areas of strength coincide with your areas of weakness, and vice versa. One effective technique is to prepare the material and "teach" it to your study partner. Teaching your partner one of your weaker areas results in a deeper understanding than just reading or listening to someone else talk about it.

Online Study Groups   If there is no one local for you to partner with, try an online study group. Join groups dedicated to the PHR/SPHR exam such as those found on `linkedin .com` or `goconqr.com`, and see if there are offerings for online study groups to help keep your efforts on track.

> I'd advise anyone to form a study group and meet on a regular basis to read, compare notes, quiz each other, and lend moral support! Not only did I learn a lot from my study partners, I gained some wonderful professional friendships—and we all passed!
>
> *—Julie O'Brien, PHR*

> Present the material yourself! Don't just listen—participate. If you teach it, you think of it much differently than if you are sitting passively and listening.
>
> *—Alicia Chatman, SPHR*

> I set up a very small study group: three people. We met once a week until a month before the test, when we met twice a week. It was good to have someone say, "Listen to the question." This made me slow down and review the phrasing and some key words like most, not, least, etc.
>
> *—Patricia Kelleher, SPHR*

Preparation Materials   Several publications are designed to prepare candidates for the exams. This book (of course!) is an intense, focused overview of material you may find on the exam.

In preparing for these exams, it is a best practice to take advantage of multiple preparation resources to ensure you get a full view of the exam content. HRCI.org dedicates a special section of their website to a list of preparation resources and offers bundled packages that include prep materials and exam fees.

In Appendix D of this book, "Resources," you'll find a list of additional materials that focus on specific functional areas, as well as many other excellent sources.

> I think there was a synergistic benefit from applying several approaches rather than using just one technique or single source of information. I used several approaches to prepare: two study guides, a review course, and flashcards. I also found that my kids enjoyed quizzing me during our times driving to school, sports, etc.
>
> —*Lyman Black, SPHR*

Self-Study   Self-study provides you with the greatest flexibility in deciding what areas to focus on. If you go this route, developing a study plan is crucial in keeping you focused. Equally important for this method is finding a study partner to share questions and ideas.

> Capitalize on your resources. Look to guidance from peers, bosses, consultants, subject-matter experts, textbooks, whitepapers, and articles, and anyone/anything else you can find that will complement your knowledge. I made my own flashcards on specific topics where my knowledge was weaker. Those helped a lot, too.
>
> —*Shirley Pincus, SPHR*

Formal Preparation Courses   A number of organizations sponsor formal preparation courses designed specifically for the exam. These are offered by colleges and universities, local network affiliations, and independent exam preparers.

Developing a Study Plan

Although many are tempted to jump in and immediately start reading books or taking classes, the best thing you can do for yourself at the outset is to identify where you are right now and what study methods have worked for you in the past, and then develop a study plan for yourself:

> The study technique that worked best for me was simply making preparation for the test a priority! I outlined a realistic study schedule for myself and stuck to it as much as possible. Plus, I studied away from my everyday environment in order to avoid distractions. For me this was a local bookstore cafe, a table covered with notes, a latte in one hand, and a pack of flashcards in the other...and it worked!
>
> —*Julie O'Brien, PHR*

Where are you right now?   The best way to answer this question is to take the self-assessment test immediately following the Introduction to this book. This will help you to see where your strengths and weaknesses lie. Based on the assessment test and on your work experience, make a list of areas you will need to spend the bulk of your time studying (your weaknesses) and the areas in which you simply need a refresher review (your strengths).

What study methods have worked for you in the past?   This may be easy or hard to determine, depending on how long it has been since you took a class. List study methods you have used successfully in the past.

Develop a study plan.   Using your list of strengths and weaknesses and the study methods that work for you, create a study plan:

> **Develop a timeline.**   Decide how much time you need to spend on each functional area of the body of knowledge.
>
> Working back from the test date, schedule your study time according to your strengths and weaknesses. You may want to leave time close to the test date for an overall review—be reasonable with yourself! Be sure to factor in work commitments, family events, vacations, and holidays so you don't set yourself up for failure.
>
> **Get organized!**   Set up folders or a binder with dividers to collect information for each functional area so you know where to find it when you're reviewing the material.
>
> **Plan the work, and then work the plan.**   Make sure you keep up with the plan you have set for yourself.
>
>> Keep up with the reading; do it every week, faithfully. Take notes on what you don't understand, then ask someone about them.
>>
>> —*Becky Rasmussen, PHR*
>>
>> Make sure you don't cram; at least a week before the test, take some days off or make extra time available to study so that you're not cramming the night before.
>>
>> —*Rose Chang, PHR*

When creating your study plan, did you do the following?

- Assess your strengths and weaknesses by taking the assessment test at the beginning of this book?
- Review the HRCI test specifications?
- Identify study methods that will work for you, such as self-study, working with a study partner, using a virtual (online) study group, or taking a formal preparation class?
- Identify useful study materials such as this study guide and website content, online HR bulletin boards, and current HR books and magazines?
- Develop a study timeline?
- Plan to start studying three to four months before the test?
- Allow more time to study weaker areas?
- Allow refresher time for stronger areas?

- Schedule weekly meetings with a study partner?

- Set up a file or a binder with space for each functional area to store all your study materials, questions, and practice tests?

- Allow two to three weeks before the test for a final review of everything you've studied?

- Simulate the test experience by finding a place to study that is free from distractions and giving yourself 1.07 minutes to answer each bonus exam question from this book?

- Challenge yourself further by setting a timer to see how well you do?

Preparation Techniques

To begin with, the best preparation for the exam is solid knowledge of human resource practices and federal employment law combined with broad generalist experience. Because it's experiential in nature, your ability to use HR knowledge in practical situations is the key to success. This isn't a test you can cram for, regardless of the materials you use.

> Rewrite the book in your words! Use your experiences to explain the lesson. It will help you remember the lesson.
>
> *—Alicia Chatman, SPHR*

Preparation materials can help provide an organized way of approaching the material. In many cases, you already have the information; you just need a refresher of where it came from and the reason it's appropriate for a particular situation.

> A friend of mine used the practice tests to give me oral exams on the material. This was very helpful because I was not reading the questions, just listening to them and answering them, marking, of course, the ones that I answered wrong to emphasize my study on that specific topic.
>
> *—Marcela Echeverria*

> I found an "SQ3R" technique (Survey, Question, Read, Recite, Review) effective in studying the materials.
>
> *—Lyman Black, SPHR*

Possibly the best advice to give you is this: Don't rely on a single source of information in your preparation. If you have a limited budget, check out books about the various functional areas from your public library. If you're financially able and so inclined, take the opportunity to build your personal HR library (and don't forget to read the books while you're at it!). Take a preparation course. Form a study group. Ask questions of your peers at work. Find a mentor willing to answer your questions. Make use of online HR bulletin boards to ask questions and to observe what others ask and the responses they receive.

 NOTE A word of caution about HR bulletin boards: Although they can be a great source of information and provide a wide range of responses, in some cases, the answers provided are *not correct*. If you make these bulletin boards part of your preparation, make sure you verify the information you receive with other sources.

None of the people who create the preparation materials for the PHR/SPHR exams have special access to the test. The best any preparation materials can do is to provide you with a review of HRCI's test specifications. It's to your advantage to utilize as many sources of information as you can to obtain the broadest possible review of the HR body of knowledge.

Answer as many questions as possible! Whether or not they're the same format as the questions on the exam, they will assist you in recalling information, and that will benefit you during the exam. Aside from the practice questions provided with this book, a great source of questions is HRCI's online assessment exams. Because the questions used are retired from actual PHR/SPHR exams, HR professionals have the opportunity to prepare for the style and types of questions they're likely to encounter when taking the actual exam. Additionally, the assessment content is weighted in accordance with the exam requirements, allowing you the opportunity to identify strengths and weaknesses by functional area, resulting in a more meaningful study plan. Purchase the two-exam package, and take one at the beginning of the study period and one before the exam itself for maximum value.

> Knowing the material isn't always enough. Many people sitting for the exam have been away from test taking for a long time. I think it helped me a lot to practice taking tests with time limits. Practice evaluating similar answers and identifying the best of the lot (not always the very best answer, but the best one presented).
>
> —*Judy Wiens, SPHR*

Taking the Exam

One of the comments heard most often by candidates as they leave the test site is that the information in their preparation materials did not bear any resemblance to what was on the test. None of the questions in this book or in any other preparation materials will be exactly like the questions on the exam. The broader your preparation and experience, the greater will be your ability to successfully answer the exam questions.

Knowing the kinds of questions that may be asked, as described earlier in this chapter, can help you focus your study and be as prepared as possible.

One of the best pieces of advice we've heard about getting ready for test day is to stop studying two or three days before the test. By then, if you've been diligent about your study plan, you will be well prepared. The night before, get a good night's sleep. Allow yourself plenty of time to get to the test site.

> Go to bed early the night before and have a light breakfast the morning before the test, so you are alert...unlike me who kept falling asleep during the test!
>
> —*Rose Chang, PHR*

On Test Day

The PHR/SPHR exams are administered as a computer-based test (CBT) by Prometric. This approach provides candidates with greater flexibility in scheduling the test and has other benefits as well.

Here are some time-tested hints and tips for exam day gathered from many who have gone before you and were willing to share some of what they learned in the process. For the day of the exam, do the following:

- Get a good night's sleep the night before the test.

- Plan to arrive at least 15 minutes before your scheduled test time.

- Bring your ID (your driver's license, your passport, or any other unexpired government-issued photo ID with a signature) and the test admission letter, along with any other required documents.

- Bring only items you must have with you. You won't be able to take anything into the testing area except your ID.

- Don't overeat in the morning or drink a lot of caffeine before the exam.

While taking the exam, do the following:

- Read the entire question carefully; don't skim it. Taking the time to do this can make the difference between a correct and an incorrect answer.

  > I am a speed-reader, and missing one little word could change the entire question. Slow down and read every word.
  >
  > —*Marie Atchley, SPHR*

- Read all of the answer choices carefully; don't skim them or select an answer before you've read them all.

- If you're unsure of the answer, eliminate as many wrong answers as you can to narrow down your choices. Remember: One of them is correct!

- Very often, your gut instinct about the correct answer is right, so go with it.

- Don't overanalyze the questions and answers.

- Don't look for patterns in the answers. A myth has been circulating for a number of years that the longest answer is the correct one—it's just not true.

- If you don't know the answer to a question, *guess*. If you don't answer, the question will be counted as incorrect, so you have nothing to lose, and you might get it right.

  > I was not surprised by the test at all. Everyone said it was hard; it was! Everyone said that it was subjective; it was! Everyone said that you will feel like you flunked; I did! (But I actually passed.)
  >
  > —*Patricia Kelleher, SPHR*

The Aftermath

The best thing about CBTs is that you will have a preliminary test result before you leave the test center. If you pass, knowing immediately relieves you of the anxiety of worrying and wondering about the results for four–six weeks until they arrive in the mail. If you don't pass the test, knowing immediately probably won't make you feel any better about it, but there are a couple of consolations:

- The time and work you put into studying has already benefited you by increasing your knowledge about your chosen profession—congratulate yourself for investing in your career.

- Although the test is important to you, put it in its proper perspective—it's only a test about HR; it's not your life. People take tests every day, and not all of them pass on the first attempt.

If you plan to take the test again, review HRCI's advice on retaking the exam at www.hrci .org. Browse the entire HRCI website—there is a lot of information about how the test is constructed and scored that may help you refine your study plan for better success.

 If you are really anxious about your ability to pass this exam on the first try, purchase the second chance insurance offered by HRCI. This insurance allows candidates to pre-purchase (at a reduced cost) the ability to retake an exam if they are unsuccessful the first time. The insurance must be purchased when you first apply to take the exam, and it is nonrefundable.

Summary

Certification for HR professionals is a process that has been evolving for more than 50 years. The *HRBoK*™ was first developed in 1975 to define the profession and provide the basis for certification. Over the years, HRCI has updated the *BOK* to reflect current business needs and trends to ensure its viability in business. Both the PHR and SPHR exams are based on federal legislation and case law and are experiential, meaning that in order to pass them, candidates need to have exempt-level experience in the field.

Questions on the exams are developed by certified HR professionals who volunteer their time to produce 50 questions per year. The questions go through two levels of review prior to inclusion as unscored pretest questions on an exam. A question that is validated in this process goes into the pool of questions available for testing purposes. Questions that don't pass this rigorous process are either discarded or returned to the writer for additional work.

A number of methods can be used to prepare for the exam. The most important preparation methods are to use as many sources of information as possible and to study with a partner or group.

Chapter 2

PHR Exam: Business Management

The HRCI test specifications from the Business Management functional area covered in this chapter include PHR-level responsibilities and knowledge. These are listed here.

Responsibilities:

✓ 01 Interpret and apply information related to general business environment and industry best practices.

✓ 02 Reinforce the organization's core values, ethical and behavioral expectations through modeling, communication, and coaching.

✓ 03 Understand the role of cross-functional stakeholders in the organization and establish relationships to influence decision-making.

✓ 04 Recommend and implement best practices to mitigate risk (for example: lawsuits, internal/ external threats).

✓ 05 Determine the significance of data for recommending organizational strategies (for example: attrition rates, diversity in hiring, time to hire, time to fill, ROI, success of training).

Knowledge:

✓ 01 Vision, mission, values, and structure of the organization

✓ 02 Legislative and regulatory knowledge and procedures

✓ 03 Corporate governance procedures and compliance

✓ 04 Employee communications

✓ 05 Ethical and professional standards

✓ 06 Business elements of an organization (for example: other functions and departments, products, competition, customers, technology, demographics, culture, processes, safety, and security.

✓ 07 Existing HRIS, reporting tools, and other systems for effective data reporting and analysis

✓ 08 Change management theory, methods and applications

✓ 09 Risk management

✓ 10 Qualitative and quantitative methods and tools for analytics

✓ 11 Dealing with situations that are uncertain, unclear, or chaotic

The current business environment, with its emphasis on the ability to compete in multiple markets and respond to rapidly changing conditions, requires more of its leaders and managers than ever before. They must seek and develop a competitive advantage in their marketplaces and continuously create new processes, products, and services to meet the ongoing challenges presented by several key forces, including economic changes, modes of service delivery, customer expectations, and the rapid changes to technology. As each challenge is met, successful managers are already forecasting the next challenge on the horizon, looking for an advantageous market position. This ongoing process of innovation, advantage, value creation, and reassessment is known as *strategic management*. PHR-level candidates must be able to use information about the business environment to influence decision-making, create and reinforce expectations, and manage risks associated with all business functions.

Organizations

Since ancient times, people have formed groups to achieve goals that they were unable to achieve on their own. Whether it was for protection, shelter, food, or profit, organizing gave people the means to achieve more than they could by acting alone. With the advent of the Industrial Revolution in the late 18th century, organizations grew larger and more complex as the goals to be achieved became more complex. As the production of goods moved from a single worker creating an entire product to multiple workers completing pieces of a single product, the need for control over the production process became greater. The modern organization evolved to coordinate the many different activities that are needed to produce the goods or services necessary to achieve its goals.

Because organizations consist of people, the HR function is impacted by everything that affects an organization, whether it's an external development (such as a competitor's technological development) or a change in a business process (such as a product design change). Whatever the impact, HR professionals are called on to implement the resulting changes.

External Business Environment

Many organizational changes occur as the result of forces outside an organization's control, and HR professionals must understand how these forces impact existing organizational strategies. These external forces affect the competition as well, and how different organizations respond to these forces plays a role in determining whether they succeed in the new environment.

Technological Developments   Historically, developments in technology have driven the growth and decline of organizations. Family farms have largely been replaced by corporate farms as a result of improved techniques and equipment, for example. Typewriters and mimeograph machines have been replaced by computers and plain-paper copy machines. Organizations that make a point of keeping abreast of these types of developments thrive, whereas others deteriorate when they ignore or dismiss the changes as insignificant.

Industry Changes   Technological developments often lead to industry changes. For example, the methods used to distribute goods have evolved over the past 100 years or so from animal power (horse-and-wagon) to railcars, trucks, and airplanes. Very few companies that began distributing goods using horse-drawn wagons were able to adapt to these changes. One company that did, the West Motor Freight Company, successfully transitioned from horse-and-wagon deliveries that began in 1907 to a regional delivery service, celebrating more than 100 years of continuous operation because it has been able to embrace industry changes.

Economic Environment   The economic environment impacts all organizations and individuals. When the economy is growing, there is a greater demand for business goods and services, and many companies are able to thrive and grow. When the economy is shrinking, companies survive, or may even prosper, when they're able to keep expenses in line with declining income. In this environment, tightly run companies (those able to eliminate redundancy and waste) are more likely to succeed.

Many factors impact economic conditions. Higher taxes mean customers have less cash to spend on goods and services and are more selective about their purchases. Stricter government regulations mean organizations must spend more of their money on mandated expenses, such as reducing the pollution created by manufacturing processes. In the United States, the availability of cash is affected by decisions of the Board of Governors of the Federal Reserve System (the Fed). When the Fed raises interest rates, organizations and individuals pay more to borrow money, which means less money is available to spend on goods and services.

Labor Pool   Another significant aspect of the general business environment that affects organizations is the availability of skilled labor. Note that the labor force population is one of the pillars of the American economy, so any shifts in hiring have significant impact on the country's economic health.

Legal and Regulatory Activity   Finally, the external business environment is affected by activities of federal, state, and local governments.

As important as the general business environment is to the health of an organization, it's equally affected by internal business operations.

Internal Business Operations

Every organization is unique in how it organizes itself, but some basic functions and structures are common to all of them. HR professionals who are focused on strategic contributions to their organizations must understand how organizations function.

Organization Functions

Every business has some common components: production and operations, sales and marketing, research and development, finance and accounting, information technology, and, of course, the people who make everything happen. Regardless of whether the business is simple or complex and whether it has one employee or hundreds of thousands, these components are all necessary for success. HR's role within an organization is to serve as business partners, so it is important for practitioners to have a general understanding of the ins and outs of all business units.

Production and Operations

The terms *production* and *operations* are, in many cases, used interchangeably. When used separately, *production* generally refers to the process by which businesses create the product or service they offer to customers. Traditionally, this meant manufactured goods, but with the growth of service and information businesses, it has come to include services as well.

The *operations* function encompasses all the activities necessary to produce the goods or services of the business. These can include such activities as the following:

Capacity   This includes determining how much of a product or service is able to be produced with the available materials, labor, and equipment (known as *inputs*) as well as what changes in inputs are required by fluctuating customer demands.

Production Layout   This is the way in which the goods or service will be produced: for example, the design of an assembly line or, in the case of a service, the process to be used in providing it, such as a model plan or protocol for a financial audit.

Scheduling   Scheduling activities make sure the products or services are available at times of peak customer demand.

Quality Management   Quality assurance (QA) ensures that the product or service meets acceptable standards.

Inventory Management   Operations managers must balance two conflicting needs related to inventory: the cost of maintaining a large inventory and the need to satisfy customers by filling orders promptly. *Just-in-time (JIT)* inventory-management systems attempt to do this by purchasing smaller amounts of supplies more frequently to reduce inventories and ensure a steady supply of products for distribution.

Technology   Increasing the use of technology can improve product quality and the amounts that are produced.

Facility Location   Evaluating the best places to locate production facilities involves many considerations: the cost of labor, distribution systems, and government regulations, to name a few.

Cost Control   As with all business functions, operations must provide products or services that meet the quality standards set by the organization at the lowest possible cost.

Sales and Marketing

Sales and marketing are closely related activities involved with creating a demand for the company's products and moving them from the company to the customer.

The *sales* function includes the near-term activities involved in transferring the product or service from the business to the customer.

Marketing incorporates functions necessary to promote and distribute products in the marketplace, provides support for the sales staff, conducts research to design products that customers will be interested in purchasing, and determines the appropriate pricing for the products. Marketing begins with an identification of the target market for the organization's product or service. Once that has been identified, decisions about the following can be made:

Product   This can be a physical product, a service, or, in some cases, both. Product development includes making decisions about what the product will do, how it will look, what kind of customer service is needed, whether a warranty or guarantee is appropriate, and how the product will be packaged to attract customers.

Price   Setting the correct price point for a product is an important marketing function. The price must attract the customer, compete with other similar products, and return a profit. Pricing looks not only at the list price but also at any discounts or allowances that will be offered.

Placement   Also referred to as *distribution*, this is where decisions are made about where the customer will find the product. Having an in-depth description of the target customer is helpful in this step: How does the customer shop? On the Internet? At the mall? By phone? These and similar questions must be answered to appropriately place the product.

Promotion   Products are promoted in many different ways, including advertising, public relations, personal selling, and providing incentives for customers to buy. Incentives such as discounts, rebates, and contests are techniques commonly used to market products and services.

Competition   Developing accurate sales and marketing plans requires knowledge about a company's key competitors. Armed with this knowledge, the company can make decisions about products to design, price points to set, the placement of products, and how best to promote products or services in the marketplace.

Competition exists for the organization's products, but also for its human capital as well. For example, if your business is located in a highly industrialized area, there will be several employers competing with you for top talent in functions such as production, marketing sales, and even human resources.

Research and Development

The research and development (R&D) function is charged with designing new product offerings and testing them to make sure they do what they're designed to do before they're offered to the public. R&D develops new products and redesigns old ones to meet changing market demands, often developing products to create demand where none previously existed. R&D works closely with marketing and production in this process. Marketing provides information it gathers from customers about their needs, whereas production provides input on the ability of the production process to create the product or the need for new processes.

In some organizations and industries, such as automobile manufacturing and pharmaceuticals, R&D is a separate function. In other organizations, it may be shared by the marketing and operations functions.

Finance and Accounting

Finance and accounting are closely related functions and include all the activities related to moving money into and out of the organization.

The *finance* function is responsible for obtaining credit to meet the organization's needs, granting credit to customers, investing and managing cash for maximum return on investment (ROI), and establishing banking relationships for the organization. The finance function also provides technical expertise for the analysis of current operations or proposals for new business directions and the projection of future financial needs.

Financial analysts work with all functions of the organization in a variety of ways. For the operations function, an analyst can provide models to predict the number of employees needed at different production levels, along with the budget impact of those different levels. Working with personnel in the operations and marketing functions, analysts compile cost data, profit margins, and pricing information to provide accurate profitability forecasts at different sales volumes and pricing levels. HR practitioners may work with analysts to project needed staffing levels or benefit costs for budget planning purposes.

The *accounting* function is responsible for activities that record financial transactions within an organization.

Transactions related to product sales and the costs related to creating the product are known as *cost accounting*; this information is critical for the operations function to manage production costs. Other accounting activities include the processing of various transactions such as payroll, expense reimbursements, and accounts receivable and payable, and the establishment of internal controls to ensure compliance with government regulations, standards set by the Financial Accounting Standards Board (FASB), and generally accepted accounting principles (GAAP). The accounting function is also responsible for preparing the budget reports managers use to maintain control of operating costs.

Under the Securities Exchange Act of 1934, Congress gave statutory authority for establishing reporting standards for publicly held companies to the Securities and Exchange Commission (SEC). In 1939, the American Institute of Certified Public Accountants (AICPA) established a committee to develop accounting standards and reports for the private sector. This committee developed GAAP for use by accounting professionals. In 1972, an independent body, the FASB, was created by the AICPA to take over responsibility for setting accounting standards. FASB standards are officially recognized by the SEC as the authority for accounting practices. These standards are essential to the efficient functioning of the economy because they enable investors, creditors, auditors, and others to rely on credible, transparent, and comparable financial information.

In 2008, the SEC began to consider allowing U.S. companies to use international accounting rules developed by the International Accounting Standards Board (IASB) instead of GAAP rules when preparing and filing their financial reports. The International Financial Reporting Standards (IFRS) would provide consistency for global financial reporting, but because this would be a fundamental change in the way financial reports are prepared, any final changes would take place over an extended period of time.

Information Technology

Information technology (IT) is the area of the business responsible for managing systems such as voicemail, computer networks, software, websites, and the Internet as well as the data collected by these systems.

As technology has become more prevalent and sophisticated, the use of IT systems has expanded from the original data storage and retrieval function. For example, the ability of new systems to increase the accuracy of scheduling requirements for operations managers by providing real-time sales and inventory tracking makes the IT function a strategic advantage in organizations. As a result, IT plays a growing role in both the operational and strategic management of organizations.

Organization Life Cycles

As organizations are established and grow, they move through four distinct phases: startup, growth, maturity, and decline. Organizations approach each of these stages with different expectations and needs:

Startup During the startup phase, organization leaders struggle to obtain funding so the organization can survive. Because employees hired during this phase must wear many different hats, there is little time for training, so they may not be fully qualified for their positions, and base pay is very often below the market rate. At this stage, outsourcing can be a cost-effective alternative for specialized functions that don't require full-time employees. There are generally few layers of management, which allows employees to work closely with the founders and leaders.

Growth In the growth phase, the founder isn't able to manage the organization alone, so additional management personnel are brought into the company. This can lead to morale issues when employees who once had access to organization leaders lose the daily contact common in the startup phase. As the organization becomes more successful, funds are available to provide competitive compensation and benefits to attract and retain qualified employees. From an operation standpoint, the growth phase presents challenges when it exceeds the ability of the infrastructure to handle it, sometimes necessitating the outsourcing of some functions to meet needs.

Not all organizations are able to make it through the growth phase and instead collapse under the weight of their good fortune or are acquired by larger entities with the infrastructure to support operations.

Maturity At the maturity phase, the organization has enough resources to provide planning and standardize policies and procedures. In this stage, it's possible to become bureaucratic and unwieldy, making it difficult for the company to change direction as rapidly as may be necessary to remain competitive. From an HR standpoint, the relative stability of this phase means that it's possible to hire less experienced personnel and provide them with training and development so that they're able to take on additional responsibilities. The compensation and benefits for executives are often enhanced during this stage.

Decline   A declining organization is characterized by inefficiency and bureaucracy. To remain viable, leaders may implement workforce reductions, close facilities, and take other cost-cutting measures. The organization's products may be outdated and unable to compete, resulting in a downward sales trend.

Organizations in the declining phase of the life cycle will need to reinvigorate themselves in order to survive. This may happen with the development of new product lines or with the redesign of existing products to bring them up to current competitive standards. When this doesn't occur, the organization may be acquired by a competitor or may cease to exist.

From this discussion, it's clear that all organizations consist of similar components. Why, then, do some organizations succeed while others either stumble along at a mediocre level or fail completely? The difference lies in how well the organization is able to position itself to take advantage of market opportunities and avoid the pitfalls present in the business environment. The strategic planning process provides a framework within which organizations are able to do this.

HR's Role in Organizations

The concept of VUCA describes the environment in which HR must be able to perform: volatile, uncertain, complex, and ambiguous. This demands sharp business focus with aligned HR initiatives that are at once stable and fluid—stable in that they always serve business strategy and fluid in that they may be adapted as needs dictate. Successful VUCA managers are characterized by an ability to align structures, processes, culture, and people with organizational objectives while responding to the external realities of the competitive landscape.

VUCA also describes a skill set, evidenced by exam knowledge requirement 09 "dealing with situations that are uncertain, unclear or chaotic." Competent HR professionals will be able to synthesize their knowledge of labor laws, the company culture, and the business needs to formulate a rapid response to the—quite often, unpredictable—nature of their day-to-day activities.

Not long ago, HR practitioners were expected to contribute to the organization in an advisory capacity, provide services to employees and others, and control employment policies and procedures in their organizations. As advisers, we were asked to provide information and guidance for managers to deal with employee issues. As service providers, HR professionals were required to answer questions and provide information for a wide range of constituents, from government agencies to candidates for employment and senior management. In the control role, HR was expected to enforce policies and ensure compliance with federal, state, and local employment regulations and laws.

Today, although the roles are ever-changing, they exist as strategic, administrative, and operational roles.

Strategically, HR professionals contribute to decisions that build on employee strengths to meet corporate goals. Establishing recruiting and retention plans to attract the best-qualified employees and keep them in the organization is a key contribution that HR is uniquely qualified to make. Developing performance-management systems to motivate employees and providing continuous development opportunities are other areas that provide strategic advantage to organizations. Managing change and leading or participating in reengineering or restructuring programs to ensure the retention of key employees furthers the organization's ability to meet its goals. As Dave Ulrich has stated, HR is not about HR—it is about the business.

Administratively, HR manages compliance issues related to government regulations, maintains employee and benefit records, and ensures the confidentiality of employee information.

Operationally, HR professionals manage the employee relations and recruiting functions that require daily attention to maintain a productive work environment.

Mission, Vision, Values

PHR practitioners must serve as the company's role model of many different behaviors. This is especially true when it comes to communicating and reinforcing guidelines for behavior. For many companies, these standards are developed as mission, vision, values statements.

Mission Statement   Effective mission statements describe the company, what it does, where it's going, and how it's different from other organizations. The message of the mission statement is generally directed at employees in the organization, and it should tell them where the company is headed in the mid to long term.

Vision Statement   A vision statement should inspire the organization and inform customers and shareholders, describing what will carry the organization into the future and what it will accomplish. In a very concise way, the vision statement should communicate what the company does, for whom it does it, and what long-range success will look like.

Corporate Values Statement   A statement of corporate values is a way for the executive team to communicate their standards for how the organization will conduct business. The values chosen for this purpose should be those that will be true regardless of changes in product lines or business processes. A question to ask in selecting an organization's values is whether the value would hold true if the organization changed its focus entirely and began doing business in a completely different way. Values such as integrity, excellence, teamwork, customer service, and mutual respect are some of those that remain constant regardless of changes in business operations.

These beliefs about the organization are usually reflected in its culture. When you are identifying corporate values, it's important to look not only at what the management team would like to see in the way of behaviors in the organization but also at the values being demonstrated in the course of business each day. When there are discrepancies between the stated, formal values and the informal values demonstrated by the workforce, the strategic plan can include goals designed to align the two.

Core Competencies   In addition to the MVV statements defined here, organizations often identify their *core competencies*: the parts of their operations that they do best and that set them apart from the competition. Many organizations believe that focusing on these core competencies makes it possible to expand their revenue streams. Competencies can be related to the technology used in operations, customer relationship management, product characteristics, manufacturing processes, knowledge management, organization culture, or combinations of these or other organizational aspects that work together synergistically and are difficult for others to replicate. When core competencies are identified, organizations can focus their strategy on ways to build related products or services instead of moving into unrelated areas. In many companies, HR becomes a core competency when it is embedded in operations rather than a segregated business unit. This involves HR leading change, fostering teamwork, developing staff, and contributing to organizational decision-making and strategic planning.

Once the vision and mission statements have defined why the organization exists, corporate goals are needed to describe how the organization will get there in the mid to long term. Effective corporate goals follow the SMART model:

Specific   The goal should be descriptive enough to guide business-unit managers in developing action plans that will accomplish the goal.

Measurable   The goal must include a method for determining when it has been met.

Action-Oriented   Goals must describe the actions that will be taken.

Realistic   The goal must be high enough to challenge the organization or individual but not so high that it's unachievable.

Time-Based   Goals must include a time frame for completion.

Once identified, these elements are combined into one strategic document, often called a *business plan*. The contents of a business plan may vary, but ultimately, it must match the purpose identified through the strategic planning process. A business plan must also consider corporate governance factors, a concept that is explored next.

Corporate Governance

Corporate governance refers to the various influences and processes that impact the way a corporation is managed and the relationship among its stakeholders, principally the shareholders, board of directors, and management. Other groups, including employees, vendors, customers, lenders, and members of the general public, are affected by the way decisions are made in the process of governance. Let's look at the roles of each of the key stakeholders:

Shareholders   Shareholders are the owners of the corporation.

Board of Directors   Members of the board of directors (BOD) are elected by the shareholders to represent the shareholders' interests with management. There are two types of directors: inside and outside. An *inside director* is a person with operational responsibilities who is employed by the organization, such as the CEO, the CFO, or another officer of the corporation. An *outside director* is someone who isn't employed by the corporation and doesn't have operational responsibilities.

Management   Management includes the officers of the corporation, such as the CEO, chief financial officer (CFO), chief operating officer (COO), and other executives who make day-to-day decisions about company operations.

A corporation is a legal entity that has rights and obligations. Although a corporation itself can't make decisions, those at top levels in the organization must make decisions on behalf of its owners. They have a *fiduciary responsibility*, or obligation to act in the best interests of the shareholders by making decisions that benefit the organization over decisions that benefit them personally. Recent events have demonstrated that this responsibility is sometimes ignored by those at the highest corporate levels. The failures of corporate executives at Enron, WorldCom, Tyco, and other public corporations to appropriately perform their fiduciary responsibilities led to the enactment of the Sarbanes-Oxley Act (SOX) in 2002.

Two of the major factors that determine how a corporation is run are the values and ethics of those who have fiduciary responsibility.

Organization Values and Ethics

Business organizations have a responsibility, and sometimes a legal requirement, to interact with employees, shareholders, and the community at large in a trustworthy and ethical manner. These responsibilities range from making appropriate decisions about pollutants that are released into the environment; to treating employees, customers, and other stakeholders honestly and fairly; to working with and training disadvantaged individuals to become productive members of society. This section describes ways to approach some of the issues in these areas.

Since the Enron scandal erupted in December 2001, the issue of business ethics has come to the forefront of discussions about the behavior of corporate executives, auditors, attorneys, and board members. Subsequent revelations about possible accounting irregularities at other multinational corporations such as AOL, WorldCom, and Global Crossing made it clear that this was not simply a case of one company that ran amok, but a pervasive problem at the top levels of major corporations. SOX made many of the practices that occurred in these companies illegal and provided penalties for violations. These are some of the requirements of Sarbanes-Oxley:

- Established the Public Company Accounting Oversight Board (PCAOB) and required all public accounting firms to register with the board, which conducts periodic inspections to ensure their compliance with audit standards

- Established new standards to ensure the independence of auditors relative to the businesses they audit, including restrictions on non-audit-related services such as bookkeeping, management, human resource consulting, or other similar services; rotation of audit partner assignments at least every five years; and a requirement that the audit report and recommendations to the management team be delivered directly to the audit committee of the BOD

- Established standards for corporate responsibility, holding the chief executive of a public company accountable for the fairness and accuracy of financial reports filed with the Securities and Exchange Commission (SEC)

- Required CEOs and CFOs to reimburse the company for incentive—or equity-based compensation in the event of a material restatement of financial reports to the SEC caused by misconduct

- Prohibited insider trading of stock during pension fund blackout periods when employees aren't able to trade the stock in their pension accounts

- Established ethical requirements for senior financial officers

- Took steps to ensure the fairness, accuracy, and independence of stock analysis

- Established criminal penalties for management officials who defraud shareholders, destroy documents, or obstruct justice

- Protected employees who report conduct that they reasonably believe violates SEC regulations or federal laws related to shareholder fraud

Ethical behavior begins at top levels in the organization. The BOD must demand it of the executive team, and the executive team must model it for all others in the organization. It would seem that this should be a pretty simple thing to do; after all, at the end of the day, ethical behavior occurs when people do the right thing. But because the values people hold are different depending on the culture they grew up in, their family background, and their personal experiences, the right thing can mean different things to different people. That is why the executive team must set the standard of behavior, communicate it, model it, and enforce it if they're serious about maintaining an ethical workplace.

Companies that are committed to ethical practices often create behavior codes as guidelines for employees to follow. In most cases, the terms *code of ethics* and *code of conduct* are used to describe these guidelines, but some organizations use other terms, such as *code of practice* or *code of professional standards*. In practice, the terms *code of ethics* and *code of conduct* are interchangeable, but each has a different purpose. A code of ethics is a statement of ideal standards that the organization is committed to uphold in its business practices. A code of conduct is a statement of behaviors that the organization expects from employees; inherent in the conduct is the idea that disciplinary action would be the result of violating the behavioral standard. In some cases, the two statements are combined, and each topic (honesty, conflict of interest, and so on) consists of the ethical statement followed by a description of expected behavior. For example, a business might write a conflict-of-interest statement in this way:

Ethics/Value Statement   It is the intent of our company to comply not only with regulatory requirements, but also to act in the best interest of our stakeholders. Our employees have a duty to disclose any real or perceived conflict of interest or financial interest when exercising their corporate responsibilities.

Conduct Statement   In the event that a conflict, or the possibility of a conflict, arises between the interests of an employee and those of the business, the employee should report the conflict to the manager or ethics officer for guidance before proceeding.

A corporate values statement created during the strategic planning process can begin to set the stage for ethical behavior, but the code of conduct, or code of ethics, is a useful tool that can inform people in the organization about what behavior is expected and what is unacceptable. Some topics to consider when creating a code of ethics include those discussed next:

Honesty   The code of ethics should set an expectation of honesty in the workplace. As with all other aspects of an ethics code, the executive team must model honesty in the representations they make to employees, customers, suppliers, and all other stakeholders in order for the message to be taken seriously within the company.

Integrity   *Integrity* is defined as a firm's adherence to a code of moral values. Integrity is demonstrated when an individual does the right thing, even when that "thing" is unpopular.

Confidentiality   In most companies, confidential information can be found in every department: marketing plans, new product development, financial statements, personal employee information, and email accounts can all contain highly confidential information. In HR, professionals work every day with confidential employee information and are sometimes pressured to share this information for one reason or another. However, information collected during the employment process, such as an employee's age, religion, medical condition, or credit history, may not be used to make employment decisions such as promotions, transfers, discipline, or selection for training. HR professionals and other employees with access to confidential information have a duty to maintain its confidentiality.

Conflicts of Interest   As mentioned at the beginning of this section, employees must put the interests of the organization before their own. Any time an employee stands to gain personally from an action taken by the employer, there is a conflict of interest (except, of course, for payment of the employee's salary). At a minimum, these situations must be disclosed to the employer, or employees should remove themselves from the situation. The ethics statement should make it clear that even the appearance or perception of a conflict of interest is damaging to the company and should be avoided.

Insider Information   Although insider information is most commonly associated with trading securities on the stock exchange, it can also apply to other areas. Insider information is any information that an employee has access to or comes into contact with that isn't available to the general public. Using this information in stock exchanges is illegal and can result in criminal prosecution and civil penalties.

The prohibitions against using insider information with regard to stock transactions apply to an employee who overhears the information as much as they apply to decision makers in the organization. Federal law requires that those with access to insider information may not act on it until the information is made public.

Gifts   An ethics policy should address the issue of gift exchanges with customers, vendors, and employees. It should describe under what circumstances gifts are acceptable and define limitations on the amounts if they're to be allowed. When the receipt of a gift unfairly influences a business decision, the gift becomes unethical and should be refused.

For companies operating outside the United States, this can be a difficult issue because in some cultures exchanging business gifts is a standard and expected practice, and the failure to do so can be seen as an insult. The Foreign Corrupt Practices Act of 1977 was enacted by Congress in response to revelations by multinational corporations of the bribes that were paid to obtain business in some foreign countries. The act prohibits the payment of bribes and requires accounting practices that preclude the use of covert bank accounts that could be used to make these payments.

Personal Use of Company Assets   A code of ethics should clearly state what the employer considers to be an appropriate and acceptable use of company assets. In some organizations, the receipt of any personal telephone calls or emails is considered inappropriate, whereas in other companies a limited number is acceptable. Copying and distributing copyright material from newspapers, books, magazines, CDs, or other company assets may also violate patents or copyrights, and employees should be made aware of the consequences if they use any of these assets inappropriately.

Workplace Privacy   Some employers feel the need to install surveillance cameras in work areas. This happens for a variety of reasons. For a retail store open late at night, for example, this practice provides a measure of security for employees. In other situations, concerns about productivity or pilferage can spur an employer to install a surveillance camera in a distribution warehouse. Whatever the reason, the employer must balance the need to manage its workforce with an individual employee's expectation of privacy.

Advances in technology have made it possible for employers to monitor Internet, email, and voicemail usage, and some employees see this as an invasion of privacy. Employers who plan to monitor employee communication and Internet usage should develop and distribute a policy clearly stating what information is subject to monitoring and under what conditions.

The code of ethics should include a statement about the use of surveillance and monitoring to reduce the risk for claims of invasion of privacy.

Fairness   Actions taken by employers have the ability to significantly impact the lives of their employees. Whether decisions are being made about hiring or layoffs, or accusations of malfeasance or inappropriate behavior are being made, employers have an obligation to treat employees fairly in all their actions. Employees who have the power to make decisions, such as selecting suppliers or evaluating employee performance, have an equal responsibility to handle these decisions fairly.

A real test of an organization's fairness occurs when an employee makes a complaint to a federal agency, claiming that illegal activity has occurred. A person who does this is known as a *whistle-blower*. Some federal statutes, such as the Occupational Safety and Health Act, Railroad Safety Act, Safe Drinking Water Act, and Toxic Substances Control Act provide protection for employees who "blow the whistle" on their employers. Even so, it's a true ethical test to see how the whistle-blower who continues to work for the company is treated in the workplace once the complaint has been made.

As important as a code of ethics is, it's equally important to be aware of situations where conflicting needs and desires make doing the right thing less clear-cut. As those responsible for maintaining the confidentiality of personal employee information, HR professionals make ethical decisions on a regular basis and are in a position to model ethical behavior in the way they respond to inappropriate requests for information.

Ethics Officers

Businesses serious about establishing meaningful ethics programs have appointed ethics officers or facilitators charged with the responsibility to ensure that the organization adheres to the ethical standards set by the executive team. Ethics officers advise employees at all levels in an organization on ethical issues and manage programs designed to allow confidential reporting of ethical concerns by employees, customers, shareholders, or others, and they also investigate allegations of wrongdoing. Ethics officers provide periodic reports for the executive team to keep them apprised of ethical issues in the organization.

Corporate Responsibility

Corporate responsibility (CR) is a business behavior that is focused on building external strategic relationships. Identifying the CR goals and resulting behaviors used for future decision-making is an element of the strategic planning process.

CR activities are interdependent on multiple department responsibilities that serve to link the external environment to the internal environment. Achieving the CR objectives often requires the active participation and commitment of the entire organization.

The emerging stakeholders with an investment in the outcomes of CR activities are often identified as those with a need for deeper participation and activity on the part of their business leaders (employees and the community), social initiatives, and the global landscape. These stakeholders typically are represented at a local, national, or global level. The former CEO of Aetna, Ronald A. Williams, had this to say about corporate responsibility:

> No single group can solve the world's problems, but public companies can move the collective needle by using their human and financial resources to innovate in ways that benefit both private interests and the public good.

From "CEOs on CSR" by Tara Weiss, Matthew Kirdahy, and Klaus Kneale, Forbes, October 16, 2008, https://www.forbes .com/2008/10/16/ceos-csr-critics-lead-corprespons08-cx_ tw_mk_kk_1016ceos.html

Sustainability

Sustainability is defined by HRCI as "the capacity to endure over time". In other words, it speaks to company behavior that doesn't deplete the resources used to achieve an outcome. These resources include time, labor, and finances, all three of which have a significant impact on the long-term health of a corporation. Sustainability first became a widely recognized principle as the result of "green" initiatives, and companies now understand that the financial benefit of sustainable business practices is a long-term strategic solution that influences factors far beyond their environmental footprint.

Sustainability issues for many companies are often functionally still only a matter of complying with regulations, but true sustainability initiatives are undertaken regardless of the political climate. Companies that care about their environmental and social impact have taken steps to embed sustainability into their corporate behavior and brand. This means that regardless of changing regulations from the Environmental Protection Agency (EPA) or the Federal Communications Commission (FCC), sustainability efforts remain firmly rooted as a function of business strategy.

Figure 2.1 shows examples of HR behaviors that support corporate responsibility and accountability efforts.

FIGURE 2.1   HR's role in CR efforts

Internet Access

The use of the Internet in business continues to provide multiple opportunities for HR professionals to emerge as business leaders. HR practitioners must be able to establish relationships with individuals both inside and outside the organization to assist in the achievement of corporate responsibility initiatives.

One issue in which a partnership would be relevant is the "digital divide." This is characterized both economically and geographically: Roughly one-third of U.S. households with an annual income of under $30,000 do not have access to high-speed Internet, and in some cases, have no access to Internet at all. These issues must matter strategically to the businesses HR serves for many reasons:

Limited Internet access affects where companies may operate.   A lack of digital infrastructure will keep companies from expanding where there is available talent and less expensive real estate. This affects the cost of goods and services, thus undermining profitability.

Access to the Internet is how many students are educated.   A lack of access results in a less educated and qualified workforce to serve future staffing needs. This also means that the competition for talent will remain fierce in some industries, such as nursing and technology.

Professional growth is limited.   The Internet provides many free and low-cost resources for individuals to develop professionally. This includes fundamentals such as reading skills, interviewing tips, and even language courses.

The Internet is a revenue stream.   With the dominance of online shopping, the Internet is a source of revenue to which people must have access in order to make purchases. It behooves companies that sell or market anything online to partner with groups to aid in getting and keeping consumers connected.

HR can lead the efforts to partner with governments, nongovernment organizations, and local community groups to bring infrastructure to underserved areas. For example, Microsoft's Affordable Access Initiatives have many partners addressing the connectivity issues that 53 percent of the world struggles with. HR may also get involved in lobbying efforts to help maintain a free Internet, allowing for innovation and fair competition.

Track the Pew Research related to the digital divide at
https://pewresearch.org.

Whistle-Blower Protection

The Sarbanes-Oxley Act requires violations of securities laws or breaches of fiduciary responsibility to be reported to either the chief legal officer or CEO of the company by in-house attorneys or outside counsel; if resolution doesn't occur, attorneys must report the concerns to the audit committee of the BOD. Section 806 of SOX provides broad protection for employees who initiate reports of what they reasonably believe are company actions in violation of SEC regulations or federal securities laws. Enforcement of these whistle-blower protections is delegated to the Department of Labor's OSHA. OSHA regulations apply to employees who provide information, assist someone else in providing information, or assist in an investigation of alleged violations of mail, wire, bank, or securities fraud, or violations of SEC regulations or federal laws protecting shareholders from fraud.

OSHA rules state that employers may not take unfavorable employment actions against employees in any of the terms and conditions of employment, such as laying off or terminating, demoting, blacklisting, denying benefits, failing to hire or rehire, intimidating, reassigning, reducing hours or pay, disciplining, and others. Employees who believe that their employment status has been unlawfully affected by the filing of an allegation must file a written complaint including their name, the name of the company that allegedly retaliated against them, and *prima facie* evidence of the violation. A *prima facie* violation includes the following four elements:

1. The employee was engaged in a protected activity.
2. The employer knew or suspected that the employee was engaged in the protected activity.
3. The employee suffered an unfavorable employment action.
4. Sufficient circumstances existed to infer that a contributing factor to the unfavorable action was the employee's participation in the protected activity.

Employees must file retaliation complaints within 180 days of the retaliatory action by the employer, and the 2015 updates to SOX allow for the complaints to be made verbally as opposed to only in writing. If a final ruling from OSHA is not received within 180 days, the employee may file suit against the employer. If OSHA finds that retaliation occurred, it first seeks to reach a settlement between the parties. If that isn't possible, OSHA has authority to order reinstatement of the employee with back pay, restore benefits, and order other actions that make the employee whole, including paying interest on back wages and compensation for attorney's fees and litigation costs.

OSHA has the authority to issue a *preliminary order of reinstatement* prior to conducting a hearing on the claim if it reasonably believes a violation occurred. If preliminary reinstatement isn't appropriate, OSHA may require economic reinstatement—that is, it may require the company to pay the employee at full pay and benefits even though the employee doesn't return to work. OSHA's final ruling specifically excluded a method by which employers may recover the pay/benefits should the report turn out to be false.

BOD audit committees have the responsibility to establish processes to facilitate confidential reports of possible violations. The elements of an effective process include the following:

- A clear policy statement or code of business conduct identifying specific steps for employees to follow if they discover unlawful or unethical activity
- Training for employees to help them recognize the difference between lawful and unlawful activity
- Training for managers on how to handle employee reports, maintain confidentiality, and prevent retaliation
- A system for tracking complaints, maintaining records of investigations, verifying follow-up activities, and resolving the complaint
- Development of an investigative process before it's needed. By identifying in advance whether the company will use internal or external investigators, how evidence will be gathered and maintained, how interviews will be conducted, specifics on maintaining confidentiality, a process to receive anonymous reports, and the range of disciplinary actions to be taken if wrongdoing is identified, investigations can begin almost

immediately upon receiving a report. The process should also describe what kind of reports will be made, if any, to employees or others who report concerns.

- A record-retention system for documents gathered during an investigation, to comply with SOX requirements for full and complete access in any legal action related to SOX

Whether an employer is publicly held and bound by SOX requirements or is a midsized, privately held company, some attorneys recommend the establishment of a formal channel for reporting possible unethical or fraudulent activities. Employees are often in a better position to observe questionable actions of co-workers and supervisors than are their managers whose multiple responsibilities may distance them from day-to-day operations. The Association of Certified Fraud Examiners conducted a study in 2016 that found that 39 percent of fraud is initially detected by tips provided by employees, vendors, customers, or other stakeholders. The report also noted that companies with whistle-blower hotlines were almost twice as likely to detect fraud through tips than companies without hotlines. A well-planned and publicized process provides an avenue for employees and others to make confidential reports of unethical or unlawful activity. This builds employee morale and establishes credibility in the marketplace, while also increasing the odds of detecting fraud that cost businesses an average loss of $2.7 million in 2016.

Check out the full fraud report at www.acfe.com.

 Real World Scenario

Whistle-Blowing in the Wake of the Enron Scandal

In the wake of the Enron scandal, and particularly during the month when congressional hearings into the bankrupt corporation's activities were televised each day, the SEC saw a marked increase in complaints. This trend has continued over the last 15 years. For example, the SEC, in their annual Whistleblower program report ,noted that "from FY 2012... to FY 2018, the number of whistleblower tips received by the Commission has grown by approximately seventy-six percent" (sec.gov).

Sherron Watkins, who is credited with blowing the whistle on the Enron accounting practices that eventually led to its bankruptcy in December 2001, may have inspired the increased reports. Ms. Watkins followed a path typical of whistle-blowers by meeting with Enron CEO Ken Lay long before she went to regulators. Her desire was to advise him of the wrongdoing so he could put an end to it. That unfortunately did not happen, and the company filed for bankruptcy a few months after their meeting.

Although some whistle-blowers have statutory protection from retaliation, courts are divided on just what whistle-blowing activity is protected; those who go to regulators are often unable to work in their chosen profession after taking the action.

One whistle-blower who paid the price for his actions is Dr. Jeffrey Wigand, a former tobacco executive who was fired by Brown & Williamson Tobacco Corporation in 1993 after the company refused to remove a known carcinogen from its cigarette products. After his termination, Dr. Wigand testified against tobacco companies in civil lawsuits and appeared in an interview on the television show *60 Minutes*; his former employers launched a campaign to discredit him. Dr. Wigand was a key witness in the lawsuit brought by 46 states against tobacco companies that was settled when they agreed to pay $206 billion to reimburse the states for medical expenses related to smoking.

The good news is that regardless of the evolution of regulations, whistleblower protection since the Enron and Brown & Williamson examples continues to gain traction, largely due to the impact of media. Consider the 2018 whistleblower report to the Wall Street Journal by Theranos employee, Tyler Shultz, of the company's potential manipulation of data. The result was, by several accounts, the beginning of the end for Theranos and company founder, Elizabeth Holmes (Wall Street Journal). In today's world, whistleblowing to the media has significant impact (often more so than to state or federal regulators) because of the viral nature of news delivered and then shared online.

Enterprise Risk Management

For some businesses, safety and security is a separate business function; for others, it is part of an HR Generalist's role. Regardless of where the task-level responsibilities lie, HR makes important contributions. *Enterprise risk management (ERM)* is a practice of forecasting possible risks to the organization and taking steps to mitigate their impact on operations. In exam content terms, objective 04 relates to HR recommending and implementing best practices to reduce risk in the workplace. The first step in accomplishing this is to identify the risks; for HR, that means conducting an audit of HR practices to identify areas of potential loss.

HR Audits

An *HR audit* identifies areas that may be out of compliance with legal requirements or that are in need of updating because of strategic changes within the organization, and it defines elements that are working well. First identifying the exposure factors and then developing an audit system to measure the current levels based on behaviors and outcomes (not the intent) are important contributions of HR within the scope of ERM.

Once possible risks are identified and analyzed, options to mitigate the risks are reviewed, and recommendations for handling the risk are made. Depending on the level of risk and its possible impact on operations, decisions can be made about how to handle each risk. When a risk has been identified, the following are examples of the types of audits HR can use to minimize exposure and to demonstrate a good-faith effort toward compliance:

Hiring Statistics at All Levels of Employees   What percentage of your management team are protected-class individuals?

Recruiting Sources   Which recruiting sources offer the most diverse pool of qualified applicants?

Data Security   Review components such as the security of confidential information, breaches in the process, and the validity of control measures.

Form I-9 Audits   Verify procedures, and conduct a review to reduce penalties associated with improperly completed forms.

Harassment Claim Management   Review training records, conduct an employee survey to ensure that claims are taken seriously, and review the policy to ensure compliance with both state and federal laws.

An experienced HR professional is capable of identifying the elements that should be audited and monitoring the process. A complete audit will include a review of policies and practices in all the functional areas of HR, including hiring, compensation, benefits, training and development programs, employee relations, records management, legal and regulatory compliance, and safety. HR audits can use a variety of methods to obtain the information needed for an assessment, including checklists or questionnaires, surveys of employees and managers, and interviews.

Insurance Policies

For some risks, the purchase of an insurance policy will adequately protect the organization. Employment practices liability insurance (EPLI) provides protection for employers to help them reduce the potential loss associated with various employment-related claims. Sexual harassment, discrimination, and wrongful discipline are some examples of the types of protection EPLI offers. In cases where the risk is low, a plan for self-insuring—that is, to pay out-of-pocket should the risk occur—may make sense. It may be possible to reduce the level of risk for some practices, such as unsigned I-9 forms, by implementing checklists or reviewing procedures. The potential exposure from other risks may be so high that eliminating the practice would provide the best protection for the organization.

Employee Handbooks

An employee handbook can be an organization's first step toward compliance with labor laws that require or recommend written policies as part of compliance efforts. A well-written policy can protect the employer against potentials risks from the following: sexual harassment, reasonable accommodations of employees with a disability, safety, wage and hour laws, and at-will employment statements and leave laws. An employee handbook should include the company's expectations, the employees' rights, and the company's legal obligations to the employees. For a more in-depth discussion regarding employee handbooks, see Chapter 6 titled "PHR Exam: Employee & Labor Relations."

Litigation Statistics

Another way to identify an organization's risk is to identify current trends based on litigation statistics. For example, the Equal Employment Opportunity Commission (EEOC) compiles a list of all charges filed with the agency related to adverse employment actions. Although a charge filed with the EEOC doesn't by default mean that a company is guilty of an illegal practice, the burden of proof rests firmly with the employer. In Table 2.1, the Total Charges number reflects the number of individual charge filings. Because individuals often file charges claiming multiple types of discrimination, the number of total charges for any given fiscal year is less than the total of the eight types of discrimination listed. Note that the total number of charges actually trended down.

 The EEOC issued its Performance and Accountability Report for 2018, noting that most harassment suit resolutions by their agency involved a hostile work environment based on sex. This and similar trends should be used by HR professionals to ensure their companies take proactive steps to avoid these types of risk. View the report in its entirety at https://www.eeoc.gov/eeoc/plan/upload/2018par.pdf.

TABLE 2.1   Types of EEOC charges filed from 2015 through 2017

	FY 2015	FY 2016	FY 2017
Total Charges	89,385	91,503	84,254
Race	31,027	32,309	28,528
Sex	26,396	26,934	25,605
National Origin	9,438	9,840	8,299
Religion	3,502	3,825	3,436
Color	2,833	3,102	3,240
Retaliation—All Statutes	39,757	42,018	41,097
Retaliation—Title VII only	31,893	33,082	32,023
Age	20,144	20,857	18,376
Disability	26,968	28,073	26,838
Equal Pay Act	973	1,075	996
GINA	257	238	206

Source: Equal Employment Opportunity Commission. Sourced on May 17, 2017 at https://www.eeoc.gov/eeoc/statistics/enforcement/charges.cfm

Other

Other examples of risk-management trending and forecasting include the following:

- Unemployment rates by geographic location

- Safety standards (for example, ergonomics and heat-illness prevention)

- Updates to labor laws referencing cultural or technological trends (such as post–September 11, 2001 religious discrimination, disaster preparedness in response to Hurricane Katrina, or Office of Federal Contract Compliance Programs [OFCCP] regulations for defining an "Internet applicant")

Legislative and Regulatory Processes

The human resource profession can play a key role in the development of legislation and regulations affecting the employment relationship between an organization and its employees. HR professionals should be aware of the ways in which they, as individual citizens and as business leaders, can affect these processes. Because the PHR exam is based on federal laws, this section will discuss how proposed legislation or regulation is handled by the federal government. A similar process is followed by state and local governments, and involvement at any level of government can benefit business organizations.

Legislative Process

The federal legislative process begins when someone has an idea. This idea can come from a senator or congressperson, an individual, a business, a church, or a professional association. Ideas for particular types of legislation may also come from citizen's groups, lobbyists, or special-interest groups concerned with solving a particular problem. If the idea comes from someone other than a member of Congress (MOC), it must be presented to a member of the U.S. House of Representatives or U.S. Senate to begin the process of becoming a law. The steps in the process are as follows:

1. When an MOC agrees to sponsor a bill and presents it to the full body of the House or the Senate, it's assigned to a committee for study.

2. The committee first determines the likelihood that the bill will be able to pass a vote in the full body; if the determination is made that it isn't likely to pass, no further action is taken, and the bill effectively dies in the committee.

3. Bills that are deemed likely to pass a vote of the full body are studied by a subcommittee, and hearings are conducted to obtain input from government representatives, subject matter experts, and citizens with points of view for or against the bill.

4. Once the bill has been studied, the subcommittee may make changes, a process known as *marking up* the bill. The subcommittee then votes on whether to return the bill to the full committee with a recommendation for further action. A bill that isn't reported back to the committee dies in the subcommittee.

5. Bills that are returned to the full committee may be subjected to further study, or the committee may vote to accept the subcommittee recommendations and "order the bill reported" to the full body.

6. When the committee votes to report a bill to the full body, a written report of the findings and recommendations of the committee is prepared, including dissenting views of members who voted against the bill.

7. Bills that are reported out of committee are placed on the legislative calendar and scheduled for a vote by the full body.

8. Members of the full body are able to present their views about passage of the bill prior to a vote. During the debate period, members may offer amendments that will take effect if the bill is passed.

9. When debate is completed, a vote is conducted.

10. If the full body passes the bill, it must go to the other body and usually the process begins again; in some cases, the other body may vote to pass the bill as it was presented. During the review process, the second body may vote it down, table it, or change the bill. Bills that are rejected or tabled at this stage are considered dead and won't become laws.

11. If the bill passes the second body, any major differences between the two bills are reconciled in a conference committee. If the conference committee can't agree on the form of the bill, it will die and not become a law. If the committee recommends a conference report incorporating the changes, both houses of Congress must vote to approve the conference report before the bill is forwarded to the president for signature.

12. When the president receives the bill, he or she has three choices: sign it into law, veto it, or fail to sign it. If the bill is vetoed, Congress may override the veto by a two-thirds vote of a quorum in each house, in which case the bill will become a law in spite of the veto.

    If the president simply fails to sign a bill, one of two things will happen. When Congress is in session, a bill that remains unsigned for 10 days will become law without the president's signature. If Congress adjourns before the 10-day period is up, the bill won't become law. This is known as a *pocket veto*.

Administrative Law

In addition to the laws passed by Congress and signed by the president, HR professionals should be aware of the process by which administrative law is developed. Three types of administrative law impact employment relationships: agency rules and regulations, agency orders, and executive orders.

Much of the legislation passed by Congress empowers and requires federal agencies to develop enforcement regulations. An example of this is the Occupational Safety and Health Act of 1970, in which Congress established the Occupational Safety and Health Administration (OSHA) and required that it develop regulations to improve the safety of American workplaces. In developing these regulations, the agencies follow an established process.

First, they develop rules or regulations and publish them in the *Federal Register* (the official daily publication for rules, proposals, and notices of federal agencies and the Office of the President) and give the public an opportunity to comment on the proposals. Once the comment period has been completed, the agency publishes final rules that take effect no less than 30 days after the date of public notice.

Some federal agencies, such as the National Labor Relations Board (NLRB) and the EEOC, have the power to order compliance with federal laws in courts known as *administrative law courts*. The orders issued by an administrative law judge (ALJ) in these cases have the effect of law, and many of these decisions are published in the Federal Register as well.

The final type of administrative law with which HR professionals should be familiar is the executive order (EO). EOs are issued by the president of the United States and become law after they have been published in the Federal Register for 30 days.

Lobbying

Lobbying is an activity in which people can participate when they want to influence new laws and regulations. HR professionals can contribute as individuals or as part of the HR profession. The Society for Human Resource Management (SHRM) has legislative affairs committees (LACs) on the national and local levels that monitor and provide information on proposed changes to employment-related legislation and regulation in addition to coordinating lobbying efforts.

HR professionals who want to influence the legislative or regulatory processes should first make sure they fully understand the topic and are able to provide sound justifications for the position they take. It's also important to gather as much support as possible—legislators are more likely to be responsive when a large number of voters feel the same way. To be an effective lobbyist, it's also important to find a senator or a congressperson who will guide you through the process and introduce you to other legislators.

There are many avenues for contacting elected officials or regulators. The House of Representatives has a website, www.house.gov, which provides information about contacting representatives; the Senate has a similar site at www.senate.gov.

HR professionals who want to stay abreast of legislative activity can find information on pending legislation in many places. In addition to the LACs mentioned previously, information about pending legislation is available at the House and Senate sites just mentioned and on the SHRM website at www.shrm.org.

Technology

As mentioned earlier in this chapter, the human resource role in organizations has evolved over the years. One area most changed by this evolution is the administrative function. Because of technological developments, there are many opportunities to reduce the amount of time required by HR staff to perform these types of tasks. Table 2.2 describes some of the functions that are more easily and accurately accomplished with the use of technological tools such as human resource information systems (HRISs) and applicant tracking systems (ATSs).

TABLE 2.2   HR technology applications

Wage and hour	HR management	Benefit administration
Timekeeping	Recruiting	Eligibility
Payroll	Employee records	COBRA administration
Tax payments	Workforce planning	Annual open enrollment
Attendance	EEO compliance	
Work schedules	Compensation management	
Garnishment orders	Performance management	
	Succession planning	

In addition to automating repetitive tasks and more accurately maintaining records, technological advances provide opportunities to improve the accuracy of information and accessibility for employees and managers by giving them direct access to the information they need. For employees, this could mean the ability to access and update personal information such as address and dependent status changes (referred to as employee self-service). For managers, this could take the form of access to performance-management or training records. Even candidates can benefit through the ability to input their résumés or applications directly into the applicant-tracking system.

Critical to implementing HR technology is aligning it to business strategy. HR professionals may do so by developing technological competence beyond what is only required for their department. By focusing on streamlining the administrative functions through technology, HR is freed up to target the more strategic elements of the business. This includes understanding emerging technology as well as the systems on which their competitors depend. If the competition can do anything faster or more efficiently, it is a threat that must be addressed.

Other issues that continue to emerge in this arena include a reliance on social networking, a concept discussed more thoroughly in Chapter 3, "PHR Exam: Talent Planning & Acquisition." The advancement of mobile devices to communicate with the workforce population must also be accounted for in HR systems and practices. The popularity of wearables in the workplace is allowing employers to stay informed on productivity or attendance.

Workforce Analytics

Of course, it is not enough to have data-gathering technology if a company fails to properly interpret and apply the data. This is a major issue in the area of workforce analytics. Gathering information on a macro scale is a field ripe for harvesting. Being able to predict turnover, design meaningful employee wellness programs, and make better hires are just a few of the positive outcomes from robust workforce analytics systems. In pursuing these matters, HR must be careful to help their employers distinguish between data that is *interesting* and data that is *impactful*. For example, a turnover report is limited in that it doesn't tell a story about why employees left—it lacks depth. Analytics is future-focused, based on predicting behavior using current and past information to improve employee engagement and organizational competitiveness. With the vast availability of information via technology, HR must help their employers invest in analytics that are best aligned with strategic objectives.

HR is also tasked with addressing corporate governance issues in general (exam knowledge objective 03). Consider the giant hedge fund The Galleon Group, whose billionaire founder was found guilty of conspiracy and securities fraud based in large part on the data-gathering activities the company used to try to predict which way the stock market was headed. HR will be instrumental in crafting governance polices to effectively manage these and other data-mining risks.

Human resource professionals at all stages of their career will need to serve as advisers for their business leaders on how to best direct the penetrating impact of technology in the workplace. This will include developing the necessary competencies to think strategically, lead change, manage risks, and maintain a "human" relationship with the people. It also requires a heavy dose of data interpretation techniques, two of which are discussed next.

Qualitative and Quantitative Analysis

Making business decisions requires accurate and reliable information; without it, for example, a decision can result in excess inventory rather than increased profits because demand for the product was less than projected. Because there are no crystal balls in the boardroom, business leaders must rely on the judgment of experienced managers and an analysis of historical data to predict possible future trends.

There are two types of research: primary and secondary. *Primary research* is original, meaning that the researcher has performed the research. *Secondary research* is based on information that has been collected or reported by others, such as books or articles by primary researchers, industry standards, or analysis of trends in an organization.

One very formal method of primary research is known as the *scientific method*, and although it isn't generally identified as such in analyzing business problems, the process is similar to the way in which business problems are analyzed prior to making decisions. There are five steps to the scientific method. Using a common business problem, absenteeism, the following analysis shows how these steps can be used in solving HR problems:

1. Identify a problem:

    Absenteeism is too high.

2. Create a hypothesis:

    The absentee rate is higher with new employees.

3. Decide how to test the hypothesis:

    A correlation analysis of length of employment and attendance data will confirm or not confirm the hypothesis.

4. Collect data to verify the hypothesis:

    Review employee files and attendance records. Correlate hire date and number of absences for each employee.

5. Draw conclusions/analyze the data:

    Does the correlation analysis verify or not verify the hypothesis?

The result of the analysis will either prove the hypothesis, that absences are higher among new employees, or disprove it. Sometimes, the process of analyzing data may shed light on other factors that contribute to the problem.

Another issue to consider is whether there will be a control group in the test. Using a control group tells the researcher whether the hypothesis being tested causes the result or whether the result is the same with both the group being tested and the control group.

In many situations, secondary research also provides valuable insights for HR professionals looking for ways to solve problems in their organizations. In the 21st century, HR pros may subscribe to publications and video feeds, or seek out case studies to identify how other companies creatively solve the day-to-day issues (such as attendance) plaguing all businesses, regardless of industry. A word of caution—be sure to consider the source of the secondary research. Pay attention to differences between state and federal labor laws, union versus non-union environments, and other factors that may influence the applicability of the information in your work environment.

Data Collection

Collecting data is an important element of the analysis process; if the proper data isn't collected, any decision based on it, regardless of the method of analysis used, won't be an accurate decision. So, how do you find reliable data to use in analyzing HR problems? Here are some sources to consider:

Personnel Records   Personnel records provide information used for analyzing trends. For the absentee example, personnel records describe how long each employee has worked for the company as well as how often the employee is absent from work.

Observations   The hypothesis for the absentee example could have been based on the observation of a general manager who noticed that several new employees were frequently absent.

Interviews   Interviews provide direct information about problems. The HR department can interview some new employees to find out how often they're absent and why. This data-collection method can provide more information than records, but its relevance depends on the frankness of the people being interviewed and their willingness to share information. In addition, interviews are time-consuming and may not be cost effective for that reason.

Focus Groups   Focus groups are often used to find out how people feel about products or advertisements. They can also be an effective method for gathering information for HR analysis, but again, they're subject to the willingness of participants to open up. In a focus group, this willingness may be inhibited by the presence of co-workers or supervisors.

Questionnaires   Questionnaires can be an effective means of gathering information from large groups of geographically dispersed employees but are limited in the types of data that can be collected.

Once data has been collected, there are two basic categories of data-analysis tools: quantitative analysis methods based on mathematical models and qualitative analysis methods based on the best judgment of experienced managers or subject-matter experts (SMEs).

Analysis Tools

A number of different tools are available for data analysis, and they fall into two basic categories: quantitative tools and qualitative tools. Both types of analysis have benefits and drawbacks; relying on a single method may not provide the most comprehensive analysis. Using several different tools helps minimize errors.

Quantitative Analysis

Quantitative analysis tools are based on mathematical models for measuring historical data. Several of these measures provide useful data for HR decisions. Some quantitative analyses commonly used to analyze HR and other business data are as follows:

Correlation   A *correlation* measures two variables to determine whether there is a relationship between them. For example, if the HR department posts a quarterly reminder of the referral bonus that is paid for new hires, a correlation analysis could be used to determine whether there is an increase in referrals in the weeks after the reminder.

Correlation Coefficient   The *correlation coefficient* describes the relationship between two variables and is stated as a number between −1.0 and +1.0.

For example, say the HR department wants to find out what factors contribute to absenteeism in the company. One of the factors they decide to analyze is length of time at the company, so one hypothesis they might use is "The absentee rate is higher with new employees."

To analyze this, they would collect two numbers for each employee: how many months employed and how many days absent. The numbers are then plotted on a graph for analysis.

If this hypothesis is correct, they would expect to see a *negative* correlation coefficient—that is, the shorter the length of time employed, the higher the absentee rate. This would be reflected by a negative number: for example, −.2. Figure 2.2 shows how this looks.

FIGURE 2.2   Negative correlation

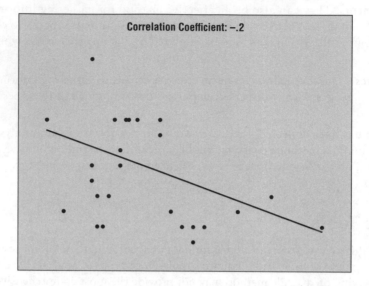

A *positive* correlation coefficient would tell HR that the opposite is true—that the absentee rate is actually higher when employees have longer tenure with the company. This would be reflected by a positive number, such as +.8. Figure 2.3 shows what this would look like.

FIGURE 2.3   Positive correlation

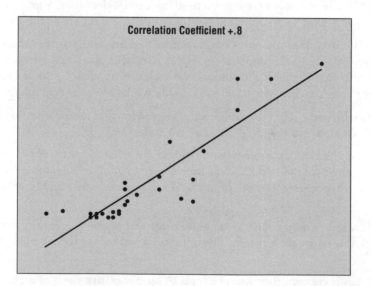

If there was no correlation at all—that is, if length of employment had nothing to do with absenteeism—the correlation coefficient would be 0.0, as shown in Figure 2.4.

FIGURE 2.4   No correlation

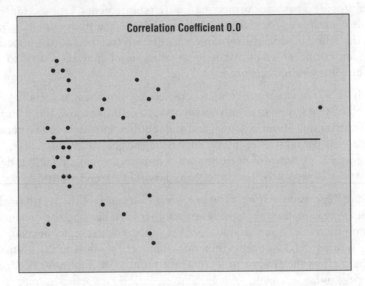

The steeper the trend line (the higher the absolute number), the greater the connection between the two variables. In the absentee example, the positive correlation (+.8) reflects a stronger connection between a longer amount of time with the company and more absences than the example of negative correlation (–.2).

Measures of Central Tendency   Central tendency is often referred to as the *average*. Several measures can be used in analyzing data:

Mean Average   The *mean average* is the sum of the values in a set of numbers, divided by the number of values in the set.

Mode   The *mode* is the number that occurs most frequently in a set of numbers.

Median   The *median* can be found by putting the numbers in a set in sequential order. The median is at the physical center, so half the numbers are below it and half are above it.

Moving Average   Sometimes called a *rolling average*, the *moving average* is used to calculate an average for a specific period: for example, to calculate the average number of new hires each month for the past 12 months. As the number for the most recent month is added, the oldest number is dropped.

Weighted Average   A *weighted average* is used to compensate for data that may be out of date; the more current data is multiplied by a predetermined number to better reflect the current situation.

Weighted Moving Average   The *weighted moving average* calculation assigns more weight to current data with the use of a predetermined number and drops the oldest data when new data is added.

Time-Series Forecasts   Several *time-series forecasts* exist that can be used to measure historic data and provide a basis for projecting future requirements. One example of how HR uses these tools is in the area of staffing levels, but they're useful in analyzing many other areas as well, including benefit utilization, compensation trends, and the effectiveness of a recruiting system. For purposes of discussion, staffing-level analysis is used to demonstrate how each of the following tools is used:

Trend Analysis   *Trend analysis* compares the changes in a single variable over time; over a period of years, they generally move upward or downward. For example, this tool can reveal information about seasonal staffing requirements, which are periods of time within a one-year period that regularly vary from the general trend. *Cycles*, periods of time during which a pattern of performance is shown (growing, peaking, declining, and plateauing at the lower level), also become apparent in a trend analysis.

Simple Linear Regression   *Simple linear regression* measures the relationship between one variable (for example, staffing) against another variable (such as production output) and allows prediction of one variable from the other. For example, measuring the number of units produced against the number of employees producing the units over a period of years would allow the analyst to forecast the number of employees needed to meet an increase in demand.

Multiple Linear Regression   *Multiple linear regression* measures the relationship between several variables to forecast another. An application of this model in workforce planning would be to determine whether there is a relationship between lower staffing levels, absenteeism, and production output.

Simulation Models   Simulation models allow several possible plans to be tested in abstract form. For example, an organization that wants to know the predicted results of different staffing alternatives can use a simulation model to determine which is the most cost effective.

Ratios   Ratios provide a benchmark based on the historic relationship of one variable to another. For example, the average HR staffing ratio is generally considered to be 1:100. As an organization's workforce increases or decreases, this ratio can provide an estimate of the number of staff required to provide services for the general employee population.

Qualitative Analysis

Qualitative analysis tools are subjective evaluations of general observations and information and include various types of judgmental forecasts. These tools can be as simple as an estimate made by a knowledgeable executive (for example, an experienced sales manager may be able to predict quite accurately by the end of the first month of a quarter whether the sales goal will be met). In other situations, the tools can be as involved as formalized brainstorming using a Delphi or nominal group technique.

The *Delphi technique* obtains input from a group of individuals who provide their expertise in succeeding rounds of questions about an issue or problem. After each round, the results are collated, prioritized, and returned to the participants in the form of additional questions for further analysis until a consensus is reached. An important factor of the Delphi technique is that the participants never meet but provide their input in written form. This technique has several benefits, including the fact that it's a viable alternative when participants are geographically separated and that it encourages a wide variety of ideas that might otherwise not be considered.

The *nominal group technique* is a structured meeting format designed to elicit participation from all members of the group in order to arrive at the best possible solution to the problem at hand. The process requires a facilitator and begins with a period of time for individuals to think about and write down all their ideas about the issue. After that, each participant presents one idea, which is recorded by the facilitator for later discussion. When all the ideas have been presented, the process of prioritizing and consensus building takes place until a resolution has been agreed on.

Choosing appropriate tools for data analysis provides the HR professional with a comprehensive view of what is needed to accomplish department and organization goals.

Change Management

The result of almost everything covered in the previous sections—developing a company's mission, vision and values statements, establishing ethical guidelines, contributing to corporate governance initiatives, engaging in meaningful enterprise risk management, managing through workforce technology functions—is *change*. Although, intellectually, many people understand the need for such changes, how they're personally affected has a direct impact on employee morale and productivity. There are two aspects to the change process: structural changes (covered in this chapter) and individual behavior (covered in Chapter 6). The discussion of methods and how they can be used to effect organizational change occurs later in the book, along with the discussion of the impact of changes on individuals in the organization. This section provides a brief look at the *structural* changes that significantly affect workforce populations today:

Reengineering   Reengineering involves looking at the entire organization to simplify or eliminate unnecessary processes with the goal of increasing customer satisfaction through improvements in efficiency.

Corporate Restructuring   Corporate restructuring looks at individual units in the organization to reduce or eliminate redundancy or bureaucratic processes in order to reduce costs and increase production.

Workforce Expansion   Workforce expansions create their own type of stress in an organization. When a large number of employees enter an organization within a short period of time, it can be difficult for them to assimilate into the existing culture and climate. The resulting clashes of operating styles (face-to-face vs. email communication, team orientation vs. individual contributors, or authoritarian vs. laissez-faire management style, for example) can create mistrust and reduce productivity.

Workforce Reduction   Workforce reductions, also known as *reductions in force* (RIFs), *downsizing*, or *rightsizing*, are used to decrease expenses by reducing the size of the workforce. One way RIFs are used is to lower expenses for short-term improvements in net profits in order to meet previously stated earnings targets for stock-market analysts.

Mergers and Acquisitions   Mergers and acquisitions (M&As) have similar results—the combining of two organizations into one—but they happen for different reasons and in somewhat different ways. A *merger* occurs when two or more organizations are combined into a single entity with the goal of leveraging the assets of both into a more successful entity. One well-known merger was that between Sirius Satellite Radio and XM Satellite Radio.

An *acquisition* occurs when one organization, generally a corporation, purchases or trades stock to gain controlling interest in another. Acquisitions can be hostile, when the management and board of directors of the company being acquired object to the takeover. Hostile takeovers are usually antagonistic, with the acquiring company purchasing shares on the open stock market. This type of acquisition can negatively affect employee morale as rumors about mass layoffs circulate among the staff of the target organization. For example, after a friendly bid by International Paper for Temple-Inland was rejected by Temple-Inland's board of directors, International Paper went directly to the shareholders and was successful with a $3.31 billion offer. This was 46 percent more than what Temple-Inland stock was trading for in the days leading up to the action.

In a friendly takeover, the management and board of the targeted company agree to terms offered by the acquiring organization, generally a cash purchase of stock or a predetermined number of shares in the acquiring company. An example of a friendly transaction was the $11 billion merger of US Airways into American Airlines in 2015. The two-year march toward full integration represented a strategic alliance designed to compete with larger industry rivals United and Delta.

HR professionals participate in the due-diligence process prior to a merger or an acquisition. There are many aspects to review in order to obtain a complete picture of the employment practices of the target company. The types of information to be collected as part of the due-diligence process include the following:

Documents

- Names of all employees and their locations
- Offer letters
- Employment contracts
- I-9 forms and visa documentation
- Benefit plans

Compensation

- Hourly wage rates by job
- Salary schedules
- Number of employees in each position

Policies and procedures

- Policy manual
- Employee handbook
- Supervisor/manager handbook

Equal opportunity compliance

- EEO-1 reports
- Affirmative Action Plans (if required)
- Government notices of compliance activity

Legal compliance

- COBRA notices and participants
- Active FMLA leaves
- WARN compliance
- OSHA compliance

Labor relations

- Collective bargaining agreements
- Ongoing negotiations
- Union activity
- Grievance history and outstanding grievances

Legal exposure

- Pending or resolved sexual-harassment claims
- Termination disputes
- Violations of state or federal laws
- Active workers' compensation claims

HR professionals also work to facilitate the successful integration of the two workforces in a merger or an acquisition. To begin with, an analysis of the workforce of the two organizations provides information on how to best use people in the new entity. This may result in transferring employees into different positions or reducing the workforce as redundant operations are identified and streamlined. Development of strategies to retain key employees is an important task, particularly during the initial period of uncertainty. In the longer term, one of the most difficult transitions is combining the two cultures into a cohesive environment that enhances productivity.

Divestitures   In a divestiture, a company asset such as a product line, a division, or another part of an organization is sold or somehow disposed of. This may occur as the result of a strategic decision to focus on core competencies or because the asset has greater value as a stand-alone operation than as part of the original organization. In some cases, there will be little change to day-to-day operations for employees because the organization remains intact with a new ownership structure.

Offshoring and Outsourcing Decisions and Management   Offshoring is the process of moving production or service processes to other countries to realize cost savings. For example, India has become a popular offshore site for U.S. service processes, such as customer support call centers.

Outsourcing contracts internal business services to outside organizations that specialize in the specific process, such as payroll processing, IT, or janitorial services.

Either decision generally results in a reduction in staff for employees who previously did the work that will now be done externally. In some cases, an outsource firm may hire those employees, who will continue to do the same work as members of the new organization.

No matter the cause, even employees who remain in the company after a change occurs are affected by it. A key contribution to be made by HR during change is to be sure the decision makers understand the difficulties that employees will face during and after the change and how those difficulties affect productivity. HR can put programs into place that mitigate the negative effects of the change as much as possible. It's simply not possible to overcommunicate in such situations. Some steps that can help reduce employee anxiety include the following:

- Keep employees in the loop about the actual situation.
- If there are actions that employees can take to remedy the situation, tell them what they can do.
- When talking to employees, be honest and truthful. Don't hide the facts.

Good or bad, the way companies handle change will be remembered long after employees have adjusted to the new way of doing business. The long-term impact of including employees in the change process through open and honest communication is to increase loyalty and productivity. If the organization has a habit of being brutal in its change processes, long-term productivity suffers, and it will be more difficult to attract and retain workers.

HR Metrics: Measuring Results

Measuring the efficacy of human resource activities is critical for all HR practitioners. The findings may influence decision-making, mitigate risk, and allow HR to make recommendations for organizational strategies that are sound. Best practice measures include the following.

Business Impact Measures

The business impact of HR plans created to support an organization's strategic plans and goals can be difficult to measure because it's hard to isolate the effect of the HR support from other factors. However, it's easier to measure whether HR achieved its specific goals; for example, if the marketing department staffing plan was to hire three marketing analysts and three were hired, HR met its target for that objective. The impact of HR initiatives designed to improve productivity, such as an engagement initiative, can be measured by using metrics such as revenue per employee or units produced per employee.

There are other ways to measure how HR is adding value, such as how well risk is being managed, measured by the presence or absence of employee complaints, injuries, or lawsuits. If functions such as benefit administration or payroll are outsourced, an analysis of employee satisfaction with service levels and cost savings realized from outsourcing versus performing the service in-house can be used to measure business impact.

Balanced Scorecard   Developed by Robert Kaplan and David Norton, the *balanced scorecard* is a management tool that ties the outcomes of each department together in one measurement system. When used properly, it improves communication between departments and measures the progress of operational outcomes that are in alignment with the strategic objectives developed through the planning process.

Kaplan and Norton found that because traditional business measurements focused only on financial results, other key elements that impacted business success weren't included in strategic management decisions. To address this shortcoming, the balanced scorecard tracks information in four key areas: financial results, customer results, key internal processes, and how people are hired and trained to achieve organization goals. The Balanced Scorecard Institute provides a complete discussion of the concept at www.balancedscorecard.org.

Return on Investment   One of the most commonly used business metrics is *return on investment (ROI)*. ROI is calculated by dividing the benefits realized as a result of a program by the total related direct and indirect costs.

Cost-Benefit Analysis   A *cost-benefit analysis (CBA)* compares all costs of a proposed program to the benefits that will be realized if it's implemented and forecasts the net impact on the bottom line. CBA can be used to evaluate the cost effectiveness of several alternatives and recommend a preferred course of action. The difference between CBA and ROI is that CBA includes soft costs in the calculation, whereas ROI generally includes only hard costs.

Tactical Accountability Measures

Meaningful measures of tactical accountability for strategic management include the following:

HR Expenses as a Percent of Operating Expenses   This metric is calculated by totaling all the direct and indirect HR costs and dividing them by the total operating expenses.

HR Expenses as a Percent of Total Revenue   This metric is calculated by totaling all the direct and indirect HR costs and dividing them by the total revenue.

Ratio of Total Employees to HR Staff   The total number of HR staff is divided by total employees in the organization to calculate this ratio.

HR Department Expenses per Employee   As the organization grows, this metric can help HR maintain costs in line with other expenses. Total direct and indirect HR department expenses are divided by the total number of employees to obtain the ratio.

Accession Rate   The accession rate measures the number of new employees against the total number of employees. This measurement is useful for determining the types of HR programs needed to manage and support the workforce. The accession rate is calculated by dividing the total number of new employees by the number of employees at the end of the previous measurement period.

Attrition Rate/Turnover Analysis   One of the most commonly used metrics is used to understand how many employees are separating from a company or department, either voluntarily or involuntarily. *Turnover analysis*, as it has been traditionally called, is calculated by dividing the average number of total employees for the measurement period by the number of employees who exited the organization. This measurement can be calculated in a variety of ways to meet specific organization needs. Some variations include calculating on a monthly or annual basis and calculating turnover for voluntary separations only or for different business units in the organization.

Quality of Hire   To calculate a quality-of-hire metric, HR must first develop criteria to identify what constitutes a quality hire. This information includes accurate job descriptions, assessment tools that accurately identify the best-qualified candidates, clear communication of expectations to new hires, and preestablished criteria to measure performance. The measurement is often based on performance ratings made by hiring managers after observing employees on the job.

Diversity in Hiring   Measuring the diversity of an employer's hiring practices can be done both internally and externally. Internally, HR measures the diversity of hires in each job group or category. For example, an almond producer may note through this metric that they tend to hire more women for the almond sorting line than men, or a hotel may find that they hire male janitors but female maids. Externally, HR may compare the diversity of their hires to the relevant geographic location. For example, a private university located in a highly ethnically diverse neighborhood could compare their hires to the diversity of their surroundings. If their hires do not reflect the demographic population, it could be an indication of lack of diversity in their recruiting sources.

Cost per Hire   Cost per hire is a common metric but is often calculated without including all the costs associated with a hire. For example, a meaningful cost-per-hire calculation includes costs for advertising; in-house recruiter time to review résumés and screen candidates, and/or recruiter fees; HR staff salary; salaries for hiring managers and other members of the interview team; assessment tests; preemployment inquiries; administrative costs; and any other costs involved in hiring a new employee. The metric is calculated by dividing the total costs by the number of hires for the measurement period.

Time to Hire   The time-to-hire metric is calculated from the date a job is posted to the date a job is accepted by the new employee.

Replacement Cost   Replacement cost per employee can be an eye-opener for managers and executives. In addition to the costs calculated for the cost-per-hire metric, this measurement includes costs for training, lost productivity, temporary replacements, overtime for employees who fill in while the position is vacant, and others. These costs can easily reach 300 percent of the annual salary for the position.

The data collected from these measures over a period of time can be examined to identify and compare internal practices to market data in similar industries or for similar activities. The results can indicate problems on the horizon and allow HR to be proactive in addressing those issues. Many organizations are utilizing visual dashboards to track and communicate HR metrics. A function of real-time reporting, they allow HR to measure progress toward key performance indicators that have significant impact on organizational issues. This serves both strategy implementation and course correction while also providing significant information to use at the evaluation stage of planning.

Building a Business Case

A business case is used to evaluate the possible consequences of taking (or not taking) a particular action. A business case is the method used by HR to achieve exam knowledge objective 05: determine the significance of data for recommending organizational strategies. A business case identifies what criteria will be used to determine success, proposes alternative ways to execute the action, and describes possible risks that could result from implementing or not implementing the proposal. An extended timeline demonstrates the impact of the program on cash flow, identifying where cost reductions or gains are to be expected. An important element is the description of the basis for quantifying benefits and costs so that those reviewing the proposal clearly understand the assumptions that led to the final recommendation or decision.

Summary

The role of HR in the 21st century is changing into one that is more strategic and involved with planning the future direction of the organization and driving the achievement of business results. As a result, it's crucial for HR professionals to have a working knowledge of other functional areas of the business in order to provide the operational and administrative support necessary to attract and retain qualified employees in each area.

PHR candidates use their knowledge to reinforce organizational values and ethics. HR professionals are responsible for modeling appropriate behaviors, and coaching employees and managers who fall short of these guidelines.

As change becomes increasingly prevalent in business, HR plays a role in advising management and counseling employees to reduce the stress that accompanies change and maintain productivity during the process. HR develops and uses their communication skills to form relationships, thus influencing organizational decision-making to serve positive outcomes and help avoid risk.

The role technology plays in business will continue to expand. HR is expected to lead the effort, advising management on best practices that improve employee engagement, increase organizational competitiveness, and protect both from risk. The rise of workforce analytics will continue to drive all human resource systems, so a competent HR team must be able to organize, analyze and report the data.

HR professionals are expected to act ethically and handle their organizational responsibilities with care and respect. Employees rely on HR practitioners to carry out their responsibilities in a professional manner, assuming a moral responsibility to preserve the integrity and personal nature of the employee information they handle. The organization relies on HR to protect its best interests by maintaining a high standard and adhering to a professional code of ethics.

Through active involvement in the development of legislation at the federal, state, and local levels, HR professionals can influence the course of proposed laws and regulations, thus providing a benefit to their employers, their employees, and the profession.

Exam Essentials

Understand different business functions.   HR professionals must understand the purpose of different business functions and how they interact with each other and with HR. Understanding the unique needs of production and operations, sales and marketing, finance, accounting, and information technology and how each contributes to the organization's success allows HR to be more effective in providing services to the organization.

Understand the importance of change management and HR's role in managing change. Change is a fact of life in organizations; reengineering, restructuring, and downsizing occur often as a result of strategic decisions and changes in the marketplace. HR can develop programs that provide a means for communication, both top-down and bottom-up, to ease the process and reduce stress in the work environment.

Understand HR's role in the organization.   The role of HR is evolving into one that provides strategic, administrative, and operational services for the organization. HR must understand the role of cross-functional stakeholders, and establish relationships to influence organizational decision-making.

Be able to describe the steps involved in the legislative process.   A bill can originate in the House of Representatives or in the Senate, where it's referred first to a committee for consideration and then, if it's reported out of committee, is ready for full floor consideration. After all debate is concluded, the bill is ready for final passage. It must pass both bodies in the same form before it can be presented to the president for signature. The president may sign the bill; veto it and return it to Congress; let it become law without signature; or at the end of a session, pocket-veto it.

Review Questions

You can find the answers in Appendix A.

1. HR participates in the legislative process by doing which of the following?
   A. Becoming as knowledgeable on a subject as they can
   B. Fundraising
   C. Picketing at state capitols
   D. Rallying support for a bill

2. Restructuring is used to do which of the following?
   A. Remove redundant operations.
   B. Assimilate employees into the organization.
   C. Simplify processes to increase customer satisfaction.
   D. Purchase stock to gain controlling interest in a competitor.

3. What is a statement that describes what an organization does that is different from others?
   A. Values statement
   B. Corporate goal
   C. Vision statement
   D. Mission statement

4. Which of the following options is one characteristic of an organization during the growth phase?
   A. Executive benefit packages are upgraded.
   B. New hires may have less experience.
   C. The compensation package is competitive.
   D. Employees work closely with founders.

5. Improvements in technology have had their greatest effect on which of the following?
   A. Employee morale
   B. Productivity
   C. Cost of living
   D. Management's span of control

6. Which of the following is a practical benefit for measuring diversity in hiring practices?
   A. The findings may allow HR to correct an issue before it is litigated.
   B. The findings may allow HR to save money on attorney fees.
   C. The findings will make HR practitioners better business partners.
   D. The findings will allow HR to comply with affirmative action laws.

7. Which of the following is an appropriate use for an HR audit?

    A. To determine which employees no longer have the skills needed by the organization

    B. To determine the employee productivity and turnover rates

    C. To determine whether the employee handbook is in compliance with current government regulations

    D. To determine the timeline for changes that are necessary in the HR department

8. The four *p*'s summarize the marketing function. Which of the following is not one of the *p*'s?

    A. Perception

    B. Price

    C. Placement

    D. Promotion

9. Which of the following is one of the elements of a SMART goal?

    A. Action-oriented

    B. Strength

    C. Technology

    D. Threat

10. What is a pocket veto?

    A. The president vetoes a bill from Congress. Congress holds a vote, but the bill does not pass.

    B. Congress submits a bill to the president and then adjourns. The president does not sign the bill within 10 days.

    C. The president vetoes a bill from Congress. Congress holds a vote but does not have a quorum.

    D. Congress submits a bill to the president, but the president does not sign the bill within 10 days.

11. Which of the following is *not* a method used by organizations to communicate expected behavior to employees?

    A. Written policies

    B. Executive behavior modeling

    C. Mentor programs

    D. Employee coaching

12. Which of the following risk-management tool or activity is *not* required by law?

    A. Employee handbooks

    B. Employer practice(s) prohibiting harassment

    C. The reporting of securities law violations

    D. EEO-1 reporting

13. An HR audit enables an employer to do which of the following?

    A. Evaluate the effectiveness of current HR practices in alignment with strategic goals.

    B. Identify exposure factors and the employer's potential risk due to compliance failures.

    C. Conduct a knowledge assessment of the current workforce.

    D. All of the above

14. What are corporate programs that focus on behaviors that minimize the depletion of time, money, and labor called?

    A. Viability programs

    B. Sustainability efforts

    C. Corporate governance

    D. Strategic planning

15. Ethics, offshoring, data security, and philanthropy are all examples of HR's role in which of the following functions?

    A. Strategic planning

    B. Workforce planning

    C. Technology development

    D. Corporate responsibility

16. A decision about outsourcing specialized labor would most likely be made at which stage of the organizational life cycle?

    A. Startup

    B. Growth

    C. Maturity

    D. Decline

17. What is the purpose of an HR budget?

    A. To determine how much cash is required to achieve a goal

    B. To hold departments accountable for outcomes

    C. To ensure that the outcomes match the strategic plan

    D. To evaluate the effectiveness of HR strategy

18. What element of an inventory-management system is defined by "purchasing smaller amounts of supplies more frequently"?

    A. Inventory allocation

    B. Just-in-time inventory

    C. Distributive inventory

    D. Blanket orders

19. Which of the following statements about whistle-blower protection is false?

    A. Whistle-blower protection is provided under Sarbanes-Oxley.

    B. Attorneys must report concerns of securities law violations to the CEO or CLO and are protected under whistle-blower law.

    C. An employee must be engaged in a protected activity such as reporting a violation to qualify for protection.

    D. The employee does not have to have suffered an unfavorable employment action to qualify for protection.

20. Salaries, payroll taxes, and benefits are all examples of which of the following HR activities?

    A. Conducting a business impact measure

    B. Creating an HR budget

    C. Creating a compensation strategy

    D. Analyzing the cost of recruiting

Chapter 3

PHR Exam: Talent Planning and Acquisition

The HRCI test specifications from the Talent Planning and Acquisition functional area covered in this chapter include PHR-level responsibilities and knowledge. Both have content focused on identifying, attracting, and employing talent while following all federal laws related to the hiring process.

Responsibilities:

✓ **01 Understand federal laws and organizational policies to adhere to legal and ethical requirements in hiring (for example: Title VII, nepotism, disparate impact, FLSA, independent contractors).**

✓ **02 Develop and implement sourcing methods and techniques (for example: employee referrals, diversity groups, social media).**

✓ **03 Execute the talent acquisition life cycle (for example: interviews, extending offers, background checks, negotiation).**

Knowledge:

✓ **12 Applicable federal laws and regulations related to talent planning and acquisition activities**

✓ **13 Planning concepts and terms (for example: succession planning, forecasting)**

✓ **14 Current market situation and talent pool availability**

✓ **15 Staffing alternatives (for example: outsourcing, temporary employment)**

✓ **16 Interviewing and selection techniques, concepts, and terms**

✓ **17 Applicant tracking systems and/or methods**

✓ **18** **Impact of total rewards on recruitment and retention**

✓ **19** **Candidate/employee testing processes and procedures**

✓ **20** **Verbal and written offers/contract techniques**

✓ **21** **New hire employee orientation processes and procedures**

✓ **22** **Internal workforce assessments (for example: skills testing, workforce demographics, analysis)**

✓ **23** **Transition techniques for corporate restructuring, mergers and acquisitions, due diligence processes, offshoring, and divestitures**

✓ **24** **Metrics to assess past and future staffing effectiveness (for example: cost per hire, selection ratios, adverse impact)**

In today's fast-paced business environment, HR professionals must be able to "turn on a dime," adjusting workforce plans and life-cycle employment activities to meet the changing needs of their organizations. Talent Planning and Acquisition is the functional area of the human resource body of knowledge (*HRBoK*™) that tests your knowledge of workforce planning and the associated employment activities of identifying, attracting, and employing talent all while following American labor laws. The talent planning process identifies skills and timelines for acquiring the employees needed to achieve organization goals; staffing is the process by which HR professionals work with line management to locate, hire/transfer, and integrate new employees into existing workgroups. Once employees are hired, activities include ensuring that talented individuals in the organization are identified, developed, and retained so they're available to move into positions of greater responsibility as organizational needs evolve. The function of talent planning and acquisition is completed once an employee has come on board with the organization (is "acquired"). This chapter reviews the responsibility and knowledge requirements for PHR-level candidates. Note that many of the functions of this area require practical knowledge of labor laws; you will find this information in Appendix C, "Federal Employment Legislation and Case Law."

Talent Planning

The goal of talent planning is to ensure that qualified employees are available when the organization needs them. An effective workforce planning process is based on the following:

- Workforce goals and objectives that forecast the organization's future workforce needs
- Job analysis and description that identifies the knowledge, skills, and abilities needed to meet future needs
- Identification of qualified employees beginning with the organization's current workforce demographics
- Translating the goals and objectives into tactical staffing plans to build the future workforce

The workforce plan resulting from this process provides the framework for targeting and prioritizing future staffing requirements, remaining flexible enough to allow HR to respond rapidly to changing business needs.

Workforce Goals and Objectives

During a company's strategic planning process, organization leaders make decisions about how to achieve business goals and objectives that provide a competitive advantage, improve the level of business performance, and add value for its stakeholders. In some cases, this requires the company to restructure some part of its business. A PHR-level candidate must be able to understand and apply transition techniques for the following business restructures:

Reengineering   The goal of reengineering is to realign operations in a way that adds value to customers. For workforce planning, this may mean eliminating jobs in some areas and adding jobs in others. Twenty-first century reengineering may also include a heavy dose of automation. For example, a McKinsey and Company report found that nursing assistants spend about two-thirds of their time collecting health information. By adopting data collection technology, this time may be reduced, allowing time for more patient interaction and care. (View the full potential of automating jobs at https://www.mckinsey.com/business-functions/digital-mckinsey/our-insights/where-machines-could-replace-humans-and-where-they-cant-yet.)

Corporate Restructuring   Corporate restructuring looks at individual units in the organization to reduce or eliminate redundancy or bureaucratic processes in order to reduce costs and increase production. For workforce planning, this means reducing the workforce or reassigning employees to new jobs.

Mergers and Acquisitions   In some cases, business leaders make a decision to acquire products and market share by purchasing other companies instead of building them internally. One result of a merger or an acquisition is reducing labor costs as economies of scale allow jobs to be combined or eliminated.

Divestitures   When the strategic plan includes a decision to divest an operating unit, this can mean eliminating jobs or transferring employees to a new operating entity. The effect on workforce planning can be twofold: reducing the workforce in the divesting organization and, if appropriate, performing due diligence to determine whether to transfer employees to the new entity.

Offshoring/Outsourcing   In most cases, *offshoring* or outsourcing decisions result in a workforce reduction or transfer of employees to other jobs. When employees are acquired by an outsource provider, they're terminated from the organization and hired by the new company.

Workforce Expansion   An organization may decide to expand its workforce in order to accomplish business objectives. For example, if the strategic plan calls for increasing sales by 15 percent, leaders may determine that achieving that goal requires increasing the salesforce.

Workforce Reduction   Whether necessitated by a restructuring, a merger, or an acquisition, or in response to a loss of market share, reducing labor costs is a painful result of some business decisions. There are many examples of workforce reductions in the business environment, including the job losses that occurred during the dot.com bust of 2000–2001 and the financial market meltdown beginning in 2008.

One thing is certain: HR professionals must be ready to respond rapidly to changes in business workforce requirements with a road map that produces employees who possess the talent needed by the business to achieve its goals. This road map is built on the jobs that need to be performed and the individuals who will perform those jobs.

Job Analysis and Description

Job analysis and job descriptions provide the foundation for much of what happens in the employment relationship. The job description compiles all the information collected during the job analysis into a document that is used for multiple purposes in the organization, beginning with the hiring process:

- Based on the job description, the recruiter screens applicants to ensure that their knowledge, skills, abilities, and other characteristics (KSAOs) are appropriate for the position.

- The applicants for the position use the job description to find out what they will be required to do if the position is offered to them.

- The job description is the basis for performance management and appraisal.

- The job description is the basis for determining the appropriate level of pay for the work that is done.

- The job description includes the essential job functions and provides a guideline for employees who request reasonable accommodation for disabilities.

Job descriptions are also used to determine competitive compensation, to classify employees properly for equal-opportunity and affirmative-action reports, and for many other aspects of employment. It's essential, therefore, that these processes produce full and complete information about the jobs in the organization.

Job Analysis

The purpose of job analysis is to define a job so that it can be understood in the context of accomplishing organizational goals and objectives. To do this, information that describes the work to be done must be collected. Information can be collected during the job analysis process in several ways:

- Interview the incumbent if available.

- Interview the supervisor or a group of co-workers.

- Complete a structured or an open-ended questionnaire.

- Complete a task inventory.

- Observe incumbents and make notes.

- Use work logs kept by incumbents.

The information gathered during the analysis is summarized in a job description that is used for the various purposes described previously.

Job Descriptions

Job descriptions are written documents that contain information about a job. The description includes the following information:

Identifying Information   The job description is identified with the title of the position, department, supervisor's title, Fair Labor Standards Act (FLSA) exemption status, salary range or grade, and the date it was created.

Supervisory Responsibilities   If the position has responsibility for supervising others, a description of those leadership responsibilities is listed in this section.

Position Summary   The summary provides a brief overview of the job and its primary purpose, usually two to five sentences.

Essential Functions   *Essential job functions* are the reason the job exists and must be performed by the incumbent. This information is required to comply with the Americans with Disabilities Act (ADA), discussed in Appendix C. Each function should include a description of the level of complexity and the frequency of tasks. As appropriate, the functions describe relationships that the incumbent will have, including supervisory, with co-workers in the work group, with co-workers in other departments of the company, and any external relationships with vendors or customers, and the level of interaction that will take place in these relationships.

Nonessential Functions   *Nonessential job functions* are those that could be performed as part of another job in the organization. For ADA purposes, these functions could be moved into other jobs as a reasonable accommodation for a disabled employee who is fully qualified to perform the essential job functions.

Equipment Operated   This section lists tools or equipment that will be used and the frequency of use. This includes use of the computer, telephone, and production equipment; any hazardous equipment or tools that will be used; and protective gear or uniforms that will be required.

Job Specifications   Job specifications state the minimum qualifications needed for successful performance. Depending on the job, some or all of the following may be required specifications:

Education, Licenses, or Certificates Required   Minimum required qualifications are described in this section. The requirements must be related to the essential job functions to comply with the ADA.

Communication Skills Required   A description of the level of communication skills necessary to do the job is included in this section. Will the position be writing reports, making presentations internally or externally, or communicating orally?

Experience Required   The minimum level of experience required to successfully perform the position is identified.

Skills   Any skills necessary for successful job performance are included in this section.

Physical Requirements   Any physical requirements must be described to comply with the ADA. The physical requirements must be related to the essential job functions.

Mental Requirements   For ADA purposes, describe the level of mental acuity required to perform essential job functions.

Work Environment   The work environment is described, whether it's in an office setting or includes any hazardous equipment or locations that will impact the employee. If stairs or ladders must be used or the job will require work in confined spaces, this must be included as well.

Approvals   The job description should be signed by the manager to verify its accuracy.

During the job analysis process, it's important to keep in mind that the analysis focuses on the *job*, not the *person*. Particularly when a high-performing employee has been in a job for any length of time, it can be difficult to separate what the employee brings to the job from the job's main purpose.

The ability to update the job competencies, essential functions, and job specifications should be a post-analysis function that is properly planned for and maintained. For example, some companies update the competencies, functions, and specifications each time the position becomes open or on an annual basis sorted by department. These types of processes account for changes or updates to job duties and outputs without having to complete an organization-wide job analysis all at once, which can be time-consuming and disruptive to day-to-day operations.

Qualified Employees

Organizations have three options for locating the talent they need to achieve business goals: internal transfers or promotions, external hires, and alternative staffing methods. HR professionals evaluate the options by deciding which option is best in a given situation. Are there sufficient skills within the organization that can be redirected to the new requirements through transfers or promotions? Is it best to bring in full-time employees? Will some other staffing alternative provide the best solution? Let's take a brief look at these alternatives and discuss the strategic implications of each source.

Internal Talent

The first place to look for qualified employees to fill future needs is among those who already work for the organization. There are a number of advantages to filling jobs internally or "promoting from within." Management has an opportunity to evaluate candidates and determine their suitability for advancement over an extended period of time as they perform current duties, and the possibility of future promotion can encourage employees to maintain a high level of performance. Investing in employees through learning and development and then providing advancement opportunities for them communicates to employees that the organization values and rewards their contributions. When promotion from within is an organization policy, most external hiring is done at the entry level; this allows employees to become acclimated to the organization culture and operating procedures early in their careers, leading to greater success when they move into positions with greater responsibility.

Of course, some disadvantages are associated with relying solely on promotion from within to fill positions of increasing responsibility:

- There is the danger that employees with little experience outside the organization will have a myopic view of the industry.

- Although the morale of those promoted will be high, employees who have been passed over or lost out on promotions may have lower morale and be less motivated in performing their jobs.

- When several people are being groomed for promotion, the competition can lead to a breakdown in teamwork and jockeying for political position.

- If the organization lacks diversity in its workforce, overreliance on promoting from within can perpetuate the imbalance.

- Reduced recruiting costs will be offset by an increase in training costs to prepare employees for positions with increased technical responsibilities or for supervisory or management positions.

External Talent

At some point, organizations need to look outside for new employees. Even if the organization has a policy or practice of promotion from within, entry-level positions must be filled as employees are promoted or transferred. There are, of course, advantages to bringing new people into the organization:

- Experienced professionals bring new ideas with them and can revitalize operations.

- It's usually easier and more cost-effective to hire individuals with highly specialized skills than it is to develop them within the organization.

- If there is an urgent need for someone with particular skills, it's usually faster to hire those skills than to provide on-the-job training.

- Looking outside the organization to fill positions provides opportunities to increase the diversity of the workforce.

Looking outside the organization also has several disadvantages:

- Current employees who have been passed over for promotion will very likely have lower morale.

- It's always difficult to know how someone from outside the organization will fit into an existing team.

- The new hire is an unknown. Until the person begins doing the job, it's very difficult to know what his or her performance level will be.

Alternative Staffing Methods

To expand the pool of available candidates with the desired skills, consider alternative staffing methods. A wide range of alternatives provides varying levels of flexibility to the organization. Particularly when staffing needs require specialized skills or when the labor market is tight, these methods can provide access to highly qualified candidates who might otherwise be unavailable to the organization:

Telecommuting   Due to advances in technology, *telecommuting*, which allows employees to work at home and connect to the office electronically, has become a viable solution for individuals who don't want to commute or who have other reasons to work at home. This option continues to grow in popularity as the United States reduces unemployment rates and the competition for talent heats up. For example, Amazon announced in 2017 they would be hiring more than 5,000 part-time, work-from-home employees. These jobs will also include benefits such as tuition reimbursement and health insurance. Amazon's strategy will allow them to find and retain talent while providing mobile work options for military spouses or college students, an often underemployed labor pool.

Job Sharing   *Job sharing* is an alternative that allows two people with complementary skills to share the duties and responsibilities of a full-time position.

Part-Time Employees   *Part-time employees* are those who work less than a regular workweek. This staffing strategy can be a cost-effective solution for organizations needing particular skills on an ongoing but not full-time basis.

Internships   *Internship programs* are usually designed to give students opportunities to gain experience in their chosen fields prior to graduation. Successful programs provide meaningful work and learning experiences for the students, including opportunities to meet with senior executives. The student gains a valuable learning experience, and the organization benefits by developing low-cost access to employees and the chance to observe the intern's performance prior to making an offer for full-time employment. In 2018 the Department of Labor (DOL) made changes to the Fair Labor Standards Act internship program requirements. All seven factors in the test of whether an employee is an intern or student are built on the premise that the "primary beneficiary" is the intern—not the employer.

Temporary Workers   The temporary worker category covers a wide range of flexible staffing options:

Traditional   In a traditional arrangement, an individual is employed by an agency that screens and tests candidates prior to sending them to a work site for variable periods of time, from short, one-day assignments to assignments lasting for long periods of time. Under certain circumstances, these assignments can be converted to a regular, open position. These arrangements allow organizations to observe and evaluate a worker's performance prior to making an offer of full-time employment.

On-Call Workers   *On-call workers* are employed by the organization, available on short notice, and called to work only when they're needed.

Payrolling   *Payrolling* allows the organization to refer to an agency those individuals they want to hire. The agency hires the individuals to work for the organization and provides payroll and tax services for either a fixed fee or a percentage of the salary, which is generally less than a traditional temp agency fee.

Seasonal Workers   *Seasonal workers* are hired only at times of the year when the workload increases, such as the Christmas shopping season or when it's time to harvest agricultural products.

Contract Workers   *Contract workers* provide another solution for acquiring talent. There are two types of contract workers:

Independent Contractors   *Independent contractors* are self-employed individuals who work on a project or fee basis with multiple customers or clients. Both federal and state governments have guidelines to determine the difference between an independent contractor and an employee. Misclassifying an employee as an independent contractor can result in substantial penalties to the employer, so it's important to ensure that the guidelines are followed.

Contingent Workforce   A *contingent workforce* is made up of nontraditional workers, including part-time and seasonal as well as temporary or leased employees. Employment agencies or brokers will typically act as the employer of record on behalf of many contract workers, providing payroll, mandated benefits, and other services to this classification of workers.

Professional Employer Organization   A *professional employer organization* (PEO) operates as the organization's HR department. The PEO becomes the employer of record and then leases the employees back to the organization. PEOs provide full-service HR, payroll, and benefit services and can provide a cost-effective solution that enables smaller companies to offer benefits comparable to those offered by much larger organizations.

Outsourcing   *Outsourcing* moves an entire function out of the organization to be handled by a company specializing in the function. For example, *human resource outsourcers* (HROs) may be used for one or more HR functions, such as benefits administration or recruiting. On a larger scale, NASA announced that Space X—an Elon Musk company that was the first privately held entity to launch an unmanned spacecraft—was awarded the contract to build a rocket ship to fly astronauts to and from the space station. This solution can be beneficial by allowing the organization to focus on its basic business operations and potentially reduce costs.

 Real World Scenario

Employee or Independent Contractor?

The Internal Revenue Service (IRS) has established guidelines for determining whether an individual can be considered an independent contractor or an employee. Recently, the IRS clarified the factors it uses to determine the appropriate status for an individual. These standards fall into three categories:

- *Behavioral controls* establish whether the organization has the right to direct and control tasks completed by the worker, including the following:

  - Instructions given by the organization to the worker as to when and where the work is done, the tools or equipment used, whether the worker must perform the task or may hire others to assist, the order or sequence of tasks, and who must perform specific tasks

  - Organizations train employees to perform services in a particular manner, whereas independent contractors determine their own methods.

- *Financial controls* establish whether the organization controls the business aspects of the individual, including the following:

  - The extent to which business expenses are *not* reimbursed

  - The extent of investment made by the worker in the business

  - The extent to which the worker makes services available to the relevant market versus a single business

  - How the worker is paid

  - The extent to which the worker can realize a profit or loss

- The *type of relationship that exists between the parties* is demonstrated by the following:

  - The existence of a written contract

  - The existence of benefits such as insurance, a pension, and vacation and sick pay

  - The permanency of the relationship—that is, an indefinite period of time (employee) or a specific project or period of time (contractor)

  - The extent to which the services performed are a key aspect of the regular business of the organization

Additional information about the IRS guidelines is available at https://www.irs.gov/pub/irs-pdf/p15a.pdf.

Many states have established their own rules for determining the appropriate status for workers. As with all employment laws and regulations, the highest standard is the one with which employers must comply, so be sure to familiarize yourself with the standards for the state(s) in which you practice.

Translating Organization Goals into Staffing Plans

Translating strategic workforce goals and objectives into a tactical action plan is accomplished with the use of a *staffing needs analysis*. This tool is used to determine the numbers and types of jobs forecasted in the organization's strategic plan. Figure 3.1 depicts a typical staffing needs assessment.

FIGURE 3.1   Staffing needs analysis

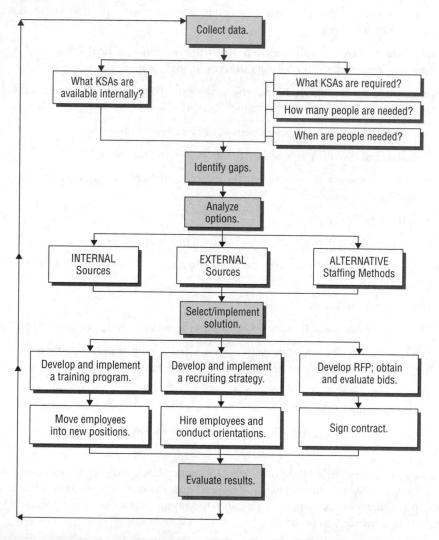

The strategic plan identifies two key pieces of information for HR: the work that needs to be done and how many people are needed to do it. That information forms the objective for the staffing needs analysis and identifies the information to be collected:

Collect data.   Talent planning provides an opportunity for HR professionals to build key relationships within their organizations, demonstrating the value they can add to the business. Business-unit managers are the ones, of course, who establish the goals and objectives for their individual work groups. During this planning phase, HR can assist these managers to identify the KSAOs that will be needed to execute those objectives as well as the number and timing of people required. At this time, HR also collects information about current employees who may be ready to assume new tasks and responsibilities and any training needed to prepare them for new roles. Organizations fortunate enough to have a robust human resource information system (HRIS) or workforce analytic tools are better positioned to collect the date for further analysis.

Identify gaps.   Building on the data collected from individual business-unit managers, HR develops a comprehensive list of the KSAOs required to meet future needs for the organization. Factored into this list should be contingencies for retirements or unexpected resignations of current employees based on prior history of turnover, transfers, and promotions. Comparing the required KSAOs with the current capabilities of the workforce identifies the gaps that will need to be filled and provides the data needed to analyze the best way to fill those needs, whether internally, externally, or by using alternative staffing methods.

Analyze options.   Once the list of numbers, types, and timing of future openings is available, HR identifies options for filling the positions, whether from internal transfers or promotions, external hires, or the use of alternative staffing methods.

Select/implement solutions.   Conducting a cost–benefit analysis of the options identified in the previous step provides a means for comparison between the available options.

Evaluate results.   After the solution has been implemented, an evaluation of its success is conducted to ensure that it meets the needs of the organization.

Labor Market Analysis

Conditions in the labor market affect the ability of an organization to hire the qualified individuals it needs. A labor market analysis looks at various economic indicators and other factors that impact the availability of those individuals:

Economic Indicators   A variety of economic measures are used in labor market analysis. The Bureau of Labor Statistics (BLS) collects data from employers throughout the United States and makes this information available on its website. Some of the measures useful in analyzing the labor market include the unemployment rate, occupational outlook, demographics, and wages by area and occupation. The BLS's Job Openings and Labor Turnover Survey (JOLTS) is published to produce data on job openings, hires, and separations.

Industry Activity   Another important factor to consider in a labor market analysis is the industry situation. Are new competitors entering the market? Is an existing competitor ramping up to produce a new product? Is a competitor losing market share and laying off employees? Activity within an industry affects an organization's ability to obtain qualified individuals to fill job openings. With the rise of e-commerce, many companies are having to rethink their strategies. For example, Walmart now offers free grocery pick-up for customers who place their orders online. Walmart has a competitive advantage over Amazon in that Walmart has a store within 15 miles of 90 percent of Americans, something Amazon does not. From a talent planning perspective, Walmart will have to consider having employees bring the groceries out to the customer, or even begin to hire delivery drivers to offer delivery services if Amazon continues to gain market share.

Labor Market Categories   Depending on specific job requirements, the labor market most often falls into one of three broad categories:

Geographic   This labor market can be local, regional, national, or international and contains individuals with a wide variety of technical and professional skills and levels of education. Selection of the geographic labor market depends on the availability of candidates with the necessary skills for the position. For example, the pool of candidates for an entry-level customer service representative opening could be quite large in the local labor market, whereas obtaining a sufficient pool of candidates to fill an open CEO position could require looking at the national or international labor market.

Technical/Professional Skills   This labor market contains individuals with expertise in a specific skill or discipline, such as accounting or information technology. These skills are often transferable between industries and can expand the available pool of candidates for openings.

Education   This labor market includes individuals with similar levels of education. In some professions, such as teaching, medicine, or science, an advanced degree may be required to fill a position.

A useful labor market analysis for a particular organization includes data that is relevant to the needs of the organization and the types of employees and skills it's seeking to hire.

Staffing Programs

The workforce plan and staffing needs analysis have identified the jobs to be filled, when they're needed, where they're located, and the KSAOs and competencies needed for successful performance. The job descriptions and specifications for successfully recruiting qualified candidates are in place. A review of internal demographics indicates if past recruiting efforts have resulted in a diverse workforce or whether it's necessary to explore alternative ways to promote diversity in the organization. Armed with this information, the process of finding qualified candidates for open positions can begin. The question now becomes where to find the appropriate people to fill the gaps.

Sourcing and Recruiting Candidates

The sourcing and recruiting of qualified candidates to fill open positions is critical to the success of any organization. Sourcing and recruiting functions may be combined into one position or, in large organizations or during periods of intense hiring, may be split. *Sourcing* provides names and contact information for potential candidates in the active and passive markets. Active job seekers are seeking work and often attracted through traditional advertising methods (see the section "External Recruiting" later in this chapter).

Passive candidates are those who aren't currently looking for work, so locating them requires additional research, such as identifying professional associations or organizations that are likely to employ individuals with similar skills. *Recruiting* is the process of creating interest about open positions in an organization and seeking candidates who possess the necessary qualifications to successfully fill them.

Recruiting Strategies

An effective recruiting strategy is ongoing. Even during times when few positions are open, continuing to communicate with potential candidates, educational institutions, search firms, and other sources can help shorten the time needed to fill positions when they do occur and result in better service to internal customers.

Employer Brands

Defining the employer's brand identity sets the stage for many aspects of the recruiting process. Each organization has a brand identity in the marketplace, whether or not it has been consciously developed. The reputation established with employees, current and former, along with the way the organization presents itself in the general marketplace, contribute to the brand. Because the information is out there, HR can take a leading role in defining the brand so that it's an accurate reflection of where the company wants to be and can be used in the recruiting process.

Simply developing a catchy PR campaign isn't enough to make an effective employer brand. For a brand to be useful in attracting high-quality employees to the organization, it must first match the reality of working in the organization and describe what is unique about it. When that happens, every employee becomes an ambassador, creating interest among friends, neighbors, former colleagues, or others in working for the organization.

Building an employer brand begins with identifying unique elements of the organization culture. This may include answering the following questions:

- What values are important to the company?
- How are employees treated?
- Is the company on the leading edge in its industry?
- Is risk-taking encouraged or frowned upon?
- Are employees involved in the decision-making process?
- Is the performance-management process perceived to be fair? Do employees receive regular feedback?
- How does the company respond to economic downturns?

Some of the considerations become part of the brand. An accurate brand message gives candidates an idea of what it would be like to work in the organization and positively influences retention. If the employer has differentiated its organization as an employer of choice with a clearly defined message about the benefits of working there, then attracting the quality of candidates desired by the organization becomes less difficult. It's critical, however, that the "official" brand message is an accurate reflection of the organization.

To ensure that this is the case, an employee survey can be conducted to find out whether current employees perceive the organization the way the brand portrays it. If there is a discrepancy, the organization can choose whether to adjust the brand message or make operational changes that address the differences between employee perceptions and the branding message.

In a tight labor market, many employers are using their brand to drive HR practices. Salesforce, for example, is known for their innovation and customer service. They have applied these characteristics to their staffing programs by treating the recruiting process as a customer service function. Résumés are submitted online, with a real-time, near-immediate response of "yes, we will proceed" or "no, not qualified." Other companies are similarly looking to embed their brand where it matters, actively seeking out employee ratings and reviews on Internet job boards.

An effective employer brand that accurately portrays the organization's culture benefits the organization in any economic climate. During times of economic growth when high-quality employees are in great demand, the brand both attracts and retains them. In an economic downturn, the brand becomes a vehicle for fostering communication and improving morale.

Total Reward Packages

An organization's total rewards philosophy affects its ability to attract qualified candidates. This strategy is a key element in the organization's recruiting strategy because it directly affects how well it will be able to attract and retain employees with the KSAOs it needs. In general terms, organizations interested in acquiring the "best and brightest" candidates, or candidates with unique and highly desirable skills, employ a philosophy of leading the market, paying a premium to attract candidates. This philosophy, of course, may require the financial ability to pay at a premium. Organizations that may not be financially able to pay a premium but want to hire qualified employees compete with a philosophy of meeting the market, meaning they pay the average market rate. Some organizations decide to lag the market by paying below the market rate. This may be a financial necessity (such as an early-stage company or a nonprofit organization) or a conscious decision on the part of management if, for example, jobs require little or no skill or training and employees are easily replaced.

Recruiting Methods

During the process of creating job competencies, descriptions, and specifications, HR works with line managers to ensure that the job requirements are accurately presented. In the recruiting process, HR works with line managers to create a candidate profile so that applicants who go through the selection process fit the requirements of the position. In developing this profile, line managers often want to describe an "ideal candidate" who possibly even exceeds the requirements of the position. It's up to HR to work with line managers in developing candidate profiles that are realistic, given the working conditions and salary range offered for the position. At the same time, it's also effective to work with line managers to develop alternatives to the candidate profile, possibly substituting years of experience for education requirements or lowering experience requirements if the experience is in the same industry. This expands the pool of available candidates and increases the chances of success in the recruiting process.

With the job description and candidate profile in hand, HR is able to determine the best sources for qualified candidates. Choosing appropriate sources for candidates depends on how available the specific KSAOs are in various labor markets, along with workforce diversity issues that need to be addressed in the hiring process. In general terms, the labor market used to recruit candidates depends in large part on the scarcity of the KSAOs needed—the scarcer the KSAOs, the larger the labor market to reach and the greater the recruiting budget.

Internal Recruiting

Once the organization has decided to fill positions internally, there are several methods for communicating information about the openings to employees. A *skills inventory* is an HR management tool used to collect and store a wealth of information that would otherwise be obtained only after many hours of research by HR staff. An effective skills inventory collects information on special skills or knowledge, performance appraisals, fluency in foreign languages, educational qualifications, previous experience in or outside of the company, credentials or licenses that may be required, and any continuing education employees have obtained through training classes, seminars, or educational institutions. When collecting this information is one of the functions of an automated HRIS system, obtaining a report with detailed information about the internal talent pool can be accomplished in minutes. When replacement and succession plans are in place, conversations with potential candidates can take place over a period of time, often during performance reviews and goal-setting sessions.

Once possible internal candidates for openings are identified using the skills inventory, replacement chart, or succession plan (both described shortly), two methods are used to publicize current openings throughout an organization:

Job Posting   A *job posting* is an internal job announcement that provides basic information about the opening, including the title; a brief description of the competencies, duties, responsibilities, and specifications; the salary range; and the application procedure.

Job Bidding   *Job bidding* provides a means by which interested employees express interest in a position before it's available. This gives the supervisor and HR department an opportunity to review the job qualifications with the employee, provide training opportunities, let the employee gain additional experience if needed to meet the position requirements, and add the employee's name to the replacement or succession plan as appropriate.

Succession Planning

A well-thought-out *succession plan* identifies individuals in the organization who have the talent and ability to move into management and executive positions in one to five years. Once these individuals are identified, development plans are created to ensure that they're mentored and have opportunities to obtain education, training, and experience in areas that will enhance their ability to move into senior positions when the organization needs them.

Organizations might also choose to develop, implement, and use a *replacement chart*. This tool is useful at all organization levels and helps HR and line managers identify staffing needs by categorizing current employees in one of four categories:

Ready for Promotion   Employees in this category demonstrate the KSAOs to assume additional responsibilities and are ready to move forward in the organization.

Develop for Future Promotion   This group includes employees who are proficient in their current positions and, with additional training opportunities and experience, will be ready to move forward in the organization.

Satisfactory in Current Position   These employees are proficient in their current positions but don't demonstrate the KSAOs or interest to assume greater responsibility in the organization.

Replace   Employees are placed in this category for a variety of reasons, such as transfer or promotion, impending retirement, short-term disability, or unsatisfactory performance.

External Recruiting

Once it has been decided that the appropriate method for filling positions is to hire from outside, a number of factors must be considered. Particularly when the skills needed by the organization are in short supply in the labor market, the organization must find ways to effectively publicize its openings to appropriate candidates.

A variety of recruiting methods can be considered for finding new employees. The appropriate method depends on the type of employee needed by the organization in a particular situation. This means that a number of methods may be used in a single organization at any given time:

Media Sources   Until the advent of Internet job boards, the most prevalent means for recruiting was newspaper advertising; for some jobs it's still the preferred method. Advertising jobs on the radio is used much less often than newspaper ads, but it can be effective if a company is trying to fill a large number of positions in a short period of time or for a targeted audience such as individuals with bilingual skills. Television advertising is rarely used to advertise individual positions; when used, it's most often by agencies that accomplish a dual purpose with the ads—attracting candidates and soliciting clients.

Internet Job Boards and Community Sites   Advertising open positions on Internet job boards such as ZipRecruiter or Dice.com has become prevalent in recent years, particularly for positions in high-technology companies. Its popularity as a recruiting source is growing because it's often more cost-effective than traditional media advertising. A downside for employers using this method is that some job seekers are indiscriminate when responding to posted jobs, which results in a large number of résumés from unqualified applicants that must be sorted through to find appropriate candidates.

Mobile Devices   In 2017, the popular Internet job board CareerBuilder found that close to half of all candidate traffic and job applications come from a mobile device. Yet many employers do not have their career pages mobilized. These numbers highlight the need for HR to take the lead in ensuring that applicants can find open jobs and easily apply online.

To view additional insights related to the candidate experience, visit https://resources
.careerbuilder.com/recruiting-solutions/candidates-searching-jobs-career-site.

Social Media Recruitment   Social media is quickly becoming a cost-effective way to
recruit for many staff positions. A 2017 Society for Human Resource Management
(SHRM) research spotlight reported that more than 80 percent of the companies polled
were using social media sites to recruit. You can view this and other results at
https://www.shrm.org/hr-today/trends-and-forecasting/research-and-surveys/
pages/social-media-recruiting-screening-2015.aspx.

Other studies have reported that organizations that posted a short video with the job information had a 34 percent higher application rate than those who posted jobs without video.
These behaviors indicate that the current and future workforce continues to be online and
mobile, marking a need for HR to respond. One example of a type of corporate response is
the use of an applicant-tracking system. This outsourced activity involves hiring a social-
media recruiting service that tracks how many times an employee refers a job through his
or her personal network. The originating employee and the final referring "friend" both
share a referral bonus.

Other examples of social-media recruiting and selection activity include the use of the
following:

- School alumni sites
- Personal networks used to mine passive and active job seekers, such as LinkedIn,
  Facebook, and Twitter
- Corporate social-media campaigns
- Search engine optimization (SEO) ranking, brand management, and career sections on
  web pages
- Mobile technology
- Job alerts and mobile-friendly web pages
- Videos
- Job postings with video
- Virtual interviewing
- Skype and GoToMeeting

Company Websites   Most companies with a web presence have a "career" or "opportunities" page on their websites where they post current openings. When combined with
recruiting software that requires applicants to enter their own information into the recruiting database, this recruiting method can greatly reduce the time spent wading through
résumés from applicants who don't qualify for positions.

Colleges and Universities   Colleges and universities are a good source for entry-level
hires in areas such as accounting, engineering, and human resources. An effective college
recruiting program capitalizes on school ties by sending alumni to the campus as recruiters.

Recruiters are carefully chosen for their enthusiasm about the students as well as for the company. Key factors for recruiting success are delivering informative presentations about the organization and being honest about the job opportunities currently available in the organization. College recruiting has become a reliable source for locating minority applicants in recent years.

Job Fairs   Job fairs are events designed to bring employers and job seekers together in a single location. This format gives employers a chance to meet many potential job applicants in a short period of time. Including line managers and other employees with HR reps in the booth gives job seekers an opportunity to talk directly to hiring managers and find out about the organization without going through a formal interview process.

Alumni Employees   Building and maintaining professional relationships with former employees who left in good standing and on good terms can be a cost-effective, worthwhile source for re-recruiting. Particularly if they enjoyed their experience in the organization, they may be enticed to return if an appropriate opportunity presents itself, and they can be good sources for referrals.

Previous Applicants   Often during the recruiting process, a recruiter may remember a candidate who wasn't the best fit for one position but left an impression as someone who would be good elsewhere in the organization. Maintaining professional contact with such individuals can pay off when an appropriate position becomes available.

Employee Referrals   Current employees are a great resource for potential candidates. Recommendations from this source can result in long-term hires, because employees will remain longer with a company where they have established a social network. Moreover, a referral program that provides nominal cash awards after the new hire has remained with the company for a specific period of time (normally 90 to 180 days) encourages such referrals and keeps cost per hire under control.

Vendors and Suppliers   Individuals who provide goods or services to the company are often aware of potential candidates for openings. Particularly when there has been a long-term relationship, the vendor is aware of the organization's culture and needs and may prove to be a good source for applicants.

Labor Unions   In union environments, the union hiring hall can be a good source for qualified employees.

Professional Associations   Relationships developed in connection with attendance at professional association functions or conferences often provide leads for qualified applicants. In addition, many associations provide job-posting opportunities on websites or sell job advertisements in their publications.

Employment Agencies   Each state has an agency dedicated to providing services to job seekers, including job counseling and training opportunities. There is no charge for employers to list job openings with the agency, which then screens, tests, and refers appropriate candidates. Contingent employment agencies generally focus on jobs in a specific profession or job category, such as accounting professionals or administrative employees. Fees, paid by the employer only when a candidate is hired, are usually based on a percentage of the first year's salary and vary widely with different agencies. The fee is often negotiable. Retained employment agencies are often referred to as *headhunting firms* or *executive search firms*. When these agencies are engaged by an organization, a fee for recruiting services is paid whether or not any of the candidates are hired. A *retained search firm* is generally used for executive-level positions; these firms specialize in sourcing candidates from the passive labor market.

Walk-in Candidates   Candidates may come into the business in person to fill out applications and apply for jobs.

Where you search for candidates depends on your analysis of the availability of the specific KSAOs in the various labor markets. Where you look for candidates also affects the cost of the recruiting effort as well as how much you must pay to attract the right candidate.

Uniform Guidelines on Employee Selection Procedures

The Uniform Guidelines on Employee Selection Procedures (UGESP) were jointly developed by the EEOC, the Civil Service Commission (CSC), the OFCCP, and the DOJ to assist employers in complying with requirements of Title VII, EO 11246 (as amended), and other federal EEO legislation. Specifically exempted from the UGESP are requirements under the ADEA and the Rehabilitation Act. The UGESP states that any selection tool that has an adverse impact against a protected class is discriminatory unless the employer can show that the tool is both job-related and a valid predictor of success in the position. The UGESP directs that if employers have access to more than one selection tool, the tool that has the least adverse impact is the one to be used. Records are to be kept by sex, race, and ethnic group, using categories consistent with the EEO-1 report (Hispanic, White, Black or African-American, native Hawaiian or other Pacific Islander, Asian, American Indian or Alaska native, and two or more races) and EEO reporting purposes.

One report required by the UGESP is a determination of whether selection procedures have an adverse impact on one or more protected groups. An *adverse impact* occurs when the selection rate for a protected class is less than 4/5ths, or 80 percent, of the selection rate for the group with the highest selection rate. This is often referred to as the 4/5ths rule or the 80 percent rule. Table 3.1 illustrates an adverse-impact calculation.

TABLE 3.1   Calculating adverse impact

Group	Applicants	Hired	Selection rate	4/5 of highest rate
Males	255	48	19%	15%
Females	395	52	13%	
Total	650	100		

In this example, the company advertised 100 openings. Applications were received from 255 males and 395 females for the position. Adverse impact is calculated as follows:

1. For each group, divide the number of applicants hired by the total number of applicants:

   Males: 48 ÷ 255 = 19%

   Females: 52 ÷ 395 = 13%

2. Multiply the highest selection rate by 80%:

   Males: 19% × 80% = 15%

3. Compare the selection for the other group(s) to determine whether adverse impact has occurred:

   Females: 13%

   Males: 15%

In this example, female applicants were adversely impacted by the selection process.

Applicant Tracking

The UGESP require employers to keep records of individuals who apply for open positions based on their sex and race/ethnicity as previously described for the EEO-1 report. In 1974, the UGESP defined an applicant as "a person who has indicated an interest in being considered for hiring, promotion, or other employment opportunities. This interest might be expressed by completing an application form or might be expressed orally, depending on the employer's practice."

As the Internet grew into an increasingly important factor in the recruitment and selection of new employees, it became clear that an additional definition was needed. In October 2005, the UGESP were amended to include the definition of an Internet applicant as meeting these criteria:

- The employer has acted to fill a particular position.
- The individual has followed the employer's standard procedures for submitting applications.
- The individual has indicated an interest in the particular position.

Candidate Selection Tools

The result of the recruiting phase of the employment process should be résumés and application forms from job seekers hoping to be selected for the position. Screening these hopeful candidates to find those who best meet the needs of the position begins with establishing procedures that ensure equal employment opportunities.

Communicating with Applicants

HR departments are often criticized for ignoring job applicants. Although a large volume of applications makes it difficult to personally contact each person who expresses interest in a position, many companies use an "autorespond" email to acknowledge receipt of electronic résumés and applications and let candidates know that they will be contacted if selected for the interview process. Mail or in-person applications can be similarly acknowledged with preprinted postcards carrying the same message.

Recruiters need to stay in contact with candidates who move forward in the process until they have been removed from consideration, and then a final, respectful communication that they're no longer being considered is appropriate. These communications can be made in writing, but candidates who have made it to the final round of interviews deserve a personal call. This allows job seekers to move forward in their job searches and leaves them with a favorable impression of the HR department and the organization.

Screening Tools

The goal of the assessment process is to narrow the candidate pool into a manageable group including those candidates most qualified for a position. A variety of tools are used to assess candidate qualifications.

Résumés

Many organizations rely on candidate résumés as a first step in the assessment process. Although they generally contain relevant information, it can be difficult to compare qualifications of different candidates because of the lack of uniformity of style and content. Résumés generally present information about the applicant in the most favorable light and don't always contain all the information necessary to determine whether the applicant is qualified for the position. For those reasons, having all applicants complete an employment application is a good practice.

Employment Applications

Because application forms are considered employment tests by the EEOC, employers must be certain that the information requested on them is both job-related and a valid predictor of success in the position. A key benefit to using a standard application form is the inclusion of a statement signed by the applicant stating that the information contained in the document is true and complete. This statement can be useful in the event that an employer becomes aware of misstatements or discrepancies subsequent to hiring a candidate.

There are four basic types of application forms to consider using; one will suit the needs of the specific position or organization:

Short-Form Employment Application   As its name implies, the short-form application is less extensive than other application forms. The term *short* is relative—it describes application forms that range from one to five pages. Short-form applications are often used by employees who are applying for transfers or promotions and are useful for prescreening candidates or for positions with minimal skill requirements.

Long-Form Employment Application   The long-form application provides space for additional information related to the job requirements, such as advanced degrees and longer employment histories.

Job-Specific Employment Application   If the organization hires a substantial number of employees for positions with similar requirements, the application form can be designed to gather specific information related to the position or profession. This type of form would be appropriate for teaching, scientific careers, or volume hiring in similar professions.

Weighted Employment Application   The weighted application form was developed to assist recruiters in evaluating candidate qualifications. The form is developed using the job description; aspects of the job that are more important for success are given higher weights than other, less critical requirements. Weighted applications tend to reduce bias in the screening process, but they're expensive to maintain because they must be redesigned whenever job requirements change.

Screening Interviews

After reviewing the application forms and choosing those applicants who meet the job specifications and candidate profile, the recruiter conducts screening interviews to decide which candidates will be forwarded to the hiring manager. The purpose of these interviews is to both discover facts about the candidate and provide information about the position. The recruiter can assess the candidate's interest in the position and begin the process of determining which candidates are the best fit for the requirements. Screening interviews may be conducted by telephone or in person, and are relatively short, lasting from 15 to 30 minutes.

Selection Tools

Once HR has screened the applicants for a position and narrowed the candidate pool to those who meet job requirements and fit the candidate profile, the next step in the process of selecting the best candidate for the position begins. This may include several elements, such as an in-person interview, a realistic job preview, an in-box test, or participation in an assessment-center process. By far the most common selection tool is an in-depth interview conducted by hiring managers and others who know what the successful candidate will need to do in the position. The best interview process begins with an interview strategy.

The purpose of an interview strategy is twofold. First, it ensures that everyone on the interview team knows the candidate profile as well as what requirements the hiring manager has for the job. Second, when several interviewers will be interviewing candidates for a position, it ensures that everyone is using the same criteria to evaluate candidates. During the strategy-development phase, HR professionals work with hiring managers to decide the appropriate type of interview for the position.

Conducting Effective Interviews

Job interviews are stressful situations for interviewers and candidates alike. The interviewer has a very short period of time to determine whether the candidate is the best choice for the position, and the candidate wants to make a good impression with the ultimate goal of obtaining a job offer. To reduce the stress and improve the chances of obtaining the information needed to make the best hiring decision, preparing for the interview is essential. HR can assist interviewers in this process by providing advice on structuring an effective interview and developing an interview strategy:

Select the interview team.   HR's role in selecting the interview team is to work with the line manager to ensure that everyone who needs to be involved in the interview process is involved. In a team environment, it may be appropriate for all members of the team to participate; in other situations, employees from other business units who have frequent contact with the person in the position may be invited to participate in the process, along with employees who are knowledgeable about the work to be done.

Hold a pre-interview strategy meeting.   Conducting a pre-interview strategy meeting with the interview team provides an opportunity for the hiring manager to share what will be required of the successful candidate and to ensure that all interviewers are on the same page for the interviews. Topics for discussion can include the job description, specifications, and competencies. At this time, a discussion of the type of interview to be conducted and of common interview biases is also appropriate. This is a good opportunity for HR to share best interview practices with interviewers, such as not making notes on the application form or résumé, and to review appropriate interview questions.

Complete candidate evaluation forms.   During the pre-interview strategy discussion, HR can review the candidate evaluation form with the interview team. This form provides consistency in the interview process by providing interviewers with a list of topics to cover during the interview. The form is useful in rating candidates on job requirements and acts as a reminder of what to discuss during the candidate-evaluation phase of the selection process.

Conduct interviews.   Interviewers should prepare to meet the candidates by reading the application forms or résumés and making notes of any items that need explanation. During the interview, the candidate should be treated with dignity and respect, beginning with starting the interview on time and giving full attention to the candidate during the course of the interview. This includes screeners putting away their phones and focusing exclusively on the candidate. Setting the candidate at ease in the first few minutes will set the stage for a productive and informative interview. Providing a clear explanation of the organization's mission, values, and culture; details concerning the position; and what will be expected of the successful candidate early in the interview gives prospective employees a context in which to answer questions. Listening carefully to the candidate's answers, taking notes as appropriate, and following up on points that need clarification indicate a genuine interest in what is being said and encourage an open and honest exchange. Be honest with candidates about the workplace environment, and give them time to ask their own questions. End the interview with an explanation of the next steps in the process.

Evaluate candidates.   When everyone on the interview team has met with all the candidates, a final meeting takes place. During this meeting, the interviewers review the candidate-evaluation forms and share their thoughts on each candidate.

Types of Interviews

Several types of interviews are available for selecting candidates. Not all of them are appropriate for every situation, and it's up to HR to counsel the hiring manager on what will work best in each situation:

Behavioral Interviews   These interviews are based on the premise that past behavior is the best predictor of future behavior. This interview type asks candidates to describe how they have handled specific situations in previous jobs or life experiences. Candidates are expected to be able to describe a situation or problem, the actions they took to resolve it, and what outcome resulted. Interviewers skilled in this type of questioning are able to drill down into the answers to determine the candidate's depth of experience.

Situational Interviews   It is helpful to note that the key distinction between behavioral and situational interviews is the past and the future. Situational interviews are future-focused, often beginning with a variation of the question "How would you address…," followed by a realistic example of a likely work encounter. For example, a candidate for a customer service position may be asked "How would you handle an angry customer who called in to complain about our product?" These types of questions are appropriate for jobs in which there are consistent situations that applicants will be required to manage in their new role. Employers are trying to predict the candidate's decision-making style, critical thinking skills, ability to probe for more information, and ultimately, how the candidate would take action.

Structured/Directive Interviews   As the name implies, a structured or directive interview is very much controlled and guided by the interviewer, with a predetermined set of questions asked of all candidates. This style allows for consistent questioning, thus reducing the potential for bias or discrimination.

Nondirective Interviews   In this interview style, the interviewer asks broad questions and allows the candidate to guide the conversation. This style may produce a great deal of information relating to the candidate's qualifications, and that can become a problem during the candidate-evaluation phase, as well as in substantiating or defending the final hiring decision.

Patterned Interviews   A patterned interview is structured to cover specific areas related to the job requirements. The interviewer covers each area with all candidates but may ask different questions of them.

Panel Interviews   In a panel interview, several interviewers interview the candidate at the same time.

Stress Interviews   In some positions, such as airline pilots, law enforcement officers, and astronauts, employees encounter highly stressful situations on a regular basis. A stress interview subjects candidates to an intimidating situation to determine how they will handle stress in the position.

Question Guidelines

Equal opportunity legislation and regulations require that questions asked of candidates during the selection process be constructed to obtain only job-related information. Some topics, such as race, may never be a consideration in a selection decision. Others, such as age, are bona fide occupational qualifications (BFOQs) that may be asked in a nondiscriminatory manner (for example, state laws may require that a bartender be at least 21 to serve alcoholic beverages). Table 3.2 illustrates appropriate and inappropriate ways to obtain job-related information in an interview.

TABLE 3.2   Appropriate and inappropriate job-related questions

Inappropriate interview questions	Appropriate interview questions
Affiliations	
What clubs or social organizations do you belong to? Do you go to church?	Do you belong to any professional or trade associations or other organizations that you think are relevant to this job?
Age	
How old are you? When did you graduate from high school?	Are you 18 or older? Can you, after employment, provide proof of age?
Arrest Record	
Have you ever been arrested?	Have you ever been convicted of _____? (Name a crime that is plausibly related to the job in question.)
Disabilities	
Do you have any disabilities? Have you had any recent or past illnesses or operations? If yes, list them and give dates when these occurred. How's your family's health? When did you lose your vision/arm/hearing? How did it happen?	After reviewing the job description, are you able to perform all the essential functions of the job, with or without accommodation? Any job offer will be made contingent on a medical exam. Are you willing to undergo one if we offer you a job?
Marital/Family Status	
What is your marital status? With whom do you live? What was your maiden name? Do you plan to have a family? When? How many children will you have? What are your child-care arrangements?	Are you willing to relocate?* This job requires frequent travel. Are you willing and able to travel when needed?* Is there anything that will prevent you from meeting work schedules?*

TABLE 3.2   Appropriate and inappropriate job-related questions *(continued)*

Inappropriate interview questions	Appropriate interview questions
Military Service	
Were you honorably discharged? What type of discharge did you receive?	In what branch of the armed services did you serve? What type of training or education did you receive in the military?
National Origin/Citizenship	
Are you a U.S. citizen? Where were you/your parents born? What is your race? What language did you speak in your home when you were growing up?	Are you authorized to work in the United States? What language(s) do you read/speak/write fluently? (Acceptable if related to essential functions.)
Personal	
How tall are you? How much do you weigh? Would working on weekends conflict with your religious beliefs?	This job requires the ability to lift a 50-pound weight and carry it 100 yards. Are you able to do that? This job will require work on the weekends. Are you able to do so?

*Acceptable if asked of every candidate

Interviewer Bias

Any interviewer may bring preconceived ideas or biases into an interview situation; these can have an unintended impact on the hiring decision. The following list includes some of the types of interview bias that can occur. Once interviewers are aware of these, it's possible to reduce their impact on the selection process:

Average/Central Tendency   The *average bias* becomes apparent when the interviewer has difficulty deciding which candidate is best and rates them all about the same.

Contrast   The *contrast bias* occurs when an interviewer compares candidates to each other or compares all candidates to a single candidate. For example, if one candidate is particularly weak, others may appear to be more qualified than they really are.

Cultural Noise   *Cultural noise bias* occurs when candidates answer questions based on information they think will get them the job—what they think the interviewer wants to hear. For example, a candidate who has been an individual contributor may tell an interviewer that she prefers working as part of a team if the interviewer stresses teamwork as a key job requirement.

First Impression   This bias can work either for or against a candidate, depending on the interviewer's *first impression*. A candidate who is very nervous and stutters during the first few minutes of the interview may be viewed as less qualified even if during the remainder of the interview he is poised and well spoken.

Gut Feeling   The *gut feeling bias* occurs when the interviewer relies on an intuitive feeling that the candidate is a good (or bad) fit for the position without looking at whether the individual's qualifications meet the criteria established by the job specifications and candidate profile.

Halo Effect   The *halo effect bias* occurs when the interviewer evaluates a candidate positively based on a single characteristic. For example, a candidate's self-confident attitude may overshadow a lack of experience in a particular requirement.

Harshness/Horn Effect   *Harshness bias*, or the *horn effect*, occurs when the interviewer evaluates a candidate negatively based on a single characteristic.

Knowledge-of-Predictor   *Knowledge-of-predictor bias* occurs when the interviewer is aware that a candidate scored particularly high (or low) on an assessment test that has been shown to be a valid predictor of performance.

Leniency   *Leniency bias* occurs when an interviewer tends to go easy on a candidate and give a higher rating than is warranted, justifying it with a rationalization.

Negative Emphasis   The *negative emphasis bias* occurs when the interviewer allows a small amount of negative information to outweigh positive information.

Nonverbal Bias   *Nonverbal bias* occurs when an interviewer is influenced by body language. For example, a candidate who frowns when answering questions could be rated negatively even though the answers were correct.

Question Inconsistency   *Question inconsistency bias* occurs when an interviewer asks different questions of each candidate. Although this is acceptable to a certain extent in order to delve more deeply into each candidate's qualifications, there is no baseline for comparison if there are no questions that were asked of all candidates.

Recency   The *recency bias* occurs when the interviewer recalls the most recently interviewed candidate more clearly than earlier candidates.

Similar-to-Me   The *similar-to-me bias* occurs when the candidate has interests or other characteristics that are the same as those of the interviewer and cause the interviewer to overlook negative aspects about the candidate. For example, an interviewer who played college football may select a candidate who did so even though the candidate's qualifications aren't the best for the position.

Stereotyping   The *stereotyping bias* occurs when the interviewer assumes candidates have specific traits because they are a member of a group. For example, an interviewer may assume that a woman would not be able to successfully perform in a job that requires frequent lifting of packages weighing 50 pounds.

In-depth interviews are the cornerstone of the selection process, used in virtually all hiring decisions. However, interviews aren't the only tool available for candidate selection. Equally important information that adds different perspectives to candidates can be obtained by using realistic job previews, in-box tests, and assessment centers.

Realistic Job Preview

A *realistic job preview* (RJP), designed to give candidates an accurate picture of a typical day on the job, provides an opportunity for them to self-select out if the job isn't what they expected it would be. This increases the chances for success on the job, thereby reducing turnover. Depending on the type of job, the RJP can take many forms, including observing a current employee doing the job (as in a call center environment, for example), a simulated experience of the job, or a video presentation about the organization, work environment, and co-workers. A tour of the workplace is another way to give candidates an idea of what it would be like to work in the organization. These techniques, either singly or in some combination, can provide candidates with realistic expectations of the job and the organization.

In-Box Test

An in-box test provides candidates with a number of documents describing problems that would typically be handled by an employee in the position, with instructions to prioritize the problems and/or decide how the problems should be handled. Candidates are evaluated on the appropriateness of their decisions as well as on the length of time it takes for them to complete the test.

Assessment Centers

Assessment centers are characterized by multiple tests designed to measure different aspects of the job. Generally used to assess candidates for management potential and decision-making skills, they have been demonstrated to be valid predictors of success on the job. Used extensively by state and local governments and large organizations for assessing internal candidates for promotion, their use is limited due to the high cost of conducting them. Typical assessments include interviews, testing and problem-solving skills, in-basket tests, leaderless group discussions, and role-playing exercises.

Candidate Testing Programs

The use of preemployment tests has become more prevalent in recent years. These tests take many forms and have a variety of purposes. The key issue to keep in mind with regard to preemployment tests is the requirement that they must be job-related and, should they be challenged by an EEOC complaint, defensible as valid predictors of success in the position. Candidates for PHR/SPHR certification should be aware of the following types of selection tests:

Aptitude Tests   These tests are designed to measure an individual's knowledge and ability to apply skills in various areas, such as mathematics, typing, language, and reasoning. Properly constructed aptitude tests have been shown to be valid predictors of job success.

Cognitive Ability Test (CAT)   CATs measure an individual's ability to analyze and solve problems and draw conclusions from a set of facts. They also measure an individual's potential for learning, thinking, and remembering.

Personality Test   Personality tests assess how a candidate will "fit" into a specific job. If, for example, an employer uses a personality test that has shown particular characteristics to be valid predictors of success—such as extroversion or conscientiousness—in sales positions, and an applicant doesn't reflect those characteristics when tested, the test would indicate an area to be explored with the candidate prior to making the hiring decision.

Integrity Tests   Also known as *honesty tests*, integrity tests assess a candidate's work ethic, attitudes toward theft and drug and alcohol use, and similar traits. According to the EEOC, professionally developed integrity tests don't create an adverse impact for protected classes as long as the tests are administered equally to all candidates.

Psychomotor Assessment Tests   A psychomotor assessment tests an individual's coordination and manual dexterity.

Physical Assessment Tests   Physical assessment tests are used to determine whether candidates are physically capable of performing specific job duties. The tests generally require that tasks be completed within a predetermined period of time and most often simulate activities that regularly occur on the job. A common physical assessment test is one that is given to potential firefighters to ensure that they're capable of lifting and carrying heavy weights for predetermined periods of time in a variety of circumstances.

As previously discussed, a key requirement for selection tools is that they be both related to specific job requirements and valid predictors of successful job performance. To determine whether a specific employment test meets those criteria, employers must ensure that tests are both reliable and valid.

 Real World Scenario

The Courts Address Employment Tests

Once Title VII of the Civil Rights Act of 1964 was enacted, employees who thought they had been subjected to unlawful employment discrimination were able to initiate lawsuits to resolve their grievances. Preemployment testing practices were the subject of a number of cases, the most prominent of which are described here.

1971: *Griggs vs. Duke Power Co.*   Duke Power Company, located in North Carolina, employed 95 workers in its Dan River Steam Station in 1964. There were five departments at the plant: Labor, Coal Handling, Operations, Maintenance, and Laboratory and Test. The Labor Department was the lowest-paid department in the company; in fact, the highest-paying job in the department paid less than the lowest-paying job in the other four. In 1955, the company began to require that employees in all departments except Labor have a high-school diploma, but prior to that time employees could be hired into any of the departments without one. On July 2, 1965, the effective date of Title VII, Duke added a requirement that all new employees must pass two aptitude tests and that an employee wanting to transfer from Labor to another department needed a high school diploma.

Willie Griggs was one of 14 black employees working in the Labor Department at the plant. There were no black employees in any of the other departments. Mr. Griggs filed a class-action lawsuit on behalf of himself and 12 of the black employees, alleging that the requirement for a high school diploma and satisfactory scores on the aptitude tests discriminated against them. The district court that first heard the case dismissed it. The court of appeals found that Griggs had not shown that there was a discriminatory purpose to the requirements and that a discriminatory purpose was required to show discrimination. The Supreme Court granted *certiorari* (agreed to review the case) and heard oral arguments in December 1970.

Because a number of the white employees who didn't have high school diplomas had been hired prior to the requirements for the diploma or the aptitude tests, and those employees performed well on the job, it was clear that the requirements didn't predict job performance, and Duke Power didn't dispute this fact. The Supreme Court found that "good intent or absence of discriminatory intent" in the face of a job requirement that adversely impacts a protected class isn't a sufficient defense against discrimination. The job requirement must be shown to be job-related in order to be lawful, and it's up to the employer to prove this.

The HR significance of *Griggs vs. Duke Power Co.* is that discrimination doesn't need to be intentional to exist. It's up to employers to prove that job requirements are related to the job.

1975: *Albemarle Paper vs. Moody*   In 1966, a group of current and former black employees at Albemarle Paper's mill in Roanoke Rapids, North Carolina, filed a lawsuit against both their employer, Albemarle Paper, and the union representing them with the company. The group asked the court for an injunction against "any policy, practice, custom, or usage" at the mill that was in violation of Title VII. When the case dragged on for several years, a demand for back pay was added to the injunction request in 1970. One of the policies in question was the employment testing practice used by Albemarle Paper. The district court denied the claim for back pay and refused to consider the testing procedure, saying that the tests had been validated.

The court of appeals reversed the ruling, finding that the absence of bad faith wasn't sufficient grounds to deny back pay and that the validation process had four serious flaws:

- It had not been used consistently.

- It had compared test scores to the subjective rankings of supervisors, which couldn't be tied to job-related performance criteria.

- The tests were validated against the most senior jobs and not entry-level positions.

- The validation study used only experienced white employees, not the new job applicants, who were mostly nonwhite.

The HR significance of *Albemarle Paper vs. Moody* is that test validation must be in accordance with the Uniform Guidelines on Employee Selection Procedures. Subjective supervisor rankings aren't sufficient for criterion validation; the criteria must be able to be tied to the job requirements.

1975: *Washington vs. Davis* In 1970, two applicants for the police department in Washington, D.C., filed suit against the city, claiming that the written personnel test given to applicants had an adverse impact on black applicants. The Supreme Court upheld the district court's finding that the test was a valid predictor of successful performance in the police-training program.

The HR significance of *Washington vs. Davis* is that tests that have an adverse impact on a protected class are lawful if they are valid predictors of success on the job.

Reliability and Validity

The UGESP requires that selection tests be reliable and valid predictors of success on the job.

Reliability

Reliability measures whether a test or other measurement produces consistent results so that, over time, the scores won't vary greatly. Test reliability is enhanced by several factors, including wording instructions and test questions clearly. Providing optimal conditions for administering the test contributes to its reliability, as does making sure it's long enough to accurately test the candidate's knowledge.

In essence, measuring reliability can be done by administering the same test to the same respondents after a set amount of time has passed, and seeing if there is a correlation between the test questions and predicted behaviors. This is called "test-retest" reliability.

Another method, called the "internal consistency" method, is used when questions from the same content domain are constructed in different ways, and the items are evaluated for respondent consistency.

Finally, a third way to measure test reliability is the "parallel forms" method, used when two tests from the same content domain are constructed and results are compared for consistency.

Validity

Validity considers the characteristics being measured by a test and whether the test is measuring the characteristics accurately:

Content Validity *Content validity* is the simplest of the three validation measures. Job analysis is a key element of the content-validity process, which confirms that a selection procedure samples significant parts of the job being tested. For example, a driving test given to a delivery person who would drive a truck 80 percent of the time if hired for the job is a test with content validity.

Construct Validity *Construct validity* determines whether a test measures the connection between candidate characteristics and successful performance on the job. According to the DOL, construct validity is a method of testing that measures an applicant's abstract future behaviors. In order for a test to be legally defensible, it must show that it measured the proper characteristic and that it accurately predicted future success on the job.

Criterion Validity A criterion is a trait or work behavior that is predicted by a test. *Criterion validity* is established when the test or measure either predicts or correlates the behavior:

Predictive Validity *Predictive validity* compares the test scores of a test given at the beginning of a job before new employees have experience to the same criterion collected at some future time. When the employees have had some experience (for example, 6 months or 1 year) with the job, the manager evaluates their performance. The original test scores are then measured against the criterion (the evaluation ratings), and the test is validated if they're similar.

Concurrent Validity The process for determining *concurrent validity* is similar to that of determining predictive validity. The difference is that the criterion measurement occurs at the same time the test is given and not at a later time.

> The concepts of testing, reliability, and validity can be confusing for students and HR professionals alike. For that reason, it is important you take your studying efforts to the next level. It is well worth your time to visit onetonline.org, and search for the guide titled *Testing and Assessment: An Employer's Guide to Good Practices* to ensure you are ready for exam day questions on these important concepts.

Preemployment Inquiries

Preemployment inquiries or background checks cover a range of activities designed to ensure that candidates who receive employment offers are who they represent themselves to be during the selection process. Information collected during these processes should be protected from inappropriate dissemination and, at the appropriate time, disposed of in a way that ensures its security. Preemployment inquiries verify information collected from candidate résumés and/or interviews during the selection process. Some of the information is relatively easy to verify, such as educational degrees and previous employment, and provides insight into earlier educational and employment experiences.

Real World Scenario

Validity in Action

What does all this validity stuff have to do with HR? Federal courts look to validation studies to determine whether specific job requirements discriminate against protected classes. A professionally developed validation test serves as proof in court that the employment requirement is a valid predictor of successful performance on the job. The following are some ways that companies can use forms of validity in various situations.

Imagine that a company needs to hire business analysts who will spend 95 percent of their time analyzing sales trends and predicting future sales. The company would want to administer a test that measures a candidate's ability to reason. In this case, a test that measures a candidate's ability to reason would have *construct validity*.

In another example, an accounting firm that has had significant turnover in its entry-level accounting positions in the past few years wants to put some measures in place that will result in new hires with a better chance of success in their positions. As a result, the HR director commissioned a test to measure analytical ability, to use in the hiring process. The firm recently hired 100 recent college graduates with accounting degrees as entry-level accountants, none of whom has ever worked in the accounting field. On their first day of work, all 100 accountants took the new test. Six months later, the accountants were evaluated by their supervisors, and the results of the evaluation ratings (the criterion) were compared to the test results. The accountants who were highly rated by their supervisors had high scores on the test, and those who scored poorly on the test had lower evaluation ratings. The test has *predictive validity*.

Here's an example to illustrate the use of concurrent validity. The owner of CADServ, a computer-aided design service bureau, recently won a large contract for design work with a nationally known real estate developer. The project will require that CADServ hire at least 20 more CAD operators within a few months. The owner would like to bring in some entry-level operators but needs to be sure they will be successful on the job. The owner contracts with a testing firm to administer an abstract-reasoning test to the candidates but wants to be sure it will be accurate. The owner decides to have the 30 CAD operators who already work at CADServ take the test. The test is given around the same time as the annual review cycle, and when the test results come in, they're similar to the ratings received by the employees—those who received high test scores also received high performance ratings. The test has *concurrent validity*, and CADServ will use it in the hiring process for the new operators.

Preemployment inquiries may also include a check of the candidate's financial records, driving record, and any previous criminal behavior, depending on the type of job. Any background or reference check conducted by a third party is considered to be a consumer report and is therefore subject to requirements of the Fair Credit Reporting Act (FCRA). When employers conduct their own reference checks, those requirements don't apply.

Reference Checks

An organization may ask for several types of references from potential employees. Types of references may include the following:

Employment References   To make an informed decision about a potential employee, employers should obtain all the information they can from previous employers. Information collected during the reference-checking process includes previous employment history, dates, job titles, and type of work performed. Many employers are reluctant to provide more information than this for privacy reasons, but as long as the information is factual and given in good faith, most states consider it "qualifiedly privileged," which protects the employer from legal action. It's desirable to obtain additional information about the employee's work habits and interpersonal skills and find out if the employee is eligible for rehire.

Educational References   Depending on the position applied for and the length of time since graduation, some employers request high school, college, and postgraduate transcripts to verify the accuracy of information presented during the selection process.

Financial References   Financial references are generally used only when candidates will be handling large sums of cash. As with all other selection tools, a financial reference must be shown to be job-related *and* a valid predictor of success in the position. When required, financial references, generally provided by credit-reporting agencies, are subject to requirements of the federal Fair Credit and Reporting Act (FCRA).

Criminal Record Checks

Criminal record checks can uncover information about substance abuse, violent behavior, and property crimes such as theft and embezzlement. Because private employers don't have access to a central database that collects information from every level of government (federal, state, county, and local), it can be difficult to do a comprehensive check. When applicants have lived or worked in several states, counties, or municipalities, records in each jurisdiction must be checked to ensure completeness.

Negative information obtained through criminal record checks should be carefully reviewed on a case-by-case basis, considering all of the relevant information:

- How does the type of crime relate to the position applied for?
- How recent was the conviction?
- How old was the applicant when the conviction occurred?
- What is the level of risk to customers, co-workers, and others in the workplace if the applicant is hired?

Criminal record checks are considered consumer investigations and must comply with related FCRA requirements.

When an employer considers making an adverse hiring decision based on negative information received in an investigative consumer report, the applicant must be notified in writing and given a chance to respond. Should the negative information be the result of a mistake, the applicant can provide information to clear the record. If the employer decides to proceed with the adverse action, the applicant must receive a second written notice stating that the adverse action has been taken.

Negligent Hiring

Negligent hiring occurs when an employer knew or should have known about an applicant's prior history that endangered customers, employees, vendors, or others with whom the employee comes in contact. Employers can prevent negligent-hiring lawsuits by carefully checking references and running background checks for all candidates. Once an employer finds out about such a history, the employer is obligated to safeguard others who come in contact with the individual during the workday by taking whatever action is necessary to maintain a safe work environment.

To defend themselves against claims of negligent hiring, employers can demonstrate that they exercised due diligence in the hiring process by taking the following steps:

- Conducting reference checks with previous employers
- Obtaining reports from the Departments of Motor Vehicles in the states where the applicant has lived or worked
- Verifying the validity of the applicant's Social Security number
- Conducting criminal record checks
- Verifying the validity of any government-issued licenses, such as a medical or engineering license issued by a state
- Conducting drug-screening tests

Medical Examinations

As with all other assessment tools, medical examinations are allowable after extending a job offer or conditional job offer if their purpose is job-related and they're required of all candidates. These exams are used to ensure that the employee will be fully capable of performing the requirements of the job and, in some cases, may be part of an employer's health and safety program. Under the ADA, employers may make a job offer conditional on a medical examination before the candidate begins working as long as all applicants for positions in the same job category must undergo the exam. If the offer is rescinded as a result of the medical exam, the employer must be able to demonstrate that the job requirement eliminating the candidate from consideration is related to a business necessity.

Drug-Screening Tests

Studies conducted by the Occupational Safety and Health Administration (OSHA) indicate that drug-screening programs reduce job-related accidents. Substance abuse is also linked to reduced productivity.

Drug-screening tests are specifically excluded from the ADA's medical-examination requirement and may be required prior to extending an offer.

Employment Offers

The postinterview strategy meeting has been concluded, the references have been checked, and results of the preemployment tests are in. The hiring decision has been made, and it's time to extend an offer. After discussion with HR, the hiring manager contacts the successful candidate and extends a verbal offer, or in some organizations, HR may be responsible for extending verbal offers. When the verbal offer is accepted, a written offer agreement is prepared.

Employment Agreements and Contracts

Employment relationships in many states are subject to the common law concept of *employment-at-will,* meaning that the relationship can be ended at any time by either party with or without a reason. As a result, few employees today work under employment contracts. In most cases, the relationship is defined in an offer letter that is composed after negotiations are complete.

Making and Negotiating Offers

One of the goals of the selection process is to collect information from candidates about their expectations for cash compensation, benefits, and other terms and conditions of employment that may be appropriate to the position. When it's time to make an offer, these expectations are incorporated into the decision-making process of crafting the offer. Prior to making the offer, any required approvals are obtained, along with approval for any "wiggle room" should the candidate come back with a request for a higher salary or increased benefits. Once the verbal negotiations are complete, the written agreement can be completed.

Offer Letters

The offer letter should be prepared immediately upon acceptance of the verbal offer by the candidate. The standard offer letter should be reviewed by the corporate attorney to ensure that its provisions don't compromise the organization and that it contains the terms of the offer as well as any contingencies that apply, such as a medical exam, a background check, or proof of the right to work in the United States. The salary offer should be stated in an hourly or monthly amount. The offer should state clearly that the organization is an at-will employer and that only the terms and conditions of the offer contained in the offer letter are valid. Finally, there should be a reasonable time frame for returning a signed acceptance of the offer.

Care should be taken to ensure that any promises of benefits or special conditions agreed on by the hiring manager are included in the offer letter so there is no ambiguity about the complete offer.

Employment Contracts

An employment contract binds both parties to the agreements contained in the contract. Contracts are generally reserved for senior-level managers and professionals such as doctors and teachers, and they can cover a wide range of topics. Any areas of the employment relationship not specifically covered in the contract are subject to common law. Some standard clauses seen in employment contracts include the following:

Terms and Conditions of Employment   This clause covers the start date and duration of the contract and, if the contract is for a set period of time, includes any automatic extension agreements.

Scope of Duties   General and specific duties and responsibilities are covered by this clause. The duties can be part of the contract, or the job description may be incorporated into the agreement as an addendum. Expectations for performance are included here as well.

Compensation   The compensation package is described in this clause, which includes the base salary, any bonus and incentive agreements, auto or telephone allowance, company car, or other agreements.

Benefits and Expense Reimbursements   Items covered by this clause include disability and health insurance benefits and retirement plans. The extent of and conditions for expense reimbursements are also described here.

Nondisclosure of Proprietary Information   Requirements for the maintenance of confidentiality with regard to proprietary information are included here, along with noncompete language and requirements for the return of company property when the employment relationship ends.

Nonsolicitation Agreement   This clause sets forth agreements that limit the employee's ability to solicit customers, vendors, and employees during the course of the contract and for an agreed-on period of time after the contract ends.

Advice of Counsel   A clause advising the employee to seek legal counsel prior to signing the contract is often included.

Disability or Death   The employer can include a clause that states what happens to the agreement in the event of the disability or death of the employee.

Termination Clause   The termination clause sets forth conditions that would lead to a termination for cause, such as inability to perform, neglecting the duties of the position, misconduct, violations of company policy, or other egregious acts.

Change of Control   A change of control clause protects the employee's job and compensation in the event of a reorganization, an acquisition, or a merger, for a specified period of time.

Post-Offer Employment Activities

When the offer has been accepted, the transition from candidate to employee begins. At this stage, employees form their first impressions about what it will be like to work in the organization. During this time, employers can take steps to begin the relationship positively by including employees in special events that may be scheduled prior to their first day, and providing them with information that will help them become productive more quickly and begin assimilating into the work group.

Relocation Practices

In some circumstances, employers may be willing to pay the costs of relocating an employee or an applicant. When that occurs, HR may manage the process. Elements of relocation packages that can be negotiated include a company-paid trip for the spouse and family to see the area and look for a new home, assistance with selling the old and/or purchasing the new home, payment of moving expenses, assistance with a job search for the spouse in the new area, and a guarantee of the sale price of the old house if it doesn't sell.

Relocation is an activity that lends itself to outsourcing. Some organizations contract with moving companies that include relocation assistance as part of the moving package, and there are also professional organizations that manage the entire process for the organization and the family. These companies can provide property-management services, home inspections, real estate attorneys or title companies, home appraisals, moving companies, and, in some cases, corporate living situations for short-term job assignments. This can be a cost-effective solution that saves time for in-house staff.

Immigration Processes

In 2003, enforcement responsibility for the Immigration and Nationality Act (INA) of 1952 and its amendments was transferred to the U.S. Citizenship and Immigration Services (USCIS), an agency of the Department of Homeland Security. The INA and its amendments control immigration policy for the United States established by the following:

INA of 1952 and Amendment of 1965   The purpose of the INA was to simplify the multiple laws that previously governed U.S. immigration policy. As established by previous legislation, immigration quotas continued to be set on the basis of national origin.

Following the trend of equal opportunity established by the Civil Rights Act of 1964, the 1965 amendment eliminated national origin, race, and ancestry as bars to immigration and changed the allocation of immigrant visas to a first-come, first-served basis. The amendment also established seven immigration categories with the goals of reunifying families and giving preference to those with specialty skills that were needed in the United States.

Immigration Reform and Control Act (IRCA) of 1986   IRCA was enacted in 1986 to address illegal immigration into the United States. The law applied to businesses with four or more employees and made it illegal to knowingly hire or continue to employ individuals who weren't legally authorized to work in the United States. Unfair immigration-related employment practices were defined as discrimination on the basis of national origin or citizenship status.

Employers were required to complete Form I-9 for all new hires within the first 3 days of employment and to review documents provided by the employee that establish identity or employment authorization or both from lists of acceptable documents on the Form I-9. IRCA requires employers to maintain I-9 files for 3 years from the date of hire or 1 year after the date of termination, whichever is later, and allows, but doesn't require, employers to copy documents presented for employment eligibility for purposes of complying with these requirements. The act also provides that employers complying in good faith with these requirements have an affirmative defense to inadvertently hiring an unauthorized alien. Substantial fines for violations of both the hiring and recordkeeping requirements were provided in the law. In 2016, increased fines took effect. Paperwork violations (including failure to complete or retain forms) may result in a penalty of $216 to $2,156 for each violation. In addition, for penalties assessed for missing or incomplete I-9 forms, IRCA established fines for unauthorized employees. Table 3.3 outlines the fines for hiring violations under IRCA.

In addition to the fines listed, employers who knowingly hire unauthorized workers are subject to fines and/or 6 months imprisonment.

Until 2005, IRCA required employers to store I-9 forms on one of three types of media: paper, microfilm, or microfiche. Passage of HR 4306, which was signed into law by President George W. Bush, allows employers to store I-9 forms in PDF files or other electronic formats.

E-Verify   E-Verify is a free service offered through the USCIS. It's a tool that helps employers comply with IRCA's requirement that employers must verify the identity and employment eligibility of new employees. The employer accesses E-Verify through the Internet, inputs basic information gleaned from the Form I-9, and receives a near-instant "employment authorized" or "tentative nonconfirmation" (TNC) reply from the website. The employer then prints the results. A TNC result gives the employee more information about the mismatch and a statement of that person's rights and responsibilities under the law. It's important to note that employers may not terminate employees for the initial TNC; it's only when they receive a final nonconfirmation that employers may terminate under E-Verify.

To get started in the program, employers must first enroll their company, sign a memorandum of understanding (MOU) reviewing their obligations and acknowledging their understanding of the terms of enrollment, and commit to using E-Verify for every new employee at the affected hiring site. Under federal law, employers may designate the use of E-Verify to certain locations, although this may be restricted under some state laws.

The USCIS provides several webinars designed to educate employers and employees about the E-Verify process. Visit their home page at www.uscis.gov/portal/site/uscis and follow the instructions to these free webinars.

Immigration Act of 1990   The Immigration Act of 1990 made several changes to IRCA, including adding the requirement that a prevailing wage be paid to H-1B immigrants to ensure that U.S. citizens didn't lose jobs to lower-paid immigrant workers. The act also restricted to 65,000 annually the number of immigrants allowed under the H-1B category and created additional categories for employment visas, as shown in Table 3.4. In 1996, the number and types of documents to prove identity and eligibility to work were reduced.

Illegal Immigration Reform and Immigrant Responsibility Act (IIRIRA) of 1996   This act reduced the number and types of documents allowable to prove identity, employment eligibility, or both in the hiring process and established pilot programs for verification of employment eligibility.

Visit www.uscis.gov, and click on the Legal Resources tab to view the full text of INA and its amendments.

TABLE 3.3   IRCA fines

Violation	Amount of fine
First	Not less than $539 or more than $4,313 for each unauthorized employee
Second	Not less than $4,313 or more than $10,781 for each unauthorized employee
Third	Not less than $6,469 or more than $21,563 for each unauthorized employee

TABLE 3.4   Employment visas

Visa	Classification
	Visas for Temporary Workers
H-1B	Specialty occupations, DOD workers, fashion models
H-1C	Nurses going to work for up to three years in health professional shortage areas
H-2A	Temporary agricultural worker
H-2B	Temporary worker: skilled and unskilled
H-3	Trainee
J-1	Visas for exchange visitors Visas for intracompany transfers

Visa	Classification
L-1A	Executive, managerial
L-1B	Specialized knowledge
L-2	Spouse or child of L-1
	Visas for Workers with Extraordinary Abilities
O-1	Extraordinary ability in sciences, arts, education, business, or athletics
	Visas for Athletes and Entertainers
P-1	Individual or team athletes
P-1	Entertainment groups
P-2	Artists and entertainers in reciprocal exchange programs
P-3	Artists and entertainers in culturally unique programs
	Visas for Religious Workers
R-1	Religious workers
	Visas for NAFTA Workers
TN	Trade visas for Canadians and Mexicans

Employee Onboarding and Orientation Programs

Formal onboarding and orientation programs consist of two elements: a general introduction to the organization as a whole and a job-specific orientation. HR often is responsible for providing the organization orientation, including information about the mission, goals, and values, and for answering general questions. The job-specific orientation is conducted or overseen by the hiring manager and provides information specific to the department and position, sets performance expectations, and ensures that the new hire knows where to go for assistance when needed. These programs are an important part of a new hire's introduction to the organization. In many organizations, daily events move so quickly that new employees are sometimes left to fend for themselves without understanding what they're supposed to do or how to get help when they need it. The onboarding and orientation programs help ensure that new employees have the support they need to be successful. HR helps to bridge the gap between the more administrative orientation activities to the more robust introduction that make up the activities of onboarding.

Orientation   An example of a short-term objective within the scope of onboarding is the *new-hire orientation*. An orientation typically includes paperwork completion; compliance training; and an introduction to policies, procedures, and rules through a review of the employee handbook. It may also include an expanded tour of the facility and email welcome to all staff. Many organizations provide benefit information and application forms with the written offer so the employee has time to review them, make appropriate selections, and include spouses in those decisions.

Onboarding   Onboarding refers to a system of organizational behaviors at the time of hire focused on the retention of new employees. It consists of both short-term and long-term behaviors that help to integrate employees into their new work environment. Onboarding programs exist to reduce the length of time it takes new employees to become productive team members.

An example of a long-term onboarding activity is *socialization*. This includes efforts such as the assignment of an internal mentor or peer-to-peer support for training. Buddy programs are sometimes used to provide additional, informal support to new employees. Buddies are employees in good standing with enough time on the job to be familiar with how things work in the organization and can answer questions or direct the new employee to a person with the answers.

As with any successful HR program, scheduled follow-up to measure successful entry is an important component of the onboarding process. Functional follow-up may include completion of enrollment in a benefits plan or the verification of receipt of an identification badge or working phone extension. A less functional but no less important follow-up activity may be to schedule a meeting within the first 30 days to discuss how the job is matching with the employee's initial expectations. The most effective onboarding activities take place over an extended period of time with regularly scheduled follow-ups that provide opportunities to check in with the employee and provide support as needed.

Electronic Storage

Technology has influenced many HR practices, not the least of which is records retention. Before deciding to electronically store records, an HR professional must consider the specific regulatory requirements of the law(s) governing record retention, security, access, and legibility. A good example of the considerations for the electronic storage of records is given by the USCIS related to storing the Form I-9 electronically:

> Instructions from the U.S. Citizen and Immigration Services
>
> Employers may use a paper system, an electronic system or a combination of paper and electronic systems to store Form I-9 records. An electronic storage system must:
>
> ▪ Include controls to ensure the integrity, accuracy and reliability of the electronic storage system.

- Include controls to detect and prevent the unauthorized or accidental creation of, addition to, alteration of, deletion of or deterioration of an electronically stored Form I-9, including the electronic signature, if used.

- Include controls to ensure an audit trail so that any alteration or change to the form since its creation is electronically stored and can be accessed by an appropriate government agency inspecting the forms.

- Include an inspection and quality assurance program that regularly evaluates the electronic generation or storage system, and includes periodic checks of electronically stored Form I-9s, including the electronic signature, if used.

- Include a detailed index of all data so that any particular record can be accessed immediately.

- Produce a high degree of legibility and readability when displayed on a video display terminal or reproduced on paper.

Summary

When strategically tied to the organization's vision, mission, and goals, planning for workforce needs is a key element of success. HR professionals must provide expertise for management in deciding whether to aggressively develop current employees for future growth in the organization, hire candidates from the outside, or use alternative staffing methods to accomplish the work that needs to be done. Understanding the implications of each approach allows HR to guide management in making decisions that best suit the organization's needs, culture, and values.

Identifying candidates who not only have the best KSAOs for the job but whose personal goals, ambitions, and qualities also complement the needs of the organization requires HR professionals to be keenly aware of the organization's strategic direction. Providing opportunities to all qualified candidates opens up the labor pool available to the organization and includes candidates with a great deal to offer who might not have been considered in the past.

An effective hiring process begins with using sources that produce a pool of candidates with diverse backgrounds who have the required KSAOs, continues with screening the candidates with a fair and equitable process designed to find the best match for the organization, and concludes by welcoming them with orientation programs that assist them in becoming productive members of the team.

HR professionals can show that they understand the fundamental needs of business by making recommendations and decisions based on quantifiable measures. Being able to show, for example, how much a bad hiring decision costs the organization in terms of the direct and indirect costs of hiring, training, and replacing employees demonstrates to management that effective HR management has a positive effect on the bottom line.

Exam Essentials

Be able to develop and implement a strategic talent plan, including methods and techniques to source candidates.   A strategic workforce plan provides a framework for HR professionals to ensure that the right people with the right qualifications are available at the right time to achieve the organization's goals.

Be able to conduct a staffing needs assessment.   A staffing needs assessment determines which KSAOs are needed to meet future strategic goals and where training efforts (if filling jobs internally) or recruiting efforts (if hiring from the outside) should be focused.

Understand the Affirmative Action Plan process.   An AAP is required to be filed by companies with federal contracts of $50,000 or more per year and 50 employees. The plan identifies how many incumbents in different job classifications are members of protected classes and compares that information to the availability of protected classes in the labor market.

Be able to develop job requirements from a job analysis.   A job analysis provides the information to develop the job competencies, job descriptions, and test specifications necessary to both identify what needs to be done on a daily basis and recruit effectively for the best candidate to fill the position.

Be able to identify recruitment methods.   Depending on the level of experience and skill being sought, there are a variety of methods to consider in the recruiting process. HR professionals must understand which methods will produce the candidates who are most appropriate to fill positions at different levels.

Be able to establish and implement selection procedures.   Effective selection procedures help ensure that candidates selected for the organization meet all the job requirements and are the best fit for the position. Interviewing, testing, realistic job previews, and assessment centers help organizations determine whether the candidate is the right fit for the job. Reference checks ensure that the candidate has performed successfully in previous positions.

Be able to conduct post-hire activities.   HR activities conducted during the post-hire phase have implications for the long-term success of new hires. It's important to understand the ramifications of employment offers and ensure that the new employee has all the necessary information to be successful. An effective orientation will make new employees feel welcome, introduce them to the company, and provide information on company policies.

Review Questions

You can find the answers in Appendix A.

1. The marketing director needs to hire a replacement for the marketing coordinator, who is being promoted. The position has changed quite a bit since the last time the job was advertised, and the director is looking to HR to assist in redefining the job requirements so the recruiting process can begin. Which of the following would *not* be used in determining the job requirements?

   A. Job competencies

   B. Job description

   C. Job specifications

   D. Candidate profile

2. Which of the following is *not* a BFOQ?

   A. A synagogue hiring a new rabbi requires that the rabbi be Jewish.

   B. A lingerie catalog hires only female models.

   C. A retail store in a predominantly Asian neighborhood advertises for Asian clerks.

   D. A swimming club requires that the men's changing-room attendant be male.

3. The court case that identified adverse impact as an unlawful employment practice was which of the following?

   A. *Griggs vs. Duke Power Co.*

   B. *Albemarle Paper vs. Moody*

   C. *Washington vs. Davis*

   D. *Taxman vs. School Board of Piscataway*

4. To determine the numbers and types of jobs necessary to realize business goals, HR must assess the KSAOs available within the organization during a staffing needs analysis. What other factor is necessary to complete the assessment?

   A. The KSAOs needed to achieve future goals

   B. The tasks, duties, and responsibilities for the work

   C. The KSAOs available in the local labor market

   D. The organization's core competencies

5. Your New Orleans plant has an opening for a controller, and four candidates have been selected for interviews. Jack, the son of a plant employee, worked as an accountant for two years to put himself through the Wharton Business School and recently earned his MBA. Richard is a CPA with eight years of experience in a public accounting firm. Susan also has a CPA and has worked as an accounting manager in the corporate office of a large corporation in the same industry. Jane does not have a CPA or MBA but has worked as controller of a smaller local competitor for eight years. After interviewing all four candidates, the general manager told you that he wants to hire Jack because he shows promise. You know from previous conversation with the GM that he also worked his way through college. Which of the following biases could be influencing the GM's decision?

    A. Knowledge-of-predictor

    B. Halo effect

    C. Similar-to-me

    D. Gut feeling

6. Please refer to the following table for this question. A company advertised for 100 sales representative positions. They received 650 applications and hired the 100 employees as follows:

Group	Applicants	Hired
Black	140	23
Asian	120	21
Hispanic	145	19
Caucasian	230	35
Native American	15	2
Total	650	100

    Which group has the highest selection rate?

    A. Black

    B. Asian

    C. Caucasian

    D. Hispanic

7. Please refer to the following table for this question. A company advertised for 100 sales representative positions. They received 650 applications and hired the 100 employees as follows:

Group	Applicants	Hired	Selection Rate	4/5 of Highest Rate
Black	140	23	16%	
Asian	120	21	18%	14%
Hispanic	145	19	13%	
Caucasian	230	35	15%	
Native American	15	2	13%	
Total	650	100		

In which groups has adverse impact occurred?

A. Hispanic and Caucasian

B. Caucasian and Black

C. Asians

D. Native American and Black

8. An Affirmative Action Plan must be completed by employers that meet which criteria?

A. Private employers with 25 or more employees

B. Government contractors and subcontractors with contracts of $10,000 or more in a 12-month period

C. Government contractors with contracts of $2,500 or more in a 12-month period

D. Government contractors with 50 or more employees and contracts of $50,000 or more each year

9. When a Reduction in Force (RIF) occurs, the ADEA allows that protected employees may waive their rights under some circumstances. For the waiver to be valid, the protected employee must be allowed how long to review and consider the agreement?

A. 7 days

B. 21 days

C. 45 days

D. 180 days

10. Which of the following is *not* required by IRCA?

A. That an I-9 form be completed for all new hires within 3 days of hire

B. That employers comply with IRCA in good faith

C. That I-9 forms be maintained for all employees

D. That copies of documents presented for employment eligibility be maintained

11. In a self-audit of your employee's I-9 forms, several errors were found. These errors included incomplete sections, questionable documents accepted for verification, and over-documentation. Of the following corrective and prevention strategies, which should you recommend to your employer?

A. Training for employees

B. Recertification of all I-9 forms

C. Enrollment in E-Verify

D. Requesting updated documents from affected employees

12. Electronic storage of records must include specific controls to ensure which of the following?

A. Online retrievability on demand

B. No unauthorized access

C. Ease of use

D. Collaboration with an HRIS system

13. Strategic recruitment activities include all of the following except which one?

   A. Labor market analysis

   B. The design of total rewards packages

   C. Employee referral programs

   D. Defining the employer brand

14. Which of the following is a requirement of the Uniform Guidelines on employee selection procedures?

   A. Any selection tool that results in discrimination based on a protected class characteristic is unlawful.

   B. All selection tools must be job-related and valid predictors of future success.

   C. Application forms must be the same for all employment classifications within the organization.

   D. Internet recruiting efforts are excluded from applicant-tracking requirements.

15. Which of the following acts requires federal contractors or subcontractors with contracts of $25,000 or more to list all nonsenior management job openings with state employment agencies?

   A. The Rehabilitation Act of 1973

   B. Executive Order 11375

   C. Executive Order 11246

   D. The Vietnam Era Veterans' Readjustment Assistance Act of 1974

16. Within the first 90 days of his employment, a security guard physically assaulted an alleged shoplifter. Upon investigation, it was found that he had been previously convicted of a violent crime, but the employer failed to conduct a background check. This is an example of which of the following?

   A. A violation of the Privacy Act of 1974

   B. Negligent hiring

   C. Failure to report

   D. A criminal act

17. Which of the following is the correct definition of "a major life activity" under the Americans with Disabilities Act?

   A. A physical or mental impairment

   B. Any activity that cannot be mitigated

   C. General activities and major bodily functions

   D. A physical or mental impairment that requires the use of supplemental medication or prosthetics

18. Professionals, craft workers, and laborers/helpers have what in common?

   A. They are all job categories on the EEO-1 report.

   B. They are all classifications for defining exempt workers.

   C. They are all examples of types of labor unions.

   D. They are all examples of protected-class individuals.

19. Which of the following definitions is correct for the term *job bidding*?

   A. An internal job announcement

   B. Allowing contractors to submit requests for proposals

   C. The means by which internal employees can express interest in a job prior to it becoming available

   D. Ranking job applicants based on their comparative qualifications

20. Which of the following interview questions is unlawful?

   A. If you were an animal, what kind of animal would you be?

   B. Are you a U.S. citizen?

   C. Tell me about a time you disagreed with your boss about a course of action.

   D. Any job offer made will be contingent on a medical exam. Are you willing to undergo one if we offer you the job?

Chapter 4

PHR Exam: Learning and Development

The HRCI test specifications from the Learning and Development functional area covered in this chapter include PHR-level responsibilities and knowledge.

Responsibilities:

✓ 01 **Provide consultation to managers and employees on professional growth and development opportunities.**

✓ 02 **Implement and evaluate career development and training programs (for example: careerpathing, management training, mentorship).**

✓ 03 **Contribute to succession planning discussions with management by providing relevant data.**

Knowledge:

✓ 25 **Applicable federal laws and regulations related to learning and development activities**

✓ 26 **Learning and development theories and applications**

✓ 27 **Training program facilitation, techniques, and delivery**

✓ 28 **Adult learning processes**

✓ 29 **Instructional design principles and processes (for example: needs analysis, process flow mapping)**

✓ 30 **Techniques to assess training program effectiveness, including use of applicable metrics**

✓ 31 **Organizational development (OD) methods, motivation methods, and problem-solving techniques**

✓ 32 **Task/process analysis**

✓ 33 **Coaching and mentoring techniques**

✓ 34 **Employee retention concepts and applications**

✓ 35 **Techniques to encourage creativity and innovation**

Learning and Development (L&D) is the functional area of human resources (HR) that seeks to affect two types of behaviors: employee and company. This is so that the organization can achieve its goals through engaged and productive employees. This chapter explores the variety of organizational development (OD) techniques that HR may use to effect change, both at the business/operations level and the individual employee level.

This chapter looks at ways that organizations implement the changes necessary to accomplish their missions and the strategies they use to align employees with the vision, mission, and goals developed by their leaders. It includes a review of learning and development activities that support positive organizational and employee outcomes.

This chapter begins by examining several different approaches to an organization's development and the ways these approaches positively impact organizational culture and climate. That discussion is followed by a review of techniques for developing employees, managers, and leaders as well as a systems model for use in developing training programs.

L&D doesn't occur in a vacuum; it occurs in the context of how the organization sees itself, how it conducts business, how it views its employees, and how it develops its leaders. L&D activities are often driven by what the employer values, what they exist to "do" as well as by external forces such as customer needs or regulatory demands. Every organization makes determinations about these issues, whether consciously, as part of an OD process, or unconsciously, as a result of the way its people operate on a day-to-day basis. Effective organizations are those in which values and beliefs are shared at all levels and are reflected in the behavior of individuals throughout the organization.

Organizational Development

Organizational development (OD) is a systematic method of examining an organization's technology, processes, structure, and human resources, and developing action strategies to improve the way it achieves desired business results. OD is a collection of theories developed by organizational scientists that are designed to be applied in the workplaces of today. This research field produced classic works such as the Hawthorne Studies (which are described in detail at https://courses.lumenlearning.com/baycollege-introbusiness/chapter/video-hawthorne-studies-at-att/) and more recent studies related to emotions and their influence in the workplace (described in Chapter 6, "PHR Exam: Employee and

Labor Relations"). As you can see, OD has penetrated all aspects of the practice of human resources.

When employers take action based on these theories, it is termed an "intervention." *OD interventions* may be directed toward structures, processes, technology, individuals, groups of individuals, or entire organizations. This section focuses on organization-wide changes to strategy, processes, and individuals.

Strategic Interventions

Strategic OD interventions are often used to implement changes made in response to changing marketplace conditions. These changes must take care to align with the company vision and mission, or in some cases, the vision and mission might need to change. These interventions are designed to align various elements in the organization with the new direction or focus established by the leaders. Some examples of strategic OD interventions are change management, knowledge management, and learning organizations.

Change Management

The result of any OD process is a change in the way things are done in an organization. Whether it's a new technology, a more efficient process, or a different reporting structure, the resulting change will have to be implemented by people—and no matter how difficult it is to create the new operating plans, implementing them successfully will be even more difficult because the people in the organization must embrace the change and be motivated and committed to making the change work.

Change Process Theory

An early model of *change process theory*, developed by a social psychologist named Kurt Lewin, described three stages for change:

Unfreezing   This stage creates the motivation for change by identifying and communicating the need for the change. In this stage, it's important to create a vision for the outcome of the change and a sense of urgency for getting to the new outcome.

Moving   During this stage, resistance is examined and managed, and the organization is aligned with the change. Communication remains an integral part of the process.

Refreezing   In the final stage of the theory, the change becomes the new norm for the organization, the outcome is evaluated, and additional changes occur to adjust the actual outcomes to those that are desired.

Human resource professionals can use change process theory to aid employees through a stressful work change. Let's take a look at some other ways HR can help employees deal with change.

Tools for Successful Change

People dislike change for a variety of reasons: Change moves them out of the comfort zone to which they have become accustomed, and they may be fearful of the unknown. The politics of the organization may make change undesirable in one group or another, and employees may perceive that they will lose status or control. Changes fail most often because the people who are expected to implement them aren't prepared to do so. Organizations can take steps to ensure the success of change initiatives, including the following:

Prepare for Change   The only constant in the current business environment is change. Organizations must be aware of situations developing in the industry or geographic areas in which they operate so they can be ahead of the curve in developing strategies that will effectively handle changes in the environment.

Communicate   To enhance the likelihood of a successful implementation, leaders must communicate effectively and repeatedly with employees well in advance of any planned implementation. Soliciting ideas from those who are closest to operations may provide insight into better solutions and increase buy-in when it's time to implement the change. Communication at every stage of the process will enable employees to get used to the idea of the change gradually, increase the level of acceptance, and build commitment for the process.

Develop a Plan   A comprehensive plan that clearly defines the goals of the change, addresses all of its implications, and includes tools for evaluating its success is essential. Scheduling training for employees who may need to upgrade skills, integrating processes from different areas of the organization, upgrading equipment, and developing a plan to address resistance to the change and reduce stress will increase the chances for successful implementation.

Have an Executive Sponsor   The CEO or another senior executive who is committed to and enthusiastic about the change must be able to inspire employees to commit to the implementation.

Motivate Direct Supervisors   Employees want to know how their supervisors feel about changes and will be influenced by what the supervisors say about the change. When direct supervisors and managers are motivated to implement a change, employees will be more likely to accept it.

Recruit Unofficial Leaders   Every organization has unofficial leaders who are able to influence co-workers; obtaining their commitment to the change will influence others. HRCI defines a *change agent* as a person or department that deliberately causes change within an organization. In OD interventions, this is at the direction of strategy.

Implement   Put the change into action. Ensure that employees have the tools needed to successfully implement the change, whether that is new equipment, facilities, training, or support.

Evaluate   Compare results to the evaluation criteria developed during the planning stage to determine whether the change was successfully implemented.

HR professionals are in a unique position to act as change agents during this process. A *change agent* must be able to balance the needs of various stakeholders in the process, listen to their concerns, and move them toward acceptance of and commitment to the change.

Knowledge Management

During the course of business each day, organizations generate data (such as sales figures) and review it to glean useful information (such as trends). Individual employees then interpret the information based on past experiences with similar circumstances and draw conclusions that are used to move the organization forward. These conclusions are referred to as *knowledge*. Although data and information can be easily replicated by other employees with the right skills, the knowledge that comes from past experiences isn't always so easily repeated. The process of attempting to retain this ability is known as *knowledge management* (*KM*). This term, while still evolving, generally encompasses activities related to the creation, retention, and distribution of organizational knowledge. For purposes of the exams, knowledge management focuses the organizing of information to improve business performance at an individual and an organizational level.

Much of the knowledge that an individual acquires over time in an organization disappears when that person leaves the company. *Tribal knowledge* is characterized by unwritten information that is closely guarded by a significant few employees. Whether because of layoffs, outsourcing, or the retirement of key employees, the loss of critical knowledge negatively impacts organizations.

 Real World Scenario

Using KM to Solve Administrative Problems

Over time, an experienced executive assistant (EA) learns shortcuts and details that enhance an executive's ability to operate more effectively by eliminating administrative concerns. Some of these details are personal preferences for individual executives, but many are useful for any executive in an organization, such as which IT support person is best at long-distance troubleshooting, or out-of-town businesses that can provide quality services in an emergency, such as printing presentation materials on short notice if they aren't delivered on time.

Sharing this information among EAs usually occurs on an ad hoc basis, but this requires that individuals with specific knowledge be available when an emergency occurs. A better solution for long-term benefits is the creation of a knowledge management database or manual that the EAs update as they learn new information that can help executives achieve organization goals and objectives.

Executives benefit because they're able to accomplish more, and the EAs benefit because they save time, whether it's locating the best travel deals, identifying restaurants that provide appropriate venues for client meetings, finding the co-worker who can be counted on to solve urgent problems, or handling other administrative details that allow the executives they support to be more effective in their jobs.

Organizations use different methods to retain and institutionalize knowledge so that it's easily accessible for improving processes and increasing profits. These methods can be categorized in one of the following ways:

Expert Registers   An expert register or directory collects the names and areas of expertise of employees and is made available to all employees, who are then able to contact internal experts to discuss problems and find solutions.

Best-Practice Standards   The term *best practice* is often used to describe methods or practices that have been demonstrated to produce desired results over a period of time. In the KM context, best practices are those that have been used in an organization by one group of employees to achieve particular results and are codified for distribution to other employees in similar jobs or groups throughout the organization with the idea that the results will be duplicated. Best practices also exist at an industry level, such as Human Resources, with a *body of knowledge* used for practitioner reference. The HR Certification Institute's™ Guide to the Human Resource Body of Knowledge™ (HRBoK), for example, describes both knowledge and competencies for practicing HR in the 21st century.

After-Action Evaluations   An after-action evaluation is sometimes referred to as a *post-mortem* and is a review conducted at the end of a project or other group endeavor. The purpose of the evaluation is to share in the group what worked, what didn't work, and what knowledge can be retained for use in future projects.

Communities of Practice   A *community of practice* (CoP) is an informal means of learning what works well in environments characterized by open communication and trust. CoPs may be spontaneous and self-organized or sponsored by the organization. In either case, they consist of people with common work interests or needs who are willing to share experiences and expertise with co-workers. These groups benefit individuals by enhancing skills, satisfaction, and productivity; benefit the work group with increased trust and learning opportunities; and benefit the organization with improvements in sales, improved product development, reduced time-to-market lead times, and, ultimately, improved market share because of improved customer satisfaction.

Technology Solutions   The information technology (IT) group can play a large role in facilitating KM initiatives. As the organization function for communication infrastructure, IT implements database management and other IT tools that encourage knowledge sharing among employees.

Knowledge Management Systems   Some business functions lend themselves to the use of a *knowledge management system (KMS)*. These systems support and collect the creation, capture, storage, and dissemination of organizational knowledge and information. The goal of a KMS is to provide employees with easy access to information that has been collected from various sources, verified for accuracy, and organized for retrieval to answer questions or solve problems. An example of an effective KM program with which many people have had some experience is customer relationship management (CRM). Customers often complain about the frustration they experience when calling a customer support or help line and having to repeat all the details of a problem with a product to each new customer service representative (CSR) who comes on the line. An effective KMS has each CSR enter facts about customer problems into a database so that, when the customer calls back, the next CSR to answer the call knows everything that has already transpired between the customer and the company. The customer doesn't need to repeat information, and the CSR can avoid going back to step one in the problem-solving process.

Learning Organizations

Learning organizations are innovative environments in which knowledge is originated, obtained, and freely shared in response to environmental changes that affect the ability of the organization to compete. Defined by HRCI as promoting ongoing employee education and innovation, these organizations are focused on improving their competitiveness through continuous learning. The atmosphere in a learning organization is one in which employees are able to solve problems by experimenting with new methods that have been observed outside the organization or that have been experienced in other parts of the organization.

Peter Senge, author of *The Fifth Discipline: The Art and Practice of the Learning Organization* (Crown Business, revised edition, 2006), identifies five disciplines, or guiding principles, that enable organizations to increase their ability to realize desired results, cultivate new ways of thinking, expand on individual ideas, and encourage continuous lifelong learning in the organization. These disciplines include the following:

Systems Thinking   *Systems thinking* describes the ability of individuals and organizations to recognize patterns and to project how changes will impact them.

Personal Mastery   *Personal mastery* describes a high level of expertise in an individual's chosen field and a commitment to lifelong learning.

Mental Models   *Mental models* refer to the deep-seated beliefs that color perceptions and can affect how individuals see the world around them and react to it.

Building a Shared Vision   Stretching beyond the corporate vision statement and building a *shared vision* encourages the organization to plan for a future that inspires commitment on the part of all individuals in the organization.

Team Learning   *Team learning*, as defined by Senge, refers to the ability of a team to share and build on their ideas without holding anything back.

Techno-Structural Interventions

OD interventions that fall into the techno-structural category address issues of how work gets done in the organization by examining the level of employee involvement and redesigning work processes. *Total quality management (TQM)*, a process that focuses all resources in the organization on providing value for customers, is an example of a techno-structural intervention, as is Six Sigma. Several other interventions that are used in this category include process mapping, job design, and high-involvement organization.

Total Quality Management

TQM is a long-term intervention requiring employees at all levels in an organization to focus on providing products that meet customer needs. This is done by continually changing an organization's practices, structures, and systems. A successful TQM implementation requires the commitment of top management to lead the process. Because TQM is focused on customer needs, market research and product development are key components of the system. Processes are reviewed to eliminate wasted time as well as materials that either don't contribute to or are obstacles to producing the end product. Teamwork is an essential function in a TQM environment; all members involved in the product or service, from front-line workers to suppliers and sales managers, must work together to solve problems for customers.

There have been a number of leaders in the quality movement; the following are four who have made significant contributions:

W. Edwards Deming   The quality movement originated in the 1940s with the work of W. Edwards Deming, who proposed that quality is defined by the consumer. Deming developed a 14-point plan that placed the burden of quality on management because they're able to control the systems in the organization. Although American business was initially cool to the quality concept, Deming's theories were warmly received in Japan during the 1950s. In 1951, the Japanese named their quality award the Deming Prize, after him.

Joseph M. Juran   Another early proponent of the quality movement was Joseph M. Juran, who, like Deming, believed that quality begins with defining customer needs. Unlike Deming, Juran proposed that once customer needs were identified, they should be translated into the "language" of the business in order to deliver a product or service that met the needs of both customers and the business. He developed the Juran Trilogy, which identified three phases in the process: quality planning, quality control, and quality improvements. *Quality planning* initiates programs by addressing quality concerns during the product- or service-development process. *Quality control* ensures conformance to the parameters established in the planning phase during the operations phase. *Quality improvements* are used to continually improve operations and reduce waste.

Kaoru Ishikawa   Kaoru Ishikawa made significant contributions to the quality movement. He provided a collection of analytical tools to use in the workplace and developed the cause-and-effect diagram that bears his name. The following list explains some of these tools and provides examples:

Check Sheet   *Check sheets* are the simplest analysis tools, requiring only a list of items that might be expected to occur. In an HR setting, a check sheet might be used to keep track of the reasons people resign from their positions. Figure 4.1 is an example of a check sheet used for that purpose. When an item occurs, a check or tick mark is placed next to it on the list. The data collected with a check sheet may be graphically represented in a histogram to facilitate analysis.

FIGURE 4.1   Sample check sheet

Reason	Number of Occurrences	Total
Lack of advancement	ꟷꟷ	5
Lack of recognition	ꟷꟷ ꟷꟷ ||||	14
Long commute	|	1
Low pay	||	2
Poor supervision	ꟷꟷ ꟷꟷ ꟷꟷ |	16
		38

Histogram   *Histograms* provide a way of looking at random occurrences to find out whether there is a pattern. Using the data from the check sheet provided in Figure 4.1, a histogram provides a visual image of the reasons for resignations, as illustrated by Figure 4.2.

FIGURE 4.2   Histogram

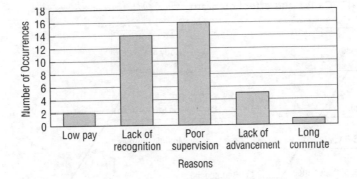

Pareto Chart   The *Pareto chart* provides a graphical representation of the 80/20 rule: 80 percent of the problems are caused by 20 percent of the causes, a principle established by an Italian economist named Vilfredo Pareto. The Pareto chart points out which areas of concern will provide the greatest return when corrected. The difference between a Pareto chart and a histogram is that the Pareto chart arranges the data in descending order and includes a cumulative percentage on the right side of the chart. Figure 4.3 uses the Pareto chart to identify the most significant causes of resignations. In this case, poor supervision and a lack of recognition cause 80 percent of the resignations.

FIGURE 4.3   Pareto chart

FIGURE 4.3   Pareto chart

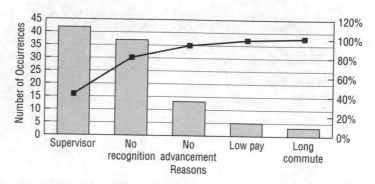

Cause-and-Effect Diagram   A *cause-and-effect diagram* aids in organizing information during brainstorming sessions. This quality-analysis tool is also known as the *Ishikawa diagram* or *fishbone diagram*. Figure 4.4 analyzes what PHR candidates can do to maximize their chances for success on the exam.

FIGURE 4.4   Cause-and-effect diagram

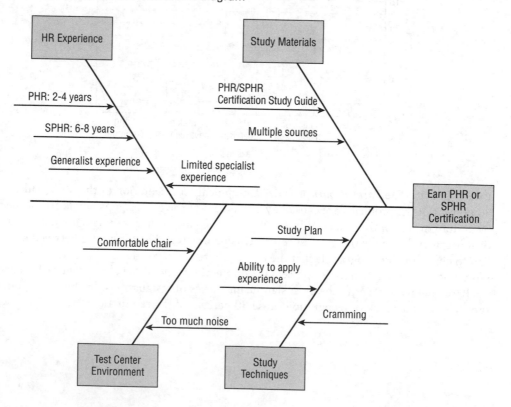

Stratification   To stratify something means to sort large amounts of data into smaller groups. *Stratification charts* show the individual components of a problem in addition to the total or summary. This aids in identifying possible strategies for correcting problems. Figure 4.5 is an example of a stratification chart. In the resignation example, the shorter bars represent components of each category, and the taller bar is the total amount. For example, the poor-supervision reasons could be broken down into categories for poor management skills and the inability to delegate. This kind of chart aids in the development of appropriate programs to solve the individual problems that make up a whole.

FIGURE 4.5   Stratification chart

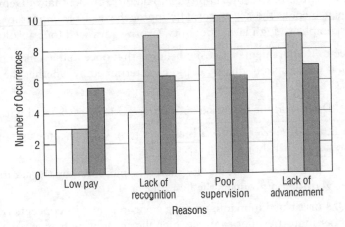

Scatter Chart   Also known as an *XY chart*, a *scatter chart* provides a graphical representation for the relationship between two sets of numbers. Information presented on a scatter chart is used for various forms of statistical analysis.

Process-Control Chart   *Process-control charts* provide a graphical representation of elements that are out of the acceptable range by setting parameters above and below the range. This tool is most effective for determining variances in production processes over time. Although this tool is generally used in a production context, to help you understand how it works, let's look at how it could be applied in an HR context. Let's say your department has established that open positions will be filled within 30 days from the date of notification to the HR department, with a 5-day grace period. The sample process-control chart in Figure 4.6 shows you that two positions were out of the normal range: One took less than 25 days, and the other took more than 35 days. Both of these are considered to be "out of control" and warrant investigation to determine what caused the variance.

FIGURE 4.6   Process control chart

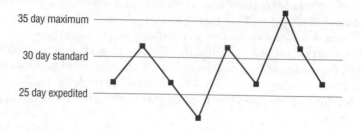

Philip B. Crosby   Philip B. Crosby's approach to quality, unlike that of Deming and Juran, focused on management as the key factor. His approach was based on strategic planning as the means to accomplish a high level of quality. Crosby advanced four absolutes of quality:

Conformance to Requirements   Crosby believed that once management clearly described what was required, quality could be determined by whether the product met the standard.

Prevention   "Do it right the first time" is a phrase Crosby associated with this absolute.

Performance Standards   *Zero defects* is another term Crosby came up with to describe the quality standard that should be met.

Measurement   In Crosby's view, quality should be measured by the additional cost of not producing zero-defect products the first time.

Although TQM originated in manufacturing environments, its concepts translate easily to service and other industries. For example, a public accounting firm can establish standards and then develop checklists and templates for accountants to follow when providing client services. By emphasizing the importance of accuracy and measuring how many corrections must be made, the firm can quantify the work of its accountants to ensure that it's up to the standards the company established.

Six Sigma

Six Sigma is a quality philosophy developed by engineers at Motorola during the 1980s, when they were looking for a more precise way to measure process defects. The Six Sigma quality standard is measured on a "defects per million" basis, unlike previous standards that were measured on a "defects per thousand" basis. The Six Sigma methodology is referred to as DMAIC: Define, Measure, Analyze, Improve, and Control:

Define   The first step is to define the customer and issues of importance to them, along with the process and project parameters.

Measure   Once the process is defined, data about defects and other measures is collected and then compared to the original parameters to identify underperformance.

Analyze   An analysis of the data is made to identify gaps between the goal and actual performance, explain why the gaps occurred, and rank possible improvements.

Improve   Based on the analysis, solutions are created and implemented.

Control   During the control phase, systems are revised to incorporate the improvements, and employees are trained in the new processes. The goal of this phase is to prevent backsliding into the previous process by ongoing monitoring.

A significant component of Six Sigma is the quality team structure used to develop, implement, and manage initiatives. In these organizations, employees who are trained and certified in the Six Sigma methodology work full-time on quality initiatives focused on continuously reviewing and revising business processes. There are requirements for certification at each level in the structure, including a specific curriculum and requirements for demonstrating effectiveness by working on quality initiatives. In addition, candidates must pass a written test prior to certification. The team structure's levels are as follows:

Quality Leader/Manager   The quality leader in an organization generally reports to the CEO or president in order to remain objective. This role represents customer requirements and focuses on continually improving operations.

Master Black Belt   Master black belts generally work with a single function, such as marketing or accounting. They work closely with process owners to implement the DMAIC methodology and ensure that projects stay on track.

Process Owner   Process owners are individuals responsible for a specific process in the organization; for example, the highest-level HR employee in the organization would be the process leader for HR initiatives.

Black Belt   Black-belt employees work full-time on quality initiatives, coaching green belts to improve their quality skills.

Green Belt   Green belts have received Six Sigma training and participate on project teams part-time while continuing to work in another role for the balance of their time.

Process Mapping

Defined by HRCI as a "process flow analysis," this is a method of assessing critical business functions. A process map is a tool that visually represents workflow. It is useful to show the end result of a process, and all the steps and people involved in getting there. Visually relaying this information can be used to improve efficiencies and make decisions about resources. Additionally, a process flow map can be used as a training tool to show others how the work gets done, provide process documentation, and improve task consistency. They are also helpful in diagnosing bottlenecks, especially for more complex processes that require many steps.

Important to the work flow mapping are standard symbols to communicate steps in a workflow or process. Figure 4.7 shows a sample of flowchart symbols and what they represent on a process map.

FIGURE 4.7   Meaning of process flow symbols

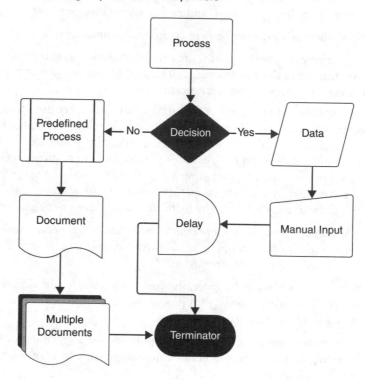

"Created in Lucidchart at www.lucidchart.com"

Job Design

Organizations that seek to promote from within are often faced with a difficult dilemma—there aren't higher level jobs available for everyone. One solution is to employ a promote-from-within strategy that develops employees within the context of their current role. There are several effective ways to do this:

Job Enrichment   When an employee shows potential and is interested in growth opportunities, employers use *job enrichment* to assign new responsibilities or tasks that challenge the employee to use existing skills and abilities in new ways or to develop new ones as they tackle new assignments. Beginning with Frederick Herzberg, many social scientists have built behavior models that help incorporate job enrichment activities into job design. This strategy is based on the theory that when certain job factors are present, positive outcomes such as improved attendance, increased productivity, and greater levels of job satisfaction are the result. J. Richard Hackman and Greg Oldham's Job Characteristics model identified five job design factors that can improve four critical psychological states, including meaningfulness of work, responsibility for outcomes, knowledge of actual results, and employee growth needs. Here are the five job design factors used to achieve these positive states:

Skill Variety   The ability of the employee to use multiple skill sets to complete a task.

Task Identity   The concept that the effort applied by the worker produces a whole identifiable unit or outcome, as opposed to a single part.

Task Significance   The inherent or perceived value of a job either internally to co-workers or externally to society.

Autonomy   The degree of independence or discretion allowed on the job.

Feedback   Communication to the employee by management related to how well the employee performs his or her duties.

Job Enlargement   *Job enlargement* is when additional tasks are added to the job without increasing the level of responsibility or skill. Job enlargement may be viewed positively by employees when it reduces job boredom by increasing the variety of tasks assigned. In other cases, employees may view this job design negatively if they perceive they're doing more work without a corresponding increase in pay.

Job Rotation   Focused on giving employees a sense of the "bigger picture." *job rotation* allows employees to cross-train for jobs within other areas of the company. This strategy allows for skill variety while increasing the task identity, and potentially, the significance of their work as a whole.

Job Crafting   In many cases, the design (or redesign) of jobs can be taken on by the employees themselves. *Job crafting* is a term that is used to describe the efforts employees take to 1) change the work itself, such as scope of job tasks, and 2) change the amount or quality of interaction with others, including co-workers and customers. Job crafting is a form of employee ownership achieved through autonomy and trust that can improve the meaning of jobs. Cautious employers may want to take a blended approach to job design and redesign, ensuring that employees have a voice while still controlling for productive outcomes.

Job Loading   Built from Hackman and Oldham's job model, *job loading* seeks to redesign work in order to better serve employee psychological needs for understanding and meaning, thus increasing ownership of work outcomes. *Horizontal loading* involves adding different tasks to a job that are equal to other tasks, whereas *vertical loading* adds decision-making responsibility to a position. For example, a nursing job can be vertically loaded by giving employees a shared governance role over scheduling.

High-Involvement Organizations

In *high-involvement organizations* (*HIOs*), employees are involved in designing their own work processes, are empowered to take the actions necessary to complete their work, and are accountable for the results. HIOs are characterized by broadly defined jobs in flat hierarchies in which continuous feedback is provided and information flows between and among self-directed work teams.

Edward E. Lawler, III, founder of the Center for Organizational Effectiveness at the University of Southern California and author of numerous books on organizational effectiveness, identified four elements needed to create an HIO:

Power   Traditional organization structures are built on a "command and control" model in which decisions are made at the top with little or no input from lower levels in the hierarchy. HIOs grant decision-making power down to the employees assigned to carry out the decision and hold them accountable for the results.

Information   "Information is power," and in traditional organizations that often means individuals hold on to information that could be used to improve results instead of sharing it with the individuals who could use it to make improvements. In an HIO, a variety of information (production statistics, sales, expenses, profits, customer feedback, and so on) is disseminated so that everyone can use it to direct their efforts toward improving results.

Knowledge   Increasing the knowledge, skills, and abilities (KSAs) available in the organization enhances the ability of all employees to contribute to bottom-line success. Providing training and development opportunities increases the organization's capability for making decisions and taking actions that improve operating effectiveness.

Rewards   Tying pay to performance compensates employees according to the level of effort they expend to accomplish their goals and objectives and contribute to organizational success. When employees know that their contributions will be recognized, they're encouraged to go "above and beyond" normal job requirements. These rewards can be based on individual or team contributions.

The return on the investment for HIOs is significant. They include higher levels of reported customer satisfaction, reduced turnover, and reduced employee complaints.

Need more information? Check out this video describing the findings of a study on the seven measures of an effective workforce. The details start at about three and a half minutes in: www.youtube.com/watch?v=T1v6YjDAfv0.

Human Process Interventions

Human process interventions are directed at developing competencies at the individual level in the organization. Common interventions in this area include team-building activities and creative problem-solving.

Team-Building Activities

For a team to function effectively, the members must know the goals they're working toward and what is expected of them as team members. Team-building exercises build relationships in the team to communicate expectations and to involve team members in developing creative and effective ways of accomplishing their goals. Team-building activities run the gamut from expensive events staged by consultants, such as wilderness adventures, to games devised by managers in their individual workgroups. The goal of any team-building activity is to put team members in unusual situations that require them to rely on one another to solve a problem. These activities can be fun and effective methods for starting the process, but to be fully effective, the team spirit built or lessons learned must be reinforced when team members are back in the normal routine. The ultimate goal for the organization, of course, is to improve results. Team-building activities can boost productivity by enhancing communication within the group and encouraging collaboration.

Although game-based team-building programs are still used in some organizations, recent research into their effectiveness indicates that the results may not last for the long term. Some organizations have turned to personality inventory models, such as the Myers-Briggs Type Indicator and the Keirsey Temperament Sorter, that help team members understand themselves, provide insight into differences in how others view experiences, and build communication skills. Other team-building methods involve role-playing situations related to actual business problems the team faces and allow team members to work through a collaborative solution together. These experiences can then be drawn on when regular challenges occur back in the real world of work.

Creative Problem-Solving

Employees and leaders who have the ability to solve problems are highly valued. Creativity is often linked with innovation, and innovation is often the result of implementing a new vision or solving existing problems for customers.

As with many initiatives, it is up to HR to understand and lead the process by creating the right conditions for creativity to thrive. This includes helping to build a culture that welcomes new ideas, cultivates open sharing, and effectively manages constructive conflict to make sure a problem is properly framed.

Basadur Applied Creativity has a framework for problem-solving that runs through three classifications that contain eight steps:

Classification 1: Formulate the problem.   Step 1—This step includes identifying what the desired outcome is, and what obstacles exist in achieving those states. It can include both current and potential threats to an issue or condition.

Consider, for example, that a company is receiving product from a vendor in India that requires a significant amount of rework before being sold to the consumer.

Step 2—Step 2 relates to active data gathering to ensure the proper perspectives are being considered. This includes historical views, facts, and tangible data that can be used toward effective decision-making.

The problem-solving team identifies that 60 percent of the defects are found in only two of the several hundred products they receive from this supplier.

Step 3—This step is where the problem is defined and the target is established.

The team identifies that the problem target are the top two defective products from this supplier.

Classification 2: Formulate the solution.   Step 4—Step 4 is about brainstorming, where problem solvers work together to identify potential solutions for their target.

In these sessions, the team realized that they could change vendors, pull the offending products off the market entirely, create quality training videos for the supplier, refuse shipments, or visit India to reiterate the quality standards and find out what was going on.

Step 5—This step is where the problem solvers synthesize all of the above to select the solution that makes the most sense.

The team decides to create training videos related to the quality manufacturing standards and needs of the products having the most issues.

Classification 3: Implement the solution.   Step 6—This is known as the action planning step; problem solvers put together an implementation plan to create the solution.

The team meets again to map out the necessary action steps for the Quality, Production, Purchasing, and Marketing departments to achieve the goal.

Step 7—This step is focused on gaining acceptance of the plan and addressing any concerns that may not have been considered in the solution planning.

The Purchasing department reached out to the vendor in India to discuss any concerns and gather their preferences on what would be the most beneficial information to include in the training videos.

Step 8—The final step is all about taking action. Any solution without action is useless, and the problem will remain unsolved.

The problem-solving team puts their plan into action, resulting in three short videos that demonstrate the quality standards and procedures India should implement to reduce defects in the products.

 Real World Scenario

Process Council and Facilitators

When organizations get employees involved with team building, leadership, and process improvement, the result can improve organizational processes as well as morale.

One San Francisco Bay Area organization has given the responsibility of process updating and building to the Process Council. Process Council members are specifically chosen for their leadership abilities, experience at the organization, and knowledge of how the organization operates as a whole. When a process issue is identified, the Process Council decides whether a team is needed to tackle the problem. With the help of upper management, the Process Council recommends team members, a team leader, and a facilitator and provides the leader with a charter outlining the council's expectations for the team. The Process Council meets quarterly to discuss process issues, appoint new teams, and discuss teams in progress.

The organization appoints several facilitators to help the Process Council teams meet their goals. Facilitators are chosen for their leadership abilities, their work with various employees across the organization, and their energetic personalities. Facilitators are specifically trained to provide a safe, objective environment in which team members can discuss the process issue at hand without judgment or criticism. Facilitators guide team members by asking pointed questions, politely interrupting "time robbers" (those who talk incessantly with no relevance to the team goal), and keeping members on track to solve the issue in a timely manner.

The Process Council and facilitators have tackled several cross-departmental problems and have even been involved with two reorganizations that occurred as a result of Process Council team decisions. Because facilitators and Process Council members are also employees who will be affected by Process Council results, they have a vested interest in team success. They're also trained to tackle day-to-day problems that may not need a team discussion.

Human Resource Management Interventions

Human resource management (HRM) interventions focus on individual interactions in the organization: human to human, human to process, or human to job.

Employees are complex beings with unique and differing needs. Effective HRM programs are those that are diverse enough to meet those needs while staying aligned with business goals and objectives. In addition to traditional HR practices such as rewards and recognition, this can be accomplished by HRM interventions that develop succession plans through leadership development, having clearly defined career plans, developing high-potential employees, career pathing, and in some cases, creating dual-career ladders.

Succession Planning through Leadership Development

The Center for Creative Leadership (CCL) describes the goal of succession planning as having the talent necessary to meet future goals and challenges. Organizations of today have had to respond to pressures from mergers and acquisitions, downsizing, layoffs, corporate restructuring, government mandates, political shifts, corrupt business practices, demographic migrations, an opioid crisis, and medical marijuana—the list seems nearly endless. Though it's impossible to predict the nature of future challenges, HR practitioners know that they will need a pipeline of future leaders to call on when the time comes. This section briefly reviews a few of the more popular and emerging strategies for building a leadership pipeline.

Developmental Networks   The CCL describes the practice of having employees create *developmental networks* so that they have mentors and coaches beyond their direct manager. In an article on Forbes Magazine.com, the CCL describes three main elements of this approach to developing leaders:

- **Diversity**—Do the leaders have a network of individuals with varying perspectives and subject matter expertise?
- **Density**—Do the leaders have a network of individuals with enough distinction to reduce the redundancy of information?
- **Strength**—Are the relationships with the network varied enough in strength for clarity on which resources to tap when needed?

Developmental Multisource Feedback   Similar to building a developmental network, HR can help leaders identify areas for development by seeking feedback from multiple sources. Tools such as the 360-degree feedback assessment provide feedback to managers about specific skills or behaviors from subordinates, peers, managers, and even outside sources such as customers or vendors. HR helps leaders navigate the process and provide the feedback necessary to then develop plans for growth. Giving performance feedback through appraisals is discussed in greater detail in Chapter 6.

Developmental Assignments   Many developmental assignments can be taken on simultaneously with existing job responsibilities. Asking future leaders to take on a new assignment or project, lead a team, or become a subject matter expert are all ways employees can develop skills for their next role. Job rotation may also work well here, particularly for future leadership teams that are focused on operational learning.

Personal Growth   So much of the research in leadership development directly relates to the human condition. Research has consistently shown that the impact a program has on people is directly linked to the quality of the emotional experience—the effect of a leadership experience is stronger when it is bound with an emotion. Some examples include Tony Robbins events, leadership workshops using Patrick Lencioni's work on vulnerability-based trust in teams, and Dale Carnegie's leadership breakthrough plans. Personal growth programs designed to increase self-awareness have many advantages, not the least of which includes emotional intelligence, personality factors, and emotional labor. All of these concepts are discussed in Chapter 6.

Management by Objectives   A *management by objectives* (MBO) intervention aligns individuals with organization goals and measures the successful attainment of objectives as well as the quality and/or quantity of performance. Because it's an effective way of tying results to goals, MBO is often used as a performance appraisal tool. Its application and acceptance results, at least in part, from its philosophy that rewarding people for what they accomplish is important.

The MBO process is built on the concepts of mutual involvement in setting performance goals, ongoing communication during the performance period (usually one year), measurement, and reward for accomplishments at the end of the period. The process identifies and clarifies expectations and provides for a broad assessment of individual performance. It usually begins in the first quarter of each fiscal year when the supervisor and the employee agree on a few significant business objectives, such as sales volume, new business development, completion of specific projects, or achievement of other specific goals. Utilizing the SMART goal process will result in goals that clearly communicate what is expected and help to ensure the outcomes are aligned with key business objectives.

The use of an MBO process to tie individual goals to corporate goals and objectives has value but must take into account the rapid pace of change in the current business environment and use goals that are broad enough to be meaningful for the entire review period or that allow for revision as business objectives change.

Supervisory Training   When the organization is successful in advancing employees, very often they end up in positions with supervisory responsibility. Some organizations make the mistake of assuming that a person who excels in a technical area will automatically be able to supervise employees in that area, but that is rarely the case. Providing training for new supervisors gives them the tools they need to succeed at their new responsibilities.

Supervisory training usually involves topics related to interactions with employees, such as performance management, progressive discipline, performance appraisals, workplace safety, interviewing, and training. New supervisors also benefit from training on topics such as legal requirements for employers (such as exemption status, leave policies, equal employment opportunity [EEO], the Americans with Disabilities Act [ADA], the Family and Medical Leave Act [FMLA], and so on) and policies and procedures specific to the organization. Other topics that help supervisors accomplish more and improve effectiveness include the following:

- Effective management skills
- Financial analysis
- Business basics
- Technology management
- Decision-making skills
- Conflict management
- Team building
- Influence and negotiation skills
- Communication skills
- Time management
- Interview skills
- Delegation
- Planning
- Motivation skill

Career Management

Career management is a term used by HRCI to describe the preparation, implementation, and monitoring of the professional development of employees while still focusing on the goals and needs of an organization. Career management is generally achieved by engaging in career planning and development.

Career planning is a process that helps employees take steps to improve professional skills and create new opportunities. It begins by identifying gaps between where an employee is currently in their career and where they wish to be. A plan, often called a path, can then be developed to help employees move forward toward their career goals.

The career planning process uses an assessment of individual strengths and weaknesses, both in their current role and in the context of a future role. From this data, individual intervention strategies, including training, coaching, and mentoring can then be put into motion.

Skills Training   Skills training provides employees with specific information that is needed to do their jobs. In some cases, skills training is job-specific; for example, to teach accounting staff how to use new accounting software, or to provide a software engineer with training in a new language that will be needed to develop a product. Training in soft skills is often used to assist employees; for example, training on meeting management might be provided to reduce the amount of time spent in meetings and make them more productive. Training for communication and time-management skills are other examples of soft skills training. Another type of skills training is provided for employees who are moving into supervisory or management positions for the first time.

Coaching Programs   Although formal training can be useful in providing information for managers, one of the best ways to develop them is by assigning a mentor or coach.

A *coach* is typically a specialist who becomes involved, often at the organization's expense, in developing an employee in a particular area: for example, to hone leadership skills or to improve communication skills. Some coaches can offer guidance in many areas.

Coaching programs can be tailored to suit many management and executive needs and are especially beneficial to L&D for training management and executives in effectively managing organizational talent. Too often, employees with strong operational skills but very little leadership skill are promoted into management. Yet with the changing workforce and increased demands on employees, the ability to influence others is rapidly becoming a benchmark of effective management techniques. Identifying strengths and weaknesses, discovering latent talent or aptitudes, personal development, and recognizing elements of the job that are most enjoyable to the individual are outcomes from successful coaching methods. Other more technical outcomes of these programs include the analysis of orientation toward learning, EI scores, cognitive processing skills, and measuring levels of motivation.

Non-skill or work-related deficiencies that are unrelated to an employee's skill set can also be addressed through the coaching process. These include issues such as work burnout, career plateaus, lack of personal accountability, and struggles with work/family balance. Coaching is a viable alternative to traditional training that can be quite effective in addressing some of these more difficult influences on management performance.

As with all training design, a needs assessment should first be conducted to evaluate the specific deficiencies to be addressed. Depending on the need, various approaches to coaching can then be applied in an effort to modify and strengthen a leader's ability. The decision of how to deliver the coaching process—internally, externally, or virtually—must then be made:

Internal Sources   Internal sources for coaching and mentoring can be effective for several reasons. Peer-to-peer coaching is useful when the values or behaviors desired are shared within a workgroup or management tier. For example, some organizations create training initiatives that focus on the achievement of strategic aims such as increasing retention or forecasting growth. Having an internal peer network that can identify with the unique company culture is helpful for managers who are having difficulty achieving specific organizational objectives. Furthermore, assigning a mentor or creating a peer group provides the opportunity for career depth and gives the participant a safe place to brainstorm when the relationships are built on trust and credibility. The facilitator chosen to lead these types of teams or groups should be someone proficient in adult learning styles and who has the ability to address specific company cultural issues such as a highly politicized workgroup, entrenched employees, or the ability to navigate a period of rapid growth or restructuring.

External Sources   External coaching sources are appropriate when the need is for a one-on-one experience or the focus of the coaching is highly technical/psychological in nature. The individual seeking the executive coaching may have a need to hone one or two specific skill sets, and the organizational hierarchy doesn't have an internal source or tools to provide meaningful, real-time feedback and analysis.

Having an objective viewpoint of the manager's knowledge, skills, and abilities in addition to the organizational roadblocks *as perceived by the participant* is often necessary to modify a manager's behavior. Quite often, a perspective change is all that is necessary to get the manager/executive to the next level of performance. Dr. Seuss was once quoted as saying, "Sometimes the questions are complicated and the answers are simple." Furthermore, multiple external resource specialists can be engaged to assess the abilities of the participant in areas such as learning assessments, career aptitudes, or personality tests. They can further be retained to analyze the manager's subordinate group to identify sources of potential conflict or miscommunication. Reaching outside the organization can provide the fresh perspective, personalized attention, and creative problem-solving that is at the core of successful coaching programs.

Virtual Coaching   Virtual coaching techniques combine the concepts of self-paced learning with typical coaching outcomes. The mode of delivery varies and can include a combination of email relationships, telephone consulting, videoconferencing, webinars, tests that simulate workplace experiences and measure reactions, discussion boards, and industry-specific forums.

An important element in a coaching relationship is the trust factor, and virtual coaching can fall short of this critical facet. And, as with many other virtual training tools, participant satisfaction rates and successful outcomes can be diminished when there is little to no face-to-face interaction. With this in mind, virtual coaching should be viewed as a tool to augment personalized coaching sessions, not replace them.

Mentoring Programs   In a business context, a *mentor* is generally an experienced individual who acts as a teacher, guide, counselor, or facilitator and provides personalized feedback and guidance to a more junior colleague. In many cases, a mentor is someone who takes an interest in an employee's career and acts as a sponsor for them, providing a sounding board for issues and decisions. Traditionally, the mentor relationship is based more on an informal personal interest than on a formal program. *Mentoring programs* formalize this concept and ensure that the benefits of mentoring are available to a diverse group of employees who demonstrate leadership potential.

Formal mentors are those approved by an organization to take on protégés after being screened to ensure that only those who are best suited for mentor relationships enter the program. Mentors in formal programs receive training to develop skills in mentoring, and both mentors and mentees receive training to ensure that everyone understands what to expect from the relationship.

A relatively new feature of mentoring is the *reverse mentor*. These are young individuals who help older co-workers understand technology and the culture of the younger generation.

Coaching vs. Mentoring

There are several definitions of coaching and mentoring in the business lexicon. For purposes of the exams, focus on HRCI's definitions as follows:

- **Coaching:** A method of developing specific skills in which a coach gives information and objective feedback to a person or group (guiding, giving information or training).

- **Mentoring:** When an experienced person shares knowledge with someone who has less experience (helping a person learn).

Career Pathing

A career path is important for every employee, not just those who are high potential or seeking a management role. Helping employees develop their personal and professional skills will lead to better business outcomes, from loyalty (retention), customer satisfaction, and productivity. There is not necessarily only one way to design a career path program for your employer, but all systems should share an outcome that gives employees skills that will transfer on the job—current or future. Figure 4.8 illustrates how one company is utilizing a bucket list format to encourage all employees to lead.

FIGURE 4.8   Career bucket list

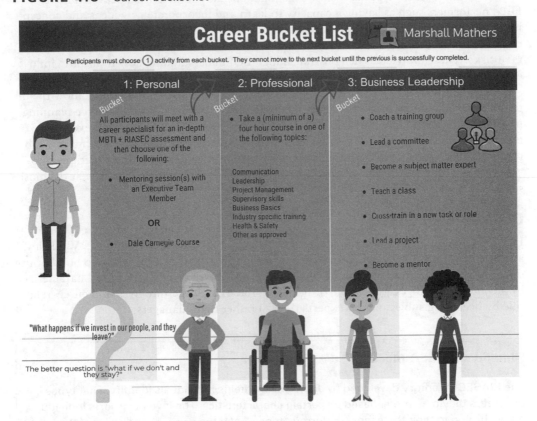

High-Potential Employees

Some of the individuals identified as future organization leaders in this process are known as *high-potential employees* (*HiPos*) and are provided with extensive training opportunities to prepare them for future roles. Identifying HiPos can be difficult, because future performance can't always be predicted from current performance (as described in *The Peter Principle*, a book written in 1968 by Dr. Laurence Peter Harper Business that describes how organizations tend to promote people until they rise to their level of incompetence and leave them in that position). Many selection procedures can be used to screen candidates for the HiPo track, including assessment centers, behavioral interviews, and observation. See the Holland's RIASEC Model to learn about how career inventories such as the RIASEC (Holland Codes, or the Holland Occupational Themes) can be useful in evaluating individuals for a HiPo development program.

The results of these types of assessments highlight the characteristics representative of HiPo performers such as having a capacity to learn and incorporate new ideas and concepts into daily performance, using feedback to improve skills and performance, and having a commitment to continuing career development. Potential HiPos are also able to assess and take risks. These individuals demonstrate a high EQ, understanding how to inspire, influence, and motivate others, qualities that are essential in effective leaders.

Once identified, HiPos receive assignments that challenge their abilities and allow them to take risks. Organizations that create succession plans as part of the workforce planning process factor HiPos into the plan. Very often they're paired with senior-level executive mentors to guide them as they take on assignments with increasing levels of difficulty. Job rotation, which moves HiPos through various divisions, departments, and functions, provides them with a broad view of the organization's needs that will be necessary at the most senior level.

Dual-Career Ladders

For some employees, the idea of moving into a supervisory role is not palatable. While loyal and talented, they may prefer to take on new responsibilities that allow them to build or use different skills. For these employees, dual-career ladders are an effective tool. Characterized by advanced training, certification, or licensing, these employees progress in their current role by becoming subject matter experts (SMEs) rather than managers.

Holland's RIASEC Model

The RIASEC inventory developed by John Holland helps individuals identify what types of careers they may prefer based on certain characteristics. The inventory sorts individuals according to their three most preferred "types," and the combination/order of the letters may help to predict satisfaction in certain careers. The groupings are:

- **R**ealistic—Also known as "the doers," these individuals prefer jobs that require the use of concrete (versus abstract) skills. They may include careers in the culinary arts or outdoor education.

- **I**nvestigative—These folks prefer to use their thinking skills at work, gravitating toward jobs where they can work with data or models. These individuals are suited for work such as counseling or engineering.

- **A**rtistic—Also known as creators, people who prefer to use their artistic skills are drawn toward industries such as graphic design or teaching.

- **S**ocial—Not surprisingly, those with a dominant social preference are usually found in careers where they may use their people skills to help others. Careers such as nursing or clergy may be well suited for these individuals.

- **E**nterprising—Enterprising individuals are most noted for both their people skills and power of persuasion. They are often working in fields such as customer service or human resources.

- **C**onventional—Those known for their preference for data and rules are most likely exercising their conventional preferences for career choice. You will find many conventional personalities in jobs such as business training and web developing.

For a look at how the RIASEC Model is used in career development, check out the Department of Labor's job database. Search onetonline.org for their career codes, and you can see how they apply to specific jobs. Click Advanced Search, and then browse by Interests for a more robust review of the RIASEC Model in action.

Employee Training Programs

Training is an effective tool for improving productivity and increasing operational efficiency, but it isn't the answer to every organizational problem. Training can solve problems related to employee skills or knowledge about a specific process, but it can't solve problems caused by structural or system issues. Before developing a training program, it's important to find out what is causing the problem and whether training is the appropriate solution.

For example, if customer service representatives are expected to handle an average of 20 calls per hour and they're handling an average of 12, it's important to find out why. One possibility is that the CSRs aren't familiar enough with the products to answer the questions easily, so they must look up answers in a manual. Another possibility is that the call volume has tripled since the call center phone system was installed and it can no longer handle the load, so it's frequently offline. The first possibility can be resolved with training, but the second can't.

Training may take place at one of the following three levels:

Organizational   *Organizational-level training* may encompass the entire organization or a single division or department. At this level, training is focused on preparing for future needs. Analyzing indicators that suggest a decline in the effectiveness of organizational operations can indicate the need for a training intervention. Some indicators that training is needed could include an increase in the number of accidents, a change in strategic direction, or the addition of a new product line. Metrics indicating a negative trend, such as a decline in employee satisfaction or productivity measures, are indicators that training is needed at this level.

Task   *Task-level training* involves processes performed in a single job category. The need for training at this level may be indicated by low productivity for a single process or poor-quality results.

Individual   *Individual-level training* involves a review of performance by individual employees and can be indicated by poor performance reviews or requests for assistance by the employee.

Employee training programs have many facets and approaches. The following sections will explore adult learning processes, instructional design models, and learning management systems.

Adult Learning Processes and Learning Styles

HR practitioners must have a foundational understanding of how adults learn as they approach the task of training design and development. The concept that adult learning processes were different from those of children was developed in the United States by Eduard Lindeman during the 1920s. Lindeman first promoted the idea that, for adults, the methods of learning were more important than what was being taught. His belief was that the most effective learning for adults took place in small groups where knowledge could be shared based on the life experience of the participants. Malcolm Knowles expanded on Lindeman's theories in the 1970s when he identified characteristics that set adult learning apart from the way children learn.

The work of Lindeman and Knowles is the basis for the study of how adults learn known as *andragogy*. The definition of andragogy evolved as researchers sought to further define adult learning; today it has come to mean education in which the learner participates in decisions about what will be taught and how it will be delivered. This approach is in contrast to *pedagogy*, the study of how children learn, which is defined as education in which the teacher decides what will be taught and how it will be delivered.

Much of Knowles's work centered on identifying characteristics of adult learning that would make the process more productive for learners. Knowles promoted the idea that, with maturity, people grow into new ways of learning, described by the following five characteristics, which form the basis of andragogy today:

Self-Concept   An individual's self-concept moves from dependency on others to autonomy and self-direction.

Experience   An individual builds a wealth of knowledge that grows with each new experience. This information reserve can then be drawn on for further learning.

Readiness to Learn   Individuals become increasingly interested in the relevance of information to specific needs and how directly it applies to their current situations.

Orientation to Learning   The ability to apply information immediately to solve current problems is increasingly important to learners.

Motivation to Learn   The motivation to learn is based more on personal needs and desires than on expectations of others.

When designing training, you must consider adult learning styles, which answer the question, "How do I learn?" There are generally considered to be three types of learners:

Auditory   *Auditory learners* process information by hearing. Individuals who are auditory learners will, for example, recite information out loud several times to memorize it.

Visual   *Visual learners* depend on their visual processing of information. Often described as "thinking in pictures," these learners prefer visual tools such as outlines and graphs.

Tactile/Kinesthetic   *Tactile/kinesthetic learners* are physical learners; they rely on their sense of touch for memory recall. These individuals are recognizable in training as the ones who periodically get up to stand in the back of the room, or tap their fingers against the table during lectures.

Because all learning styles are represented in the workforce, it's important to incorporate elements of each style when designing training. Other factors to consider include the following:

- These styles are often innate; you can train employees to use multiple styles, but their default method of learning will often yield the best results.
- Trainers often unintentionally discriminate. They design training to their own personal learning style instead of accounting for the blended needs of their audience.
- The study of these categories of learning styles continues to evolve, via the use of music, logic, videos, virtual reality, pictures, and simulation.

Several websites offer free or low-cost tools to inventory your personal learning characteristics. Go online to discover your learning style, and then use the results to create your study plan for the PHR exam.

These basic characteristics of adult learners are important concepts with implications beyond traditional training and development. Learning is, of course, the point of training, so understanding the best ways to provide information in work situations can enhance productivity and job satisfaction for the workforce.

Knowing how adults learn will help HR prepare and manage the talent for successful implementation of OD interventions, but also as they prepare to design training.

Instructional Design Models

Although development programs address long-term organizational needs, training programs are designed to address short-term needs. Training activities are more technical in nature and include such topics as new-hire orientation, safety, and skill development, among others. This section will examine the ADDIE model in depth and then will explore several other models.

The ADDIE Model

The design and development of training programs follows an instructional design model known as the *ADDIE model*. ADDIE is an acronym that describes the five elements of instructional design:

- Analysis
- Design
- Development
- Implementation
- Evaluation

The ADDIE model is discussed here in the context of training at the task level, but the principles of the model can be used to develop training programs at the organizational or individual levels as well.

Training needs are often identified by managers who notice a problem in their departments and determine that training is needed to correct it. This determination may be based on a drop in the production rate, installation of new machinery or equipment, or the addition of a new line of business. Once the need for training has been identified, a needs assessment determines whether training will solve the problem and, if it will, proposes possible solutions.

Analysis

Figure 4.9 demonstrates how a needs assessment model can be used in assessing training needs. Using the model, the following process will provide the information to determine what type of training is necessary to solve the problem:

FIGURE 4.9 Training needs assessment model

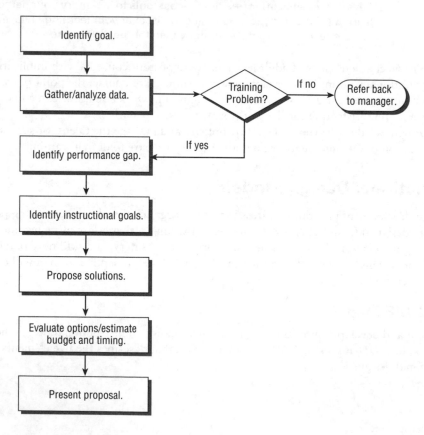

1. Identify goal.

    The needs assessment begins by identifying the desired outcome. In the preceding example, the customer service manager determined that the CSRs should handle an average of 20 calls per hour, which is the desired outcome. The desired outcome forms the basis for several other steps in the analysis process, including what data is collected, the identification of instructional goals, and development of solutions.

2. Gather and analyze data.

    Once you know the desired outcome, you can begin to collect relevant information that will be used to determine the cause of the problem. Information may be gathered in a number of ways from a variety of sources:

    - **Review Documents:** Many types of documents can be used to gather information about training needs. These include measures of organizational effectiveness such as production records and records of customer complaints, a review of the human resource succession plan to determine what training is needed to prepare individuals for future needs based on skills inventories and performance-appraisal forms, and an analysis of the organizational climate based on HR metrics such as turnover rates and the results of exit interviews.

    - **Labor Law Review:** Compliance with various labor laws often involves the training of supervisors and workers to the standards. For example, in establishing an affirmative defense against a sexual harassment claim, employers must demonstrate not only that they had a written policy, but that employees and supervisors were properly trained to the requirements. Understanding which labor laws apply to an employer is a necessary component to establishing both short- and long-term training needs.

    - **Ask Employees:** Training often is a function of reaction: reacting to changing market demands, poor performance, or the demands of legal compliance. While all three of those examples are necessary to analyze when assessing training needs, it is also helpful to ask your employees what types of training or development opportunities would be most beneficial. Clearly defining the outcome is necessary in order to ensure the most relevant response from employees. When the data has been gathered and analyzed, a determination can be made as to whether training is the appropriate solution. If it is, the needs analysis continues; if not, L&D can report the results of the analysis to the requesting manager with a recommendation for an appropriate solution.

3. Identify the performance gap.

    Once all the data has been gathered, it's possible to compare where the organization is to where it wants to be. At this stage, the L&D professional begins to have a sense of the type of training that will be required.

4. Identify instructional goals.

    The performance gap is the starting point for identifying the corrections that need to be put into place.

5. Propose solutions.

At this stage in the needs assessment, all possible means for filling the gap should be identified and considered to find the solution that best meets the organization's needs.

6. Evaluate options, and estimate the budget impact and training timeline.

Once a comprehensive list of possible solutions is available, it's possible to conduct a cost–benefit analysis (described in Chapter 2, "PHR Exam: Business Management") to estimate the cost of implementing each of them and the benefits that will result from the training. It's important to include both direct and indirect costs associated with the program in the estimated budget. This includes the cost of the trainer, facility, preparation of materials, use of equipment, transportation, meals and lodging, wages and salaries of the participants for the time they spend training and in traveling to the training, lost production time due to the training, and incidental office support. It's also important to consider potential savings from increased productivity, reduced errors, higher product quality, and other similar gains that will result from the training and, finally, what it will cost the organization if the training doesn't occur.

At the same time, an estimate of the time required to implement the solution can be made.

The result of the needs assessment is a proposal that describes the desired outcome, the current situation, and the gap between the two. The proposal should include as many alternative solutions as is feasible, with an estimate of the cost and time needed to implement each of them and L&D's recommended solution.

During the assessment phase, a key consideration is whether the program will be created internally, whether a prepackaged program will be used, or whether the process will be outsourced. These decisions are based on a variety of factors unique to every organization and include the size of the organization, the training expertise and availability of in-house staff, the uniqueness of the subject matter, and the availability of prepackaged programs on the topic. For example, sexual-harassment training may be best conducted by a trainer specializing in the subject matter who is able to answer in-depth legal questions and "what-if" scenarios. Conversely, a training program that is specific to a proprietary manufacturing process may be better developed in-house.

Design

When the appropriate decision makers concur that training is the appropriate solution for the problem, the design phase begins. During this phase of a training project, the program begins to take shape. The data gathered during the needs analysis phase will be useful in this stage as well:

1. Compile a task inventory.

To complete the design process, the trainer must know what tasks are required for the job in question. A *task inventory* lists all tasks included in the job. Each task description should contain an action verb, an object, and a function: for example, "Answer phone to assist customers."

The inventory can be compiled from information collected during the needs-assessment process, or additional information can be acquired during the design phase. The inventory may also be gleaned from a job description if it was written as a result of a job analysis.

2. Identify the target audience.

Knowing who will be attending the training will be of great use in designing a program that will keep the audience interested. Preparing a training program about the proper completion of expense reports for a group of middle managers from the accounting department will look very different from the same presentation to the salesforce.

In identifying the audience, it's important to keep in mind the three learning styles that impact an individual's ability to learn:

- *Visual learners* retain information better when they can see or read it.
- *Auditory learners* retain information more easily when they hear it.
- *Kinesthetic learners* retain information best when they're able to have a hands-on experience during training.

Incorporating elements of all three learning styles in a training program helps ensure that all individuals attending the program will benefit from the information presented.

3. Develop training objectives.

Training objectives are statements that describe a measurable outcome of the training and are developed based on the target audience and task inventory. Objectives help the L&D professional during the development process and during implementation communicate to employees what they will learn. They're also useful during the evaluation phase to determine whether the training was successful.

A useful training objective is a precise description of what is to be accomplished in normal job circumstances. For example, a training program for carpenters may include a session on how to build straight walls. The objective begins with a description of a normal job situation, uses an action verb to describe a measurable behavior, describes the conditions under which the behavior will occur, and finally describes the criteria that will be used to measure the results. An objective that includes all these elements could be something like this: "Given the necessary materials and tools, build a wall that is perfectly plumb."

This objective leaves no doubt about what is to be accomplished and includes the basis for determining whether the training was successful.

4. Develop the course content.

Based on the training objectives, the trainer can begin to design the course, identifying what material should be included to best prepare the attendees to take the information back to their jobs and begin using it immediately.

An important consideration for this aspect of training design is the learning curve associated with various subjects. A *learning curve* is a graphical representation of the rate of learning over time. Let's look at some examples of various learning curves:

- **Negatively Accelerating Learning Curve:** A *negatively accelerating learning curve* is characterized by rapid increases in learning at the beginning that taper off as the learner becomes more familiar with the process or task. Negative learning curves are representative of routine tasks, such as operating a cash register. Figure 4.10 provides an example of this learning curve.

FIGURE 4.10 Negatively accelerating learning curve

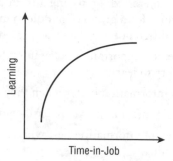

- **Positively Accelerating Learning Curve:** A *positively accelerating learning curve* is characterized by a slow start in learning that increases as the learner masters different aspects of the process or task. Positive learning curves are representative of tasks that are complex, such as a junior accountant learning to use an accounting software program. The accountant must first know basic accounting practices in order to become proficient in using the program. Figure 4.11 shows a positive learning curve.

FIGURE 4.11 Positively accelerating learning curve

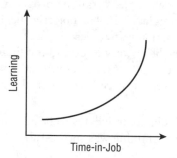

- **S-Shaped Learning Curve:** The *S-shaped learning curve* is a combination of positive and negative learning curves. It begins with a slow learning process that accelerates over time and then slows again. This learning pattern can be found in software-conversion projects. Learners must understand how the new system works before they're able to become as proficient at it as they were with the older system. Figure 4.12 is an example of an S-shaped learning curve.

FIGURE 4.12   S-shaped learning curve

- **Plateau Learning Curve:** A *plateau learning curve* begins with a rapid increase in knowledge that levels off after a period of time, and no additional progress occurs for an extended period of time. A plateau curve might occur when an employee performs a task irregularly, not often enough to become proficient. Figure 4.13 shows a plateau learning curve.

FIGURE 4.13   Plateau learning curve

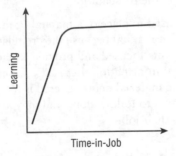

5.   Develop evaluation criteria.

Now is the time to develop the evaluation criteria for the program. The initial evaluation will be based on whether the trainees are able to perform the task described by the objective within the parameters that it sets forth. The real evaluation of training effectiveness is whether the trainees are able to maintain the level of proficiency that was developed during the training and improve operating results.

Development

During the training development phase, the program design is translated into the presentation format. The program developer creates a strategy for the presentation, deciding on the materials, instructional techniques, and program-delivery methods that will be used. The trainer may conduct a pilot presentation during this phase to work out the kinks and, if necessary, will revise the program based on the results of the pilot.

TRAINING MATERIALS

One of the activities occurring during the development phase of the training process is the collection of appropriate training materials. It's often tempting to use work created by others, particularly if the material is perfectly suited to the topic of the training. The two federal laws protecting the rights of writers, artists, and inventors with regard to unauthorized use of their original works, the Copyright Act of 1976 and the U.S. Patent Act, are discussed in Appendix C, "Federal Employment Legislation and Case Law."

Aside from considerations related to the use of copyrighted material, training materials created in the development phase should be appropriate to the subject matter and the needs of the participants. Some types of materials to consider include the following:

Leader Guide   When more than one trainer will be presenting the training sessions, a leader guide ensures consistency in the presentations. These guides may provide notes to assist the trainer in presenting the material, timing information, and questions for use in facilitating discussion during the session. The guide provides a basic road map for the presentation.

Manuals   Manuals can provide a reference to assist in reinforcing the information covered during the training session when participants return to their jobs. In addition to an agenda or a schedule, they can contain handouts and copies of slides for note-taking purposes as participants follow along during the presentation.

Handouts   Handouts may be used in place of a manual or included with the manual. For presentations that don't require a manual because they're relatively straightforward, a handout can help keep participants focused and provide a place to take notes. In addition, handouts can provide additional information that isn't covered during the presentation but is related to the topic. When the material being covered is technical in nature, a handout can make it easier for participants to follow along and may also be used as a handy reference when employees return to their jobs.

INSTRUCTIONAL METHODS

You can choose from a variety of instructional methods when designing a training program, and selecting the appropriate one for a given situation can add to the success of the training:

Passive Training Methods   *Passive training methods* are those in which the learner listens to and absorbs information. These methods are instructor-focused and require little or no active participation from the learner:

Lecture   *Lectures* are used to inform and to answer questions, often in combination with other training methods such as demonstrations.

Presentation   A *presentation* provides the same information to a group of people at one time.

Conference   *Conferences* are generally a combination of lecture or presentation with question-and-answer sessions involving the participants.

Active Training Methods   *Active training methods* are those in which the learning experience focuses on the learner:

Facilitation   Facilitation is a moderated learning situation led by a facilitator who leads a group to share ideas and solve problems. Facilitators generally have skills in moderating group discussions and may be experts in the subject of discussion.

Case Study   A *case study* reproduces a realistic situation that provides learners with the opportunity to analyze the circumstances as though they were encountered in the course of business. Case studies let learners investigate, study, and analyze the situation and then discuss possible solutions with the group. Solutions are developed and presented to fellow learners.

Simulation   *Simulation training* is an interactive training method that provides the learner with opportunities to try new skills or practice procedures in a setting that doesn't endanger the inexperienced trainee, co-workers, or the public.

Vestibule   *Vestibule training* is a form of the simulation method. It allows inexperienced workers to become familiar with and gain experience using equipment that either is hazardous or requires a level of speed that can be attained only with practice. Vestibule training is commonly used to train equipment operators in the construction industry and to help retail clerks gain speed at the checkout counter.

Socratic Seminar   Socratic seminars are based on the method of instruction used by the Greek philosopher Socrates in which ideas are examined in a question-and-answer format. A question may be posed by the seminar leader at the beginning of the seminar and discussed by participants to gain a full understanding of the topic.

Experiential Training Methods   *Experiential training methods* provide experience in real-time situations:

Demonstration   The *demonstration* method of training can be used as part of an on-the-job training program or combined with a lecture program. The method involves the trainer explaining the process or operation, demonstrating it on the equipment, and then having the learner perform it under the guidance of the trainer.

One-on-One   In *one-on-one training*, an inexperienced worker is paired with an experienced supervisor or co-worker who uses a variety of techniques to provide the worker with the information and hands-on experience necessary to do the job.

Performance   *Performance-based training* (PBT) is most often used to correct performance problems in highly technical or hazardous professions. The trainee is provided with opportunities to practice and demonstrate the necessary skill or knowledge until the required level of proficiency is mastered.

PROGRAM DELIVERY MECHANISMS

Devising suitable delivery methods for training programs is subject to a number of factors, including what information is to be covered, who will be attending the training, the experience level of the participants, the availability of technology, and so on:

Classroom   Classroom training provides the same content to a group of employees in a classroom setting. It's effective for small groups when providing the same information to everyone in the group.

Self-Study   A program of self-study is directed entirely by the learner, who determines what, when, and where learning will occur. It may be based on a defined program and involve a trainer or mentor, but it's controlled by the learner.

Programmed Instruction   *Programmed instruction*, also referred to as *self-paced training*, is the forerunner of computer-based training (CBT). In this method, the learner progresses from lesson to lesson in a predesigned course of instruction as mastery of the objectives is attained. This method allows learners to progress at their own rate. Programmed instruction is effective for disseminating facts and concepts, refreshing previously learned skills or expanding a learner's knowledge in a field that is already familiar.

Virtual Training (VT)   Deciding whether to conduct training in a classroom setting through the use of virtual tools or use the tried and true on-the-job training (OJT) is one of the first steps taken in training design. In response to the advance of technology and the generational preferences of the emerging workforce, virtual learning is evolving into a viable method for training delivery.

The virtual classroom has grown in importance in many areas, not the least of which has been in the application of training. As one technique in the category of electronic learning (e-learning), virtual classrooms or virtual reality systems are gaining in popularity despite their expense. Other e-learning tools include web-based training (WBT), CBT, self-directed learning (SDL), mobile learning (m-learning), videoconferencing, simulation, multimedia and social networking sites, and discussion boards. These techniques can be *synchronous* (occurring at the same time with the instructor) or *asynchronous* (self-paced), depending on the content, the training goals, and an analysis of training barriers.

E-learning encompasses several types of electronically based training delivery systems that are generally cost-effective, self-directed methods for training employees:

Electronic Performance Support Systems   An electronic performance support system (EPSS) is a training tool integrated in the computer system used by employees on the job. It allows instant access to information that helps them complete tasks more effectively.

Computer-Based Training   *Computer-based training* is an interactive training method that combines elements of the lecture, demonstration, one-on-one, and simulation methods, thus allowing the learner to have a real-world learning experience. Well-designed CBT programs ensure consistency of training across a company that is geographically dispersed. CBT is based on the programmed instruction method.

Distance Learning   Sometimes referred to as a *virtual classroom*, this is similar to lectures and allows simultaneous training to occur in geographically dispersed multiple locations. *Distance learning* provides participants with the ability to communicate with presenters and participants at other locations.

Microlearning   Microlearning is characterized by short bursts of information, mostly in the form of online videos. This method is a highly efficient way to deliver narrowly tailored content to users. It is also more easily updated, as shorter videos have less to edit/refine than longer, mixed-content series.

Blended Learning   Blended learning uses multiple delivery methods to enhance the learning experience. The term is currently used to describe different ways of combining delivery methods, such as multiple web-based learning methods, a combination of instructor-led delivery with some form of technology, or combining learning technology with the performance of actual job tasks.

Online Bulletin Boards   Online bulletin boards allow trainees to post questions and share information with one another. They may be supervised or facilitated by a leader who is knowledgeable in the subject matter and acts as a resource for the participants.

One successful example of virtual reality training is the Bus Ride, a VT tool developed by Janssen Pharmaceuticals, Inc. This simulation gave mental health professionals a glimpse into a schizophrenic episode from a patient's perspective. The use of headphones, auditory recordings, and video were developed using years of research and descriptions by psychiatrists and their patients. The goal of this tool was to help practitioners in the diagnosis and treatment of the illness and its symptoms. Other high-profile uses of virtual reality training include military field training, flight simulations, and training for surgeons through the use of highly realistic performance-based training and multisensory learning tools.

According to one report referenced by the American Society for Training and Development, U.S. companies spent $16.7 billion on self-paced e-learning. For the human resource professional, this means the ability to demonstrate the return on investment for e-learning initiatives such as VT is a critical stage in the development of strategic training solutions.

Implementation

Implementation is the phase of training where all the preceding work comes together for the presentation. The trainer or facilitator sets up a program schedule, creates the agenda, and notifies participants about the training. At this time, it may be necessary to conduct "train the trainer" sessions to ensure that those who will implement the trainings are themselves fully trained to proceed.

The process begins with selection of the facility and trainers or facilitators:

Facility   The facility selected for the training will depend on the type of training to be conducted, the number of participants attending, and the amount budgeted for the program. Although individual-level training may best be conducted at the employee's workstation, training for larger groups of people is best conducted away from the distractions of the workstation. A conference room at the worksite may provide an adequate training facility if the size of the group is small (or the room is large enough). It may be necessary for a variety of reasons to conduct the training off-site. Although the cost will be greater to rent a facility, the reduction of distractions may result in a more effective training experience with longer-lasting results.

The amount of space needed for the training depends largely on what training activities will take place. Passive training that requires little more of participants than listening requires the least amount of space. More space is required for situations in which participants will be taking notes or practicing work activities. Figure 4.14 through Figure 4.19 depict some of the more common seating styles for trainings and the types of training for which each is most appropriate.

FIGURE 4.14 Theater-style seating

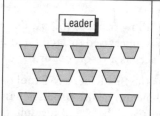

Theater-style seating is best for training when lectures, films, or video presentations are used. This seating style accommodates the largest number of people in any space.

FIGURE 4.15 Classroom-style seating

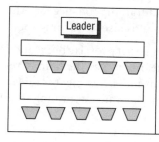

Classroom-style seating is best for training situations when participants will be listening to presentations, using manuals or handouts, and taking notes.

FIGURE 4.16 Banquet-style seating

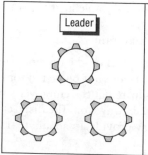

Banquet-style seating is best for training situations in which participants will be taking part in small group discussions and interacting with each other in addition to participating in activities as a single group.

FIGURE 4.17   Chevron-style seating

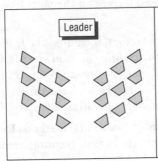

The chevron arrangement is appropriate for training situations in which participants will be interacting with the instructor and each other. This seating style is able to accommodate larger groups than some other seating styles. Useful for situations in which participants will be engaged in several activities: lectures, films, or video presentations, in addition to interacting with others in the room. Chevron-style seating can be used with tables or without, depending on the particular training and space available.

FIGURE 4.18   Conference-style seating

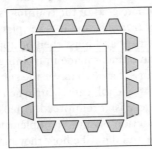

Conference-style seating is used when participants are of equal status and the training is led by a facilitator instead of an instructor. This arrangement provides for maximum interaction between individuals, but is not conducive to the use of visual aids.

FIGURE 4.19   U-shaped-style seating

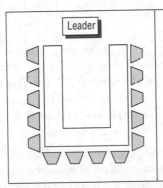

U-shaped-style seating is an effective seating style for collaborative training situations when presentations and discussions will take place. The center area may be used for additional seating or for role-playing.

Another very important step in preparing the facility is to ensure that the physical environment is conducive to learning. For example, the room temperature should be comfortable for most people, sufficient restroom facilities should be available to accommodate the number of participants, and beverages and/or food should be available as appropriate.

Trainers   Trainers may be selected based on their mastery of the subject matter or for their ability and skill in training. This decision will be based largely on the nature of the training being conducted.

Schedule   The training schedule is affected by many factors, including the feasibility of shutting down operations entirely for the length of the training session so that all employees are trained at the same time or whether it's more cost effective to conduct multiple sessions in order to maintain operations. Sessions may need to be broken into segments and scheduled over a period of days or weeks to accommodate operational needs.

The selection of program-delivery mechanisms and instructional methods for various types of training needs are related to the size of the group, type of training needed, and geographic location of the participants.

Evaluation

Training evaluation occurs both before and after the training takes place and is based on criteria established in the assessment phase. The ultimate goal of the training is to improve performance on the job. This is known as *transfer of training*, and it takes place when learning occurs away from the regular work environment and must then be applied to the real job situation. It's obviously important that the investment made in training employees provides a return in increased productivity, quality, or safety (whatever the subject of the training) on the job. A failure of training to transfer to the job can occur when the new skill isn't applied in the work environment and therefore isn't reinforced. A technique that can overcome this problem is the development of an action plan to be implemented after training. This approach requires trainees to visualize and describe how they plan to apply the training when they're back on the job so they're more likely to use their new skills. An effective evaluation will include provisions for measuring job performance for a period of time after the training has been completed to ensure that the new skills have been transferred to the job.

FORMATIVE EVALUATION

Formative evaluation is a process used in the design phase of training. It involves testing or previewing the content prior to final delivery to ensure that it will result in the desired behaviors. Designed primarily to elicit feedback from participants, it's a useful tool when used to modify design elements and content prior to the actual delivery. Formative evaluations are designed to identify what the participants want, know, and need. Examples of strategies used in the formative evaluation process include the following:

Needs Assessment   This is a review of who needs the program, what elements must be addressed, and the best method of delivering the message. Asking potential participants for their wants and needs will help to ensure a program designed toward effective transfer of training.

Asking People   There are many methods for gathering information from people, including observations; interviews with employees, supervisors, or subject matter experts (SMEs); attitude surveys; questionnaires; focus groups; and advisory committees. See Chapter 2 for more information on these techniques.

Analyzing Jobs   In some cases, it may be necessary to conduct a full job analysis as described in Chapter 3, "PHR Exam: Talent Planning and Acquisition," to determine where training is needed.

Pilot Test   Pilot tests are used once the training design and content have been developed. They involve a focus group of participants used to evaluate the relevance of the content and delivery methods to the stated training objectives, followed up by their feedback and influence on the final delivery.

Pretest   A pretest can be used to measure participant knowledge prior to the design of the training. In addition to content-specific questions, it should also ask for feedback related to "the muddiest point"— the content that seems most unclear to the end user. Other options for testing employee knowledge include assessment centers, knowledge tests to measure what people know, and practical tests to determine whether they're able to apply what they know.

SUMMATIVE EVALUATION

A common model for summative training evaluation was developed by Donald Kirkpatrick. He proposed four levels of evaluation for training programs: reaction, learning, behavior, and results. Measurements at each level are based on the objectives developed during the design phase:

Reaction   The *reaction evaluation method* measures the initial reaction of the participants. This is most commonly determined by a survey completed by participants at the end of the training. Although this level of evaluation doesn't measure the organization impact, it does provide feedback for the trainer in terms of the presentation of the information.

Learning   The *learning evaluation method* uses a test to measure whether the participants learned the information that was presented. Although this level of evaluation provides more information about the effectiveness of the training, it still doesn't provide feedback about the application of the information on the job.

In some cases, learning evaluation uses an experimental design known as the *pretest/ posttest comparison*:

1. A group of employees is selected for training.
2. The employees are randomly assigned to two different groups.
3. An identical pretest is administered to both groups of employees.
4. One group receives the training, also known as a *treatment*.
5. An identical posttest is administered to both groups of employees.
6. The results are compared to see whether the training resulted in improved performance.

Behavior   The behavior evaluation method attempts to measure the behavioral changes that occurred as a direct result of the training. It is often viewed as an attempt to measure the successful application of the new knowledge. This category includes the introduction of new processes or systems that help trainees apply the knowledge.

Results   The results evaluation method measures the impact training had on the initial training targets. Because training initiatives are often looked at as investments in future results, many organizations focus this level of training evaluation solely on the final outcomes. However, HR can support positive outcomes by tracking shorter-term milestones as predictors of results. In this way, HR may intervene and adapt where necessary.

The pretest/posttest comparison is appropriate when an organization wants to isolate the impact of training on productivity. To make a legitimate comparison, all other factors that could affect performance must be equalized. For example, all employees in the group should have similar KSA's, be using similar equipment, and have access to similar resources. If other factors are dissimilar, it isn't possible to isolate the training impact on performance.

Other Instructional Design Models

While ADDIE continues to be used in many organizations today, there are a few other more project-oriented instructional design tools. They include the following:

AGILE   The acronym AGILE stands for *align, get set, iterate and implement, leverage, and evaluate.* It is used to accomplish "content chunking," a concept that seeks to break up large amounts of training content into more manageable modules. Whereas the ADDIE model is applied to entire training programs, the AGILE model will be used repeatedly to build out training content in silos, rather than once in a whole piece.

SAM   The Successive Approximation Model (SAM) is an instructional design technique that relies on repetition and collaboration. Designers engage in a collaborative cyclical design process that begins with analyzing the training needs and gathering information, designing the project plan and brainstorming for input, and then developing the content with real-time changes as identified.

Learning Management Systems

It can sometimes be difficult to convince senior management of the benefits of training. As with any other HR initiative, it's important to demonstrate how a training program will add value to the bottom line. As part of the Workforce Investment Act (WIA), the federal government will fund some training programs that are managed by state workforce agencies. Some states use these funds to reimburse training costs to employers who want to hire, retain, or upgrade the skills of employees. In Maine, for example, the governor's initiative reimburses employers who provide technical, on-the-job, or workplace safety training to workers, in addition to higher education, high performance skills, or competitive retooling training programs. Employers must submit a comprehensive application to be approved for participation in the program and maintain accurate, detailed documentation to receive reimbursement. Implementation of a learning management system can simplify the reporting and is an effective use of HR technology.

A *learning management system* (LMS) is computer-based software that administers, tracks, and reports employee training and development activities. An LMS helps to streamline the administration of employee training programs. The components included in an LMS depend on organization size and the complexity of training needs. These systems can be used to automatically enroll students in required courses (such as safety trainings required by OSHA) and notify managers when employees don't attend. The programs can provide managers with access to approve training requested by employees and to identify skill-development needs in their departments or for individual employees. An LMS can maintain curriculum for required (or optional) courses and provide access on an individual, functional, or organizational basis. Other administrative functions performed by LMS programs include course calendars, facility assignments, pre- and posttesting, and report generation. An LMS can also include self-service functions that eliminate tedious administrative chores from daily HR tasks, such as registering employees, notifying participants, obtaining approvals, and maintaining waitlists. Table 4.1 summarizes the functions available in an LMS system.

TABLE 4.1   LMS system functions

HR Tasks	Training Tasks	User Benefits
Streamline process (automate recordkeeping, notices, and reminders).	Manage resources: facilities, instructors, and equipment.	Employees: self-registration, web access, online learning
Automatic enrollment for mandated courses	Manage course calendar.	Managers: Approve employee requests, access to online assessment tools, plan department trainings.
Verify qualifications.	Self-registration	
Manage waiting lists.	Web-based delivery	
Generate reports.	Deliver/score tests, including pre- and posttests. Score and record course work.	

An LMS is capable of managing the organization's learning tasks in a wide range of situations, from tracking attendance, maintaining training calendars, and generating reports to delivering web-based content to participants, administering and scoring tests, and providing planning tools for managers.

The next step in LMS development seems to be learning and performance management systems (LPMSs) that incorporate functions for managing performance (including 360-degree assessments, self-evaluations, succession planning, and manager feedback) and that track individual rewards. These functions improve a manager's ability to assess performance, assign training to address areas of improvement, and prepare employees for the next level in their career growth.

Organizations that develop their own content use learning content management systems (LCMSs) to create, deliver, and modify course content. These systems allow trainers to develop content, often in a module format so that a single module can be used in multiple training courses. For example, a geographically dispersed organization may create an orientation program with different modules for corporate information, employee benefit options, expense reporting, and other information common to employees throughout the organization, along with modules for each geographic location. This allows an HR professional in a regional office to provide a customized orientation that includes information specific to that office along with relevant information about the corporation at large.

Metrics: Measuring Results

The most important measure for learning and development activities is how (or whether) an intervention affected business results. For example, if a training program was implemented to improve call center response times, did that occur? If so, was the result immediate, or did improvement occur more slowly as CSRs gained confidence from experience implementing the training?

Business Impact Measures   Metrics that validate the impact of training programs on results are the ones that provide useful information to management. Depending on the situation, some of these metrics may be appropriate:

Production Measures   Metrics that provide measures taken prior to training and several months after training takes place demonstrate how well the program solved the business issue. There are many applications of this for production issues, such as increased speed, number of rejected items, and increased output. A similar measure can be used for other types of training. For example, measuring the number of incidents of sexual harassment prior to training and then again six months to one year after training occurs demonstrates whether the training was effective.

Learning Measures   Learning measures such as Kirkpatrick's training evaluation seeks to measure what behaviors were changed as the result of training or other intervention methods.

Return on Investment   A key measurement for any HR function is, of course, return on investment. Measuring the ROI of L&D programs provides objective information about how they're increasing productivity or providing other benefits to the organization that justifies investing in them.

Tactical Accountability Measures   A number of established metrics are used to measure HR's tactical accountability in L&D. Some of the more common include the following:

Training Cost per Employee   Training cost per employee is calculated by collecting all costs related to training, including design and development, materials, equipment rentals, time spent by HR staff and managers or others who aided in development, participant time to attend the training, facilities, beverages, food, and so on. The total cost is then divided by the number of full-time equivalent employees.

Employee Satisfaction Surveys   Employee satisfaction surveys can provide general information about the effectiveness of these programs, such as whether employees are satisfied with the amount and types of training and development provided. This question can be tailored to individual organizations by making it specific with regard to programs provided.

Learning Surveys   Surveying attendees 30, 60, or 90 days after training can provide significant information about how many of the training skills they actually applied in their daily jobs, how impactful such training has been, what was helpful, and what skills were never used.

Summary

Learning and development (L&D) is tied closely to organizational development (OD). One really cannot exist without the other. A company seeking to manage change and achieve business goals through OD interventions will have to rely on activities of L&D to achieve the desired outcomes. L&D activities will result in a higher return on investment when closely aligned with business goals, often defined as part of the OD process.

L&D/OD interventions address organizational challenges with such programs as learning organizations, total quality management, and management by objectives that are designed to align the workforce with the leaders and the organization strategy. These programs must fit in with the culture and strategy of the organization to be successful.

Employee-development programs prepare talented individuals to accept positions of greater responsibility and authority in the organization and aid the retention of individuals who are key to its long-term success. This includes succession planning to meet future needs and challenges.

Training is an important aspect of L&D. The ADDIE, AGILE, and SAM models are used to develop training programs that address the needs of the organization and of individuals in the organization.

HR practitioners play a key role consulting with managers and employees on all intervention activities, and apply their understanding of adult learning principles to engage the workforce.

Exam Essentials

Understand and be able to describe organizational development intervention strategies. OD interventions address strategic objectives through a series of interventions. Built on a strong change management and knowledge management foundation, HR contributes to techno-structural, human process, and human resource management interventions to achieve desired results.

Be able to create and sustain employee career and development plans.   Advising employees on their professional development activities is critical to retaining qualified talent to meet current and future organizational needs. Doing so requires that employees have a clear understanding of their individual strengths and weaknesses and have a plan to help them achieve growth.

Understand and be able to describe instructional design models.   The ADDIE, SAM, and AGILE models are instructional design tools used for creating training programs. The ADDIE model is distinct in that it applies to building training content as a whole, whereas AGILE and SAM chunk training into smaller units for easier consumption and revision.

Be able to identify the four types of training evaluation.   The four types of evaluation are reaction, which measures immediate feedback; learning, which measures what was learned through testing; behavior, which measures job performance six months or more after training; and results, which measures whether the training had a positive impact on the bottom line.

Understand the connection between change management and OD.   OD *is* change management. It seeks to address issues that prevent organizations from becoming fully effective and introduces interventions to align the workforce with the organization strategy.

Review Questions

You can find the answers in Appendix A.

1. _____ is one of several learning organization characteristics.
    - **A.** An assessment center
    - **B.** Massed practice
    - **C.** Systems thinking
    - **D.** Programmed instruction

2. Which of the following should be included in a supervisory training program?
    - **A.** Conflict management
    - **B.** Budgeting
    - **C.** Rotation through various divisions
    - **D.** Internal controls

3. In the evaluation phase, the _____ evaluation method focuses on how well the training resulted in learning new skills and competencies.
    - **A.** Reaction
    - **B.** Learning
    - **C.** Behavior
    - **D.** Results

4. Which of the following factors can adversely affect transfer of training?
    - **A.** The trainer's expertise
    - **B.** A lack of job reinforcement
    - **C.** The subject of the training
    - **D.** None of the above

5. A _____ learning curve begins slowly, with smaller learning increments, but increases in pace and with larger increments as learning continues.
    - **A.** Positively accelerating
    - **B.** Negatively accelerating
    - **C.** S-shaped
    - **D.** Plateau

6. The most common reason for the failure of organizational-change initiatives is which of the following?
    - **A.** The strategic plan was not communicated to employees.
    - **B.** Organization leaders did not support the change.
    - **C.** No training system was in place.
    - **D.** Employees were not prepared for the change.

7. The best-quality tool to use for gathering information about a specific problem is which of the following?

   A. A Pareto chart

   B. An Ishikawa diagram

   C. A stratification chart

   D. A histogram

8. Which employee growth and assessment program is characterized by performance objectives?

   A. Behavioral-based performance assessment

   B. Skills-based performance assessment

   C. Management by objectives (MBO)

   D. Continuous-feedback program

9. An employer uses short bursts of content delivered via video to train employees on new product designs. This is the *best* example of which of the following instructional design models?

   A. ADDIE

   B. SAM

   C. AGILE

   D. Virtual

10. Mentoring involves which of the following?

    A. Someone who monitors an employee's performance in doing their job

    B. Someone whose goal is to develop an employee in a particular area

    C. Someone who takes a personal interest in an individual's career and who guides and sponsors the individual

    D. Someone who provides training in areas of interest to an employee

11. Melissa recently facilitated company-wide diversity training through a series of webinars. Prior to designing the training, she surveyed a sampling of employees to identify their experiences in the organization related to harassment, promotion opportunities, and equitable treatment. This is an example of which of the following?

    A. Summative evaluation

    B. Knowledge banking

    C. Attitude assessment

    D. Formative evaluation

12. Wine Cellar Barrels recently became aware of several negative reviews online related to the company's customer service. Management has tasked HR with designing a strategic training initiative to address the interpersonal skills of the call center staff. Using the ADDIE model, HR's first step should be which of the following?

    A. Design the training.

    B. Conduct a needs assessment.

    C. Identify training participants.

    D. Schedule the training.

13. Task identity, task significance, and feedback are all examples of what?

    A. Job enrichment

    B. Job enlargement

    C. Key productivity indicators

    D. Performance appraisal criteria

14. Allowing employees to participate in the redesign of their work is an example of which of the following?

    A. Ownership

    B. Job crafting

    C. Autonomy

    D. All of the above

15. Participants in a training program are asked to log into a website at their convenience, watch a video lecture, and take a quiz. This is an example of which of the following types of training?

    A. Vestibule

    B. Mobile learning

    C. Asynchronous

    D. The Delphi technique

16. Which of the following types of evaluations are designed to identify what the participants want, know, and need?

    A. Reaction summaries

    B. Formative evaluations

    C. Summative evaluations

    D. Trainer evaluations

17. People Logistics recently began scheduling off-site meetings for its management team to review the operational realities of implementing elements of the strategic plan. This is an example of which of the following development activities?

    A. Peer-to-peer coaching

    B. Assigning a mentor

    C. Hiring an executive coach

    D. Strategic planning

18. Calculate the training cost per employee using the following data: $2,000 for the training design and facilitator; $2,500 for the facility; 20 full-time employees (40 hours per week) and 10 part-time employees (20 hours per week).

    A. $150

    B. $180

    C. $200

    D. $300

19. A training session involved asking a group of participants to answer questions related to how Aflac Insurance used a duck to successfully launch its brand. This was an example of which of the following types of training?

    A. Vestibule

    B. Facilitation

    C. Case study

    D. Socratic seminar

20. Which of the following types of OD interventions would be *best* to help a company that is struggling with inefficiencies on the production line?

    A. Process flow mapping

    B. Learning organization

    C. Six Sigma

    D. TQM

Chapter

5

PHR Exam: Total Rewards

The HRCI test specifications from the Total Rewards functional area covered in this chapter include PHR-level responsibilities and knowledge. They are listed here.

Responsibilities:

✓ 01 Manage compensation-related information and support payroll issue resolution.

✓ 02 Implement and promote awareness of non-cash rewards (for example: paid volunteer time, tuition assistance, workplace amenities, and employee recognition programs).

✓ 03 Implement benefit programs (for example: health plan, retirement plan, employee assistance plan, other insurance).

✓ 04 Administer federally compliant compensation and benefit programs.

Knowledge:

✓ 36 Applicable federal laws and regulations related to total rewards

✓ 37 Compensation policies, processes, and analysis

✓ 38 Budgeting, payroll, and accounting practices related to compensation and benefits

✓ 39 Job analysis and evaluation concepts and methods

✓ 40 Job pricing and pay structures

✓ 41 Non-cash compensation

✓ 42 Methods to align and benchmark compensation and benefits

✓ 43 Benefits programs policies, processes, and analysis

The Total Rewards function of the PHR exam accounts for 15 percent of exam content. In terms of total weight, that equates to about 27 questions that you will see related to this subject on exam day. Although this may not seem to be much, it is impossible to anticipate what those 27 questions will be about, so it is critical you are thoroughly prepared in two primary areas: employee compensation and employee benefits. In addition, the exam content outline notes a particular focus for PHR candidates in the area of payroll. Wage and hour and employee benefits labor laws are also particularly fraught with risk, so you should become extremely proficient in the total rewards labor laws covered in Appendix C, "Federal Employment Legislation and Case Law." However, for this chapter we begin by defining total rewards.

Total Rewards Defined

At the broadest level, *total rewards* can be described as an exchange of payment from an employer for the services provided by its employees. In today's economy a competitive total rewards program is vital to attracting, retaining, and motivating employees. In many organizations, compensation and benefits costs are the single largest operating expense and therefore an extremely important component of the human resource program. A total rewards package includes all forms of rewards, which are generally categorized into one of two components: monetary and nonmonetary compensation. Let's look now at what goes into each of these components:

Monetary Compensation   Monetary compensation includes any costs the organization incurs for the benefit of employees, such as all forms of cash compensation, 401(k) matching, medical care premiums, pension plans, and paid time off. Other kinds of rewards include benefits that support the organization's culture such as stock options, employee stock ownership programs (ESOPs), and incentive plans.

Nonmonetary Compensation   It's important to recognize that just as monetary rewards are a critical component of a global total rewards program, so are nonmonetary rewards. This chapter focuses primarily on tangible rewards, but providing an environment that supports intrinsic and extrinsic nonmonetary rewards is a very important part of the total rewards package.

An *intrinsic reward* is one that encourages individual employee self-esteem, such as satisfaction from challenging and exciting assignments. An *extrinsic reward* is one in which esteem is achieved from others, such as fulfillment from working with a talented team of peers. The relationship employees have with their supervisors, recognition of accomplishments, development and career opportunities, and teamwork are a few examples of nonmonetary rewards. Nonmonetary rewards also include nontraditional work–life balance benefits such as telecommuting, on-site childcare, and flex time.

Other terms used throughout this chapter are direct and indirect compensation:

Direct Compensation   *Direct compensation* includes payments made to employees that are associated with wages and salaries. This includes base pay, variable compensation, and pay for performance.

Indirect Compensation   *Indirect compensation* consists of any employee payments not associated with wages and salaries. This includes fringe benefits such as vacation, sick, and holiday pay; insurance premiums paid on behalf of employees; leaves of absence; 401(k) or other pension plans; and government-mandated benefits such as Social Security or Family and Medical Leave Act (FMLA) and other benefits.

The mix of components included in a total rewards package is unique to the compensation and benefits philosophy, strategic direction, and culture of each organization. Ultimately, the goal of a total rewards package is to maximize the return on investment (ROI) of resources spent on employee rewards.

For PHR candidates, it is important to focus on implementing, promoting, and managing legally compliant compensation and benefits programs. This includes understanding best practices as they relate to budgeting and accounting.

Budgeting and Accounting for Total Rewards

Employee wages and benefits make up a large portion of an employer's cost of doing business. For this reason, HR professionals must work closely with line managers and finance professionals to build the total rewards budget for the organization. Compensation and benefit budgets are projected during the annual budget process and must consider increases to base salaries as well as adjustments to the salary structure to keep salary ranges competitive with current labor market trends. At this time, budgets are also projected for incentive pay programs and planned promotions. Salary surveys are particularly helpful in forecasting changes to base salaries and salary structure adjustments. To best perform salary surveys, it is necessary to conduct compensation benchmarking to identify job responsibilities and external market value.

Salary Surveys

Salary surveys allow organizations to gather compensation and benefits data that reflects current trends in the labor market. Surveys are often provided by professional services' vendors or compensation consulting firms. The vendor provides a confidential data-collection process by administering the survey and compiling data into a usable, aggregated format. Salary surveys identify trends in labor costs and are integral in ensuring that compensation and benefits programs continue to attract, retain, and motivate employees. There are different types of salary surveys for an organization to consider:

Employee Surveys   Polling the internal workforce is one method companies can use to gauge employee satisfaction with their pay structures, measure perceptions of pay equity, and identify the needs of the current workforce as it relates to compensation and benefit offerings.

Government Surveys   A great source for compensation data is the Bureau of Labor Statistics (BLS), an independent national statistical agency whose mission is to collect, analyze, and distribute statistical data. The BLS is a statistical resource to the Department of Labor (DOL) as well as a source for salary survey data.

Industry Surveys   For certain jobs, it may be important to consider industry-specific salary surveys for greater validity. For example, the high-tech and hospitality industries are two that provide specific surveys for companies in their sectors.

Commissioned Surveys   Many organizations operate in industries with very specific skill requirements that may be difficult to match in readily available surveys, or they may want to find out how their compensation practices stack up against several specific competitors. This information can sometimes be collected by commissioning a third party to conduct a survey, aggregate the data, and supply the results to the participating organizations. Commissioning a survey can be very costly and time-consuming but may provide the best data for building a competitive salary structure.

An alternative way to collect some of this data is to use an informal process where HR professionals exchange information on pay practices with their counterparts in other organizations. Another informal option is to work with a local/regional HR or compensation association and have the group facilitate the collection of pay practice data from participating members.

When conducting or participating in a salary survey, one of the first decisions to be made is which jobs will be priced in the survey. The most accurate data would be obtained by including all the organization's jobs, but this may not be practical. Generally, including 65 to 70 percent of organization jobs in a survey provides a solid base for use in creating a salary structure.

It's important for HR professionals and employees to keep salary survey data confidential in order to comply with legislative mandates. Over the years, there have been a number of lawsuits against organizations and individuals who are not properly managing their pay scales.

A notable example occurred in the Silicon Valley, where large tech firms were accused of wage collusion when they secretly agreed to not poach talent from each other by offering higher wages. This had the effect of interfering with the natural wage-setting mechanism of the talent market.

Pay History Bans

Several states including Massachusetts and Oregon are addressing pay inequity by passing laws banning employers from asking applicants about their salary history. This means that HR will need to base compensation offers on the value of the jobs in the marketplace, not on what an applicant was making at their previous job. This makes an even stronger case for a systematic approach to creating wage bands using market data and the need for HR practitioners to understand the unique laws of the states in which they pay employees.

Benchmarking

Before embarking on the salary survey journey, HR must have a thorough understanding of the tasks, duties, and responsibilities of each job being priced. Compensation benchmarking is the process of validating existing job descriptions in order to identify the external market rate for each position. It is not enough to search based on job titles; benchmarking requires the data obtained through the job analysis process defined in Chapter 3, "PHR Exam: Talent Planning and Acquisition."

It is considered a best practice to use three-to-five sources to ensure you have accurate descriptions from which to conduct market research. Reliable sources for job and salary data includes O*NET OnLine, the job database maintained by the DOL. The job descriptions on O*NET are linked to Career One Stop, which will sort salary data by state. This and other local and regional resources are also valid sources to access pay trends by geographic location.

For example, say a local manufacturing company needs to hire a sourcing specialist for their R&D department. HR begins the search by building a job description from the data on O*NET. As she searches for the proper job duties, she finds that the O*NET title for the job she will be recruiting for is "procurement clerk." The HR practitioner can then use the industry classification code to conduct market-based research on pay scales in her area, thus ensuring the job is competitively priced.

Compensation

Deciding how best to compensate employees for the work they do is based on various factors including internal value (the importance of jobs relative to each other), external value (economic factors, such as supply and demand), and the knowledge, skills, and abilities (KSAs) individual employees demonstrate on the job.

Organizations must be aware of a variety of external factors when developing programs and administering compensation, including economics, the labor market, competition in the product market, and other pressures such as those related to tax and accounting requirements and government legislation and regulations:

Economic Factors   The ability of an organization to find qualified employees is affected by a number of economic factors at the local, national, and global levels, including economic growth, inflation, interest rates, unemployment, and the comparative cost of living. These factors influence the *cost of labor*, or the cost to attract and retain individuals with the skills needed by the organization to achieve its goals. Organizations recruiting employees with a particular skill set create a competitive environment for individuals with those skills, resulting in an increase in the cost of labor. For example, when two large companies in the same metropolitan area are hiring large numbers of experienced manufacturing technicians, the supply of individuals with this skill set is in demand, and the availability of qualified individuals decreases. This combination of increased demand and decreased availability raises the competitive compensation rate for this skill set, thereby increasing the cost of labor.

With the increasingly competitive global economy, many industries are constantly assessing how to increase quality, accelerate time to market, and improve productivity. This increased intensity has resulted in a creative approach to organizing and redesigning work that, in turn, affects the skill sets needed by the organization and the cost to employ individuals with those skills.

Labor Market   Organizations may need to revise their compensation programs to meet the demands of changing labor markets. The *labor market* is made up of any sources from which an organization recruits new employees; a single organization may find itself recruiting from several different labor markets, depending on the availability of skills for different positions. Ultimately, the combination of supply and demand for a certain skill set in the labor market impacts what the employers competing for those skills must pay to individuals who possess them. For example, the Bureau of Labor Statistics estimates that by the year 2022, there will be a shortage of nurses in the labor force population. When attrition is factored in, it is estimated that the United States will have to produce over a million more registered nurses by 2022. From a forecasting perspective, HR professionals in the healthcare industry should be brainstorming on how to recruit for and retain talented nurses, and these strategies should be included in a total rewards review.

Labor markets vary by region and industry. Urban areas provide a greater pool of candidates with a wider set of skills from which to select. Because there are more businesses in urban areas competing for this pool of candidates, urban environments may be more competitive, leading to an increase in the cost of labor. As a result, the cost of labor for a single skill set may vary widely between the areas in which an organization operates. To offset these differences, many companies use regional pay structures to reflect the market conditions of the different areas in which they have business locations. For example, a company that is headquartered in the southeast may have a different pay structure for their regional offices in New York City and in the Silicon Valley in California to reflect the higher cost of labor in those areas.

Over the years, the way people look at pay has changed because of the increased mobility of the workforce, the shift from a manufacturing economy to a knowledge-based economy, and fluctuating economic conditions. During the technology boom of the late 1990s, job hopping and generous compensation packages were prevalent, particularly for individuals with sought-after technological skills. Organizations recruited at a national level and were willing to relocate candidates because the labor market was so competitive. When the technology bubble burst and the unemployment rate increased, organizations were able to recruit for many positions locally, reducing the cost of labor. As the economy improved, competition for talented employees again led to increased labor costs. As this cycle repeats over time, HR professionals must be aware of changing economic factors that impact the labor market and adjust compensation strategies in their organizations to maintain their competitive edge in the labor market.

A 21st century consideration is the emergence of a "gig economy," where the traditional workforce is being replaced with independent contractors and freelancers. It is estimated that as much as a third of the working population is employed in some sort of part-time, adjunct, or flexible job. The continued growth of a gig economy has changed the way jobs are priced. Jobs can no longer be budgeted in the traditional way based on annual pay, benefits, and burden. Pricing the work as projects or by busy seasons are now factors HR must consider.

Additionally, the Internal Revenue Service (IRS) and state governments continue to clarify the definition of who is legally an independent contractor and who must be classified as an employee. Specifically, the IRS identified three factors to determine the degree of control and independence:

- **Behavioral:** Does the company control or have the right to control what the worker does and how the worker does his or her job?

- **Financial:** Are the business aspects of the worker's job controlled by the payer? (These include things like how worker is paid, whether expenses are reimbursed, who provides tools/supplies, and so on.)

- **Type of Relationship:** Are there written contracts or employee type benefits (for example, pension plan, insurance, vacation pay, and so on)? Will the relationship continue and is the work performed a key aspect of the business?

Misclassifying workers is a costly mistake for employers, so HR must be up-to-date on these definitions and apply the knowledge by auditing their workforce and then advising executive management on any changes that should be made.

Product Market Competition   Competitive product markets place financial pressure on an organization and challenge its ability to attract and retain qualified employees. Increased competition creates pressure to do everything faster, better, and cheaper. These added pressures place a strain on the employee population. In a climate epitomized by strong competition between organizations accompanied by a decrease in demand, issues related to the financial health of an organization will likely surface. Some of the repercussions of these pressures for employees can include wage freezes, which may result in skipping a merit-review process, eliminating promotions, and/or not paying incentives. In a strong economy, increased competition can mean growth for the organization because of increasing demand resulting in increased financial rewards for employees. HR professionals must be aware of the implications of changes in the competitive environment to ensure that the programs they propose are in line with these pressures.

Tax and Accounting   Several external factors affect compensation and benefit decisions including regulations by many state and federal agencies. These include the Securities and Exchange Commission (SEC), the Financial Accounting Standards Board (FASB), and the IRS. These agencies affect compensation and benefits issues through the enforcement of federal tax legislation, such as Social Security and Medicare taxes, pension regulation, and enforcement of rules about some benefit programs. When an organization wants to make changes to compensation or benefit programs, it may want to find out how the IRS will view the changes for tax purposes before it makes them. In some situations, it may be beneficial to request a *private letter ruling* from the IRS before the changes are made. These rulings apply only to the specific taxpayer and circumstances included in the request and are used to find out what the tax implications of a complex or unusual financial transaction will be.

In addition to tax regulations, the DOL has established strict rules regarding minimum wage, overtime, and compensable time for employees, so PHR candidates must be well versed in up-to-date laws regarding compensation and benefits practices (these are discussed in Appendix C).

Types of Compensation

Compensation comes in many forms. The topic of this section is all forms of direct compensation, from base pay to differentials, variable-pay plans, and commissions and bonuses. The backbone of a compensation program is base pay—the salary or hourly wage paid to employees for the work they do.

Base Pay

Whether paid as a salary or as an hourly wage, *base pay* is the amount of compensation that the employer and the employee agree will be paid for the performance of particular job duties. Base pay both reflects the internal value of jobs while striving to recognize their external market value.

HR professionals take a variety of factors into consideration when making base-pay determinations: The KSAs that employees bring to the job, previous earnings, and internal equity are all part of the decision-making process. Once an employee is hired, changes in base pay may be based on various factors, including performance in the job, seniority, and increased skills.

Base pay is typically evaluated on an annual basis, through a performance- or seniority-based process, discussed in more detail later in this section. When employees take on new roles and responsibilities, base pay can increase through the promotion process. Other changes in base pay can occur as the result of demotions or changes in job duties.

When determining a new hire's base pay, the length and type of previous experience are key factors to consider. Years of experience in a certain profession, a certain industry, or total experience may be relevant to the job. Type of experience may also be relevant to a certain position. How well the new hire will perform in the job is an unknown variable and will be taken into account once the employee begins work.

The federal government establishes a minimum wage that must be paid to employees. As of 2019, the federal minimum wage continues to be $7.25. In 2017, executive order 13658 was passed mandating that individuals working on or as part of a federal contract be paid a minimum wage of $10.35 per hour. The EO also required that tipped employees working on or in connection with federal contracts no longer may be paid less than the federal minimum wage of $7.25. These changes went into effect in 2018.

The company's compensation philosophy drives the type of compensation program that is used. These are categorized as either performance-based or seniority-based programs.

Performance-Based Compensation

Performance-based pay programs, which may include merit increases or promotions, are based on how well individual employees perform against the company's process for measuring performance. The performance ratings earned by employees determine the eligible range of increase for the review period.

Differentiating pay based on performance means the base salaries of employees in the same classification or salary range may vary from one another. When using a performance-based compensation system, it's important to keep accurate records that justify the reasons for disparity in salaries between employees in the same positions. This documentation will be useful in defending against claims of unfair pay practices should they occur.

Seniority-Based Compensation

Organizations that use *seniority-based compensation* systems make pay decisions based on the length of time employees have been in a position and on years of related experience. A seniority-based compensation system is representative of an entitlement compensation philosophy where employees feel "entitled to" certain pay or benefits based on length of service as opposed to individual performance.

A good example of seniority-based compensation is an organization with a union representing its workers. In a union context, long-term and short-term compensation decisions are the result of negotiations between the union and the employer. Because of this, they aren't necessarily driven by an organization's compensation philosophy. In a union environment, annual increases are typically determined by seniority.

Pay Differentials

Some organizations use pay differentials to encourage employees to perform work that is uncomfortable, out of the ordinary, inconvenient, or hazardous. Pay differentials serve as incentives for employees to work on tough assignments or to be available to respond at inconvenient times. A *pay differential* provides additional pay for work that is considered beyond the minimum requirements of the job. For example, multinational employers who require employees to travel and work in potentially dangerous parts of the world may use hazard pay to make those jobs more attractive to employees.

Examples of pay differentials include overtime, shift pay, on-call pay, call-back pay, reporting pay, hazard pay, and geographic pay.

Overtime

Although the Fair Labor Standards Act (FLSA) requires payment only for overtime exceeding 40 hours in a week, some states have overtime laws that exceed federal requirements, and employees are paid at the more generous state rate. Federal law allows employers to require unlimited overtime as long as employees are paid at the required wage rate. It isn't common practice to pay overtime to exempt employees, but doing so isn't prohibited by the FLSA; however, doing so by definition requires employees to keep track of their hours. Requiring exempt employees to keep track of their time isn't prohibited by the FLSA as long as it doesn't result in a reduction of their pay based on the quality or quantity of work produced.

It's important for employers to take a leadership position in managing overtime costs. To prevent abuse, it's ideal for overtime work to be approved in advance. Employers may also want to develop a process or policy when scheduling overtime work for large groups of employees, such as scheduling employees for overtime based on their skill sets, seniority, or shift, depending on the needs of the employer. Overtime is an area that is commonly cut when employers face financial and/or economic challenges.

Shift Pay

The days and hours of a typical work week vary by industry—the most common work schedule is one in which employees work Monday through Friday. A *shift* is any scheduled block of time during the work week when employees perform job-related duties. Shifts have a specific start and end time and are most applicable to nonexempt employees but can also affect exempt employees. There are three commonly recognized shifts: the day shift, with hours from 8 a.m. to 4 p.m.; the evening, or *swing shift*, with hours from 4 p.m. to 12 a.m.; and the *graveyard shift*, with hours from 12 a.m. to 8 a.m. Shift work is necessary in industries with 24-hour operations, such as hospitals, airlines, law enforcement, and some manufacturing operations.

In some cases, employers pay more than what is required by the state or federal government for shifts or other time spent at work, such as paying employees for rest or meal periods. Compensating employees in excess of FLSA requirements typically reflects common practice in an industry or market segment. Employers may decide to pay for these items in order to maintain a competitive advantage to more effectively attract, motivate, and retain employees.

A *shift premium* is additional compensation provided for employees who work other than the day shift. Shift premiums may be paid as a percentage of base pay or may be factored into the hourly rate. For example, in high-tech manufacturing, it's common to pay a 10 percent shift premium for shifts that overlap 6 p.m. to midnight and 15 percent for shifts that overlap the midnight to 6 a.m. time period. Although it's most common for non-exempt employees to be paid shift premiums, they may also be paid to exempt employees.

Shift-premium calculations can be a little tricky. Here's an example: Laura works as a nonexempt manufacturing technician at MonoCorp, working an 8-hour shift, 5 days a week, resulting in a 40-hour workweek; she makes $10 an hour. Laura also works some hours on the second shift, from 4 p.m. to midnight, Monday through Friday. The second shift at MonoCorp pays a 10 percent shift premium. Table 5.1 illustrates the base pay and overtime costs for Laura's work.

TABLE 5.1   Laura's schedule: hours worked

Day	Shift/scheduled hours	Overtime
Monday	8	0
Tuesday	8	2
Wednesday	8	0
Thursday	8	2
Friday	8	2
Total hours worked	40	6

As you can see, Laura worked a full 40-hour week and put in 6 hours of overtime. Table 5.2 illustrates Laura's pay based on her $10/hour salary and her 10 percent shift premium.

TABLE 5.2   Laura's pay schedule

Category	Hours	Pay
Regular	40	$400
Overtime at 1.5 times regular rate	6	$90
Subtotal	46	$490
Shift Premium @ 10 percent		$9
Total		$499

On-Call Pay

Although the FLSA establishes minimum requirements for on-call time, employers may decide to provide *on-call pay* that is more generous. Employees who are required to respond to work-related issues on short notice, typically emergencies, and who must be available via pager, telephone, or email, may be paid an hourly or daily premium. In certain professions, being on call is part of the job, and on-call premiums aren't paid.

Call-Back Pay

Some companies may provide *call-back pay* to employees who are called to work before or after their scheduled hours. Nonexempt employees who are called into the facility or who work from home are paid their regular rate of pay and any other applicable premiums.

Reporting Pay

When an employee is called into work and there is no work available, the employer may be required by state law or employment agreements to pay for a minimum number of hours of work. This is called a *reporting premium* and ensures the employee receives compensation for showing up for their regular shift or when called to the worksite.

Hazard Pay

Hazard pay is additional pay for dangerous and/or extremely uncomfortable working conditions. Hazard pay may be needed to attract candidates to jobs that require contact with hazardous elements such as radiation, chemicals, or extreme conditions. Firefighters commonly receive hazard pay, because they deal with extreme conditions and physically demanding duties. Examples of other professions that may receive hazard pay include medical positions that work with infectious diseases, police officers, and federal employees who are posted to assignments in countries that are considered dangerous because of wars and/or active hostilities. Although certain jobs may have risks, they may not provide a hazard pay premium, and their compensation is instead reflective of the labor market. FLSA doesn't require hazard pay, but it does require employers who provide hazard pay to factor it into overtime calculations.

Geographic Pay

Organizations use *geographic pay* to ensure that employees in different locations are paid at rates competitive in the labor market for specific jobs and locations. Geographic structures are put into place to make sure the employees are paid competitively and aligned with the organization's compensation philosophy. It's common to find nonexempt pay structures that vary by city and/or state because of the local cost of labor.

Exempt structures may be adjusted by region to reflect regional labor markets. Having an exempt salary structure specific to the Northeast, Pacific Northwest, or Southeast may be appropriate for some labor markets. As an example, if a manufacturing organization is headquartered in the Silicon Valley in Northern California and has manufacturing plants in San Francisco, St. Louis, and Boston, it would be appropriate to have a salary structure specific to each location.

Variable Compensation

Increasingly, organizations are designing compensation programs that include individual or group incentives as a significant component of the total compensation package. According to several salary surveys, almost two-thirds of U.S. companies include some sort of variable compensation in the pay packages offered to employees. Known as *variable compensation*, *incentive pay*, or *pay for performance*, these programs reward employees for individual and/or organizational results. When aligned with the organization's compensation philosophy, this form of compensation can help shape or change employee behavior or organizational culture by rewarding behaviors that are valued by the organization. An effective variable-pay program motivates employees to achieve business objectives by providing a line of sight between desired performance and the reward.

Another reason incentive pay has become a key component of compensation packages is that the broad spreading of merit dollars may not always reinforce performance. Merit budgets have become smaller, on average, which can make it difficult to provide meaningful rewards that differentiate between levels of performance. Providing meaningful rewards to employees through the merit process, given the average merit budget, requires many employees to be passed over for annual merit increases so the dollars can be spent on top performers.

Once an organization determines the type of employee performance or behavior it wants to encourage, an appropriate incentive plan can be selected. Whether the incentive plan is based on individual or group performance, or on some type of special incentive, depends on the organization's specific needs.

Individual Incentives

Individual incentives reward employees who achieve set goals and objectives and can be powerful tools for motivating individual performance. Incentives are prospective in that they state specific objectives that need to be achieved over designated periods of time and include payout targets stated either as a percentage of base pay or as a flat dollar amount.

Successful incentive-plan programs have three critical phases:

Plan Design   Plan design should be kept simple and should make it as easy and convenient as possible for employees to understand and recall performance goals (for instance, an employee or group needs to increase production by 10 percent or decrease defective parts by 5 percent). Complicated incentive plans tend to create confusion and distrust and may not produce the desired results.

Research on incentive programs has found that a minimum bonus target of 10 percent is required to influence and change behavior. Bonus targets of less than 10 percent of base pay may not provide sufficient motivation for employees to put forward the effort or spend the additional time to achieve the plan objectives and as a result may not produce the desired results.

Review Process   Typically, bonus review and payment corresponds to the end of the organization's fiscal year. In some cases, incentives may be paid more frequently if employees have a direct influence on revenue generation. As with most compensation programs, the *ability to pay* (the company affordability factor) is critical to any incentive program. Many bonus-based incentive programs define desired financial metrics that must be achieved before incentives are paid.

Communication and Implementation   Individual incentive-plan objectives are ideally communicated before or at the beginning of the review period. For example, annual, calendar-based plans are usually communicated in January. Targets for incentive plans are commonly part of an offer package but can be modified as needed. When bonus targets are modified, whether they're increased or decreased, great care should be taken in communicating the rationale. Legal counsel and/or local HR representatives should be involved in making these changes to ensure legal compliance with state and local law, particularly in global environments when modifying bonus targets may require new employment contracts.

Communication of an incentive-plan program is key to ensuring that employees understand the metrics of the plan. As part of a communication strategy, some organizations may choose to create and publish a plan document that describes the incentive program in detail.

Organization or Group Incentives

Organization incentives or *group incentives* have many of the same characteristics as individual incentives. A sure step to a successful organization or group incentive plan is that the plan objectives align with the organization's compensation philosophy. Organization or group incentives are commonly used to increase productivity, foster teamwork, and share financial rewards with employees. Benefits that are common to all group incentives include increased awareness of and commitment to company goals. As the name implies, group incentives aren't used to reward individual performance. There are several types of group incentives, including the following:

Gainsharing   *Gainsharing* programs involve employees and managers in improving the organization's productivity and sharing the benefits of success. The key components of gainsharing include the following:

- Employees and management work together to review organizational performance.
- When measurable improvements are achieved, employees and managers share the success.
- The organization and the employees share the financial gains.

Some of the organizational benefits derived from gainsharing include the following:

- Teamwork, sharing knowledge, and cooperation
- Increased motivation
- Employee focus and commitment to organizational goals
- Greater employee acceptance of new methods, technology, and market changes
- Perceived fairness of pay, which results in increased productivity at all levels

Improshare   *Improshare* was developed in the 1970s by Mitchell Fein. It's differentiated from other group incentive plans because a key part of the program is the establishment of a baseline for organization productivity and a baseline for productivity costs. The difference between the baseline productivity and the new output is used to calculate the group's or organization's performance.

Scanlon Plan   The *Scanlon plan* is one of the earliest pay-for-performance plans. In the 1930s, Joseph Scanlon created his plan to increase productivity and decrease costs through employee involvement. Employees receive a portion of cost savings achieved through productivity gains and cost savings. This type of group incentive requires the disclosure of financial information and productivity metrics to employees. Scanlon plans are administered by committees that are representative of the employee population.

Profit Sharing   Very similar to the Scanlon plan, profit sharing is an incentive-based program that shares company profits. Profit-sharing plans are typically qualified plans found across many industries and available to employees at all levels, from individual contributors to senior management. Profit-sharing plans distribute pretax dollars to eligible employees, typically based on a percentage of an employee's base salary. Distribution of profit-sharing dollars typically occurs annually, after the close of the fiscal year. The set formula for a profit-sharing plan defines individual contributions and distributions. It's typical for the plan to have a vesting schedule, described in the plan document. The document details when and how distributions occur and what happens at milestone events, such as employee termination, leave of absence, death, retirement, and so on. Because most profit-sharing plans are a form of defined-contribution plan, they're covered by regulations of the Employee Retirement Income Security Act (ERISA).

Employee Stock Ownership Plans (ESOPs)   An *employee stock ownership plan (ESOP)* is a tax-qualified, defined-contribution plan that allows employees to own shares in a company. An employer sets up a tax-deductible trust that accepts tax-deductible contributions made by the company. Employee eligibility can be based on a formula that may include base salary, length of service, or other factors. At the time of termination, retirement, or death, employees are able to receive the vested portion of their ESOP, which becomes taxable at the time funds are distributed.

Employee Stock Purchase Plans (ESPPs)   ESPPs allow employees to use after-tax payroll deductions to purchase company stock at a discounted price. Typically, there is an offering period in which the employee deductions are accumulated until the purchase date, when the money is used to purchase company stock at a discounted rate of up to 15 percent. These types of benefits programs serve a culture of employee ownership, help develop employee loyalty, and can provide a direct line of sight from employee inputs to rewards.

Special Incentives

In some cases, an organization may decide to provide incentive plans to address specific circumstances. For example, as part of an acquisition, the acquiring company may want to make sure specific executives or other key employees from the company being acquired stay with the new organization long enough to ensure a smooth transition. A financial incentive, often referred to as a *retention bonus*, is one way to do this. Retention bonuses are generally structured so that the full bonus is paid if the employee remains with the company through a certain date, but the entire amount is forfeited if the employee leaves before that date. Retention bonuses are also used in situations when an organization is closing its doors. Some employees, such as an accounting manager, will be needed to complete final tasks, and a retention bonus can be used to make sure those employees don't accept new jobs until the necessary tasks are completed.

Special incentive plans can also be included as part of executive compensation packages to reward top executives for achieving established financial goals, such as a percentage of increased sales, a predetermined stock price increase, and other performance goals established by a board of directors.

Commissions and Sales Bonuses

Commissions provide incentives to sales employees by paying them a percentage of the sale price for products and services sold to a customer. Commissions may serve as the entire cash compensation package, or they may be used in combination with a base salary. When sales employees receive a base salary, it's usually a portion of their target cash compensation. The incentive or variable component is intended to drive sales objectives. Compensation for sales employees paid on a commission-only basis must meet at least the minimum wage.

An alternative to a commission plan is a sales bonus plan, in which a percentage of base pay compensates the employee for sales targets achieved. The difference between commission and bonus plans is the method of calculation, and this has many implications for the design of sales compensation programs. For example, Joaquin sells new cars and has an annual quota of 100 cars. For every car Joaquin sells over 100, he receives a bonus of 1 percent of his base salary.

When performance targets are clearly communicated, commissions and bonuses are an excellent way to motivate sales employees to perform desired behaviors and achieve desired results.

Bonus Plans

A *bonus* is additional compensation for performance above and beyond expectations and is paid in addition to an employee's base salary or hourly rate. Unlike incentive plans communicated when an assignment is made and conditional upon successfully completing the assignment, most bonuses are considered discretionary. This means the bonus is optionally offered and isn't based on established objectives. An example of a *bonus plan* is the holiday bonus that some organizations distribute at the end of the year. It's up to the employer to decide whether a bonus will be paid each year, which employees are eligible to participate, and how much each individual receives. Another example is a spot-bonus plan, which provides an immediate reward for outstanding performance, such as an employee who makes sure a critical customer proposal is completed in time to make the delivery cut-off schedule. Bonuses also take the form of a sales-performance bonus paid to salespeople who exceed their quotas, employee-referral bonuses paid to employees who refer candidates hired for open positions, patent awards, employee-of-the-month rewards, and so on.

Traditional Pay Structures

Traditional pay programs have existed relatively unchanged for more than 50 years. The way an organization develops pay structures and uses them to administer pay on a day-to-day basis is known as *salary administration*, *compensation administration*, or *pay administration*. Figure 5.1 represents the steps in this process.

FIGURE 5.1   Salary administration

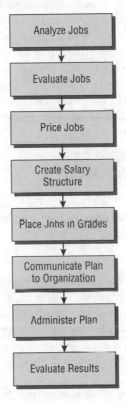

Analyze Jobs

Evaluate Jobs

Price Jobs

Create Salary Structure

Place Jobs in Grades

Communicate Plan to Organization

Administer Plan

Evaluate Results

Each step in this process is aligned with the organization's compensation philosophy, and a description of the process may be kept in its policy manual. The first step in salary administration is the job-analysis process described in Chapter 3. Job analysis is the process used to collect information about jobs and create job descriptions. Accurate job descriptions are an essential element of the job-evaluation process.

Compensation administration includes concepts and tools used on a regular basis to manage compensation decisions. These include job evaluation, job pricing, designing a pay structure aligned with organization goals, administering the compensation plan, and handling pay increases and nontraditional pay structures.

Job Evaluation

Job evaluation is the process used traditionally to determine the value of jobs relative to each other in the organization. It's an inexact science that attempts to remove subjectivity from the process as much as possible by replacing opinions and preconceived ideas with more objective criteria. Job evaluations are normally conducted when a job is developed, when the job duties change, or as part of a routine job-evaluation process. HR professionals partner with line management when conducting job evaluations; defined job-evaluation methods allow for a repeatable process for this key component of the compensation system.

Job-evaluation methods identify and define the compensable factors of each job that are most relevant for the organization. *Compensable factors* are characteristics that define and distinguish jobs from one another. For instance, a junior-level engineer's compensable factors might include the following:

- Bachelor's degree in electrical engineering
- Two years of industry-related experience
- Two years of experience testing products for quality and reliability

The two methods discussed in this chapter for job evaluation include the ranking method and classification method. Let's examine each of these in greater detail.

Ranking Method

The *ranking method* requires evaluators to compare the value of jobs to one another. Because this is a subjective method for evaluating jobs, evaluators can be influenced by any preconceptions they may have about different positions or job duties, and this impacts the way in which jobs are ranked. Although ranking is a simple and cost-effective method for use in small organizations, it can become a very complicated process in a complex organization with many positions to evaluate. In this method, it's also difficult to compare unrelated jobs.

Here is an example of the ranking method in action: SkyLine Healthcare uses the ranking method to compare Judy, an administrative assistant, to Leonard, a file clerk. Both Judy and Leonard are administrative-level employees. Judy's job requires higher or more advanced qualifications and experience than Leonard's; therefore, Judy's position is ranked higher than Leonard's.

Classification Method

The *classification method* involves identifying key *benchmark positions*. Benchmark positions are jobs common to organizations regardless of size or industry, such as accountants or administrative assistants. Once a job is matched to a benchmark position, it may be classified according to value on a vertical scale. Benchmark positions are then associated with a grade on a hierarchical salary structure. Positions with similar characteristics are slotted into the same grade or level, which are identified by a similar level of knowledge, skills, and abilities.

To use the classification method, companies must determine *internal equity*, or the value of jobs to each other relative to their value to the organization. There are several ways to measure and assess internal equity, including broadbanding (discussed in the section "Nontraditional Pay Structures" later in this chapter), the point-factor method, and the HAY system:

Point Factor   The *point-factor method* provides organizations with a system of points that are assigned to the position being evaluated. Based on the total number of points a position receives, a pay grade/range is assigned to the position. Each company that uses this complicated method for evaluating jobs may have abstract or very specific factors that broadly fall under five categories: education, skill, effort, responsibility, and working conditions.

HAY System   In 1943, Edward Hay, founder of the Hay Group, a professional services organization and consulting agency, developed the *HAY system*, a classification method that uses a complex point-factor system. Jobs are evaluated using three factors: knowledge, problem-solving, and accountability. Using the points from the evaluation, the jobs are matched to a profile.

Job Pricing

Job pricing occurs when a new job is created or an existing job has undergone changes and is a common practice when administering compensation. Many organizations, especially those going through high growth periods, use job pricing to ensure pay is competitive. A four-step process is used to determine the appropriate pay level for a position:

1. Review the job description, and understand the level and scope of the job and its required responsibilities and skills.

2. Select a salary survey. When selecting a salary survey, it's important to consider the type and number of survey participants. For example, if you're pricing a job in Austin, Texas, it may not be appropriate to use data from a salary survey if most of the participants are located in Silicon Valley. Most compensation managers like to see several competitors or other premier employers as part of the survey so that the data is perceived as valid.

3. Review compensation components, such as base pay, variable pay, equity pay, and so on. At this time it's also important to review a number of matches for a certain position. The more matches, the better, because the data will be more reliable and less likely to be skewed by outliers (jobs that are paid significantly above or below the average).

4. Recommend a salary range. The recommendation should be in alignment with your organization's compensation philosophy of leading, matching, or lagging the market. In addition to a salary range, it may be appropriate to recommend incentive pay or special pay programs.

It's important for HR professionals to review job-pricing results with management to validate that the survey positions and data match the job. Once a job is priced, it's appropriate to slot the job into the appropriate pay range and grade.

Salary Structure Development

A salary structure provides an organized, systematic way of identifying base pay for employees in different jobs throughout the organization. The structure consists of a specified number of salary grades with a range of compensation attached to each. Developing a salary structure requires an analysis of both internal equity and external labor market conditions obtained through the job-pricing process. Jobs are grouped using the data collected during job evaluation and pricing. During the pricing process, job descriptions are matched to comparable benchmark positions that provide a market range for each.

In most cases, the market median or fiftieth percentile is used as the data-comparison point for each job. There may be times when an organization decides to use a higher point of comparison for some jobs (highly skilled positions that are in short supply in the labor market, for example) or for all jobs (if the compensation philosophy is to lead the market). Jobs are grouped according to the data points established by the survey. These groups of jobs with similar market levels provide the basis for determining the number of job grades to include in the structure.

Using the grouped jobs as a starting point, midpoints are established for each job grade. The *midpoint progression*, or difference between the midpoints of consecutive grades, is generally narrower for lower grades and increases for higher grades. Typically, the midpoint progression ranges from 12–15 percent at lower grades to 25 percent at higher grades. Once grades are established, a pay range is developed for each grade.

A *pay range* (also known as a *salary range*) is the spread between the minimum and maximum pay for the job grade. Ranges can be stated as an hourly amount for workers paid on an hourly basis or a monthly, semimonthly, biweekly, or annual amount for salaried workers. The spread of traditional pay ranges is typically narrow and varies depending on level. At entry-level grades, ranges are the narrowest based on the assumption that employees in those grades will gain KSAs and progress to higher job grades. At the highest grades, the spread is quite wide to provide salary progression for highly valued employees who remain in positions for longer periods of time. The spread for entry-level job grades usually begins at 15 percent and can go as high as 25–30 percent for the highest job grades. The spread is calculated based on the midpoint established by the market.

For example, the pay grade for a group of midlevel professional positions might have an 18 percent spread. At a midpoint of $50,000, the minimum would be 82 percent of the midpoint, or $41,000, and the maximum would be 118 percent of the midpoint, or $59,000.

Placing Jobs in Grades

Initially, jobs are placed in pay grades based on the grouping done to develop the grades. If market data was collected only for benchmark positions, the rest of the jobs will need to be placed in the ranges based on internal equity with the benchmark positions. At this point, the placements are reviewed with senior management to ensure they make sense in the context of the organization's strategic direction. By providing a chart or spreadsheet that shows the jobs in each job grade by business unit, executives can determine whether changes are necessary. Once agreement is reached, the structure is finalized and communicated to employees.

Real World Scenario

Comparable Worth

Comparable worth, or *pay equity*, describes the concept of minimizing pay disparities between jobs traditionally held by women, such as teachers, with higher-paying jobs traditionally held by men, such as carpenters. This concept suggests that jobs with similar duties and responsibilities requiring similar levels of knowledge, skill, and ability should be paid similarly. Comparable worth doesn't reflect supply and demand in the labor market because it's about the inherent value of the job's content to society. The issue is complex because value is a subjective measure and how jobs are valued often depends on who is valuing them. Those opposed to this concept argue that the price of a particular job in the labor market is based on the supply and demand for its skills and that social engineering isn't an appropriate role for business.

Communicating the Structure

The goal of the communication plan is to have buy-in at all levels of the organization so that the salary structure accomplishes what it needs to do: provide a fair and equitable structure for making pay decisions. To do this, communication about the pay structure takes place at two levels: employee and manager. Employees need to understand how the structure was developed so they feel fairly compensated for their work and have a line of sight from their performance to their compensation. Explaining how the structure was created should alleviate any concerns about political influence or favoritism in the decision-making process.

Managers need to understand how the salary structure can be used to influence behavior in a way that encourages employees to accomplish their goals and objectives. They need to be well versed in how the structure works so they can effectively explain pay decisions to employees.

Administering the Compensation Plan

Once a pay structure is created, managers must have the tools they need to administer pay for their work units. Compiling a salary-administration handbook helps managers throughout the organization apply the system consistently. A typical handbook contains the following kinds of information:

- The organization's compensation philosophy
- The roles played by HR, line managers, and executives in salary administration
- Basic information about pay increases
- A description of how salaries or wages for new hires are determined

If variable compensation is part of the compensation mix, information about bonuses and other incentives is included as well.

Range Placement

Up to this point, the pay-structure discussion has concentrated on jobs, not on the employees in the jobs. The focus now turns to using the pay structure to make decisions for individual employees. One of the key factors to consider when making individual pay decisions is the employee's place in the pay range. Table 5.3 illustrates how ranges are used to make individual pay decisions.

TABLE 5.3   Using ranges in pay decisions

Placement	Use for...
Minimum	Entry-level employees
	Employees new to the organization or the position
	Employees performing below standard
Midpoint	Fully proficient employees
Maximum	Employees highly valued by the organization based on technical skill level, company-specific experience, and/or consistently outstanding level of performance

When changes are made to an existing salary structure, pay for some employees may fall outside the new range. Pay that falls below the minimum of the salary range is referred to as a *green circle* rate of pay. Employees may also be green-circled because their experience and/or skills don't meet the requirements of the position or as a result of performance issues. Conversely, *red-circle* pay refers to employees whose pay falls above the maximum of the salary range. This may occur when an employee is demoted without a corresponding decrease to base pay, because of a transfer or for some other unusual circumstance.

Wage Compression

Wage compression occurs when new employees are hired at a rate of pay greater than that earned by incumbent employees for similar skills, education, and experience. These situations are usually the most challenging during high-growth economic times or when there is high demand for certain skill sets. Compression may also occur if the organization's pay practices, merit increases, and promotional budgets aren't in line with the market. One way to reduce compression is to provide salary adjustments for the incumbent population.

Compa-ratios

A *compa-ratio* is a simple formula used to compare employee salaries. It is calculated as a percentage by taking the employee's base pay and comparing it to the midpoint of the pay range. This measure is commonly used for comparison against a group of employees and is especially useful when providing recommendations for pay increases for promotions, merit increases, and so on.

Here's the formula for finding the compa-ratio:

Base Salary ÷ Midpoint of Salary Range × 100

Here's an example of a compa-ratio in action:

120,000 base salary ÷ 100,000 midpoint × 100 = 120

A compa-ratio of 100 percent indicates that the base pay equals the midpoint of the salary range. For example, say an HR manager, Elena, is evaluating the new base pay for Joseph, an executive who is about to be promoted to the next pay grade. Elena determines that incumbents in the new position have an average compa-ratio of about 110 percent. Because Joseph is entering this level for the first time, a compa-ratio of less than 100 percent may be most appropriate for him.

Increases to Base Pay

Base pay can be increased for a variety of reasons: cost-of-living adjustments, annual reviews, and promotions are some of the most common.

Cost-of-Living Adjustments (COLAs)

Cost-of-living adjustments are generally used during periods of high inflation to reduce the effects of wage compression. These adjustments happen more often in public sector jobs than in the private sector, which generally relies on survey data to maintain compensation at a level that is competitive with the appropriate labor market, whether at the local or the national level. Many employers tie the percentage of increase to the Consumer Price Index (CPI) recommendations.

Annual Reviews

Calculating increases for annual reviews can be simple or complex. In a seniority-based compensation system where increases are based on time in the job, the calculation is relatively simple—the most common methods use a fixed dollar amount or percentage of base pay. In a performance-based system, where *merit increases* are based on demonstrated performance, the calculation is usually more complex.

Merit programs are often aligned with a performance-management system. When this is the case, an annual performance rating is the key determining factor for the amount of a merit increase. Reviews may be conducted on an employee's anniversary date or during a *focal review* period when all employees are reviewed at the same time.

A merit matrix is commonly developed by HR as a tool for managers to use in planning increases for their work units. A merit matrix combines a performance rating with the employee's position in the salary range to recommend the amount of increase. The matrix shown in Table 5.4 demonstrates that in addition to differentiating employees based on performance, it's important to differentiate based on their positions in the salary range. For example, employees at the midpoint of the salary range are considered to be fully trained and able to perform all job duties. Employees on the low end of the salary range who are moving up the learning curve quickly may warrant a higher merit increase than an employee at the midpoint or maximum of the salary range.

TABLE 5.4   Merit increase matrix, assuming 5 percent annual merit budget

Performance/position in range	Minimum	Midpoint	Maximum
Exceeds expectations	8–10 percent	6–8 percent	3–6 percent
Meets expectations	5–7 percent	4–6 percent	0 percent
Doesn't meet expectations	0 percent	0 percent	0 percent

There are several things to consider before giving a merit-based salary increase:

Employee's Position in the Salary Range   Before providing a merit increase, consider the employee's current salary and where it fits into the range for the job title. For example, Tanya and Maurice are both customer service representatives. They perform the same job equally well. Tanya is at the high end of the salary range, and Maurice is on the low end. In order to keep Tanya and Maurice within the same range, Maurice, with his salary on the low end, should receive a higher merit increase than Tanya. Typically, the midpoint of the salary range is the ideal place in the salary range for a fully trained, solidly performing employee.

Tenure in Position (Hire Date/Date of Last Promotion)   It's important to consider how long an employee has held a job, the amount of time since the employee's last promotion, and the date of the last increase. For example, an employee who was recently promoted may still be learning a position and not performing all job requirements at a fully qualified level. The impact of this situation on the amount of increase would be to reduce the amount of the award so that the employee's salary is between the low and midpoints of the salary range. This would reflect the level of performance being delivered.

Skill Set and Performance Compared to Peer Group   HR managers and supervisors should be aware of the marketable skills and current compensation of an employee relative to the employee's peers. Employees have access to market data via the Internet, and many are very aware of their worth in the marketplace. From the employer's perspective, this places employees at risk for recruitment by competitors if they believe their pay is substandard.

In addition to merit matrices, some organizations require managers to use some sort of forced-distribution calculation when awarding merit increases. This helps to manage the salary increase budget and forces managers to differentiate between varying levels of performance by employees in their work units. To reward outstanding performers with a meaningful increase, increases for poor performers are minimal or nonexistent. This approach is designed to send a message to employees in both categories.

Managers should understand how to connect merit increases to performance and explain the connection between the two to employees. When it's unclear, employees can begin to view merit increases as COLAs. Connecting the two will help managers avoid an atmosphere of entitlement in their work units.

Promotions

Promotions occur when employees are moved into new positions with different duties and greater responsibilities or when they develop a level of experience and skill enabling them to assume added responsibilities in their current positions. Typically, a promotion is accompanied by a change in title and salary level. In organizations with traditional pay structures, this also means an increase in salary grade.

When determining how much of an increase to provide for a promotion, several factors are considered. These include how long the employee has been in the current position, how recently a merit increase was awarded, whether the new position is in the same area of the organization or a different one, and where the new salary will place the employee in the new salary range. Generally speaking, an increase of 10–15 percent is provided for promotions.

Nontraditional Pay Structures

In the more than 50 years that traditional pay structures have been used, significant changes in the way businesses operate have taken place, and many compensation professionals think that traditional, job-based systems don't serve current employer needs. Some organizations may strongly consider skill sets as determining factors for pay decisions, awarding increases to employees who possess skills that are critical to the organization's success. Other organizations may provide additional compensation for the development and acquisition of new skills. An example of this can commonly be found in manufacturing environments, where an entry-level operator who acquires additional skills for the position receives additional compensation for these skills. One method for doing this is competency-based compensation.

Although traditional pay programs focus on job requirements, a *competency-based compensation* program is salaries based on demonstrated skills and knowledge. Competency-based pay programs place responsibility for advancement on each employee: the greater the level of competence, the higher level of pay is available. The underlying concept for organizations is that as employees gain competence in their jobs, fewer employees are needed to achieve organizational goals, and employers can afford to pay them more.

As the information and knowledge economies replaced the industrial economy, many organizations found the bureaucracy of traditional pay programs an impediment to the rapid changes necessary for responding to changing market conditions. Instead of conducting a job analysis and evaluation so that a new job description can be created each time an employee's duties change, competency-based programs encourage employees to hone their current KSAs and develop new ones, rewarding them for their increased abilities instead of for specific job duties that may change over time.

Competency profiles replace job descriptions in these programs. A competency profile consists of 10–12 key competencies identified by those who know the job requirements best—in most cases, job incumbents who are performing at a high level. A career ladder then identifies specific levels of competency required at various stages (usually three or four, beginning at entry level and advancing to a senior, highly skilled level). The profile describes the level of fully functional competence expected from employees at each stage and the corresponding pay for each level. Competency profiles include technical skills specific to individual jobs and softer skills identified as valuable to the organization, such as communication skills, teamwork, or adaptability. Because competency-based compensation doesn't reward performance in the way traditional programs do, it's often combined with cash incentive programs to reward desired performance.

Competency-based compensation is used most effectively with broadband salary ranges to maximize flexibility as employees attain greater levels of competence in current KSAs or add new ones. Range levels are generally tied to the different stages of the competency profile.

This type of pay program communicates organizational focus to employees by selecting competencies that support strategic goals. For example, creating competencies that reward teamwork will help to change the culture from highly competitive to one that is more team-based by rewarding those employees who work effectively in teams. Clearly defined competencies help employees see that increased competence results in higher compensation and places responsibility for advancement on individual employees.

Traditional salary structures don't support the needs of competency-based pay, so some organizations have used broadbanding in conjunction with this pay program. *Broadbanding* splits positions in the company into just a few specific pay ranges. Each range includes a variety of jobs. For example, a broadband classification structure may have four levels, such as individual contributor, manager, director, and VP. All jobs in the company fit into one of the four classifications. Broadbanding helps organizations remain flat and facilitates lateral career movement. In contrast, narrowbanding or traditional pay classifications have many levels and are organized in a hierarchical and vertical fashion. Narrowbanding may not facilitate lateral movement and can create an employee focus on the organizational structure rather than job responsibilities. One benefit of broadbanding is that it can lead to greater collaboration by limiting employee focus on hierarchical differences between jobs.

Benefits

Employee benefit programs are an integral part of a company's total compensation plan and represent a significant cost to employers. Of equal importance to compensation in the total rewards mix, employee benefit programs are varied and designed to meet specific employee needs. There are two basic types of benefit programs: those that are legally mandated and those that are voluntary. The purpose of this section is to explore how HR professionals, working with senior management, can determine the mix of benefits that will attract and retain the type of employees needed by the organization to achieve its goals.

When most employees think about their benefit packages, they think of medical and dental insurance, vacation and sick leave, and the retirement plan; however, employers provide many other benefits that employees often overlook. These include nonmonetary benefits such as the location of their facilities, the length of the daily commute for employees, "dress down" days, and monetary benefits such as paid volunteer time or tuition assistance. These are all factors taken into consideration by candidates when determining whether to accept an offer. However, without specific effort on the part of employers, employees are often unaware of the value of the benefits provided for them because they rarely consider these costs when they think about their total income. Decisions about these facets of the employment relationship in each company can either help or hurt the efforts of the organization to attract and retain employees.

HRCI's glossary of terms has at least four separate entries related to the term "benefits." Though slightly redundant, this is a useful way to understand the term through the filter of exam content:

- **Benefit programs:** Workers' entitlements in addition to base salary. Examples include health insurance, life insurance, disability pay, retirement pension, and so on.

- **Benefits:** Compensation that the employee receives in addition to base salary. Examples include health insurance, company housing, company meals, clothing allowance, pensions, and gym memberships.

- **Employee/employer benefits:** Payments or allowances that organizations give to their employees (for example, medical insurance, Social Security taxes, pension contributions, education reimbursement, and car or clothing allowance)

- **Healthcare benefits:** Company-sponsored medical plans that help employees pay for the cost of doctor visits, hospitalization, surgeries, and so on

Two main categories of benefits may be offered: involuntary and voluntary.

Involuntary Benefits

The first involuntary, or legally mandated, employee benefits were introduced as part of President Franklin Delano Roosevelt's (FDR's) New Deal programs during the mid-1930s to aid the millions of Americans who lost their jobs and were unable to find work during the Great Depression. Unemployment reached 25 percent at the low point of the Depression in 1933, leaving many families destitute, homeless, and living in shantytowns throughout the nation. In response to this economic crisis, when FDR was elected in 1932, he set about creating protections for American workers to provide a safety net during economic downturns.

Once again, keep in mind that legal requirements in your state may differ in some respects from the federal requirements. For the PHR examination, you must be familiar with the *federal* requirements. They include Social Security, Medicare, unemployment insurance, family and medical leave (eligibility based on number of employees in the organization and individual hours worked), workers compensation, and COBRA benefit continuation. All of these are discussed in great detail in Appendix C.

It is also worth noting that many states are exploring (and adopting) paid sick leave requirements. New York, for example, passed the Earned Sick Time Act, which requires that workers earn one hour of paid sick time for every 30 hours worked. For PHR exam preparation purposes, you don't need to know or understand the specifics of state laws—the exam is based on federal acts. You do need to understand that when there are competing laws between the federal and state government, you generally must comply with the law that gives the greatest benefit to the employee.

Voluntary Benefits

The kinds of benefits that organizations may voluntarily provide are significantly more complicated. Table 5.5 provides some examples of voluntary benefits.

TABLE 5.5   Voluntary employee benefits

Types of benefits	Benefit details
Deferred compensation	Qualified pension plans
	Nonqualified pension plans
Health and welfare benefits	Dental insurance
	Vision insurance
	Life insurance
	AD&D insurance
	Short-/long-term disability insurance
	Long-term care insurance
Work–life balance	Vacation leave
	Sick leave
	Paid time off
	Paid holidays
	Childcare
	Fitness
	Elder care
Other voluntary benefits	Employee assistance plans
	Relocation assistance
	Tuition reimbursement
	On-site schooling
	Student loan help
	Flexible spending accounts
	Cafeteria plan
	Adoption assistance
	Section 529 plans
	Commute assistance

Employers attract qualified candidates with different types of skills by offering cash compensation that leads or matches the labor market for those skills. They can also use the mix of their benefit packages to attract and retain segments of the labor market with characteristics that align to their particular business values and goals. For example, an organization interested in attracting employees focused on maintaining a high level of knowledge in their chosen fields may offer a generous educational reimbursement benefit and provide training opportunities as a way of attracting and retaining those employees.

Making decisions about the voluntary benefit package that is most appropriate for a particular organization's workforce requires consideration of many factors: demographics, industry standards, local area practices, the financial situation of the company, and the organizational culture among them. A needs assessment provides insight into which benefits are most attractive to the organization's current workforce and provides a starting point for evaluating options. There are many choices, and finding the right mix can significantly affect an employer's ability to attract and retain employees with the desired qualifications. For example, Amazon has a Career Choice program that will reimburse up to 95 percent of employee tuition and fees to train employees in high-demand fields such as nursing and machining. Amazon noted that participants in this program have one fourth of the attrition rate for nonparticipants. It also allows for workforce planning because they have data related to employees who will be exiting the company within the four years or so that that the benefit is available.

Voluntary benefits programs also need to address the lifestyle needs of all employees, not just some. LinkedIn, for example, heard from employees without kids who were frustrated that they did not get the same benefit from the paid parental leave policy as their co-workers with children. In response, LinkedIn started a pilot program called PerkUp, which provided up to $500 a quarter for employees to spend on lifestyle perks, including dog walking and massages.

To aid in understanding the discussion of benefits in this section, candidates for the PHR exam should be familiar with the following list of terms:

Defined Benefit   A *defined-benefit plan* is a traditional pension plan in which the employer provides a specific benefit upon retirement. The funds in these plans aren't accounted for individually.

Defined Contribution   A *defined-contribution plan* is an individual plan in which the amount of funds contributed is known but the amount of the benefit that is eventually paid out isn't known because it depends on the investment returns that are earned. The funds are accounted for in individual accounts for each participant.

Nonforfeitable   A *nonforfeitable claim* is one that exists because of a participant's service. Nonforfeitable claims are unconditional and legally enforceable.

Party in Interest   A *party in interest* may be a fiduciary, a person or an entity providing services to the plan, an employer or employee organization, a person who owns 50 percent or more of the business, relatives of any of the above, or corporations that are involved with the plan in any of these functions.

Plan Administrator   The *plan administrator* is the person designated by the plan sponsor to manage the plan.

Plan Sponsor   The *plan sponsor* is the entity that establishes the plan. This may be a single employer, a labor organization, or, in the case of a multiemployer plan, a group representing the parties that established the plan.

Qualified Plan   A *qualified plan* meets ERISA requirements and provides tax advantages for both employees and employers. To be classified as a qualified plan, a pension plan can't provide additional benefits for officers, shareholders, executives, supervisors, or other highly compensated employees—all employees in the organization must be eligible for all plan benefits.

Nonqualified Plan   A *nonqualified retirement plan* is one in which the benefits exceed the limitations of qualified plans or don't meet other IRS requirements for favorable tax treatment. These plans aren't required to include all employees, so they may provide additional benefits to officers, shareholders, executives, supervisors, or other highly compensated employees.

Voluntary benefits fall into four main categories: deferred compensation, health and welfare benefits, work–life balance benefits, and other benefits. Although there are no federal laws requiring employers to provide any of these (with the exception of the mandates of the Affordable Care Act covered in Appendix C), some federal laws regulate pensions or benefits when employers choose to include them in their total rewards packages.

Deferred Compensation Benefits

Deferred compensation is a type of employee pension that is tax-deferred, such as individual retirement accounts (IRAs), 401(k) programs, or traditional employer pension plans. HRCI defines deferred compensation programs as those that "allow an employee to contribute a portion of income over time to be paid as a lump sum at retirement when the employee's income tax rate will be lower." This employee benefit was first offered in the late nineteenth century by business owners who wanted to reward long-term employees. Early pension plans were defined-benefit plans with all funds being provided by the employers. The payments owed to retirees weren't set aside specifically for them but were made from business operating funds. As a result, a company that went out of business was no longer able to make the pension payments, and employees didn't receive the benefits that had been promised to them. To encourage businesses to provide pension benefits, in 1935 the Social Security Administration (SSA) allowed employers who provided pension plans to deduct the full amount of the payments they made to employees, but there were no laws to govern how the plans operated or to require that the funds to pay pensions be set aside to ensure their availability for retirees. In 1958, Congress made its first attempt to exert some control over private pension plans when it passed the Welfare and Pension Plans Disclosure Act (WPDA) requiring the administrators of health insurance, pension, and supplemental unemployment insurance plans to file descriptions of the plans and annual financial reports with the DOL.

As the number of pension plans provided for employees by American businesses grew, some companies found ways to obtain tax benefits from pension plans while denying benefits to employees. There were no requirements for communicating information to plan participants, so many employees were unaware of eligibility requirements. There was also little oversight of the ways the plans were operated. Vesting schedules were inadequate, and many long-term employees found themselves ineligible to receive pension benefits as a result. There were no established standards to ensure the viability of plans to pay promised benefits. The result of this was that many employees found themselves without pensions when they were ready to retire. Furthermore, some businesses set lengthy vesting schedules to obtain tax benefits but terminated long-term employees just before they vested in the plan.

Qualified Deferred Compensation Plans

A qualified deferred compensation plan is one that meets all ERISA requirements and protects employees from loss of benefits due to employer mismanagement of pension funds. Within the broad description of a qualified plan, employers have a number of options to choose from when designing a plan that meets the needs of their particular workforce:

Defined-Benefit Plans HRCI defines a *defined-benefit plan* as "a retirement plan that tells participants exactly how much money they will receive on a specific later date (usually the day they retire)." A defined-benefit plan is based on a formula. The formula looks at two factors: salary and length of service with the company. In most traditional defined-benefit plans, the retirement benefit is based on the salary earned during the last 5 to 10 years of earnings, but it may also be based on career average earnings, a flat dollar amount for each year of service, or a unit benefit plan in which the benefit payment is based on a percentage of earnings multiplied by the years of service.

 Real World Scenario

Retirement Before ERISA

In 1963, nearly 7,000 employees of the Studebaker Corporation lost all or most of their pension benefits because of a plant closure in Indiana. More than 4,000 of these employees had served an average of more than 22 years with the company and, at the time of the plant's closure, were an average of 52 years old. The pension fund failed largely because there was no legal precedent requiring organizations to set aside adequate funds with which to pay retirement benefits; plans at that time were still being funded from current operating funds in the Studebaker Corporation.

Although the failure of the Studebaker Corporation fund wasn't unique, the large number of workers deprived of benefits focused national attention on the problem and led eventually to the passage of the Employee Retirement Income Security Act. ERISA replaced the WPDA, increasing the reporting requirements, requiring that pension funds be separated from the operating funds of the business, establishing vesting schedules for plan participants, requiring employers to provide summary plan descriptions of the plans to employees, and setting minimum standards for fund management.

In these plans, the company is committed to pay a specified benefit amount when an employee retires. How much the company must accrue each year may fluctuate based on the return earned on the invested funds. If the funds are invested in high-growth investments, the company will need to transfer less cash from its operating funds to the pension trust. But if the return earned on the investment drops, the company may have to play catch-up with larger-than-anticipated transfers of cash to maintain the viability of the plan. During the stock-market boom of the late 1990s, many companies didn't need to transfer large sums to fund their pension accounts, but when the stock market dropped, much of the value of the pension funds was lost. This required larger transfers to be made to maintain availability of the pension funds for employees. In defined-benefit plans, employers take the risk for paying out the promised benefit at retirement.

Cash-Balance Plans   *Cash-balance plans* (CBPs) have become increasingly popular since they were approved by the IRS in 1985. It is estimated that CBPs now account for more than 25 percent of all defined-benefit plans. Although some companies see them as a hybrid of the defined-benefit and defined-contribution plans, they're subject to the regulations placed on defined-benefit plans. CBPs are less costly for employers; in 1999, IBM revised its defined-benefit plan to a CBP and projected savings of $500 billion over 10 years as a result of the change.

In a CBP, benefits are determined by using a hypothetical personal pension account (PPA); each month, this account is increased by a set rate—for example, 5 percent of the employee's salary. The account also accumulates interest, typically related to the interest rate on Treasury bills. Think of it as an individual employee savings account in which the employer makes deposits based on a defined formula.

For employees, the benefit of the CBP is that it's portable; when an employee resigns, the funds may be withdrawn in a lump-sum payment, may be converted to an annuity, or may remain in the employer's account and be withdrawn at a later time. CBPs also have higher contribution limits, which can be attractive for employees who are behind on retirement savings.

Defined-Contribution Plans   A defined-contribution plan relies on contributions from employees and employers to fund IRAs. In these plans, the amount of the contribution is fixed, but the amount of the benefit available upon retirement can vary based on the type of investments made and the returns earned on them. In these plans, the employee takes the risk for having funds available at retirement. There are several types of defined-contribution plans:

Profit-Sharing Plans   Also known as *discretionary contributions, profit-sharing plans* allow employers to contribute deferred compensation based on a percentage of company earnings each year. A maximum contribution of 25 percent may be made for an individual employee each year. The maximum contribution amount was indexed to inflation in increments of $1,000 beginning in 2003. For 2012, the maximum contribution is the lesser of $50,000 or 25 percent of compensation. When calculating contributions, employers may only use the first $245,000 of an employee's compensation; this amount is also indexed to inflation and adjusted annually in increments of $5,000. The percentage of the contribution may vary from year to year, and the company may elect to make no contributions in some years. The maximum tax deduction for contributions that can be taken by the employer is 25 percent of total employee compensation. Because the contributions may vary from year to year, profit-sharing plans work well for companies with erratic profit levels.

Money-Purchase Plans   A *money-purchase plan* uses a fixed percentage of employee earnings to defer compensation. This type of plan works well for organizations with relatively stable earnings from year to year because the percentage is fixed and, once established, contributions must be made every year. The contribution limits are the same as the limits for profit-sharing plans.

Target-Benefit Plans   A *target-benefit plan* is a hybrid plan with similarities to a defined-benefit plan and a money-purchase plan. Instead of using a fixed percentage of employee salaries to determine annual contribution amounts, actuarial formulas calculate the contribution amount needed to reach a predetermined benefit amount at retirement. Because this amount takes into consideration the current age of each employee, different amounts will be contributed for employees with equal compensation packages. As with other deferred-contribution plans, the amounts are distributed to individual employee accounts, and the contribution limits are the same as the limits for profit-sharing plans.

401(k) Plans   A common type of deferred compensation is the *401(k) plan*, established by the Revenue Act of 1978. A 401(k) plan allows for contributions from both employees and employers. Employees may defer part of their pay before taxes up to predetermined limits. Employers may make contributions as well; the limits for these are the same as those for profit-sharing plans. Plans similar to the 401(k) are available for nonprofit workers [403(b) plans] and for public employees (457 plans). Any earnings or losses that accrue in the account impact the funds available for retirement, and employees are ultimately responsible for ensuring that the funds are properly managed and available for use when they're ready to retire.

One requirement of 401(k) plans is that they may not provide greater benefits to *highly compensated employees* (HCEs) than other employees. An HCE is defined as a plan participant who, during the current or prior year, earned $115,000 (if preceding year is 2018, $125,000 if the preceding year is 2019) or more, owns 5 percent or more of the company, and, at the company's discretion, is one of the top-paid 20 percent of employees. Each year, an *actual deferral percentage (ADP) test* must be conducted to ensure that the plan is within limits set by IRS regulations. When the ADP test indicates that HCE participants are realizing greater benefits from the plan than non-HCE participants, the company must take action to correct this or lose the tax benefits of the plan. To correct the problem, a company may refund the excess contributions to HCE participants, which will increase their taxable income for the prior year, or the company may increase matching contributions to non-HCE employees in order to pass the test. Another option to correct imbalances is to aggregate the plan with other plans sponsored by the employer, if available.

Nonqualified Deferred Compensation

Nonqualified deferred-compensation plans aren't protected by ERISA and are generally made available only to a limited number of employees at the executive level. Known as *top-hat plans*, these benefits provide retirement funds that supplement qualified retirement benefits and aren't subject to ERISA discrimination testing requirements. These plans allow highly compensated employees to defer income in excess of limits placed on qualified plans. Two types of nonqualified plans are as follows:

Grantor or Rabbi Trusts   Commonly known as *rabbi trusts*, *grantor trusts* are nonqualified deferred-compensation plans established to provide retirement income for officers, directors, and HCEs. The funds are unsecured and therefore subject to claims made by the organization's creditors. Benefits are taxable as ordinary income at the time they're paid to beneficiaries.

Excess Deferral Plans   An excess deferral plan allows the organization to make contributions to a nonqualified plan in order to reduce the impact of discrimination testing on HCEs. This is done by making up the difference between what the executive could have contributed to the plan and what was actually allowed because of limits required by the qualified plan.

Health and Welfare Benefits

Health and welfare benefits have come to be expected by most American workers. The benefits that fall into this category are described in this section.

Medical Insurance

The cost of medical insurance is substantial for employers and employees. The costs can be controlled to a certain extent by the type of plan selected. These are some plans to consider:

Health Maintenance Organizations (HMOs)   HMOs are a type of managed-care plan that focuses on preventive care and controlling health costs. HMOs generally use a *gatekeeper*, most often the patient's primary care physician (PCP), to determine whether the patient need to be seen by a specialist.

Preferred Provider Organizations (PPOs)   PPOs use a network of healthcare providers for patient services and don't require patients to be referred by a primary care physician. Employees who use healthcare services within the network make copayments. Out-of-network providers may be used, but the insured will have to pay the difference between the fees negotiated by the plan and those charged by the provider.

Point-of-Service (POS) Plans   A POS plan is a hybrid between an HMO and a PPO where the employee gets to choose which service to use each time they see a provider. POS plans include network physicians but allow for referrals outside the network. Like HMOs, these plans require employees to select a primary care physician (PCP) from doctors in the network. The PCP generally refers employees to specialists in the network when needed, but like PPOs, an employee may see specialists outside the network as well. When employees see physicians outside the network, they must submit reimbursement claims to the insurance company themselves. Payment is covered by the plan, but when the employee sees a care provider outside the POS network, the employee usually pays a higher percentage of the cost than for in-network physicians.

Exclusive Provider Organizations (EPOs)   An EPO consists of a network and includes a hospital. Unlike physicians who participate in a PPO, EPO physicians may see only those patients who are part of the EPO. Patients in an EPO may see only those healthcare providers in the network; they receive no reimbursement for healthcare obtained outside the network.

Physician Hospital Organizations (PHOs)   In a PHO, physicians join with a hospital and together rely on the PHO structure to develop and market their services and to negotiate and sign contracts. PHOs are unique in that they contract directly with employer organizations to provide services.

Fee-for-Service (FFS) Plans   An FFS plan is typically the most expensive to employers and employees because it places no restrictions on the doctors or hospitals available to the patient. These plans require patients to pay for services out-of-pocket and submit claims to be reimbursed for expenses.

In managed-care settings, providers often determine premiums based on the costs incurred by the group during the current coverage period. The costs are analyzed by type, and premiums for the following period are adjusted based on this *experience rating*. Some organizations have implemented wellness programs to improve the experience rating and lower premiums.

Most carriers use a standard coordination of benefits (COB) process when an employee is also covered as a dependent on another plan, such as that of a spouse or parent. When this occurs, the employee's primary coverage pays according to the plan benefits. The secondary coverage will then pay up to 100 percent of the allowable expenses, including deductibles and copayments for the claim. The secondary plan will pay only up to the amount it would have paid as the primary carrier, so the total insurance payout may still be less than 100 percent of the claim.

Other Health Benefits

In addition to medical insurance benefits, many companies offer other health-related benefit options. These include dental, vision, and prescription coverage insurance, among others:

Dental Insurance   Employers may choose dental insurance plans to provide varying levels of coverage for preventive or restoration work such as fillings, major restoration work such as bridges, and orthodontia.

Vision Insurance   One of the lowest-cost benefits available, vision insurance provides employees with reduced costs for eye examinations and contact lenses or glasses.

Prescription Coverage   Even though most medical plans include some form of coverage for prescription drugs, these plans are also offered separately. The cost of the plans is managed by controlling the amount of the required copayment and requiring the use of generic drugs instead of name brands.

Life Insurance   Many insurance companies bundle basic life insurance with medical or dental insurance for a very low rate and offer supplemental insurance for employees who are willing to pay an additional premium for the coverage.

It's important to keep in mind that the IRS views group life insurance in excess of $50,000 as *imputed income* (any indirect compensation paid on behalf of employees) when the premiums are paid by employers. The calculation of imputed income for group life insurance is based on a table provided by the IRS. The table assigns a small amount per month for each $1,000 of coverage that exceeds $50,000 based on an employee's age. The amounts range from $.05 for employees who are 25 years old to $2.06 per month for employees age 70 and older.

You can find a complete guide for employers on imputed income and fringe benefits at www.irs.gov/pub/irs-pdf/p15b.pdf.

Accidental Death and Dismemberment Insurance (AD&D) Insurance   AD&D insurance can provide insurance for employees and their dependents in the event of an accident that results in the death of the covered person or the loss of a bodily function. AD&D doesn't pay benefits in the event of death due to an illness.

Short- and Long-Term Disability Insurance   Disability insurance protects employees from income loss because of disability caused by illness or accident. Disability protection generally begins with sick leave provided by employers. When employees exhaust their sick leave, they may become eligible for short-term disability insurance, which can be in effect for anywhere between 3 and 6 months. Employees still disabled when short-term disability ends become eligible for long-term disability coverage, which can last for anywhere from 2 years until age 65.

Because these benefits are so common, businesses seeking to use them as recruiting and retention tools must find some way to differentiate their plans from those of their competitors. This need must be balanced with the skyrocketing cost of medical insurance and its impact on the bottom line. Companies looking for a way to increase the attractiveness of their benefit packages may want to reduce or eliminate the employee contribution toward premiums for themselves or for their families or include coverage for domestic partners in the package. A *domestic partnership* is a legal or personal relationship between two people who aren't legally married or in a legally recognized civil union. State and local governments vary in how they view and recognize domestic partnerships.

Health Benefit Cost Management

Regardless of the health plan selected, it's crucial for HR professionals to manage the cost of benefits by selecting the most cost-effective method for funding those benefits. There are several choices, and determining the most appropriate choice for a particular organization depends on factors such as the size of the organization and claim history.

One common funding method for smaller organizations is to purchase insurance coverage for the plan. The organization pays premiums for all participants in the plan, and the insurance company manages payment to the service provider and manages claims issues. In this funding method, the insurer assumes the risk for any unusual claims that may result in claim costs exceeding premiums received. Insurers keep track of the claim history and adjust premiums in subsequent years to recover any losses.

In larger organizations, it may make sense to self-fund the insurance plan. A *self-funded plan* or *captive plan* is one in which the employer creates a claim fund and pays all claims through it. Self-funded plans must conduct annual discrimination tests to ensure that HCEs aren't using the plan disproportionately to non-HCEs. In this case, the employer assumes the risk for unusual claims that may exceed the amount budgeted for the plan.

Another option is for organizations to implement a *partially self-funded plan*. These plans use *stop-loss insurance* to prevent a single catastrophic claim from devastating the claim fund. The employer agrees on a preset maximum coverage amount that will be paid from the claim fund for each participant before the insurance company begins to pay the claim.

Self-funded organizations may decide to contract with an insurance company to manage and pay claims, which is known as an *administrative services only (ASO) plan*. A third-party administrator (TPA), which provides claim-management services only and isn't part of an insurance company, may also be used for self-funded plans.

To take advantage of economics of scale, smaller employers may form *health purchasing alliances* (HPAs) with other employers in the geographic area. The HPA negotiates and contracts for the plans on behalf of all members of the group.

Work–Life Benefits

Work–life benefits help employees manage the conflict between work demands and family responsibilities and develop a healthful balance for the many areas of their lives. Some of the benefits in this category include time-off programs, wellness benefits, and assistance with childcare or eldercare needs.

Time-off Programs

Paid time off, like health insurance coverage, is a benefit that employees have come to expect. Over the years, businesses have developed different programs to accommodate various needs for time off, such as those described here:

Vacation Pay   Vacation pay is generally earned as employees complete time on the job. Many companies require employees to work a specific period of time, usually 3 to 6 months, before they're eligible to use any accumulated vacation pay. Some companies allow employees to accumulate vacation pay year-to-year; others have a "use it or lose it" policy, although some state laws prohibit companies from forcing employees to forfeit time off that has been earned. In those cases, companies may decide to pay employees for the leave that would otherwise be forfeited.

Most vacation-pay policies require employees to schedule time off in advance and obtain approval from their supervisors before scheduling vacations.

Sick Pay   Sick pay is provided for employees to use when they're ill or when they need to care for a sick child or other family member. Some states such as California are now mandating sick time, so HR practitioners must stay up-to-date on how state requirements may differ from the voluntary nature of sick pay at the federal level.

Holiday Pay   Many companies provide paid time off for a variety of national holidays including New Year's Day, Presidents' Day, Martin Luther King Jr.'s birthday, Memorial Day, Independence Day, Labor Day, Columbus Day, Veterans Day, Thanksgiving, and Christmas.

Paid Time Off (PTO)   Many companies have combined all forms of time off into a single PTO bank that employees can use as they see fit to handle illnesses, personal needs, vacations, and other matters. This provides greater flexibility for employees but can add to employer costs because of the way state laws view vacation and sick pay. Vacation pay is usually viewed as earned leave, meaning that employees must be paid for the leave if they don't use it (for example, if they resign from the company). Sick leave is usually viewed differently, and employees aren't compensated for sick time they don't use. Because PTO combines the two, it's viewed as earned leave, and employees must be compensated for all leave they have earned but not used.

Unlimited Paid Time Off   Unlimited time off programs have received a lot of recent attention thanks in large part to high-profile companies such as Netflix and Virgin Airlines adopting unlimited vacation time for their employees. While still very few employers offer unlimited time-off benefits, it is an emerging trend for which HR practitioners should be prepared. Often combining both vacation and sick pay, employers with unlimited time-off policies have the advantage of not having to track accruals as well as the positive employee morale that is associated with such programs. The expectation is that trusted employees will manage their time effectively and not take time off that will negatively impact the business. The downside to these programs is that some jobs cannot be structured to allow employees to miss days, making these programs difficult to apply consistently and with precise fairness. Defining just what "unlimited" means can also back employers into a corner when complying with medical and other leave policies or collective bargaining agreements.

Sabbaticals and Leaves of Absence   In educational institutions, sabbaticals are a long-standing benefit provided for educators in which, after working for a specified period of time, they receive a year off with pay to pursue further education, conduct research, or write books in their field of study. Some companies have adopted this benefit for long-term employees to encourage professional development.

Jury Duty Pay   Employers are required to provide time off for employees who are called to jury duty, although most states don't require employees to be paid for this time. Many employers pay the difference between the employee's regular earnings and the amount they're paid for performing jury duty.

Bereavement Leave   Most companies allow employees time off with pay to attend funeral services for close relatives.

Parental Leave   Some companies provide paid leave for parents of newborns or newly adopted children.

Volunteer Time Off (VTO)   Another growing trend in time off benefits is allowing employees to take paid or unpaid time off to volunteer. A 2016 study by SHRM found that at least 21 percent of employers are offering this benefit. That number significantly increases based on employer size; more than 60 percent of the 250 world's largest employers are offering this benefit.

Volunteer time-off policies are able to attract socially conscious and committed employees as well as increase their loyalty over the long term, and can be easily absorbed into the administration practices of existing time-off systems.

Wellness Benefits

Some employers have developed *health and wellness programs* to prevent employee illnesses and to lower healthcare costs. As with any program proposal, it's essential that HR professionals show management how the company will benefit from the program, how much it will cost, and what return the company can expect on its investment. Being able to provide specific costs and savings demonstrates HR's ability to develop programs that serve the long-term strategic goals of the business. Table 5.6 illustrates some of the benefits and costs to consider in analyzing the advantages of a wellness program for the company.

TABLE 5.6   Costs and benefits of wellness programs

Benefits	Costs
Increased productivity	Program implementation
Reduced turnover	Ongoing vendor costs
Reduced medical costs	Administrative costs
Reduced absenteeism	Liability issues
Enhanced ability to attract top-quality employees	
Reduced workers compensation premiums	

A typical wellness program must be voluntary for employees and includes a physical screening to assess each employee's current fitness level and needs. The program may include nutrition counseling; education programs for weight control, smoking, and stress reduction; and a program of physical exercise. Other programs could include education about substance abuse, spinal care, and prenatal care, depending on the needs of the particular employee population. Health and wellness programs can take many forms, depending on the budget of the employer, the needs of the employees, and the availability of services in the local area.

Employees like wellness programs because they provide convenient opportunities to make healthful lifestyle choices that result in more energy and less stress, both on and off the job.

The size of the budget available for a wellness program will obviously dictate how the program is offered. Some large companies provide fitness centers on-site, along with employee cafeterias that serve healthful meals. Smaller organizations may engage a wellness vendor to provide the educational piece of the program and offer employees subsidies for gym memberships or develop walking or sports programs for employee participation.

An important consideration for programs that include on-site fitness centers will be to analyze the total costs, including not only the space and equipment but also fitness personnel and liability for injuries suffered while an employee is working out. Recommendations for on-site programs should therefore include an assessment of the possible risks involved as part of the cost analysis.

Childcare and Eldercare

Depending on an employer's size and resources, on-site childcare opportunities may be available for employees. Although this is an ideal situation for parents, not all companies have the resources to provide this service. If this isn't an option, HR can identify resources that help parents find suitable childcare arrangements by developing the resources internally or by contracting with an *employee assistance program* (EAP) that may have broader access to information in the commute area for the company.

Eldercare support is generally provided in the form of resources made available to employees so that they can find suitable programs for elderly parents requiring ongoing care.

Other Voluntary Benefits

Other voluntary benefits available to employers are limited only by the creativity of the workforce and willingness of the employer to provide. They can include commuter assistance, on-site gourmet meals, concierge services, relocation assistance, flowers, chair massages, adoption assistance, Section 529 educational savings programs, online schooling, student loan assistance, tuition reimbursement, "bring your pet to work" programs, game rooms, and pool tables—there is no limit to what some employers provide. Some of the more common benefits are described here.

Flexible Spending Accounts

FSAs were authorized by the Revenue Act of 1978. Also known as *Section 125 plans*, they allow employees to set aside pretax funds for medical expenses they plan to incur during the calendar year. Employees should be cautioned to be conservative when projecting the amounts they plan to spend during the year because any funds left in the FSA after all expenses for the year have been paid will be forfeited and may be used by the employer to pay the administrative costs of the plan. For employers, a downside to offering an FSA account is that employees may be reimbursed for expenses before the funds have been withheld from their paychecks. If they leave the company before the funds have been withheld, they aren't required to reimburse the company for those expenses.

Expenses that may be included for reimbursement are the costs of any copayments and deductibles from medical, dental, or vision-care plans and other medical expenses approved by the IRS for reimbursement. Other allowable expenses include acupuncture treatments, orthodontia, psychiatric care, wheelchairs, physical therapy, Braille books and magazines, and a variety of other medical expenses. Some expenses that aren't included are monthly premiums, memberships to fitness clubs or gyms, babysitting, elective cosmetic surgery, weight-loss programs, and nonprescription drugs. To receive reimbursement for covered expenses, employees must provide receipts for expenditures.

A similar *dependent-care account* is authorized by Section 129. Employees may set aside a maximum of $5,000 to be used to care for dependent children or elders. To obtain reimbursement for dependent-care expenses, employees must provide an itemized statement of charges from the caregiver. Unlike the FSA for medical expenses, employees may not be reimbursed for expenses in excess of the amounts that have been withheld from their paychecks.

For employees to use either of these accounts, they must sign up at the beginning of the year, at the time they join the company, or during an open enrollment period. Once the contribution amount has been set for the year, it may be changed only if a qualifying event occurs, such as the birth or adoption of a dependent, death, divorce, or a change in employment status for the employee or the employee's spouse.

The IRS requires employers to conduct annual discrimination tests to ensure that FSA plans are being used consistently. Two types of tests are used to determine this: eligibility tests and utilization tests such as the key-employee-concentration test and dependent-care test. A plan that doesn't pass the test may lose its favorable tax treatment.

There are no federal laws requiring employers to offer any of these benefits; when they're offered, amendments to ERISA, COBRA, HIPAA, and the Mental Health Parity Act (MHPA) of 1996 have implications for administering them.

Cafeteria Plans

Large employers with diverse employee populations may offer cafeteria plans with a wide variety of benefit options in response to various needs of different employee groups. At the beginning of each plan year, employees select the benefits that best meet their needs. For example, a parent with young children may select dependent coverage as a benefit to cover daycare needs. Once children no longer need daycare, another benefit, such as 401(k) matching, may be selected.

Employee Assistance Programs

An EAP is sponsored by the employer as a benefit. EAPs are often as advantageous for employers as they are for employees because they're generally a low-cost benefit that provides a resource for employees with problems that aren't work-related and can't be solved in the work context. In some cases, this assistance allows people who might not otherwise be able to remain employed to stay on the job.

EAPs offer a variety of counseling services for problems ranging from alcohol and drug abuse to legal assistance or financial counseling. Many EAPs are a source for outplacement counseling during a layoff, and some programs offer on-site smoking cessation. During times of crisis, such as after the death of an employee or an incident of workplace violence, the EAP can be a resource for employees to come to grips with their feelings so that they're able to continue with their jobs.

EAP services are most often provided through a third party to ensure the confidentiality of employee information, but some employers have in-house programs with counselors on staff. Smaller businesses may join together in a consortium and jointly contract with an EAP to lower costs.

Payroll

In many organizations, payroll is administered as a function of the finance department, but in others it's an HR responsibility. Although an in-depth knowledge of payroll systems and administration isn't required for the PHR exams, candidates should have basic knowledge of payroll activities and how they interact with HR responsibilities.

Payroll Systems

Whether an organization employs one person or hundreds of thousands, a payroll system must meet some basic requirements:

- It must accurately calculate payments that are due to employees.
- It must accurately calculate statutory and voluntary deductions.
- It must track payroll tax payments owed to federal and state agencies.
- It must provide accurate reports of payroll costs to management.
- It must provide security for payroll information.

In a small organization with a few employees, all of these requirements may be met with a manual system in which a qualified bookkeeper manually calculates the payments that are due to employees, uses federal and state tax publications to look up withholding information, and prepares checks. This process can be streamlined with the addition of an off-the-shelf accounting software program that makes the calculations, prints the checks, and tracks tax payments owed to federal and state agencies. As organizations grow, manual systems are no longer feasible and may be replaced by a service bureau, which performs the necessary calculations, prints the checks or deposits them electronically, and submits payroll tax payments on behalf of the organization. Very large organizations may develop proprietary software designed to handle their specific needs.

Because payroll systems collect some of the same information that is entered into human resource information systems (HRISs), HR managers can benefit from systems that are able to interact and share information to reduce or eliminate the double entry of information into separate systems.

Payroll Administration

Payroll administration is the function in the company that is responsible for calculating employee earnings and deductions and maintaining records of those payments. Administering payroll is one of the most visible functions performed in any organization because it affects every employee from the CEO to the most junior assistant. Not only is it visible to everyone, but a payroll error has the potential to profoundly affect an employee's life, if only until the error can be corrected.

Employee Earnings

The payroll department is responsible for preparing employee paychecks and ensuring that earnings are calculated correctly. To calculate nonexempt earnings, the payroll department must know the employee's base pay rate, shift differentials, tips, and bonuses; how many hours the employee worked during the pay period; and whether any paid leave was used. With this information, the *gross pay*, or earnings before taxes, can be calculated.

To calculate earnings for exempt employees, payroll needs to know the base salary, any bonus amounts, and any paid leave used during the pay period.

Statutory Deductions

Before employees receive their paychecks, various deductions are made from the gross earnings. These deductions include the following:

- Social Security
- Medicare
- Federal income tax
- State income tax
- Unemployment insurance (in some states)
- Disability insurance (in some states)
- Other state and local taxes

These amounts are withheld from employee earnings. Employers match the amount of Social Security and Medicare taxes that are withheld from employees. These amounts, along with the federal income tax withheld, are remitted to the IRS at regular intervals. Failure to remit taxes on time results in substantial penalties for employers. State and local taxes are remitted separately to the appropriate government agency according to payment schedules established by each agency.

At the end of each calendar quarter, reports of gross payroll and withheld taxes are filed with the federal, state, and local taxing authorities. These reports reconcile the amount of tax withheld to the amounts deposited during the quarter. At the end of the year, W-2 forms are prepared for each employee and submitted to federal and state tax agencies.

Voluntary Deductions

A number of other deductions may be made from an employee's paycheck. These include medical, dental, and other health benefit contributions; 401(k) contributions; union dues; and, in some cases, contributions to charities designated by employees.

Involuntary Deductions

From time to time, employers may be required by a court order or tax levy to withhold additional funds from employee paychecks. These withholdings are known as *wage garnishments* and are issued to satisfy a debt owed by the employee. Garnishments may come in the form of a court order (for example, an order to pay child support or another debt) or from a government agency such as the IRS or other taxing authority to collect unpaid back taxes. Wage garnishments aren't voluntary, and employers have no discretion as to whether to honor them.

The Federal Wage Garnishment Law is found in Title III of the Consumer Credit Protection Act (CCPA) of 1968 and applies to all employers and employees. Employers are required to withhold funds from an employee's paycheck and send the money to an entity designated in the court order or levy document.

Title III of the CCPA protects employees in three ways:

- Prohibits employers from terminating employees whose wages are garnished for any one debt, even if the employer receives multiple garnishment orders for the same debt

- Sets limits on the amount that can be garnished in any single week

- Defines how disposable earnings are to be calculated for garnishment withholdings

The law doesn't protect employees from termination if the employer receives garnishments for more than one debt.

Disposable earnings are what is left in an employee's paycheck after all legally mandated deductions have been made, such as federal and state income tax, Social Security, state and local taxes, disability insurance, and so on. Title III provides separate garnishment calculation methods for debt garnishments and child-support orders:

Debt Garnishment Calculations   Title III defines two methods for calculating the maximum weekly garnishment. The first method allows garnishment of up to 25 percent of disposable earnings. Disposable earnings are the amount of earnings left after legally required deductions have been made. The second method is calculated by multiplying the federal minimum wage ($7.25 per hour as of 2018) by 30 ($217.50). The total is subtracted from the disposable earnings. Any disposable earnings that exceed that amount must be sent directly to the recipient designated in the order and not to the employee.

The maximum amount of garnishment allowed is the lesser of those two calculations.

Child-Support Garnishment Calculations   Title III allows child-support garnishments of up to 50 percent of an employee's disposable earnings if the employee is currently supporting a spouse or child and up to 60 percent if not. If support payments are more than 12 weeks in arrears, wages may be garnished an additional 5 percent. There are no restrictions on child-support garnishments.

Depending on the nature of a violation, employers who violate the CCPA may be required to reinstate a terminated employee, pay back wages, and refund any improper garnishments. Whenever possible, the DOL tries to resolve garnishment violations informally. If that isn't possible, they may take legal action. Willful violators are subject to criminal prosecution and may be fined or imprisoned.

Personal Responsibility and Work Opportunity Reconciliation Act of 1996

This legislation requires employers to report all new hires within 20 days of their hire date to the State Department of New Hires. The law requires only that employers forward the W-4 form to the state, but some states have developed their own forms for this purpose. As a side benefit for employers, the new hire reporting database has reduced and prevented fraudulent or erroneous unemployment payments that would otherwise be charged to the employer's unemployment insurance account. The database also crosschecks against workers compensation claims, which has reduced fraud and errors in those programs as well.

Payroll-Related Information

The data collected throughout the life cycle of the employee's tenure with the organization must be adequately accounted for and managed. This data generation begins at the time of hire when basic information is gathered, such as tax withholdings, and continues with pay adjustments to account for benefits enrollment, wage increases, or exceptions such as garnishments. It ends at the time of termination when accrued benefits are calculated, health insurance and retirement benefits are rolled over or cancelled, and final wages are paid to the employee.

Outsourcing Compensation

Many organizations are turning to outsourcing groups to help navigate the complexities of managing the various components of compensation and benefits plans. In fact, one of the most common outsourced HR functions is that of processing payroll. The services offered by various companies include payroll, COBRA administration, quarterly reporting, tax filings, and HR expertise in other functions. Outsourcing payroll is a strategic decision that allows the internal talent to focus on the core competencies required for successful operations. However, managing the vendors is still an important function of HR, because the hiring company typically retains liability in the case of errors or omissions in compliance.

Finding the right provider(s) is the first step toward effectively managing the outsourcing process. Clearly defining expectations and needs, clarifying the frequency of contact, and agreeing on set deliverables are all methods of effective vendor management.

Communicating Compensation and Benefits Programs

Taking the time to develop a compensation philosophy, participate in salary surveys, and develop new compensation programs doesn't help the organization unless results and objectives are clearly communicated to employees and managers.

For example, when rolling out the annual merit-increase process, it's important to have timely, effective, and frequent communication geared toward both management and employee populations. Management typically receives different or additional information designed to facilitate their role as evaluators. Sharing salary survey results with management continues the dialogue about attracting, retaining, and motivating talent through existing or new programs. Furthermore, training management in corporate policies and compensation philosophies allows them to properly respond to employees when questions arise. Emotions can run high when employees have questions about their pay or benefits, so it's important that front-line supervisors have the information necessary to meet employee needs. Answering questions about deductions, understanding leave policies, and justifying pay rates are all examples of information that can be shared through systematic management training.

Communicating compensation programs or philosophy involves a series of written communications. Updating the company intranet, the employee handbook, and plan documents are a few examples of written information that serve as great resources for employees.

Employee self-service options are gaining in popularity. These interactive, online services allow employees to gather relevant data based on their specific needs. Forms requests, online benefits enrollment, and access to payroll data are all examples of the convenience of robust self-service programs for employees. Benefits for employers also exist through the use of self-service programs. Time is saved by allowing employees to update their own personal information; reports such as benefit-utilization reviews can be gathered, wage statements including the value of employee benefits can be generated and communicated, and surveys and polls can be conducted to identify the needs of the real-time workforce.

Ultimately, communication of compensation programs should be simple, and the alignment to compensation philosophy should be visible.

Metrics: Measuring Results

Compensation and benefits costs are significant in virtually all organizations. Using metrics to monitor whether total rewards programs are delivering the type of qualified employees needed by the organization is therefore key to demonstrating how HR professionals add value to their organizations:

Business Impact Measures   One of the clearest indications that there is a problem with the total rewards package in an organization is an increase in turnover and exit interviews that indicate employees are easily able to find higher compensation and/or a richer, more appropriate benefits package with other employers.

Tactical Accountability Measures   Two metrics that may provide useful information about compensation and benefits programs are as follows:

   Compensation as a Percentage of Operating Expenses   This metric provides information about the cost of human capital relative to other operating expenses for an organization. The higher the compensation costs are, the more impact HR programs can have on the bottom line. To calculate this metric, divide the total compensation costs (base salary, variable pay, and any deferred compensation) by the total operating expenses.

Benefits as a Percentage of Operating Expenses   This measure helps view increased benefit costs in the context of other expenses. Tracking the cost of benefits relative to other operating expenses can help organizations make decisions about the appropriate mix of benefits to offer as costs rise and to view increasing benefits costs in the context of other expense increases. This metric is calculated by dividing the cost of benefits (health and welfare, paid time off, and so on) by the total operating expenses.

Summary

Compensation and benefits packages are a key factor in virtually every organization's quest to attract and retain employees who are best qualified to achieve its goals. The total rewards package is guided by the corporate mission and goals and reflects its organizational culture. The culture in particular impacts the intrinsic and extrinsic rewards that employees derive from their work. Total rewards philosophy drives the organization's ability to attract, retain, and motivate its employees to meet strategic objectives.

HR practitioners must apply their knowledge of budgeting and accounting principles to their employer's compensation programs. This includes conducting market research on salaries in order to build wage structures that can be used to inform decision-making. Skilled practitioners are also able to administer legally compliant payroll practices.

The first mandatory benefits, Social Security, Medicare, and unemployment insurance, were developed to provide a safety net for American workers. More recent benefits such as FMLA and COBRA require employers to actively participate in and administer programs.

The mix of voluntary benefits chosen by an organization can help it attract and retain employees with particular characteristics. For example, a generous educational reimbursement benefit will help the company attract employees who are committed to continuous learning and skill development.

Exam Essentials

Be aware of the components of compensation.   Base pay is the foundation of an employer's compensation program because it reflects the value placed on individual jobs by the organization. Differentials such as overtime and hazard pay motivate employees to spend longer hours at work or to accept assignments that may be unpleasant or hazardous. Incentive pay motivates and rewards employees when they achieve corporate goals.

Understand the job-evaluation process.   Job evaluation is an objective mechanism used to determine the worth of different jobs to the company. Compensable factors distinguish jobs from each other and are used in determining their value to the organization.

Understand the purpose of salary surveys and how they're conducted. Salary surveys are used to determine current market trends and competition for different skills and knowledge and assist the employer in setting pay levels that lead, meet, or lag the market. Surveys are conducted by gathering information about specific jobs in a large number of companies in an industry, a profession, or a geographic area and summarizing the data by job.

Understand how HR interacts with payroll systems. Whether HR interacts with or administers payroll, HR professionals are involved in ensuring that changes to employee pay and deductions are accurate.

Be able to communicate the compensation and benefits program to employees. An effective communication program informs employees about the total rewards package so they're able to take advantage of benefits that are offered and have an understanding of the full cost to the employer of providing the different programs.

Be aware of the wide variety of benefits that are available. With an awareness of the various and sometimes unusual benefits that are available, employers are able to develop a benefit mix that meets the needs of employees at the lowest cost to net profits.

Be aware of mandatory benefits. Mandatory employee benefits are determined by Congress and affect employers with varying minimum numbers of employees. Social Security, Medicare, unemployment insurance, FMLA leave, and COBRA continuation benefits are required by statute.

Understand how voluntary benefits influence employees. Voluntary benefits fall into four categories: deferred compensation, health and welfare, work–life balance, and other benefits. Some benefits, such as medical insurance and paid time off, have come to be expected by employees, whereas others will attract and retain different types of employees with different needs.

Review Questions

You can find the answers in Appendix A.

1. What impact does a gig economy have on an employer's compensation plan?

   A. Gig workers usually have a higher base pay.

   B. HR must budget compensation costs differently.

   C. HR must ensure they are not discriminating against gig workers.

   D. Gig workers may still be entitled to mandated benefits.

2. The employer you work for has a marketing specialist who is an independent contractor. She is required to work three days a week, from 8:00 a.m. to 5:00 p.m. You have advised your employer that she is improperly classified and should be hired as an employee. Which IRS factor are you most likely basing this on?

   A. Behavioral

   B. Financial

   C. Type of relationship

   D. None, her classification is legally compliant.

3. Which of the following is an example of an intrinsic reward?

   A. Recognition of accomplishments

   B. The satisfaction of a job well done

   C. A great supervisor

   D. An exciting assignment

4. A total rewards philosophy can help achieve an organization's strategic goals by doing which of the following?

   A. Attracting and retaining employees with the necessary KSAs

   B. Establishing a pecking order for jobs in the organization

   C. Positioning the company to lead the competition for employees

   D. Maintaining an entitlement culture

5. An entitlement culture is appropriate for a business that needs what type of workforce?

   A. One that continues to show productivity increases over time

   B. One that has a line of sight to retirement

   C. One that is highly competitive in completing daily assignments

   D. One that has a skill set that's in high demand

6. A company that wants to reduce the cost of its unemployment insurance should do which of the following?

   A. Aggressively fight unjustified claims for unemployment.

   B. Establish an effective performance-management program.

   C. Terminate employees who violate company policy.

   D. All of the above

7. An unlimited time-off plan has which of the following advantages for the employer?

   A. Employers are better able to schedule workflow.

   B. The employee does not have to worry about timecards.

   C. The employee is better able to achieve work–life balance goals.

   D. The employer does not have to track time-off accruals.

8. The state in which you practice HR requires a higher minimum wage than the federal government. Your employer only wants to pay the federal minimum wage. What should you do?

   A. Make all employees exempt from overtime to reduce hourly wages.

   B. Conduct market research and create wage bands so he can see what his competitors are paying.

   C. Tell your employer that paying the federal minimum wage would be unlawful and that the company is required to pay the state minimum wage.

   D. Agree to pay the federal minimum wage rate, but gradually increase employee pay to the state minimum.

9. What is the primary purpose of paying employees commission?

   A. To keep employee wages at risk

   B. To reward employees who work harder than others

   C. To keep labor costs low

   D. To incentivize employees to behave in a certain way

10. A summary plan description is not required for which of the following?

    A. Defined-contribution plans

    B. Defined-benefit plans

    C. Flexible spending accounts (FSAs)

    D. All of the above

11. Which of the following expenses may generally not be used against a flexible spending account?

    A. Gym membership

    B. Durable medical equipment

    C. Acupuncture

    D. Psychiatric care

12. ESOPs, ESPPs, and profit-sharing are all examples of which of the following?

    A. Deferred compensation

    B. Gainsharing strategies

    C. Group incentives

    D. Sales bonus options

13. When several workers at a nuclear power plant call in sick with the flu, the manager calls James and asks him to come in three hours early. James will be paid a premium on top of his normal pay rate for these hours. This is an example of what?

    A. On-call pay

    B. Call-back pay

    C. Reporting pay

    D. Hazard pay

14. Cost-of-living adjustments are generally tied to which economic factor?

    A. Consumer price index

    B. Social security index

    C. Employment cost index

    D. Producer price index

15. In a merit matrix, where would be the best position to place a fully trained employee that is meeting performance expectations and who has been with the company for about three years?

    A. The minimum for the range

    B. The mid-point of the range

    C. The maximum point for the range

    D. Somewhere between the mid-point and maximum.

16. Prescription coverage is an example of what type of employee benefit?

    A. Deferred compensation

    B. Perquisites

    C. Health and welfare

    D. Long-term care insurance

17. Which of the following is *not* an example of a voluntary benefit?

    A. Medicare

    B. Vision insurance

    C. Qualified pension plan

    D. Sick pay

18. Which of the following would be the best choice of a profit-sharing plan if the employer wishes to improve organizational productivity through shared management and employee efforts?

    A. Employee stock purchase plan

    B. Bonuses

    C. Gainsharing

    D. Improshare

19. Job fulfillment from working with a talented peer group is an example of which of the following types of compensation?

    A. Monetary

    B. Intrinsic

    C. Extrinsic

    D. Total rewards

20. Earnings before taxes are most commonly referred to as which of the following?

    A. Gross pay

    B. Net pay

    C. Employee burden

    D. Wages, salaries, and tips

Chapter

6

PHR Exam: Employee and Labor Relations

The HRCI test specifications from the Employee and Labor Relations functional area covered in this chapter include PHR-level responsibilities and knowledge.

Responsibilities:

✓ 01 Analyze functional effectiveness at each stage of the employee life cycle (for example: hiring, onboarding, development, retention, exit process, alumni program) and identify alternate approaches as needed.

✓ 02 Collect, analyze, summarize, and communicate employee engagement data.

✓ 03 Understand organizational culture, theories, and practices; identify opportunities and make recommendations.

✓ 04 Understand and apply knowledge of programs, federal laws, and regulations to promote outreach, diversity and inclusion (for example: affirmative action, employee resource groups, community outreach, corporate responsibility).

✓ 05 Implement and support workplace programs relative to health, safety, security, and privacy following federal laws and regulations (for example: OSHA, workers' compensation, emergency response, workplace violence, substance abuse, legal postings).

✓ 06 Promote organizational policies and procedures (for example: employee handbook, SOPs, time and attendance, expenses).

✓ 07 Manage complaints or concerns involving employment practices, behavior, or working conditions, and escalate by providing information to appropriate stakeholders.

✓ 08 Promote techniques and tools for facilitating positive employee and labor relations with knowledge of applicable federal laws affecting union and nonunion workplaces (for example: dispute/conflict resolution, anti-discrimination policies, sexual harassment).

✓ 09 Support and consult with management in the performance management process (for example: employee reviews, promotions, recognition programs).

✓ 10 Support performance activities (for example: coaching, performance improvement plans, involuntary separations) and employment activities (for example: job eliminations, reductions in force) by managing corresponding legal risks.

Knowledge:

✓ 44 General employee relations activities and analysis (for example, conducting investigations, researching grievances, working conditions, reports, etc.)

✓ 45 Applicable federal laws and procedures affecting employment, labor relations, safety, and security

✓ 46 Human relations, culture and values concepts, and applications to employees and organizations

✓ 47 Review and analysis process for assessing employee attitudes, opinions, and satisfaction

✓ 48 Diversity and inclusion

✓ 49 Recordkeeping requirements

✓ 50 Occupational injury and illness prevention techniques

✓ 51 Workplace safety and security risks

✓ 52 Emergency response, business continuity, and disaster recovery process

✓ 53 Internal investigation, monitoring, and surveillance techniques

✓ 54 Data security and privacy

✓ 55 The collective bargaining process, terms, and concepts (for example: contract negotiation, costing, administration)

✓ 56 Performance management process, procedures, and analysis

✓ 57 Termination approaches, concepts, and terms

The Employee and Labor Relations (ELR) function includes the tasks and responsibilities necessary to sustain effective employment relationships in both union and nonunion environments. Because this topic makes up about 39 percent of PHR content, it is important to prepare for ways to manage the employee experience through the employment life cycle. This chapter reviews the rights and responsibilities of both employers and employees in this relationship and HR's role in those processes.

The study of organizational behavior is not necessarily new, but many of the theories continue to gain traction outside of academia and in the applied setting of the workplace. While many theories will be explored throughout this chapter, one theory in particular serves nicely as an introduction to the functional area of ELR.

The open systems theory developed by Daniel Katz and Robert L. Kahn proposes that organizations are highly dependent on their environment just as a living creature is; if a living thing ignores its environment, it will die. In other words, an organization is an organic, fluid, living entity with both a climate and a culture that is built on operating systems made up of inputs (raw materials, human resources), throughputs (production processes, training processes), and outputs (products, services, knowledge).

It is helpful to view the function of ELR in the context of the open systems theory in that a business is highly dependent on the HR subsystems of the organizational core competencies, specifically those that occur within the employee life cycle. This includes recruiting, selection, compensation, employee development and performance management, retention, the exit process, the relationship with a union, and risk management. In fact, one of the major changes to the 2018 exams was the integration of what was formally a functional area of *Risk Management* into the functional content of *Employee and Labor Relations*. This speaks to the shifting nature of HR practice in the field as well. Many practitioners understand that any time an employee issue is explored and acted on, the component of risk must be considered and managed. For this reason, the second half of this chapter deals exclusively with risk management.

Interestingly, the life cycle has more recently been expanded to include the formation of *alumni groups*, networks designed to keep in touch with former employees. Alumni groups can serve multiple purposes, including re-recruiting former talent, providing referrals from past employees who understand the company job and culture, and even scoring competitive market data as these workers move from job to job. One example is that of Chevron. Their Bridges program allows alumni to sign up for contract work. Chevron gets access to vetted talent, and alumni have the opportunity to expand their skill set or make more money. Look at https://alumni.chevron.com to learn more about how this program works.

Underlying all of this is the idea that PHR-level candidates must be able to support positive human relations, and so, we begin there.

Human Relations

The concept of human relations covers a broad spectrum of ideas that concentrate on the importance of the human element at work, including interpersonal characteristics and organizational behavior.

This approach to workplace relationships, introduced in the 1920s, challenged traditional assumptions that people work only for economic reasons and that monetary incentives provided sufficient motivation for increased productivity. Human relations theories recognized that businesses are social as well as economic systems and looked at the impact of formal (management) and informal (workgroup) social connections in the workplace and the impact these connections have on work processes. For the first time, there was recognition that employees are complex individuals, motivated at different times by different factors, and that increased productivity could be tied to employee job attitudes, including job satisfaction, organizational commitment, and engagement.

One notable contribution to the study of human relations and organizational behavior were the findings of the Hawthorne Studies. A group of researchers convened at Western Electrics Company in the 1920s and 1930s to study the impact of environmental factors—such as lighting—on employee productivity. They found that regardless of whether they increased or decreased lighting, worker efficiencies improved. These researchers stumbled on a fundamental truism of human relations—that simply paying attention to employee morale and well-being had a positive effect on employee productivity.

There are excellent videos of what has been dubbed "The Hawthorne Effect" on YouTube.

In addition to the interaction between employees and the environment, human relations theories build on innate characteristics such as intelligence. These theories classify intelligence into several types. Of interest here are the two types of personal intelligence: intrapersonal and interpersonal. *Intrapersonal* intelligence refers to self-knowledge or how well individuals know themselves. *Interpersonal* intelligence refers to emotional intelligence and social aptitude.

Emotional intelligence (EI) is characterized by individuals who are aware of their emotions and are able to control how they react to them. Emotionally intelligent individuals are able to motivate themselves to achieve goals and are sensitive to the emotion of others. EI is considered to have three main aspects: being able to recognize emotions when they occur (self-awareness), being aware of the emotions of others (other awareness), and being able to consciously gain control of emotions when they are experienced (emotion regulation).

The advancement of EI studies in the field of industrial-organizational (I-O) psychology has provided HR practitioners with other factors to manage. Consider, for example, the job of a fast-food clerk who works for a chain that believes "the customer is always right." Absolutes are rarely true, and the customer may not actually always be right. But the job of the service employee is to regulate their emotional response, even in the face of discourteous customers. This is called *emotional labor*, when employees have to suppress how they really feel on the job. Emotional labor may be linked to increased burnout and job stress. Furthermore, employees who aren't able to express their real feelings may take to sharing their negativity with others in their workgroup, potentially infecting their attitudes as well. This is called *emotional contagion* and can result in entire departments being perceived as having a negative collective affect.

Finally, studies are now showing that factors of emotional intelligence are increasing creativity and innovation in the workplace. For example, a longitudinal study of more than 200 employees across 7 companies found a strong relationship between a positive mood and creativity on a project (Amabile, T. M., Barsade, S. G., Mueller, J. S., & Straw, B. M. [2005]. "Affect and Creativity at Work." *Administrative Science Quarterly*, 50[3], 367–403). Other studies have shown that a leader with a positive attitude is most effective at influencing follower behavior on creative projects, whereas leaders with a negative affect were better at influencing analytical tasks (Van Kleef, G. A., Wisse, B. [2013], "How Leader Displays of Happiness and Sadness Influence Follower Performance: Emotional Contagion and Creative versus Analytical Performance," *The Leadership Quarterly*, 24, 172–188).

Several aspects of human relations to consider are how personality affects the workplace, the importance of psychological capital, and motivational concepts theories. The following sections explore each of these.

Personality at Work

Over time, a number of assessment tools have been developed to identify how individuals react in different situations; for example, is an employee confrontational, or do they attempt to mediate situations? Do they prefer extroversion or introversion? These personality assessment tools are used in some organizations to help employees work together more effectively. For example, the *Myers-Briggs Type Indicator (MBTI)* inventory identifies personality types with four-letter codes; the explanation of the code provides a description of individuals' preferences in areas of where they direct their energy (Extroversion/Introversion), the type of information they are most likely to value and trust (Sensing/Intuition), how they prefer to make decisions (Thinking/Feeling), and how they are most likely to organize their outside world (Judging/Perceiving). The MBTI instrument may be used in organizations to improve organizational effectiveness and increase understanding between co-workers.

Another theory proposes that certain individual traits are predictive of success in different environments. Perhaps one of the most well-known examples of this is "The Big Five" (using the acronym OCEAN for openness, conscientiousness, extroversion, agreeableness, and neuroticism):

- **Openness:** Being naturally curious and open to exploring new ideas. This trait is characterized by being flexible.

- **Conscientiousness:** Being achievement-oriented and dependable. This trait is positively correlated with overall career success.

- **Extroversion:** Different from the MBTI definition of extroversion, the Big Five describes those with this trait as outgoing and sociable. Individuals with high degrees of extroversion generally are successful in sales careers.

- **Agreeableness:** Individuals with this trait are described as being approachable and warm, and naturally easy to get along with.
- **Neuroticism:** Perhaps the Big Five trait correlated mostly with lack of professional success, individuals with high levels of neuroticism are notable for their anxious, mercurial behaviors.

Psychological Capital

Promising new studies regarding the concept of psychological capital (PsyCap) are emerging. PsyCap refers to the individual differences and transitions of employees. PsyCap is made up of both who a person currently is and who the person is in the process of becoming. PsyCap is especially intriguing in the area of improved job satisfaction, which in turn improves employee productivity. While still developing, the four basic elements of PsyCap include (using the acronym HERO for hope, efficacy, resiliency, and optimism):

- **Hope:** Employees have the drive to succeed and are able to identify the path to success.
- **Efficacy:** Employees believe in their own ability to achieve success.
- **Resiliency:** Employees are able to rebound from setbacks and carry on (progress, not perfection).
- **Optimism:** Employees believe that positive outcomes are achievable and are motivated to perform because of those beliefs.

Human resource professionals should find ways to stay actively engaged in the science of organizational behavior or I-O psychology as part of their ongoing professional development. These activities should focus on both emerging human relations studies and the foundational theories; we explore these foundational theories next.

Motivational Concepts

From the beginning of the industrial revolution, business owners have sought the key to improving productivity. This search prompted scientists to study the work environment, businesses, and the relationship of people to organizations. These studies led to many theories about work, some related to the physical environment or organization structures and others that looked at why people work and what motivates them.

The traditional theories of motivation discussed next center either on the need for employees to be self-motivated or on the need for managers to motivate them. They provide a basis for understanding what drives employees to perform at peak levels of productivity, which can help managers understand the reasons for lowered productivity. Each functional area of the exam content is impacted by whether employees are motivated or demotivated at work. Incorporating these concepts into the planning stage of HR programs and initiatives can increase the value of the end result.

Abraham Maslow: The Hierarchy of Needs (1954)

Abraham Maslow, a behavioral scientist, developed his *Hierarchy of Needs* to explain how people meet their needs through work. This theory describes needs that begin with the most basic requirements for life—food, shelter, and basic physical comforts—and progresses through stages of growth as people strive to fill higher-level needs. Maslow identified five levels of needs that motivate people:

Physiological Needs These are the most basic needs. Individuals striving to find enough food to eat or a place to live are motivated by attaining those things. People at this level are motivated by actions that provide the basic necessities of life.

Safety Needs Once people have food and shelter, they look for ways to ensure that they're safe from physical and emotional harm.

Social Needs At this level, people are motivated by the desire for acceptance and belonging in their social group.

Esteem Needs At this level, people are motivated by recognition for their achievements.

Self-Actualization Needs When people are confident that their basic needs have been met, they become motivated by opportunities to be creative and fulfill their own potential. They don't look outside themselves for these opportunities but depend on themselves to find and act on them.

B. F. Skinner: Operant Conditioning (1957)

The results of B. F. Skinner's work on *behavioral reinforcement* are more commonly known as *behavior modification*. His basic theory is that behavior can be changed through the use of four intervention strategies:

Positive Reinforcement Encourages continuation of the behavior by providing a pleasant response when the behavior occurs.

Negative Reinforcement Encourages continuation of the behavior by removing an unpleasant response to a behavior.

Punishment Discourages future occurrence of the behavior by providing an unpleasant response when the behavior occurs.

Extinction Discourages future occurrence of the behavior by ceasing to reinforce it. For example, when a parent praises a child for doing his homework each night and the child starts doing it without being reminded, the parent may stop praising the child. If the child then reverts to the previous behavior of forgetting to do his homework, the behavior has become extinct.

Frederick Herzberg: Motivation/Hygiene Theory (1959)

Frederick Herzberg's *motivation/hygiene theory* (also known as the *two-factor theory*) began with a study on job attitudes that he conducted in Pittsburgh in the 1950s. He began the study believing that the causes of job satisfaction would be the opposite of the causes of job dissatisfaction. However, his review of several thousand books and articles on job attitudes didn't prove his premise; in fact, the results were so vague that it wasn't possible to draw any conclusions. This led Herzberg to conduct a study in which he asked the participants to identify the work experiences that resulted in positive feelings about their jobs and the ones that resulted in negative feelings.

The result, as Herzberg himself described it in an interview, was that "What makes people happy is what they do or the way they're used, and what makes people unhappy is the way they're treated" ("An Interview with Frederick Herzberg: Managers or Animal Trainers?" *Management Review*, 1971). Both factors can motivate workers, but they work for very different reasons. The satisfaction (motivation) factors motivate by changing the nature of the work so that people are challenged to develop their talents and fulfill their potential. For example, adding responsibilities that provide learning opportunities for a receptionist performing at a substandard level can result in improved performance of all duties assigned if the poor performance is related to boredom with repetitive tasks. The dissatisfaction (hygiene) factors motivate to the extent that they allow people to avoid unpleasant experiences. For example, as long as employees continue to perform their assignments at an acceptable level, they continue to receive a paycheck. Hygiene factors provide only short-term benefits to employers, whereas factors related to motivation lead to longer-term job satisfaction.

A result of Herzberg's theory is the concept of job enrichment in which the significance of the tasks in a job is increased to provide challenging work and growth opportunities.

Douglas McGregor: Theory X and Theory Y (1960)

Douglas McGregor expanded on Maslow's work to describe the behavior of managers in their relationships with their employees. McGregor identified two distinct management approaches, *Theory X* and *Theory Y*.

Theory X managers have a worldview of employees as lazy and uninterested in work and needing constant direction to complete their assignments. Theory X managers believe that employees don't want to take responsibility and are interested in job security above all else. Theory X managers are generally autocratic, utilizing a top-down management style.

In contrast, Theory Y managers believe that, given the opportunity, people will seek out challenging work and additional responsibility if the work is satisfying. Theory Y managers are more likely to invite participation in the decision-making process from their subordinates.

David McClelland: Acquired Needs Theory (1961)

The premise of David McClelland's *acquired needs theory* is that experiences acquired throughout their lives motivate people to achieve in one of three areas:

Achievement   Those motivated by achievement take moderate risks to achieve their goals, respond to frequent feedback, and generally prefer to work as sole contributors or with others interested in achieving at the same level.

Affiliation   Individuals who need affiliation look for acceptance in the workgroup and need regular interaction with their co-workers or customers.

Power   These individuals are looking for either personal power or institutional power. Those interested in institutional power are often effective managers who are motivated by coordinating workgroups to achieve organization goals.

J. Stacey Adams: Equity Theory (1963)

The basic concept of J. Stacey Adams's *equity theory* is that people are constantly measuring what they put into work against what they get from work. If their perception is that it's a fair trade, they're motivated to continue contributing at the same level. When they perceive there is an imbalance and they're putting in more than they're getting back, they become demotivated and lose interest in their work, decreasing productivity and quality.

Victor Vroom: Expectancy Theory (1964)

Victor Vroom's *expectancy theory* maintains that people are motivated by the expectation of the reward they will receive when they succeed and that each individual calculates the level of effort required to receive a particular reward to determine whether the reward is worth the effort that is required to attain it. Vroom uses the following terms to explain this theory:

Expectancy   According to Vroom's theory, motivation starts with an assessment by individuals about their capabilities to successfully complete an assignment.

Instrumentality   If individuals believe they're capable of completing an assignment, they next ask "What's in it for me?"—that is, will their effort to complete the work be the instrument for obtaining a reward for the work?

Valence   This is the result of calculations as to whether the possible reward is worth the effort required to successfully complete the work.

Clayton Alderfer: ERG Theory (1969)

The *ERG theory* developed by Clayton Alderfer builds on Maslow's work as well. Alderfer identifies three levels of needs:

Existence   This relates to Maslow's definition of physiological and safety needs as those that are required to maintain basic life needs.

Relatedness   This is similar to Maslow's descriptions of social needs and the esteem we find from others.

Growth   This is based on the self-esteem and self-actualization concepts Maslow described.

The premise for Maslow's theory was that people move sequentially through the levels one at a time. Alderfer's theory allows for the possibility that people can work on multiple levels simultaneously. It also describes the concept of frustration-regression, which occurs when an individual falls back to a lower level in frustration at the difficulty of a higher level.

Real World Scenario

Operant Conditioning in Customer Service

The customer service manager at Wright Sisters, Inc. (WSI), Susan Sherwood, has a problem employee, David Rogers. David can be charming and has a knack for calming down disgruntled customers on the phone. In fact, his co-workers often rely on him for assistance with unhappy customers who are difficult to please. David has worked for WSI for three years and is for the most part productive and cooperative. At times, however, he has snapped at co-workers, and he is often disruptive in staff meetings. Recently, Susan has observed him being rude to some customers during customer support calls. She has also noticed that co-workers have stopped giving him work that he is supposed to be doing; instead, they're doing it themselves to avoid dealing with him. Susan, who has been working on her MBA, just finished a course in industrial psychology and decides to try Skinner's theory of operant conditioning to see whether it will work in a practical application. She comes up with the following interventions to use with David:

Positive Reinforcement   At the end of each meeting in which David exhibits professional behavior, Susan will thank him publicly for his contribution during the meeting.

Negative Reinforcement   When David behaves professionally during the day and doesn't create any disruptions, he won't have to meet with Susan at the end of the day.

Punishment   Whenever David is rude to a customer or co-worker, Susan will reprimand him.

Extinction   Co-workers will no longer do his work for him when David becomes confrontational with them.

Organization Climate and Culture

For many, the terms *organization climate* and *culture* are used interchangeably. Researchers trying to identify and describe how organizations work and what influences productivity and other organizational behaviors define the difference as one between a quantitative description (climate) and a qualitative one (culture).

The sharing of values and beliefs and the behavior related to them is known as the *organizational culture*. The culture of an organization, combined with leadership and management styles and the level of bureaucracy, creates a work environment or climate that will either inspire and motivate employees to achieve the corporate mission or inhibit employees' motivation and enthusiasm for their jobs, thereby limiting the success of the organization. Organizational culture and climate determine the level of employee involvement in the decision-making process and provide the unwritten ground rules on which decisions can be based in the absence of relevant policies.

The *organizational climate* describes how people feel about an organization based on a number of factors, including observable practices and employee perceptions. Climate is strongly influenced by organizational structure as reflected in the organization chart—is it hierarchical and bureaucratic or flat and open? The management style of organization leaders also has significant influence over its climate. Are employees encouraged to take risks or punished for doing so? How are employees held accountable for their successes and failures? Are there opportunities for growth? The climate is built on the way leaders manage and interact with employees.

If climate is reflected by *how* people feel, culture reflects *why* they feel the way they do. Both are often communicated by what efforts are rewarded and what behaviors are disciplined.

Although it's possible for businesses to earn a profit without considering the needs of their employees (and some do), this approach is not recommended for 21st century employers. Results of job-satisfaction surveys consistently show that employees are motivated to perform at a high level of productivity by a variety of factors that can be influenced by culture and climate. The presence of multiple generations in the workforce, socially progressive movements, progress in scientific research, and the very nature of work itself has prompted many employers to stage OD interventions to address employee engagement. Challenging work, respect, work–life balance, and flexibility are often of equal or greater importance to employees than the amount of money they earn in determining their level of satisfaction, commitment, engagement, and productivity. Although it's important to keep in mind that businesses exist to earn a profit rather than to merely provide a satisfying work experience for employees, organizations that are able to create atmospheres including trust, respect, and challenging work are generally rewarded with higher rates of productivity and increased revenue and profits than organizations that are focused only on cost reduction and efficiency.

Additionally, community outreach programs can help build an employer brand that aids in both recruiting and retention efforts because employees want to work for companies that they trust and that share similar values. By partnering with local agencies or supporting specific causes, the employer communicates who they are as a business. Community outreach as a cultural component also has an effect on corporate social responsibility.

Culture Factors and Job Satisfaction

"Once a person reaches an income level where they can live comfortably, the relationship between income and job satisfaction goes away" (Scandura, 2016, p. 92). In fact, research suggests that the strongest links to employee job satisfaction (and retention) are the nature of the work itself, the quality of supervision, and the relationship employees have with their co-workers. In short, elements of the company culture and climate.

Scandura, T. (2016). *Essentials of Organizational Behavior*. Sage Publications, Thousand Oaks, CA.

Organizational culture has a significant effect on employee job attitudes, which include job satisfaction, organizational commitment, and employee engagement. The following sections will examine key organization climate and culture factors such as employee engagement, employee involvement strategies, communicating with employees, and positive employee relations (ER) programs.

Another key component of organization climate and culture is its diversity and inclusion. While some aspects of diversity and inclusion are discussed throughout this chapter, an entire section is devoted to it in Chapter 11, "SPHR Exam: Employee Relations and Engagement."

Employee Engagement

A critical development both in academics and in human resource best practices is the concept of *employee engagement*, described by researchers as an individual's total immersion into their work: socially, physically, and mentally. Others view employee engagement as the degree of individual "investment" employees have in the success of their companies. Many leaders may not be able to describe precisely what this means, but they certainly recognize lack of employee engagement when they see it!

For purposes of applied theory, employee engagement describes individuals who report higher levels of job satisfaction and organizational commitment. Engaged workers have less absenteeism, lower turnover, and fewer injuries. Engaged employees are also more productive and feel valued by their employer. These reported outcomes demonstrate clearly that employers must understand how to better engage their workforce if they wish to remain competitive. HR can influence these outcomes by building performance feedback systems, improving peer-to-peer relationships, and working with supervisors to improve the quality of their relationships with subordinates.

Another positive outcome from employee engagement strategies are employees with better *organizational citizenship behaviors (OCB)*. OCB is positive employee behavior that goes above and beyond the transactional nature of the job tasks. One study found three characteristics that were linked to OCB:

- **Altruism:** Defined as a moral attitude that includes voluntarily helping others without regard for personal gain
- **Courtesy:** Showing care for and interest in others' priorities and needs
- **Conscientiousness:** Acting in accordance with personal and professional guidelines

OCB improves the quality of relationships between people, the social connectedness of a team, and the overall performance of the organization.

Appendix E, "Summarizing the Summaries: What Meta-Analyses Tell Us About Work Engagement," explores several meta-analyses of employee engagement.

Employee Involvement Strategies

A significant factor in effective employee relations is the extent to which employees are involved in making decisions that affect them on a day-to-day basis. This requires a commitment from senior management to both ask for and listen to what employees have to say and, whenever possible, implement changes suggested by employees. It's also important that management communicate to employees that the changes were implemented. Employee involvement can be simple, such as a suggestion box, or complex, such as a self-directed work team. The next section discusses a number of communication strategies that are a key aspect of effective employee involvement programs. Other strategies for involving employees include the following:

Technology   Virtual feedback programs such as Officevibe and Slack allow management to gather feedback and respond in real time. These and other programs are especially useful when a team is geographically spread out. Companies may also use technology for onboarding groups, assigning members to an immediate team with a mentor, coach, or other person responsible to socialize new members to their work environment and the company culture.

Digital badges are also gaining in popularity, allowing for recognition of senior staff members or subject matter experts on social networking pages or email signature lines.

Suggestion Boxes   A suggestion box provides an anonymous means by which employees can provide management with ideas for improvements. As with any method of soliciting information from employees, it's important that suggestions be acted on in a timely manner, or the concept of the suggestion system loses its credibility.

Delegating Authority   Management demonstrates respect for its employees by trusting them to make the decisions necessary to do their jobs. To do this effectively, management needs to delegate a sufficient level of authority to employees for making decisions or incurring expenses so that they're free to act without waiting for approval to take necessary action.

Task Force   A task force is brought together to research and recommend solutions for a significant undertaking or problem; once the solution has been determined, the task force disbands. A task force might be created to analyze technological improvements in a manufacturing plant and recommend improvements that will meet the long-term strategic objectives of the organization.

Committees   Committees are often formed to address ongoing issues in the organization and may be permanent, such as a safety committee, or ad hoc, such as a group appointed to plan a company function.

Work Team   A work team consists of employees who work together each day to accomplish their assignments. The team can be composed of members in a single functional area, or it can have members from several functions that are needed to accomplish the goal. A functional work team might consist of employees in the marketing department who develop collateral pieces for company products. A cross-functional work team might consist of employees from the research and development, manufacturing, marketing, operations, and accounting departments who are responsible for developing, launching, and marketing a specific product.

Virtual Work Team   A virtual work team operates in much the same way as a work team, with one major exception: Team members aren't located in the same building but may work anywhere in the world and connect through the Internet to accomplish team assignments.

Employee-Management Committees   Employee-management committees are used to solve problems in a variety of areas, such as production schedules, safety, and employee social events. The inclusion of employees on these committees helps to bring all the information to the table for making decisions and provides employees with input into how they do their jobs. From this point of view, they make positive contributions to operations.

Employers should use care when creating committees to address issues related to any terms and conditions of employment such as wages, safety, training, scheduling, and overtime, because they can be viewed as "employer-dominated unions" by the National Labor Relations Act (NLRA). The NLRA prohibits employers from creating mock unions with no real power to bargain on behalf of employees. In 1992, the National Labor Relations Board (NLRB) found that committees established by Electromation, Inc. were employer-dominated unions.

Self-Directed Work Team   A self-directed work team is a group of employees who are jointly responsible for accomplishing ongoing assignments. Team members set the work schedules, determine who will do which jobs, and hold each other accountable for accomplishing goals.

Communicating with Employees

The role of open and honest communication in organizations can't be underestimated. Communication must be both top-down and bottom-up; management must be willing to hear and act on information that may be contrary to its decisions. To be effective, management must solicit information from those employees closest to the issue being discussed in order to make fully informed decisions. Employees must feel comfortable in approaching management with relevant information when they're aware it has not been included in the decision-making process.

Effective communication programs incorporate multiple and repeated methods of providing information to employees. Depending on the size of the organization, communication may be as simple as an "all-hands meeting" in which the owner talks to the whole company about issues, or it may be as complex as a simultaneous web broadcast for a multinational corporation. The most effective communication methods are those that occur between employees and their direct supervisors because they provide the best opportunities for a meaningful exchange of information. Some common communication methods include the following:

Open-Door Policy   Open-door policies are an effective means for managers to keep their fingers on the pulse of operations and stay in touch with employee concerns. Giving employees access to the decision makers who can provide support, answer questions, and address concerns also shows a commitment from management to the needs of employees.

Management by Walking Around   Publicized in the 1980s by Tom Peters in his book *In Search of Excellence*, management by walking around (MBWA) is a practice first used at Hewlett-Packard in which management provided employees with goals and then spent time with them observing their progress and listening to their concerns or ideas.

Department Staff Meetings   Regularly scheduled meetings in which direct supervisors meet with their staff for updates and coordination of activities, as well as to disseminate information about organization policies and changes, provide a vehicle for employees to voice their questions and concerns and have input into their schedules.

All-Hands Staff Meetings/Town-Hall Meetings   From time to time, employees like to hear from senior management to find out what's really going on with the company. The all-hands meeting is a means by which executives can update employees on the state of the company and answer questions about its future direction, new products, or stock prices. Depending on the size of the company, these meetings can occur in person, via video teleconferencing, or as a web broadcast.

Brown-Bag Lunches   A brown-bag lunch program provides an informal setting for a small group of employees to meet with a senior manager to learn more about the company or a specific goal and ask questions. These informal meetings get their name from the fact that they occur over a lunch period on company premises, with employees bringing their own lunches.

Newsletters   Newsletters can provide employees with regular updates on company projects, profits, and goals. They're an effective means for introducing employees to other areas of the organization, reporting on financial issues, and soliciting input for changes in the employment relationship.

Intranet   An employee intranet can be an effective, easily updated source of information for employees. In many organizations, the employee handbook is available on the intranet, as are the company newsletter and updates on company goals.

Word of Mouth   In many organizations, word of mouth is the main means by which employees obtain information. This, of course, has drawbacks. Although word-of-mouth communication based on accurate information from management can be an effective way to "get the message out," the information tends to be distorted by the employee grapevine.

Email   Email provides a virtually instantaneous means of communicating information to large groups of employees at the same time. However, email, by its very nature, can be the source of problems—for example, when an executive inadvertently sends a confidential communication about pending layoffs to all staff instead of to the executive team. Particularly with regard to human resource issues, email should be used cautiously to avoid embarrassment and legal complications, because it's discoverable in the event of legal action.

Instant Messaging   Most employer digital platforms include some sort of employee communication tool, one of which is instant messaging (IM). IM is useful for the sharing of more immediate information; conversely, it is less effective for longer correspondence or for detailed reviews. Additionally, it is important that HR establish expectations for this kind of communication, specifically to follow professional guidelines for when to use IM, etiquette, and content.

Company Videos   Videos are another method that is growing in popularity to communicate with employees. CEOs may record business updates to inform employees at all locations. Marketing may use videos to help HR capture the employer brand for use in social media recruiting. Trainers can document standard operating procedures or provide how-to videos to educate customers on how to use their products. In short, videos are a useful communication tool to disseminate information but not necessarily to receive feedback, an important concept covered next.

Employee Feedback

A key component of effective ER programs is staying in touch with how well employee engagement programs are meeting the needs of employees. Measuring the needs of the employees and their levels of engagement can be achieved by gathering feedback from employees. Some of the communication techniques previously described gather this information in an informal way; however, there are also several more structured methods to do this:

Employee Surveys   Employee surveys can be used to gather information on any number of issues and are often the most effective means for obtaining information from large numbers of employees.

Exit Interviews   Many experts report that companies still use exit interviews to measure employee engagement. Generally, an exit interview can be used to gather information from the departing employee related to their "real" reason for leaving the organization. The findings—better pay elsewhere, a difficult manager, the perception of stalled career growth—can help an organization direct its ER programs toward meaningful results. Although there is little research correlating exit interviews with retention, several studies tie employee engagement to retention. This means that the data gathered from an exit survey—when properly and promptly acted upon—provides employers with the opportunity to engage their remaining talent.

Employee Focus Groups   An employee focus group consisting of a cross-section of employees from various departments and levels in the organization can be used to involve employees in decisions.

Skip-Level Interviews   A *skip-level interview* process in which employees are interviewed by their manager's manager provides insight into employee goals and job satisfaction, as well as an opportunity for career counseling.

When an organization undertakes a feedback initiative, it's critical that the results be reported to both management and employees. The HR professional should carefully review the data to ensure that it's accurate. If the results are quantified, they should be viewed critically to ensure that they make sense and accurately reflect what is truly happening in the organization. Any quantitative analyses should be carefully reviewed for data-entry errors or inadvertent misrepresentations of the information. For example, if only a representative sample of the employee population was surveyed, are the results skewed because the members of the group weren't truly representative of the entire population? If the entire workforce was surveyed, did the phrasing of the questions influence the results? There are many ways in which statistical data can be misinterpreted, intentionally or unintentionally. Before reporting any survey results, it's important to ensure that they're accurate.

Finally, it is not necessary for human resource practitioners to reinvent every wheel. The Job Descriptive Index developed at Bowling Green State University is an excellent, free tool that can be used to measure elements of job satisfaction. Figure 6.1 shows a sample. The complete version can be downloaded free of charge from www.bgsu.edu. Search for "The Job Descriptive Index."

FIGURE 6.1   Sample Items from the Job Descriptive Index (JDI) and the Job in General (JIG) scales

In the blank beside each word or phrase below, write
<u> 1 </u> for "Yes"
<u> 2 </u> for "No"
<u> 3 </u> for "?"

Work on Present Job	**Opportunities for Promotion**
How well does each of the following describe your work?	How well does each of the following describe your opportunities for promotion?
_____ Fascinating	_____ Good opportunities for promotion
_____ Routine	_____ Opportunities somewhat limited
_____ Satisfying	_____ Promotion on ability
_____ Boring	_____ Dead-end job
Present Pay	**Supervision**
How well does each of the following describe your present pay?	How well does each of the following describe your supervision?
_____ Income adequate for normal expenses	_____ Supportive
_____ Fair	_____ Hard to please
_____ Comfortable	_____ Impolite
_____ Bad	_____ Praises good work
Coworkers	**Job in General**
How well does each of the following describe the people you work with?	How well does each of the following describe your job most of the time?
_____ Stimulating	_____ Pleasant
_____ Boring	_____ Bad
_____ Slow	_____ Great
_____ Helpful	_____ Worthwhile

Source: Bowling Green State University (©1975–2009)

Positive Employee Relations Programs

An effective ER program is based on mutual respect, open and honest communication, fair and equitable treatment, and mutual trust. These characteristics begin at the top. If the executive team behaves autocratically, expecting adherence to strict and restrictive policies, procedures, and work rules, this demonstrates a lack of trust in the ability of employees to do competent work. When the executive team supports employees in making decisions and taking risks, it demonstrates trust in the competence of its employees. Employees who are empowered to take ownership of the work they do, accepting the rewards of good work and consequences of errors, are more productive.

An organization characterized by mutual respect is one in which management listens to employee ideas and concerns and acts on them and in which employees feel they're partners with management in the workplace. Management can demonstrate respect for the workforce by actions such as promoting from within, providing training for employees to prepare them for increased responsibility, and providing opportunities for employees to demonstrate their capabilities. Employees demonstrate respect for management and one another by listening to differing points of view and supporting decisions that are made.

Open communication is essential to establishing productive work relationships, and the most effective communication programs use multiple methods of conveying and receiving information.

The concept of fair and equitable treatment goes beyond that which is required by legal statute and common-law doctrine. An effective ELR program is one in which favoritism doesn't exist and where employees can see that employment decisions, even the ones they may not agree with, are based on objective criteria and equitable treatment. When disputes occur, an effective ER program has a nondiscriminatory process for adjudicating them, and it provides a means for employees to appeal unfavorable decisions to an impartial party. Dispute-resolution methods are discussed later in this chapter.

Finally, none of the preceding concepts work effectively in the absence of an atmosphere of mutual trust in the organization. Trust is built over time, when management continuously demonstrates that its actions are based on fairness and equity and gives employees input into decisions that affect them. A key element of building trust occurs when management communicates not only the "rosy scenario" but an honest evaluation of problems and challenges being faced by the organization. This accomplishes two goals: It encourages employees to come up with creative solutions to the problem or challenge, and it demonstrates that management both respects and values employees and trusts them to handle the information appropriately. The role of the HR professional in employee relations is to provide the change-management expertise needed to develop programs containing these elements and to develop methods for measuring the impact of ER programs on the bottom line. Examples of programs that promote a positive organizational culture include the following:

Recognition Employee-recognition programs are designed to acknowledge the efforts of employees and encourage that same behavior in the future. Length of service, safe work practices, and going "above and beyond" the expectations of the job are common behaviors acknowledged through these programs. One challenge in administering employee-recognition programs is that the measures of success continually change, making the return on investment (ROI) difficult to evaluate. However, programs that are designed to be closely aligned with desired organizational outcomes tend to be the most effective behavior management/employee relations technique.

Special Events "Events coordinator" is a common job responsibility of the HR department, but it does not deserve the negative connotation it has garnered. Employee events provide a significant opportunity for the company—and HR—to communicate specific outcomes and see people face-to-face. In short, employee events can "humanize" human resources. From organizing the company holiday party to sending emails on employee birthdays, these activities can be important in supporting the culture of an organization. While coordinating a company BBQ or planning a holiday party may seem relatively simple, it can be fraught with pitfalls such as sexual harassment, the role of alcohol, and the need to include all employees. For this reason, many companies have shifted from celebrating specific holidays or events to hosting an annual or quarterly all-employee meeting where recognition and achievement awards are given, and business details such as forecasted sales are shared.

One goal of effective ER programs is to retain employees. An effective ER program that includes the components discussed in this chapter—mutual respect, open and honest communication, fair and equitable treatment, and mutual trust—contains the building blocks for retention. In addition to these components, employee-friendly or work–life balance policies and programs can enhance the employer's ability to retain employees.

The need for employers to consider the impact of family issues on an employee's performance has been increasing in the United States, because of pressure from dual-income families, childcare responsibilities, an aging population, and government regulations. Employers respond to this in different ways. At one end of the spectrum are employers who comply with legal requirements but don't provide any additional leeway for employees who must deal with family issues. At the other end of the spectrum are companies such as SAS, a software company in North Carolina that provides on-site childcare, an eldercare information and referral program, wellness programs, recreation and fitness facilities, and other benefits designed to assist employees in managing the balance between their work and the rest of their lives. These types of programs provide resources for employees so that they're better able to stay focused on work needs while they're at work. Making resources available on-site or through an employee assistance program (EAP) also reduces the need for employees to take time off to deal with family or other personal needs. Some of the tools that add to flexibility include the following:

Telecommuting Globalworkplaceanalytics.com reported that more than half of the jobs being done by U.S. workers today have some compatibility with telecommuting (2018). Additionally, more and more of the work being done in schools is virtual or online, meaning that the workforce of tomorrow is being conditioned from an early age to be successful in a self-directed, virtual setting. For components of jobs that do not depend on geographic proximity, progressive employers should consider building in this type of flexible arrangement both to serve employee needs and to capitalize on the skill sets of the future workforce.

Employees who telecommute connect to the company network via the Internet and communicate with co-workers and managers via email, fax, and telephone, all from their homes. The telecommuting solution for organizations that are willing to embrace it has many benefits for the organization, the employee, and the community. The organization is able to hold on to employees who might otherwise choose to leave, maintaining the knowledge, skills, and abilities (KSAs) and training that have been invested in the individual. The employee is able to continue working while remaining available to handle personal needs, such as caring for an ill child or parent. The community benefits from reduced rush-hour traffic congestion.

Flextime   Flextime allows employees to work the hours that enable them to take care of personal business, such as taking children to school, attending classes, or avoiding heavy commute traffic. Many organizations set core hours during which all employees are required to be at work but other than that allow employees to determine what hours meet their needs.

Compressed Workweeks   Some organizations allow employees to work four 10-hour days or a 9/80 schedule in which the employee works nine 9-hour days in each 2-week period and has a day off every other week. There are a number of variations to these schedules; employers must be aware of FLSA overtime requirements for nonexempt employees and ensure that the compressed workweek doesn't violate those requirements.

Part-Time Work   Occasionally, employees may want to reduce their hours for a variety of reasons such as attending school or caring for elderly parents or young children. Employers who agree to a regular part-time schedule will retain qualified employees who would otherwise need to leave the organization.

Job Sharing   Job sharing is a situation where two part-time employees share one job. The employer can benefit from this practice in several ways. First, it allows accommodation of an employee's request for a part-time schedule yet maintains full-time coverage for the job. Second, it can allow the employer to hire two people with complementary skills that enhance results.

Nontraditional work arrangements such as these that weren't possible in the past are available now because advances in technology have made them feasible.

Employee Rights and Responsibilities

Employment rights developed over time from legal statutes and common-law doctrines. Just as these doctrines and statutes establish rights and responsibilities for employers, they provide employees with protection.

The statutory laws governing the employee relations (ER) function provide employees with the right to fair treatment and the expectation of equal opportunity in a workplace free from discrimination or harassment, and they protect employees' rights to join together in negotiating the terms and conditions of employment. Another legal concept with relevance to employee relations is the constitutional guarantee of due process.

Due process as a legal concept was established in the Magna Carta in 1215 and incorporated into the U.S. Bill of Rights to protect citizens from arbitrary acts of the federal and state governments. It isn't a legal requirement for private employers, but the concept is a practice that is in the best interest of employers. *Due process* in the employment context means that employment actions are taken in accordance with established procedures, including notifying employees of pending actions and providing the opportunity to respond to any allegations prior to making a final adverse employment decision.

The common-law doctrine of employment at-will provides employees with the right to leave a job at any time, with or without notice. Other common-law doctrines place responsibilities on employees in the employment relationship as well:

- The *duty of diligence* requires an employee to act "with reasonable care and skill" in the course of performing work for the employer.

- The *duty of obedience* requires employees to act within the authority granted by the employer and to follow the employer's reasonable and legal policies, procedures, and rules.

- The *duty of loyalty* requires that employees act in the best interest of the employer and not solicit work away from the employer to benefit themselves.

A couple of key factors that relate to employee rights and responsibilities include workplace policies and procedures and the life cycle of records management. The following sections will take a look at those concepts.

Workplace Policies and Procedures

Employers need a consistent and understandable means to communicate important information about how the company operates and what is expected of employees. This is best done through *policies*, which are broad guidelines developed by the employer to guide organizational decisions. *Procedures* provide further explanation and more details on how the policy is to be applied, and *work rules* state what employees may or may not do to comply with the policy. For example:

Policy   Employees will conduct business in a manner consistent with the highest standards of business ethics.

Procedure   Employees should avoid situations in which the best interest of the company conflicts with the employee's self-interest.

Work Rule   Employees may not own, in whole or in part, any venture that seeks to do business with, or is a competitor of, this organization.

Some employment policies are required by law, such as a sexual-harassment prevention policy. Other policies help ensure the consistent application of employment practices throughout the organization, and still others serve to motivate employees, such as education reimbursement, recognition, or telecommuting policies. The number and type of policies in each organization should be reflective of the mission, values, and culture of the organization and seek to promote successful employment relationships. Regardless of how policies are used in any organization, it's important that they be reviewed and updated periodically to ensure that they're still relevant for the organization.

HR policies, procedures, and work rules are developed in conjunction with line management. The role of HR in this process is to advise management on current best practices and legal requirements and work with management to develop policies that are consistent with organizational goals, easily communicated, and viewed by employees as equitable. Once these documents are developed, HR is responsible to advise management on appropriate ways to administer the policies, procedures, and work rules, as well as provide training when needed.

Employee handbooks can be useful as a way of communicating policies, procedures, and work rules to employees in an organized fashion by providing a reference. However, poorly worded handbooks have, in some cases, been found by the courts to create implied contracts. When this happens, courts have required employers to abide by the contract implied in the handbook. If the organization wants to maintain its status as an at-will employer, it's important to clearly state this in the handbook and, more important, to have the handbook reviewed by legal counsel to ensure that it accomplishes the purpose intended without a negative impact.

Handbooks generally begin with a welcoming statement from senior management and a statement of the organization's ER philosophy. Some handbooks provide a history of the organization to give new employees a feel for the type of organization they have joined. Handbooks also contain legally required policies, such as statements of the organization's compliance with equal employment opportunities, prohibitions against unlawful harassment, and information about federally mandated leaves such as the Family and Medical Leave Act (FMLA). The employer then has the opportunity to describe the terms and conditions of employment in the organization, including such things as work hours, safety, ethics, employment status, eligibility for benefits, and benefit programs. The handbook is a good place to inform employees of workplace privacy considerations; if the organization has a policy of monitoring the workplace or places restrictions on Internet usage, clear descriptions of those policies can prevent future problems.

It's advisable to include a tear-out acknowledgment form for employees to sign, or, if the employer uses an online handbook, an electronic acknowledgment. The acknowledgment should include statements that employment is at-will, that the employer has the right to unilaterally change the terms and conditions described in the handbook, and that the employee has received, read, and understands the contents of the handbook. Although some of this language may be viewed negatively by employees, it provides documentation for the employer in any future disciplinary or legal actions that may occur.

Two other methods of communicating the more functional of the employer expectations are reference guides and standard operating procedures (SOPs). A reference guide is a tool used to organize large amounts of data into a single source document. Reference guides can be as simple as an employee phone list or company product list or more elaborate user guides and troubleshooting manuals. SOPs are tools used to capture processes that typically follow a sequence of events. Capturing step-by-step procedures through the use of definitions, charts, and screen shots allows for the application of uniform business activities regardless of who is doing the work. Both reference guides and SOPs are tools that help to reduce errors, streamline processes, communicate employer expectations, and serve as an effective means of managing the knowledge of the organization.

Many employers are able to effectively address the current needs of the company through the use of handbooks, reference guides, SOPs, and other communication tools but fail to update them as the business evolves. Therefore, regularly verifying, updating, and communicating the changes is just as important as the initial effort.

Records Management: The Life Cycle

Every employment-related activity in the scope of human resources receives or generates a record. The specific retention, storage, and destruction of these records make up the *records life cycle.*

Establishing the Policy

An effective records-management policy should be focused on defining controls. This includes controlling the creation, access, legibility, retrieval, use, retention, and destruction of each record.

A records-retention policy should include a description of the employment documents covered by the policy (defining what is a record), a control system for limiting access and ensuring availability upon demand or need (description of maintenance or use), and a schedule for retention and eventual destruction by record type.

An HR professional should have a firm understanding of theory and application related to developing and implementing a records-retention process. In addition to being a best practice, records retention is required by several federal laws. For example, the Civil Rights Act of 1964 requires that employers with at least 15 employees must retain applications and other personnel records relating to hires, rehires, tests used in employment, promotion, transfers, demotions, selection for training, layoff, recall, terminations, and discharge for one year from making the records or taking the personnel actions. See Table 6.1 for more examples of the types of records that are generated by functional area of HR.

TABLE 6.1   Types of records generated by HR

Functional area of HR	Examples of types of records created or received	Laws or rules governing recordkeeping or retention requirements
Equal Employment	Medical certifications, training selection procedures, applicant tracking, Affirmative Action Plans/results	FMLA ADA ADEA EPA CRA 1964 VEVRAA Uniformed Services Employment and Reemployment Rights Act (USERRA)
Staffing	Applications, pre-employment test results, selection notes, EEO-1 reports, I-9 forms, job postings, reference check information, credit reports, basic employee data	IRCA CRA 1964 ADA UGESP FCRA Federal Unemployment Tax Act (FUTA)
Compensation and Benefits	Payroll records, tax records, benefits administration records, summary plan descriptions, leave of absence (LOA) records, copies of employee notices describing benefits, records of insurance premium payments	Employee Retirement Income Security Act (ERISA) HIPAA FMLA PDA Fair Labor Standards Act (FLSA) IRS tax code
Training and Development	Participant records, description of tools used in training	OSHA ADA
Employee Relations	Performance reviews, adverse employment actions, investigative reports	CRA 1964 ADA ADEA
Risk Management	Workplace injury and illness records, records of exposure to hazardous material	OSHA

Proper Disposal

In June 2005, the FTC issued a disposal rule related to the destruction of consumer information. This rule covers employment records related to sensitive personal information (Social Security numbers, medical history), consumer credit, references, and background searches. It directs affected companies to destroy covered records in a manner that protects against "unauthorized access to or use of the information." The FTC describes the following as acceptable methods for compliance. Employers may:

- Burn, pulverize, or shred papers containing consumer report information so that the information cannot be read or reconstructed.

- Destroy or erase electronic files or media containing consumer report information so that the information cannot be read or reconstructed.

- Conduct due diligence and hire a document destruction contractor to dispose of material specifically identified as consumer report information consistent with the rule.

You can find the final Rule in its entirety on the FTC's website: www.ftc.gov/os/2004/11/041118disposalfrn.pdf

Electronic Storage

Technology has influenced many HR practices, not the least of which is records retention. Before deciding to electronically store records, an HR professional must consider the specific regulatory requirements of the law(s) governing record retention, security, access, and legibility. A good example of the considerations for the electronic storage of records is given by the U.S. Citizen and Immigration Services (USCIS) related to storing Form I-9 electronically. The following is an excerpt from the USCIS website (www.uscis.gov/i-9-central/retain-store-form-i-9/storing-form-i-9):

> Employers may use a paper system, an electronic system or a combination of paper and electronic systems to store Form I-9 records. An electronic storage system must:
>
> - Include controls to ensure the integrity, accuracy and reliability of the electronic storage system.
>
> - Include controls to detect and prevent the unauthorized or accidental creation of, addition to, alteration of, deletion of or deterioration of an electronically stored Form I-9, including the electronic signature, if used.
>
> - Include controls to ensure an audit trail so that any alteration or change to the form since its creation is electronically stored and can be accessed by an appropriate government agency inspecting the forms.
>
> - Include an inspection and quality assurance program that regularly evaluates the electronic generation or storage system, and includes

periodic checks of electronically stored Form I-9s, including the electronic signature, if used.

- Include a detailed index of all data so that any particular record can be accessed immediately.
- Produce a high degree of legibility and readability when displayed on a video display terminal or reproduced on paper.

U.S. Citizen and Immigration Services (USCIS);
www.uscis.gov/i-9-central/
retain-store-form-i-9/storing-form-i-9

Performance Management Programs

Performance management is an ongoing process of providing feedback for employees about their performance to develop them into increasingly productive contributors to the organization. Although only one element of a robust talent management program, *performance management programs* begin by defining employee jobs and end when an employee leaves the organization. The performance management process provides for an employee's professional development in the context of organizational needs.

Effective performance management must be based on an agreement between the manager or supervisor and the employee about what the job requires. This information comes from the organization's strategic plan, the manager's goals and objectives, and the employee's essential job functions as contained in an accurate job description. With these elements, the parties can develop individual goals and objectives and agree on the standards of performance to be used in measuring results.

Meaningful feedback that can be used to improve performance is specific, describing the behavior so the employee is clear about what is being done correctly or incorrectly. For example, instead of saying "Good job," you can tell an employee, "The way you handled Bob Kent's complaint yesterday was professional and effective. I was impressed with how quickly you were able to calm him down by remaining calm yourself and solving his problem." Feedback should also focus on behaviors, not personal attributes. Telling an employee "You have a bad attitude" is open to interpretation and doesn't help them to see where they need to improve. Instead, say, "Sally, I noticed that you were scowling at your desk this morning, and when Joe asked you a question, you told him to find the manual himself. That isn't an appropriate way to respond to questions. Part of our job is to assist our co-workers in finding the reference materials we maintain." This response provides actionable information for the employee. It's also important for the feedback to be as timely as possible and at least within the same day as the observed behavior.

Corrective feedback should be given privately to avoid embarrassing the employee—the point of feedback is to improve behavior, not to alienate the employee. The employee should also be able to respond, explain, or ask for clarification.

On the other hand, positive feedback given more publicly can motivate the recipient and observers to repeat the positive behavior and receive additional recognition.

Performance management isn't a once-a-year proposition—for maximum effectiveness, it must be an ongoing process that enables a manager to intervene in the early stages if an employee is getting off track.

The following sections will take a closer look at the elements, timing and methods of conducting performance appraisals, training performance evaluators, and how to improve performance and deal with workplace behavior issues.

Performance Appraisal

One important aspect of performance management is the *performance appraisal, performance evaluation,* or *performance review* process. These three terms are used interchangeably to describe the process of reviewing how well employees perform their duties during a specified period of time. The appraisal process has the potential to be a powerful tool for building the important relationship between supervisors and their direct reports.

When used well, appraisals provide a structured means for communication, helping to build working relationships. This structure provides for positive performance feedback, recognition of accomplishments during the review period, honest discussion of areas for improvement, and development opportunities for the future. You can find more information about this in the section "Training Performance Evaluators" later in this chapter.

Another important function of the performance appraisal process is the documentation it provides for employment decisions—positive or negative. For example, appraisals that document a history of achievement and positive contribution provide the basis for promotion decisions or inclusion in a high-potential employee (HiPo) development program. Conversely, appraisals that document a history of mediocre or below-average performance are crucial when making adverse employment decisions. Contemporaneous performance documentation can be essential in defending employment actions at either end of the spectrum if challenged by disgruntled employees.

Three factors in the appraisal process are important to understand: the elements included in an appraisal process, the timing of review cycles, and the methods used.

Elements of a Performance Appraisal

Several elements should be included as part of an effective annual review:

Supervisor Assessment   The supervisor's assessment begins with a review of the goals and objectives set at the beginning of the review cycle and whether the anticipated results were achieved. The supervisor must then evaluate whether any deficiencies occurred because of inadequate performance by the employee or whether they were the result of circumstances outside the employee's control, such as a change in the organization's direction. The supervisor must then develop a plan to address the discrepancies.

Employee Self-Assessment   Because this process is meant to be a two-way conversation, employees should be asked to assess their own performance as part of the appraisal. Giving employees advance notice of the scheduled review meeting allows time for reflection about their past performance as well as goals they may have for the future and areas of professional development that are of interest to them.

Assessment from Others   It's important for supervisors to obtain feedback from those with whom the employee has contact each day to find out whether there are areas of concern or outstanding performance about which the supervisor may not be aware. This includes *360-degree feedback*, which HRCI defines as "employee appraisal data gathered from internal and external sources (such as peers, subordinates, supervisors, customers and suppliers); also known as *multi-rater* feedback."

Goal Setting   A key component of the review is planning for the future using changes to the strategic plan and the supervisor's goals and objectives to help plan the employee's goals. It's important for employees to participate in the setting of their own goals to facilitate their commitment to achieving them.

Development Goals   As part of the review, supervisors can provide development opportunities for employees to address any areas of deficiency or to prepare them for the next level.

Timing Performance Appraisals

Performance appraisals can be conducted either on employee anniversary dates or during an organization-wide focal review period. In organizations that time reviews to coincide with employee anniversary dates, managers conduct individual reviews throughout the year. The advantage of this process is that there are fewer reviews to conduct at one time; disadvantages occur when awarding salary increases and when using comparative appraisal methods. Managers who don't plan adequately for salary increases or other compensation awards may find that rewards for high performers don't exceed—or, worse, are lower than—what average performers received earlier in the year. It's also difficult to use comparative appraisal methods when appraisals occur on individual employee anniversary dates because the manager will need to consider the performance of employees not up for review at the same time.

During a *focal review period*, all employees in the organization are reviewed at the same time. This is more difficult for managers, as well as for HR, because of the sheer volume of reviews that must be completed. On the other hand, the focal process provides managers with an opportunity to allocate salary increases, equity grants, bonuses, and other rewards in a way that appropriately reflects individual performance levels. Comparative appraisal methods are more easily conducted during a focal review as well.

Performance Appraisal Methods

Employee performance appraisal may be based on quantitative data, such as whether specific goals were accomplished, or on more qualitative factors. There is currently much discussion in the HR field about the effectiveness of traditional performance appraisal processes. Some HR texts suggest that appraisal systems be abolished and replaced with more effective methods of providing feedback and developing employees.

A number of methods have been developed for use in evaluating employee performance; all of them can be placed in one of four basic categories: comparison, rating, essay, and behavioral.

Comparison Methods

Comparison appraisal methods compare the performance of individuals or employees to each other. The most common methods of comparison are ranking, paired comparison, and forced ranking:

Ranking   In the *ranking* method, employees are listed in order from the highest to the lowest performer. This method works well for small groups of employees but becomes increasingly difficult as the size of the group increases.

Paired Comparison   In the *paired comparison* method, all employees in the group are compared to one employee at a time. For example, if there are three employees in the workgroup—Susan, Jack, and Rachel—then Susan's performance is compared to Jack's and Rachel's, Jack's performance is compared to Susan's and Rachel's, and finally, Rachel's performance is compared to Susan's and Jack's.

Forced Ranking   Also known as *forced distribution* or *forced choice*, *forced ranking* requires managers to rank employees according to the bell curve, rating a small group of employees at the high end, a small group at the low end, and the bulk of the employees in the average range. This appraisal tool can be used as part of any of the appraisal methods to reduce the effects of the leniency or harshness biases discussed in detail in Chapter 3, "PHR Exam: Talent Planning and Acquisition."

Rating Methods

Common rating methods for performance appraisal include the use of rating scales and checklists:

Rating Scales   Rating scales may be numeric, with scales ranging from 3 to 10 ratings to differentiate levels of performance, or may use phrases such as "exceeds expectations," "meets expectations," or "does not meet expectations." Rating scales attempt to quantify what is a very subjective process, but because of the different ways in which the descriptors are interpreted by raters, these scales aren't as objective as they may appear at first glance.

Checklists   A performance checklist is a list of statements, phrases, or words that describe levels of performance, such as "always finishes work on time." The reviewer checks off those that best describe the employee. The various descriptions may be weighted and used to calculate a rating score.

Narrative Methods

Narrative methods of appraisal require managers to describe the employee's performance. These include critical incident, essay, and field reviews:

Critical Incident   The *critical incident review* process requires that during the review period supervisors make notes of successful and unsuccessful performance issues for each employee. At the time of the review, the supervisor is able to review these critical incidents and present them to employees in a written narrative.

Essay   An *essay review* requires the reviewer to write a short description of each employee's performance during the year. This format provides maximum flexibility for managers to cover areas they see as most important to improving employee performance.

Field Review   A *field review appraisal* may be conducted by someone other than the supervisor. This can be an HR practitioner or someone from outside the organization.

Behavioral Methods

The best-known behavioral review method is the *behaviorally anchored rating scale (BARS)*. This is defined by HRCI as "a type of performance rating scale designed to combine both qualitative and quantitative data to the employee appraisal process. The BARS compares an individual's performance against specific examples of behavior that are attached to numerical ratings." The BARS method uses the job description to create dimensions that represent the most important requirements of the job. For each dimension, anchor statements are created to represent varying levels of performance behaviors that describe rating numbers on a scale. For example, a job dimension for a receptionist might be greeting customers. Table 6.2 shows the anchors that could be used to measure the behaviors associated with this job dimension.

TABLE 6.2   Sample BARS anchor statements

Rating	Anchor statement
5	Greets customers warmly and makes them feel welcome
4	Pleasant to customers and answers their questions
3	Courteous to customers
2	Finishes other work before greeting customers
1	Rude to customers when they approach the desk

Regardless of the review method used in an organization, raters should be aware of the various biases that can impact the fairness of a review. It's also important to keep in mind that the same biases and errors described in Chapter 3's discussion of interviewer bias, such as the halo/horn effect, leniency, harshness, and similar-to-me errors, can influence a review. Supervisors should be cognizant of this when preparing the review. When bias is a concern, organizations can use a process known as *inter-rater reliability*, which uses multiple raters to reduce the possibility of rating errors due to bias. The scores of all raters are averaged, with the goal of providing a review that is as free from bias as possible.

Training Performance Evaluators

It's unfortunate that the performance appraisal process is disliked by so many supervisors and employees, because when well used it provides a structure for building positive, productive working relationships. One of the concerns many employees have about the appraisal process is their perception of its fairness, or lack of fairness. Some employees may think their boss is much tougher than other managers, and some managers have developed reputations for being "easy graders." Those perceptions may never go away entirely, but providing training for those who conduct appraisals will at least ensure that everyone is beginning from the same place. Evaluators should be made aware of the purpose of performance evaluations (it's not just for wage increases), the methods of providing feedback (formal and informal), the behaviors being rated (and how to tell the difference between employees), and the common rater errors such as leniency and bias that can affect the appraisal process (as discussed in Chapter 3).

The training should provide information for activities before, during, and after the actual appraisal meeting.

Before the Meeting

Preparation prior to meeting with employees helps alleviate some of the stress and discomfort that many evaluators feel, particularly when they're new to providing feedback. The goal of the process is to make sure employees know they're valued team members and to motivate them to continue positive performance and improve any areas in which they may be deficient:

- Schedule the meeting for a mutually convenient time, and allow sufficient time for an open conversation. Give the employee advance notice—ideally one week minimum. Don't schedule the meeting for a time when other pressures, such as deadlines or other commitments, will be a distraction.

- Provide the employee with a self-appraisal form or questionnaire to complete prior to finalizing the evaluation to ensure that the employee's input is considered; at least one day before the meeting, provide the employee with a copy of the completed appraisal. If reviewing multiple employees in the same job category, use the same appraisal criteria for all of them.

- Prepare for the meeting by reviewing the job description, performance standards, goals set during previous appraisals, and the critical-incident log or other notes about specific performance issues (positive and negative) that occurred during the review period.

- Complete the review form using specific, job-related comments to describe positive and negative performance issues. This helps the employee see what to continue doing that is successful and how to improve other areas as needed.

- Make sure the appraisal is balanced. Keep in mind that few employees are all good or all bad; in most cases, even those with serious performance deficiencies are usually doing some things right, and outstanding performers can improve in some area.

- Whenever possible, use quantitative measurements, such as on-time project completions, missed deadlines, production data, and so on. Describe how the behaviors impacted the organization.

- If improvements are needed in some areas, provide specific information on what is expected from the employee and how feedback will be given. Don't sugarcoat problems—appraisals that neglect to document performance problems make future adverse employment actions difficult and expose the organization to litigation.

▪ Arrange a private area to conduct the meeting; even if the evaluator has an office, the use of a conference room may be advisable to eliminate interruptions and create a neutral atmosphere conducive to open dialogue.

During the Meeting

Adequate preparation is essential and demonstrates that the supervisor values the employee. It's equally important for evaluators to make full use of that preparation during the meeting. This is an opportunity to communicate about issues that are important to both participants—feedback, expectations, goals, and, in some cases, rewards.

Most employees enter an appraisal meeting wanting to know how they're doing, what the supervisor expects from them, and what their reward for previous performance will be. Some will approach the meeting as though it were a guillotine, whereas others see it as an opportunity to learn the positive and negative information provided to continue developing their careers.

The evaluator's goal during the meeting is to acknowledge the employee's value to the organization and provide them with constructive feedback to enhance their productivity. Training for evaluators should include the following information:

▪ Set a tone of mutual respect. It's up to evaluators to ease anxiety by creating an open atmosphere and giving employees their full attention.

▪ Discuss the appraisal forms that were exchanged prior to the meeting. If there are areas of disagreement, seek to understand the employee's perspective; be willing to revise the appraisal if warranted due to any oversights or misunderstanding of the facts. Don't, however, change an appraisal to avoid confrontation about accurate facts.

▪ Discuss training options and development needs. Find out what career direction the employee wants to take, and provide realistic guidance about how that may be achieved.

▪ Set goals for the next review period. Be sure to include the employee in developing the goals instead of merely assigning them. Keep in mind that the goal of the appraisal is to enhance performance; giving employees a voice in setting their goals helps them to feel invested in the outcome.

▪ Communicate expectations clearly. If attendance or tardiness is an issue, say so flat out—don't leave anything to interpretation.

▪ Give the employee an opportunity to ask questions about the appraisal, expectations, or goals so that when they leave the meeting they're clear about any next steps.

▪ Once the appraisal part of the meeting is completed, in many organizations the discussion turns to rewards, whether that is a salary increase, a bonus, a promotion, or another reward.

▪ Have the employee sign any necessary paperwork required for the appraisal or reward.

After the Meeting

Provide information to supervisors about how to complete the appraisal process. In most cases, this will include submitting paperwork to HR for retention and processing salary changes. In addition, encourage supervisors to make continuous feedback part of their daily interaction with employees. This reduces the level of stress involved in annual appraisals because the feedback becomes a regular part of the daily routine instead of an annual review of what should have been done differently during the year. An appraisal with no surprises is easier on supervisors and their employees.

Training those individuals who conduct appraisals is one way to make the experience, if not pleasant, at least more effective.

Nonsupervisory Evaluators

Evaluators are generally supervisors or managers, but in the case of 360-degree appraisal systems, co-workers may be asked to provide feedback as well. These evaluators should receive training on the organization's appraisal process and the importance of keeping the feedback related to job activities. They should also be made aware of the biases that can affect the appraisal process.

Performance Improvement

As in any relationship, there are times when disagreements occur; in the employment relationship, these disagreements are usually related to some form of performance issue and can result in a disciplinary action. Much has been written about this topic, because it can become a source of legal action if the employer doesn't act appropriately. HR's role in the disciplinary process is to provide the expertise needed to set up a fair and equitable process that is applied consistently throughout the organization.

 Real World Scenario

Weingarten Rights

Leura Collins was employed by J. Weingarten, Inc., a company that operated a chain of retail stores. Collins worked at the lunch counter at store #2 for about 9 years and was then transferred to store #98. After Collins had been working at the second store for about two years, an undercover member of Weingarten's security department investigated a complaint that Collins was stealing money by observing her at work for two hours; during this time he found nothing to substantiate the complaint. He met with the store manager, who told the investigator that a co-worker reported that Collins had just underpaid for a box of chicken. Collins was called to the office and interrogated by the investigator and the store manager. Collins asked several times that her union representative be included in the meeting, but each time her request was denied. Collins explained what had happened. The investigator confirmed her story with the co-worker, found that the complaints were caused by a misunderstanding, and determined that Collins had not violated any company rules. Collins informed the shop steward of the incident, and the union filed an unfair labor practice complaint with the NLRB.

The NLRB found that employees are entitled to have a union representative present at any investigatory interview that the employee believes could result in disciplinary action. Employers aren't required to inform employees of this right, but if an employee requests that a co-worker be present, the employer has three options:

- Discontinue the interview until the co-worker arrives.

- Decide not to conduct the interview at all, and make any disciplinary decision based on other facts.

- Give the employee the choice of voluntarily waiving the Weingarten rights and continuing the interview or having the employer make disciplinary decisions without an interview.

Weingarten appealed the finding, and the case was eventually heard by the Supreme Court. In 1975, the Court upheld the NLRB's decision.

The NLRB has extended Weingarten rights to and withdrawn them from *non*union workers several times since then. The rights were first extended in 1982 and withdrawn in 1985. In July 2000, the NLRB reinstated Weingarten rights to nonunion employees based on a case involving the Epilepsy Foundation of Northeast Ohio. In its decision, the Board determined that nonunion employees invoking Weingarten rights are entitled to the presence of another co-worker but aren't entitled to have a family member or attorney present. In a case involving IBM Corp. in June 2004, the board reversed its Epilepsy Foundation decision, once again denying Weingarten rights to nonunion employees.

So, what should nonunion employers do? First, understand that employees still have the right to *ask* for a co-worker's presence, so employers should not take disciplinary action based on such a request. Although employers currently have no obligation to allow co-workers into these meetings, it may be prudent to act cautiously in this area given the unsettled nature of the law.

Workplace Behavior Issues

Employees are human beings whose behavior at work is influenced by many factors, including experiences and situations that exist outside the context of the workplace. Regardless of the source, these factors influence the way employees behave while they're at work. Employee behavior and management's response (or, in some cases, lack of response) affects the productivity and morale of the entire workgroup and may spill into other parts of the organization. Some employee behaviors that can lead to disciplinary action include the following:

Absenteeism   Employees call in sick for many different reasons—sometimes they themselves are ill or perhaps a child or parent needs care. Some employees have been known to call in sick to go surfing, hang out with friends, go shopping, or have a "mental health" day. Regardless of the reasons that employees give for absences, more often than not the unanticipated absence causes problems for the workgroup. At the very least, another employee usually must take on additional tasks or responsibilities for the duration of the absence. When one employee has an excessive number of absences that aren't protected under FMLA, an absentee policy provides the basis for disciplinary action. An effective policy includes a clear statement of how much sick leave is provided, whether each day off work is counted as one absence, or whether several days off in a row for the same illness is considered one absence. The policy should also tell employees whether the absences are counted on a fiscal, calendar, or rolling-year basis, and when a doctor's note is required before sick leave may be used.

Dress Code Dress-code policies let employees know how formal or informal their clothes need to be in the workplace. Some types of clothing may not be appropriate for safety reasons (such as to prevent a piece of clothing from getting caught in a machine) or to ensure a professional appearance throughout the organization. A policy should describe what type of clothing is appropriate for different jobs, give examples to clarify, and let employees know the consequences for inappropriate attire. If appropriate, the policy may also describe functions or situations in which employees are expected to dress more formally than normal.

 Real World Scenario

Jespersen vs. Harrah's Operating Co.

Darlene Jespersen worked for more than 20 years as a bartender with an exemplary performance record at Harrah's Reno casino. Harrah's implemented a comprehensive uniform, known as the "Personal Best" program, with revised standards for all its bartenders, male and female. The standards established a standard work uniform: black pants with white shirt and bow tie and comfortable black shoes. In addition, women were required to wear facial makeup, and men weren't permitted to do so. Men's hair length was required to be above the collar; women were allowed to have long hair. The standards also included other gender-specific requirements for appearance, jewelry, and nail care.

Jespersen objected to the makeup requirements, stating that "it would conflict with her self-image." She complied with all the other requirements but was unwilling to wear makeup and left Harrah's when there were no other openings for which she qualified. She obtained a right to sue notice from the EEOC and filed suit, claiming that the "Personal Best" policy discriminated against women by "(1) subjecting them to terms and conditions of employment to which men are not similarly subjected and (2) requiring that women conform to sex-based stereotypes as a term and condition of employment." Harrah's requested summary judgment based on its defense that the standards created by the new policy imposed similar requirements for males and females and that the differences in the requirements placed similar burdens on both sexes. The district court granted the motion.

The appeals court upheld the summary judgment, agreeing with the lower court that Jespersen didn't demonstrate that the policy was motivated by stereotyping based on sex.

Insubordination   Insubordinate behavior can be as blatant as employees refusing to perform a legitimate task or responsibility when requested by their managers. It can also be subtler, such as employees who roll their eyes whenever a manager gives them direction. It's not only disrespectful to the manager or supervisor on the receiving end of the behavior, but it can also create morale problems with other members of the workgroup. Although few organizations have specific policies for insubordination, a code of conduct that describes the organization's expectations for appropriate behavior, such as treating all employees with dignity and respect, provides managers with the tools they need to correct unacceptable behavior.

Discipline is a performance management tool that is designed to modify employee behavior through the use of negative consequences. Many companies have a formal code of conduct that is used to communicate examples of expected employee behavior, and when an employee fails to behave in accordance with policy, discipline may be used. HR is responsible for creating the discipline policy, communicating the code of conduct, and ensuring that the administration of the policy doesn't violate the law. A good discipline policy doesn't necessarily have to tie an employer to specific steps in the discipline process (often called progressive discipline), but rather makes a statement about the employee's responsibilities and the consequences for failing to execute those responsibilities in accordance with company guidelines. With wrongful-termination and wrongful-discipline lawsuits on the rise, it's imperative that HR is up-to-date on the standards pertaining to employee discipline. A seemingly neutral code of conduct that negatively impacts a protected-class group may be found to be discriminatory. Furthermore, disciplining or terminating an employee for exercising their leave rights, for reporting harassment, or to avoid paying a sales commission are all examples of wrongful discipline/discharge.

When discussing performance issues with employees, managers should be encouraged to focus on describing the unacceptable behavior as specifically as possible instead of using general terms such as *bad attitude*, *insubordinate*, or *poor performance*. The more specific the description, the easier it will be for the employee to understand and improve. Specific descriptions of performance issues make any adverse actions easier to defend if an employee decides to take legal action.

Organizations with effective ER programs work to prevent the need for disciplinary action. The establishment and publication of clear policies, procedures, and work rules combined with clearly communicated expectations for individual employees are the cornerstones of prevention. With regular feedback, both positive and negative, employees are better able to improve performance issues when they're easily remedied. If a performance problem can't be resolved at this level, HR may need to step in and manage the exit process.

No-Beard Policy

A pizza-delivery restaurant has an inflexible no-beard policy. The restaurant fires Jamal, one of its African American drivers, for failing to remain clean shaven. Jamal has a severe case of pseudofolliculitis barbae (PFB), an inflammatory skin condition that occurs primarily in African American men and that is caused by shaving. The severity of the condition varies, but many of those who suffer from PFB effectively can't shave at all. If Jamal or EEOC were to challenge the no-beard policy as unlawful because it has a significant negative impact on African Americans, the employer would have to prove the policy is job-related and consistent with business necessity.

Organization Exit/Off-Boarding Processes

Organization exits happen in one of two ways: Employees choose to leave of their own volition (resignations and retirements), or they're asked to leave in one way or another (termination, downsizing, or layoff). Organization exits are stressful. Even when the employee has chosen to leave and is exiting on good terms, issues arise for the organization in replacing the employee or allocating duties to remaining co-workers. Co-workers can be affected by the change as well, so developing an exit process that reduces stress and builds a smooth transition will pay off in many ways. Most significant for HR is the positive message a smooth transition sends to employees who remain in the organization.

The following sections will explore both voluntary and involuntary exit processes, dispute resolution, arbitration, mediation, and constructive confrontation.

Voluntary Exit Processes

Employees voluntarily exit the organization by either resigning or retiring. Resignations occur when an employee decides to leave the organization and pursue other opportunities. For HR, resignations present few legal issues, but they do require decisions about replacement or reassignment of work that may lead to promotions or transfers of other employees, all of which affect the workforce planning process. Resignations require HR to ensure that any outstanding loans or advances are repaid to the organization or arrangements are made for that to happen. If the employee provided 72 hours' notice, final payment of all wages due, including any unused accrued vacation or PTO, must be paid at the time of departure. In addition, Consolidated Omnibus Budget Reconciliation Act (COBRA) and Health Insurance Portability and Accountability Act (HIPAA) notices must be provided for departing employees. (COBRA and HIPAA requirements are covered in detail in Appendix C, "Federal Employment Legislation and Case Law.")

Planned retirements occur when an employee decides to stop working full time and pursue other interests. HR can provide preretirement counseling to prepare employees for the transition from the structure provided by full-time work to unstructured time for pursuing other activities in leading a full and rewarding life. Employee assistance programs (EAPs) are excellent sources for this type of counseling and assistance.

Before an employee leaves the company, an exit interview should be conducted to gather relevant feedback. An effective exit interview provides an opportunity for employees to communicate information to the organization about why they decided to leave, what improvements the organization could make to enhance the employment experience, and any specific issues that need to be addressed. If the employee is one who has been a significant contributor and whom the organization would consider rehiring in the future, this would be the time to leave the door open for that possibility. Ideally, a third party conducts exit interviews so that employees feel free to be candid. Some organizations provide this service, most often as a telephone or online interview. Collecting and evaluating this data over time will help identify possible problem areas that, if resolved, can reduce unwanted and costly turnover.

Involuntary Exit Processes

Involuntary exits occur as the result of either performance problems or changing business needs. This section will examine many aspects of involuntary terminations, including disciplinary terminations, termination meetings, wrongful terminations, the Worker Adjustment and Retraining Notification (WARN) Act, layoff decisions, layoff meetings, and programs that can ease the transition.

Disciplinary Terminations

In progressive disciplinary situations, if informal coaching and the initial stages of the disciplinary process don't remedy the performance problem, it's time to move to the termination stage. When this becomes necessary, the manager should work with HR to ensure that, to the extent possible, all necessary steps have been taken to prevent legal action as a result of the termination. Due process isn't required in employment actions taken by private employers, but ensuring that employees are informed of the issues and given the opportunity to tell their side of the story demonstrates that the employer treats them in a fair and equitable manner.

In cases where employee actions create a dangerous situation for the employer, as in theft of company property or violence in the workplace, the employer should move immediately to the termination phase of the disciplinary process. When this occurs, the best course of action is to suspend the employee pending an investigation, conduct the investigation in a fair and expeditious manner, and should the results of the investigation support termination, terminate the employee. Terminations are always difficult situations, and HR professionals need to be able to provide support for managers who must take this action. There are two areas in which HR's expertise is critical: counseling supervisors before the termination meeting and providing information so that managers avoid wrongful-termination claims.

The Termination Meeting

Termination meetings are among the most difficult duties any supervisor has to perform. When termination becomes necessary, HR should meet with the supervisor to ensure that there is sufficient documentation to support the action and to coach the supervisor on how to appropriately conduct the meeting. By this stage in the process, the employee should not be surprised by the termination, because it should have been referred to as a consequence if improvement didn't occur. The meeting should be long enough to clearly articulate the reasons for the termination and provide any final papers or documentation. Managers should be counseled to be professional, avoid debating the action with the employee, and conclude the meeting as quickly as possible.

The timing of termination meetings is a subject of disagreement as to the "best" day and time. Taking steps to ensure that the termination occurs with as little embarrassment for the employee as possible should be the guiding factor in making this decision.

Once the meeting is completed, and, of course, depending on corporate policy and the circumstances surrounding the termination, the employee may be escorted from the building. Company policies differ on this part of the process: some companies have a security officer escort the employee from the building; others allow the employee to pack up personal items from the desk with a supervisor or security officer present. While the supervisor is conducting the termination meeting, facilities and IT personnel are often simultaneously taking steps to prevent the employee from accessing the company network or facilities once the termination has been completed.

In any situation with the possibility of the employee becoming violent, HR should arrange for security personnel to be nearby or, in extreme cases, ensure that the local police department is advised of the situation.

Wrongful Termination

Wrongful terminations occur when an employer terminates someone for a reason that is prohibited by statute or breaches a contract. For example, an employee may not be terminated because they're a member of a protected class. If an employer gives a different reason for the termination but the employee can prove that the real reason was based on a discriminatory act, the termination would be wrongful. Similarly, an employee may not be terminated as retaliation for whistle-blowing activity or for filing a workers' compensation claim.

Worker Adjustment and Retraining Notification (WARN) Act of 1988

The WARN Act was passed by Congress in 1988 to provide some protection for workers in the event of mass layoffs or plant closings. The act requires that 60 days' advance notice be given to either the individual workers or their union representatives. The intent of Congress was to provide time for workers to obtain new employment or training before the loss of their jobs occurred. The WARN Act is administered by the DOL and enforced through the federal courts.

Employers with 100 or more full-time employees or those with 100 or more full- *and* part-time employees who work in the aggregate 4,000 hours or more per week are subject to the provisions of the WARN Act. The employee count includes those who are on temporary leave or layoff with a reasonable expectation of recall.

The WARN Act established that a *mass layoff* occurs when either 500 employees are laid off or 33 percent of the workforce and at least 50 employees are laid off. A *plant closing* occurs when 50 or more full-time employees lose their jobs because a single facility shuts down, either permanently or temporarily. In cases where the employer staggers the workforce reduction over a period of time, care must be taken that appropriate notice is given if the total reductions within a 90-day period trigger the notice requirement.

The WARN Act also established rules on notice. For instance, notice is required to be given to all affected employees or their representatives, the chief elected official of the local government, and the state dislocated worker unit. Notice requirements vary according to which group they're being sent to, but they must contain specific information about the reasons for the closure, whether the action is permanent or temporary, the address of the affected business unit, the name of a company official to contact for further information, the expected date of closure or layoff, and whether bumping rights exist.

The WARN Act provides for three situations in which the 60-day notice isn't required, but the burden is on the employer to show that the reasons are legitimate and not an attempt to thwart the intent of the act:

- The *faltering company* exception applies only to plant closures in situations where the company is actively seeking additional funding and has a reasonable expectation that it will be forthcoming in an amount sufficient to preclude the layoff or closure and that giving the notice would negatively affect the ability of the company to obtain the funding.

- The *unforeseeable business circumstance* exception applies to plant closings and mass layoffs and occurs when circumstances take a sudden and unexpected negative change that couldn't have reasonably been predicted, such as the cancellation of a major contract without previous warning.

- The *natural disaster* exception applies to both plant closings and mass layoffs occurring as the result of a natural disaster, such as a flood, an earthquake, or a fire.

Once the organization has determined whether compliance with WARN Act requirements is necessary, decisions regarding a reduction in force (RIF)—also commonly referred to as a *layoff*—can be made. Planning and conducting an RIF is stressful for managers, who must decide which employees will be asked to leave the organization, and even more so for employees, who usually figure out that layoffs are coming long before the management announcement. Maintaining productivity in a workforce that is waiting to find out whether they will have jobs is a challenging prospect. During these times, honest communication with employees is essential, and management should provide as much information as possible before actual layoff decisions are complete. Once the layoff has occurred, open and honest communication is still essential, because remaining employees struggle with feelings of anger that their co-workers had to leave the company, "survivor guilt" because they're still employed, and dissatisfaction or work overload if they're now asked to take on the work of the employees who left the company.

 Some states have enacted WARN Acts with more stringent requirements than the federal WARN Act. Be sure to know the federal requirements when you take the exam.

Making Layoff Decisions

As managers struggle with decisions about who will go and who will stay, the focus of those decisions must be on what is necessary for the business. Documenting the business reason for the decision clearly and unambiguously is essential in case the decision is challenged on the basis of disparate impact or other equal opportunity requirements.

Managers often look to layoffs as a way to remove low performers. If this is the route taken, documentation of the method used to determine who these employees are is necessary. Performance appraisals are often used for this purpose.

Severance   Offering a severance package to departing employees helps ease the shock of unemployment. Severance packages must be consistent, based on a rationale that ensures equity to all departing employees. Severance amounts can be based on seniority, employee classes, or some combination of the two.

Outplacement   *Outplacement* services are used to transition employees who are leaving the company, most often as the result of a downsizing or layoff. These services assist employees with updating résumés, preparing for interviews, and searching for new jobs. They're often provided in a group-seminar setting for individuals who have been terminated as part of a mass layoff.

 Real World Scenario

Taxman vs. Board of Education of Piscataway (1993)

In 1989, the Piscataway Board of Education found it necessary for budgetary reasons to reduce the faculty. According to state law, the board was required to conduct the layoffs based on seniority. Two teachers had the least seniority: Sharon Taxman and Debra Williams. Both had been hired on the same day in 1980, had equivalent educational qualifications, and had received equally outstanding evaluations. In essence, the board felt they were both equally qualified to be retained. In making previous layoff decisions in similar cases when there were no differences in qualifications, the board had drawn lots to determine which teacher to lay off. In this case, however, there was one difference between the teachers that the board considered: Taxman was white, and Williams was black. The board decided it was in the interest of the school to demonstrate the importance of diversity in the workplace and retained Williams because she was black.

There was no evidence of past discrimination that needed to be rectified based on an Affirmative Action Plan; in fact, blacks were employed in the school district at about twice the rate of the applicable labor pool. Sharon Taxman sued the school board for racial discrimination in violation of Title VII. The federal district court that heard the case found in favor of Taxman, and the school board appealed to the Third Circuit Court of Appeals, which also found in favor of Taxman. The school board then appealed to the U.S. Supreme Court but agreed to settle the case before the Supreme Court hearing.

State or local unemployment offices, as well as Workforce Investment agencies, may provide outplacement assistance as well, including on-site meetings with impacted employees.

Executive outplacements may occur as the result of a merger or an acquisition and may include additional benefits, such as headhunting services and one-on-one counseling. Providing outplacements for other employees can be a great help in finding new jobs or in coping with the change in circumstances. Continuing the EAP for a finite period of time for laid-off workers is another way to assist them in coming to terms with a job loss.

Unemployment Insurance   If the RIF or layoff meets WARN notice thresholds, the state unemployment office will be aware of the pending layoff. Whether or not that is the case, HR should ensure that employees are clear about their eligibility for unemployment benefits and how to apply for them. Most states provide pamphlets explaining the requirements, which are distributed at the time of the layoff.

Conducting the Layoff Meeting

During the layoff meeting, managers should communicate the message unambiguously and with compassion. If the layoff decision is a permanent one, employees should be advised that they won't be called back to work; if there is a possibility for rehire, they should be advised of the time frame in which that may occur. Employees should be given adequate time to gather personal items prior to leaving but shouldn't be allowed to hang around indefinitely, because this negatively impacts productivity and is hard on the morale of employees who will be staying with the organization. Once the termination meetings have been conducted, it's important that management meet with the remaining employees to answer questions and provide reassurance.

Easing the Transition

Whether a termination decision will affect a single employee or a group, it's one of the most difficult decisions managers face. Even so, the difficulty and discomfort experienced by management is far less than that of the employees who are losing their jobs and wondering how long it will take to find a new job and how they will make ends meet in the meantime.

Many state governments provide programs through the agencies designated to provide employment or reemployment services. The federal government contributes to these efforts with funding for training or retraining displaced workers. Two of these programs are the result of the Workforce Investment Act and the Trade Adjustment Assistance Act:

Workforce Investment Act (WIA)   The creation of WIA was a collaborative effort between the DOL and Congress, resulting in a job-training program designed to improve worker skills for jobs in the twenty-first century. WIA programs are designed to achieve three goals:

- Improve workforce quality
- Enhance national productivity and competitive ability
- Reduce reliance on welfare

The foundation of the program is its One-Stop service-delivery centers, which were established to provide a full range of services for workers and employers. These centers can include education services, skills assessment and training, job-search counseling and support, mentoring, and access to job-search information, and are generally managed by state and local governments.

Trade Adjustment Assistance (TAA)   In 2002, Congress established the Trade Adjustment Assistance (TAA) program to assist workers who lose their jobs as the result of an increase in imported goods. Eligibility for the program requires a group of three or more workers to submit an application to the DOL Division of Trade Adjustment Assistance (DTAA). DTAA determines whether the group meets eligibility requirements and, if so, issues a certification. The group must meet three requirements to be certified:

- Workers must have been laid off or had their hours and pay reduced by 20 percent or more.
- The employer's sales and/or production levels must have declined.
- The loss of jobs must be due in large part to increased imports.

Once DTAA certifies that a group is eligible for the program, individual workers may apply for services and benefits that are available at one of the local One-Stop service centers established by WIA. Retraining and reemployment services available under the TAA program include up to 104 weeks of training, trade readjustment allowances (TRAs) for up to 52 weeks of training after unemployment benefits are exhausted, reimbursement of job-search expenses, and relocation allowances.

Tools for Dispute Resolution

Most employment disputes are resolved within the organization, but on some occasions that isn't possible. Complaints can be filed with federal agencies such as OSHA and the EEOC, with the burden of proof often falling on the employer to demonstrate that it didn't violate a law related to working conditions of terms of employment. Using impartial third-party resources such as legal counsel and investigators is often the first step toward avoiding a court-ordered resolution—a very long and expensive process for all parties.

Alternative dispute resolution (ADR) covers a range of methods used to solve disagreements without litigation. These alternatives are often able to resolve problems with less animosity than occurs when a lawsuit is filed, and at far less cost to the parties.

Several different ADR methods can be used in resolving disputes before they reach the level of court action. Initially, the parties involved in a dispute may attempt a cooperative problem-solving meeting, where they work together to find a solution to the problem. Another internal ADR technique is known as a *peer-review panel*, which consists of management and nonmanagement employees who are trained in company policies, procedures, and work rules. The panel hears disputes and makes decisions that, depending on the individual program, can be final and binding on both parties to the dispute. Some companies establish an *ombudsman* or ombuds, an impartial person not involved in the dispute, who speaks with both parties and suggests alternative solutions. An ombudsman can be someone in the company or an outsider.

Some common approaches to dispute resolution are arbitration, mediation, and constructive confrontation. These are each explored in the following sections.

Arbitration

Arbitration is a means of resolving conflicts without using a judge or the courts; in short, without a lawsuit. *Voluntary arbitration* occurs when both parties to a disagreement agree to submit the conflict to an arbitrator for resolution. *Compulsory arbitration* can be a contract requirement or may be mandated by a court system as a means of reducing the backlog of civil lawsuits or by legal statute, as with public employee unions, which are prohibited from striking. If arbitration is part of an employment contract, it's important to have such agreements periodically reviewed by legal counsel; the law regarding validity of arbitration clauses in employment agreements continues to evolve through judicial decisions.

Arbitration decisions may be either binding or nonbinding. In *binding arbitration*, the parties agree to accept the arbitrator's decision as final. In *nonbinding arbitration*, either party may reject the decision and continue the dispute by filing a lawsuit.

A number of organizations throughout the country offer arbitration services; most of them have a roster of individuals with expertise in a variety of business and legal disciplines so that the arbitrator assigned to a particular case will be knowledgeable in its requirements and common practices. These organizations develop standards for those selected as arbitrators to ensure that they have the qualifications necessary to make fair and impartial decisions in the matters they hear. For example, the oldest of these organizations, the American Arbitration Association (AAA), requires that its arbitrators have a minimum of 10 years of senior-level experience and educational degrees and/or professional licenses in their area of expertise as well as training in arbitration or dispute resolution. In addition, the AAA wants its arbitrators to demonstrate professional recognition for excellence in their field and memberships in professional associations.

Arbitration proceedings begin by selecting the arbitrator. The arbitration service provides a list of individuals with relevant expertise, and each party to the arbitration has an opportunity to eliminate those who may have a conflict of interest in the proceedings.

There are three types of arbitrators:

- An *ad hoc arbitrator* is selected to hear only a single case.

- A *permanent arbitrator* is one who both parties agree is fair and impartial to resolve any disputes arising between them.

- A *tripartite arbitration panel* consists of three arbitrators who hear the issues and reach a joint decision in the matter.

In an arbitration proceeding, each party makes an opening statement describing its case for the arbitrator. The parties then present evidence, in the form of documents or witnesses, to support their case. The arbitrator asks questions of both sides to obtain additional information, and then each side makes a closing statement to sum up the evidence that was presented. The arbitrator then weighs the evidence and renders a decision, notifying the parties by mail.

As of 2017, class action waivers as part of an arbitration agreement are still enforceable. However, this practice has been challenged by the National Labor Relations Board (NLRB). The NLRB states that requiring employees to waive their right to class action suits violates their right to engage in "concerted protected activity" under the National Labor Relations Act. The Supreme Court is expected to rule on this, so it is important for students of HR to take note of the outcome.

Mediation

Mediating a grievance involves having the parties work together with the aid of a mediator to devise a solution for a problem. The decisions of a mediator aren't binding on the parties, and if the process fails, the parties may continue to the arbitration process. Mediation is an informal undertaking without evidentiary rules, and no formal record of the proceedings is retained. Mediators assist the parties by using a variety of problem-solving skills to move the disagreement to a resolution.

 Real World Scenario

Davis vs. O'Melveny & Myers

In June 1999, Jacquelin Davis began working as a paralegal at the firm of O'Melveny & Myers, LLP. Three years later, in August 2002, O'Melveny implemented an ADR program, stating the following: "This dispute resolution program…applies to and is binding on all employees (including associates) hired by—or who continue to work for—the firm on or after November 1, 2002." The document included contact information for employees who had questions about the program. Davis continued to work for the firm until July 14, 2003, and during that time asked no questions about the program.

Seven months after leaving the firm, Davis filed a lawsuit claiming that O'Melveny had violated the FLSA as well as other federal and state employment laws by withholding overtime pay and denying breaks and meal periods. O'Melveny responded by claiming that the ADR program required Davis to submit her claim to arbitration. The district court sided with O'Melveny, upholding the ADR program, and Davis appealed to the Ninth Circuit Court of Appeals.

In its finding, the Ninth Circuit found the ADR program to be procedurally unconscionable because it didn't allow employees to opt out of the program—basically requiring them to "take it or leave it." Another clause in the agreement, prohibiting mention of the mediation or arbitration "to anyone not directly involved," was also found to be unfavorable to the employee because it restricted the employee, for example, from "contacting other employees to assist in litigating (or arbitrating) an employee's case." The court also ruled that the company's unilateral ability to enforce such confidentiality requirements was "one-sided and unconscionable."

Finally, the court held that the agreement's preclusion of employee complaints to agencies such as the DOL was contrary to public policy and therefore again unconscionable.

Because arbitration agreements continue to be challenged in court and continue to evolve over time, it's important that legal counsel periodically review any form agreements to ensure that they will pass muster with the courts' latest rulings.

The mediation process has several steps, described in the following list:

Structure   Before the parties meet, the mediator develops a structure for the mediation, deciding on the time, place, and attendees for the session.

Introductions   The mediator makes introductions, explains the mediation process, and sets expectations and goals for the mediation.

Fact-Finding   During the mediation, each party presents its side of the issue in a joint session. Generally, the mediator meets with each party individually as well, to ask questions and ensure that everyone has the same facts and that the issues are clearly identified.

Options   As the parties present their facts and listen to those of the other side, alternative solutions may become clear; the mediator may guide the parties to these options as well.

Negotiating   Once the possible alternatives are on the table, the mediator facilitates negotiations during which the parties come to an agreement. Depending on the steps identified in the employer's policy, binding arbitration is often the next step taken in the ADR process.

Writing the Agreement   The mediator or the parties write the agreement that has been reached, and the parties sign it.

Mediation is a cost-effective solution that successfully resolves many employment disagreements. In mediation, the parties are in control of the decision-making process and resolving the conflict; the mediator facilitates the process that allows this to occur.

In either mediation or arbitration (unless it's a binding arbitration), either party may choose to continue the dispute by taking the matter to court if they're dissatisfied with the decision. In most cases, the use of either of these methods results in an agreement that is acceptable to both sides.

Constructive Confrontation

Constructive confrontation is a form of mediation developed by Guy Burgess, PhD, and Heidi Burgess, PhD, to resolve long-standing, deep-rooted conflicts about difficult, significant issues in organizations. This method is based on the idea that conflict can be healthy and is designed to move those in conflict from a focus on solving a large problem to removing the nonessential elements from the conflict until only the core issue remains.

Constructive confrontation begins with identifying the fundamental issue causing the conflict, the stakeholders, and their positions about the issue. The process then looks at other conflicts that arise as a result of the fundamental disagreement and how interactions between the parties, including their beliefs about the problem and how to handle it, limit their ability to resolve the conflict. These ancillary issues usually serve to increase the level of hostility surrounding the conflict without adding any benefit. The ancillary issues, when separated from the core issue, can be more easily resolved when treated as single issues. Once the ancillary issues are resolved, the core issue can be seen objectively and resolved more easily. Sometimes, the way the core problem or facts about the problem are stated causes one party to react harshly, further limiting resolution of the conflict. One party to the conflict may not like the process being used; others may believe that their points of view are being ignored. These and other issues can cause misunderstandings between the parties, escalating hostility, or can force participants to take sides, making it increasingly difficult to have meaningful discussions about the core issues. Constructive confrontation identifies ways in which the parties are exacerbating the problem and provides tools to help the parties work through the conflict, such as training, mediation, and facilitation.

Once the ancillary issues have been resolved, the parties can move on to the core issue. At this stage, the core issue can be seen more clearly, and the parties can seek alternative solutions that weren't readily apparent earlier in the process. The goal of constructive confrontation isn't necessarily to have the parties agree but to find a way to work together.

Labor Relations

The history of American labor relations begins with the formation of the Knights of Labor in 1869. This organization was an advocate of the 8-hour workday when 12 or 14 hours per day was the norm. By the end of the nineteenth century, unions became powerful enough to threaten business profitability, and federal antitrust laws were used to hinder their growth. In reaction, Congress enacted labor legislation that supported union growth. The pendulum swung back and forth until the 1960s, when the political focus turned to civil rights legislation. Although labor unions grew in importance for more than a century, in recent years they have lost some of their appeal to working people. The various labor laws that were enacted had a significant impact on business-labor relations in the United States.

The following sections explore such important aspects of labor relations as labor laws and organizations, employee rights, and union organization.

Collective bargaining can be a key aspect of labor relations. Some relevant aspects of collective bargaining, strikes, and approaches to dealing with them are discussed throughout this chapter, and the "Labor Unions" section in Chapter 11 explores these subjects in further detail.

Labor Laws and Organizations

While the body of labor laws related to unions is discussed in Appendix C, an examination of them is necessary here to understand the context of how employee rights within union membership is established.

The first piece of legislation to impact the labor movement was the Sherman Antitrust Act, passed in 1890. This legislation was originally intended to control business monopolies that conspired to restrain trade in the United States. The act allowed *injunctions*, court orders that either require or forbid an action by one party against another, to be issued against any person or group that conspired to restrain trade. It was first used against a labor union to obtain an injunction against the American Railway Union in 1894 to end its strike against the Pullman Palace Car Company.

The Clayton Act, passed in 1914, limited the use of injunctions to break strikes and exempted unions from the Sherman Act.

In 1926, Congress enacted the Railway Labor Act, the intention of which was to avoid interruptions due to strikes, protect the rights of employees to join a union, and allow for a "cooling-off" period of up to 90 days if the president deemed a strike to be a national emergency. Originally intended to cover the railroad companies, today this act applies to airlines as well.

The Norris-La Guardia Act was passed in 1932 and protected the rights of workers to organize and strike without the interference of federal injunctions. It also outlawed *yellow-dog contracts*, which employers had used to prevent employees from joining unions by requiring them to sign an agreement that the employee wasn't a member of a union, that the employee wouldn't become one in the future, and that joining a union would be sufficient grounds for dismissal.

In 1935, the NLRA, or Wagner Act, was passed as part of President Franklin Roosevelt's New Deal. At the time, it was referred to as *labor's bill of rights* and represented a marked change in government attitudes toward unions. The NLRA allowed employees to organize, bargain collectively, and engage in "concerted activities for the purpose of collective bargaining or other mutual aid or protection." The right to engage in concerted activities applies not only to union employees but to nonunion employees as well. The NLRA went on to identify five employer unfair labor practices and created the NLRB to enforce provisions of the act. The NLRB is charged with conducting elections and preventing and remedying unfair labor practices. The NLRB doesn't instigate actions on its own; it only responds to charges of unfair labor practices or petitions for representation elections filed in one of its offices.

In 1947, when a Republican majority was elected to Congress, the Taft-Hartley Act, or Labor Management Relations Act (LMRA), was passed in response to employer complaints about union abuses. Not surprisingly, union leaders decried the act as a "slave labor" law. The LMRA prohibits closed shops and allows union shops only with the consent of a majority of employees. It also provides that states have the right to outlaw closed shops and union shops by passing "right to work" laws. Jurisdictional strikes and secondary boycotts were also prohibited. When employers bring replacement workers in during an economic strike, the LMRA allows that they may permanently replace union workers; however, if the strike is in response to unfair labor practices committed by the employer, the union members will be reinstated when the strike ends. The LMRA established the Federal Mediation and Conciliation Service to "prevent or minimize interruptions of the free flow of commerce growing out of labor disputes" by providing mediation and conciliation services.

An important feature of Taft-Hartley is the power granted to the president to obtain an injunction ending a strike or lockout for an 80-day cooling-off period if, in the president's estimation, the continuation of the strike could "imperil the national health or safety." This power is rarely invoked because its record of leading to successful long-term agreements is mixed.

The Labor Management Reporting and Disclosure Act (LMRDA) of 1959, also known as the Landrum-Griffin Act, placed controls on internal union operations. Congress said this was necessary because of "a number of instances of breach of trust, corruption, disregard of the rights of individual employees, and other failures to observe high standards of responsibility and ethical conduct" on the part of union leadership. The act provided a bill of rights for union members that required equal rights for all members to participate in the union, granted freedom of speech and assembly for union members to gather and discuss union issues, and restricted increases in dues and assessments to those that were approved by majority vote of the union. Landrum-Griffin gave employees the right to sue the union and provided safeguards against retaliatory disciplinary actions by the union. The act also prohibited "extortionate picketing" by unions and required that union leadership elections be conducted no less often than every 3 years for local unions and every 5 years for national or international officers.

Employee Rights

The NLRA grants employees the right to organize, join unions, bargain collectively, and engage in other "concerted activities" for mutual aid or protection, as well as the right to refrain from doing so.

The NLRA also protects the right of employees to strike and identifies lawful versus unlawful strikes:

Lawful Strikes   One type of lawful strike is an economic strike in which the union stops working in an effort to obtain better pay, hours, or working conditions from the employer. In an economic strike, employers may hire permanent replacements for striking employees and aren't required to rehire the strikers if doing so means the replacement workers would be fired. If employees make an unconditional request to return to work, they may be recalled at a later time when openings occur.

The other type of lawful strike is one that occurs when the employer has committed an unfair labor practice and employees strike in protest. In this case, strikers may not be discharged or permanently replaced.

Unlawful Strikes   Strikes can be characterized as unlawful for several reasons:

- Strikes are unlawful if they support union unfair labor practices.
- Strikes are unlawful if they violate a no-strike clause in the contract.
- Lawful strikes can become unlawful if the strikers engage in serious misconduct.

Unfair Labor Practices

An *unfair labor practice (ULP)* is an action by an employer or a union that restrains or coerces employees from exercising their rights to organize and bargain collectively. Congress has identified ULPs for both employers and unions.

Employer Unfair Labor Practices

Employers who attempt to restrain or otherwise interfere with the right of employees to organize and bargain collectively can, in a worst-case scenario, be ordered by the NLRB to bargain with a union even if an election didn't take place or if the union loses an election. For that reason, it's extremely important for employers to be certain that all supervisory personnel are aware of what constitutes an unfair labor practice. An acronym that is helpful in avoiding prohibited activity is *TIPS*: employers may not threaten, interrogate, promise, or spy on employees.

Employer ULPs defined by the NLRA are as follows:

Interfere with, Restrain, or Coerce Unionization Efforts   Employers may not interfere in any way with attempts to unionize the workplace, including organizing activity, collective bargaining, or "concerted activity" engaged in by employees for mutual aid or protection. Interfering also includes inhibiting the free speech of employees who advocate unionization.

Dominate or Assist a Labor Organization   Employers are precluded from forming company unions that are controlled by management and, therefore, don't allow employees an independent representative. Employers are also prohibited from showing favoritism to one union over another.

Discriminate Against Employees   Employers may not discriminate against union members in any of the terms and conditions of employment. This includes taking disciplinary action against employees for participating in union activities.

Discriminate Against NLRB Activity   Employers may not retaliate against employees who have filed charges or participated in an investigation conducted by the NLRB.

Refuse to Bargain in Good Faith   Employers must bargain with a union once it has been designated by a majority of the employees and the union has made a demand to bargain.

Enter into a Hot-Cargo Agreement   It's unlawful for employers and unions to enter into a *hot-cargo agreement* in which, at the union's request, employers stop doing business with another employer.

Union Unfair Labor Practices

The LMRA identified the following union actions that were considered ULPs:

Restrain and Coerce Employees   Union conduct that interferes with an employee's right to choose a representative or to refrain from participating in organizing or collective bargaining activity is a ULP. The act identifies some of the coercive behavior that is unlawful, including assaults, threats of violence, and threats to interfere with continued employment. Unions are also held responsible for coercive acts committed by union members in the presence of union representatives if the representatives don't renounce the actions.

Restrain or Coerce Employers   Unions may not refuse to bargain with representatives chosen by the employer to negotiate with the union, or fine or expel from the union a supervisor based on the way the supervisor applies the contract during the course of business.

Unions may not insist that employers accept contract terms the union has negotiated with other bargaining units.

Require Employers to Discriminate   Unions may not require the employer to terminate an employee for working to decertify the union, or require employers to hire only union members or others of whom the union approves.

Refuse to Bargain in Good Faith   Unions must meet and confer with employer representatives at reasonable times to negotiate the terms and conditions of the contract.

Engage in Prohibited Strikes and Boycotts   Unions may not engage in hot-cargo actions or secondary boycotts.

Charge Excessive or Discriminatory Membership Fees   Membership fees must be reasonable and in line with the members' wages and industry standards.

Featherbedding   Unions may not require employers to pay for services that aren't rendered. For example, unions may not require employers to continue to pay employees to do jobs that have been rendered obsolete by changes in technology. An example of this is the fireman on a train who fed coal into the fire on a steam engine to keep the water hot enough to run the train. When diesel trains came along, the fireman was no longer needed to run the train. If a union insisted on keeping the firemen on the trains even though they weren't necessary, this was known as *featherbedding*.

Organizational and Recognitional Picketing   Although sometimes organizational and recognitional picketing are done lawfully, there are three instances in which they're unlawful:

- When another union has been lawfully recognized as the bargaining representative for the organization
- When a representation election has been held within the previous 12 months
- When a representation petition isn't filed within 30 days of the start of the picketing

Picketing is discussed more fully later in this chapter in the "Union Campaign Tactics" section.

Consequences of Unfair Labor Practices

If, as the result of an investigation, an employer or a union has been found to have committed a ULP, the NLRB can order remedial actions to be taken. The NLRB goal is to eliminate the ULP and to undo the effects of the illegal action to the extent possible. One of the requirements is that the offending party post notices in the workplace advising employees that the ULP will be discontinued and describing the actions to be taken to correct the offense:

Employer Remedies   The NLRB may require that the employer disband an employer-dominated union, reinstate employees to positions they held prior to the ULP, or engage in the collective bargaining process and sign a written agreement with the union.

Union Remedies   Unions may be required to agree to reinstatement of employees it caused to be terminated or rejected for employment, refund excessive dues with interest to members, or engage in the collective bargaining process and sign a written agreement with the employer.

Filing an Unfair Labor Practice Charge

ULP charges can be filed by an employee, an employer, or a union representative (the charging party) on a form available from the NLRB. Charges may be filed in person, by fax, or by mail at the regional office of the NLRB where the alleged violation occurred. The statute of limitations for ULPs requires that they be filed within 6 months of the incident.

Once the case has been received by the NLRB, the charged party is notified, invited to submit a written statement of the facts and circumstances about the case, and advised that they have the right to counsel. The case is then assigned to a board agent for investigation.

The board agent conducts interviews with all parties to the action, as well as with any witnesses, and makes a recommendation to the regional director for the disposition of the case. At this stage, the charges may be dismissed if unwarranted or result in a complaint if valid. Depending on the nature and severity of the offense, the complaint may result in an informal or formal settlement agreement. An informal settlement agreement requires that the charged party will take specified actions to remedy the ULP and doesn't involve a board order or court decree. A formal settlement involves a complaint issued by the NLRB against the charged party and results in a board order or court hearing.

An administrative law judge (ALJ), who conducts a hearing on the evidence, reviews the record and issues a "decision and order" for charges that aren't settled. If a party isn't satisfied with the order of the ALJ, they have 28 days to file an exception with the NLRB office in Washington, DC, which will issue a final order concurring with or amending the finding of the ALJ.

If the charged party isn't satisfied with the NLRB findings, an appeal can be filed with the U.S. Court of Appeals in the appropriate jurisdiction.

Union Organization

At the initial stages of a union-organizing campaign, signs of union activity are difficult to detect. By the time management notices something unusual is taking place, the organizing process may already be well underway.

One early indication that an organizing campaign has begun is a noticeable change in employee behavior. For example, employees may begin to challenge management decisions using union terminology related to benefits or employee rights. The earliest signs of a union presence are characterized by sometimes subtle changes in workforce relationships. First-line supervisors, those closest to rank-and-file employees who are the target of organizing efforts, are the ones most likely to notice that something about those relationships is different. How these changes manifest themselves is different in every company, but some signs that raise concern include the following:

- Groups of employees begin to congregate in unlikely places, scattering or ending their conversation when a supervisor or another manager appears.
- Employee behavior during meal and rest periods changes noticeably; instead of "hanging out," some employees are obviously occupied with nonwork activity.
- Absenteeism increases significantly in a short period of time for no apparent reason.

- Groups of employees challenge supervisors or managers with questions about benefits and employment practices in an uncharacteristically antagonistic manner.

- Former employees or newcomers approach employees in the parking lot or at public entrances to the building.

- People are observed taking down license numbers on employee cars.

- Employees who normally hang out with one group of co-workers befriend others, jumping from one group to another during meal or rest periods.

- Union slogans in the form of graffiti begin to appear in locations where employees congregate.

As organizing activity intensifies, the union may instigate a confrontation with the employer by coaching one or a group of employees to defy instructions for reasons that are protected by the NLRA, such as refusing to work because they aren't paid enough to do a particular job. If the refusal is based on an activity protected by the NLRA, employees may not be fired and must be treated as lawful strikers. An uninformed or unaware supervisor may unknowingly commit a ULP by disciplining employees for this behavior.

The Organizing Process

The recognition process has seven basic elements, but not all of them occur in every situation. The process consists of authorization cards, a demand for recognition, a petition to the NLRB, an NLRB conference, a preelection hearing, a campaign, and finally the election.

Authorization Cards

The goal of the union during the organizing process is to obtain signed authorization cards from employees. An *authorization card* is the means by which the NLRB determines that there is sufficient support for a union to hold an election. The NLRB will hold an election if 30 percent of the eligible employees in the anticipated bargaining unit sign the authorization cards. In practice, the union would like to have far more signed cards before submitting a petition for an election—generally it would like to have signed cards from at least 50 percent of the eligible employees.

Demand for Recognition

When the union has a sufficient number of signed authorization cards, it's ready to approach the employer with a demand for recognition. This usually comes in the form of a letter to the employer in which the union claims to represent a majority of workers and demands to be recognized by the employer as the exclusive bargaining agent for employees. The demand may also be made in person when a union representative approaches any member of the management team, including a first-line supervisor, offering proof that a majority of employees want the union to represent them. It's crucial that whoever is approached doesn't respond in a way that could be construed as recognition by the union, politely referring the union to the HR department or a senior member of the management team.

Union representatives may also approach employers requesting a neutrality agreement or a card-check election. In a neutrality agreement, an employer agrees not to say or do anything in opposition to the union. A card-check election means that the employer agrees to recognize the union based on signed authorization cards. At a minimum, agreeing to either situation limits the employer's ability to resist unionization efforts. Agreeing to one of these alternatives may be interpreted as voluntary recognition of the union.

An employer may choose to recognize a union voluntarily under some circumstances, but this should be done only after conferring with legal counsel. One-way unions may seek voluntary recognition is to approach management with signed authorization cards to have management witness its majority status by accepting the cards. A number of NLRB cases have involved union claims that management has witnessed majority status by counting the authorization cards, so supervisors and management should be made aware of the consequences of handling the cards.

Petitioning the NLRB

If management refuses to grant voluntary recognition, the union files a petition for an election with the NLRB, along with evidence of employee interest in union representation. The NLRB reviews the petition to determine that it represents an appropriate level of interest in union representation and that signatures on the petition or authorization cards are valid.

NLRB Conference/Preelection Hearing Issues

When the NLRB is satisfied with the legitimacy of the petition, it schedules a conference with the employer and employee representatives. During the conference, an NLRB representative reviews any jurisdictional issues, the makeup of the bargaining unit, the eligibility of voters in the proposed unit, and the time and place of the election. If either party disputes issues related to the bargaining unit, legitimacy of the authorization cards, or timing of the election, a formal hearing is held by the NLRB to resolve those issues.

Bargaining Units

The makeup of the bargaining unit is a critical factor to both union and employer points of view. The union wants the unit to be as large as possible and include a majority of employees who are in favor of the union. Management, of course, wants to limit the size of the unit and include a majority of employees who choose to remain union-free.

The NLRA grants broad discretion for bargaining unit determinations to the NLRB. Guidance in the act is that "...the unit appropriate for the purposes of collective bargaining shall be the employer unit, craft unit, plant unit, or subdivision thereof." Aside from that, the only specifics provided are that a bargaining unit may not consist of both professional and nonprofessional employees unless the professional employees vote to be included in the unit, and that individuals hired as guards to protect the employer's premises or property may not be included in a unit with other employees. The NLRB looks at several objective criteria to devise a bargaining unit that is appropriate for the individual situation, beginning with determining whether there is a "community of interest" in the unit—that is, that the interests of members of the unit are sufficiently similar to preclude disagreements during the bargaining process. The NLRB looks as well at factors such as how the employer administers its business (whether it uses standard policies across the entire company or diverse policies in different locations), geography (how far apart the locations are in the proposed unit), whether the unit is made up of employees involved in a major process of the company, whether employees are cross-trained or frequently transfer between locations, what unit the employees want to be part of, and any relevant collective bargaining history. Finally, the NLRB considers the extent to which employees are already organized, although the act makes it clear that this may not be the determining factor.

Bargaining units may consist of two or more employees in one employer location or employees in two or more locations of a single employer. If there is an employer industry association, the bargaining unit may include employees of two or more employers in several locations.

Some employees aren't eligible for inclusion in a bargaining unit. These include confidential employees, supervisors, and management personnel. The act also excludes independent contractors and some agricultural laborers from bargaining units.

Temporary Workers

In August 2000, the NLRB made a significant change to its previous rulings on the inclusion of temporary workers in an employer's bargaining unit in a case involving M. B. Sturgis, Inc. Sturgis is a gas hose manufacturer in Missouri that was the target of an organizing campaign. When the union petitioned for an election, Sturgis wanted to include the temp workers on its site in the bargaining unit, but the union didn't want them included. The NLRB reversed two longstanding positions in this case by deciding that the determining factor in this decision is whether a community of interest in wages, scheduling, and working conditions exists between the regular employees and the temp workers, and that a unit including temp workers isn't considered a multiemployer unit needing the consent of both employers.

Union Campaign Tactics

At their peak in 1953, unions represented 35.7 percent of the private sector workforce. According to the Bureau of Labor Statistics, unions represented only 7.8 percent of the private sector workforce in 2005. However, unions are far more prevalent in today's public sector: 36.5 percent of public sector employers are unionized. As unions struggle to maintain membership levels, they have had to reexamine their strategies for attracting new members.

As the economy in the United States moved from a manufacturing to an informational base, the workforce changed from predominantly blue-collar workers who were the traditional union members to white-collar workers who haven't traditionally been attracted by union membership. Although the strategies vary with each union, the general trend is to find ways of attracting white-collar workers to union membership. Once potential members indicate interest in unionizing their place of work, a number of methods are used to organize the employees:

Internet   Many unions have sophisticated websites that provide information for employees who are interested in forming a union. The sites contain information on labor laws, information on unfair labor practices, advice on beginning a campaign, and opportunities for interested workers to contact union personnel.

Home Visits   This tactic is most often used when the union is trying to gain initial supporters in the company. It provides an opportunity for organizers to have private conversations with potential inside organizers. Because home visits are expensive for the union and can be viewed as an unwanted invasion of privacy, they aren't widely used.

Inside Organizing   The most effective organizing process occurs when one or more employees work from within the organization to build support for the union. Insiders can use their influence on co-workers, identify those most likely to respond to the effort, and encourage participation.

Salting   *Salting* occurs when a union hires a person to apply for a job at an organization they have targeted. Once hired, the employee acts in much the same way as an inside organizer who was already employed by the company.

Meetings   Union-organizing meetings bring together experienced organizers, inside organizers from the company, and employees who are undecided about supporting the organizing process. Meetings provide opportunities to communicate the benefits of membership and exert peer pressure on potential members.

Leafleting   The goal of union leaflets is to point out the advantages the union will bring to the workforce and to counter information that management provides to employees about the benefits of remaining union-free. Leaflets are generally used when the organizing campaign is well underway.

Media   Unions have developed expertise in getting their message out. When management commits a ULP or takes any action the union perceives as unfavorable, the union will issue a press release that interprets the action in the most favorable way for the union. For example, in 1999, the Union of Needletrades, Industrial, and Textile Employees (UNITE) was conducting an organizing campaign at Loehmann's Department Store in New York City. With little more than a month before the scheduled NLRB election, the store fired one of the leaders of the organizing campaign. UNITE issued a press release that concentrated on the fact that the employee had an exemplary work record at the store and was a single mother. The union went on to allege that the store had spied on the employee during her lunch break in order to find a reason to fire her. The union used this as the basis for encouraging the public to boycott the store.

Picketing   *Picketing* occurs when a group of employees patrols the entrance to a business in order to inform customers and the public about disputes or to prevent deliveries to a business that the union is trying to influence in some way. It can also occur to advise the public about ULPs the union believes the employer has committed. The NLRB recognizes three types of picketing:

Organizational Picketing   *Organizational picketing* occurs when the union wants to attract employees to become members and authorize the union to represent them with the employer.

Recognitional Picketing   *Recognitional picketing* occurs when the union wants the employer to recognize the union as the employees' representative for collective bargaining purposes. The NLRA places a limit of 30 days on recognitional picketing, after which a petition for an election must be filed.

Informational or Publicity Picketing   *Informational* or *publicity picketing* is done to truthfully advise the public that an employer is a union-free workplace.

There are three instances when picketing is prohibited: when another union has been lawfully recognized as the bargaining representative for the organization; when a representation election has been held within the previous 12 months; and when a representation petition isn't filed within 30 days of the start of the picketing.

NLRB Elections

The purpose of an NLRB election is to determine whether a majority of employees in the unit desire to be represented by the union. During the time between the NLRB decision and election day, both management and the union present the case for their point of view to employees in the bargaining unit. The employer is required to post notices of the election in "conspicuous" locations frequented by employees in the bargaining unit. Within two days of the consent or direction to hold an election, the employer must provide an *Excelsior list* in electronic format containing the full names, work locations, shifts, job classifications, and "available" contact information including the personal emails and phone numbers of all employees in the proposed bargaining unit to the union.

A preelection hearing will be scheduled within eight days from the date of service of the Notice of Hearing. The purpose of the hearing is to determine if a question of representation exists. The company must complete a Statement of Position form that identifies any issues they wish to raise at the hearing. The NLRB in their 2015 updates identified what must be addressed at the preelection hearing. These include:

- Jurisdiction
- Labor organization status
- Bars to elections
- Appropriate unit
- Multifacility and multiemployer issues
- Expanding and contracting unit issues
- Employee status (for instance, if the classification of independent contractors concerns more than 20 percent of the unit)
- Seasonal employees
- Inclusion of professional employees or guards with other employees
- Eligibility formulas
- Craft and healthcare employees

The NLRB's new rules specifically list the existence of a joint employer relationship as one of the issues that must be litigated at the preelection hearing. However, except for jurisdiction, the employer will waive these issues if not raised in the Statement of Position.

The regional director of the NLRB will schedule the election for the earliest date practicable. On the day of the election, neither the employer nor the union may conduct campaign activities in or around the polling area.

To be eligible to vote in the election, an employee must have worked during the pay period prior to the election and must be employed by the business on the day of the election. Employees who are sick, are on vacation, are on military leave, or have been temporarily laid off may vote subject to rules established by the NLRA. Economic strikers who have been replaced by bona fide permanent employees may vote in any election that takes place within 12 months of the beginning of the strike.

The NLRB representative counts the votes at the end of the voting period and provides the vote count to the parties at that time. If the union receives 50 percent plus one vote, the union is certified as the bargaining representative for the unit. In the event of a tie vote, the union isn't certified.

After a vote, the party that lost the election may file charges that the prevailing party interfered with the election results by committing ULPs. The party filing the charge must also include a written offer of proof in support of their claim, in addition to providing the names of any witnesses to the ULP. The NLRB will investigate the charges in accordance with its administrative procedures and, should they be justified, will take remedial action against the offending party.

Norma Rae

For those unfamiliar with the organizing process, the 1979 movie *Norma Rae* provides dramatic insight into the unionization of a garment factory in the South. Based on a true story, the movie follows the efforts of a union organizer from New York to build support for a union in a textile factory in a small southern town. The organizer begins by visiting the homes of some of the workers, distributing leaflets at the front gate of the factory, and enlisting the support of one of the workers who becomes the inside organizer. This insider lends credibility to the union representative by introducing him to co-workers, sponsoring organizing meetings, and obtaining signed union-authorization cards. In the course of the campaign, management commits several ULPs. One of the final scenes dramatizes the vote count: As the NLRB official observes, representatives for management and the union count each vote.

(Fields, Sally. *Norma Rae*. Film. Directed by Martin Ritt. Los Angeles: Twentieth Century Fox, 1979).

Bars to Elections

The NLRA won't allow elections in some circumstances. The following are known as *election bars*:

Contract Bar   Except in very limited circumstances, the NLRB won't direct an election while a bargaining unit is covered by a valid collective bargaining agreement.

Statutory Bar   The NLRA prohibits an election in a bargaining unit that had a valid election during the preceding 12-month period.

Certification-Year Bar   When the NLRB has certified a bargaining representative, an election won't be ordered for at least one year.

Blocking-Charge Bar   An election petition will be barred when there is a pending ULP charge.

Voluntary-Recognition Bar   If an employer has voluntarily recognized a union as the representative for a bargaining unit, an election will be barred for a reasonable period of time to allow the parties to negotiate a contract.

Prior-Petition Bar   When a union petitioning for an election withdraws the petition prior to the election, then no elections will be approved for six months.

Union Decertification

Employees may petition the NLRB for *decertification* if they're dissatisfied with the union's performance. A decertification petition requires signatures of at least 30 percent of the employees before the NLRB will act on it. Employees may want to decertify the union for a variety of reasons, including poor performance by the union in its representation of the employees or the desire of the employees to be represented by a different union. Decertification may also occur because the employee relationship with management is a good one, and employees no longer feel the need for union representation. It's critical for HR professionals and management to understand that the employer may not encourage or support employees in the decertification process. Doing so constitutes a ULP and may well result in employees being compelled to continue to be represented by the union.

Union Deauthorization

Employees may want to maintain the union but remove a union security clause, such as union-shop, dues check-off, or maintenance of membership clause (discussed in the next section). The NLRB will approve *deauthorization* based on a petition by 30 percent or more of the members of the bargaining unit. As with decertification, employers must not participate in the effort to deauthorize the union, because doing so is considered to be a ULP.

Risk Overview

Risk management (RM) activities touch all functional areas of human resources (HR) as well as activities in virtually all other business functions. Risk is inherent in legal compliance, employee safety and health, and security, not to mention business continuity, workplace privacy, and other issues.

The following sections provide an in-depth look at identifying, assessing/analyzing, and managing risks in the HR function. For HR professionals, the focus of these activities is on managing those aspects of risk that impact the people, assets, and functioning of an organization.

Risk Identification

An argument could be made, and often is, that risk is inherent in any activity. The magnitude of the risk often determines whether an activity is pursued, and this of course is true for human resource activities. HR risks can be classified into one of the following five areas:

Legal Compliance   Employers are at risk for potential lawsuits arising from employment practices that are out of compliance with laws and regulations designed to protect employees from unlawful activities such as discrimination, wrongful termination, and sexual harassment. Failure to comply with legal requirements has the potential to cost employers millions of dollars in legal expenses, judgments, penalties, and fines.

Safety and Health   Risks for illness and injury exist in virtually every workplace, not just those involving the operation of heavy equipment or dangerous situations such as those faced by first responders. Employees who work in pleasant, climate-controlled environments face the possibility of repetitive stress injuries (RSI), emotional and physical stress, and ergonomic strains.

Security   Security risks can affect financial operations and practices, physical assets such as buildings and equipment, information assets such as documentation and data storage, and the people who work in organizations. At times, people may be the source of risk, as in the case of a hacker or an embezzler; at other times, they may need to be protected from a risk, such as a fire or natural disaster.

Business Continuity   The ability to continue operating a business can be adversely affected by environmental disasters, organized or deliberate disruptions, loss of utilities and public services, equipment or system failures, serious information security incidents, or other emergencies. The HR responsibility for mitigating risks in this area is to develop programs that protect human assets.

Workplace Privacy   In most organizations, HR is responsible for maintaining the privacy of highly confidential employee information. Risks to this information range from identity theft to the release of private health information and improper workplace-monitoring procedures.

The process of identifying and assessing risks makes it possible for organizations to take steps to mitigate or prevent losses. The following sections examine the assessment of risk in each of these areas. Following them, the "Risk Management" section discusses methods for managing and reducing risks in each area. But first you will look at tools that can help identify risk.

HR Tools to Identify and Assess Risk

One way for HR professionals to identify and assess risks is to ask questions of executives, managers, and employees and to learn what challenges they face in the course of doing their jobs. Often, informal conversations provide a wealth of useful information that can improve HR services as well as provide insight into potential risks facing the organization. Two more formal HR tools are used to identify and assess potential HR risks: the HR audit and the workplace investigation. Both tools have multiple purposes but easily adapt to risk management purposes.

HR Audits

An HR audit is one of the most useful and versatile tools available for HR professionals. An audit can be used to see what HR functions need to be done, to identify opportunities for improving business results, and to identify organizational risks. A comprehensive audit is one that reviews HR activities in all functional areas. The following is a brief overview of some components included in an audit:

Organization of HR Function An audit begins by looking at the structure of the HR department and reviewing the organization chart. It verifies the existence of current job descriptions for all department positions and ensures the existence of clear accountability for different functions. The audit should evaluate the size and effectiveness of the HR team, ratio of HR staff to total employees, commitment to professional development for the team, and how well the team meets ongoing customer needs.

The audit examines whether HR programs align to organization goals, reviews the human capital management plan if one exists, evaluates the department mission statement, and analyzes the budget.

Workforce Planning and Employment An HR audit examines the recruiting philosophy and process, whether the company promotes from within, job-posting and candidate-sourcing procedures and the approval process, and the existence and status of affirmative action and diversity programs. A review of the staffing needs analysis and its use in projecting the availability of candidates for future needs is based on labor market demographics. The audit verifies the job analysis process and determines whether job descriptions include essential job functions.

The selection process is examined for HR's level of involvement and how interviews are conducted, whether there are seasonal or other periodic hiring cycles, how many people interview candidates, and whether interviewers receive training. The audit also analyzes any preemployment tests that are used and ensures that they're valid and reliable. The use of alternative staffing methods and hiring cycles is reviewed as well. The existence, accuracy, consistency, and legality of reference and background checks are examined.

HR Development An HR audit looks at learning and development practices and programs, the existence of regular training programs, and performance-management practices. The performance evaluation process is assessed for adequacy, equity, and content.

Compensation and Benefits   The compensation philosophy is reviewed for consistency with the practices and level of communication of the organization. The adequacy of compensation procedures is examined, and the frequency of salary survey comparisons is analyzed. Salary administration practices, including pay ranges, compression, salary budgets, and incentive pay practices, are reviewed.

The benefits program philosophy and policies are reviewed for comparability to competitor programs. Healthcare programs are analyzed for cost containment and plan content. Programs for controlling absenteeism, unemployment, and other costs are analyzed. Time-off policies and accrual practices are also examined as part of the audit.

Employee Relations   An HR audit assesses the organization's employee relations (ER) philosophy for alignment with corporate goals and reviews practices for conflict resolution and disciplinary procedures. The existence of an employee communication philosophy is reviewed, and written communication tools, such as the handbook, policies, procedures, work rules, code of conduct, and behavior expectations, are examined. Orientation programs are assessed for content and frequency.

Absentee rates and turnover demographics are analyzed; exit interview practices and reporting are examined. Procedures for voluntary and involuntary organization exits are reviewed. Diversity practices are analyzed.

Labor Relations   The existence of labor unions, collective bargaining agreements, and union avoidance practices are examined.

HR Risk Management   Legal compliance for all applicable federal, state, and local governments is reviewed. Safety, health, and wellness programs are analyzed.

HR audits result in a comprehensive review of current practices and can highlight areas in need of improvement. Audits can also identify opportunities to design service improvements that align HR programs with organizational goals and add value to the business.

Workplace Investigations

When management receives complaints about inappropriate or unlawful behavior; identifies a potential financial loss from embezzlement or pilferage; receives accusations from co-workers, customers, or members of the public about an employee; or becomes aware of some other type of loss, one important tool for assessing the risk is a prompt and thorough *workplace investigation*. When the loss involves employees or an issue of noncompliance with employment laws or regulations, the responsibility for conducting investigations often falls on HR professionals. It's important for investigations to be seen as credible by all stakeholders, so they must be conducted in a way that protects the employees who make accusations and the individuals accused or suspected of wrongdoing. It's equally important that workplace investigations are conducted in a way that protects the organization from liability.

The best way to prepare for an investigation is to establish a procedure at a time when no investigation is pending so that when it's necessary, the HR professional has a guide to ensure that all necessary steps are taken. Using the same protocol for all investigations provides consistency in the process and assures the subjects of investigations (and the courts, if an employee takes legal action) that the investigator acted with integrity and the process treated everyone involved in a fair manner. An effective, prompt, thorough workplace investigation includes the following steps:

1. Begin planning the investigation immediately upon receiving the complaint.

2. Determine whether an employee or third-party investigator would be the most appropriate for the situation. For example, if the situation involves executives, or employees on the HR team are too close to the parties or situation to remain objective, a third-party investigator may be required.

3. Develop a clear strategy before beginning to collect evidence or conduct interviews.

4. Compile a list of individuals to be interviewed and documentation to be collected.

5. Prepare a list of questions based on the information presented by the complainant.

6. Conduct interviews, taking contemporaneous notes; ask each interviewee to provide a signed, written statement, or have them review and sign notes at the conclusion of the interview:

   - Interview the complainant first and obtain names of possible witnesses.

   - Interview witnesses.

   - Interview the accused.

7. At the conclusion of each interview, make note of the interviewee's demeanor and openness, keeping the notes free from personal opinions and judgments.

8. With each interviewee, stress the importance of confidentiality for the integrity of the investigation, and reiterate company policy with regard to retaliation against accusers and witnesses.

9. At the conclusion of the interview with the accused, clearly state that retaliation or intimidation of those interviewed during the investigation isn't acceptable and that the accused shouldn't attempt to discuss the situation with the complainant or witnesses.

10. If the accused provides an alternate description of events, completely investigate the new information, re-interviewing witnesses as necessary.

11. Conclude the investigation:

    - Make a finding of fact based on the evidence obtained and observations during the interviews.

    - Include any relevant documentation that supports the finding.

    - Evaluate possible reasons for false accusations and the credibility of those involved.

    - Notify the complainant and the accused of the results of the investigation.

12. As appropriate, take disciplinary action consistent with organizational policy.

13. In some cases, there will be no clear finding; when that occurs, explain this to the complainant and accused, and document the finding.

14. Compile and close the investigation file, including signed statements from witnesses, complainant, and accused; relevant documentation; and the original handwritten notes with transcribed copies.

15. Communicate resolution only to those who need to know the information, and maintain the investigation file in a secure location.

16. If necessary, and without violating confidentiality of those involved, take appropriate action to subdue rumors about the situation.

Workplace investigations, properly conducted, document actions taken by the employer to respond to accusations of wrongdoing. Particularly in sexual harassment investigations, this can make the difference in whether the employer will be held liable if a lawsuit is filed.

Taking clear, relevant notes in investigations is crucial, but it's essential that those notes be free from any comments or observations that could be construed as prejudicial. It's important to keep in mind that investigatory notes are discoverable in lawsuits unless they involve communication with legal counsel.

Risk Assessment

Risk is inherent in virtually any area of HR practice, so how does an HR professional ensure that those risks are minimized? *Risk assessment* is the process used to determine the likelihood that an organization will be affected by a particular risk, such as an employee injured as the result of unsafe working conditions or a case of identity theft resulting from a breach of confidential employee information. An assessment estimates the cost of the loss if one should happen and the impact it would have on the ability of the organization to continue operations. With this knowledge, it's possible to identify which losses are most likely to occur and what controls must be in place to prevent them. Identifying and ranking risks provides organizations with the opportunity to be proactive and implement controls to prevent losses.

Some useful tools for assessing risk were introduced earlier in the "HR Tools to Identify and Assess Risk" section. This section will discuss more specifically assessing legal compliance, health and safety, and security risks.

Assessing Legal Compliance Risks

Mitigating or preventing losses occurring as the result of noncompliance with the legal requirements for employment practices isn't solely the responsibility of the HR function, but it's HR's responsibility to ensure that members of the management team are aware of the laws, regulations, and potential costs to the organization for failing to comply.

Table 6.3 summarizes the federal legislation that affects risk management activities for which you must be prepared on the PHR exam. All are included in Appendix C.

TABLE 6.3 Federal legislation governing risk management activities

Type	Enforcement agency
Civil rights	Equal Employment Opportunity Commission (EEOC) and/or Office of Federal Contract Compliance Programs (OFCCP)
Corporate governance	Securities and Exchange Commission (SEC), Occupational Safety and Health Administration (OSHA)
Work/Life Discrimination	EEOC
Health and safety	OSHA, Mine Safety and Health Administration (MSHA)
Privacy	Civil litigation
Security	SEC
Substance abuse	Drug-free Workplace Act, contracting government agency

Assessing Safety and Health Risks

Any discussion of managing safety and health risks must begin with the Occupational Safety and Health Administration (OSHA), because it sets standards that exert overwhelming influence on those issues in the workplace. OSHA statistics, developed through the recordkeeping requirements of the Occupational Safety and Health Act of 1970, show significant improvements in workplace safety and health since 1971; fatalities have been reduced by 62 percent, and injury and illness rates have been reduced by 42 percent, even though the workforce has more than doubled during the same time period. These improvements in working conditions are a result of many factors—the change from a manufacturing to a service economy and improvements in technology among them—but underlying them all has been OSHA, with its unwavering focus on establishing standards to improve health and safety in the American workplace.

The Bureau of Labor Statistics (bls.gov) reported that there were more than 2.8 million nonfatal workplace injuries and illnesses reported by private employers in 2017. The purpose of assessing risk for environmental health and safety issues is to prevent those illnesses and injuries from occurring in the first place, to protect workers, and in the long run, to reduce the costs of turnover and workers' compensation, as well as to increase productivity and eliminate OSHA fines and penalties.

Environmental Health Hazards

Environmental health hazards in the modern workplace come in many forms, from physical hazards such as noise and extreme temperatures to chemicals used for everything from making copies to manufacturing products to biological hazards from viruses and bacteria. The effects of these various hazards differ between individual employees—some are more affected than others—so employers must take steps to prevent serious health consequences in the workplace. Table 6.4 lists some of the more common environmental health hazards.

TABLE 6.4   Examples of environmental health hazards

Chemical	Physical	Biological
Asbestos	Ergonomic design	Bacteria
Battery acid	Stress	Contaminated water
Corrosives	Extreme temperatures	Dusts
Gas fumes	Light, noise	Fungi
Pesticides	Electrical currents	Molds
Polyurethane foam	Radiation	Plants
Solvents	Vibrations	Viruses

Chemical Health Hazards

Many of the OSHA standards deal with specific *chemical health hazards* in the workplace. Every chemical present in the workplace should have a *safety data sheet (SDS)* from the chemical manufacturer to provide information on how to both prevent and treat an injury. The SDS identifies the ingredients in the substance, how the substance reacts to changes in the atmosphere (such as at what temperature it will boil or become a vapor), and information about its explosive and flammable qualities. The SDS tells employees whether the substance is stable or unstable, what materials it must not be in contact with, and what additional hazards are present when it decomposes or degrades.

Most importantly for safety programs, the SDS provides information about how the chemical may be absorbed by the body; whether it can be inhaled, can be ingested, or can enter through the skin; whether it's carcinogenic; and what protective equipment is required to prevent illness when handling the substance.

Some chemicals, known as *teratogens*, have no effect on a pregnant woman but do affect an unborn child. Some employers, concerned about the health of the employee and her child as well as about potential liability, have developed policies to protect the fetus. These policies, although well-intentioned, violate the Pregnancy Discrimination Act (PDA), which prohibits sex-specific fetal protection policies.

Physical Health Hazards

Many *physical health hazards* are easy to identify and remedy. One such hazard would be an open hole without any warning signs or barriers to prevent someone from accidentally falling. Another would be an electrical or telephone cord that isn't covered or secured to prevent someone from tripping. Another physical hazard would be a walk-in freezer storage unit that couldn't be opened from inside the unit. Other physical hazards occurring in the workplace are less obvious:

Ergonomics   In 1700, Bernardino Ramazzini published his "Discourse on the Diseases of Workers," which sought to connect illnesses with environmental conditions in the workplace. One of the connections he made was to identify "irregular" or "unnatural" body movements that affect the safety and health of workers. We know this concept today as *ergonomics*—the science that addresses the way a physical environment is designed and how efficient and safe that design is for the people in the environment.

Poor ergonomic designs can cause *musculoskeletal disorders (MSDs)*. An MSD is the result of repeated stress to various parts of the body (including the back, arms, shoulders, and other areas) that is caused by the way tasks are performed. MSDs are referred to by several other names as well, including *repetitive stress injuries (RSIs)* and *cumulative trauma injuries (CTIs)*. MSD injuries that can result from poor ergonomics in the workplace include tendonitis, bursitis, and carpal tunnel syndrome. According to the Bureau of Labor Statistics (BLS), these and other MSD injuries account for one-third of workplace injuries and illnesses each year, which makes them the largest job-related health and safety problem in the United States. Factors that contribute to MSDs include awkward postures; forceful lifting, pushing, or pulling; prolonged repetitive motions; contact stress; and vibration, such as that which occurs while using power tools for an extended period of time.

 Real World Scenario

Automobile Workers vs. Johnson Controls, Inc.

Johnson Controls, Inc., manufactures batteries, a process in which lead is a primary ingredient. Occupational exposure to lead can have serious health consequences, including posing a risk to the health of an unborn child. Prior to 1964, Johnson Controls didn't employ women in any of the battery-manufacturing jobs in its plant. After passage of the Civil Rights Act in 1964, women were given the opportunity to work in those jobs.

In June 1977, Johnson developed its first fetal protection policy, which stated, "Protection of the health of the unborn child is the immediate and direct responsibility of the prospective parents. While the medical profession and the company can support them in the exercise of this responsibility, it cannot assume it for them without simultaneously infringing their rights as persons." Although this policy didn't exclude women from the manufacturing jobs, the company discouraged women who wanted to have children from taking these jobs and required them to sign a statement that they had been advised of the risks of lead exposure to a fetus.

In 1982, after eight women became pregnant while maintaining high levels of lead in their blood, the policy changed: "Women who are pregnant or who are capable of bearing children will not be placed into jobs involving lead exposure or which could expose them to lead through the exercise of job bidding, bumping, transfer, or promotion rights." The policy went on to define lead levels that would make a job inaccessible to women and required that women who wanted to work in those positions supply medical proof of their inability to bear children.

In 1984, a class-action petition challenging the fetal protection policy was filed. Among the individuals in the class were Mary Craig, who had chosen to be sterilized so that she could keep her job; Elsie Nason, a 50-year-old divorcee who had been transferred out of a job where she was exposed to lead to a job that paid less; and Donald Penney, who had requested and been denied a leave of absence so that the lead level in his blood could be lowered in order for him to become a father.

Johnson Controls argued that its policy was a business necessity.

Both the District Court and the Federal Court of Appeals found for Johnson Controls. The case was then appealed to the U.S. Supreme Court in 1990, where the lower court decisions were reversed. The Supreme Court found that there was clear bias because the policy required only female employees to prove that they weren't capable of conceiving children, and it was therefore in violation of the PDA.

The Supreme Court ruled that "Decisions about the welfare of the next generation must be left to the parents who conceive, bear, support, and raise them, rather than to the employers who hire those parents."

Development of an ergonomics program provides a means by which employers can determine whether MSDs are a problem in their workplaces. An effective ergonomics program requires management support and involves employees in the process. After a review of OSHA logs and workers' compensation claims for injury patterns, an analysis of job tasks, beginning with an observation of the work area while work is being done, is needed to determine whether the risk factors for potential injury exist. Jobs with poor ergonomics may be redesigned to make them less hazardous and reduce injuries.

OSHA has developed tools to assist employers in reducing potential ergonomic hazards. The tools are provided in a checklist for various activities that are statistically prone to ergonomic injury, including handling baggage, sewing, and working at a computer workstation. The checklists provide guidance in the form of basic principles that can be used to reduce ergonomic injuries. For example, the computer workstation checklist provides guidelines for the placement of the monitor, keyboard, mouse, desk, chair, and telephone and discusses some common problems that can occur. You can view the checklists online at www.osha.gov/dts/osta/oshasoft/index.html#eTools. In addition to those currently available, OSHA is in the process of developing similar checklists for specific industries and jobs.

Job-Related Stress In 1999, the National Institute for Occupational Safety and Health (NIOSH) published the results of a study entitled *Stress at Work*, which defined job *stress* as "harmful physical and emotional responses that occur when the requirements of the job do not match the capabilities, resources, or needs of the worker." When job stress is added to personal factors in an employee's life, such as a sick child or financial concerns, the effect on job performance can be magnified. Dr. Hans Selye, an endocrinologist, is generally credited with identifying stress as an influencer of health and well-being. He identified three stages of stress: arousal, resistance, and exhaustion. Table 6.5 describes the three stages of stress and some of the related symptoms.

TABLE 6.5 Stages and symptoms of stress

Stage	Physical	Emotional	Mental
Arousal	Teeth grinding Insomnia	Irritability Anxiety	Forgetfulness Inability to concentrate
Resistance	Fatigue without a cause	Mood swings Social withdrawal Resentment Indifference Defiance	Procrastination Indecision
Exhaustion	Headaches Chronic fatigue Indigestion Intestinal problems	Chronic depression Hostility Isolation	Disorganization Poor judgment Disillusionment

Stress-related illnesses such as allergies, heart disease, panic attacks, and other diseases affect productivity, as does burnout, which can be the result of long-term, unrelenting job stress.

High levels of job stress can result in increased turnover, low morale, increased tardiness and absenteeism, reduced productivity, poor product quality, and increased accidents on the job. All of these negatively affect the bottom line.

The NIOSH study identified six circumstances that can lead to job stress. Table 6.6 explains these circumstances.

TABLE 6.6   Job stressors identified by NIOSH

Stressor	Characteristics
Task design	Heavy workloads and infrequent rest breaks
	Long, hectic hours
	Shift work
	Routine tasks with little inherent meaning
	Tasks that don't use employee skills
	Little or no control over daily work
Management style	Lack of participation in decisions that affect employees
	Poor organizational communication
	Lack of family-friendly policies
Interpersonal relationships	Poor social environment
	Lack of support or help from co-workers and supervisors
Work roles	Conflicting or uncertain job expectations
	Too much responsibility
	Too many "hats to wear"
Career concerns	Job insecurity
	Lack of opportunity for growth, advancement, or promotion
	Lack of preparation for rapid changes
Environmental conditions	Unpleasant or dangerous physical conditions such as crowding, noise, or air pollution
	Ergonomic problems

Source: NIOSH "Stress at Work" booklet

The NIOSH study recommends a two-pronged approach to reducing job stress: organizational change and stress management. Organizational changes can take the form of employee-recognition programs, career development, a culture that values individual employees, and employer actions consistent with the organization's stated values. Stress management programs are, to a certain extent, dependent on the needs of individual employees, because people react differently to job stressors. These programs include training for employees about the sources of stress and how it affects health and teaching stress reduction skills. Managers can encourage employees to reduce the effects of stress by balancing their work with private activities, maintaining an exercise program, and building a support network at work and at home.

The full NIOSH study is available free of charge at www.cdc.gov/niosh/topics/stress/?.

Biological Health Hazards

Biological health hazards come in many forms, from unsanitary conditions in a food preparation area to serious diseases contracted through needlestick injuries. Infectious diseases are spread by different means to employees, but the resulting impact on the health of the workforce or the community can be substantial. Although the healthcare and food-preparation industries are at greater risk than other industries, HR professionals should understand the implications of infectious disease in all workplaces:

HIV/AIDS   Human immunodeficiency virus (HIV) and acquired immune deficiency syndrome (AIDS) are blood-borne pathogens transmitted through blood or other bodily fluids. For this reason, transmission to co-workers in workplaces other than in the healthcare industry is relatively unlikely. Persons with HIV/AIDS are protected by the ADA; as long as they're able to perform their essential job functions, they're entitled to remain employed.

HBV   The hepatitis B virus (HBV) is another blood-borne pathogen posing risks to healthcare workers. Because transmission chiefly occurs as the result of an accidental needle stick, healthcare workers are at the greatest risk of infection in the workplace. The CDC recommends that healthcare workers at a high risk of infection be vaccinated to prevent them from contracting the disease.

Tuberculosis   Tuberculosis is a lung disease that is spread through the air. Exposure occurs when someone with TB coughs or sneezes, expelling pathogens. Those at higher risk for contracting TB in the workplace are people who share the same breathing space, such as co-workers or healthcare workers, particularly in nursing homes.

Severe Acute Respiratory Syndrome (SARS)   According to the CDC, there have been no outbreaks of SARS since 2004. Between the initial outbreak in November 2002 and the last known outbreak in April 2004, it affected business travel and had a negative effect on some industries, particularly the travel industry. SARS appears to be transmitted by close person-to-person contact when an infected person coughs or sneezes. Preventing the spread of SARS in the workplace requires frequent hand washing and the use of common household cleaners to frequently clean surfaces.

Avian Influenza   Avian influenza (H5N1) is a more current global health concern. At this time, H5N1 mainly affects wild and domesticated birds in parts of Asia, Europe, the Near East, and Africa, with only a small number of cases of human infection. A few cases in Asia have been the result of human-to-human transmission, and healthcare practitioners are concerned that if this type of transmission increases a global pandemic will ensue. The CDC advises travelers to avoid contact with live birds, wash their hands often with soap and water, and cover their noses and mouths when coughing or sneezing.

Preparing for a Pandemic   HR professionals can play a role in preparing their organizations to cope with a pandemic by establishing plans to maintain essential functions if a large number of employees are absent from work. The CDC encourages employers to prepare guidelines for minimizing face-to-face contact; secure vaccines for employees to prevent outbreaks; modify sick-leave policies to allow ill employees time to recover so they don't spread the disease; use telecommuting, flexible work hours, and work shifts to minimize contact; and establish knowledge-management programs to ensure business continuity during a health crisis. Additional information on preparing for a pandemic is available at www.pandemicflu.gov.

Employees with infectious diseases who don't pose a threat to co-worker health and safety are protected by ADA requirements for reasonable accommodation and may not be subjected to adverse employment actions because of their disease.

Environmental Safety Hazards

Although the Occupational Safety and Health Act didn't clearly define workplace hazards, it did empower OSHA to define *occupational safety and health standards* that would result in improved workplace safety and health as quickly as possible. Wherever possible, the act encouraged OSHA to use previously existing federal standards or industry standards that already had substantial agreement in the industry. The resulting standards range from those that are job- and industry-specific, such as standards for handling toxic chemicals used in manufacturing processes, to those that apply to businesses in many different industries.

Let's review some of the more generally applicable standards. Each standard is identified here with the OSHA title and the number assigned to it in the Code of Federal Regulations (CFR):

The General Duty Standard, Section 5   The *general duty standard* requires employers to provide jobs and a workplace environment that are free from recognized safety and health hazards that could potentially cause death or serious physical harm. This standard also requires employers to comply with all OSHA rules, regulations, and standards.

Employees are required to comply with OSHA standards and rules that apply to their own conduct in the course of performing their duties.

Emergency Action Plans, 1910.38   Employers are required to have *emergency action plans* in place to inform employees of appropriate procedures to follow during a fire or evacuation. The plan must designate employees who will remain behind during an evacuation to maintain or shut down critical operations. Employers must also develop a process to account for all employees after an evacuation and identify those employees who are responsible for carrying out rescue and medical duties in the event of an emergency. Employers must provide training for employees when the plan is first developed, when new employees are hired, and when an employee is assigned new responsibilities for execution of the plan.

The plan must also identify the person responsible for maintaining it who can be contacted by employees when they have questions about the plan.

Fire Prevention Plans, 1910.39   An OSHA-required fire-prevention plan must describe the major fire hazards and appropriate procedures for handling and storing hazardous materials to prevent fires. The employer must develop and implement procedures to control the accumulation of flammable or combustible refuse and ensure that devices on heat-producing machinery designed to prevent ignition of fires are adequately maintained.

The fire prevention plan must also inform employees about any fire hazards they will face when first assigned to a new job and what actions they should take to protect themselves in the event of a fire.

Occupational Noise Exposure, 1910.95   This standard establishes permissible noise levels for the workplace, establishes measurement procedures, requires implementation of hearing-conservation programs when average noise levels reach 85 decibels or greater, and requires audiometric testing for employees who work in environments with noise at those levels. Audiometric test results indicating a hearing loss of 10 decibels must be reported on OSHA form 300.

Personal Protective Equipment, 1910.132   OSHA established standards for personal protective equipment (PPE) to be used for jobs in which employees come in contact with hazardous materials, compressed gases, explosives and blasting agents, liquid petroleum, and ammonia. The standard requires PPE to protect the eyes and face, respiration, head, feet, and hands. It also requires employers to provide gear that protects employees from electrical shocks or other injuries. The standard requires that PPE be provided, used, and maintained in working condition. Employers are required to train employees in the appropriate use of PPE and are responsible for ensuring that employee-owned equipment is adequately maintained for use in hazardous situations.

Sanitation, 1910.141   This standard requires that the workplace be clean to the extent the type of work allows and sets forth specific guidelines for maintaining sanitary conditions.

Specifications for Accident Prevention Signs and Tags, 1910.145   OSHA has developed specifications for hazard signs and tags and requires that all workplace signs conform to the OSHA specifications. These specifications describe the colors to be used for different levels of warning and, in some cases, such as biohazard and slow-moving vehicle signs (among others), provide specifications for size, color, and design of the sign.

In general, OSHA defines red as the background color for danger, yellow for caution, orange for warning, and fluorescent orange or orange-red for biological hazards. Lettering or symbols on the signs is specified as being of a contrasting color to the background.

Permit-Required Confined Spaces, 1910.146   OSHA requires permits for employees to enter spaces that may become filled with a hazardous atmosphere that is immediately dangerous to life or health. The atmosphere in confined spaces must be tested prior to an employee's entrance into them, and other personnel are required to be in close proximity to the entrance to render assistance if needed. Employees who will be entering the space have the opportunity to observe the testing process if they desire to do so.

The Control of Hazardous Energy (Lockout/Tagout), 1910.147   The lockout/tagout standard applies to machinery that may start unexpectedly when a guard or other safety device must be removed to perform a service or maintenance process and any part of an employee's body may be subjected to injury in the course of the process.

Medical Services and First Aid, 1910.151   OSHA requires that employers provide adequate first-aid supplies and either have medical personnel available or ensure that one or more workers are trained in first aid to assist injured employees in an emergency.

General Requirements for All Machines (Machine Guarding), 1910.212   OSHA requires that woodworking machines; cooperage machinery; abrasive wheel machinery; mills; power presses; forging machines; portable power tools; welding, cutting, and brazing tools; and tools for specific industries such as paper, textile, bakery, and sawmill, among others, use guards to protect employees from injury. These guards can be barrier-type guards, two-hand tripping devices, electronic safety devices, or other guards or devices that effectively prevent injuries.

Selection and Use of Electrical Work Practices, 1910.333   Employers must ensure that employees who work on or around electrical equipment or circuits are protected from injury that could result from direct or indirect contact with electrical currents.

Blood-Borne Pathogens, 1910.1030   Blood-borne pathogens are pathogenic microorganisms in human blood that can cause disease in humans. HBV and HIV are examples of blood-borne pathogens but are not by any means the only ones. Workers in the healthcare industry are those most at risk for exposure to blood-borne pathogens, and OSHA regulations require employers to take steps to prevent exposure, including a written exposure-control plan that informs employees of preventive steps, post-exposure evaluation and follow-up, recordkeeping, and incident evaluation procedures.

Hazard Communication Standard (HCS), 1910.1200   The HCS requires employers to provide employees with information about physical and health hazards related to the use of any chemicals in the workplace. Employers must develop and maintain an ongoing written HCS plan that is to be updated as changes occur in the materials used in the workplace. The safety data sheets (SDSs) provided by chemical manufacturers provide sufficient information for communicating to and training employees.

You can access the comprehensive list of OSHA standards at www.osha .gov/law-regs.html.

From MSDS to SDS

In 2013, OSHA updated the hazard communication requirements for documents that relayed information about chemical exposures in the workplace. The updated standard required all employers to switch to the international version of the material safety data sheets (MSDSs), known simply as safety data sheets (SDSs). The main purpose of the change was to create a simpler and more consistent way for employers in all industries and geographic locations to communicate the hazards of a chemical.

The new format requires the following (in this order):

Section 1, Identification includes product identifier; manufacturer or distributor name, address, phone number; emergency phone number; recommended use; restrictions on use.

Section 2, Hazard(s) identification includes all hazards regarding the chemical; required label elements.

Section 3, Composition/information on ingredients includes information on chemical ingredients; trade secret claims.

Section 4, First-aid measures includes important symptoms/effects, acute, delayed; required treatment.

Section 5, Fire-fighting measures lists suitable extinguishing techniques, equipment; chemical hazards from fire.

Section 6, Accidental release measures lists emergency procedures; protective equipment; proper methods of containment and cleanup.

Section 7, Handling and storage lists precautions for safe handling and storage, including incompatibilities.

Section 8, Exposure controls/personal protection lists OSHA's Permissible Exposure Limits (PELs), ACGIH Threshold Limit Values (TLVs), and any other exposure limit used or recommended by the chemical manufacturer, importer, or employer preparing the SDS where available as well as appropriate engineering controls; personal protective equipment (PPE).

Section 9, Physical and chemical properties lists the chemical's characteristics.

Section 10, Stability and reactivity lists chemical stability and possibility of hazardous reactions.

Section 11, Toxicological information includes routes of exposure; related symptoms, acute and chronic effects; numerical measures of toxicity.

Section 12, Ecological information*

Section 13, Disposal considerations*

Section 14, Transport information*

Section 15, Regulatory information*

Section 16, Other information, includes the date of preparation or last revision.

***Note:** Since other Agencies regulate this information, OSHA will not be enforcing Sections 12 through 15 (29 CFR 1910.1200[g][2]).

As with the former MSDS, chemical manufacturers are required to produce these documents, and employers must keep them up-to-date and make them accessible upon demand.

Assessing Security Risks

Security in the workplace covers a broad spectrum of topics related to protecting the company from threats of one kind or another, including fires, earthquakes, hurricanes, tornadoes, and other natural disasters and man-made threats such as terrorist attacks, computer hackers, workplace violence and theft, or unintentional release of trade secrets or confidential information. Many of these threats aren't ultimately the responsibility of

HR professionals, but a working knowledge of the impact they have on the workforce is essential to understanding the ways HR interacts with other business functions in the organization.

Risk assessment is the process used to evaluate the likelihood that losses will occur. Before an employer can put plans in place to reduce security risks, the threats (external forces) and vulnerabilities (internal weaknesses) must be evaluated for the degree of risk to the organization. This knowledge is needed to determine appropriate controls to protect the company and which emergencies are most likely to occur so that preventive measures can be taken.

A security risk assessment is most often a collaborative effort between internal managers and outside consultants with expertise in security issues. Depending on the nature of the business, consultants with different types of expertise will be required; for example, a software company developing a new product will have significantly different needs than a manufacturing plant whose employees belong to a labor union and may go on strike. Risk assessments are most frequently accomplished using a qualitative analysis, where all the possible emergencies are listed along with the potential financial costs and impact on operations. The emergencies can then be prioritized to address those with the greatest possible impact on the business first.

Identifying and ranking risks provides management with the opportunity to be proactive and implement controls to prevent damage to the assets of the business. There are four basic types of company assets: financial assets, such as cash, securities, and accounts receivable; physical assets, such as buildings, machinery, and equipment; information assets; and human assets, including the effects of workplace violence and substance abuse. Table 6.7 displays some of the common risks associated with each of these asset types.

Let's examine the asset types and associated risks in more depth:

Financial Assets   Financial assets, including cash, inventory, accounts receivable, and securities, are vulnerable to theft and embezzlement. Implementing policies and procedures to protect financial assets is generally the responsibility of a company's chief financial officer (CFO).

Physical Assets   Physical assets consist of buildings, manufacturing machines and equipment, vehicles, furniture, and office equipment. HR responsibility for risk assessment on these assets is related to how people are impacted by risks associated with them. For example, a possible risk to physical assets could be fire. HR assessment of risks for physical assets focuses on protecting people from these risks. In most cases, these risks are managed through the safety plans described in the "Injury and Illness Prevention Programs" section of this chapter.

Information Assets   Risks to information assets come in different forms. Employees may release confidential information to an unauthorized person unintentionally or, in some cases, intentionally. Information stored on servers may be compromised because of unauthorized access by hackers or unintentional release by employees. Regardless of the cause, the risks from information loss can range from a minor disruption of operations to a catastrophic loss of trade secrets or financial records that damage an organization's credibility in the marketplace or its ability to continue operations.

TABLE 6.7 Types of risks and assets impacted

Type of risk	Financial	Physical	Information	Human
Accidents	x	x	x	x
Computer hackers	x	x	x	
Corporate espionage	x	x	x	
Embezzlement	x			
Fire	x	x	x	x
Human error	x	x	x	x
Identity theft			x	x
Lawsuits	x	x	x	x
Loss of confidential information			x	x
Natural disasters	x	x	x	x
Pilferage		x		
Breach of private information			x	x
Sabotage		x	x	x
Substance abuse				x
Terrorism	x	x	x	x
Theft	x	x	x	
Workplace violence				x

Human Assets   Providing protection for employees takes many forms. Many of the security measures that protect physical assets also protect employees; in addition, an ongoing safety training program can include information on ways in which employees can protect themselves in different situations. Protecting employees working outside the United States presents different issues for employers. Issues of political stability and animosity toward American companies and citizens require programs and vendors that specialize in protecting them abroad. Large corporations must often take special security precautions to prevent executives from kidnapping, particularly when they travel overseas. Executive security may take several forms, including bodyguards and vendors that specialize in corporate protection.

Employees must also be protected from the effects of workplace violence and substance abuse in the workplace.

Assessing Business Continuity Risks

Ensuring an organization's ability to continue despite a disruption is one of the many challenges facing business leaders today. Whether the threat to operations is natural or man-made, accidental or intentional, the goal of business continuity planning is to protect the organization from unforeseen emergencies and other circumstances. Risks to business continuity can generally be classified as natural, man-made, or biological. In some cases, disasters such as fires or floods can be either natural or man-made, but response is similar in either situation:

Environmental Disasters   Environmental disasters come in many forms, from extreme weather conditions as in hurricanes, tornadoes, or blizzards, or from other causes such as floods, earthquakes, fires, volcanic eruptions, toxic gas releases, and chemical spills. For some environmental disasters, such as volcanic eruptions and floods, there is usually some advance warning, such as rising water levels in a river or gradually increasing volcanic activity. In these cases, businesses are able to take precautionary steps to secure people, data, and physical assets. At other times, natural disasters are unexpected, such as a major earthquake or toxic gas release. At those times, people must react instantly to save lives and business assets; the best way to do this is with a preestablished plan for people to follow so they don't have to make decisions under stressful conditions.

Organized or Deliberate Disruptions   Organized and/or deliberate disruptions can be the result of acts of terrorism, major thefts, sabotage, or labor disputes. Major thefts and acts of sabotage come with little or no warning and can disrupt operations and, in the case of sabotage, potentially injure people. Terrorism also comes with little or no warning. In addition to the devastation to people and infrastructure, this disruption has the additional element of creating fear in people who may not have even been on the same continent where the attack occurred. In addition to the loss of life and infrastructure, management must be able to calm employee fears to continue operating the business.

On the other hand, labor disputes generally occur after a period of notice by a union and provide an opportunity to plan for continued operations. Even so, the disruption is costly and can be dangerous for employees who cross picket lines.

Loss of Utilities and Public Services   The loss of utilities can occur as the result of a demand for electricity that exceeds the capacity of the power grid as the result of an oil shortage or as the result of a failure of the communication system, any of which can be caused by an environmental disaster or an organized disruption. In some cases, such as excessive demand on the power grid, the utility company may have a system in place to notify business owners of a potential loss of power prior to the loss. At other times—as the result of a terrorist act, for example—the disruption could be immediate and unexpected.

Equipment or System Failures   Equipment breakdowns, such as a failure of production equipment or water pipes bursting and causing a flood, can halt production and disrupt operations unexpectedly. Other internal systems, such as the company's Internet service, communication system, or building power, can fail as well, disrupting operations.

Serious Information Security Incidents   Cyberattacks by hackers, or the unleashing of a major email virus, can compromise sensitive and confidential information, shut down the customer-ordering website, or cause the IT system to fail.

Other Emergencies   Other emergencies vary widely in the amount of disruption caused to business operations. At one extreme, a biological disaster such as a serious epidemic could affect much of the workforce, reducing the ability of the company to function. Biological disasters can be either natural, such as the swine flu outbreak in 2010, or man-made, as the result of a bioterror attack. These types of disasters pose different challenges than some others because they affect the people who would otherwise be available to reduce the impact of the emergency. The unexpected loss of a key employee might not have an immediate impact but could cripple an organization's forward movement, regardless of the cause. In some cases, such as a resignation, there is some opportunity for transitioning to a replacement, including the transfer of essential knowledge. At other times, because of an accident, terrorist attack, or other type of disaster, the circumstances would rule out any time for transition, and remaining employees would need to reconstruct critical information in order to move forward. A public transportation strike or gas shortage is another situation that could either prevent employees from getting to work at all or significantly increase commute times.

Assessing Workplace Privacy Risks

Many employees are surprised and angry when subjected to electronic monitoring, physical property searches, or video surveillance of their activities in the workplace. Employers use electronic surveillance to monitor email, voice mail, and telephone conversations and to access call logs, monitor Internet use, or inspect computer files. Organizations may conduct property searches in cubicles, offices, file cabinets, employee lockers, or in some circumstances, personal employee belongings. In some cases, employers may conduct video surveillance by installing cameras in the workplace to protect employees or monitor behavior. There can be compelling reasons for employers to monitor employee activities, including concerns about theft, employee safety, improper use of equipment, loss of confidential proprietary information, productivity, and other issues. Employers may be accused of knowingly allowing employees to disseminate harassing or inappropriate communication, and implementing some form of electronic monitoring may protect them from liability. Add to this mix concerns about identity theft, and employers have legitimate reasons to take protective actions. In doing so, it's important to balance these concerns with the effect monitoring has on employee rights, morale, and productivity and then assess the risks inherent in those programs.

Risk Management

In general, risks can be managed in one of the following ways:

- *Mitigation:* The company minimizes the risk.
- *Acceptance:* The company manages the risk if it occurs.
- *Avoidance:* The company eliminates the risk.
- *Transfer:* The company uses insurance to cover the risk.

Now that we've identified and assessed many of the risks related to the workplace, the following sections describe some of the possible choices for minimizing, managing, transferring, and even eliminating HR risks.

Managing Legal Compliance Risks

Members of the management team look to the HR function for guidance in complying with employment laws and regulations. HR also takes the lead in establishing compliant policies and procedures and is responsible for ensuring that members of the management team are aware of laws and regulations governing employment practices and the potential costs to the organization for failing to comply.

Americans with Disabilities Act

Preventing losses from the mishandling of ADA claims can be accomplished by developing and implementing guidelines for employees to follow when requesting an ADA accommodation. Documenting the steps in this process demonstrates an employer's good-faith participation in an interactive process to provide a reasonable accommodation for a disabled employee.

Sarbanes-Oxley Act

Although the background and intention of SOX is to ensure the accuracy and fairness of financial reporting for public companies and its specific requirements for key executives and board members, there are also requirements that are relevant to HR practice.

Concepts that are explored in more detail in the labor law index include whistleblower protections, internal controls of accounting practices, board of director audits, and disclosures of potential lawsuits or employee settlements on financial statements.

Of specific interest are the standards related to ethical conduct. The SEC rules define a code of ethics for these purposes as written standards designed to deter wrongdoing and to promote the following:

- Honest and ethical conduct, including the ethical handling of actual or apparent conflicts of interest between personal and professional relationships
- Full, fair, accurate, timely, and understandable disclosure in reports and documents that a registrant files with, or submits to, the SEC and in other public communications made by the registrant
- Compliance with applicable governmental laws, rules, and regulations

- The prompt internal reporting to an appropriate person or persons identified in the code of violations of the code

- Accountability for adherence to the code

Managing Safety and Health Risks

Other than OSHA compliance, what exactly is workplace safety? In a word (or two), it's accident prevention. *Safety* is about identifying possible hazards in the workplace and reducing the likelihood that an accident will happen by correcting the hazard. Management and employees are partners in this process. Because employees are close to the possible hazards, they should feel empowered to take the steps necessary to reduce hazards that are within their control, whether that means correcting the hazard themselves or reporting the hazard to management with suggestions on how to correct it.

Workplace accidents negatively impact the bottom line in many ways. They reduce productivity because an injured employee must be given time to recover from an injury. A high accident/injury rate increases insurance costs and, when employees sense that management is unconcerned about their safety, lowers morale and increases turnover. Employees who aren't satisfied with their work care less about what kind of job they do, which has a negative impact on quality. Poor-quality products tarnish the company's reputation, which makes it more difficult for the company to compete against other products. All of these consequences of poor safety policies reduce the company's ability to earn a profit, which reduces the value of the company to its owners. All of this can happen when employers don't think safety matters!

Accident prevention begins with a commitment from the top that safety does matter and that the health and well-being of employees is important to the company. Employers need to provide safe operating procedures, train workers to use those procedures, and then enforce the procedures by rewarding positive safety actions and disciplining employees who fail to comply with procedures.

Because the employees doing the job know best what is safe and what is unsafe, they must be involved in developing safe operating procedures. Working in partnership, management and employees can identify the hazards present in the workplace and develop strategies to reduce or eliminate them. An added benefit of including employees in this process is that they will have a greater stake in maintaining safe operations that they were part of creating. As safe operating procedures are identified, they become part of a safety and health-management plan.

Employers that have developed effective safety-management programs have safer work environments for their employees. Over the past 30 years, through workplace investigation and analysis of injury and illness statistics, OSHA has determined that effective safety and health-management plans have four common characteristics:

- Senior management is committed to a safe work environment, and employees are involved in the decisions and activities to make it happen.

- The company is engaged in an ongoing worksite analysis to identify potential safety and health hazards.

- The company has active hazard prevention and control programs in place to correct hazards before injury or illness occurs.

- Safety and health training is an ongoing process in the company.

An effective plan identifies the person who is responsible for its overall implementation and creates a safety committee with representatives from both management and labor to address safety concerns and develop workable solutions to safety problems. An effective plan identifies hazards that exist in the work environment, whether they're physical, chemical, or biological, and provides guidance in the form of OSHA safety standards on the appropriate way to work with each hazard. The plan provides a mechanism for employee complaints so that they reach the appropriate management level for speedy resolution to prevent injuries. If the work environment requires the use of machinery, equipment, tools, or PPE, the plan spells out the appropriate methods for using and maintaining them and includes consequences for failing to comply with the standards.

The plan describes how to report accidents, who must be notified, and the time frames in which the notifications must occur and provides an accident investigation procedure, identifying who will conduct the investigation, what records must be kept, and how and where they should be filed. When an investigation takes place, the plan should include a process that ensures all employees are advised of the accident circumstances and what steps should be taken to avoid similar accidents in the future.

Part of an effective plan is ongoing training for employees that addresses previous accidents and ways to prevent similar occurrences in the future.

Injury and Illness Prevention Programs

Injury and illness prevention plans (IIPPs) are required by OSHA and designed to protect employees from preventable workplace injuries and illnesses. OSHA describes several plans with different purposes. This section describes each of these plans. Some elements are present in all of the plans, and others are related only to individual plans. OSHA requires the following plans:

- Safety and health management plan (also known as an *injury and illness prevention plan*)

- Emergency action plan (also referred to as an *emergency response plan*)

- Fire prevention plan

Generally, employers with 10 or fewer employees aren't required to provide written plans unless they have been notified by OSHA to do so.

To ensure the safety of employees and business assets, an emergency action plan, combined with ongoing employee training, is essential. By developing a plan and having regular drills to reinforce the steps to be taken, employers can improve the chances that all employees will be safe in an emergency.

The OSHA emergency action plan standard requires, at a minimum, that the employer define the preferred method for reporting fires and other emergencies, an evacuation policy and procedure, and floor plans or maps that define escape procedures and assign evacuation routes. The plan must have contact information for individuals who can provide additional information during an emergency and provide procedures for employees who will remain behind to perform essential services during the emergency. Employees who will perform rescue and medical duties are to be included in the plan as well. The plan requires alarm systems to notify all employees, including those who are disabled, of the need to evacuate.

 Real World Scenario

Sample Emergency Action Plan

Section 1: Responsibilities   In this section is a description of everyone who has a role to play during an emergency. Who will make the decision to evacuate the building? If critical machinery must be shut down, who will do that? Who is responsible to "take roll" and ensure that all employees have been safely evacuated from the building? Which employees are certified to perform first aid until medical personnel arrive on the scene? How will the emergency be reported to authorities, and who is responsible for doing that? Finally, this section should include the names of those who have been designated to answer questions and explain duties required by the plan.

Section 2: Emergency Escape Procedures   This section of the plan identifies the emergency escape procedures that employees are to follow and provides a diagram of the building showing escape routes from each floor and each area. In this section, special procedures for evacuating persons with disabilities, visitors to the building, and others with special needs should be spelled out. A safe meeting area should be designated so that all employees know where they should go in the event of an evacuation.

Section 3: Critical Plant Operations   Particularly in manufacturing operations, there are processes that must be shut down according to specific protocols. This section should identify these processes, along with instructions for employees on recognizing when they must evacuate themselves, even if the operation is not yet complete.

Section 4: Accounting for Employees   In the event of an evacuation, it's critical that rescue personnel know whether people are trapped in the building. Equally important is that rescue personnel not endanger themselves if everyone has been successfully evacuated. This section of the plan should describe the procedures to be followed, including where employees will meet and who will account for employees and visitors to the area.

Section 5: Reporting Emergencies   This section describes how emergencies are to be reported to the appropriate authorities.

Section 6: Identifying Emergency Contacts   In this section, the plan should identify who should be contacted for specific information. This may be a single person, or it may be several individuals who are responsible for different sections of the plan.

Section 7: Alarm System   This section of the plan should describe how employees will be notified of an emergency, where alarms are located, if there are different alarms for different emergencies, what they sound like, and whether the alarm system automatically notifies emergency personnel.

Section 8: Types of Evacuations   If the building is located in an area in which the potential for different types of emergencies exists, such as fires, tornadoes, and floods, this section of the plan describes the evacuation plan for each type of emergency.

Section 9: Training Requirements   In this section, the plan should describe how employees will be trained in emergency procedures and how often. The person responsible for training employees should be identified, along with a schedule for emergency drills.

Section 10: Recordkeeping   In this section, the plan should include documents that might be required in an emergency. This could include information on SDSs for chemicals in the worksite, maintenance records for safety equipment, equipment inspection records, building plans, and OSHA forms.

Elements Common to All Plans

Some elements are important enough for inclusion in each of the plans:

- A clear statement of the company policy regarding the program
- The commitment and full support of senior management
- A process for including employees in the process, whether through the establishment of a safety committee or some other means
- Identification of those with responsibilities under the plan, including employees, vendors, and public health and safety officials, and contact information for those individuals
- A clear, unambiguous process for reporting hazards or concerns to the responsible parties
- A description of the process to be used in training employees
- Procedures for maintaining records required by OSHA

Safety and Health Management Plan

In addition to the elements common to all plans, a safety and health management plan will include the following:

- A process to ensure two-way communication between management and labor
- An assessment of known hazards
- Procedures to correct known hazards
- A procedure to ensure that the company engages in an ongoing analysis of workplace hazards and conducts updated training on changes

- Maintenance procedures for any equipment, machinery, tools, or PPE used in the workplace
- An accident investigation procedure
- An accident reporting procedure

Emergency Action Plan

The emergency action plan begins with the common elements described previously and adds the following:

- Emergency escape procedures, including a floor plan or diagram for employees to follow
- Procedures for shutting down critical plant operations
- A process to account for employees after an evacuation
- A description of the alarm system that will notify employees of an emergency, including how persons with disabilities, visitors, and temporary employees will be notified
- Procedures to follow for different types of emergencies, such as fires, tornadoes, earthquakes, and terrorist attacks

Fire-Prevention Plan

The fire-prevention plan may be included as part of the emergency action plan. Whether the plan is included with it or separate, it must provide information about the following:

- All major fire hazards, how they should be handled and stored, a description of possible causes of igniting them and how to prevent that from happening, and a description of the appropriate equipment to suppress each hazard
- The location of fire-extinguishing systems or portable fire extinguishers
- The procedure describing how waste materials that are flammable or combustible will be stored before disposal

Injury and Illness Compensation Programs

As long as there have been workers and employers, there has been a debate about financial responsibility for injuries suffered on the job. The first written record of this is in the Hammurabic Code, written some 4,000 years ago by the king of Babylon. Of course, at that time, the workers were slaves and compensation for injuries was paid to their masters, but nonetheless, there was recognition of financial liability when injuries occurred.

Over time, three common-law doctrines developed that were applied to workers who were injured on the job:

- The *fellow servant rule* absolved employers of responsibility if a co-worker's actions caused the injury.
- The *doctrine of contributory negligence* was used to mitigate the employer's responsibility if the worker's actions contributed in any way to the injury.

- *Voluntary assumption of risk* said that workers who knew the dangers of the job when they took it assumed the associated risks, and the level of pay they accepted reflected the amount of danger involved, so the employer had no responsibility when death or injury occurred.

For workers, these doctrines presented many problems. First, they assumed the employer and the worker were equals in the labor market, so the law treated employment relationships the same as it did contracts between business owners. They also assumed that if the terms and conditions of employment weren't agreeable to the worker, the worker could simply seek other employment.

Second, these doctrines required workers injured on the job to seek recompense through the court system. Employers for the most part could afford the best attorneys to represent them, whereas few employees could afford a lengthy legal battle.

These common-law doctrines became known as the *unholy trinity* because the results were almost always in favor of the employer; only 50 percent of cases brought on behalf of workers killed or injured on the job resulted in any kind of compensation, and of those who did receive compensation, it was rarely more than a few months' pay. As governments recognized the blatant unfairness of the lopsided way these doctrines were applied, states began enacting workers' compensation laws to level the playing field for workers. Wisconsin was the first state to pass a workers' compensation act in 1911, and New Jersey followed in the same year.

Federal Workers' Compensation Requirements

Workers' compensation laws for private employers are in most cases the purview of state government; however, there are a few industries with federal legislation to protect injured workers. These include the federal government, the longshoring industry, coal mines, and the Department of Energy. Legislation pertaining to these industries is covered by the following laws:

Federal Employees Compensation Act (FECA) of 1916   FECA is administered by the DOL and is the federal employees' equivalent of workers' compensation, providing similar benefits for workers injured during the course of performing their jobs.

The Longshore and Harbor Workers' Compensation Act (LHWCA) of 1927   LHWCA provides workers' compensation benefits for maritime workers whose injuries occur on the navigable waters of the United States or on piers, docks, or terminals.

Black Lung Benefits Act (BLBA) of 1969, Amended in 1977   The BLBA provides benefits to coal miners who have been disabled by pneumoconiosis as a result of their work in the mines. Benefits are also paid to surviving dependents if the miner dies from the disease.

Energy Employees Occupational Illness Compensation Program Act (EEOICPA) of 2000   This act was created to provide compensation for employees and contractors of the Department of Energy who were subjected to excessive radiation while producing and testing nuclear weapons.

Safety Training Programs

OSHA has developed guidelines to assist employers in developing effective training programs that reduce work-related injury and illness. The following guidelines can be modified to fit the specific industry and work site requirements for individual businesses:

1. Determine whether training is needed. In other words, is the safety problem something that can be corrected with training or is another correction necessary?

2. Identify the training needs. What should employees be doing that they aren't doing? The program should inform them of appropriate methods for doing the job.

3. As with any other training program, develop objectives for the training.

4. When the learning needs and objectives have been identified, methods for delivering the training can be developed. Will classroom training be best? One-on-one training with an experienced employee? Demonstration and practice? This will depend on the specific training needs for the organization.

5. Conduct the training.

6. Evaluate how well the training worked, using training evaluation methods discussed in Chapter 4.

7. Based on the evaluation, adjust the training to improve its effectiveness.

Managing Security Risks

HR professionals must provide the expertise to appropriately handle suspected inappropriate conduct by employees in order to protect the company from liability.

Workplace security measures are those taken by employers to ensure the safety of the people and assets of the business and begin with assessing the possible risks. When the potential risks have been identified, plans for protection of the people and the assets of the organization can be made and implemented. The following sections briefly review security issues with which HR professionals may become involved.

Financial Assets

CFOs are responsible for implementing *internal controls* to ensure that cash and negotiable securities aren't mishandled, along with inventory controls to reduce employee pilferage or customer theft. In most organizations, CFOs implement processes to ensure that purchase commitments at certain dollar levels are reviewed and approved by senior-level managers to prevent the misappropriation of funds. One common control used to ensure the security of financial assets is to define accounting jobs so that more than one person handles different aspects of transactions. For example, the job with responsibility for preparing customer invoices would not also be responsible for opening the mail or making bank deposits. Separating these duties makes it more difficult for an employee to embezzle money.

The internal control requirements of SOX have a major impact on finance operations. These more stringent reporting requirements affect other business functions, including

HR, where business processes must be more consistent, reliable, and efficient to conform to internal controls. HR also plays a role in helping companies manage the cultural transformation to higher levels of transparency and financial accountability with change initiatives.

Physical Assets

HR responsibility for managing physical asset risks focuses on two areas: protecting people from injury and protecting assets from theft or damage. Managing risks from injuries caused by physical assets was described earlier in the chapter. Methods for protecting physical assets from theft or damage can include building security measures such as guards, security cameras, keys or card-key lock systems, and entry barriers such as fences or security gates. The size, nature, and cost of the asset, along with the budget of the organization, determine appropriate methods for protecting these assets.

Information Assets

Managing risk for information assets includes maintaining the confidentiality of information and protecting the loss of personal employee data.

Protection of Confidential Information

The most effective way to protect confidential information from intentional or unintentional distribution by employees is to ensure that they know what the company considers confidential before they're hired. An *intellectual property agreement (IPA)* and/or *nondisclosure agreement (NDA)* is used for this purpose. Because the types of confidential information vary widely between different organizations, it's important that an attorney develop an agreement to meet specific needs. An IPA should identify what the company considers to be confidential information (such as customer lists, financial information, or trade secrets) and how its use is limited by the agreement, as well as how long the information must remain confidential after the agreement expires. The agreement may contain a "nonsolicitation" clause limiting the ability of employees who leave the organization to hire co-workers. IPAs should contain clauses that require employees to describe any discoveries or inventions they may have made prior to entering into the agreement and require that they don't share confidential information from other companies with the new employer or disclose who owns the inventions or discoveries made during the course of employment. Finally, the agreement should state that materials containing confidential information are the property of the company and may not be removed from a given location.

These agreements help prevent employees from sharing confidential proprietary information with other companies or individuals. For these documents to be effective, the organization must advise employees on a regular basis that even inadvertently sharing this information can cause damage.

Although this discussion has been limited to the use of IPAs and NDAs in employment relationships, these documents are equally important when sharing proprietary information with others outside the organization. This can include business partners or others with whom the company shares the information in the course of doing business, such as candidates for jobs during the interview process.

Preventing Data Loss

Data loss can occur as the result of an intentional act (such as hacking, data theft, or sabotage); through the failure of equipment (storage media or hardware), software errors, or inadequate operating procedures; or by accident. Preventing the loss of critical data is the responsibility of the IT function, which ensures the safety of the hardware and software systems used in an organization. The use of enterprise-wide databases that store massive amounts of data from all functions can make data protection a complex process. Many organizations use data-sharing technology to streamline operations internally and, in some cases, to share data externally. This efficiency carries with it greater risk for the unauthorized release of data and has led to the creation of security measures, such as firewalls, that ensure the integrity of the data. A *firewall* is a hardware device or a software program that restricts access to an organization's computer network based on criteria established by the IT function.

Human Assets

Many of the risk management activities that protect human assets have already been described, including health and safety plans, injury- and illness-prevention plans, and emergency-response plans. Two areas of risk apply almost exclusively to people for discussion here: workplace violence and substance abuse.

Workplace Violence

Workplace violence occurs when an employee with poor behavior control becomes highly stressed. The stress may or may not be work-related, but it's often set off by an incident in the workplace. Under OSHA's General Duty Clause, employers are required to be aware of employees exhibiting the signs of possible violent behavior and take steps to prevent its occurrence. Employees who commit acts of violence in the workplace frequently show recognizable signs of stress before they commit the acts. It's up to employers to train managers and supervisors to identify these signs so that employees who are having difficulty can be referred to an employee assistance program (EAP) for counseling or directed to social services if needed. Training managers to recognize and prevent workplace violence is becoming a more common topic for inclusion in management training curricula, along with supervisory skills, sexual harassment prevention, and other issues.

Some of the more common signs of stress include a change in work habits, a decline in productivity, conflicts with co-workers, depression, and refusing to take responsibility for individual actions.

Even though not everyone who exhibits signs of stress is likely to become violent, any employee who exhibits these signs should be counseled and referred to appropriate professional assistance. As part of the emergency response plan described in the "Managing Business Continuity Risks" section, a plan for responding to an incident of workplace violence should be developed and communicated to employees. This plan, in addition to other requirements, can include code words to be used when employees feel threatened so they can alert co-workers to call for help, along with a resource book for managers and supervisors that contains referral agencies for different types of issues to assist employees who are troubled.

Substance Abuse

Government statistics indicate that more than 70 percent of substance abusers have jobs. They're all working in someone's business—some of them might work in your organization. Substance abusers increase costs for employers due to tardiness and absenteeism, increased errors, accidents, and increases in healthcare costs and workers' compensation claims. When a substance abuser's job is to drive a semi-trailer or operate heavy equipment, an employer also faces increased costs for injuries or damages that occur as a result of an accident. If the employer is a federal contractor subject to the Drug-Free Workplace Act, continued substance abuse at the workplace could result in the loss of the contract.

There are six components for an effective substance abuse program in the workplace:

- Support for the substance abuse policy from top management (As with any policy, this is the most important component.)

- A written policy clearly stating that substance abuse won't be tolerated in the workplace

- Training for managers and supervisors to ensure that they understand and can explain the policy, are able to recognize the signs of substance abuse, understand the importance of documenting poor performance, and know what steps to take when they become aware of a substance abuser

- Education programs for new hires and employees to inform them of the policy and explain the consequences for violations. If the organization has a drug-testing program, it should be explained prior to employment and during orientation. Employees should be made aware of resources in the community or through the EAP, as well as the effects of substance abuse on themselves, their families, and the costs to the employer.

- An EAP that provides confidential counseling for substance abusers as needed

- An ongoing, fair, and consistent drug-testing program that complies with federal, state, and local laws and union contracts. The program should identify who will be tested, when tests will occur, which drugs will be tested for, and what happens if the test is positive.

Drug-Testing Programs

There are several decisions to make when a company decides to implement a drug-testing program. First, the program must be implemented in a fair and consistent manner to avoid charges of discrimination. Next, the company must decide what type of testing will be done:

Preemployment Testing   Lawful only after an offer of employment has been made. Before beginning a testing program, the employer must decide which applicants will be tested. This decision may be based on the type of work done in different jobs; for example, a company may decide to test all employees who operate machinery. The test must be conducted fairly and consistently on all applicants for the designated jobs.

Random Drug Testing   Done on an arbitrary, unscheduled basis. To make the testing truly random and reduce the risk of legal challenges, employers may want to use a computer program that randomly selects employees. Random drug testing should be implemented with legal counsel to avoid violating privacy rights unnecessarily.

Scheduled Drug Testing   Can be useful when monitoring the rehabilitation progress of employees but has limited value because employees who may be currently using drugs are generally able to stop long enough before the test to clear their systems of the drugs.

Reasonable-Suspicion Drug Testing   Can be used any time there has been an accident in which an employee's actions contributed to the cause of the accident in the workplace or when a supervisor suspects, based on behavior, that an employee is under the influence of drugs.

Regardless of the substance abuse testing schedule that is used, it's important to keep in mind that implementation must be fair and equitable to avoid charges of discrimination. If employers choose to test specific job categories, then all employees in those categories must be subjected to the testing process. If random testing is used, all employees in the selected category must be included in the selection group.

HR professionals must also keep in mind that, under the ADA, current users of illegal drugs are specifically excluded from protection, while current abusers of alcohol aren't automatically denied protection. Regardless, employers may take adverse action if the behavior negatively affects an employee's ability to do the job. Entering recovery is a trigger for protection under the ADA for both groups.

Return-to-Work Programs

Whether the absence was the result of a work-related illness or injury or another cause, a return-to-work (RTW) policy can reduce the risk of re-injury. Some organizations develop a comprehensive policy that includes accident reporting procedures, definitions of various terms, types of leaves covered by the RTW program, and administrative procedures in their procedures, whereas others develop separate policies and procedures for different aspects. Organizations will develop policies tailored to their specific needs, but all should include a clear statement of compliance with specific legal requirements of Family and Medical Leave Act (FMLA) medical certifications, workers' compensation, or other laws that may apply. The procedure should answer basic questions for supervisors and employees, such as the following:

- What is the goal or objective of the RTW program?
- Who is eligible?
- Are there policy or procedure differences between a work-related medical leave of absence (MLOA) and a non-work-related MLOA?
- What is the impact of an MLOA on employee compensation and benefits?
- Under what conditions will the organization accommodate modified work assignments that allow employees to transition back to work before they have recovered completely?

- What are the employee's responsibilities with regard to the leave and RTW?
- What are the employer's responsibilities with regard to the leave and RTW?
- What are the responsibilities of the HR department with regard to the leave and RTW?
- What type of medical release does the organization require prior to accepting workers back on the job?

Once the previous questions have been adequately addressed, designing the elements of an RTW process becomes necessary. Examples include the following:

Modified Duty Assignment   Because many injured workers are quite willing and able to perform some but not all of the essential duties of a job, modifying specific tasks or functions may be necessary to allow an employee to return to work. In fact, workers' compensation studies have shown that employees who are offered modified/light duty assignments return to full duty more quickly than injured workers who incur lost time. This translates into a lower overall injury cost and allows the employee to get back into the routine of work much more quickly. Modified duty may include eliminating essential functions or creating a short-term job for the employee until they're able to return to full duty.

Having accurate job descriptions is necessary to engage in this process, as the employee and doctor will use them to return the employee to work with the proper restrictions.

Reasonable Accommodations   Reasonable accommodation is similar to modified duty, with two very major distinctions. Modified duty is typically a short-term option used for injured workers who are expected to be able to return to full duty, and an employer need not create a light-duty position for a "non-occupationally injured employee" as part of reasonable accommodation efforts. The process of identifying reasonable accommodation includes discussing options such as a reduced schedule, additional unpaid time off, and reassignment to a vacant position for which the disabled individual is qualified. It very well could also be modifying the essential functions of the job if that action wouldn't impose undue hardship on the employer.

Independent Medical Exam (IME)   Fit-for-duty exams are effective tools to use to determine if an employee is capable of returning to work without causing harm to themselves or others. These types of exams allow for an impartial review of the injured employee's medical status. For employers, IMEs can help to prevent fraud and deal with excessive extensions of time off due to lack of a proper diagnosis or treatment. For employees, these types of exams are helpful when there are conflicting reports of their needs or an employee doesn't agree with a doctor's findings.

A clear, legally compliant RTW policy mitigates the risk of inadvertent errors by managers and helps ensure that all employees are treated equitably when returning from medical leaves. In addition, requiring a medical release prior to an employee's return reduces the risk of re-injury.

Sexual Harassment

Recent events have shown a spotlight on industry and workplace incidents of egregious acts of sexual harassment. In particular, they have highlighted how confidentiality agreements can suppress the natural reporting mechanism of claims, creating systemic issues that are far deeper than single employer incidents.

And yet, this type of behavior has been prohibited since 1964 by Title VII of the Civil Rights Act subsequent amendments. Issues such as same-sex harassment, the implied obligation of supervisor-employee propositions, and whistleblower protections will continue to be important HR practices to be managed. The heart of the law remains however, in which employers have an obligation to prevent two forms of sexual harassment: quid pro quo and hostile work environment.

Quid pro quo is a legal term that means, in Latin, "this for that." Quid pro quo harassment, therefore, occurs when a supervisor or manager asks for sexual favors in return for some type of favorable employment action. *Sexual favors* is a broad term that covers actions ranging from unwanted touching to more explicit requests.

A *hostile work environment* has been defined by the EEOC as one in which an individual or individuals are subjected to unwelcome verbal or physical conduct "when submission to or rejection of this conduct explicitly or implicitly affects an individual's employment, unreasonably interferes with an individual's work performance, or creates an intimidating, hostile, or offensive work environment." When investigating these charges, the EEOC looks at many factors. In most cases, a single incidence of inappropriate and unwelcome behavior doesn't rise to the level of a hostile work environment, but in some cases when the actions or behavior are particularly offensive or intimidating, the EEOC may find that harassment has occurred. A hostile work environment can also be found to exist for victims who have been affected by unwelcome offensive conduct toward someone other than themselves.

> Unlike the quid pro quo form of harassment, a hostile work environment can be created by co-workers, suppliers, customers, or other visitors to the workplace.

Courts have held employers responsible for the harassing actions of their employees, whether or not the employer was aware of the harassment. Beginning in 1986, the Supreme Court issued a number of rulings to clarify employer responsibilities in the prevention of sexual harassment. The most commonly cited of these for HR purposes are *Meritor Savings Bank vs. Vinson* (1986), *Harris vs. Forklift Systems* (1993), and two cases decided at the same time in 1998, *Burlington Industries vs. Ellerth* and *Faragher vs. City of Boca Raton*:

Meritor Savings Bank vs. Vinson **(1986)** Mechelle Vinson applied for a job at a branch of Meritor Savings Bank in 1974 when Sidney Taylor was a vice president and manager of the branch. Taylor hired Vinson, who worked at the branch for four years, starting as a teller trainee and working her way up to assistant branch manager, based on her performance in the jobs she held. Once she passed her probationary period as a trainee, Vinson claims that Taylor began to harass her, requesting that they go to a motel to have sexual relations. Although Vinson refused Taylor's advances initially, she gave in eventually because she believed she would lose her job if she didn't. Vinson claims that Taylor's harassment escalated to the point that she was fondled in front of other employees and expected to engage in sexual relations at the branch both during and after work. In September 1978, Vinson took an indefinite medical leave, and the bank terminated her in November 1978.

The Supreme Court issued its opinion in June 1986, finding that a claim of "hostile environment" sex discrimination is actionable under Title VII. The Court rejected the idea that the "mere existence of a grievance procedure and a policy against discrimination" is enough to protect an employer from the acts of its supervisors. The opinion indicated that a policy designed to encourage victims of harassment to come forward would provide greater protection.

Harris vs. Forklift Systems (1993)   In April 1985, Teresa Harris was employed by Forklift Systems, Inc. as a manager, reporting to the company president, Charles Hardy. Hardy insulted Harris frequently in front of customers and other employees and made sexually suggestive remarks. When Harris complained in August 1987, Hardy apologized and said he would stop the conduct. But in September of that year, Hardy once again began the verbal harassment, and Harris quit on October 1.

Harris then filed a lawsuit against Forklift, claiming that Hardy had created a hostile work environment on the basis of her gender. The district court found that although Hardy's conduct was offensive, it didn't meet the required standard of severity to seriously affect her psychological well-being.

The Supreme Court agreed to hear the case in order to resolve conflicts in the lower courts on what conduct was actionable for a hostile work environment. The Court found that the appropriate standard is one that falls between that which is merely offensive and that which results in tangible psychological injury. Although this isn't a precise guideline, it does allow courts to take into consideration a number of factors about the work environment, the frequency and severity of the conduct, the level of threat or humiliation to which the victim is subjected, and whether the conduct interferes unreasonably with performance of the employee's job.

Faragher vs. City of Boca Raton (1998)   Beth Ann Faragher and Nancy Ewanchew were two of six females out of more than 40 lifeguards for the city of Boca Raton in Florida from 1985 to 1990. During their tenure, they were verbally and physically harassed by two supervisors, Bill Terry and David Silverman. They both complained to a third supervisor, Robert Gordon, about the harassment but didn't file a formal complaint, and no corrective action was taken. Ewanchew resigned in 1989 and wrote to the city manager in 1990 to complain about the harassment. The city investigated and (when it found that both Terry and Silverman had acted inappropriately) reprimanded and disciplined both supervisors.

The Supreme Court found that employers are responsible for actions of those they employ and have a responsibility to control them. Going further, the Court determined that a supervisor need not make an explicit threat of an adverse *tangible employment action* (TEA), which the Court defined as "a significant change in employment status, such as hiring, firing, failing to promote, reassignment with significantly different responsibilities, or a decision causing a significant change in benefits" in order for harassment to be actionable. The Court determined that subordinates know that the possibility of adverse supervisory actions exists whenever requests are made, even if the adverse actions aren't stated.

Burlington Industries vs. Ellerth (1998)   Kimberly Ellerth worked for Burlington Industries in Chicago as a salesperson from March 1993 to May 1994. During that time, Ellerth claims that she was subjected to ongoing sexual harassment by Ted Slowick, who wasn't her direct supervisor but did have the power to approve or deny a TEA with regard to her employment. Although Ellerth was aware of Burlington's policy prohibiting sexual harassment during her employment, she didn't complain about the harassment until after she resigned. After resigning, she filed a complaint with the EEOC and, when she received a right-to-sue letter in October 1994, filed suit against Burlington.

A key issue in this case was that of *vicarious liability* (an element of the legal concept of *respondeat superior*), which, in this context, means an employer may be held accountable for the harmful actions of its employees, whether or not the employer is aware of those actions. The Supreme Court decided in part that "An employer is subject to vicarious liability to a victimized employee for an actionable hostile environment created by a supervisor with immediate (or successively higher) authority over the employee."

 Real World Scenario

Oncale vs. Sundowner Offshore Services, Inc.

In late October 1991, Joseph Oncale was a roustabout employed by Sundowner Offshore Services on an oil rig in the Gulf of Mexico. During the time he worked on the rig, three of his male co-workers, including two who had supervisory authority over him, humiliated him in front of other employees on the rig using sexually explicit words and actions. At one point, Oncale was physically assaulted and threatened with rape. When Oncale complained to other supervisors about the harassment, no corrective action was taken, and one of them, the company's safety-compliance clerk, told him that he too was subjected to similar treatment by the three. When Oncale quit his job, he gave his reason for leaving as being "due to sexual harassment and verbal abuse."

Oncale filed a complaint against Sundowner, alleging discrimination on the basis of his sex. The district court denied the complaint, and on appeal, the Fifth Circuit Court of Appeals upheld the district court. Oncale then appealed to the U.S. Supreme Court. The Court heard oral arguments in the case in December 1997, and comments of the justices during the arguments gave a rare early indication of the way they were leaning: Chief Justice Rehnquist commented, "I don't see how we can possibly sustain the holding."

In March 1998, Justice Scalia wrote the majority opinion, referencing in part the Court's opinion in an earlier sexual harassment case that "When the workplace is permeated with discriminatory intimidation, ridicule, and insult that is sufficiently severe or pervasive to alter the conditions of the victim's employment and create an abusive working environment, Title VII is violated" (*Harris vs. Forklift Systems, Inc.*).

Scalia went on to say that even though the intent of Title VII was to protect harassment of women in the workplace, "sexual harassment of any kind that meets the statutory requirements" must be covered as well.

EEOC Guidelines for the Prevention of Sexual Harassment

The EEOC has developed detailed guidelines titled "Enforcement Guidance: Vicarious Employer Liability for Unlawful Harassment by Supervisors" to assist employers in developing policies that clearly express the employer's prohibition against harassment and conducting investigations that meet EEOC standards.

To summarize the guidelines, employers are encouraged to develop antiharassment policies, along with complaint procedures for those who believe they have been harassed. The policy should clearly explain unacceptable conduct and reassure employees who complain that they will be protected against retaliation. The complaint process should describe multiple avenues for reporting harassment and provide assurances of confidentiality to the extent it's possible. Investigations of allegations should be prompt and impartial, and if the investigation finds that harassment did indeed occur, the policy should provide for immediate corrective action.

These guidelines are fully described at www.eeoc.gov/policy/docs/harassment.html.

 Real World Scenario

Medina Rene vs. MGM Grand Hotel, Inc.

Even though federal law doesn't expressly prohibit discrimination based on sexual orientation, the courts have applied Title VII protections to complainants in these cases.

For two and a half years, Medina Rene worked as one of a group of male butlers for high-profile guests of the MGM Grand Hotel in Las Vegas. He alleged he was subjected to a hostile work environment by his supervisor and co-workers, and he provided extensive documentation of inappropriate behavior over a two-year period. According to the evidence he provided to the court, the behavior included inappropriate touching, caressing, and being forced to look at sexually explicit photographs. At one point, Rene was asked why he thought his co-workers were behaving that way toward him, and his answer was that it was because he was gay.

Attorneys for the MGM Grand argued that this case was different from Oncale because Rene was openly gay and Title VII didn't provide protection for sexual orientation. The district court granted summary judgment for the hotel, and Rene appealed to the Ninth Circuit Court of Appeals. The appellate court found that sexual orientation wasn't a pertinent fact in this case and remanded the case because Rene was singled out and subjected to offensive sexual conduct, the conduct was sexual in nature and discriminatory, and he was treated differently based on his sex.

As described previously in the discussions of the *Ellerth* and *Faragher* cases, the Supreme Court found that employers always have vicarious liability for unlawful harassment by supervisors when it results in a TEA, but when there is no TEA, liability may be avoided with an affirmative defense including two elements:

- The employer exercised reasonable care to prevent and correct promptly any harassing behavior.
- The employee unreasonably failed to take advantage of any preventive or corrective opportunities provided by the employer or to avoid harm otherwise.

LGBTQ Rights

There has been a rapid evolution of the particular issues faced by the lesbian, gay, bisexual, transgender and queer (LGBTQ) communities in the workplace—as well as what employers are required to do. While antiharassment laws have existed since 1964 to discourage unlawful discrimination against protected class groups, it wasn't until 2015 that the Equal Employment Opportunity Commission formally recognized that sexual orientation is protected under the law. This recognition, however, has not been enough to resolve the headlines. For example:

- In 2016, the Supreme Court upheld the rights of employers to engage in some forms of discrimination for religious reasons (*R.G. & G.R. Harris Funeral Homes vs. EEOC & Aimee Stephens*).
- In 2017, the Justice Department disagreed with the EEOC's inclusion of LGBTQ as a form of sex discrimination. They issued a friend-of-the-court brief that stated, in part, that sexual orientation is not a form of sex discrimination and that an amendment to Title VII of the Civil Rights Act needed to go through Congress.

The above may illustrate why a 2018 study published by the Human Rights Campaign (HRC) Foundation found that more than half of LGBTQ individuals remain closeted at work. The study also found that:

- One in five LGBTQ workers report having been told or had co-workers imply that they should dress in a more feminine or masculine manner.
- 53 percent of LGBTQ workers report hearing jokes about lesbian or gay people at least once in a while.
- 50 percent of non-LGBTQ workers don't think there are any LGBTQ employees at their place of work.

Many LGBTQ employees don't report negative behaviors toward them at work because they lack faith in the accountability processes from HR and they don't want to harm their relationships with co-workers. The lack of reporting by this community is significant. It implies that HR departments and executive management may be underestimating the presence of discrimination, bullying, loss of employment, and in extreme cases, physical violence against these workers.

Regardless of the status of the law, many companies prohibit discrimination against LGBTQ individuals in the same way they protect other groups. Some companies, such as Macy's department stores, publish policies, such as transgender bathroom and fitting room use. Other companies create LGBTQ resource groups to provide support to these employees. Still others create LGBTQ-friendly policies, such as equitable benefits, and engage in workplace education. Regardless, by creating an inclusive culture, all employees will feel that their employer values and accepts differences. This will reduce stress and improve organizational commitment overall.

Managing Business Continuity Risks

As noted throughout this chapter, many identified risks have the potential to disrupt business operations. Planning for these eventualities is a process known as a *business continuity plan (BCP)*, which results in a written document used to describe possible disruptions to operations and actions to be taken to minimize those disruptions and assign responsibility for executing the plan to specific individuals.

A BCP is often an umbrella term that includes other emergency plans, such as the emergency response plan and disaster recovery plan. In some organizations, these terms are interchangeable, whereas in others each describes a specific process. For the purposes of this discussion, the BCP is treated as an umbrella term covering different aspects of the business continuity process.

A successful BCP begins with a commitment from the CEO so that sufficient resources are provided for the process. When the CEO is committed to the process, a planning committee that includes representatives from each business function is appointed and defines the scope of the plan. At this point, the committee assesses the risks facing the organization:

Assess and prioritize organizational risks.   By their very nature, emergencies occur with little or no warning and can devastate individuals, single organizations, or whole communities. There are several different types of emergencies to consider when planning response, recovery, and continuity processes:

- Environmental disasters such as earthquakes, fires, tornadoes, hurricanes, toxic gas releases, chemical spills, and so on
- Organized and/or deliberate disruptions such as theft, labor disputes, sabotage, terrorism, and so on
- Loss of utilities and services caused by power failures, oil shortages, communication system failures, and so on
- Equipment or system failure such as a breakdown in the production line, equipment failure, or internal loss of power
- Serious information security incidents such as loss of customer data to hackers or failure of the IT system
- Other emergency situations such as workplace violence, legal problems, the unexpected loss of key employees, public transportation strikes, violations of health or safety regulations, and so on

The BCP planning process identifies those risks most likely to occur based on the organization's location, industry, and other considerations. The risks are then assessed for the level of disruption each would cause and the impact on different business functions, as well as an estimate of the cost to reestablish or maintain them in the event of each risk. Information systems are so integral to operating ability that most businesses will need to assess the impact of each risk on information and communication systems. Finally, each identified risk is evaluated and prioritized for its impact on operations.

Identify vital processes and key employees.   Another element of the BCP is a review of each functional business area. This review identifies vital business processes, key employees necessary to maintain operations in each critical area, and records essential for the continuation of the business. If emergency plans currently exist, the planning team will review them at this time and determine what revisions are needed for different risks. At this stage, the BCP team will identify critical vendors and suppliers and how to move forward if one or more of them are incapacitated. Alternative locations and equipment resources for use in the event that the building is destroyed are also identified.

Create an emergency response plan.   An important piece of the planning process is to develop an *emergency response plan (ERP)* describing how the organization will react to different emergency situations or natural disasters if they occur. The OSHA emergency action plan (described earlier in the "Environmental Safety Hazards" section) will be part of the ERP, describing how employees and visitors who are on-site during an emergency will be evacuated or, in cases where it's safer to remain at the workplace, sheltered in place until it's safe to leave the worksite. The ERP identifies a response team, assigning specific responsibilities to each team member; describes how vital records and information will be protected; and establishes an emergency communication plan. Depending on the type of emergency, the communication plan can include a public relations component and identify individuals who will represent the organization to customers, vendors, suppliers, and the media.

The ERP describes how computer systems and information will be protected and accessible. Prudent business practice includes ongoing off-site storage system backups and copies of records and legal documents needed to maintain operations in an emergency.

Develop a disaster recovery plan.   A *disaster recovery plan (DRP)* describes activities that take place once the initial response to the emergency is over.

Planning for this phase develops alternatives for reestablishing operations when property, processes, information systems, and people have been disrupted. If the building is unusable, what are the arrangements for temporary facilities? If the computer systems are inoperable, how and where will the off-site backups be reinstalled to continue operations? If transportation systems and roadways are damaged, how will employees get to work?

One important factor to consider in the DRP is compliance with SOX requirements for information safety. This requirement is discussed in Chapter 2, "PHR Exam: Business Management."

Another element to include in the DRP is a list of alternative vendors, suppliers, and service providers that can provide materials or support when normal sources are affected by emergencies and unable, either temporarily or permanently, to continue in the aftermath. This may make the difference in an organization's ability to continue servicing customers after an emergency.

Prepare a continuity of operations plan. The *continuity of operations plan (COOP)* generally refers to plans created to move from the disaster recovery phase, during which critical business functions are maintained but normal operations may not be taking place, back to pre-emergency service operating levels.

Maintain business continuity plans. Too often, organizations go through the process of creating plans and, once they're completed, never look at them again, assuming that the plans will work when needed. A critical component of a BCP is the need to test the plan, train employees to use the plan, and revisit it annually to keep the information current. An evaluation of the test results provides information about any necessary changes so that the plan can be refined.

Many of the threats to continued business operations described throughout this chapter can be managed in the framework of the BCP process. A few of the threats may be handled in different ways or require additional consideration:

Unexpected Loss of Key Employees Ensuring that the business survives the unexpected loss of a key employee is the point of a *succession plan*. These plans identify employees with leadership potential and prepare them for senior and executive management roles through the use of high-potential employee (HiPo) programs or other development plans. These matters are discussed further in Chapters 4 and 5.

Biological Threats An additional consideration for a plan to maintain operations during a serious pandemic is that many of the people who would, in other disasters or emergencies, be the ones called on to maintain the business may themselves be incapacitated. One strategy that was used during the SARS outbreak of 2002–03 to reduce the impact of SARS on the workforce was to create redundant employee teams and isolate them from each other, assigning each team to a different work location and rotating the teams between sites on a schedule that coincided with the incubation period of the virus. For the duration of the threat, personal contact between members of the different teams was prohibited to enhance the chances that at least one of the teams would survive intact during the outbreak without one or more members being subject to quarantine.

Terrorism In the aftermath of a terrorist attack, many employees may be fearful of returning to normal activities such as commuting or traveling. A company that is the target of a terrorist attack or is directly affected in another way may want to include some form of counseling for employees who lost friends or co-workers during the attack or who live or work where the attack occurred.

Clearly, a wide range of situations will benefit from the preplanning of the BCP process. HR professionals can play a key role in managing emergencies by participating in planning activities and maintaining accurate employee information that will be needed during the execution of the plans.

Once the risks have been identified and plans have been developed, it's imperative that the affected employees have a clear understanding of the plan components through communication and training. Effective and frequent communication of the BCP allows the employees to respond to emergency situations properly, mitigate the risks associated with the crisis, and handle emergency situations when the owner/manager isn't present. Methods include classroom training of the procedures, hands-on training such as drills, and simulation of disasters such as data breaches and loss of power.

Managing Workplace Privacy Risks

There are many legitimate reasons for employers to monitor workplace activities—to ensure the safety of employees, for example, or to maintain security of trade secrets. There are risks to doing so, including lower morale among employees, abuses of the surveillance by unethical employees, and damage to personal employee belongings from physical searches. Employers must balance security needs against employee privacy concerns to avoid an atmosphere of distrust that negatively impacts productivity. Creating this balance requires employers to communicate with employees about the need for any type of monitoring activity and to clearly explain what activities are subject to monitoring, when they will occur, and how the information will be used.

Whatever type of monitoring program is established, it's important for employers to preserve employee dignity. This may not make monitoring popular with employees but should help reduce the lack of trust that may be created by the program. To avoid legal issues, a written policy describing the employer's practices is needed and should include compliance measures identified through court interpretations and the Electronic Communications Privacy Act of 1986.

Electronic Communications Privacy Act of 1986 (ECPA) The ECPA updated Title 18 of the U.S. code to bring an older law current with technology by adding electronic communication to the list of prohibited interceptions. Although the original law was enacted to control law enforcement wiretaps, the ECPA amendment added civil penalties that affect an employer's ability to monitor employee communication. The law permits employers to monitor communication that occurs in their normal course of business and when employees give consent.

Reasonable Expectation of Privacy A key consideration for courts in cases involving workplace searches is whether employees had a *reasonable expectation of privacy* based on factors such as whether there was a privacy policy in place and how an employer handled similar situations in the past. The combination of a legitimate business reason to conduct the search and a clearly stated policy that the employer can demonstrate was communicated to employees will help justify a search.

Privacy Policies An effective privacy policy makes an unambiguous statement that the employer reserves the right to search, describes the activities and resources the organization will monitor, and tells employees that there should be no expectation of privacy. Specific information about what could trigger a search and how the employer will proceed should be included as well. The policy should be specific about the following:

Monitoring Telephone Calls   Generally, employers aren't required to provide notice before monitoring business-related calls (although some states require that both parties to a call be aware of any monitoring that occurs). The monitoring must terminate as soon as the employer becomes aware that the call is personal.

Monitoring Email or Instant Messages   When accessing employee emails or instant messages (IMs), it's best to have a legitimate business reason for doing so. Policies should make it clear that email and IMs sent using the employer's equipment are the property of the employer and may be monitored or reviewed at any time. In addition, protecting customer data and information should be one component of an email privacy policy. For example, the ability of an employee to forward confidential financial or medical information should be controlled.

Some attorneys consider an email policy important enough to be a separate policy that is signed by every employee.

Monitoring Internet and Computer Use   Many issues affect employee use of the Internet, including demand for bandwidth during peak hours of operation, access to inappropriate websites, and downloading viruses, spyware, or other potentially harmful files. The Internet use policy should include a statement of acceptable uses, reasons to restrict access or use, and whether the employer allows personal use. The policy should also state that the employer reserves the right to review data stored on hard drives and require that employees provide any current password information to a designated employee.

Monitoring the Use of Social Media   Prohibiting use of social media while employees are at work is difficult at best. Smartphones allow near-instant access, so making a statement to employees about their reasonable expectation of privacy (or lack thereof) on company-issued phones and laptops is a step toward control. Furthermore, it's important to issue guidelines for acceptable social media site use, both on and off the job. For example, discouraging the use of company-specific information or the sharing of confidential corporate data in posts is reasonable. The key is to be clear on what the expectations are for the employee.

Monitoring the Use of Cell Phone Cameras   The use of personal cell phones in the workplace can be disruptive and difficult to monitor in general, and the advent of camera phones presents even more challenges for employers. Cell phone cameras can be used surreptitiously to take inappropriate photographs of co-workers that expose the employer to harassment claims, make copies of confidential documents, or photograph proprietary work processes or new product development.

An outright ban of cell phone cameras in the workplace is difficult to enforce, but stating clearly situations the employer considers inappropriate (such as in bathrooms, on customer premises, or in sensitive work areas) can be effective.

Video Surveillance   In some workplaces, installing cameras may be viewed as a necessity: for example, in small, all-night retail stores where one employee works alone late at night. In other situations, the need for video surveillance may not be as clear. Employers who determine that video surveillance is necessary for their business operation should clearly state the reasons for the surveillance, the circumstances in which tapes will be reviewed, and how the information will be used.

Video surveillance of bathrooms or locations where employees may change their clothes isn't appropriate.

Searching Property   As with other privacy policies, searches should be conducted for a legitimate business reason, because random searches conducted for no apparent reason are difficult to justify in court. Narrowing a search to employees suspected of theft, or to those who had an opportunity to commit the theft based on other information such as video surveillance tapes, is preferable. Although some employers may be tempted to search an employee's body, this is inappropriate. If this is believed to be necessary, law enforcement should be brought in to conduct the search.

A search policy should clearly state what types of situations will trigger a search, how it will be conducted, what types of property are liable for search (for example, company property such as a desk, an office, a cubicle, a locker, and so on, or personal property such as a purse or car).

Table 6.8 provides some questions to consider before conducting a search.

TABLE 6.8   Questions to ask before searching

Question	Yes	No
Is there a legitimate business reason to search this employee?	X	
Does the employee have a reasonable expectation of privacy?		X
Is there another way to find out if this employee engaged in an improper activity?		X
Is there a workplace search policy in place?	X	
Are all employees aware of the search policy?	X	
Is this a random search?		X

If the answer to any of these questions is different in a particular situation, it may be advisable to look for another way to collect the information needed.

Real World Scenario

Email Monitoring: *Fraser vs. Nationwide Mutual Insurance Company*

Richard Fraser was employed as an independent insurance agent for Nationwide Mutual Insurance when he was terminated in September 1998. Nationwide claimed it terminated Fraser for disloyal activities—contacting competitors and asking whether they would be interested in acquiring some of Nationwide's policyholders. When it learned of the contacts, Nationwide searched Fraser's email records on its main file server and found evidence of additional disloyalty. On the basis of this information, Nationwide terminated him.

Fraser filed an action claiming the search was a violation of two restrictions of the ECPA. First, he claimed that interception of email is prohibited by the act. The court found that because the email wasn't intercepted during transmission, no violation occurred. He also claimed that the search of his email violated ECPA prohibitions against access of electronically stored communication. The court found in this instance as well that because Nationwide provided and administered the email service on which Fraser's email was stored, the search of the email was allowable.

The Third Circuit Court of Appeals upheld summary judgment in favor of Nationwide.

Employers must be aware of legal restrictions on workplace-monitoring policies. In addition to the federal ECPA controls and state laws enacted to protect individual privacy rights, common-law torts for invasion of privacy must also be considered when making the decision to implement a monitoring program. These common-law torts use the "reasonable person" standard to measure whether an intrusion is highly offensive and causes harm, is publicized without a legitimate reason, or knowingly puts an individual into a false light in public. The courts often support an employer's right to monitor their employees in the workplace.

Metrics: Measuring Results

Measuring the effectiveness of risk management activities can be challenging. The key, as with measurement in all other HR functional areas, is to determine what kind of meaningful information can be provided to management in order to improve the effectiveness of risk management programs:

Business Impact Measures The effectiveness of risk management programs can be measured with a return on investment (ROI) calculation to validate the program's benefits.

Evaluating risk management programs can be a relatively simple matter: Compile statistics on a regular basis, and compare them over time. For example, if employees are lax about following safety procedures, establishing a baseline number of violations occurring before implementing a training program and then compiling statistics on a regular basis to determine whether the training reduced violations indicates whether the training was successful. The same metric can be used to keep track of whatever risk management issues are of greatest concern in any organization. Whether it's incidents of sexual harassment before and after a prevention program, the number of cyberattacks before and after improvements to the network firewall, or warehouse losses before and after installing a surveillance system, these simple measures validate the benefits of the program or indicate areas requiring adjustment or further prevention activities.

Another useful measurement for risk management purposes might be to track the reasons for employee resignations from the company. This provides information for improvements to whatever area is the source of resignations by valued employees to reduce future recruiting and training costs and prevent unwanted turnover.

Another example of a useful metric that measures program effectiveness is OSHA's recordable case rate formula to calculate the incidence rate of ergonomic injuries before the program is implemented and taking periodic measures as the program progresses to determine the reduction in injuries. The recordable case rate formula uses a base of 100 full-time employees working 40 hours per week, 50 weeks per year, or 200,000 hours. Figure 6.2 illustrates the formula for calculating the ergonomic injury rate before implementation of the program, when 53 injuries occurred, and after implementation, when the injuries were reduced to 35. The example assumes that an individual employee works 2,000 hours per year (40 hours per week times 50 weeks per year).

Tactical Accountability Measures   Areas for HR accountability in the risk management function could include a measure of the number of job descriptions that include ADA physical and mental requirements to total job descriptions in the company as a predictor of risk for ADA discrimination claims.

FIGURE 6.2   Quantitative analysis of ergonomic injury program

$$\text{Ergonomic Injury Rate} = \frac{\text{Number of Ergonomic Injuries} \times 200,000}{\text{Total hours worked by all employees during the period}}$$

Total number of employees: 350 FTE
Number of Ergonomic injuries = 53

$$\text{EIR} = \frac{53 \times 200,000}{350 \times 2,000} = \frac{10,600,000}{700,000} = 15.15\%$$

Total number of employees: 350 FTE
Number of Ergonomic injuries = 35

$$\text{EIR} = \frac{35 \times 200,000}{350 \times 2,000} = \frac{7,000,000}{700,000} = 10\%$$

Measuring Risk   Metrics addressing risk can occur before the risk happens (through risk assessments and HR audits), and in retrospect, after an exposure has come to light. Both approaches require a focus on education and prevention. Tracking items such as injury rates, days without a recordable injury, and workers' compensation experience modifiers are all ways in which HR can keep attention on organizational performance in regard to safety. HR audits such as audits of employee personnel files for completion, calculating adverse impact to measure diversity in hiring, and reviewing employment practice liability and other type of insurance coverage are all measurable ways in which HR may contribute to an employer's risk management efforts. Consider other types of exposure as well. In some cases, HR may spearhead the effort to have financial records audited on a quarterly basis by an outside auditor to ensure the proper checks and balances are in place for fraud protection and embezzlement.

Summary

Human relations continue to increase in importance for employers seeking to build depth in their employee engagement activities. There are opportunities for this at every stage of the employee life cycle. In recruiting, for example, the employer has the opportunity to communicate how people are treated, sending a message about what individuals may expect if they come to work there. Onboarding processes are another opportunity to build upon human relations principles, when employers help to acclimate a new hire to their job and the organization. Even how people are treated once they separate matters, because the remaining employees draw conclusions about how they would be treated if they left and the consequences of doing so.

Performance management is another area rich with systems that may enhance—or detract from—the human relations efforts of an employer. Taking a whole view that considers an employee's current skill set and future potential, along with an equitable and effective performance feedback system, creates a sense that the employee is a unique individual who is valued by the employer.

The role of organizational culture is another element that may be threaded throughout all HR activities. The way people treat one another, written policies as well as unwritten practices, leadership styles, and organizational values all serve to guide employee behaviors—including productivity, loyalty, and conscientiousness.

Finally, HR leaders must take care to create measurement systems that track employee engagement, and make recommendations to respond accordingly once the data is analyzed. Gathering feedback and communicating actions taken will increase the employee's belief in the employer as a place to remain.

These efforts must all be filtered through regulatory compliance and labor law in order to manage organizational risk.

As an HR function, Risk Management identifies, assesses, manages, and reviews people-related organizational risks related to legal compliance, safety and health, security, business continuity, and workplace privacy. A number of tools are available for assessing and managing risk, such as HR audits, workplace investigations, and plans such as safety and health-management plans that provide guidance for workplace hazards. Occupational health and safety has been a source of concern to workers and physicians for centuries, but employers weren't always required to protect workers from dangerous environments and were rarely held accountable when death, injury, or illness occurred as a result of hazards in the businesses they managed. The Occupational Safety and Health Act of 1970 was the first comprehensive, effective legislation that required employers to provide safe and healthful workplaces for their employees and provided an enforcement process that penalized employers who didn't comply with safety standards. Where other attempts to do the same thing have failed, OSHA has been successful because Congress provided strong enforcement powers to the agency.

In the past, employers were also not willing to compensate workers who were injured during the course of their jobs and made full use of the "unholy trinity" of common-law doctrines to avoid financial responsibility for injured workers. In 1911, Wisconsin was the first state to provide workers with a more equitable process for determining compensation due to them for injuries suffered during the course of their work by passing the first workers' compensation law. This enabled workers to receive compensation for injuries and illnesses without having to use the court system, which was, at that time, heavily weighted in favor of employers.

OSHA has been a key proponent and motivator in identifying workplace health and safety hazards and in developing processes designed to protect workers in a variety of situations. Once employers realized the financial benefits of creating safer working environments, they developed employee benefits designed to enhance health and safety programs, such as employee assistance and wellness programs that serve employee needs as well as add value to the business bottom line.

Security—of information, individuals, and organizations—becomes more complex and challenging each day as new technologies are developed. HR professionals must be able to provide employers with the tools needed to protect them without infringing on employee privacy rights. In the aftermath of devastating natural disasters and acts of terror, preparing to continue business operations is an essential responsibility of leadership teams in every organization. HR professionals contribute to this process through their awareness of the issues involved and participate by providing information necessary to respond, recover, and return to normal operations.

Exam Essentials

Understand the three main measures of job attitudes.   Employee engagement, job satisfaction, and organizational commitment are job attitudes that, if measured, can be managed. While all three contribute to positive organizational and employee outcomes such as improved attendance, lower turnover, and increased productivity, they are distinct constructs. For this reason, they should be managed independent of one another to maximize impact.

Be aware of the impact of an effective employee relations program on the bottom line.
An effective ER program provides a workplace environment in which employees are treated with dignity and respect, are involved in making decisions that affect them each day, and have work that is satisfying and challenging. This benefits employers because employees who feel respected and valued are more productive and loyal to the company and, in the long run, have a positive impact on the bottom line.

Be aware of employer unfair labor practices.   Employers may not interfere with attempts of employees to organize unions or assist a union in organizing, and they can't discriminate against employees who advocate for the union or who engage in protected NLRB activities.

Be able to establish fair and effective disciplinary processes.   The most effective disciplinary process is one that prevents performance problems by providing clear performance expectations and regular feedback, both positive and negative, on how the employee is meeting those expectations. A fair and effective process tells employees clearly what the problem is, allows the employee to respond, and involves the employee in developing a solution to the problem.

Be able to identify various methods for alternative dispute resolution.   Lawsuits are costly and time-consuming for employers and generally disruptive to operations. Establishing alternative methods of resolving employment disputes demonstrates that an employer has provided due process to employees. An effective ADR program involves successively higher levels of management in resolving disputes.

Know how to identify and respond to union-organizing activity.   Union-organizing activity is most effective when conducted by employees in the organization. Some signs that an organizing effort is underway include employees who begin challenging management in staff meetings, employees who start talking with employees they haven't had contact with before, and newly hired employees who are very vocal about perceived management abuses toward employees.

Understand the risk management process.   Risk management activities begin with identifying potential risks; each identified risk is then assessed for the level of risk to the organization and cost of mitigation, transfer, or avoidance. Risks are prioritized and managed to reduce exposure and financial impact in the event a loss occurs.

Be familiar with federal legislation and regulations for workplace health and safety.   The major federal legislation for this functional area is the Occupational Safety and Health Act of 1970. This law created OSHA, which develops and enforces workplace health and safety standards.

Understand the safety needs of organizations, and be able to design, implement, and evaluate a safety program; train employees; and evaluate program effectiveness.   Employers are responsible for ensuring that those who work for them have a workplace that is free from danger. To provide this, employers must be committed to a safe workplace, involve employees in meeting safety standards by giving them the information they need to be safe in the workplace, and provide training for the equipment and materials employees will use to perform their jobs.

Understand business continuity plans, and be able to contribute HR's perspective when creating a plan.   Being prepared to protect organizational assets during natural or man-made disasters can mean the difference between an organization's survival or demise when an emergency occurs. One of the key assets to be protected during an emergency is the workforce. HR can contribute valuable input with regard to employee communication plans and develop training programs that will help to keep the workforce intact in an emergency.

Understand the purpose of an emergency response plan, and be able to design and implement one and evaluate its effectiveness.   The emergency response plan is created in advance of an emergency. It describes what roles are to be played in the emergency and who will play them, communicates to all employees a place to meet in the event of an evacuation, and assigns responsibility for implementing the plan in the event of an emergency.

Understand organizational and workforce security needs, and be able to develop, implement, and evaluate workplace security plans.   Both employers and employees must feel secure in the work environment. Employees must be safe in order to work productively; employers must feel secure that the assets of the business will continue to be available for use in the business.

Review Questions

You can find the answers in Appendix A.

1. A supervisor has called an employee in for an interview about an inventory shortage. When the supervisor begins asking questions, the employee invokes his Weingarten rights. The supervisor has the option to do which of the following?

   A. Stop the discussion while the employee calls an attorney.

   B. Stop the discussion until the shop steward is available upon return from vacation in four days.

   C. Discontinue the interview, and make the determination based on other evidence and documentation.

   D. Continue the interview while waiting for a co-worker to return from lunch.

2. During a unionizing campaign, management may do which of the following in response to union allegations?

   A. Point out the consequences of unionization based on past facts.

   B. Encourage nonunion employees to talk about the reasons they don't want the union.

   C. Tell employees that the company will have to move the jobs to another country if the union is elected.

   D. Ask employees what the union is saying about the company.

3. The customer service manager at your organization has recently begun displaying evidence of job burnout, not participating in meetings and missing important deadlines. When asked, she told you that she is really getting frustrated at the amount of customer complaints she receives about a defective product that the company has known about but failed to fix. Her burnout is most likely related to which of the following?

   A. Emotional labor

   B. Lack of job satisfaction

   C. A negative attitude

   D. Lack of organizational commitment

4. If employees no longer want the union to represent them, they may petition the NLRB for which of the following?

   A. Decertification

   B. Deauthorization

   C. Contract bar

   D. Statutory bar

5. Under what conditions are organizational and recognitional picketing considered to be unlawful?

   A. If a representation election has been held within the past 12 months

   B. If a representation petition isn't filed within 30 days of the start of the picketing

   C. When another union has already been lawfully recognized as the bargaining representative for the organization

   D. All of the above

6. When managers rank employees using a bell curve, this is which type of comparison appraisal method?

   A. Ranking

   B. Forced ranking

   C. Paired comparison

   D. All of the above

7. The 360-degree feedback is best described as a form of what type of performance appraisal?

   A. Employee self-assessment

   B. Supervisor assessment

   C. Assessment from others

   D. Non-assessment

8. Which of the following describes salting?

   A. The union hires an individual to publicize its reasons for targeting an employer for unionization.

   B. The union hires an individual to distribute leaflets to employees as they are leaving work at the end of the day.

   C. The union hires an individual to picket the employer's business.

   D. The union hires an individual to apply for a job with an employer and begin to organize the company.

9. Which of the following communication strategies would be best used to measure employee job satisfaction?

   A. Exit interviews

   B. Brown bag lunches

   C. Employee committees

   D. Suggestion boxes

10. Which of the following is *not* one of the three goals of Workforce Investment Act (WIA) programs?

    A. Reduce reliance on welfare.

    B. Reform Social Security practices.

    C. Improve workforce quality.

    D. Enhance national productivity and competitive ability.

11. Which of the following is *not* a sign of union organizing activity by employees?

    A. An employee complaining of harassment by a co-worker

    B. An increase in employee groupings in the parking lot

    C. The use of union terms at an all-employee meeting

    D. An increase in requests for copies of the employee handbook

12. The Occupational Safety and Health Administration is to the Occupational Safety and Health Act as the National Labor Relations Board is to which of the following?

    A. The Labor Management Relations Act

    B. The Labor Management Reporting and Disclosure Act

    C. The National Labor Relations Act

    D. The Norris-La Guardia Act

13. Employee Weingarten rights established which of the following?

    A. Employers have the right to deny the presence of a co-worker in an investigatory interview.

    B. Employees have the right to consult with an attorney post-discipline.

    C. Union employees have the right to have a union representative present at an investigatory interview.

    D. Employers may not deny a nonunion worker's request for representation during an investigatory hearing.

14. Which of the following is *not* a form of alternative dispute resolution?

    A. Mediation

    B. Discipline

    C. Arbitration

    D. Peer-review panel

15. The company receptionist has always been cheerful and warm when greeting customers and has taken the initiative to do what needed to be done without waiting to be told. She has always kept the front desk tidy and presentable for visitors. Over the last few weeks, the receptionist has become moody and called in sick several times complaining of headaches, and the reception area looks disorganized all the time. This receptionist is showing classic signs of which of the following?

    A. Stress

    B. Job dissatisfaction

C. Substance abuse

D. SARS

16. The Big Five personality trait that is most characterized by flexibility is which of the following?

    A. Conscientiousness

    B. Agreeableness

    C. Extroversion

    D. Openness

17. An employee assistance program will *not* assist employees with what?

    A. Outplacement counseling

    B. Substance abuse

    C. Union organizing

    D. Stress counseling

18. Which of the following is not an IIPP plan required by OSHA to protect employees?

    A. Antidiscrimination plan

    B. Emergency response plan

    C. Safety and health management plan

    D. Fire prevention plan

19. An effective safety and health management plan does *not* include which of the following?

    A. Senior management support

    B. Ongoing worksite analysis

    C. Regular OSHA inspections

    D. Active hazard prevention program

20. How can an employer determine whether a job creates an ergonomic hazard for an employee?

    A. Review and analyze the OSHA logs.

    B. Review and analyze the workers' compensation records.

    C. Review the SDS.

    D. Observe the incumbent performing the job duties.

Chapter

7

SPHR Exam: Leadership and Strategy

The HRCI test specifications from the Leadership and Strategy functional area covered in this chapter include SPHR-level responsibilities and knowledge.

Responsibilities:

✓ 01 Develop and execute HR plans that are aligned to the *organization's strategic plan* (for example: HR strategic plans, budgets, business plans, service delivery plans, HRIS, technology).

✓ 02 Evaluate the applicability of federal laws and regulations to organizational strategy (for example: policies, programs, practices, business expansion/reduction).

✓ 03 Analyze and assess organizational practices that impact operations and people management to decide on the best available risk management strategy (for example: avoidance, mitigation, acceptance).

✓ 04 Interpret and use business metrics to assess and drive achievement of strategic goals and objectives (for example: key performance indicators, financial statements, budgets).

✓ 05 Design and evaluate HR data indicators to inform strategic actions within the organization (for example: turnover rates, cost per hire, retention rates).

✓ 06 Evaluate credibility and relevance of external information to make decisions and recommendations (for example: salary data, management trends, published surveys and studies, legal/regulatory analysis).

✓ 07 Contribute to the development of the organizational strategy and planning (for example: vision, mission, values, ethical conduct).

✓ 08 Develop and manage workplace practices that are aligned with the organization's statements of vision, values, and ethics to shape and reinforce organizational culture.

✓ 09 Design and manage effective change strategies to align organizational performance with the organization's strategic goals.

✓ 10 Establish and manage effective relationships with key stakeholders to influence organizational behavior and outcomes.

Knowledge:

✓ 01 Vision, mission, and values of an organization and applicable legal and regulatory requirements

✓ 02 Strategic planning process

✓ 03 Management functions, including planning, organizing, directing, and controlling

✓ 04 Corporate governance procedures and compliance

✓ 05 Business elements of an organization (for example: products, competition, customers, technology, demographics, culture, processes, safety and security)

✓ 06 Third-party or vendor selection, contract negotiation, and management, including development of requests for proposals (RFPs)

✓ 07 Project management (for example: goals, timetables, deliverables, and procedures)

✓ 08 Technology to support HR activities

✓ 09 Budgeting, accounting, and financial concepts (for example: evaluating financial statements, budgets, accounting terms, and cost management)

✓ 10 Techniques and methods for organizational design (for example: outsourcing, shared services, organizational structures)

✓ **11** **Methods of gathering data for strategic planning purposes (for example: Strengths, Weaknesses, Opportunities, and Threats [SWOT], and Political, Economic, Social, and Technological [PEST])**

✓ **12** **Qualitative and quantitative methods and tools used for analysis, interpretation, and decision-making purposes**

✓ **13** **Change management processes and techniques**

✓ **14** **Techniques for forecasting, planning, and predicting the impact of HR activities and programs across functional areas**

✓ **15** **Risk management**

✓ **16** **How to deal with situations that are uncertain, unclear, or chaotic**

Developing the human resource professionals of today into robust business partners is more important than ever. Competing in the 21st century not only requires high levels of adaptability, but the pace of change demands highly agile, competent professionals with a senior level understanding of the business framework within which we conduct our craft.

The acronym *VUCA* has become a mantra, defining the environment in which HR practitioners must operate. Circumstances tend to be Volatile, subject to changing needs and priorities at any given moment. HR practitioners operate with high degrees of Uncertainty, especially when managing risk and anticipating the effects of regulatory mandates and management trends. Navigating Complex situations is often the norm, with HR requiring to respond to the chaotic dictates of the unplannable. And senior leaders must become adept and maneuvering the Ambiguous, making decisions based on fact and reason but the obscure as well.

The functional area of Leadership and Strategy is especially grounded in these principles. This is evidenced by HRCI's assertion that senior HR leaders are responsible for "leading the HR function by developing HR strategy, contributing to organizational strategy, influencing people management practices and monitoring risk." Exam content related to this domain makes up 40 percent of the SPHR, so it is well worth a deep dive into the related concepts.

As with all chapters, note that there are some content redundancies between the PHR and the SPHR exam. These include the following:

- Mission, vision, values, and ethics

- Business elements

- Corporate governance

- Change management processes

- Risk management

For this reason, this chapter and those going forward will refer you to the relevant PHR chapters where appropriate for more information.

Ethics is discussed in Chapter 11, "SPHR Exam: Employee Relations and Engagement," particularly in the context of employee relations and engagement and performance management.

It is unclear from the exam content outline alone just how much specific labor law will be on the SPHR exam. However, understanding labor law as it relates to this functional domain is fundamental to HR leader competencies. Additionally, this is the *only SPHR domain* with a reference to labor laws (see Responsibility 02 and Knowledge Requirement 01), making it exceptionally noteworthy in the context of Leadership and Strategy. For this reason, we recommend that you rigorously study Appendix C, which covers the major legislation related to all domains of human resources.

Organizational Planning and Strategy

Alignment is a word that is important to understand in the context of leadership and strategy. HRCI defines it as making something line up, or making them parallel or organizing items in a similar way. Specifically, the SPHR exam calls upon senior leaders to align HR plans and programs with business strategy and results. In this sense, it is not enough to simply have a plan. HR is responsible for achieving the goals that cascade down from the organization's mission, vision, and values. For example, if the company's mission is to provide the "best customer service experience in the world," HR's strategic plan may include elements of employee training and development that support this mission. This often includes designing organizational interventions that execute goals through change management efforts.

At a macro level, HR must design, implement, and evaluate their policies and programs within the structural framework of the business. This is explored next.

Organizational Structures

Keeping a large group of people with different perspectives and assignments moving in the same direction is a challenge for organizations. *Organizational structures* were designed to provide a framework that keeps information flowing to departments and the employees who need it to do their jobs. In some cases, organizations may use different structures in different business units. For example, the vice president of sales in an organization with a functional structure reports to the CEO, but the sales organization may be organized with a geographic or product structure for the most efficient management of the sales operation. The general types of structures are:

Functional Structure   The *functional organization structure* is represented by the traditional pyramid-shape organization chart with which most people are familiar. It's a hierarchical structure in which communication moves from the top down and from the bottom up. These structures are more formal and rigid than some other structures and are appropriate for businesses with a single product line where specialization is an advantage. In this structure, each functional area reports to the CEO. Functional organizations are generally very centralized.

Product-Based Structure   A *product-based organization structure*, also known as a *customer-oriented structure*, is organized by product line and is appropriate when the company has well-defined product lines that are clearly separate from each other. In this structure, each product line reports to the CEO; these structures lend themselves to either centralized or decentralized decision-making processes.

Geographic Structure   In a *geographic organization structure*, executives of regional areas are responsible for all the business functions in their assigned region; the regional executives report to the CEO. Structuring an organization in this way is appropriate when there are common requirements in the region that are different from the requirements in other regions. Geographic structures are decentralized, with most decisions being made at the local level.

Divisional Structure   A *divisional organization structure* has characteristics similar to that of the geographic structure, but the divisions may be based on criteria other than geography, such as the market or industry. Like the geographic structure, divisional structures are characterized by decentralized decision-making.

Matrix Structure   In a *matrix organization structure*, employees report to two managers. Generally, one manager is responsible for a product line and the other has functional responsibility. For example, the VP of marketing and the production manager for a specific product would both supervise the marketing coordinator who is creating collateral for the product. A matrix organization is advantageous because it encourages communication and cooperation; it requires a high level of trust and communication from employees at all levels to ensure that contradictory instructions are minimized.

Seamless Organization   A *seamless organization* is one in which the traditional hierarchies don't exist—it's a horizontal organization connected by networks instead of separated by the boundaries that characterize other organization structures. The purpose of this structure is to enhance communication and creativity. Seamless organizations wouldn't be possible without the technology that allows employees to connect with each other via email and the Internet from anywhere in the world. This technology enables employees to meet with co-workers who have specialized knowledge without the expense of traveling.

Shared Services and Outsourcing of HR Functions

In some cases, it may be strategically advantageous for an organization to outsource individual HR systems, such as payroll and benefits administration; to outsource the entire function to an HR *business process outsource* (BPO) provider; or to lease employees through a *professional employer organization* (PEO). When this is the case, selecting the appropriate vendor for an organization is crucial. As with any other strategic decision, the first step is to clearly define the services required of the provider as well as the organization's service expectations to ensure that business needs are met. It's also important to identify the responsibilities of both parties so that there is a framework for addressing situations that aren't specifically covered in the agreement.

Considering that virtually all HR processes have the potential to affect every member of an organization, it's crucial that HR ensures a smooth transition to the provider and clearly communicates process changes to the organization.

Third-Party Contract Management

A *contract* is a legally enforceable agreement between two or more parties in which all parties benefit in some way. Generally, one party makes an offer to do or provide something of value (a product or service), and the other agrees to do or provide something in return (payment). Contracts can be formal or informal, oral or written, and implied or explicit. Although oral and implied contracts can be legally enforceable, written contracts provide more clarity and protection for the parties involved.

In a *third-party contract*, some part of the transaction is provided by an entity other than those who have signed the contract. For example, businesses may utilize third parties in functions related to accounting, payroll, or IT services. For purposes of exam preparation, this topic and related competencies are reflected in questions related to the return on investment of outsourcing as a strategic objective in any business function, not just HR. This includes helping their businesses select vendors, measure ROI, and identify alternatives.

As an increasing number of HR functions are outsourced, the need for practitioners to understand the issues involved in effectively managing third-party contractors becomes more important. A critical factor for a successful contractor relationship is a clear understanding of the product or service to be provided, along with clearly defined expectations for quality and service levels. This information is best communicated through a process known as a *request for proposal* (*RFP*) or a *request for quote* (*RFQ*).

In many organizations, the RFP process is handled by a purchasing group or is outsourced to someone who specializes in preparing RFPs, but it's important to understand what information is needed to develop an RFP that satisfies both parties. A well-constructed RFP serves as the basis on which the product or service is obtained, a guide to ensure that the delivery meets the organization's requirements, and a means of evaluation at the end of the project. Although there is no standard RFP format for use in all situations, the elements for developing one are similar:

Conducting a Needs Assessment   Whether you're requesting bids for a one-time project or an ongoing outsource relationship, you must be able to describe your objectives and budget clearly so that vendors will provide an accurate and appropriate proposal.

As part of the needs-assessment process, a client may conduct informal pre-proposal meetings with possible vendors. This is particularly useful when the client has little direct experience with the project or wants to learn more about the product or service in order to describe it more clearly in the RFP. This is sometimes known as *scoping* the project and can become a more formal process with the use of a scoping document that solicits information from a variety of possible vendors before the RFP is written.

Developing the RFP   The format of an RFP varies with each organization. In general, the following components are included:

- A brief description of the organization, including information that will help vendors provide an accurate bid, such as number of employees and locations

- An overview of the project summarizing what is needed

- Administrative details about the process, including submission deadlines, how to request an extension, the format requirements for submissions, and what happens if there are errors or omissions in the RFP. Information about how the proposals will be evaluated should be included here as well (for example, will the project be awarded to the lowest bidder, or will other criteria be more important?). Any penalties for late delivery and how to handle work that is beyond the scope of the RFP are also included in this step.

- A clear, complete, and detailed project description (also referred to as the scope of work, technical description, or project specifications) that contains information significant to the ability of the vendor to prepare a bid and that can be measured during the evaluation phase

- The name of the contact person for additional information about preparing the proposal

Proposal Formats   The RFP should provide vendors with a format to follow when submitting proposals. This serves two purposes. First, it makes evaluating the proposals easier, and second, it ensures that vendors provide all the relevant information for an evaluation of the project. Although the format will vary between organizations and different projects, the following elements will make it easier to compare and evaluate the proposals:

Executive Summary   A brief overview of the vendor's qualifications to provide the product or service needed by the client

Vendor Qualifications   Includes references from other clients

Project Management Plan   Describes specifically how the vendor intends to supply the product or service

Project Team   Includes personnel who will be supplied by the vendor as well as the client's employees who will be involved

Roles and Responsibilities   Includes information about members of the project team

Delivery Schedule   Provides a timeline and milestones for the completion of specific events

Pricing Information   Includes how the project will be billed and whether the price is based on project completion, time and materials, or completion of specific milestone events. The vendor should also provide pricing information for any requested work that is beyond the scope of the proposal.

Evaluating the Proposals   Once the proposals have been submitted, the evaluation process can begin. There are many factors to consider, including the reputation of the vendor, the qualifications and experience of the project team, the size of the company and whether it has the capability to complete the project, how flexible the vendor can be in terms of schedule or other issues, the proposed cost, whether the schedule submitted meets the needs of the organization, and whether the vendor's approach to the project is compatible with the organization's culture.

Selecting a Vendor   When the evaluation has been completed, notify the successful vendor, along with those whose proposals weren't accepted.

Negotiating the Contract   Formalize the agreement, and sign a contract with the successful vendor.

Executing the Agreement   Implement the project. Initially, gathering together all the members of the project team, both those who work for the vendor and those who work for the organization, is important to ensure that the project gets off to a good start. It's also important to maintain contact with the vendor during the implementation phase to ensure that it stays on track and meets your expectations.

Evaluating the Project   Whether this is an ongoing outsource function or a one-time project, an evaluation ensures that the project continues to meet organizational needs and provides useful information for future projects.

Strategic Planning

Global competition requires business leaders to use many tools to give them an advantageous position in the marketplace. One such tool is known as *strategic planning*. Broadly defined, strategic planning is a systematic way of setting the direction for an organization and developing tactics and operational plans to ensure its success. HRCI defines strategic planning as "the process of defining a company's direction for the future in 4 stages: analysis, development, implementation and evaluation." Strategic planning is a dynamic process—it's not something an organization does one time to produce an attractively bound booklet that sits on the shelf gathering dust. By its very nature, strategic planning requires that organizations constantly revisit the plan to make sure it's still viable in the face of changes within the organization and in the marketplace. The strategic planning process answers four essential questions:

- Where are we now?
- Where do we want to be?
- How will we get there?
- How will we know when we arrive?

Because strategic planning has been a popular topic for business writers, consultants, and academicians during the past decade, there are a number of planning models from which to choose.

The specific model selected for use in an organization will depend on the structure and culture of that organization. The elements of all the models fall into four very broad categories: environmental scanning, strategy formulation, strategy implementation, and strategy evaluation.

You should be aware of how all these elements contribute to the strategic planning process.

> **NOTE**   The steps are described here in a logical sequence. In real life, the process may not occur in a straight-line progression; if new information that will affect results is uncovered at any stage, previous steps may be revisited so that the information can be incorporated into the plans and goals.

Planning to Plan

Very often, a strategic planning initiative is led by a consultant experienced in the process. This is helpful for many reasons, not least of which is that during the course of determining the future of the organization, disagreements about the long-term direction of the company may surface, and these are more readily resolved with a neutral third party who is better able to facilitate a resolution and move the process forward than someone with a vested interest in the outcome. When a consultant is used, the preplanning process is generally part of the service they provide.

The *preplan* includes decisions about who will be invited to participate and at what stages in the process, a time frame for completing the plan, and a determination of the tools to be used in collecting data for the plan. Spending this additional time at the beginning of the process could prevent costly errors or omissions from being made and can assist in making the resulting strategic plan more accurate and meaningful.

The result of this stage should be an agreement about the process to be followed, a list of those who will be involved at various stages in the process and the type of information they will be asked to provide, the timeline for completing the plan, and a list of the planning tools to be used in gathering information to be used in the planning process.

Let's begin by defining the terms that will be used to discuss the strategic planning process:

- A *strategy* uses the strengths of a business to its competitive advantage in the marketplace.

- A *goal* describes the direction the business will take and what it will achieve. Goals are set at the corporate and business-unit levels of the organization.

- An *objective* is a specific description of the practical steps that will be taken to achieve the business goals. Objectives are set at the functional level of the organization.

To effectively determine the future direction of a company, it's necessary to know what is going on within the organization, industry, and marketplace and to know what the technology developments will mean for operations. Beginning the strategic planning process with this information can help to focus management on a plan that will avoid pitfalls and take advantage of existing opportunities.

Environmental Scanning Concepts

To develop a strategic plan and set the future direction of a company or develop human resource programs to support its growth, leaders need to know what is going on in the organization, in the industry, and in the marketplace, and they need to know how technological developments will affect operations. An *environmental scan* provides the framework for collecting information about factors relevant to the decision-making process and can help management make decisions that take advantage of existing opportunities and avoid pitfalls. There are two elements to the scanning process: internal assessment and external assessment. A number of planning tools are available to collect the information.

Conducting a comprehensive environmental scan can be a challenge; a great deal of information is available from many sources, and finding the information that is relevant to the specific business can be time-consuming. In addition to the information available from industry associations, government agencies, and trade organizations, customers and suppliers are excellent sources of information for a specific business. Many business-focused cable television channels present in-depth program segments on pertinent topics such as unemployment and inflation (among others), and business publications also provide in-depth examination of some topics. A wealth of information is available—the challenge comes in finding what is most appropriate for a specific organization's needs.

A number of tools are available for use in the scanning process. Let's take a look at some that are commonly used:

SWOT Analysis   A *SWOT analysis* looks at the strengths, weaknesses, opportunities, and threats that are facing the organization. Strengths and weaknesses are internal factors that can be controlled by the organization; opportunities and threats are external factors that may impact an organization's plans:

Strengths   Strengths are internal factors that will support the organization's plans. These can include people, such as a workforce that is highly trained in a unique skill not available to other businesses in the market. Machinery and equipment can be a strength: for example, when a recent upgrade of manufacturing equipment allows the company to produce more high-quality products at a lower cost. Developments in technology, such as a state-of-the-art order-processing system, and other factors that give the organization an edge in the marketplace are also considered strengths that contribute to organizational success.

Weaknesses   Weaknesses are also internal factors, but these represent obstacles to the organization. Weaknesses can include workforce issues such as poorly trained workers, old machinery or equipment that is inefficient and costly to operate, outdated technology, and any other factors that make it difficult for an organization to achieve its goals.

Opportunities   Opportunities are external factors that will aid the organization in the marketplace. These can include a wide variety of circumstances such as economic upswings, demand for the product, or a competitor whose product quality has declined.

Threats   External factors that the organization must overcome or turn to an advantage are threats to its ability to achieve success. These can include strong product competition, economic problems, low unemployment rates, and other factors that make it more difficult for the organization to compete.

PEST Analysis   A *PEST analysis* (also sometimes referred to as a *STEP analysis*, depending on how the letters are arranged) scans the external environment to identify opportunities and threats as part of the SWOT analysis. PEST is an acronym for political, economic, social, and technological factors. PEST is discussed in more detail in the "External Assessment" section. Some business experts refer to this as PESTLE, with the "L" reflecting the legal climate and the "E" referring to environmental issues, both of which may influence a company's planning outcomes.

Porter's 5 Forces   *Porter's 5 Forces* is an analytical tool created by Michael E. Porter, a professor at Harvard Business School who has written extensively on business planning and strategy. In his book *Competitive Strategy: Techniques for Analyzing Industries and Competitors* (Free Press, 2008), he described five forces that are found in all industries. These forces include new competitors, suppliers, buyers, alternative products available to consumers, and the type and level of competition in the industry. The importance of these factors in strategic planning is discussed more fully in the "External Assessment" section.

Internal Assessment

Leaders need a firm grasp of the talent and resources currently available in the organization. Some areas to consider in an assessment of strengths and weaknesses are the following:

- Credibility of executive team
- Market penetration
- Strength of management team
- Customer service reputation
- Organization culture
- Market share
- Workforce diversity
- Customer loyalty
- Current product quality
- Level of sales
- Time to market
- Employee loyalty
- State of technology
- Turnover rate

The areas to be reviewed depend to a certain extent on the nature of the business but should include an assessment of performance in every function of the business.

This information can be collected in a number of ways: questionnaires, qualitative analyses, focus groups, surveys (of customers, suppliers, and employees), stakeholder interviews, and other information-collection techniques as discussed earlier in this chapter.

External Assessment

Scanning the external environment presents more challenges than does an internal assessment because the vast amounts of information available must be sought in a wide variety of locations. Tools such as the PEST analysis and Porter's 5 Forces analysis can assist in narrowing down what kind of information needs to be collected. The PEST analysis provides a guide for collecting information related to the general business environment:

Political   The political environment includes such things as increased government regulations and events that influence them, such as massive business frauds. One example of this is the impact of the Sarbanes-Oxley Act of 2002 (SOX), enacted by Congress in response to the Enron and WorldCom scandals. Other equally important considerations for business planning purposes include changes in employment regulations such as the Patient Protection and Affordable Care Act passed under former President of the United States Barack Obama and the immigration debate under President Donald Trump.

For multinational corporations, consideration must be given to political situations in each country of operation, including the stability of the government in some countries, restrictive trade policies, and the friendliness of the government to foreign investment.

All countries and businesses are now faced as well with the threat of terrorism that has negatively impacted sales in the travel industry; however, products related to security have a wider market in this situation.

Economic   The most obvious example of economic concerns has to do with the strength of the economy—can customers afford the organization's products? The unemployment rate is a key factor here, along with interest rates, inflation, and changes in fiscal policy.

Another economic factor employers must consider is the cost of living in the locations where they operate. For example, California state passed a law designed to increase the minimum wage to $15.00 per hour by the year 2020. The cost of living in the epicenter of the tech industry—the Silicon Valley—is so high that the U.S. Department for Housing and Urban Development classified a 6-figure salary (above $100,000) as low income for San Francisco and San Mateo counties.

For investment and expansion purposes, the stock market impacts the ability of a business to raise capital, and the price of real estate can add to the cost of purchasing or leasing new facilities. The strength of the dollar and the rate of inflation must both be considered when creating a long-term strategy.

Social   The demographics of the target market must be considered in long-term planning as well. If an organization's products are targeted at young adults, for example, and that population is static or decreasing, the organization must either change its products or find new markets for them. For multinational corporations, analyzing the social factors of widely diverse markets around the world can prove challenging, but it's essential to ensure that the long-term planning will result in a strategy that increases the success of the business.

Technological   The rate of change in technology varies in different industries, as does the cost of purchasing new technology. Technology affects the level of automation in an organization, and that impacts the overall cost of products. In 2015, the fast-food giant McDonald's announced that it would begin rolling out self-service kiosks in more than 14,000 restaurants from which their customers may place their order. McDonald's combined this with a digital locator that will allow for table service by their employees, and the development of an app that will allow patrons to both order and pay from their mobile device. Restaurants such as Panera, Olive Garden, and Wendy's have followed suit. From cell phones to handheld computers and robotics on production lines, advances in technology affect how work is done and must be considered in the environmental scanning process.

Although the PEST analysis provides a guide for scanning the general business environment, Porter's 5 Forces analysis hones in on issues specific to the industry in which the organization operates. It's critical to understand these industry-specific factors and address them during the planning process. The following questions gather the information necessary to conduct the analysis:

How likely is it that new competition will enter the market?   A market with great demand for a product that is inexpensive to produce and requires little initial investment will encourage new competition. This puts pressure on the organization to maintain a competitive price or to differentiate its product on some basis to maintain market share.

How reliant is the organization on its suppliers?   When an organization produces a product requiring a unique part that can be obtained from only one supplier, the organization may find itself at the mercy of the supplier should it decide to raise the price of the part, discontinue it, or change it substantially.

How diverse is the organization's customer base?   A company reliant on one or only a few customers may find itself being pressured to lower prices, particularly if the product is easy to obtain from other sources.

Are comparable replacement products available to customers at a reasonable cost?   A serious threat to the organization's customer base will be present if a product is generic and similar products made by competitors are easy to obtain at a similar or lower price.

What is the level of competition in the marketplace?   The level of competition in the market will, to a certain extent, limit the strategies available to an organization wanting to enter that market. A market dominated by one or two large competitors holding the bulk of the market share presents quite a different challenge than a new, untapped market with a few small competitors.

Strategy Formulation

Having scanned both the internal and external environments and gathered data relevant to the strategic planning process, the executive team is ready to create the vision, mission, and core value statements, which guide the organization over the long term. Once these long-term guidelines have been established, corporate goals are developed to provide direction during the implementation phase:

Vision Statement   A *vision statement* should inspire the organization and inform customers and shareholders, describing what will carry the organization into the future and what it will accomplish. HRCI notes that a vision statement is a "declaration of what an organization wants to become."

Mission Statement   The *mission statement* gets a bit more specific, describing where the organization is in the present. Specifically, HRCI notes that a mission statement is "a short description of the main purpose of an organization, which does not change (unlike strategy and business practices, which can change frequently)."

Core Competencies   During the formulation of a strategic plan, organizations often identify their *core competencies*: the parts of their operations that they do best and that set them apart from the competition. Here also HRCI provides direction by defining core competencies as "the skills or knowledge that an organization needs to do its work." Many organizations believe that focusing on these core competencies makes it possible to expand their revenue streams. Competencies can be related to the technology used in operations, customer relationship management, product characteristics, manufacturing processes, knowledge management, organization culture, or combinations of these or other organizational aspects that work together synergistically and are difficult for others to replicate. When core competencies are identified, organizations can focus their strategy on ways to build related products or services instead of moving into unrelated areas. In many companies, HR becomes a core competency when it is embedded in operations rather than a segregated business unit. This involves HR leading change, fostering teamwork, developing staff, and contributing to organizational decision-making and strategic planning (all represented in the exam content for both the PHR and the SPHR).

Corporate Core Values Statement   A statement of *core values* is a way for the executive team to communicate their standards for how the organization will conduct business. Core values are "the basis upon which the employees of an organization make decisions, plan strategies and interact with others" (HRCI). The values chosen for this purpose should be those that will be true regardless of changes in product lines or business processes. A question to ask in selecting an organization's values is whether the value would hold true if the organization changed its focus entirely and began doing business in a completely different way. Values such as integrity, excellence, teamwork, customer service, and mutual respect are some of those that remain constant regardless of changes in business operations.

These beliefs about the organization are usually reflected in its culture. When identifying corporate values, it's important to look not only at what the management team would like to see in the way of behaviors in the organization but also at the values being demonstrated in the course of business each day. When there are discrepancies between the stated, formal values and the informal values demonstrated by the workforce, the strategic plan can include goals designed to align the two.

Once the vision and mission statements have defined why the organization exists, corporate goals are needed to describe how the organization will get there in the mid to long term. Effective corporate goals follow the SMART model:

Specific   The goal should be descriptive enough to guide business-unit managers in developing action plans that will accomplish the goal.

Measurable   The goal must include a method for determining when it has been met.

Action-Oriented   Goals must describe the actions that will be taken.

Realistic   The goal must be high enough to challenge the organization or individual but not so high that it's unachievable.

Time-Based   Goals must include a time frame for completion.

Once identified, these elements are combined into one strategic document, often called a *business plan*. The contents of a business plan may vary, but ultimately, it must match the purpose identified through the strategic planning process. Exam objective 01 offers insight into the competency that a senior leader must have: Plans must align with company strategy. This includes correlating HR and other plans with the organization's strategic plan's performance expectations to include growth targets, new programs/services, and net income expectations. It's from this document that strategy implementation may begin.

Strategy Implementation

The strategy implementation phase further defines the corporate goals for implementation at the business-unit and functional levels of the organization. It's at this stage that most of the short-range goals are developed:

Develop tactical goals.   Whereas the strategic goal broadly defines direction, the tactical goal describes what will be accomplished to achieve the strategy.

Develop action plans.   The action plan breaks down the tactical goal into steps to be taken by an individual, a team, or an operating group to accomplish the tactical goal.

Strategy implementation may also drive organizational interventions to help prepare the environment for the "new" normal. This often requires that HR professionals act as change agents, helping their teams adapt to both short- and long-term initiatives. For those unfamiliar with change management theories, a study of Chapter 2's section "Change Management" is advisable.

Additionally, it may be necessary to build a *business case* to persuade executive management to take action. A business case takes into account the findings from the internal and external assessments, company goals, and current and desired future states, and it then clearly defines the risk of taking/not taking the proposed action. Most often, a business case serves as an analytical justification for taking a prescribed action.

Real World Scenario

Wright Sisters, Inc. Strategic Plan

Wright Sisters, Inc. (WSI) is a fictional company with 3,000 employees that has been recently challenged by the appearance of a new manufacturing plant in the small Midwestern city where it's located. The unexpected impact of this seemingly small change in the external environment has made senior management and the board of directors realize how unprepared they are to respond rapidly to changes in their business sector. They've decided to be proactive and implement a strategic planning process to discover what other unexpected changes could be lurking in the future.

Over the years, there have been many changes in the market for WSI's products, both technological and demographic. Because WSI has always maintained strong relationships with the hardware stores that distribute its products, WSI has been able to meet the changing needs of its customer base.

As a result of the strategic planning process, the WSI board has settled on the following statement of their vision for the company:

"Bringing the joy of gardening to new generations of gardeners."

To accomplish this vision, WSI has developed a mission to guide its operations over the next five years:

"We are the home-gardening source. The quality of our products allows busy families to enjoy gardening together. Our gardening education programs grow 'gardeners for life' by teaching adults and children to make gardening easier and more enjoyable."

Based on the company's history and its vision and mission statements, the board created a corporate value statement to set expectations for how employees and managers interact:

"WSI values integrity and excellence in its products and its people. We treat ourselves, our customers, and our suppliers with dignity and respect. We believe in and encourage new ideas to make our products better and help our business grow, and we acknowledge and reward those who present these ideas. We are accountable for our actions, and when mistakes occur, we focus on preventing future errors and moving forward. We are passionate about achieving our goals, and we are passionate about gardening."

As a result of the environmental scan, the WSI board learned that one of its underutilized strengths is the popularity of "Ask Lydia," a gardening column written by one of its founders, Lydia Wright. Because of this, they have decided to capitalize on Lydia Wright's knowledge of and passion for gardening. To do this, they have developed the following corporate goal:

"Within three years, create a nationally recognized gardening education program based on the 'Ask Lydia' columns."

In order to accomplish this midrange goal, the marketing department has developed a short-range tactical goal and action plan:

Tactical goal: "Increase the number of newspapers in which 'Ask Lydia' appears by 25 by the end of the fiscal year."

The marketing action plan looks like this:

1. Identify newspapers to target.

2. Create a sales pitch.

3. Contact editors.

4. Draw up contracts.

5. Submit weekly columns.

With the goals in place, the marketing department is now able to develop a budget and implement the plan.

Strategy Evaluation

The ability of a company to accomplish its mission and conduct business in accordance with its core values largely depends on the behavior modeled by upper management. Employees are quickly able to observe any disconnect between what the employer says and what the employer does. Reinforcing values through corporate behavior is accomplished by modeling value-based behavior, communicating successful missions (celebrating success), and coaching employees using the mission, vision, and values as performance benchmarks. These activities help the organization achieve positive outcomes while reinforcing its strategic plan.

Evaluating the strategy tells the planners whether the organization is achieving the desired goals and moving the strategy forward. This stage is important because if the action plans aren't working or if conditions in the marketplace change, the organization must be prepared to respond immediately and adjust the tactical goals and action plans. In some cases, the corporate goal may need to be revisited and adjusted to adapt to the change in conditions.

Once the action plans, including the methods for evaluation, are developed, it's possible to determine how many and what kind of resources will be required to implement the strategy. The plan may require additional employees, funds to outsource some components of the plan, or the purchase of new technology or new equipment; if so, these elements determine how much cash is required to achieve the desired goal. At this point, those involved in the planning process have the information necessary to analyze the cost of achieving the goals against the potential benefits before committing resources to implement the strategy. For this reason, budgeting and accounting are explored next.

Basic Accounting and Budgeting

The finance function is responsible for creating and maintaining accounting records and managing organization budgets. HR professionals at the management level are often expected to participate in the budgeting process not only for HR-specific expenses but also by providing compensation and benefit information that is incorporated in the overall organization budget. Although closely related, accounting and budgeting activities have different goals.

Accounting

The accounting function creates reports to summarize the results of business activity, including the balance sheet, income statement, and statement of cash flows. All accounting reports are produced at the end of accounting periods, which are generally monthly, quarterly, and annually. The annual reporting period can be defined as any 12-month period and doesn't necessarily coincide with a calendar year (January through December). An annual reporting period that is different from a calendar year is known as a *fiscal year*. Many companies, for example, have fiscal years that begin on July 1 and end on June 30 of the following calendar year. This function is guided by the Generally Accepted Accounting Principles (GAAP) that govern financial recordkeeping and establish checks and balances to discourage fraud and improve record accuracy.

The *balance sheet* is a picture of the financial condition of the organization on a specific day, usually the last day of the accounting period. Information on the balance sheet includes the company's assets, liabilities, and equity. This report is known as a balance sheet because the total of the liabilities and the equity must equal the total of the assets as represented by the balance sheet formula:

$$\text{Assets} = \text{Liabilities} + \text{Equity}$$

The *income statement*, sometimes referred to as the *profit and loss statement (P&L)*, provides information about the financial results of operations during the reporting period. The report informs readers how much revenue was produced from various sources, how much it cost to produce the goods or services, what the overhead expenses were, and what the profit or loss for the period was.

The *statement of cash flows* provides important facts about the money that flowed through the business during the accounting period: where it came from and what it was used for. This statement shows how much cash was a result of sales, how much was spent to produce the products that were sold, how much money was borrowed or came in as a result of new capital investments, and how much was invested in assets.

HR professionals need to understand some basic accounting terminology and be able to read and understand financial reports in order to be effective strategic partners in their organizations. Table 7.1 provides definitions for some common accounting terms.

TABLE 7.1 Common accounting terms

Term	Definition/description
Accrued expense	Expenses, such as vacation leave, that have been incurred but not yet paid
Accounts payable	Money owed by the business to its suppliers
Accounts receivable	Money owed to the business by customers
Assets	Tangible or intangible items of value owned by the business
Audited financial statements	Financial statements that have been examined by an independent auditor (not affiliated with the company) to determine whether they fairly represent the financial condition of the business
Budget	A projection of revenue and expenses used to control actual expenses
Cost of goods sold	Money spent on supplies and labor to produce goods or services
Equity	Value of the business to owners after all liabilities have been paid
Expense	Money spent to operate the business
Generally accepted accounting principles (GAAP)	Standards established by the Financial Accounting Standards Board (FASB) for recording financial transactions
Gross profit	Sales revenue less cost of goods sold
Liability	Money owed by the business to others, such as lenders or the government (for payroll taxes withheld), or to employees (for unused vacation time)
Net profit	Gross profit fewer operating expenses
Profit	Money earned by the business after all expenses have been paid
Retained earnings	Net profits that aren't distributed to owners but remain in the business as equity
Revenue	Money received from customers for products or services

Budgeting

The budgeting process determines how many and what kind of resources will be required to accomplish goals and objectives generated by the strategic plan. Whether the plan requires additional employees, funds to outsource elements of the plan, new technology, or new equipment, these elements determine how much cash is needed to achieve the goal. There are two basic ways to create a budget; the first is based on historical budget information, and the second is known as *zero-based budgeting* (ZBB):

Budgets Based on Historic Information   A historic budget bases the current budget on the prior year's budget. Past budgets and expenditures are reviewed and the new budget is based on the historical trends. In some cases, the amounts in the budget are increased by a flat percentage rate, based on inflation or anticipated salary increases. This method assumes that, operationally, nothing will change from the last budget.

Zero-Based Budgeting (ZBB)   The concept behind ZBB is very simple: Assume you're starting from scratch, and determine what is needed to achieve the goals. How many people will be required? How much will you need to spend on outsourcing? What will be the cost of new technology or equipment? Unlike the historic budget process, ZBB requires that the need for each expenditure be justified in terms of the new goals and action plans.

As part of a zero-based budget planning process, HR examines all the programs offered to employees to determine whether they're still adding value to the organization. Programs that no longer add value are dropped and replaced with those that do add value or, if cost cutting is required, are dropped and not replaced.

Regardless of the way in which the budget is developed, it can be created from the top down, from the bottom up, or with a combination approach:

Top-Down Budgeting   The *top-down budget* is created by senior management and imposed on the organization. Managers with operating responsibility have little input on how much money they will have to achieve their goals. This process is advantageous to senior management because they have complete control of how and where the money is spent. The disadvantage is that those creating the budget are generally far removed from actual operations and may not have full knowledge of what will be needed to achieve the goals they establish. This method often results in political battles as mid- and lower-level managers lobby senior management for additional funds for their particular departments.

Bottom-Up Budgeting   The *bottom-up budget* includes all managers with budget responsibility in the budget-creation process. Managers with direct operating responsibility for achieving goals develop a budget based on their knowledge of operating costs and provide the information to senior managers who have a view of the big picture for the organization. One advantage of this process is the commitment of operating managers to a budget they helped to create. Disadvantages include the amount of time required, the lack of awareness of the organization's big picture on the part of operating managers, and initial budget requests that may be unrealistic.

Parallel Budgeting A *parallel budget* includes elements of both the top-down and bottom-up approaches: senior management provides broad guidelines for operating managers to follow in creating budgets for individual departments. This approach gives operating managers a context for developing individual budgets that are more realistic.

The end result of the budget process is a projection of expected revenue and costs needed to generate the revenue. Budget reports also include a cash flow projection that is used to prepare for short- or long-term shortfalls of cash, such as might occur in a seasonal business when the cash that comes in during the sales period (such as Christmas or Mother's Day) must support expenses that occur over a longer period of time. A separate report, known as a *capital budget*, is used to project asset purchases, such as buildings, machinery and equipment used in manufacturing, or computers.

Strategic Management

As organizations developed and grew ever larger, the need for controlling large numbers of workers in geographically diverse locations presented a challenge for business owners, who responded by creating bureaucracies to ensure that operations were conducted in accordance with the direction set by senior management. These bureaucracies, developed by American businessmen in the mid-19th century, enabled the dominance of American products throughout the world for 100 years and were emulated by businesses in other countries. As long as the demand for products was greater than the number of products available, this model, in which business dictated what it would produce to the customer, worked extremely well.

When business conditions changed and customers became more demanding, this "one size fits all" approach was not as successful. Japanese manufacturers gave customers an alternative, and customers responded by purchasing those companies' products. American businesses, because of their bureaucratic methods, were slow to respond. The need for constant innovation to satisfy changing customer needs was a difficult transition, and it continues to affect American business.

It's up to management to ensure that the strategies and plans developed to meet changing customer needs are implemented and accomplished. Four basic management functions are used for this purpose: planning, organizing, directing, and controlling. These functions ensure that organization resources are used in the best way to achieve corporate goals. The planning function has been covered extensively; let's talk briefly now about the other functions.

Organizing Managers are responsible for providing a structure within which employees are able to complete their work. Many factors must be considered, including what work needs to be done, how employees interact and with whom, the decision-making process in the organization, and how work is delegated. Issues to be considered in developing an organization structure are whether management is centralized or decentralized, the nature of the functions, and the span of control for each manager.

A *centralized organization* is one in which the decision-making authority is concentrated at higher levels in the organization; in a *decentralized organization*, the decision-making authority is delegated to lower levels.

Business functions are classified as either *line functions*, such as operations and sales, which make decisions about operating needs, or *staff functions*, such as human resources and finance, which don't make operating decisions but do advise line managers.

Finally, *span of control* refers to the number of employees that one manager can directly supervise. Depending on the nature and complexity of the task, this number varies. Managers responsible for very complex tasks requiring closer supervision are able to supervise fewer employees than managers responsible for those performing less complex tasks.

Directing   Managers must establish relationships with the employees they supervise to encourage and support them in accomplishing their goals. Management style contributes to the development of these relationships.

Controlling   The control function is used by managers to ensure that the strategies, tactics, and plans developed during the planning process are implemented. As discussed earlier in "Strategy Evaluation," this is an ongoing process. In addition to evaluating individual goals and action plans as described in that section, management must have a "big picture" view of overall progress.

Other strategic management responsibilities covered on the SPHR exam include managing risk to protect the organization's assets and ensure continuity of operations in extreme conditions. Risk management concepts are discussed at length in Chapters 6 (including the strategies of accepting, avoiding, mitigating, or transferring) (PHR level) and 11 (SPHR level). Additionally, all HR professionals are responsible to develop, implement, and manage corporate governance procedures. These procedures, along with the Sarbanes-Oxley Act that governs them, are covered in detail in Chapter 2, "PHR Exam: Business Management."

Strategic Relationships

If the purpose of business strategy is to plot the course for organizational success, what is meant by a *strategic relationship*? For HR professionals, strategic relationships are those that advance the contribution of the HR function toward achieving organization goals. Strategic relationships reflect the business plan and are important enough to make any strategic-planning tool succeed or fail. Strategic relationships are built between individuals defined as *stakeholders*, who are the employees, the management hierarchy, the shareholders, and the community. In addition, these relationships create a subculture of the very identity of the brand—both internally from the perspective of the management team and their employees and externally, driven by the forces of the business climate.

It could be argued that the success of any strategic or business planning outcomes depends on the quality of the internal and external relationships:

Internal Relationships   Internal relationships that move HR toward the accomplishment of organization goals are built over time as the HR function establishes its credibility with the executive team, management, employees, and vendors. Credibility is established when the HR function provides solutions to organization workforce problems at all levels. Often identified through an organizational chart, the relationships that exist within the corporate framework reflect both personal and professional connections. The ability of individuals to work with each other helps create the culture that drives business outcomes and often is the target of HR efforts defined under the function of employee and management relations. Communication, goal-setting, and project-management skills are representative of the types of behaviors that can be addressed through strategic employee relations activities.

These labor-management relationships are at the core of many of HR's responsibilities, because HR defines the structure from which management takes employment-related action. The following are examples of the HR activities that define these relationships:

- Creating policies, procedures, and rules
- Complying with legal and regulatory directives
- Analyzing jobs from which job descriptions and performance metrics are developed
- Employing strategic HCMPs to ensure that the workforce has the appropriate skill set to achieve the corporate objectives identified through the strategic planning process

External Relationships and Data Sources   A network of individuals whose work influences or intersects with an organization's goals brings long-range benefits to HR professionals. Frequently, the ease with which you can obtain information about the best service providers, find employees with critical skills, or build partnerships that add value to human resource programs and influence the bottom line is enhanced when relationships are established before they're needed.

Note that senior HR leaders are often plugged into external sources for information that may be used to inform decision-making throughout the organization. For this reason, the ability to discern what is credible or incredible becomes a sought-after skill. For example, the Internet has available a multitude of sites with salary data that may be used by HR to build pay scales. These sites range from the formal, published salary surveys to user self-reports. Sites that allow users to self-report (such as Glassdoor.com) contain data that may—or may not—be scientifically credible. Another example of external sources for information is the study of employee engagement. Much has been written about this management trend because increased employee engagement is positively correlated with desired outcomes such as retention and productivity. From a psychological perspective, employee engagement refers to the level of investment an employee has in the *job tasks*—not their level of commitment to the organization. This distinction is important in that if companies expect human resources to increase employee engagement, the HR plan will address job tasks, not necessarily the organizational culture as a whole. HR leaders must be able to evaluate the credibility of surveys, management trends, and even legal analysis *before* recommending their companies base decisions on it. At a minimum, HR should be sure that the intervention being recommended is a valid predictor of the desired outcome.

In addition, identifying reliable, high-quality service providers for organization workforce needs, such as recruiting agencies, benefit brokers, and others with expertise in areas of importance to the organization, ensures the availability of needed services when they're required. These workforce needs are often expressed through the design of human capital management plans, discussed next.

Human Capital Management Plans

During the strategic planning process, HR, along with all other business functions, develops tactical goals and action plans designed to meet the needs of the organization. For HR, the result is known as a *human capital management plan (HCMP)*. Also known as a *strategic HR plan*, an HCMP answers the same four questions addressed during the strategic planning process previously described:

- Where are we now?
- Where do we want to be?
- How will we get there?
- How will we know when we arrive?

To be effective and credible, the HCMP must align with the corporate strategy and goals and help achieve the desired business results. So, the answer to the question "Where do we want to be?" is based on the human capital requirements of the goals in the organization's strategic plan. From there, the HCMP lays out the HR contribution to those goals. The most impactful HCMP is as critical as any marketing plan or R&D road map—something that creates a competitive advantage for the organization.

The specific requirements of an HCMP will differ in various organizations, but some common components need to be addressed, as described in Table 7.2.

TABLE 7.2   Human capital management plan

Component	Description
HR statement of strategic direction	The HR team gathers information from the organization's strategic plan, external sources (such as labor market demographics), and internal sources (other functional areas of the organization), and so on, to clearly understand the workforce requirements for organization goals, what resources are available to achieve those goals, and the timing of deliverables.

TABLE 7.2 Human capital management plan *(continued)*

Component	Description
Desired results or goals	Broadly stated, what will the HR function contribute to the organization's strategic goals? For example, "Attract and retain skilled workers to assemble the new product line."
Objectives	What, specifically, will HR do to achieve its goals? For example, "Reduce time to hire."
Action plans	Identify the steps to be taken to achieve the objectives. For example, "Hire contract recruiter with expertise in sourcing candidates with required skills."
Communication plan	If necessary to achieve the objective, describe how HR will notify the organization of changes. For example, "Conduct workshop for production supervisors on hiring for retention."
Measurement	The means used to measure success of the HCMP coincide with other measures used by the organization. For example, if the technical workforce in the production department needs to be increased to accommodate a new product line, a hiring target of x number of employees can be used. For other types of objectives, metrics such as retention rate, ROI, and so on may be more appropriate.

Information developed during the HCMP is necessary for creating the HR function budget—the basic budgeting elements already covered are used in creating this as well as the organization budget process. As with any functional area budget, some standard expense items are under the control of the head of the HR functions, such as the following:

- Salaries
- Payroll taxes
- Benefits
- Equipment and supplies
- Repairs and maintenance
- Training and development (for HR team)
- Travel
- Professional services
- Outsourced services (human resource information systems [HRISs], payroll, and so on)

The budget may also include expenses that are allocated from budgets created in other functional areas, such as the following:

- Liability insurance (often managed by the accounting or finance function)
- Software (often purchased through the IT function)
- Computer hardware (often purchased through the IT function)

In some organizations, the HR function creates budget items that are then allocated to other functional business units, such as the following:

- Training and development
- Employee awards
- Performance increases
- Temporary replacements
- Recruiting fees

Positioning HR as a strategic partner also requires scrutiny of current HR practices with an eye toward streamlining them to increase organizational productivity and to provide better service to internal customers. This could mean replacing the HR department head count with outsourced services, implementing an employee self-service system, or implementing an HRIS that provides managers with access to information about their direct reports. These and similar process changes can reduce HR department costs and free professionals to spend more time on other organization issues.

Human Capital Projections

The "human" in human resources refers to the people getting the work done on behalf of the organization. *Human capital projecting* is a budgetary activity in which HR attempts to measure the value of these resources. These projections take into account the elements of the HCMP, creating depth by identifying the current competencies of the existing internal workforce. Further creating the competitive advantage, the process analyzes the skill set of the current employees and matches it to the skill sets necessary to accomplish the strategic objectives. From here, the gap is documented, and a plan is created to develop the competencies necessary to meet performance targets. These projections take into consideration the following:

- The necessary skill set of the workforce to achieve both short-term and long-term objectives as communicated through the strategic plan
- The current skill set of the workforce, measured through the performance management system
- The creation of a plan to address any deficiencies
- The decision to build or buy/develop the talent in-house or hire from the external labor force
- The cost of implementation
- The return on the investment in the human resource

One example of a strategic consideration related to human capital management is the national unemployment rate. It's often a great moment to "buy" talent from outside the organization in times of high unemployment, because the surplus of available labor and knowledge resources allows companies to compete at far less cost than in a healthy economic climate. In times of low unemployment, organizations may need to increase their learning and development budgets in order to "build the talent from within." Although it may seem at first glance that freezing hiring in times of economic stress is a good strategy, HR must make the argument for hiring when the right conditions exist, calculate the ROI, and align the hiring behavior with the organizational objectives.

Service Delivery and Technology

The impact of technology on business strategy cannot be understated. With the rapid evolution of digital tools, it is even more important for human resource professionals to understand both the risks and benefits of using technology to manage team members or drive service delivery. Consider these tales of three different companies, in three different industries, using emerging technology in three highly unique ways.

- **Company 1:** In 2017, a Wisconsin-based company began offering to implant rice-size microchips into their employee's hands. The RFID device is then used to access the building, log on to computers, and even buy snacks. As of 2018, more than half the company's employees had the devices implanted under their skin.

- **Company 2:** A financial institution in London installed heat- and motion-sensing devices at the desks of their investment bankers. Designed to record how long each employee is spending at their desks, the OccupEye may be used for workspace utilization reviews. Although the company noted that the devices were not intended to monitor individual performance (it is about space utilization), the union is "keeping an eye on the situation."

- **Company 3:** A San Francisco boutique burger outlet was the first to introduce a hamburger made entirely by robotics. The machine contains 20 computers and 350 sensors that are used to assemble custom burgers that are delivered on a conveyer belt in less than five minutes.

These and similar practices may seem inadvisable due to risks such as privacy, employee health, and the cost associated with untested robotic work processes. Yet companies such as Three Square Market, Barclays PLC, and Creator are broadening the boundaries of the use of technology at work. For this reason, it is up to HR to partner with their executive teams to find ways to mitigate the risk of technology, as opposed to simply saying "no."

Operationally, human resource technology serves the needs of multiple business units. The most common systems are explored next.

HRIS Systems

With the reams of paper generated during the course of an employment relationship, the advent of the *human resource information system* (*HRIS*) was a clear benefit for HR professionals. An HRIS serves two purposes: first, as a repository of information, and second, as an aid to the operational efficiencies of an HR department.

As a repository of information, the HRIS provides an electronic means of storing employment documents, thereby reducing the need to maintain physical files. In firms with multiple locations, both national and global, the ability for employees to access information through the company's intranet or via the World Wide Web reduces delays in payroll-processing tasks and ensures instant access to the information for those with the authority and need to access it. For companies required to produce reports for the Equal Employment Opportunity Commission (EEOC) or the Office of Federal Contract Compliance Programs (OFCCP), electronic access to the data needed to compile reports has increased accuracy and reduced the time required to produce them.

As an effective decision-making tool, the HRIS provides access to a wealth of information needed to make strategic decisions, such as analyzing turnover trends, creating succession plans, and projecting staffing needs. The HRIS also allows human resources to streamline services, eliminating wasted or redundant efforts in the execution of the many administrative tasks of a high-functioning HR department.

Selecting an HRIS

As with any project, the first step in selecting an HRIS is to conduct a needs analysis and identify the following:

- What information will be converted to the HRIS, and how is it currently maintained? Table 7.3 lists some uses to consider for an HRIS.

- Will the system need to integrate or share data with other company systems?

- Who will have access to the information, and how many levels of access will be needed (for example, to view and change individual records, view and change workgroup records, view payroll information, and so on)? Table 7.4 displays what a typical access hierarchy could look like.

- What kinds of reports will need to be produced based on the information?

- Will the HRIS be accessible via the intranet or the web? If so, what security will be in place to protect the privacy of employees and prevent identity theft?

TABLE 7.3   Uses for HRIS

Applicant tracking	COBRA administration
Automated benefit administration	EEO/AA reporting
Tracking recruitment efforts	Administering training programs
Eliminating duplication of data entry	Compensation administration
Tracking service awards	Tracking time and attendance
Sharing payroll information with the finance department	

TABLE 7.4   Typical HRIS access hierarchy

HR access (global information)

Maintain employee records	Coordinate payroll administration
Administer employee benefits	Administer labor relations programs
Post jobs	Administer safety programs
Administer compensation plan	Administer employee relations
Administer FMLA leaves	Manage recruiting
Track attendance/vacation time	Complete EEO/AAP reports
Track applicants	Administer training programs
Manage relocations	

Payroll access (restricted information)

View payroll information	Administer payroll

Management access (restricted to workgroup)

View budget/forecast reports	Manage performance
View succession plans	Administer service awards
Track attendance/vacation time	View compensation
Manage training needs	View recruiting status
Change emergency contact, address, telephone numbers, and family status	Change payroll tax withholding
View company policies	View attendance/vacation tracking
View benefit enrollment information	Open enrollment benefit changes
Bid for internal job openings	Obtain and view paycheck stubs

Once this information has been collected, research can begin on the availability and cost of a system that fulfills the requirements. This analysis should include the purchase cost for the system with a comparison to the cost of continuing to use the current system.

Implementing an HRIS

Once the HRIS installation project has been approved, some practical considerations need to be worked into the implementation schedule. If the HRIS software vendor or a third party will be handling the implementation phase, the RFP should include information about this phase of the project. If the implementation is to be done with internal IT staff, it's important to establish a timeline that works for both departments and allows the organization's HR information needs to be met during this stage.

When implementation is complete and the system has been tested to ensure that it's functioning correctly, the new service can be rolled out to those who will be using it. If an employee self-service component is included, this means providing the necessary level of training for all employees.

Employee Self-Service

Employee self-service (ESS) allows employees to access their own records through some type of automated system. This could be through a company intranet, the Internet, a mobile device, an automated phone system, or a computer kiosk. Providing employees with the ability to access and make changes to routine information frees HR staff to perform other mission-critical functions and gives employees 24/7 access to their information. Self-service, cloud-based software such as Bamboo HR (bamboohr.com) can help reduce the administrative burden of HR activities such as new hire orientation by allowing employees to enter their data directly.

Table 7.4 identifies the kinds of access typically provided in employee self-service applications. ESS systems are evolving as technical capability continues to improve and the workforce becomes increasingly knowledgeable about computer and web use. Access to information such as skills profiles, learning opportunities, and goal-setting guidelines empowers employees and their managers to take charge of their personal development and career planning and facilitates successful communication in these important relationships. Advances in ESS technology also reduce repetitive administrative HR tasks, freeing professionals to concentrate on other important tasks and projects.

Applicant Tracking Systems

An *applicant tracking system* (ATS) provides an automated method for keeping track of job applicants from the time they first apply to an organization to the point when the position is filled—and beyond, if the database is searched as new openings occur. These systems range from Excel spreadsheets to sophisticated database systems that track applicant qualifications, are easily searchable based on different criteria, and provide reports that can be used for annual EEO-1 reports or Affirmative Action Plans (AAPs). Table 7.5 presents the types of information typically captured in an ATS.

TABLE 7.5   Typical ATS capabilities

Applicant information	Open positions	Recruiter needs
Résumé upload	List of open positions	Applicant contact information
Application upload	Job descriptions	Search by applicant information
Applicant profile	Hiring manager access	Search by qualifications
Applicant auto-response	Job posting	Information security
Comments		EEOC report information
Link résumé to profile		Report generator

Hiring Management Systems

If ATS systems ease the administrative burden of the hiring process, *hiring management systems (HMSs)* take the technology to the next level. An HMS uses technology to carry the employer brand throughout the application process. It integrates with corporate recruiting websites to simplify the candidate's experience by moving data directly from candidate input to the database. This reduces errors and improves relationship management with faster response times. HMS systems can prescreen by providing questions that will help candidates self-screen out of the process if they don't meet minimum qualifications, thus reducing the time recruiters spend reviewing résumés of unqualified candidates.

An HMS also provides additional recruiter support with templates to standardize candidate communication and facilitate communication between recruiters in large organizations. Most HMS systems include customizable report writers that can be used to answer questions about specific jobs or the recruiting system in general.

Learning Management Systems

A *learning management system* (LMS) streamlines the administration of employee training programs. The components included in an LMS depend on organization size and the complexity of training needs. These systems can be used to automatically enroll students in required courses (such as safety trainings required by OSHA) and notify managers when employees don't attend. The programs can provide managers with access to approve training requested by employees and to identify skill-development needs in their departments or for individual employees. An LMS can maintain curriculum for required (or optional) courses and provide access on an individual, functional, or organizational basis. Other administrative functions performed by LMS programs include course calendars, facility assignments, pre- and post-testing, and report generation. An LMS can also include self-service functions that eliminate tedious administrative chores from daily HR tasks, such as registering employees, notifying participants, obtaining approvals, and maintaining wait-lists. Table 7.6 summarizes the functions available in an LMS system.

TABLE 7.6   LMS system functions

HR tasks	Training tasks	User benefits
Streamline process (automate recordkeeping, notices, and reminders).	Manage resources: facilities, instructors, and equipment.	Employees: self-registration, web access, online learning
Automatic enrollment for mandated courses	Manage course calendar.	Managers: approve employee requests, access to online assessment tools, plan department trainings
Verify qualifications.	Self-registration	
Manage waiting lists.	Web-based delivery	
Generate reports.	Deliver/score tests, including pre- and post-tests. Score and record course work.	

An LMS is capable of managing the organization's learning tasks in a wide range of situations, from tracking attendance, maintaining training calendars, and generating reports to delivering web-based content to participants, administering and scoring tests, and providing planning tools for managers.

The next step in LMS development seems to be learning and performance management systems (LPMSs) that incorporate functions for managing performance (including 360-degree assessments, self-evaluations, succession planning, and manager feedback) and that track individual rewards. These functions improve a manager's ability to assess performance, assign training to address areas of improvement, and prepare employees for the next level in their career growth.

Organizations that develop their own content use learning content management systems (LCMSs) to create, deliver, and modify course content. These systems allow trainers to develop content, often in a module format so that a single module can be used in multiple training courses. For example, a geographically dispersed organization may create an orientation program with different modules for corporate information, employee benefit options, expense reporting, and other information common to employees throughout the organization, along with modules for each geographic location. This allows an HR professional in a regional office to provide a customized orientation that includes information specific to that office along with relevant information about the corporation at large.

Project Management Concepts

Project management (PM) describes the process of initiating, planning, executing, controlling, and closing an assignment that is temporary in nature. It is described by HRCI as a methodical approach to planning projects that includes goals, timetables, deliverables, and procedures. The assignment may involve designing a new software program, constructing a building, implementing a new marketing strategy, or doing any other activity that isn't part of the ongoing operations of a business. In *Project Management Jumpstart* (Sybex, 2018), author Kim Heldman, a certified project management professional (PMP), describes the five phases of a project life cycle:

Initiation   During the initiation phase, project requests are evaluated and selected for implementation. Those who will be affected by the project—the *stakeholders* such as the project manager, sponsor, team members, customers, and others—meet to discuss the proposed project. Once a project is selected, the sponsor creates a project charter to sanction the project and commit resources to its completion. The charter also identifies the goals and appoints the project manager.

Planning   The planning phase is led by the project manager (PM) and lays out how the project will be accomplished. The plan describes the deliverables, budget, and scope of the project and then develops specific activities and identifies the *knowledge, skills,* and *abilities* (KSAs) required to execute the activities. Finally, a timeline for completing the project is created.

Executing   During this phase, the project plan is implemented. A project team is created, and other resources are acquired. Activities identified in the planning phase are completed during this time, and the PM manages the timeline, conducts status meetings, and disseminates information to the sponsor and other stakeholders as needed.

Controlling   The PM keeps the project on course and on budget by comparing accomplishments to the original plan and making course corrections as needed. As the project progresses, stakeholders may request changes to the original scope, and the PM will review and incorporate them into the project as appropriate.

Closing   The closing phase is the point at which the sponsor/customer acknowledges achievement of the project goals. The PM collects information from stakeholders to improve future projects, stores documentation of project activities, and releases resources for use in other projects or activities.

For HR professionals, the ability to manage projects is critical to success. The following list shows how HR projects can occur in any of the functional areas:

Leadership and Strategy   Integrating the cultures of two organizations after a merger

Talent Planning and Acquisition   Developing a new-hire socialization program

Learning and Development   Creating a career-development program

Total Rewards   Developing a stock option program

Employee Relations and Engagement   Developing an employee handbook

Each of these activities is a short-term assignment that will result in a program that will become part of the organization operations when it's complete, but the process of designing the program isn't an ongoing operation.

The Project Management Institute maintains a website with additional information about projects and how they're managed at www.pmi.org.

HR Data and Metrics

Senior HR leaders must be able to not only interpret data related to the effectiveness of human resource activities, but organizational outcomes as well. Each functional area of the SPHR exam covers its own types of business metrics; for purposes of Leadership and Strategy, exam candidates should understand and be able to apply the following tools for analysis:

Key Performance Indicators (KPI)   KPIs are defined by the Human Resource Certification Institute as measures that help employers track progress and identify ways to improve their business practices. The Balanced Scorecard Institute has several examples of this tool that may be adapted to individual business outcomes: www.balancedscorecard.org.

Workforce Indicators   Workforce indicators are measures that are designed to evaluate the effectiveness of staffing and other activities. For purposes of strategy, they include the following:

- **Turnover rates:** Used to identify how many employees leave the organization or departments at any given time. This data is not diagnostic, meaning that it can only inform HR that there may be an issue requiring further analysis.

- **Cost per hire:** A financial measure, cost per hire is evaluative in that it helps HR identify the expense of new hiring, often by position type. This data may then serve overall workforce plans and budgets, particularly for companies in a growth phase.

- **Retention rates:** Similar to turnover, retention rates is a singular data point that HR may use to track employee satisfaction and commitment.

A detailed discussion of the differences between qualitative and quantitative analysis tools exists in Chapter 2. SPHR candidates unfamiliar with these techniques would be well served to study these concepts as part of their overall preparation activities.

Summary

The leadership role of senior-level human resource professionals is directly tied in with business strategy. HR professionals functioning as business partners requires a deeper view of business operations, including the components of how businesses are structured and practices are managed.

Leading the strategic planning process is an essential competency for HR leaders. Scanning the internal and external environment is a data gathering effort that will be used to inform many business practices. Understanding key elements of budgeting and accounting is also an important consideration when planning a business strategy. Metrics designed to evaluate interventions such as key performance indicators and other workforce measures are critical when making evidence-based decisions.

HR plans, business plans, and human capital management plans should cascade down from business strategy and be aligned with the company's mission, vision, and values. From these plans, decisions may be made about how to deliver HR programs. This includes managing change when business must be done differently and developing key relationships in order to achieve strategic goals and objectives.

The role of technology as a business and HR practice should not be underestimated. Staying current with trends while building innovation solutions for employee and customer service should be a priority for an HR business partner. Another priority is managing the risks associated with these and other strategic objectives.

Exam Essentials

Understand different business structures.   HR professionals must understand the purpose of different structures and how they drive business and human resource outcomes. Understanding the unique needs of each structure allows HR to be more effective in managing risk and making recommendations on elements such as workflow and growth.

Understand the uses of a third-party contract.   Third-party contracts are used for various functions in the HR department. Choosing a third-party contractor begins with a needs assessment to determine how best to serve the needs of the organization. The RFP process provides an organized way to select the best option for the needs of the business.

Understand the strategic planning process.   The strategic planning process consists of four broad elements: scanning the environment; formulating the corporate strategy with the vision, mission, values, and corporate goals; implementing the strategy with tactical goals, action plans, and budgets to accomplish organization goals; and evaluating the strategy to ensure that it can be adjusted to accommodate changes in the organization or the external environment.

Apply environmental scanning tools.   Evaluating internal strengths and weaknesses and external opportunities and threats (SWOT), as well as the political, economic, social, technological, legal and environmental (PESTLE) factors are used to evaluate the climate in which an organization will build a strategy to compete.

Be able to describe and design a human capital management plan.   HR creates an HCMP to describe how it will contribute to achieving the organization's strategic plan. The HCMP clearly describes the strategic direction for the HR function, states the desired results to be achieved, states the objectives for achieving the results, creates action plans, and describes how the goals will be communicated and measured.

Understand metrics and how they're used in HR practice.   Metrics provide a means for quantifying HR programs and activities to exhibit the value added to organizations. The best metrics are those that provide relevant information to management and add value to the decision-making process.

Review Questions

You can find the answers in Appendix A.

1. HR participates in the strategic planning process by doing which of the following?
   A. Formulating the strategy
   B. Scanning the environment
   C. Providing expertise
   D. Identifying strategic goals

2. What is a statement that describes what an organization does that is different from others?
   A. Values statement
   B. Corporate goal
   C. Vision statement
   D. Mission statement

3. What is the purpose of an HR budget?
   A. To determine how much cash is required to achieve a goal
   B. To hold departments accountable for outcomes
   C. To ensure that the outcomes match the strategic plan
   D. To evaluate the effectiveness of HR strategy

4. Salaries, payroll taxes, and benefits are all examples of which of the following HR activities?
   A. Conducting a business impact measure
   B. Creating an HR budget
   C. Creating a compensation strategy
   D. Analyzing the cost of recruiting

5. Based on an analysis of the industry and labor market trends, a VP of Human Resources has determined that the best course of action for her company is to change from a narrow to a broadband salary structure. The current structure has been in place for more than 15 years, and the VP is anticipating strong resistance to making the change. Which of the following tools should the VP use to convince the executive team to make the change?
   A. Calculate the return on investment.
   B. Build a business case.
   C. Calculate the cost–benefit analysis.
   D. Conduct a SWOT analysis.

6. Which of the following is *not* an appropriate use of an HRIS?
   A. Tracking applicant data for the EEO-1
   B. Tracking time and attendance

    C. Tracking employee expense reports

    D. Maintaining employee records

7. The best way for HR to contribute to the development of an organization's strategic plan using internal business operational factors is to do which of the following?

    A. Interpret and apply internal operational information such as the relationships between departments.

    B. Scan the legal and regulatory environment.

    C. Analyze industry changes.

    D. Stay informed of technological development.

8. Which of the following is another term for a profit and loss statement?

    A. Income statement

    B. Statement of cash flow

    C. Balance sheet

    D. Fiscal year summary

9. Which of the following organizational structures would be *most* effective for a company with three distinct commodities for sale?

    A. Functional structure

    B. Product-based structure

    C. Divisional structure

    D. Flat-line structure

10. The retail restaurant for which you are Regional HR is dependent upon low-wage workers for their entry-level positions. For this reason, there is high turnover. This is the best example of which of the following SWOT elements?

    A. Strength

    B. Weakness

    C. Opportunity

    D. Threat

11. The cost of living in the Silicon Valley of California has made it difficult for educational institutions to recruit teachers. This is because teachers cannot typically afford the housing costs in the areas where the schools are located. This is the best example of which of element of a SWOT audit?

    A. Strength

    B. Weakness

    C. Opportunity

    D. Threat

12. Being granted a United States patent for an invention protects against which of Porter's five forces of competition?

    A. Barrier to entry

    B. Threat of substitutes

    C. Bargaining power of customers

    D. Bargaining power of suppliers

13. In which of the following is a statement about what the company believes in likely to be found?

    A. Vision statement

    B. Values statement

    C. Mission statement

    D. SMART goals

14. Total liabilities + equity is most likely to be reflected in which of the following?

    A. Assets on a balance sheet

    B. Cash flow

    C. Forecasted budget

    D. Income statement

15. What is the purpose of the Generally Accepted Accounting Principles (GAAP)?

    A. To create the body of knowledge for accounting professionals

    B. To guide the competencies required of certified public accountants

    C. To establish consequences for accounting professionals who behave in an unlawful manner

    D. To create checks and balances within accounting departments

16. You are the Director of HR responsible for building the Learning and Development budget for the new fiscal year. You decide to take whatever you spent in this fiscal year and add 10 percent. This is an example of which budgeting technique?

    A. Zero-based

    B. Historic

    C. Top down

    D. Parallel

17. The corporate office in which you work is located in Peoria, Illinois. The company has distribution centers located on the East and the West coasts, and each location has its own budget, balance sheet, and profit-and-loss statements. This is an example of what type of structure?

    A. Regional

    B. Bureaucratic

    C. Decentralized

    D. Centralized

18. The advisement role of the accounting department is best reflected by which of the following?

    A. Line management

    B. Staff functions

    C. Span of control

    D. Controlling

19. In which stage of project management are the plan deliverables and timelines most likely to be established?

    A. Implementation

    B. Evaluation

    C. Initiation

    D. Planning

20. What is the primary way a human capital management plan may be effective?

    A. If it aligns with the company's strategic plans

    B. If it properly forecasts the talent necessary to achieve company goals

    C. If it creates a competitive advantage for organizations

    D. All of the above

Chapter 8

SPHR Exam: Talent Planning and Acquisition

The HRCI test specifications from the Talent Planning and Acquisition functional area covered in this chapter include SPHR-level responsibilities and knowledge. These are listed here.

Responsibilities:

✓ **01** Evaluate and forecast organizational needs throughout the business cycle to create or develop workforce plans (for example: corporate restructuring, workforce expansion, or reduction).

✓ **02** Develop, monitor, and assess recruitment strategies to attract desired talent (for example: labor market analysis, compensation strategies, selection process, onboarding, sourcing and branding strategy).

✓ **03** Develop and evaluate strategies for engaging new employees and managing cultural integrations (for example: new employee acculturation, downsizing, restructuring, mergers and acquisitions, divestitures, global expansion).

Knowledge:

✓ **17** Planning techniques (for example: succession planning, forecasting)

✓ **18** Talent management practices and techniques (for example: selecting and assessing employees)

✓ **19** Recruitment sources and strategies

✓ **20** Staffing alternatives (for example: outsourcing, temporary employment)

✓ **21** Interviewing and selection techniques and strategies

✓ **22** Impact of total rewards on recruitment and retention

For SPHR candidates, the functional area of Talent Planning and Acquisition makes up 16 percent of exam content related to a senior leader's ability to "forecast organizational talent needs and develop strategies to attract and engage new talent." It centers around the need for HR to align talent availability with organizational needs—having the right people in the right jobs and at the right time to execute business strategies.

As with all chapters, note that there are some content redundancies between the PHR and the SPHR exam. These include:

- Planning techniques
- Staffing alternatives (outsourcing and temporary employment)
- Interviewing and selection techniques
- Impact of total rewards on recruitment and retention
- Transition techniques for corporate restructures, including due diligence
- Measurements of effectiveness

It is unclear from the exam content outline alone just how much specific labor law will be on the SPHR exam. However, understanding labor law as it relates to Talent Planning and Acquisition is fundamental to HR leader competencies. For this reason, we recommend that you rigorously study Appendix C, "Federal Employment Legislation and Case Law" which covers the major legislation related to the field of Human Resources, much of which is relevant to Talent Planning and Acquisition.

Recruiting and Selection

The recruiting and selection process, known collectively as *staffing*, is ultimately about predicting fit—person to job and person to organization. Fit is determined using many data inputs, including the following:

- The organizational culture and norms (the work environment)
- The tasks, duties, and responsibilities of the job identified through job analysis
- The characteristics of people identified in the selection process through preemployment testing
- Ensuring compliant practices with relevant labor laws

Person-to-Organization Fit

Predicting person-to-organization fit includes the identification and communication of the cultural norms and social mores of a company and its climate. In some cases, it is about the specific product or services offered. Many individuals, for example, would prefer not to work for vice businesses such as alcohol or tobacco, whereas others are not bothered by it. In other examples, the norm of 80+ hour workweeks may be prohibitive to individuals seeking work–life balance, whereas others would find the workload stimulating.

Person-to-Job Fit

Offering a *job preview,* defined by HRCI as "a strategy for introducing job candidates to the realities of the position, both good and bad, prior to making a hiring decision," may help improve person-to-job fit. Job previews must be realistic in that they clearly and honestly portray the organizational culture and expectations. This will aid in that critical retention period of the first 30–90 days. Predicting fit during the recruitment process is dependent on the identification of the characteristics of people (discovered during the recruiting and selection process) and the characteristics of jobs (identified through job analysis).

Job Analysis—Characteristics of Jobs

Fundamental to all human resource practices is analyzing jobs for the knowledge, skills, and abilities (KSAs) and tasks, duties, and responsibilities (TDRs) necessary to successfully perform the work. The job analysis process is systematic and should be applied consistently to all bodies of work within an organization. The process cascades down from the organizational structure, clearly defining how each job within all business units relates to each other. Specifically, for exam purposes, HRCI defines *job analysis* as "a study of the major tasks and responsibilities of jobs to determine their importance and relation to other jobs in a company." The study most often documents the purpose of why a job exists. From the job analysis, decisions about performance evaluations, compensation structures, and the recruiting and selection process may be made.

Preemployment Tests—Characteristics of People

Once the TDRs of the job and the KSAs necessary for successful performance have been established, it becomes necessary to find nondiscriminatory methods to predict an applicant's ability to perform. This is done through the use of preemployment tests. Note that EEO laws define any preemployment requirement as a test that must be job-related and nondiscriminatory in both intent and effect. This includes employment applications, interview questions, psychological tests, in-box tests, and any other requirement of the selection process.

Face-to-face or virtual interviews continue to be the go-to method for making hiring decisions. The different types of interviews are reviewed in Chapter 3, "PHR Exam:

Talent Planning and Acquisition." Regardless of the type of interview, for strategic professionals an interview may sometimes be more art than science. This is often contrary to the operational notion that the only legally defensible way to conduct interviews is to use the structured format. Although it is true that the structured interview certainly reduces the chances of a charge of discriminatory behavior, it is sometimes not a business reality for employers. For example, consider businesses hiring for creativity or innovation, traits that by their very nature are difficult to define. Finding other ways to measure a candidate's ability to perform that remain job-related and nondiscriminatory is often the charge of senior leaders. This leads to a systems-thinking view of hiring in which an interview is perhaps a weighted factor in the process but not the only factor used to make the decision.

Is the résumé outdated? Many companies such as Tesla are looking beyond work experience as a predictor of future success on the job. They are replacing it with game-playing scenarios scientifically designed to measure candidates' abilities in problem-solving, multitasking abilities, conscientiousness, and altruism—all factors of success on the job.

Personality tests continue to be used by many employers to predict fit. Senior HR leaders must be sure that the type of personality test has been statistically validated as a predictor of success on the job. The MBTI assessment, for example, is useful in building an awareness of team member preferences, but it has not been validated for use as a pre-hire tool. Others, which are assessments based on the Big Five (such as NEO-PI R), are specifically designed to be predictive. For example, social extraversion on the Big Five is considered predictive of success in a sales position, whereas on the MBTI, extraversion is simply a measure of how individuals are energized.

Physical tests and drug screens are used by employers to manage risk, and yet, improper use of these tests can actually increase an employer's risk for discriminatory practices. HR professionals must lead the effort to ensure that what is being measured in these tests is correlated with future success on the job. HR must also keep up with emerging law in this area, such as legalized marijuana on a state-by-state level.

Predictive analytics is one method employers are increasingly leveraging to improve their quality of hires. Built from models using specific hiring criteria, these types of analytics can help larger employers sift through the thousands of résumés received each year, targeting the selection process to maximum effect. Smaller employers may also benefit from streamlining the hiring process using technology. The sharp rise in the use of the Internet and social media to recruit for talent is an indication that online recruiting has replaced the more traditional sources for candidates. However, the efficiency of technology has in many cases compromised the candidate experience. Many job applicants report frustration at applying for jobs online and then never hearing back. Progressive companies recruiting in a tight labor market know that improving the applicant experience sends a message about how the company values its employees—even before they are hired.

The role of technology—a broad concept in the scope of all that HR has responsibility for at the best of times—has a particular application for the talent acquisition process. Many companies are using chatbots, for example, to allow candidates to have a conversation with a computer without even realizing it. Other companies are leveraging technology by building databases that allow applicants to complete preassessments that do not require face-to-face interaction. While many companies use technology to enhance the customer experience, so also must HR use technology to enhance (not erode) the applicant experience.

Candidate Sourcing

From a strategic perspective, HR leaders are responsible for the overall *sourcing* (defined by HRCI as "identifying candidates who are qualified to do a job by using pro-active recruiting techniques") strategy. This is different from the operational efforts of recruiting and selection activities. HR leaders are called upon to help organizations clearly define both the need for the job and the qualifications necessary to successfully perform it. In some cases, HR will advise managers on the need to build the talent; in others, it may be best to externally recruit.

HR may also advocate for job restructuring. Redesigning jobs is an effective way to capitalize on existing skill sets while potentially making a job simpler. This, in theory, should increase the talent pool and make the recruit quicker and more effective. This approach will not work where there is a shortage of entry-level workers or where entry-level pay rates are cost prohibitive.

Internal *talent pools* continue to emerge as a strategic source for leadership roles. Some define talent pools as a 21st century alternative to the traditional succession plan. This is because most organizations across the globe can no longer offer a "career for life" track for any worker, and many workers no longer value that as a retaining factor. A talent pool instead tracks the availability of people from diverse sources that may be used to backfill multiple roles as opposed to a linear option. In a pool approach, instead of a single successor for a single role, three or more potential candidates are identified, all with various levels of readiness for promotion. Often, criteria-based organizations with proper tracking mechanisms may also recruit externally for the talent pool should the size, skill set, or availability of internal candidates shrink. HRCI has a bit more specific definition of a talent pool that reads as "a group of available skilled workers, or database of resumes, that a company can use to recruit in a particular location." This definition reflects that both internal and external sources may be necessary to populate a talent pool.

In the current climate with low levels of unemployment, many senior leaders are looking for alternative methods for staffing. In Wisconsin, for example, the unemployment rate was just 2 percent. This prompted manufacturers to hire inmates at full wages to work, even while they serve their prison sentences. This example shows that in a tight labor market, employers must be both innovative and flexible.

Hiring from Within

Many organizations find the practice of filling open positions from within to be preferred. This is so that current employees are given the opportunity to develop their skills and grow with the company. *Job bidding* is an HR practice that allows employees to indicate an interest in future openings, whereas *job posting* is the practice of notifying employees of current openings within the company. Job postings should include the job qualifications as well as any significant dates—such as when the company will begin to recruit externally—for maximum effect. One challenge for senior leaders when sourcing from within is how to address employees who are not selected. This can lead to lower morale if the "why" of the nonselection is not properly communicated. Additionally, the rejected employee should be given a clear picture of what knowledge, skills, or abilities should be developed in order to be prepared for a future opportunity.

In some cases, supervisors are unwilling to promote a high performer as the job the promoted employee leaves behind may not be done as well by a new employee. In these cases, senior leaders would need to engage in some leadership development. It may be wise to help the supervisors see that their high performers may leave the organization altogether if their talents, skills, and career desires are not supported.

Salary Negotiations

It is becoming unlawful in some states for employers to ask about salary history. This is due to the practice of perpetuating systemic discrimination, as employment offers based on past discriminatory practices only furthers unequal pay. Regardless of whether you live in a state with salary history bans, it is an HR best practice to have a plan in place for offering and negotiating pay.

Here the behavioral sciences may be of help. In one study, candidates spun a wheel to select a number between 0 and 100. The participants were then asked to adjust that number to reflect how many African countries were in the United Nations. Those who spun a high number gave high estimates, and those who spun a low number gave lower estimates, an indication that the participants were using their original number as the anchoring point for their decision. *Anchoring bias* occurs when a candidate (or recruiter) makes a decision from an anchoring point. When the initial anchor figure is set high, the final negotiated salary is often higher as well. Having market-based wage ranges and a strong compensation philosophy will help organizations avoid overpaying for talent due to anchoring bias.

Senior HR leaders should also ensure that recruiters have the proper amount of authority in negotiating salaries so that the recruiters can make autonomous decisions in a timely fashion to avoid losing critical talent.

Finally, some organizations offer recruiting bonuses that are calculated as a percentage of the new hire's base pay. This can be a powerful incentive to get critical positions filled quickly. In these cases, however, proper checks and balances should exist to avoid a recruiter offering higher salaries to receive a higher bonus. In this case, salary ranges should be set and approved prior to the final offer being made.

Candidates Not Selected

Another area rich with opportunity for HR improvement exists in handling candidates who have not been selected for hire. Strategic HR pros know that *how* candidates are notified that they have not been selected can leave only one of two impressions—positive or negative. For this reason, it is an HR best practice to notify the "no" candidates as soon as possible in a professional manner. This can be in accordance with how far the candidate has progressed through the process. For example, an email to a candidate whose résumé was received but who a company declined to interview would be reasonable. However, for a candidate who got through the entire interview process but was not selected, a personal phone call from the recruiter would be more appropriate.

Additionally, in a tight labor market, an organization may make an offer to a candidate who accepts and then—for a variety of reasons—decides to renege on the acceptance, leaving HR to make the offer to the next most qualified person. If the next qualified candidate was treated rudely, or ignored for a period of time, they may be unmotivated to accept the offer, leaving HR to begin the process anew.

Labor Law Compliance

Seasoned HR professionals understand the impact of labor law on the work of business—it is pervasive, ongoing, and ever-changing. We recommend that for purposes of the exams, you rigorously study Appendix C of this book. If there are time constraints in your study window, focus less on dates and authors and more on interpretation and application. This may be achieved by having a clear understanding of the operational nature of benchmark labor law in order to advise organizations on best practices.

Staying up-to-date with major changes at both a state and a federal level is necessary for all human resource talent, from the entry level to the executive. The degree to which the understanding is applied professionally is what will vary. Senior leaders will most likely be called upon to understand how labor laws will impact company goals and objectives. For example, for a company with unpredictable payroll runs due to changing business needs, HR could recommend adopting a fluctuating workweek to make payroll more of a fixed, predictable cost. This assumes, of course, that HR understands the various risks associated with these types of strategies, vetting them at a state level and through their attorney where appropriate.

For strategic professionals, it is not only about what currently is law, but also what is being proposed. For example, the Legal Workforce Act was introduced in 2017, proposing to amend the Immigration and Nationality Act. It advocates for mandating employers use of the E-verify system for new hires. This will need to be closely watched by HR for any movement to ensure their employer's practices remain compliant. Another example is that at a state level, such as with California's minimum wage increasing to $15 per hour by the year 2020. In this example, HR can help lessen the impact by gradually increasing employee pay over a period of years, rather than in a single month. Although the overall burden does not change, the impact on cash flow is more manageable. Ultimately,

HR professionals must keep their eye on the progress of this type of legislation and react accordingly to prepare their employer for compliance.

Strategic Workforce Planning

The goal of strategic workforce planning is to ensure that qualified employees are available when the organization needs them. An effective workforce planning process includes the following:

- Forecasting business needs
- Assessing employee skill
- Building plans that bridge the gap between business needs and available talent
- Embedding ways to engage to retain employees

HRCI defines *human capital* as the "employees' knowledge, talent and skills that add to the value of the organization." In strategic planning, the term *human capital management* is a staffing-planning approach that views individuals as assets to be utilized in achieving business outcomes. In this way, employees are resources that must have a strategic, planned-for use in order to not be wasted. This is most often organized through a human capital management plan.

Human Capital Management Plans

During the strategic planning process, HR, along with all other business functions, develops tactical goals and action plans designed to meet the needs of the organization. Forecasting is related to having a deep-level understanding of the organization's current and future staffing needs. This is often done by building *a human capital management plan* (HCMP).

Also known as a *strategic HR plan*, an HCMP answers four key questions:

- Where are we now?
- Where do we want to be?
- How will we get there?
- How will we know when we arrive?

To be effective and credible, the HCMP must align with the corporate strategy and goals and help achieve the desired business results. So, the answer to the question "Where do we want to be?" is based on the human capital requirements of the goals in the organization's strategic plan. From there, the HCMP lays out the HR contribution to those goals. The most impactful HCMP is as critical as any marketing plan or R&D roadmap—something that creates a competitive advantage for the organization.

The specific requirements of an HCMP will differ in various organizations, but some common components need to be addressed, as described in Table 8.1.

TABLE 8.1 Human capital management plan

Component	Description
HR statement of strategic direction	The HR team gathers information from the organization's strategic plan, external sources (such as labor market demographics), and internal sources (other functional areas of the organization), and so on, to clearly understand the workforce requirements for organization goals, what resources are available to achieve those goals, and the timing of deliverables.
Desired results or goals	Broadly stated, what will the HR function contribute to the organization's strategic goals? For example, "Attract and retain skilled workers to assemble the new product line."
Objectives	What, specifically, will HR do to achieve its goals? For example, "Reduce time to hire."
Action plans	Identify the steps to be taken to achieve the objectives. For example, "Hire contract recruiter with expertise in sourcing candidates with required skills."
Communication plan	If necessary to achieve the objective, describe how HR will notify the organization of changes. For example, "Conduct workshop for production supervisors on hiring for retention."
Measurement	The means used to measure success of the HCMP coincide with other measures used by the organization. For example, if the technical workforce in the production department needs to be increased to accommodate a new product line, a hiring target of x number of employees can be used For other types of objectives, metrics such as retention rate, ROI, and so on may be more appropriate.

Information developed during the HCMP is necessary for creating the HR function budget. As with any functional area budget, some standard expense items are under the control of the head of the HR functions, such as the following:

- Salaries
- Payroll taxes
- Benefits

- Equipment and supplies
- Repairs and maintenance
- Training and development (for HR team)
- Travel
- Professional services
- Outsourced services (human resource information systems [HRISs], payroll, and so on)

The budget may also include expenses that are allocated from budgets created in other functional areas, such as the following:

- Liability insurance (often managed by the accounting or finance function)
- Software (often purchased through the IT function)
- Computer hardware (often purchased through the IT function)

In some organizations, the HR function creates budget items that are then allocated to other functional business units, such as the following:

- Training and development
- Employee awards
- Performance increases
- Temporary replacements
- Recruiting fees

Positioning HR as a strategic partner also requires scrutiny of current HR practices with an eye toward streamlining them to increase organizational productivity and to provide better service to internal customers. This could mean replacing the HR department head count with outsourced services, implementing an employee self-service system, or implementing an HRIS that provides managers with access to information about their direct reports. These and similar process changes can reduce HR department costs and free professionals to spend more time on other organization issues.

Human Capital Projections

The "human" in human resources refers to the people getting the work done on behalf of the organization. *Human capital projecting* is a budgetary activity in which HR attempts to measure the value of these resources. These projections take into account the elements of the HCMP, creating depth by identifying the current competencies of the existing internal workforce. Further creating the competitive advantage, the process analyzes the skill set of the current employees and matches it to the skill sets necessary to accomplish the strategic objectives. From here, the gap is documented, and a plan is created to develop the competencies necessary to meet performance targets. These projections take into account the following:

- The necessary skill set of the workforce to achieve both short-term and long-term objectives as communicated through the strategic plan

- The current skill set of the workforce, measured through skills inventories/assessments and the performance management system
- The creation of a plan to address any deficiencies
- The decision to build or buy/develop the talent in-house or hire from the external labor force
- The cost of implementation
- The return on the investment in the human resource

One example of a strategic consideration related to human capital management is the national unemployment rate. It's often a great moment to "buy" talent from outside the organization in times of high unemployment, because the surplus of available labor and knowledge resources allows companies to compete at far less cost than in a healthy economic climate. Although it may seem at first glance that freezing hiring in times of economic stress is a good strategy, HR must make the argument for hiring when the right conditions exist, calculate the ROI, and align the hiring behavior with the organizational objectives.

Many state and local resources are available to help employers make strategic hiring decisions. Analyzing the labor market using these resources can yield data such as the availability of training reimbursement dollars from government agencies, the unemployment rate, cost of living, wage data, the skill set of the labor force population in the area, and hiring support, such as through state unemployment agencies.

Another example of a strategic need is that of global staffing. While there are other exams that deal with multinational corporations and operating on an international scale, U.S. employers are more and more often seeking talent from global sources. A 2017 Harris poll found that more than 50 percent of U.S. companies expect to hire more foreign workers in the coming years. This is primarily due to the idea that employers want to attract and hire the best talent in order to compete in their industries, regardless of where they were born. A strategy of global sourcing for talent will require changes in all functional areas of HR. From a staffing perspective, the use of technology and virtual interviewing skills and the management of employment visas- such as the H1B- become part of the process. On a compensation level, immigration-related perks such as housing may become necessary. Cultural awareness for both the new hires and existing employees through diversity initiatives would also be useful for this staffing strategy to be successful.

Finally, with the shift of U.S. labor output from manufacturing to service, it has become necessary to measure knowledge and mind competencies rather than only the objective, such as physical output.

The Impact of the Business Life Cycle

Talent forecasting is much more than guesswork. In this way, the business life cycle may help inform decisions.

The business cycle refers to the stages a company goes through from infancy (startup), to growth, through maturity and then decline. Holistically, how a company does business is significantly influenced by HR behaviors at each stage. From a talent acquisition perspective, it is narrower in focus.

The ability of HR to forecast staffing needs at each stage of the business life cycle is imperative. For example, companies needing costly talent during the infancy stage may need HR to create total rewards packages that include equity compensation at the expense of higher base pay, for example. By adding a vesting component, HR may also use this same approach to increase retention as the company works to survive the early years.

During periods of growth, HR programs may make the difference between engaging and retaining key workers; here also the growth strategy matters. For example, a company with a growth strategy achieved by mergers and acquisitions will need to focus on retaining key talent and integrating the cultures. According to HRCI, a merger is when "2 or more organizations come together through a purchase, acquisition or sharing of resources. Usually the new company saves money by eliminating duplicate jobs." For example, one trend to watch is that within the cannabis industry. As regulations of the industry become less restrictive, many large corporations in industries such as food and pharmaceuticals may take action by acquiring the smaller, independent entities that grow, process, or sell cannabis. *Due diligence* will be an important element to these mergers and acquisitions. HRCI defines due diligence as "the gathering and analysis of important information related to a business acquisition or merger, such as assets and liabilities, contracts, and benefit plans." Additionally, risk management enters the picture as a need to review past tax and legal history as well as banking records. Although the gathering of data is certainly important, many senior leaders may also be called upon to help interpret the data and analyze risk, making recommendations in the process for the longer term.

Building shorter term replacement charts and longer-term succession plans is also important in the event that key personnel are lost through the transition.

A company choosing to grow by starting a *greenfield operation* (defined by HRCI as a "new business facility built in a new location") will most likely need to staff it from the ground up. Conversely, a *brownfield operation* is the "reuse of land previously used for industry or manufacturing."

It is also possible for an organization to need multiple staffing strategies at once. For example, Amazon in 2018 announced the location of their second headquarters (HQ2) in New York City and Northern Virginia, generating an estimated 50,000 new jobs. In that same year, Amazon threatened to move their Seattle operations in response to a proposed tax of $275 per employee per year to address affordable housing. For a company with 45,000 employees at the Seattle location, this would have prompted the need for simultaneous termination and talent acquisition strategies. They most likely considered a separation strategy of a *reduction in force*, defined by HRCI as a type of temporary or permanent layoff due to lack of funding or change in work requirements. It may also have resulted in HR offering *relocation services* for qualified employees willing to move to a new location. Relocation services can include offering pre-departure orientation, home finding, tax and legal advice, and other country-specific support. While the HQ2 New York deal eventually fizzled, HR teams worldwide may use it as an example of how staffing strategies can change as quickly as morning headlines. This illustrates the importance of being agile and able to work in volatile and sometimes uncertain environments.

Still other companies are choosing to downsize due to factors other than poor organizational performance. Consider McDonald's, the popular hamburger restaurant, who in 2018 restructured their corporate offices resulting in layoffs at all levels of the business. This was an effort to cut more than $500 million in general and administrative expenses.

Divestitures are another element that will dictate the talent needs of an organization. In some cases, a parent company may not have the proper resources necessary to take the business unit to the next level, so selling it off or "divesting" from it makes the most sense. In other cases, a business unit may be consuming a disproportionate amount of company resources—time, labor, and financial—making a divestiture the best way to free up these resources and bolster cash flow. As with mergers and acquisitions, retention of key talent is HR's priority throughout the event. This can be accomplished through typical retention efforts, but it may be necessary to narrowly focus the efforts on accountability. This may include a management development program to actively engage managers in the retention process. As many HR pros already know, managers may be the most influential link to whether an employee stays or leaves.

A *severance* package may be used as a risk-management tool to help employers avoid employment discrimination claims. Defined by HRCI as "an additional payment (other than salary) given to an employee when employment termination occurs," a severance package may also help to reward separating workers for years of service and offset lost employee wages due to other downsizing events.

All of these examples require that senior-level HR leaders evaluate the current organizational structure and make recommendations on restructuring options using job and labor market analysis techniques.

Strategic Analysis

Chapter 2, "PHR Exam: Business Management," includes a robust discussion of both quantitative and qualitative analysis methods. For purposes of the SPHR and workforce planning, it is important to understand three main types of analysis:

- **Supply analysis:** Internally, *skills inventories* are a useful tool to use when conducting a supply analysis. Skills inventories are typically described by HRCI as a "listing of the capabilities, experiences, and goals of current employees as a tool for meeting the organization's human resource goals and objectives." Other factors to consider include the current cost of labor plus burden, and the capacity for in-house training. This step also requires an extensive analysis of the labor market for current skills and trending labor shortages.

- **Demand analysis:** Focused on the future, a demand analysis seeks to identify needs based on organizational strategy.

- **Gap analysis:** HRCI describes a gap analysis as being used by organizations to "compare its actual performance with its potential performance." In strategic analysis, a gap analysis identifies the missing KSAs between supply and demand of labor.

Once HR has collected and sorted the data, they are ready to present their findings and recommend solutions.

Employee Retention and Engagement

While Chapter 6, "PHR Exam: Employee and Labor Relations," and Chapter 11, "SPHR Exam: Employee Relations and Engagement," deal extensively with the topic of employee relations and engagement, SPHR exam content for the functional area of Talent Planning and Acquisition focuses the topic specifically on new employees. This includes new hires, promotions, and integrations through mergers and acquisitions.

The exam content also links retention and engagement strategies to downsizing, which is important because it refers to keeping engagement levels high with employees who remain after a layoff, reduction in force, or *divestiture* (the sale of a company's assets). Employee morale and productivity for survivors of these types of events often hit all-time lows, so HR must take care to include retention strategies in any downsizing event. For companies that experience a merger or acquisition, for example, it may be prudent for HR to spearhead an employee mentoring or buddy program, where current employees are "assigned" to those just coming onboard to help navigate the company culture. Under HR leadership, mentors may be asked to help the new employees navigate simple logistics such as the process for ordering office supplies, to the more complex, such as management personalities or communication protocols.

Much has been written lately about the impact of Learning and Development activities on retention. Explored in both Chapter 4, "PHR Exam: Learning and Development," and Chapter 9, "SPHR Exam: Learning and Development," from a developmental/training perspective, some employees see professional growth differently. Rather than training or promotion, these employees may prefer a senior title, access to executive leadership, or even just more autonomy to perform their existing work.

One study by Jobvite in 2018 found that of the 1500 individuals surveyed, 8/10 of them were willing to consider new job opportunities. Additionally, more than half of those polled expect to change jobs about every 1–5 years. Perhaps more striking was that nearly 30 percent reported leaving a new job within the first 30 days of employment. Of those, more than 70 percent reported the new role as not being what they expected and company culture as being the reason they left a new job so quickly. These numbers highlight why the new-hire onboarding process is critical to preventing turnover.

 Find the entire study online at www.jobvite.com. Search for the 2018 Job Seeker Nation Study.

The behavioral sciences give us a view of the topic of *employee acculturation*, also called *employee socialization*. Acculturation occurs when new members learn the social and task expectations of their role. For companies that focus strictly on task orientation, the value of the social aspect gets lost or underutilized. It has long been understood that humans are social creatures, ones with emotions and a need to belong. Consider, for example, the last time you started a new job. What feelings existed? If you are like many, there was a mix of both excitement and anxiety. The socialization process can be a valuable time to help individuals navigate these feelings while also exposing them to the company mission, vision, values, and culture.

Some studies have found that new employees make the decision to stay or leave a company within the first three weeks of employment. When the labor market is tight, or when difficult-to-find skill sets are required, it becomes critical for HR to help the organization manage the engagement experience of their newest members.

Of special note are onboarding and engaging a workforce of virtual employees. Since the use of technology is critical to the success of these work structures, videoconferencing may be a successful strategy to begin with face-to-face encounters. Other companies tackle engagement of remote or virtual workers through the use of boot-camp style events, where members are brought together for immersion sessions on topics ranging from company culture to performance expectations.

The Impact of Wages

The holiday season of 2018 was anticipated to be record breaking for online retailers. This presented a challenge for airlines needing to keep pilots in the air to deliver packages across the globe. In response, freight companies such as FedEx Corporation offered retirement-age pilots bonuses of up to $100,000 to stay on through the holiday season. This is but one example of how companies are using their total rewards programs to respond to the critical skill shortages happening on an international scale.

Strategically, the short-term solution of FedEx is but a single response to a much larger talent shortage issue throughout many professions, including IT, nurses, and truck drivers. A blended approach using total rewards to improve retention, along with other workforce planning strategies such as partnering with universities and in-house training programs, are ways senior-level HR leaders can help their employers in a tight labor market. Competitively, this may mean that employers will need to pay above the 50th percentile of market wages and then manage issues such as *pay compression* within their employee wage bands. Pay compression occurs when incumbent pay rates do not keep up with market conditions.

Developmental rewards may also be part of overall strategy. Attracting candidates through policies such as tuition reimbursement for future education, paying off student loans, and offering paid volunteer time are all ways HR is using total rewards programs to attract (and keep) talent.

Retaining senior leaders is another area for SPHR candidates to have a general understanding. Executive compensation levels have long been understood to be complex, with many boards expressing the need to understand and communicate how C-suite performance is linked to large, six-figure-and-above salaries. This not only has an internal impact, but can affect the brand as well. The negative press received by the U.S. Department of Veterans Affairs in response to executive bonuses of upward of $100 million amidst the scandal of patient care required a rapid revamp of the executive pay program. More often than not, senior-level HR professionals will need to influence the development of total rewards strategies that link executive pay to performance. HR may also be called upon to develop the "golden" strategies (such as golden handcuffs) described in Chapter 10, "SPHR Exam: Total Rewards," in order to retain executives through a merger and acquisition.

Building the Employer Brand

Phrases such as "employer of choice" and "best places to work" are designed to communicate to potential employees (and others) the *employer brand*. HRCI defines the employer brand as "the image the employer presents to its employees, stakeholders and customers." Branding is a form of labor market positioning that communicates a message about what it is like to work for the employer. Employer branding is essential and ongoing, meaning that what the employer does in their marketplaces at any given time—not just when recruiting—has a significant impact on its reputation. For this reason, the brand messaging should be positive and honest, highlighting an employer's corporate responsibility and how they behave toward employees. Often, the brand is not only communicated by the employer; many employees via word of mouth and through social media are telling a story about what the employer values. Consider the transportation company Uber, when a video of their then CEO went viral of him berating a driver for asking questions about the future of the company. Or the story of a Zappos employee spending more than nine hours on the phone with a customer—and the company supporting it. Consumers as well as passive job seekers take in this information, and both consciously and unconsciously develop judgments based on it.

The brand is not only communicated through actions that affect employees; it also sends a message about what the employer values as an organization. For example, when a popular airline was fined over $1 million for leaving passengers stranded on the tarmac for more than three hours during the busy holiday travel season, the negative press fundamentally hurt the brand. Compare that to the perception of Virgin Airline's CEO Richard Branson, who is known for valuing his passengers (and employees). Which culture would most people prefer to work for?

Targeted messaging efforts may also be part of a senior leader's role. The reason for this is that not all individuals are looking for the same thing from an employer. By building applicant profiles, and then targeting messages through marketing efforts, the employer is most likely to achieve a stronger job and organizational fit by "hiring right."

An *employee value proposition* (EVP) is also part of the branding effort. HRCI defines an EVP as "the balance of benefits and rewards an employee receives in return for their performance on the job. In addition to compensation, intangible rewards may include development opportunities, challenging and meaningful work, or an attractive organizational culture." This may include tangibles such as pay and benefits and intangibles such as brand awareness and reputation. An example of providing an intangible benefit is the company Which Wich Superior Sandwiches (a *franchise* business model, defined by HRCI as a business that sells and receives ongoing payments for licenses to use a trademark, product, or service). The company hosts an annual event each summer where patrons and employees decorate sandwich bags with patriotic drawings. The finished bags are put on display and eventually filled with goodies and sent to active and veteran military service members. This event communicates to employees and customers some of what the company values. This effort would be attractive to individuals (customers, applicants, potential franchise owners) who share those same values.

Senior-level HR leaders must understand how the brand affects employees and other stakeholders while serving as advisers to management. Ways to manage the branding process are varied, but many experts agree that a significant portion of it occurs online. The 2018 Jobvite survey noted earlier in the chapter found that almost 60 percent of applicants for open positions first research the company on their websites before an interview. Other more traditional ways to build the employer brand include participating in job fairs, presence at community events or sponsorships, and media advertising, even when not hiring for open positions. Other examples include hosting developmental workshops on college campuses, sponsoring local college sports teams, and building apprenticeship programs for difficult-to-fill roles. These activities help individuals become familiar with the brand, a form of continuous recruitment to the organization as opposed to recruitment for a specific job.

Actively managing the brand requires that the company first understands how the brand is perceived in the relevant markets. This is followed by taking an objective look at what the company says it values and what HR programs support those values. Where there is a gap, interventions may be designed to build programs or embed practices that support the company values and increase congruency. Lastly, transparency about where the company is currently and where they want to be can be key. Employees (and customers) are increasingly coming to value transparency as a driver of business outcomes. In this way, the employer brand may serve as an employee retention tool as well.

Metrics: Measuring Results

There are several important metrics by which HR may assess the effectiveness of Talent Acquisition strategies. They include:

- **Functional vs. dysfunctional turnover:** Not all turnover is created equal, but all turnover is costly. For this reason, HR should have measures in place that evaluate both the direct and indirect costs of separating employees. This includes costs related to the loss of the employee, for example, increased overtime for other workers and costs associated with hiring a replacement, such as advertising and labor of the recruiting and selection team. Turnover may be measured for the company overall or for hires within their first six months and attrition of key talent.

- **Demographics:** Understanding demographic-diversity factors including race, age, gender and ethnicity can help HR make informed decisions about more than just EEO compliance. An older workforce reaching retirement age, for example, will inform decisions about succession planning and/or the leadership pipeline.

- **Headcount:** The number of payrolled employees at a given time, head count, is also known as "full-time equivalents" (FTEs). This informs several HR-related decisions, not the least of which is knowing which labor laws apply to the organization.

- **Cost per hire:** This metric is critical in understanding the true cost of turnover and when budgeting for growth. The cost per hire can be calculated for each job category or as an overall metric for generalizations.

- **Adverse impact:** Also known as the 4/5ths rule, adverse impact is used to determine whether there is statistical evidence of unlawful discrimination in the workplace. It is dependent on the calculation of selection ratios for each protected class group (see a complete list of those identified for protection from unlawful discrimination in Chapter 3). The first step is to calculate the selection ratio for both groups, such as for men and women. To find the selection ratio, divide the number of women considered for hire or promotion by the number of women selected, then do this for the non-protected class group (in this case, men) as well. If the selection ratio for women is less than 80 percent of the rate for men (or 4/5ths), discrimination may have occurred. For example, one company interviewed 40 men and 20 females for an open position in their hotel. Of the men, 20 were hired. Of the women, 4 were hired. To determine whether adverse impact occurred, follow these steps:

  1. Identify the selection rate for each group. For the men, 20 / 40 = 50 percent. For the women, 4 / 20 = 20 percent. The majority group is that with the highest selection rate, in this case, the men. The women make up the minority group.

  2. Divide the minority group by the majority group. 20 / 50 = 40 percent.

  3. Adverse impact is presumed to have occurred if the selection rate for the minority group is less than 80 percent of the selection rate of the majority group. 80 percent of the selection rate for the males is 40 percent (40 / 50). Therefore, the female selection rate must be at least 40 percent. Because this is not the case, adverse impact may have occurred.

Summary

The role of senior leaders in talent planning and acquisition continues to grow in importance. Factors driving this need include competing in a global market, a shift from manufacturing to service, and a volatile economy that drives supply and demand for product and services and thus talent.

Senior leaders take responsibility for creating a strategic workforce plan that will fill the gap between current employee skill sets and available talent within the labor market with business goals and objectives. From this, a staffing strategy that identifies effective talent acquisition sources will help employers fill open positions.

Fundamental to talent planning is ensuring that organizations don't lose existing talent. In this way, human resources lead the effort to engage and retain a functional, cohesive workforce.

Part of attracting and keeping talent is communicating the employer brand and value proposition, functions that help individuals understand the tangible and intangible benefits of working for the company.

Finally, senior leaders must be able to collect and analyze data related to this functional area in order to inform decision-making and advise executive management.

Exam Essentials

Lead the efforts of strategic workforce planning.   The primary focus of a strategic workforce plan is that it is strictly tied to company goals and objectives. This requires the abilities of senior-level HR leaders to forecast labor needs and identify gaps, using a human capital management plan to outline action steps and metrics. This may also require the development of short-term replacement plans and longer-term succession planning.

Organize and implement the staffing process.   While highly operational in nature, the recruiting and selection process is the means by which the strategic workforce plan is implemented. Senior leaders must take into account factors such as the current skill set of employees, the availability of talent in the labor market, the impact of wages on hiring and retention, as well as the current and proposed labor laws at both a federal and a state level. These and other factors are influenced by how a business and corresponding jobs are structured.

Engage and retain employees.   Part of a senior leader's talent acquisition strategy is to reduce the need for hiring through employee retention efforts. While typically a function of employee relations and engagement strategies, there are specialized needs for retention efforts at the various stages of the business life cycle. For new hires, this is managed through employee socialization and acculturation efforts.

Communicate the employer brand.   The employer brand continues to be a decisive force in attracting and retaining a talented workforce. HR may help the executive team objectively analyze the brand and how it is perceived, then build HR programs and policies to shape a healthy brand image in their relevant labor markets.

Make decisions using metrics.   Making informed decisions in the talent acquisition function of HR requires that senior leaders are able to interpret and apply data for strategic effect. This often means that data collection is more about quality than quantity. For example, understanding turnover rates (measure of retention) and hiring (measures of selection) costs allow HR to strategically deploy resources for maximum effect.

Review Questions

You can find the answers in Appendix A.

1. The olive oil producer that you work for has 43 warehouse positions to fill for the harvesting season. Out of the 105 applications received, 45 were women and 60 were men. After the selection process was completed, offers were made to 16 women and 27 men. Using the 4/5ths rule, what is the selection ratio for the female candidates, and did adverse impact occur?

   A. 30 percent, yes

   B. 30 percent, no

   C. 35 percent, yes

   D. 35 percent, no

2. Which of the following best defines the characteristics of jobs in order to measure candidate fit?

   A. Job analysis

   B. Job descriptions

   C. Validity studies

   D. Preemployment tests

3. Human capital projecting is a form of which of the following?

   A. Budgeting

   B. Planning

   C. Analyzing

   D. All of the above

4. Which of the following is an external example of data used to make human capital projections?

   A. Skills inventory

   B. Relevant labor market data

   C. Availability of off-the-shelf training software

   D. The organization's core competencies

5. The corporate offices for which you direct human resources has decided to explore opening a plant in Sparks, Nevada. They have heard that companies such as Tesla and Chewy.com have opened centers there, and they want to identify whether this is a business strategy they should follow. They have asked you to put together an analysis of the labor market. Which of the following resources would be the best place to start?

   A. The local newspaper

   B. Nevada Chamber of Commerce

   C. Nevada Department of Employment and Training

   D. A real estate broker

6. The company you work for is in an industry with a national unemployment rate of less than 5 percent. Your company projects that you will need to begin hiring for skilled labor within the next six months. What strategies should you consider?

    A. Building a training program to promote from within

    B. Budgeting for engagement programs to retain key talent

    C. Redesign of jobs

    D. All of the above

7. Which of the following best describes the focus of employee acculturation?

    A. Educating the new hire about the social aspects of the workplace

    B. Having employees complete the required new hire paperwork

    C. Touring the facility and introducing the employee

    D. Helping the employee succeed in the first 90 days

8. Which of the following workforce planning activities serves as the foundation for all other human resource systems?

    A. Recruiting

    B. Job analysis

    C. Strategic planning

    D. Employee socialization

9. During salary negotiations, a candidate requested a base pay amount that was higher than the recruiter expected to pay. The recruiter went to the hiring manager and asked to pay more for the role in order to keep the candidate. This may be an example of which of the following?

    A. Mirror bias

    B. Halo effect

    C. Anchoring bias

    D. All of the above

10. Which of the following is an HR best practice when notifying candidates that they have not been selected for a job?

    A. A standard email sent to all candidates not selected

    B. Personal phone calls to all those rejected for hire

    C. A hybrid approach depending on how far the candidate made it through the process

    D. It is not necessary to notify candidates that have not been selected for hire.

11. An employee applied for a current job opening in another department. Her supervisor is reluctant to make the recommendation. When pressed, you discovered that it was because the employee was particularly talented in her current role and the manager did not want to have to replace her. How should you address the issue?

    A. Allow the employee to go through the application process just like all other candidates.

    B. Promote the employee if she is truly qualified.

    C. Respect the manager's concern and do not promote the employee.

    D. Discipline the supervisor for holding an employee back.

12. When is job bidding an appropriate HR activity?

    A. For highly competitive jobs

    B. When the company wants to promote from within

    C. To create a pipeline of future candidates for a specific role

    D. All of the above

13. Human capital management activities include all of the following except which one?

    A. Analyzing the labor market

    B. Designing total rewards packages

    C. Freezing hiring

    D. Conducting skills inventories

14. What is the primary purpose of conducting a skills inventory?

    A. To analyze jobs for core competencies

    B. To develop a legally compliant workforce plan

    C. To identify skills redundancies in a merger or acquisition

    D. To assess talent to use in a gap analysis

15. In which of the following scenarios would the use of a severance package be appropriate?

    A. To offset lost income to employees due to company reductions in force

    B. To avoid a wrongful termination claim

    C. To reward a retiring worker for years of service

    D. All of the above

16. The company you work for will be shutting down a non-corporate location and moving some employees back to headquarters. The executive team has asked you to design a program to help the transferring employees sell their current homes where applicable and find housing in the new area. You have also been tasked with helping spouses of the affected employees write résumés and providing other job and school support as the families transition as well. This is an example of which type of HR program?

    A. Relocation services

    B. Workforce plans

    C. Job searching

    D. Replacement planning

17. Analyzing the future hiring needs for an annual strategic plan is the best example of which of the following?

    A. The Delphi technique

    B. The nominal technique

    C. Forecasting

    D. Cost–benefit analysis

18. In what succession plan approach are three or more potential candidates identified, all with various levels of readiness for promotion?

   A. Co-sourcing

   B. Labor market

   C. Replacement plans

   D. Talent pool

19. The large chocolate manufacturing plant in your town recently moved its operations to Mexico, leaving a large food-grade manufacturing plant sitting empty. The local paper announced that another chocolate factory will be purchasing the land and moving its operations there by the end of the year. This is the best example of which of the following?

   A. A brownfield operation

   B. A greenfield operation

   C. A workforce plan

   D. An acquisition

20. The large auto parts manufacturer for which you work has recently purchased land in an adjacent city and plans to build an additional warehouse. This is the best example of which of the following?

   A. A brownfield operation

   B. A greenfield operation

   C. A workforce plan

   D. An acquisition

Chapter 9

SPHR Exam: Learning and Development

The HRCI test specifications from the Learning and Development functional area covered in this chapter include SPHR-level responsibilities and knowledge.

Responsibilities:

✓ 01   Develop and evaluate training strategies (for example: modes of delivery, timing, content) to increase individual and organizational effectiveness.

✓ 02   Analyze business needs to develop a succession plan for key roles (for example: identify talent, outline career progression, coaching and development) to promote business continuity.

✓ 03   Develop and evaluate employee retention strategies and practices (for example: assessing talent, developing career paths, managing job movement within the organization).

Knowledge:

✓ 30   Training program design and development

✓ 31   Adult learning processes

✓ 32   Training and facilitation techniques

✓ 33   Instructional design principles and processes (for example: needs analysis, content chunking, process flow mapping)

✓ 34   Techniques to assess training program effectiveness, including use of applicable metrics

✓ 35   Career and leadership development theories and applications

✓ 36   Organizational development (OD) methods, motivation methods, and problem-solving techniques

Many aspects of Learning and Development activities must be managed, and this is often done under the umbrella of *talent management* systems. Talent management is a holistic approach that uses HR systems in, according to HRCI, "recruiting, integrating, and developing new workers, developing and keeping current workers, and attracting skilled workers." For purposes of the SPHR, the L&D exam content outline (ECO) directs senior-level HR professionals to "develop training, development and employee retention strategies." Additionally, though the exam objectives do not mention *organizational development* (OD) specifically, the knowledge requirements underscore the importance of understanding and being able to apply OD principles such as using training as an intervention strategy and employee problem-solving. HRCI defines OD as a planned process designed to improve an organization. Specifically, the OD process "uses principles of behavioral science to improve the way an organization functions."

Chapter 7, "SPHR Exam: Leadership and Strategy," took a detailed look at the structural, procedural, and technological aspects of an organization's systems through an OD lens. This chapter builds on that information but looks at it through an employee development (as opposed to organizational development) perspective. Note that content related to L&D activities makes up only 12 percent of total SPHR exam content, tied for the lowest number of questions with Total Rewards at approximately 21 questions on exam day.

As with all SPHR exam content, there are significant areas of overlap with the PHR exam, especially that which is related to the following:

- Training design and delivery
- Adult learning theories
- Instructional design principles
- Assessing training program effectiveness
- Organizational development principles
- Career pathing, coaching and mentoring
- Employee retention
- Creativity and innovation

Although this chapter will touch on some of these topics, you should read Chapter 4, "PHR Exam: Learning and Development," for a refresher of some of the content redundancies between exams.

It is unclear from the ECO alone just how much specific labor law will be on the SPHR exam. However, understanding labor law as it relates to Learning and Development is fundamental to HR leader competencies. For this reason, we recommend that you rigorously study Appendix C, "Employment Legislation and Case Law," which covers the major legislation related to all of the functions of Human Resources.

Learning and Development Defined

Integration is a recurring theme of the SPHR exam. The L&D function is no exception. Chapter 8, "SPHR Exam: Talent Planning and Acquisition," was a precursor to the L&D discussions you will review in this chapter. This is because a Talent Management System begins with a workforce plan and the ability to attract and retain key talent aligned with organizational goals. L&D then focuses an organization's attention on training and developing a workforce to meet said organizational goals. Similarly, this current chapter, which discusses L&D, serves as a precursor to Chapter 10, "SPHR Exam: Total Rewards." This is because once you have attracted and hired the talent and designed jobs (Talent Planning & Acquisition) and then developed the skill sets and defined organizational competencies (L&D), you must design pay systems that reward efforts and keep talent (Total Rewards).

Learning and Development is also closely tied to employee retention. This is because the demands of today's workforce are not solely structured around base wages. Today's workforce desires career development, meaningful feedback, and work that has significance. These three outcomes fall under the umbrella of L&D. L&D activities should be focused on building training and other learning systems to meet the career goals of employees and prepare the workforce for future organizational needs. This will help populate replacement and succession plans to ensure the organization has the talent necessary to achieve future goals.

Strategic Learning and Development

In order to become (and remain) true business partners, senior-level human resource professionals must take care to build HR systems that are aligned with business strategy. The L&D function is no exception. Lance and Dorothy Berger in their excellent book titled *The Talent Management Handbook* (McGraw-Hill Education, 2017) describes L&D activities as investments. This makes sense in that as with any other business goal, a company must invest resources (labor, time, finances) toward the achievement of these goals. Berger goes on to note that a talent management strategy includes investments related to training, rewards, education, assignments, and development (TREAD) activities. This is a useful acronym to filter through the exam objectives in that it demonstrates that L&D activities are not simple "training" initiatives. L&D efforts are tied to retaining 21st century employees by offering opportunities to continue their education and giving challenging assignments. Retention efforts should also include designing rewards that are tied to a career path and providing an environment where new skills may be practiced and developed.

Training ROI is another strategic consideration that falls on the shoulders of senior-level HR. The ROI Institute dedicates its own significant resources to studying the application of ROI in all aspects of business. As it relates to L&D activities, the ROI Institute noted in their report titled "How to Show the Business Value of Training and Learning in Ten Simple Steps" (January, 2018 from roiinstitute.net) that more than 74 percent of CEOs want to know the ROI of L&D activities, and yet only 4 percent do so. This startling number provides senior-level HR with a call to action— adding strategic value to an organization's L&D investments by becoming experts in understanding the return. This can be done using simple calculations such as dividing the benefits by the total cost and then converting the result into a percentage, or it can be done using the more complex process of tying training outcomes to business results using a balanced scorecard. HR's role is to clearly identify and understand the objectives for L&D activities and then build ways to convert them into quantitative or qualitative results.

NOTE Chapter 2 "PHR Exam: Business Management" and Chapter 4: "PHR Exam: Learning & Development include a thorough review of both qualitative and quantitative methods of data gathering and analysis. They are recommended reading for professionals who do not regularly apply these methodologies or who want an academic refresher.

L&D activities must clearly align with the mission, vision, and values of an organization. One CEO of a California manufacturing plant noted that "you can never have enough good people." This seems simple conceptually, but it is not so simple in application. Many companies struggle to find and retain the talent necessary to achieve business goals. In some cases, a particular skill set is underrepresented in the labor force population; in other instances, the talent does not yet even exist. Consider Apple founder Steve Jobs, who had been noted for hiring people with a passion and talent for innovation and then trusting them to build that which was only imagined. In other cases, particular skill sets do indeed exist but are in high demand, such as with nurses or IT professionals.

One current example of a company using L&D to achieve organizational goals is Google. Google's mission "To organize the world's information and make it universally accessible and useful" is giving their strategic HR business partners quite the task to live up to. One reason this is challenging is because the Bureau of Labor Statistics predicts that "employment of computer and information technology occupations is projected to grow 13 percent from 2016 to 2026, faster than the average for all occupations" (bls.gov). Google is getting ahead of this in part by partnering with local historically black colleges/universities (HBCUs) to develop programs that help to train future science, technology, engineering, and math (STEM) talent. Google places engineers on-site at universities such as Howard, Hampton, and Xavier to train and influence a future workforce. They also offer internships and *job shadowing* (observing another person's work practices to learn a new job) programs, both of which are focused on education and training. Significantly, this program supports Google's Diversity and Inclusion initiatives, with senior Google executive Yolanda Mangolini stating that "our mission is to organize the world of information. We cannot be universally useful and accessible if we only look one way" (https://blavity.com/success-google-partnering-hbcus-recruit-top-talent/). This is another example of how the Talent Planning and Acquisition function of HR is closely tied to Learning and Development activities. It is also a reminder that L&D systems may be structured to support organizational values, something many employees are now considering in their employment choices.

The Role of the Behavioral Sciences

As with so much of the practice of human resources, there are several distinctive contributions from the world of research. The adult learning principles introduced by Malcolm Knowles and referenced in Chapter 4 direct HR professionals to understand how adults learn differently from children (andragogy versus pedagogy). Training outcomes often are improved for adults when distinctions such as the following are considered:

- How relevant the training is to a person's job
- How interactive the training delivery is
- How the training builds on previous knowledge

This is a reminder that senior leaders must have highly developed communication and presentation skills that go beyond the traditional Microsoft PowerPoint presentations. Making training interactive and communicating context when training makes a difference for the trainee. The behavioral sciences have also found that adult learners prefer to be involved in establishing both the training needs and objectives. This knowledge may inform an HR best practice of engaging employees at a deeper level during the training needs assessment phase of instructional design.

Continuing with the theme of adult learning, the sciences have explored the critical role that individual motivation plays in learning outcomes. For example, a key tenet of self-determination theory (SDT) of motivation is that motivation is not just about quantity (such as an employee being more motivated or less motivated), but also about the quality and type of motivation. Perhaps not too surprising to a seasoned trainer, employees with high degrees of autonomy, self-efficacy, and drive (intrinsic motivators) typically have better learning results from training than those being motivated by pay or peer pressure (extrinsic motivators).

Additionally, adults process behavioral changes differently than children. Employees often must first "unlearn" past behaviors before they can begin to create new neural pathways to lead them to adopt new behaviors. Until the old behavior is unlearned and the new behavior cognitively embedded, sustainable change is unlikely to take place.

 Be sure to read Appendix F, "Neuroscience Principles and Applications for HR Leaders," the excellent contribution from Reut Schwartz-Hebron.

Deep learning is another emerging research area for HR practitioners, although the term is used in two ways. In the first way, deep learning may be applied as a means to evaluate training program effectiveness. It is related to the collection of data to help improve training outcomes. Strategic training considerations such as modes of delivery, timing, and content may be evaluated using deep-learning techniques. Training that is delivered through online portals lends itself especially well to these kinds of measurements. Data can be collected about how long employees spend in a training module or the percentage of employees that pass a certain quiz. This allows for content refinement and, ultimately, improved training results.

The second way that deep learning is used is as a reference to an individual's learning preference. Surface-level learners prefer that trainers "tell me just what I need to know to do my job." Conversely, deep learners need a larger understanding of the training material in a whole context. For example, an employee with a preference for deep learning who is seeking to become certified in Myers-Briggs Type Indicator (MBTI) assessments may need to understand the *why* of the process but also need to study the whole of Carl Jung's work, the source data for the MBTI. Deep-level learners often require more time, effort, and context before they are able to change behaviors based on training content.

Furthermore, researchers are beginning to understand that the neurosciences have an impact not only on individual behaviors, but on group dynamics and organizational behaviors as well. For example, the study of unconscious bias and how it drives employee behavior creates a framework for HR to follow when tasked with building content for diversity and sensitivity training that will guide and ultimately change employee behaviors. This occurred when Starbucks closed its thousands of stores for employee training on the topic of unconscious bias. Conflict is also being studied by the neurosciences, with findings, for example, that demonstrate that individuals have a "mirror neuron" (mirror neuron system) in the brain that causes people to unconsciously mirror the actions of others. Using this principle, supervisors, for example, may be coached to remain calm in conflict situations with the expectation that keyed up employees will take the neural cue and mimic the calmer behavior.

The new exam content outlines for both the PHR and SPHR exams challenge HR pros to understand techniques related to encouraging creativity and innovation. Some studies note that creativity and innovation are the basis for human evolution. If this is true, it is reasonable to assume that creativity and innovation are also fundamental to an organization's survival. Researchers on the relationship between creativity and neuroactivity define creativity as the development of the unique or novel that is applied in a useful manner. Creativity has long been considered a cognitive process that works in phases: 1) preparation, 2) incubation, 3) illumination, and 4) verification (Wallas, G. 1926, *The Art of Thought*. London: Jonathan Cape). These stages allow for data collection and synthetization of creative outcomes that may be applied toward desired outcomes. Other definitions use terms such as idea fluency (innovation by building one idea upon another), memory, and sustained attention spans, all of which are being studied by the behavioral sciences within organizations. Allen Gannett, in his book *The Creative Curve: How to Develop the Right Idea at the Right Time* (Currency, 2018), argues that creativity is not only the "province of genius" but that all people can learn to "engineer" the moments necessary to drive innovation.

Creativity as a cognitive process may also influence problem-solving. For example, researchers have documented that for many human minds, problems are resolved through flashes of insights whereas others prefer a more logical, algorithmic approach. If organizations are able to find ways to measure these preferences and pair them with the needs of a job or organization, these abilities may be managed toward strategic effect. Practices such as brainstorming sessions, and the Delphi and nominal techniques may also help organizations encourage creative processes as part of supporting and building an innovative culture. The *Delphi technique* is described by HRCI as when a group of experts provide confidential, individual opinions on a subject that are later collated by a facilitator to achieve consensus. The *nominal technique* is when experts meet, similar to a brainstorming session. Ideas and solutions are first written down, and then a leader facilitates a discussion until a consensus is achieved.

The Great Place to Work Institute has conducted several studies in which trust emerged as a critical factor for building a creative and innovative workforce. An outcome from one study found that nearly a quarter of those surveyed would be willing to offer more ideas and solutions toward organizational problems if they simply trusted their leaders (The Business Case for a High-Trust Culture, 2016. Greatplacetowork.com). Employee reluctance to offer their insights is often because the company (or its leaders) has not created a culture that encourages failure. The creative process will require trial and error, and some ideas will result in significant changes whereas others will simply die on the vine. A culture that encourages true creativity is most likely to adopt a mantra of "fail early" in order to succeed more quickly. In terms of retention—a critical factor for the SPHR exam—this same study found that transparency and leaders who keep their promises have a significant effect on tenure.

The findings of Geert Hofstede on dimensions of culture both globally and organizationally have application for the SPHR exam as well. Hofstede described the dimension of "uncertainty avoidance" as the extent to which an individual feels threatened by situations that are unclear or unknown. Individuals with high uncertainty avoidance will prefer clear, formal rules.

Hofstede and his team used a survey that included the questions about how often a person feels stressed at work. The statement "company rules should not be broken—even when the employee thinks it is in the company's best interest"—was strongly correlated with self-reports of high levels of work stress (Hofstede, G., Hofstede, G., Minkov, M. 2010. *Cultures and Organizations. Software of the Mind.* McGraw-Hill). Cultures and individuals that score high on the uncertainty avoidance index may be less likely to embrace innovation for the sake of being innovative. An employee may even find continuous improvement or breakthrough behaviors stressful enough to leave the job.

Finally, the behavioral sciences have made significant contributions in the field of the psychology of leadership. While many of the theories of leadership are covered in Chapter 7, "SPHR Exam: Leadership and Strategy," the context for the L&D function of the SPHR exam is to identify future leaders as part of succession planning. For this reason, we cover this exam content next.

For a snapshot of how an innovation process is used to tackle the ordinary, take a look at this video about IDEO, a company who endeavored to improve the design of a shopping cart: www.youtube.com/watch?v=M66ZU2PCIcM.

Succession Plans

Succession planning is an HR activity that is future-focused; it includes identifying and developing employees for the organization's future success. For this reason, it requires that HR participates in and understands the strategic direction of the company over a two-to-five-year planning horizon. Succession strategies are often part of a *business continuity plan*, defined by HRCI as "the creation of a strategy to protect an organization from certain risks." This includes the risk of losing key talent. When integrated with the full talent management program, succession planning is rooted in the job analysis process. *Job analysis* (a study of the major tasks, duties, and responsibilities of jobs) allows for the identification of how a career may develop for employees that increases their knowledge, skills, or work experience. For example, some jobs done in the United States may have a different or extended application overseas. Part of a career path then could be expatriate assignments that are strategically aligned with the future need for global leadership. This is in alignment with the opening of this chapter on TREAD activities as a means to invest in talent that will stay put.

Succession planning may also be integrated into a recruiting plan. In this application, internal promotions are identified as the source for future talent based on specific developmental activities for employees.

From a coaching and development perspective, the SPHR exam objective is specific in the context of preparing the internal workforce for the future by first analyzing business needs. This is an element of a *career management* process that is focused on the needs of an organization, different from a *career plan* that is unique to the individual. Business analysis in the context of career management requires human resources to identify the future staffing needs of the company. From this, an individual career development program may be designed that includes training, coaching, and development activities that are specific to the employee yet aligned with future organizational needs. For clarity, here are the distinctions from HRCI:

- **Career management:** Planning and controlling the professional development of an employee. Preparing, implementing, and monitoring the career path of employees, with a focus on the goals and needs of the organization.

- **Career planning:** Managing professional goals. Taking steps to improve professional skills and create new opportunities.

Aligning a succession and career management plan with the business needs will also require budgeting activities. Note that this is not simply forecasting how much a training program will cost. True budgeting for succession and career management requires a deeper view of labor, both of the trainee and the talent management professional, as well as the labor necessary to cover for employees who are away from their regular responsibilities. The budget may also need to include new-hire salaries, both to replace employees moving up and to add staff to the talent management team to manage an increasingly robust program. It is a mistake to underestimate the time resource that this type of program will utilize, so senior-level HR professionals are wise to manage executive expectations using financial projections and ROI where possible.

Finally, strategic alignment will involve evaluation and measurement to determine if the succession plan achieved business goals. Part of this can be achieved during the planning phase if benchmark criteria are collected. For example, let's assume that the goal of a succession plan program is to develop the internal talent necessary to fill leadership positions over a two-to-three-year period. Prior to designing and implementing the program, HR should identify the percentage of leadership positions that are filled with internal candidates. This criterion may then be compared with the same data periodically to determine whether the plan is effective and to make real-time adjustments as needed.

Integrated Talent Management

Several L&D activities occur within the context of an integrated talent management program. In fact, the three exam responsibilities in the L&D function relate to each other in one significant way—they require integration into other functions. For example, responsibility 01 relates to the develop of training strategies to "…increase organizational effectiveness," meaning that training strategies must align with business goals. Responsibility 02 directs senior professionals to "analyze business needs…" to accomplish several things, including addressing career progression, coaching, and development. This implies that senior HR leaders must be able to integrate employee development activities with organizational development interventions such as restructuring or job crafting. Finally, responsibility 03 reminds you that "retention strategies and practices…assessing talent, managing job movement" must integrate with rewards and recognition systems that meet the needs of a diverse workgroup.

So, where to begin? As with many other HR functions, the first step is to conduct a needs assessment or analysis. Usually defined as a process, a needs analysis assesses "…the present situation to determine the steps necessary to reach a desired future goal" (HRCI). The process begins by identifying an organization's strategic goals and is followed by an analysis of the individual, group, or organizational competencies that will be necessary to achieve those goals. Those first two steps will drive the third, which is conducting a gap analysis in order to compare current state to desired future state, and then design an appropriate intervention plan to bridge the gap.

A needs analysis may be narrow in scope, such as with a training needs or skills assessment, or broader in scope, such as analyzing future business needs that will drive the decision of whether to "build" talent through training and development programs or "buy" talent through acquisition efforts. Both examples require integration of efforts with other

HR structures because, as noted in *Chief Learning Officer* magazine, "If talent management involves employee recruitment, development and management—from the time they are identified as candidates until they leave the company—learning becomes a vital thread that binds this entire system" (*Chief Learning Officer*, "What Is Learning's Role in Talent Management?" 2017).

Consider as part of your training resources subscribing to *Chief Learning Officer* magazine. It is free of charge, and you can choose a digital format or print magazine. See www.clomedia.com.

L&D integration is also highly dependent on the needs of the organization. For example, does your company have need for employees who are innovative and highly skilled at problem-solving? Does the company structure call for individuals who are able to work independently, such as within a virtual environment? These are examples of what can be discovered through the use of an individual needs assessment to identify what type of training or development activities may be necessary to build an employee up for success within the organization. Additionally, there appears to be a shift away from a development strategy that focuses solely on high-potential employees. True talent management involves all employees in the process, from the CEO down to the newest hire. For many organizations, identifying training and development needs is included as part of the performance management and appraisal process, an exam objective covered in detail in Chapters 6.

As a reminder, a training needs assessment and an individual assessment are both tools that should (in the context of supporting business needs) cascade down from the organizational needs identified through the strategic planning process. As discussed in Chapter 7, part of the strategic planning process is to decide what types of interventions may be necessary in order to prepare the workforce or work environment to achieve goals.

Training as an Intervention Strategy

When training is selected as an organizational development intervention, it is usually because the company has identified a skills gap in the workforce. When aligned with a company's strategic goals, training as an intervention can support powerful outcomes. The fast-food restaurant chain McDonald's is one example of this. The company partners with local colleges to offer voluntary, free English language classes specifically to prepare current employees for customer-facing roles. Part of a larger "Archways to Opportunity" program, McDonald's pays employees to attend the classes. The return-on-investment of this program is significant when the following program outcomes are considered:

- The program improves customer service and removes language barriers to productivity.
- The program increases employee loyalty and thus retention in a typically high turnover industry.
- The program communicates a commitment to a diverse workforce.

- The program builds skills that results in greater lifetime earnings' potential for the individual, which in turn impacts the communities where they do business.

- The program allows for greater connection with others, which in turn builds stronger relationships, a fundamental human relations activity.

The design and development of training programs will need to take into consideration several factors. In the McDonald's example, the company used a *blended learning* (a method that combines face-to-face teaching with online learning) approach where classes were offered both in person and virtually. This was important, as so much of language learning is dependent upon interaction with others. The classes were offered off-site and over a period of 8 to 22 weeks to ensure employees had the support system and proper environment to reinforce the learning. The content (in accordance with Knowles's adult learning principles) was built around work interactions, with titles such as "shift basics" or "shift conversations." McDonald's also designed content for managers around delivering performance feedback. This increased the relevance and applicability of the training content to their jobs.

As you can see by this example, training as part of a larger L&D intervention program can support a company's mission, vision, and values while at the same time providing practical support to the achievement of business goals.

Summary

The Learning & Development function of test-day content may only make up 12 percent of the exam, but it is fundamental to the effectiveness of other HR activities. L&D activities for SPHR candidates share themes with other content areas related to strategic integration. These activities form the thread that binds together recruiting and selection activities with total rewards, helping employers build employee relations strategies that will improve retention over time. This occurs in tandem with binding L&D activities to a company's strategic direction and values systems.

L&D activities must be designed to meet needs at both the organizational and individual levels. Organizationally, this means that senior-level HR professionals will be able to design and develop training content that is relevant and measurable. It also requires that HR aids in the development of career paths, specifically so that employees know that the company is contributing to their individual professional growth. Activities such as offering challenging assignments and increasing the depth of job responsibilities can have great impact on employee engagement and retention. HR must take care to build programs that result in a workforce that is prepared for the future needs of the company while also mitigating external forces that drive talent availability. This includes taking ownership of the succession and replacement planning process.

Senior-level HR must also stay up-to-date on emerging knowledge in the area of L&D. Understanding how adults learn, and the psychology of conflict, creativity and leadership behaviors are all areas for HR to explore when designing learning and development systems.

As more and more companies are required to adapt to a rapidly changing competitive landscape, the need for creative, innovative employees becomes great. Human resources can contribute to this skill set by becoming subject-matter experts on how creativity may be predicted, stimulated, applied, and measured.

Exam Essentials

Understand and be able to develop and evaluate training strategies.   Learning and development programs tie together the elements needed to attract and retain key employees. To do this, senior-level HR professionals will be well-versed in program basics such as modes of delivery, timing, and content development.

Be able to analyze business needs to align employee development programs with business goals.   Developing career paths for employees serves many purposes. It helps employers identify where succession plans will need to be built. It offers employees meaningful feedback on the gap between where they are and where they hope to be. The career pathing process also improves retention by helping employees see the bigger picture of their role at the company and how they can develop to contribute. Conducting needs assessments is a critical tool in career pathing.

Develop, implement, and evaluate L&D activities that are designed to increase retention.   Retention is a critical activity for human resource business partners. In fact, activities related to L&D activities run through all other HR functions. HR staff use L&D to ensure that new hires are properly on-boarded and trained. L&D activities are focused on preparing a workforce to be ready for growth—both individually (through career development and coaching) and organizationally (through strategic interventions such as assessing talent and managing employee movement).

Review Questions

You can find the answers in Appendix A.

1. _____ is (are) a critical component to an effective learning and development system.
   A. Design of training
   B. Mode of delivery
   C. Integration with other business outcomes
   D. Cost savings initiatives

2. Career management and planning are two L&D activities that *best* promote which of the following outcomes?
   A. Business continuity
   B. Retention
   C. Return on investment
   D. Employee training

3. Why are L&D activities attributed to increased employee retention?
   A. The employees of today only want to learn new skills to move on to other opportunities.
   B. The employees of today are less motivated than other generations.
   C. The employees of today value career development along with competitive pay.
   D. The employees of today can't afford traditional education, so they seek to learn on the job.

4. Identifying the value that training created for an employer is the main purpose of which of the following business impact measures?
   A. Break-even analysis
   B. Return-on-investment
   C. Tactical accountability
   D. All of the above

5. Andragogy refers to which of the following?
   A. How children learn
   B. How adults learn
   C. Cognitive functioning
   D. Behavioral sciences

6. One of your senior leaders has come to you with a career development plan for her employees. She would like your feedback to ensure that she has covered the future needs for the employee's development. The senior leader is displaying high degrees of what?

    A. Dependence

    B. Extroversion

    C. Autonomy

    D. Self-determination

7. A sales employee is having a hard time understanding why he is required to "get off the phones" to attend classroom-based training on company culture. What is most likely missing in getting him motivated?

    A. Whole context

    B. A positive attitude

    C. Financial incentives

    D. Proper scheduling

8. Innovation by building one idea on top of another is the premise of which of the following?

    A. Creativity

    B. The Delphi technique

    C. Idea fluency

    D. The nominal technique

9. Which of the following statements is *true* about an employee who scores high uncertainty avoidance?

    A. The employee is an introvert.

    B. The employee may be uncomfortable with change.

    C. The employee is probably not creative.

    D. The employee has low levels of stress.

10. Where is the natural starting point for succession planning?

    A. Selecting employees for promotion

    B. Setting business goals

    C. Conducting performance reviews

    D. Conducting job analysis

11. What is the purpose of identifying the percentage of internal candidates that fill leadership positions prior to implementing a leadership development program?

    A. Doing so allows for effectiveness to be measured.

    B. Doing so will determine whether the program is necessary.

    C. Doing so allow for a baseline comparison after an initiative has been implemented.

    D. Doing so will increase participation.

12. The company that you work for has asked HR to build a training program to improve decision-making at all levels of the organization. What should your HR team do first?

    A. Conduct a needs analysis.

    B. Research off-the-shelf options.

    C. Hire a new trainer.

    D. Determine the ROI of the intervention.

13. Which of the following would be the *most* likely reason a company has chosen training as an intervention strategy?

    A. There is a high turnover rate in certain departments.

    B. There is a lack of motivation within the workforce.

    C. There is a gap between worker skills and organizational needs.

    D. The employees do not have the proper resources to do their jobs.

14. Which of the following is an example of return-on-investment for a company training program?

    A. Improved customer experience

    B. Profit that is the result of training outcomes

    C. Reduced employee turnover

    D. All of the above

15. HR is being asked to consider a program that will track employees engaged in computer-based training. One feature is that HR will know precisely which quiz questions employees are missing. This is an example of which of the following?

    A. Workforce analytics

    B. Deep learning

    C. Program evaluation

    D. All of the above

16. The need for adult learners to first unlearn old behaviors before they may replace them with new behaviors is the premise of which of the following sciences?

    A. Clinical psychology

    B. Applied psychology

    C. Neuroscience

    D. Biology

17. Which theory of motivation is built on the premise that the quality of motivation is just as important as the act of being motivated itself?

    A. Self-determination

    B. Hierarchy of Needs

    C. Theory X and Y

    D. Acquired needs

18. Why has trust emerged as a significant theme for leaders desiring to increase creativity in the workplace?

    A. Without trust, employees will be afraid for their ideas to fail.

    B. Without trust, employees fear they will not be rewarded for their innovation.

    C. Without trust, employees fear they will be ridiculed for ideas that are unconventional.

    D. Without trust, employees will not care enough to contribute to creative outcomes.

19. In what ways are succession plans tied to talent acquisition?

    A. A replacement employee may need to be groomed into a new position.

    B. A succession plan may require the need for a new hire.

    C. A succession plan will fail if not properly integrated with the talent acquisition process.

    D. A succession plan must be tied to business needs.

20. Which of the following should be included in a career management budget?

    A. Employee salaries

    B. HR salaries

    C. Training costs

    D. All of the above

Chapter 10

SPHR Exam: Total Rewards

The HRCI test specifications from the Total Rewards functional area covered in this chapter include SPHR-level responsibilities and knowledge.

Responsibilities:

✓ 01 **Analyze and evaluate compensation strategies (for example: philosophy, classification, direct, indirect, incentives, bonuses, equity, executive compensation) that attract, reward, and retain talent.**

✓ 02 **Analyze and evaluate benefit strategies (for example: health, welfare, retirement, recognition programs, work-life balance, wellness) that attract, reward, and retain talent.**

Knowledge:

✓ 41 **Compensation strategies and philosophy**

✓ 42 **Job analysis and evaluation methods**

✓ 43 **Job pricing and pay structures**

✓ 44 **External labor markets and economic factors**

✓ 45 **Executive compensation methods**

✓ 46 **Non-cash compensation methods**

✓ 47 **Benefits program strategies**

✓ 48 **Fiduciary responsibilities**

✓ 49 **Motivation concepts and applications**

✓ 50 **Benchmarking techniques**

The exam content related to Total Rewards for the SPHR accounts for only 12 percent of the exam, making it tied with the L&D function in terms of having the least amount of exam content. The ECO summarizes this function as the ability for a senior-level professional to "monitor the effectiveness of compensation and benefit strategies for attracting, rewarding, and retaining talent." Note that some of this content is similar to that covered in the PHR function area of Total Rewards. This is because there are some redundancies across the content for both exams, especially that which is related to the following:

- Job analysis, job evaluation, job pricing, and pay structures
- Non-cash compensation
- Benchmarking
- Types of benefits

For this reason, there will be directives throughout this chapter to review operational content found in Chapter 5, "PHR Exam: Total Rewards."

It is unclear from the ECO alone just how much specific labor law related to Total Rewards will be on the SPHR exam. However, understanding labor law as it relates to compensation issues such as Equal Pay laws and the Affordable Care Act is critical for all HR leaders. For this reason, we recommend that you rigorously study Appendix C, "Employment Legislation & Case Law," which covers the major legislation related to the field of Human Resources.

Total Rewards Defined

Total rewards is defined by HRCI as the "financial and non-financial benefits that the employee sees as valuable." Additionally, HRCI notes that *total compensation* reflects the complete pay package that is made up of both compensation and benefits. As with all areas of human resources, the compensation and benefits function of an organization can be understood as having administrative, operational, and strategic activities. The administrative and operational components are covered at length in Chapter 5, but they should not be undervalued by those seeking to pass the SPHR exam. The fundamentals serve to inform strategic decision-making, and strategic decision-making affects organizational competitiveness. Perhaps this is simply another way of stating the directive from the ECO that Total

Rewards (TR) strategies must be built around "attracting, rewarding, and retaining talent." In order for organizations to compete, they must be able to attract qualified people, reward them through monetary and nonmonetary rewards, and then keep them satisfied—in short, balancing a desired workforce with one that is affordable. This chapter is focused on the TR strategies that help organizations achieve that competitive advantage. It begins with a look at the ethical and legal responsibilities an HR professional has when administering compensation programs.

Fiduciary Responsibility

The dictionary defines *fiduciary responsibility* as one that requires confidence or trust. HRCI takes that definition further, describing it as a "legal duty to act solely in the interest of another person without benefit, profit, or conflict of interest unless expressly permitted to do so by the other person." HR professionals who have responsibility for advising, managing, and/or administering TR programs find themselves in a role that legally requires them to act in a way that inspires confidence and trust of both management and employees to be effective.

In a legal context, a fiduciary relationship has one of the highest, if not the highest, standards of care imposed on the individual acting on behalf of another individual or entity. In the context of compensation and benefits, this most often applies to activities related to pensions and other benefit programs. Although the legal standard may not be as high in other TR functions, such as establishing salary ranges, recommending salary offers, or establishing merit budgets, these activities require HR professionals to act ethically and with integrity on behalf of their organizations. To establish and maintain a high level of trust and confidence, care must be taken to avoid even the appearance of conflicts or favoritism.

An HR professional could breach this responsibility in three ways:

- *Acting in your own self interest*—HR professionals must always act in the best interest of the entire organization, not simply their own or their department's interest.

- *Conflicting duties*—In some situations, an HR professional may need to give equal priority to two responsibilities. For example, when placing an HR position into a salary range, responsibility to the HR team may need to increase the wage band to attract qualified talent. The conflicting responsibility is to ensure the integrity of the salary ranges across the organization as a whole, which may simply equate to transparency by seeking higher approval. Relying on market data to make these and similar decisions can help eliminate such conflicts.

- *Profiting from your HR role*—It may be tempting to take advantage of the unique access to surveys and other information HR is privy to, but doing so to ensure personal gain destroys the trust of management and employees in the HR function.

Those tasked to act as a fiduciary must be aware of the above in all elements of compensation and benefits administration.

Total Rewards Philosophy and Strategies

The *Total Rewards philosophy* is a high-level mission statement used to guide the development and implementation of compensation and benefits' programs that attract, motivate, and retain employees. Typically, HR works closely with the executive management team to develop and implement the organization's TR philosophy as it must be aligned to an organization's purpose in order to be effective.

During the development or revision of a TR philosophy, the HR management team facilitates the process by gathering input from and building consensus with key stakeholders such as members of the Executive Team, Board of Directors, or Compensation Committee. Creating a TR philosophy in this way provides an opportunity to look at the whole package offered to employees and analyze which combination of programs will best achieve the organization's hiring, retention, and performance objectives. In smaller organizations or new startups that may not take the time to proactively define a TR philosophy, one may develop organically over time as a result of compensation programs implemented to meet specific needs or accomplish organizational goals. The danger in relying on this type of de facto philosophy in the long term is that it isn't likely to provide a framework that supports organization-wide goals and objectives as the company grows. Instead, business units may develop compensation practices designed to satisfy their individual needs but that conflict with programs implemented by other units. Senior-level HR has probably seen this play out in random job title assignments or disjointed duties that make benchmarking to external sources more difficult. Finally, as with any other HR function, the *development* of the program is equally as important as the *evaluation* of the program. Identifying whether the TR philosophy is resulting in the desired outcomes requires a long-term focus and strategy.

Trend analysis can be an excellent way to help organizations keep pace with emerging needs and cutting-edge practices, particularly in the domain of Total Rewards. Consider, for example, that the title of this functional area has changed three times in the last 15 or so years, from Total Rewards to Compensation and Benefits and now back to Total Rewards. What can this small piece of information tell us about this field of practice? For one, it tells us that the workplace and the workforce is ever-changing and that our reward practices must respond. The recent decision to revert back to the Total Rewards title alerts us to the idea that the practice of attracting, retaining, and rewarding employees is not only about items such as base pay or health insurance. The workforce of today demands innovation and value from their employment. This includes more flexibility, rapid career growth, and the ability to gain a sense of purpose and meaning from their work.

Employees today see rewards as going beyond traditional compensation and benefits programs, and their tenure behaviors reflect this. The Bureau of Labor Statistics reported that as of January 2018, the average employment tenure of all wage workers was about 4.2 years (unchanged since 2016). Because this is not an exact science, it is more important that you understand the average tenure rate of employees within your company, preferably sorted demographically and by department. Workforce analytics is one way that you can use technology to help predict employee movement. Surveying employees on what they believe to be the most valuable in their Total Rewards offerings is another example of the use of analytics to inform TR decision-making. HR can support technological solutions that are relevant and effective in retaining talented workers.

In this section, we explore the driving needs and potential solutions to the new workplace, structured in accordance with the SPHR exam content outline.

Competing in the Market

Fundamental to an organization's compensation philosophy is the decision to *lead the market, lag the market,* or *match the market*—meaning the median pay in the relevant external labor market. HRCI defines these terms as strategies:

- **Lead the market:** A compensation strategy that is higher than the average pay rate

- **Lag the market:** A compensation strategy that is lower than the average pay rate

- **Match the market:** A compensation strategy that seeks to match the average pay rate

Employers who choose to lead the market pay above median, employers who choose to lag the market pay below median, and employers who choose to match the market pay the equivalent of the median. This decision has many implications, including pay equity, cost of labor, and the ability to attract and keep talented workers.

A 2017 survey collaboration by Deloitte and Empsight on Total Rewards found that most employers' goal is to be at market median (https://www2.deloitte.com). That may be fine for some industries in some geographic locations and for some positions. However, as mentioned in the introduction, the workforce of today is incredibly diverse, and as a result, different organizations have different priorities and values. This may be driven by the size of the employer as well. The same Deloitte survey found that of those employers who desired to be *above* market median for their compensation philosophy, one third of those were small employers (fewer than 500 employees).

The economic climate is another factor that employers use to inform their compensation philosophy. In strong economics, there may be lower levels of unemployment, meaning that employers may need to lead their industries in TR. Geography also plays a role. Some geographic locations have higher concentrations of certain types of skill sets, meaning an employer can afford to lag the labor market for certain jobs. The cost of living in many areas plays an important role in an employer's TR philosophy. For example, the housing market in the San Francisco Bay area is so costly that pay rates and other cash and non-cash offerings (transportation, housing allowances, flexible commute schedules) must track with this and other cost-of-living factors.

A philosophy is driven by much more than just market conditions; it must also be aligned with the business's core strategy.

Strategic Alignment

Strategic Total Rewards programs are built from very similar components as business strategy. Compensation experts must consider internal and external conditions as well as external opportunities and threats that affect their ability to use compensation to attract, reward, and retain talent. Companies must consider their core values and the type of employer they wish to be (or be perceived as being). For example, companies with growth plans will need to conduct skills inventories and regularly audit incumbent pay rates for competitiveness. Where gaps in skills or shortages in labor markets exist, they will then need to make decisions about whether to attract and "buy" the talent from outside the organization or to invest in training programs to "build" the talent up from within.

Senior-level HR professionals will also need to be up-to-date on emerging pay laws. An example of this includes the Department of Labor's new factors test for unpaid internships that will make it easier for employers to access talent. In short, the factors must show that the unpaid intern is the "primary beneficiary" of the unpaid internship—not the employer. The factors include whether or not the job duties are tied to the intern's educational program, the degree of scheduling in alignment with the academic calendar, the length of the internship, the degree to which the internship supplements as opposed to replaces an existing job, and the extent to which the intern understands that the job is unpaid.

HR will also need to consider the systems that must be built to deliver pay and where a self-service system can be successfully implemented. This includes determining how pay will be calculated in accordance with performance goals as well as the regulatory requirements of the locations where they do business. Finally, a compensation philosophy that is aligned with strategy will need to consider how Total Rewards will be allocated.

Strategic Allocation

The reality for many employers is that compensation and benefits account for the largest expense on their profit and loss statements. Many employers rely on senior human resources professionals to help them find ways to stabilize what has been an increasing cost of doing business for the last several years. For this reason, a major consideration of rewards allocation is affordability. As a general rule, organizations use a two-year planning horizon when budgeting how much in compensation it can afford to commit. From this, a forecast that includes pay increases, incentives, and other factors can be created.

The mix of TR components is an important consideration when deciding how to allocate organizational resources. Once an employer has decided what it can afford, it must then make a choice about how to allocate toward cash and non-cash rewards. For example, $1 per hour in base pay is taxable, whereas an additional $1 in health benefits is not. Employees at different stages of life will often value very different things; millennials may be seeking relief from student loan debt, young parents may prize childcare offerings, and older workers may more appreciate part-time work options that retain health benefits. A *conjoint analysis* is a statistical survey that asks participants to assign a value to presented options. It allows employers to interpret what trade-offs employees may be willing to make in their TR plans. There are a few key advantages to this type of analysis. One is that it allows employers to use the resulting data to offer a total compensation mix that is most valued by their specific workforce instead of trying to "guess" what employees would prefer or try and follow their competitors.

Senior-level HR professionals must prepare for the coming skills shortage that is partially due to the baby boomer generation reaching retirement age. Even though older workers are staying in the workforce longer, one SHRM report noted that 63 percent of baby boomers plan to work part-time, 25 percent intend to stop working altogether, and a mere 11 percent plan to continue working full-time once they reach retirement age. This same report noted that in the manufacturing industry alone, the skills gap due to retirements and other labor shortages will result in more than 2 million unfilled jobs between 2015 and 2025.

(Agovino, T. [2018]. Shifting patterns. HR Magazine. June/July/August 2018. SHRM.Org.)

With an aging population exploring employment options past the age of retirement, the need for retiree savings may be a priority for your workgroup. Some 2017 reports found that more than half of all Americans had less than $1,000 in their savings accounts, and a startling 47 percent of millennials have $0. Although there is debate about whether this is an issue for employers to solve, it does matter. For example, employers who allow employees to take loans out against their 401k plans create an administrative burden on their HR technicians and vendors, while at the same time eroding employee savings.

One solution may be found in the behavioral sciences. The Department of Labor (DOL)'s Chief Evaluation Office has been testing various approaches to how behavioral sciences can influence positive outcomes for employees. In our retirement savings example, the DOL tested whether simple emails, or emails plus reminders, would have an effect on savings behaviors. Their research found that:

- "Receiving an email more than doubled the percentage of workers who had not been contributing 5 percent of their pay to do so.

- Those who received an email raised their contribution by an average of about $3,000 annually.

- If maintained over 20 years, this would translate into about $11,500 in additional retirement income."

For a full review of the DOL's program, go to www.dol.gov and search for "Behavioral Insights."

Integrative Approach

An integrative approach as a TR best practice is used to help employers align their Total Rewards strategies to three needs: 1) achieve business goals, 2) meet the needs of a diverse workgroup, and 3) manage costs. The Deloitte survey referenced earlier noted that many employers *know* that they must transform their TR strategy and delivery, but they are uncertain how to do so. As a result, *cost* continues to be the primary factor driving the design of Total Rewards. A truly integrated approach, however, must expand its focus to include what people want, what people need, customization, and flexibility. Companies that wish to attract and retain scarce or unique talent will need to structure their TR systems to allow for rewards based on the value that the individual adds to the company while not overpaying for certain roles.

A holistic approach should also account for employee career goals. For example, many talented workers in fields such as science and technology do not wish to go into management yet still want the opportunity to optimize their status, title, and earnings. A dual-career structure is one method that can help. A dual-career ladder allows employees to choose a management path or a path with increasing recognition and rewards based on professional achievements such as leading research or being published.

Employers are increasingly becoming aware of the value that generous leave and other time-off policies can bring. Google, for example, increased its paid maternity leave benefit from 12 weeks to 18 weeks and reported a 50 percent decrease in the number of new mothers who quit (Rice, S. [2018]. What the Gates Foundation learned by offering 52 weeks of paid parental leave. Quartz at Work. www.qz.com).

In an industry where women in STEM jobs experience significant barriers to success, this strategy is effective.

Flexible work arrangements are another element of an integrative TR approach. With more than 40 percent of the millennial generation reporting that they plan to leave their jobs after just two years, flexible work arrangements and other work/life balance initiatives may be a viable solution to retention problems.

Effectively pricing dual-career and other career path models and designing flexible work arrangements that still allow for productivity are dependent on many factors, including the need for job analysis and job pricing. This is the focus of the following sections.

Job Analysis

The process of building job families is generally a feature of the workforce planning function of HR. In the context of compensation, however, it is also reliant on the structural drivers of the function of business management. How a company is structured will drive how jobs are structured, which in turn will drive how jobs are compensated.

Building job families is a classification technique used to group jobs according to business units. Job families are organized by titles, usually from the senior level on down to the entry level. This sorting requires analysis to determine what makes each job unique from the others, including levels of knowledge, skills, abilities, and other performance measures. Once this has been accomplished, the salary structures can be built. Options include the following:

- **Traditional:** Useful for larger, more bureaucratic organizations that are hierarchical in nature and where jobs are structured to allow for progression in both responsibility and pay. Narrow-graded structures may have 10 or more grades in a job family and are dependent on job evaluation to define each grade. Pay ranges are then attached to each grade.

- **Broad-banded:** Perhaps the most useful to organizations that desire maximum flexibility in deciding pay rates, broad-banding has a greater spread between high and low pay, in some cases between 70 and 100 percent. This allows employers to reward employees for reasons other than grading or other market-driven controls.

- **Broad-graded:** Useful in organizations that desire a blended approach, broad-graded structures reduce the number of grades from 10+ down to 5 or 6. These employers also adopt a broader wage spread than traditional structures, usually of around 30–80 percent.

Job grading (also known as leveling) is a type of compensation structure that provides the basis for assigning pay ranges. Leveling is a relatively new job evaluation method that is helping HR evaluate jobs based on the knowledge and skills as well as the cultural behaviors that are necessary to perform the job. This assists in the creation development of career and development plans. For example, entry-level IT professionals may be paid at the lower end of a pay grade, but if they add skills or knowledge, they can become eligible to move up the pay grade. Leveling uses comparable worth to determine the relative value of a job within an organization. Many employees believe that their jobs should be worth more to the organization than internal comparisons or external market value dictates. HR can control this message by educating employees on the processes used to price jobs, including how job descriptions and salary ranges are developed.

As you can see, salary structures are dependent on factors other than simply market rates; salary structures are a place where employers may embed what they value. However, in order to build a coherent salary structure, HR must have completed the process of evaluating and pricing jobs.

There are several relevant key terms in this section that are specifically defined by HRCI. They include the following:

- **Job analysis:** A study of the major tasks and responsibilities of jobs to determine their importance and relation to other jobs in a company

- **Job evaluation:** The process of measuring how much a job is worth (for example, in order to set the salary and other benefits)

- **Job grade:** A means of determining different job levels and pay scales based on the required knowledge, skills, and abilities

Job Evaluation and Pricing

The purpose of job evaluation is to help employers determine the worth of jobs within an organization when compared to internal data. Job worth is based on the principle that some jobs are more valuable to an organization's effectiveness and thus its ability to compete. Although traditional evaluation methods focus mostly on internal criteria, many scholars agree that employers must include external market factors in the evaluation process. This external data is used to establish internal *salary ranges,* which identifies the lowest and highest wages paid to employees who work similar jobs. Job pricing is achieved by calculating the floor and ceiling in relation to the *salary mid-point*—the amount of money between the highest and lowest amount paid for a particular job. The mid-point is often used to forecast salary budgets in strategic planning as well.

Job evaluation methods can be quantitative, such as evaluating job content to identify responsibilities, or nonquantitative, such as ranking jobs in order of importance to the company's core competencies.

Choosing which job evaluation method to use is dependent on the goals of a compensation program. For a smaller business, the most important consideration may be ease of development and use. Larger corporations may be more interested in perceptions of equity. For still other companies, it may be more realistic to blend one or more method in order to achieve organizational goals.

 If you are unfamiliar with the operational aspects of job evaluation such as ranking and classification, you can refresh your knowledge by reviewing these sections in Chapter 5.

Job benchmarking is the process of comparing internal jobs with similar jobs in the relevant labor market. This creates an anchor point from which to determine whether to lead, lag, or match the market in pay rates.

Job ranking compares jobs to each other based on their importance to the organization.

Job classification is an arrangement of different types of employment or grades within an organization according to skills, experience, or training.

Job-content-based job evaluation is a method used to estimate how much a person should be paid based on what they do.

Salary surveys are another element of job evaluation and pricing that senior-level HR candidates must be familiar with. While the technical processes are covered in Chapter 5, SPHR candidates should understand that all compensation surveys are not created equal, nor are organizational structures. Senior-level HR professionals will need to determine what type of surveys to access considering a variety of elements. For example, many non-profit agencies cannot use general market salary information because they simply cannot afford to pay the market rate; it is more realistic for nonprofit agencies to benchmark their jobs against other nonprofit agencies.

Additionally, pricing jobs based on survey data requires that the source of the data is highly credible. HR should be sure to consider how the survey administrators match the jobs that will be used for comparisons. For example:

- Is it only by job titles, or is a more robust method used to ensure an accurate comparison of job responsibilities and tasks?

- Do the survey administrators offer descriptions of each job used in the comparisons?

- Are HR professionals the ones validating job descriptions, or are line managers involved as well?

- Does the survey administrator publish the names of the employers who participate in the survey?

These important considerations will help HR draw in the relevant data to craft pay structures that result in competitive job pricing. This in turn will improve hiring and retention.

There are some legal concerns in sharing compensation information. *Wage setting* or *price fixing* is a violation of antitrust laws that can get employers into trouble. For example, in 2017, Animation workers reached a $100 million settlement with Disney and affiliates for wage setting (*Nitsch vs. DreamWorks Animation SKG Inc., 14-cv-04062*). The charges addressed competitors in the industry agreeing to not poach each other's talent by cold calling or counter-offering higher wages if an employee gave notice. In a similar case dealing with high-tech employers in the Silicon Valley, the complaint noted that these types of agreements "interfered with the proper functioning of the price-setting mechanism that otherwise would have prevailed in competition for employees" (The Unites States Department of Justice, 2010). This is another reason to participate in formal surveys as opposed to attempting to gather the data through more informal (and less expensive) methods.

Collective Bargaining and Contract Costing

Decisions about how to structure job families is dependent on many of the variables that affect the structure of TR programs. One factor to this is the presence of a union and formal collective bargaining agreement that dictates a large part of how TR will be designed and implemented, sometimes over several years. In fact, wages and benefits are a mandatory subject when negotiating a collective bargaining agreement. A feature of bargaining is how pay will be structured.

For example, in a two-tiered system, the union may agree to pay less for new hires performing work for which more senior employees are paid a higher wage. In some cases, wages for new members can be as much as 30 percent lower than their senior peers. Or less senior employees may receive lesser benefits or lesser protections against layoffs. Debatable as discriminatory or unfair representation, they nevertheless exist in many industries, including manufacturing and auto.

Another compensation issue that relates to collective bargaining includes using lump sum payments for annual increases. Lump sum payments do not increase base wages, which are what is used to calculate overtime and pension benefits. For this reason, lump sum payments are often used in negotiations by employers wishing to keep labor costs steady.

Two-tiered wage systems and lump sum payments both contribute to the total cost of a labor contract. For that reason, it is important for senior leaders to understand how to estimate how much a negotiated labor contract is worth. To do so, experts advise that they first focus on data collection. This must include total hours worked by both union and non-union members and cost of total compensation, including non-cash and other rewards. HR must also have access to forecasts for the term of the contract and an average breakdown of labor costs by worker classification. HR should be well versed in basic accounting and budgeting principles and should have access to company financials such as income statements, balance sheets, and any other contracts that influence profitability.

> It is beyond the scope of this section to cover in detail the methods used for total costing of a collective bargaining agreement. However, there are several detailed accounts available, such as ones provided at www.calperla.org, that we recommend if you wish to be more familiar with the concept.

Basic Budgeting and Accounting

The finance function is responsible for creating and maintaining accounting records and managing organization budgets. HR professionals at the management level are often expected to participate in the budgeting process not only for HR-specific expenses but also by providing compensation and benefit information that is incorporated in the overall organization budget. Although closely related, accounting and budgeting activities have different goals.

Accounting

The accounting function creates reports to summarize the results of business activity, including the balance sheet, income statement, and statement of cash flows. All accounting reports are produced at the end of accounting periods, which are generally monthly, quarterly, and annually. The annual reporting period can be defined as any 12-month period and doesn't necessarily coincide with a calendar year (January through December). An annual reporting period that is different from a calendar year is known as a *fiscal year*. Many companies, for example, have fiscal years that begin on July 1 and end on June 30 of the following calendar year.

The *balance sheet* is a picture of the financial condition of the organization on a specific day, usually the last day of the accounting period. Information on the balance sheet includes the company's assets, liabilities, and equity. This report is known as a balance sheet because the total of the liabilities and the equity must equal the total of the assets as represented by the balance sheet formula:

$$\text{Assets} = \text{Liabilities} + \text{Equity}$$

The *income statement*, sometimes referred to as the *profit and loss statement* (P&L), provides information about the financial results of operations during the reporting period. The report informs readers how much revenue was produced from various sources, how much it cost to produce the goods or services, what the overhead expenses were, and what the profit or loss for the period was.

The *statement of cash flows* provides important facts about the money that flowed through the business during the accounting period: where it came from and what it was used for. This statement shows how much cash was a result of sales, how much was spent to produce the products that were sold, how much money was borrowed or came in as a result of new capital investments, and how much was invested in assets.

HR professionals need to be familiar with some basic accounting terminology and be able to read and understand financial reports in order to be effective strategic partners in their organizations. Table 10.1 provides definitions for some common accounting terms.

TABLE 10.1 Common accounting terms

Term	Definition/description
Accrued expense	Expenses, such as vacation leave, that have been incurred but not yet paid
Accounts payable	Money owed by the business to its suppliers
Accounts receivable	Money owed to the business by customers
Assets	Tangible or intangible items of value owned by the business
Audited financial statements	Financial statements that have been examined by an independent auditor (not affiliated with the company) to determine whether they fairly represent the financial condition of the business
Budget	A projection of revenue and expenses used to control actual expenses
Cost of goods sold	Money spent on supplies and labor to produce goods or services
Equity	Value of the business to owners after all liabilities have been paid
Expense	Money spent to operate the business
Generally accepted accounting principles (GAAP)	Standards established by the Financial Accounting Standards Board (FASB) for recording financial transactions
Gross profit	Sales revenue less cost of goods sold
Liability	Money owed by the business to others, such as lenders or the government (for payroll taxes withheld), or to employees (for unused vacation time)
Net profit	Gross profit less operating expenses
Profit	Money earned by the business after all expenses have been paid
Retained earnings	Net profits that aren't distributed to owners but remain in the business as equity
Revenue	Money received from customers for products or services

Budgeting

The budgeting process determines how many and what kind of resources will be required to accomplish goals and objectives generated by the strategic plan. Whether the plan requires additional employees, funds to outsource elements of the plan, new technology, or new equipment, these elements determine how much cash is needed to achieve the goal. There are two basic ways to create a budget; the first is based on historical budget information, and the second is known as *zero-based budgeting* (ZBB):

Budgets Based on Historic Information   A historic budget bases the current budget on the prior year's budget. Past budgets and expenditures are reviewed and the new budget is based on the historical trends. In some cases, the amounts in the budget are increased by a flat percentage rate, based on inflation or anticipated salary increases. This method assumes that operationally, nothing will change from the last budget.

Zero-Based Budgeting (ZBB)   The concept behind ZBB is very simple: Assume you're starting from scratch, and determine what is needed to achieve the goals. How many people will be required? How much will you need to spend on outsourcing? What will be the cost of new technology or equipment? Unlike the historic budget process, ZBB requires that the need for each expenditure be justified in terms of the new goals and action plans.

As part of a zero-based budget planning process, HR examines all the programs offered to employees to determine whether they're still adding value to the organization. Programs that no longer add value are dropped and replaced with those that do add value or, if cost cutting is required, are dropped and not replaced.

Regardless of the way in which the budget is developed, it can be created from the top down, from the bottom up, or with a combination approach:

Top-Down Budgeting   The *top-down budget* is created by senior management and imposed on the organization. Managers with operating responsibility have little input on how much money they will have to achieve their goals. This process is advantageous to senior management because they have complete control of how and where the money is spent. The disadvantage is that those creating the budget are generally far removed from actual operations and may not have full knowledge of what will be needed to achieve the goals they establish. This method often results in political battles as mid- and lower-level managers lobby senior management for additional funds for their particular departments.

Bottom-Up Budgeting   The *bottom-up* budget includes all managers with budget responsibility in the budget-creation process. Managers with direct operating responsibility for achieving goals develop a budget based on their knowledge of operating costs and provide the information to senior managers who have a view of the big picture for the organization. One advantage of this process is the commitment of operating managers to a budget they helped to create. Disadvantages include the amount of time required, the lack of awareness of the organization's big picture on the part of operating managers, and initial budget requests that may be unrealistic.

Parallel Budgeting A *parallel* budget includes elements of both the top-down and bottom-up approaches: Senior management provides broad guidelines for operating managers to follow in creating budgets for individual departments. This approach gives operating managers a context for developing individual budgets that are more realistic.

The end result of the budget process is a projection of expected revenue and costs needed to generate the revenue. Budget reports also include a cash flow projection that is used to prepare for short- or long-term shortfalls of cash, such as might occur in a seasonal business when the cash that comes in during the sales period (such as Christmas or Mother's Day) must support expenses that occur over a longer period of time. A separate report, known as a *capital budget*, is used to project asset purchases, such as buildings, machinery, and equipment used in manufacturing, or computers.

Motivating and Retaining through Total Rewards

Many employers (and employees) believe that higher pay equals higher performance. The truth of the matter is that there is a limitation on what money can do. Monetary compensation can certainly help employees run through Maslow's Hierarchy of Needs (see Chapter 6, "PHR Exam: Employee and Labor Relations" for a refresher of this and other theories of motivation). For example, base wages and cash incentives meet individuals' basic needs, allowing them to purchase food and shelter. It allows employees to go on vacation with family, or make financial contributions to religious or community organizations, which are both social needs tied to belonging. Higher pay and incentives that are tied closely with status may also meet an employee's esteem needs, both on and off the job. And one CEO of a cosmetics company was quoted as saying, "It took me a long time to learn that people do what you pay them to do, not what you ask them to do." However, this seems contrary to much of the 21st century claims that employees seek recognition, praise, and appreciation above all else.

 There is an excellent TED talk on the topic of motivation and rewards by Dan Pink. The title of the 2009 video is "The Puzzle of Motivation." View it to learn about the candle problem and how it is related to the true impact of incentive pay on creative thinking and problem-solving. Find it at https://www.ted.com/talks/dan_pink_on_motivation?language=en.

Regardless, there are limitations to what wages and other monetary incentives can do. This has been a focus of the organizational behavior sciences over the last several years, resulting in empirical evidence related to the topic. Several of these findings are reviewed next.

Efficiency vs. Empathy Wages

There are two important terms to understand in this section. *Efficiency wages* are above-market pay rates used specifically to attract talent in a competitive market. *Empathy wages* refer to the effect the pay premiums have on employee behavior when tied to feelings of gratitude and loyalty. Studies show that the effect efficiency wages have on employee performance is dependent on whether employees feel gratitude for the premium. Researchers noted that "non-star" employees, those described as being economically disadvantaged and lower on the performance scale when compared to others, are more likely to be appreciative of the additional pay and thus, motivated and loyal. Note that this does not mean they are poor performers or not able to do their jobs; they are simply rated lower when compared to others. In contrast, star performers are more likely to believe that they are deserving of the pay premium and thus feel less gratitude. This, in theory, means that the effect the pay premium has on driving high performer behaviors is less. When considered in the context of commission-based pay, this has very real implications for employers that are potentially overpaying for labor.

The source of much of the content in the "Efficiency vs. Empathy Wages" section was a journal article published in *Research in Organizational Behavior* and written by James N. Baron. The title is "Empathy Wages? Gratitude and Gift Exchange in Employment Relationships (2013)." Check it out for more on this emerging topic. Check out the full report at https://www.sciencedirect.com/science/article/pii/S0191308513000087.

Other Studies

The design of incentive programs also has significant influence on creating intrinsic motivation—that is, behavior that is driven from within. One scientific survey found that *publicizing* recognition as a work incentive is effective. They found that publicly recognizing an employee's efforts in a ceremony or online seems to increase the motivating value of the reward regardless of whether it was monetary or nonmonetary. This is due in part to the social reinforcement that naturally occurs when behavior is made public. The study also found that the *scarcity* of rewards increased positive feelings in employees. The authors attributed this to the attachment of an emotional reaction individuals have when they "win" something that is limited to a certain amount. This is in contrast to base pay as a motivating reward, because all employees receive wages.

For more on the findings related to publicity and scarcity of rewards, take a look at the original study published in the *Journal of Socio-Economics* titled "And the Winner Is…? The Motivating Power of Employee Rewards" (2013) conducted by Susanne Neckermann and Bruno S. Frey. Find the report at https://papers.ssrn.com/sol3/papers.cfm?abstract_id=2369372.

Another consideration in this realm is employee need. Some reports have shown that the effect that pay has on the job attitudes of employee engagement, job satisfaction, and organizational commitment is limited. Once employees exceed a certain pay threshold relative to their baseline needs, the effect of higher pay on job attitudes decreases, eventually having little to no effect on employee performance.

Finally, the sciences remind us that in order for rewards to be effective as motivational tools, employers must take care to manage pay equity issues. Environments where employees receive different pay for individual efforts without clear reasons for doing so may create feelings of unfairness or jealousy. Unequal pay dispersion can also increase negative organizational citizenship behaviors, from lack of teamwork to the more serious effect of sabotage. At its worst, if the unequal pay is based on discriminatory reasons, employers may be found guilty of violating Civil Rights laws.

What does this all mean in terms of attracting and retaining talent? Remember that a compensation philosophy is tied to decisions about whether to lead, lag, or match market rates. In a highly competitive industry, it may be valuable for employers to increase base wages (lead their market) to retain the talent necessary to operate. Perhaps more significantly the reverse is also true: Paying more for the highly talented may not be enough to bind them to your company, leading you back to the concepts of the integrative pay practices and application of fundamental theories of motivation.

Best Practices

The organizational sciences also give us insights into how to create TR best practices that increase rather than decrease employee motivation. Researchers found that money and incentives:

- **Do not improve job-related knowledge, skills, or abilities.** Unless the monetary incentive is invested in training and development activities, the money alone does not improve an employee's KSAs.

- **Do not necessarily improve the quality of jobs.** Plenty of research exists that shows that money is only part of the equation, that the 21st century workforce craves autonomy, meaning, recognition, and feedback in addition to work–life balance.

- **Cannot improve ethical behaviors.** There is the possibility that monetary incentives may actually increase unethical behavior in some employees. For example, the authors of a study that presented an article in *Science Direct* recounted a story at a large frozen vegetable production facility, where the company incentivized employees for every insect they found on the line. It was later discovered that employees were bringing *in* insects, placing them in the vegetables, then removing them to receive the incentive (Aguinis H., Joo R., Gottfredson. What monetary rewards can and cannot do: How to show employees the money. Business Horizons).

The authors of this study noted that there are five fundamental principles to consider when designing successful monetary reward systems. These include that an organization should do the following:

1. Define and measure performance accurately. This includes both what employees should and should not do.

2. Make rewards contingent on performance. Ensure there is enough variance between performance levels to actually motivate behaviors.

3. Reward employees in a timely manner. Provide regular, ongoing feedback and rewards rather than relying on an appraisal system.

4. Maintain justice in the reward system. Consider the process used to determine pay (procedural justice) and for whom the rewards are available (distributive justice).

5. Use both monetary and nonmonetary rewards. Survey or conduct focus groups with your employees and then build reward systems that they value.

Equity Compensation

Equity (ownership in a business) is a valuable retention tool in many industries, particularly for the manager level and above. Most commonly understood to occur through stock options and grants (discussed in the upcoming sections), equity compensation is highly regulated. Equity as part of a total compensation package does tend to get a lot of negative attention. In many cases, this is because there is no clear link between reward and performance. For that reason, and in order to ensure the incentive is effective, senior leaders must take care to do the following:

▪ Understand the business strategy for which equity will be used to achieve.

▪ Define both short- and long-term performance measures to balance decision-making.

▪ Create criteria for which to evaluate success and/or failure.

▪ Tie a portion of the reward to the adherence to company values and ethics.

Blockchain tokens as equity incentives is also an emerging trend being used to reward and retain employees. The Society for Human Resource Management (SHRM) noted that employers are using blockchain technology to reward employees in the following ways:

> They are being used like equity or phantom-equity awards, granted as compensation for past or future services.
>
> They may be subject to vesting based on continued service or achievement of performance targets, and acceleration of vesting can be triggered based on designated events, such as the occurrence of a change of control transaction, the termination of an employee without cause, or the achievement of technical milestones.
>
> If an employee quits, the employer has the right to repurchase any remaining restricted tokens that have not yet vested.
>
> Johnson Y., Rathjen K. (2018). Blockchain tokens as compensation treated like equity awards. Society for Human Resource Management. SHRM.org.

Senior-level HR professionals must stay up-to-date on this emerging issue, especially as it relates to how this and alternate currency is to be regulated.

Executive Compensation

As the complexity of managing organizations in a global environment increases, the need to attract and retain executives with the skills and talent to lead a company is even more critical for success. Executive compensation is a controversial subject for shareholders and, since the collapse of major corporations in the finance industry in 2008, is the focus of increasing scrutiny by federal and state regulators.

The responsibility for negotiating executive compensation packages belongs to the board of directors (BoD). The BoD is expected to negotiate with executive candidates and incumbents "at arm's length," meaning that the negotiations are conducted with objectivity and in the best interest of the company. Because executive candidates and incumbents are, almost by definition, skilled negotiators, the conventional wisdom is that they will push hard for packages that they view as competitive and in their own interests. In practice, many boards develop close relationships with executive staff, particularly CEOs, which has called into question the degree to which the negotiation can realistically be viewed as objective. Shareholders are increasingly active in challenging excessive compensation, particularly when executives receive massive compensation when business results are falling or employees are being laid off in large numbers as the result of poor decisions made by executives.

There have been many suggestions about how to develop compensation packages in a way that attracts and retains qualified, talented executives while maintaining the objectivity necessary to satisfy shareholder concerns. Some that are being considered or implemented include the following:

- Reporting transparency of executive compensation packages in annual reports and SEC filings
- Board compensation committees that consist only of outside directors (those without paid positions in the company) and that establish internal guidelines for executive compensation
- Use of independent data on competitive executive pay practices in developing internal guidelines
- Linking executive pay to long-term business results instead of quarterly or annual results (performance-based pay)
- Tying a significant piece of total compensation to achievable stretch goals that include profit goals in addition to share price
- Shareholder approval of executive stock-option plans
- Inclusion of nonmonetary performance goals, such as "green" goals, ethical behaviors, or community investment in the rewards package.

A typical compensation package for an executive can include elements from five categories: base salary, bonuses or short-term incentives, long-term incentives, employee benefits, and executive perks.

The composition of packages for individual executives varies by industry and company culture, with some having more pay at risk than others. In an effort to motivate executive performance and address shareholder concerns, BoDs construct packages that place the majority of executive compensation at risk in the form of short- and long-term incentives. The main theory at play in the use of incentive pay for executives is that, because they will benefit personally from decisions that achieve positive results for the company, they're more likely to act in ways that benefit the company than in ways that benefit them personally. One way this connection is achieved is that the size of the executive bonus pool is usually related to the profitability of the company, which by definition ties executive pay to business results.

Federal legislation has also impacted executive pay. In 1993, the Omnibus Budget Reconciliation Act (OBRA) was an attempt to reduce executive compensation by limiting employer tax deductions for executive pay to $1,000,000 annually. Employers were allowed to deduct only what was deemed reasonable compensation. Prior to the new tax bill signed into law in 2017, there was an exception to this. Companies were able to deduct performance-based compensation in excess of $1,000,000. Under the 2017 law, this exception is no longer allowed. The definition of who is considered a covered executive was also expanded to include chief financial officers (CFOs), meaning the deductibility of their compensation is also subject to the $1,000,000 limitation. SPHR candidates should know that employment contracts in effect prior to November 2017 are subject to a grace period for compliance with the new regulations. For these reasons, HR should be familiar with other, non-cash methods for which to reward and retain senior-level employees.

Executive benefits often include benefits available to employees throughout the organization, such as flexible work schedules, deferred compensation, tuition-reimbursement programs, or health club memberships. In some cases, benefit levels for executives may be expanded; for example, a flexible work arrangement for an executive may provide reimbursement for travel between the corporate office and the family home in another state, while the benefit available to nonexecutive employees allows telecommuting several days each week.

One unique element of executive compensation is *perquisites*. Perquisites, often referred to as *perks*, are additional benefits that provide comfort and luxury to the work and/or personal environment, usually intended for senior management and executives. The following are some of the perks provided to executive employees:

- Stock options
- Personal/spouse travel expenses
- Personal use of company aircraft
- Tax preparation and financial counseling
- Tax payments for benefits
- Supplemental retirement plans
- Housing allowances
- Home security services

- Company cars/chauffeurs
- Life insurance above company plan
- Medical plans above worker coverage
- Annual physicals
- Interest-free loans
- Company-paid legal advice

This element of an executive compensation package is often the least transparent and an area of increased interest to shareholders and regulators. At the beginning of 2007, the SEC requirements for reporting executive perks were reduced from $50,000 to $10,000, forcing companies to provide detailed lists of perks received by their executives. In some cases, the resulting exposure of payments outraged stockholders and employees and embarrassed BoDs. As a result, there is a growing trend of eliminating or reducing the numbers and types of perks previously provided. For example, in 2006, the Lockheed-Martin BoD eliminated perks including club memberships and fees and company-paid financial counseling and tax services for executives and adjusted executive salaries to reflect the cash value of the perks to maintain the value of their compensation packages.

Other benefits that can be found in executive compensation packages include the following:

Golden Parachute   A *golden parachute* provides significant benefits to an executive whose employment is terminated, usually under specific conditions such as a change in control of the company. Benefits can include severance pay, bonuses, options, continuation of medical coverage, and other types of benefits.

Golden Handshake   A *golden handshake* is most often used when a CEO takes a position that entails a high risk of termination due to restructuring or a change in direction, or sometimes as an incentive to retire early.

Golden Handcuffs   *Golden handcuffs* are a form of retention pay designed to keep key employees from leaving a company. They can take the form of stock options that vest over a period of years or a written agreement to pay back bonuses or other types of compensation if the employee resigns within a specified period of time.

Golden Life Jacket   A *golden life jacket* is sometimes offered to executives of a company being acquired, to ensure that they remain with the reorganized company.

Finally, senior-level HR professionals should work with other resources such as tax and legal experts to review existing executive employment contracts. These advisers will be able to provide feedback and make recommendations on how to enhance contracts and take advantage of tax considerations while still managing the risk of this compensation activity.

Stock Options

A *stock option* is the right to purchase an employer's stock at a certain price (the strike price), at a future date, within a specified period of time. Options provide an employee with an opportunity to purchase shares but don't require that the employee do so. The *grant price* or *strike price* of the stock is based on the market price at the time the options are issued. It's common to find stock options vesting over a three-to-five-year period as a retention tactic; they can be exercised for up to 10 years. Stock options are valuable only if the stock price rises over time, so their value to employees depends on the company's financial performance. Although stock option plans vary between companies, all plans must be operated within parameters established by the SEC or IRS.

There are two types of stock options: *incentive stock options* (ISOs) and *nonqualified stock options*. The difference between the option types is the tax treatment for the employer and employee:

Incentive, or Qualified, Stock Options   ISOs are stock options that can be offered only to employees; consultants and external members of the BoD aren't eligible. The tax treatment for ISOs is often favorable for employees because they don't face taxes at the time the stock option is exercised—they don't have income to report until the stock is sold at a later date. When an ISO is sold, however, it's likely that capital gains taxes will be due and subject to the alternative minimum tax under certain conditions. Use of ISOs isn't as favorable to employers because the company receives a tax deduction only if certain conditions are met.

Nonqualified Options   Nonqualified stock options can be used for consultants and external members of the BoD as well as for employees. The organization receives a tax deduction when the options are exercised, and employees pay tax on any gain they realize from the sale. Income from the stock is treated as compensation, and when the stock is sold there are further tax implications.

Two other types of stock ownership employers provide to employees are restricted stock and phantom stock:

Restricted Stock   *Restricted stock* is common stock offered to employees, typically executives or employees who demonstrate outstanding performance. Restricted stocks are actual shares, not the option-to-buy shares, like stock options. Restricted stock usually follows a vesting schedule designed to reward retention. Employees may be motivated to stay with the organization to realize the full benefit of their restricted stock, which is why employees perceive these as golden handcuffs, or a financial benefit that will be lost if they leave the organization.

Phantom Stock   *Phantom stock* is used in privately held companies to provide the benefits of employee ownership without granting stock. Organizations use phantom stock to motivate and retain employees without granting equity or sharing ownership in the company. Phantom stock can generate the kind of payoffs that stock options or restricted stock can yield. Executives and outside members of the BoD are the most common recipients of phantom stock. There is usually a vesting schedule based on length of service and performance (individual or company). Like common stock, phantom stock follows the company's market-price movements. A valuation formula determines the value of the stock. When the phantom stock yields a payout, the employer is eligible to receive a tax deduction for the amount paid.

Board of Directors/Outside Directors

The BoD is elected by shareholders to oversee the management of the corporation on behalf of its stockholders. Members of the BoD can be executives of the organization (known as *inside directors*) or external to the organization (known as *outside directors*).

Inside directors receive executive compensation packages consisting of stock options, benefits, and base pay, to which they're entitled based on their roles as corporate executives. Outside directors commonly receive cash for meeting fees and retainers.

Benefits

As with the compensation exam responsibility, SPHR candidates are directed to understand benefits strategies in the context of how they influence an organization's ability to attract, reward, and retain talent. In further context, the exam responsibility also outlines the need to apply principles related to health, welfare, retirement, recognition programs, work–life balance, and wellness. These directives form the basis for these benefits.

A detailed description of traditional employee benefits programs can be reviewed in Chapter 5. This section instead focuses on the exam directive to design benefits programs to attract, reward, and retain critical talent using creative techniques.

There are several elements of an employer's benefits offerings that must be strategically considered. These include programs that are compliant with the many labor laws that govern Total Rewards (covered in Appendix C). Benefits must also be considered through the filter of an organization's purpose. Let's use REI, the outdoor supply retailer, as an example of this alignment. Their purpose (mission) statement is:

> We inspire, educate and outfit for a lifetime of outdoor adventure.

REI also has a Total Rewards statement that is in alignment with their purpose:

> REI is committed to recognizing and rewarding our employees with a Total Rewards package that includes competitive base pay, incentives and comprehensive benefits, generous employee discounts and other perks, as well as programs that support good health and work/life balance.

This philosophy is creating expectations in employees of the types of benefits REI will offer. Fortunately, REI is a good example of aligning benefits offerings with their commitment, and employees enjoy discounts on merchandise, a paid day off specifically to go on an outdoor adventure, tuition reimbursement, and healthcare for both part-time and full-time employees, just to name a few.

Other strategic considerations include the nature of the competitive landscape. Consider the healthcare industry, with the Bureau of Labor Statistics reporting a 2.3 percent unemployment rate as of May 2018. HR professionals in the healthcare industry understand all too well the challenges of turnover rates reflecting very high "quits" and very low layoffs. Combine this with the barriers to entry for high-skilled positions such as nurses (impacted university nursing programs, for example), and it is easy to understand why using Total Rewards to retain talent is such a priority for employers. In response, many companies are offering "other" types of benefits such as paid time off to volunteer, on-site fitness facilities, and professional development funds to offset the cost of continuing education while making an investment in their core services.

Employers must of course be cost-conscious, especially because healthcare insurance for employees has increased almost every year in the last decade, in some cases by as much as 13 percent per year. Rather than cutting benefits, however, strategic employers are looking for more creative ways to maintain their benefits levels. These include the following:

- **Insurance captives:** These are employer self-funded health insurance plans. Group captives are those in which the employer enrolls in an insurance co-op to leverage size, often being owned by employers in similar industries. The group captive receives a portion of all premiums and pays for claims up to a certain amount. Employers direct-pay the rest of the claims, and often purchase stop-loss insurance to limit financial exposure in the event of a catastrophic claim. There are some instances where employers may use unused premiums as dividends, another strategic reason middle-sized companies are considering this option.

- **Cost sharing:** Many employers are increasingly shifting part of the increased cost of benefits to their employees. This includes covering only a portion of the monthly premium and making the employee responsible for the difference. Complying with regulations is an important consideration to ensure the employer is offering affordable care.

- **Health insurance stipends:** Usually offered as a flat amount, stipends are a cash offset to the cost of employee health insurance. Employees may use the stipend to purchase the benefits of their choice. Note that in most cases, the employer may not require that the employee use the stipend to purchase health insurance, nor may they require proof of insurance. Additionally, this stipend results in an increase in the taxable income of the employee, which can erode the attractiveness of this option.

- **Selecting medical providers equipped for telemedicine:** Offering appointments over the phone or through video is increasing in popularity. This is because (1) it helps reduce exposure to contagions resulting in missed days at work, and (2) many minor issues do not require an expensive clinic visit. This approach not only cuts down on the cost of delivering services, but also reduces the amount an employee has to expend in co-payments.

- **Selecting private physician or "concierge" services:** Concierge services provide employees access to private medical care. It can be offered on an ad hoc basis, such as for employees who travel for work. It may also be service-driven, such as adding holistic medical providers to enhance the value of traditional healthcare offerings. Concierge services may also be a total care platform, where a clinic or physician is put on an annual retainer and provides a high level of personal patient interaction and longevity/preventive care planning. In some cases, employers may also "pay as they go," meaning they do not have to prepay for services that are not used.

Many employers still use the cost of health and wellness benefits to make strategic decisions about which programs to offer. While understandable, relying solely on this factor to make decisions about benefits is becoming increasingly short-sighted as a method to attract and keep talent in a competitive labor market.

Summary

The role of Total Rewards and the resulting compensation and benefits programs have a significant effect on an employer's ability to compete for talent. Human resource professionals have a fiduciary responsibility to administer TR programs in accordance with the highest degree of ethics and regulatory compliance, but also to serve the needs of both the employer and employee.

HR is often tasked with the development of a Total Rewards philosophy that should be tied to a company's mission or purpose. Doing so allows employees to have a clear view of what the company values. A clear philosophy also demonstrates that the employer is committed to providing base pay, health, wellness, work–life balance, time off, and retirement benefits in addition to training and career pathing as part of an integrative system. This system is used to meet employee needs in order to attract, retain, and reward the desired workforce.

Building an integrative TR system requires employers to access both internal and external resources for data. Surveying employees, benchmarking jobs, and conducting salary surveys are all sources that should be used to build effective TR programs.

Senior-level professionals should also be familiar with basic accounting and budgeting principles. This knowledge is used for many HR tasks, including forecasting labor costs and costing out labor contracts. They also serve to inform decisions when building executive compensation packages that go beyond base wages and are compliant with tax implications. Understanding these basic principles and applying them to the operational activities of day-to-day human resource tasks helps develop HR into true business partners.

Finally, the organizational sciences have made significant progress in helping us understand how Total Rewards can—and cannot—motivate workers. Findings include the threshold that base pay has on creating loyalty and commitment, as well as the influence of Total Rewards programs on employee job attitudes.

Exam Essentials

Be aware of the high degree of financial responsibility of senior-level human resource professionals. Understanding what it means to have fiduciary responsibility underscores all human resource activities but is especially significant in Total Rewards. Acting in one's own self-interest, navigating the presence of conflicting duties, and profiting from the level of decision-making authority are all ways HR may breach their fiduciary obligations.

Understand the importance of having a Total Rewards philosophy. A TR philosophy will serve as the basis for creating the entire TR system. Fundamental to this is the employer's decision to lead, lag, or match the labor markets in which they compete for talent. The philosophy is driven by both internal and external considerations that influence an organization's ability to attract, retain, and reward employees.

Align TR programs with organizational strategies using an integrative approach. Aligning pay and benefits programs goes beyond base wages and health insurance. Senior-level HR professionals will also need to be able to use their TR programs to respond to external factors such as changing market conditions, economic factors, and geographic factors. Internally, HR will need to deliver pay systems that have the proper mix of options to address the rising cost of TR, the diverse needs of the workgroup, and the skills shortage many industries are now experiencing.

Be familiar with job analysis, evaluation, and pricing activities. Fundamental to the building of formal pay structures is the ability to group jobs into families. Doing so allows HR to accurately benchmark jobs and access wage data to offer competitive pay. Job analysis is also helpful when designing TR programs that offer career growth as a reward for staying with a company.

Know basic budget and accounting principles. Particularly when HR is called on to calculate the cost of a collective bargaining agreement and the tax implications of executive compensation packages, understanding basic business financials will inform many TR-related decisions.

Have up-to-date, empirical knowledge of how TR serves to motivate employees. The organizational and other sciences have made important contributions in understanding the relationship between pay and performance and other motivational aspects of TR programs. Senior-level HR professionals should understand these principles and use them to create programs that meet the needs of the company and the workforce.

Be familiar with the use of equity compensation and the complexity of administering executive compensation programs. Historically, employers have used equity compensation as a major portion of executive compensation. In recent years, however, equity as a form of compensation is also increasing in popularity with industry start-ups. Therefore, it is important that HR has a competency-based, thorough understanding of this in practice.

Design other benefits programs that balance employee needs with increasing costs. The design of benefits programs that are strategically aligned with organizational goals, employee needs, and cost management should be the focus of senior-level HR activities. This includes creative problem-solving that helps manage risk while offering nontraditional benefits discussed throughout the entire TR structure.

Review Questions

You can find the answers in Appendix A.

1. Senior HR professionals are called upon to design TR systems that balance the need to find and retain qualified talent with which of the following?

    A. Complying with the Fair Labor Standards Act

    B. Meeting the needs of an older workforce

    C. Designing a TR program that is affordable

    D. Provide health insurance for all employees

2. In which of the following scenarios has a human resource professional breached his fiduciary responsibility?

    A. Selecting a benefits plan that best fits his family of four

    B. Moving an open position to a higher salary grade to make it easier for his team to recruit

    C. Choosing an insurance broker because they give generous gifts during the holidays

    D. All of the above

3. A travel agency has decided they will pay less than their competitors for reservation agents as there is an abundant supply in the labor market. This is an example of what TR philosophy?

    A. Lagging the market

    B. Leading the market

    C. Matching the market

    D. None of the above

4. In strong economies which of the following is likely true?

    A. Companies will need to pay more for labor.

    B. There are many talented workers from which to hire.

    C. There are high levels of unemployment.

    D. There are low levels of unemployment.

5. Which of the following is the fundamental factor for creating unpaid internships?

    A. The individual must be the primary beneficiary of the internship.

    B. The company may be the primary beneficiary of the internship.

    C. The company cannot benefit by having the intern do critical work.

    D. The intern must be in an active semester at school.

6. About how long should employers project out their cost of Total Rewards programs?

   A. 6 months

   B. 1 year

   C. 2 years

   D. 5+ years

7. Which of the following is a best representation of an integrative approach to Total Rewards programs?

   A. Providing retiree benefits through pensions

   B. Not overpaying for talent

   C. Creating reasonable executive compensation packages

   D. All of the above

8. The school district for which you work has requested that your team upgrade the pay structures. Currently, the plan has 12 grades sorted by job families. The current grades are best represented by which of the following types of salary structures?

   A. Traditional

   B. Open system

   C. Broad-banded

   D. Broad-graded

9. What is the main purpose of evaluating and pricing jobs?

   A. To properly group jobs into families

   B. To determine job worth when compared to internal and external factors

   C. To advise senior executives on effective variable pay plans

   D. To build pay programs that are competitive with the external labor market

10. Which of the following would be a best practice when selecting salary surveys?

    A. Line managers are involved in validating job responsibilities.

    B. Senior leaders participate in the job description comparisons.

    C. The cost of the survey is not prohibitive.

    D. Only those who participated in the survey are eligible to purchase the survey.

11. Jamie is an "HR department of one" at a small tech company start-up with fewer than 30 employees. She has been tasked to begin the job evaluation process in order to build competitive pay systems. Which of the following is most likely going to be a top priority for her choice of evaluation method?

    A. Ensuring the method is legally compliant

    B. Clear criteria to ensure equity

    C. Perceptions of distributive justice

    D. Ease of development and use

12. The collective bargaining process is underway and one wage proposal is to increase incumbent pay by 12 percent but create lower new hire wages for the contract period. This is an example of which wage system?

    A. Banding

    B. Grading

    C. Two-tiered

    D. Lump sum

13. Costing out labor rates over a two-year planning horizon is a feature of which function?

    A. Job costing

    B. Forecasting

    C. Financing

    D. Accounting

14. The small business you work for has approximately 800 hours of employee unused vacation time. This is an example of which of the following?

    A. Accrued expenses

    B. Accounts payable

    C. Accounts receivable

    D. Expenses

15. You have reached the point in the job analysis process where you are reviewing the Accounting department roles and responsibilities. Which of the following principles should govern how you distribute the tasks and duties of each job within the department?

    A. Authority principle

    B. Ethical principles

    C. Good Manufacturing Practices (GMP)

    D. Generally Accepted Accounting Principles (GAAP)

16. What is the main advantage of using a zero-based budget methodology?

    A. It is relatively simple to build.

    B. It minimizes the impact a new budget can have on cash flow.

    C. It allows for gradual progression of expenses that are more easily absorbed.

    D. It allows for real-time financial adjustments to technological, economic, or other forces that influence operations.

17. "People want what they can't have" is an example of which incentive technique designed to increase employee motivation?

    A. Scarcity

    B. Efficiency

    C. Public recognition

    D. Socioeconomics

18. Which of the following occurs when an employee has enough money for which to meet their baseline needs?

   A. Base pay increases employee motivation.

   B. Base pay decreases employee motivation.

   C. Base pay has no effect on employee motivation.

   D. It depends on the employee.

19. What type of compensation are stock options?

   A. Holistic

   B. Intrinsic

   C. Executive

   D. Equity

20. Which of the following is often used to build an executive total rewards package?

   A. Base pay

   B. Equity

   C. Perks

   D. All of the above

Chapter

11

SPHR Exam: Employee Relations and Engagement

The HRCI test specifications from the Employee Relations and Engagement functional area covered in this chapter include senior-level responsibilities and knowledge. The content is focused on a candidate's ability to "develop and/or monitor strategies impacting employee satisfaction and performance including diversity and inclusion, safety, security, and labor strategies." Responsibilities related to this functional area follow.

Responsibilities:

✓ **01 Design and evaluate strategies for employee satisfaction (for example: recognition, career path) and performance management (for example: performance evaluation, corrective action, coaching).**

✓ **02 Analyze and evaluate strategies to promote diversity and inclusion.**

✓ **03 Evaluate employee safety and security strategies (for example: emergency response plan, building access, data security/privacy).**

✓ **04 Develop and evaluate labor strategies (for example: collective bargaining, grievance program, concerted activity, staying union-free, strategically aligning with labor).**

Knowledge:

✓ **51 Strategies to facilitate positive employee relations**

✓ **52 Methods for assessing employee attitudes, opinions, and satisfaction**

✓ **53 Performance management strategies**

✓ **54 Human relations concepts and applications**

The Employee Relations and Engagement function includes the tasks and responsibilities that focus on senior-level activities. Most are designed to improve employee satisfaction, performance, and safety. As you can imagine, there are several HR-related programs and activities that frame the way this is accomplished in both union and nonunion environments. This chapter reviews job attitudes in general, and the systems that influence employee performance such as performance feedback, diversity and inclusion, safety and security, and formal labor relations strategies. This functional area makes up 20 percent of the SPHR exam, and, when combined with Leadership & Strategy, represents more than 60 percent of exam day content.

Note that some of this content is identical to that which is covered in the PHR function area of Employee and Labor Relations. This is because there are some redundancies between exam content, especially that which is related to the following:

- Human relations concepts and applications
- Methods for assessing employee attitudes, opinions, and satisfaction
- Workplace safety and security risks
- Emergency response, business continuity, and disaster recovery strategies
- Internal investigation, monitoring, and surveillance techniques
- Data security and privacy
- The collective bargaining process

Human Relations

The science of human relations studies the behavior of people in groups. It includes a broad spectrum of ideas that concentrate on the importance of the human element at work, including interpersonal characteristics and organizational behavior.

This approach to workplace relationships, introduced in the 1920s, challenged traditional assumptions that people work only for economic reasons and that monetary incentives provided sufficient motivation for increased productivity. Human relations theories recognized that businesses are social as well as economic systems and looked at the impact of formal (management) and informal (work group) social connections in the workplace, and the impact these connections have on work processes. For the first time, there was recognition that employees are complex individuals, motivated at different times by different factors, and that increased productivity could be tied to employee job attitudes that include job satisfaction, organizational commitment, and engagement.

One notable contribution to the study of human relations and organizational behavior were the findings of the Hawthorne Studies. A group of researchers convened upon Western Electrics Company in the 1920s and 1930s to study the impact of environmental factors such as lighting on employee productivity. They found that regardless of whether they increased or decreased lighting, worker efficiencies improved. These researchers stumbled upon a fundamental truism of human relations—that simply paying attention to employee morale and well-being had a positive effect on employee productivity. Expanded studies also theorized that the Hawthorne effect was not only due to increased attention; the fact that productivity was being measured contributed to increased performance as well.

It is recommended that you pause here and refer to Chapter 6, "PHR Exam: Employee and Labor Relations," content related to human relations, specifically regarding intelligence, personalities, and psychological capital.

For a deeper look at the Hawthorne studies, go to YouTube and search for the video titled "AT & T Archives: The Year They Discovered People."

Motivation

In addition to the benchmark theories of motivation from Maslow, Herzberg, Adams, and others (also found in Chapter 6), SPHR candidates must understand other, more intrinsic theories of motivation. They include psychological empowerment and cognitive evaluation theory.

Psychological empowerment is a form of intrinsic (from within) motivation that has four identified dimensions:

- **Meaning:** Refers to the relationship between an individual's values and the nature of the work

- **Competence:** Refers to what an employee "knows"—knowing why (self-awareness, career goals), knowing whom (networks, mentors), and knowing how (skills, abilities)

- **Self-determination:** Is reflected by degrees of autonomy and choice

- **Impact:** Refers to the ability of an employee to influence work outcomes

Psychological empowerment increases intrinsic motivation because employees themselves increase their:

- Belief that they can succeed (self-efficacy)

- Self-esteem, confidence, and determination

- Career identity and learning

Psychological empowerment should matter to senior-level HR professionals, as research shows it is positively correlated to managerial effectiveness, innovation, and organizational commitment.

Cognitive evaluation theory (also called self-determination theory) is focused fundamentally on a person's need for autonomy, relatedness, and competence—desires that are driven from within. This theory supports the idea that employees are motivated by extrinsic rewards only to the degree to which they *allow for autonomy, relatedness, or increased competence*. Some researchers noted that this theory helps to explain the generational differences of motivation, finding that older workers have higher levels of achievement when they have more face time with their boss or are trusted with more responsibility. In other words, the rewards of management attention and trust increases their intrinsic desire to achieve.

Job Attitudes

Employee engagement has achieved all the elements of a buzzword, molded and shaped both by sciences of organizational behavior and high-profile application of what the field "thinks" engagement should be measured by. Management thought leaders and the Internet have exploded with resources defining engagement by how satisfied, customer-driven, happy, productive, and tenured engaged workers are. And this is true—the organizational sciences support the idea that engaged workers are linked to the aforementioned positive outcomes. However, work engagement is but one of the three main job attitudes listed here, and all have distinct constructs:

- **Work engagement:** This is the degree to which employees have invested their physical, emotional, and cognitive (mental) energy and thus experience an emotional connection with their work. This includes the *tasks* themselves (as opposed to the organization as a whole) serving as a motivational force that drives employee behaviors. Engaged employees find meaning in the work itself.

- **Job satisfaction:** Job satisfaction continues to be one of the most researched job attitudes in the behavioral sciences. A job attitude exists as a positive or negative "state," meaning the state of the attitude may change at any time. Job satisfaction can be understood using J. Richard Hackman and Greg R. Oldham's job characteristics' model, which includes skill variety, task identity, task significance, autonomy, and feedback as influencers for satisfied workers.

- **Organizational commitment:** Second only to job satisfaction in terms of I/O research, organizational commitment is much broader in scope than the above job attitudes. Organizational commitment is less state-like, meaning it tends to be a more stable employee attitude than job satisfaction. Researchers have defined organizational commitment to include an employee's level of attachment and identification with a particular company. Organizational commitment has subsets, including emotional attachment and loyalty, the employee's need for employment, and the degree the employee believes they have a moral obligation to stay.

Conversely, actively disengaged employees can be highly destructive. Two examples come to mind: (1) the employee who failed to get a promotion at Tesla that allegedly engaged in sabotage by making unspecified code changes to the manufacturing operating system, and (2) the CIA employee who believed the government was overreaching in its surveillance efforts and so leaked confidential information to the press. While these examples seem extreme, actively disengaged employees can and do cause harm. It is simply a matter of degree.

Dr. Erin Richard provides a meta-analytic breakdown of job attitudes in Appendix E, "Summarizing the Summaries: What Meta-Analyses Tell Us About Work Engagement." She cites research that gives specific indications of how organizational interventions can influence employee job attitudes. While more detail is given in the appendix, here are a few examples:

- **Personal resource-building interventions:** These focus on increasing employees' optimism, resilience, or positive views of themselves (e.g., self-efficacy). For example, the healthcare provider Kaiser Permanente surveys their employees using a program called People Pulse. They use the feedback they receive to design programs that will increase what they refer to as the three R's: recognition, resources, and respect. Specifically, they ask questions related to supportive managers (recognition), physical, psychological and social job support (resources), and improved teamwork (respect).

- **Job resource building interventions:** These focus on increasing work resources, such as autonomy, social support, or feedback. For example, Amazon has the estimated second-largest workforce population in the United States. They take steps to measure employee job attitudes *daily* using a program called Connections. Amazon has a dedicated "people science" team that analyzes the data and makes recommendations for improvements and action. Another technological solution implemented by Amazon is a program called Forte, used specifically to supply meaningful feedback to employees as part of the appraisal process.

- **Leadership training interventions:** These attempt to build job resources and motivate employees indirectly by increasing the knowledge and skill of their leaders. For example, perhaps one of the most well-known professional research groups, Gallup, estimates that *managers* are primarily responsible for building an engaged workforce. For this reason, successful companies within this domain focus their engagement efforts on training and coaching for managers that support other engagement factors such as feedback and autonomy.

- **Health-promoting interventions:** These attempt to increase engagement by promoting healthier lifestyles aimed at building and sustaining personal resources. For example, at Salesforce, employees are "empowered to perform meaningful work with good people in a great environment, and will be fairly rewarded for it." Their culture development programs build on technology applications that help employees access the necessary resources to do their jobs, develop the interpersonal skills necessary to succeed, and promote wellness initiatives for themselves and their families.

Positive Employee Relations

An effective engagement program is highly dependent on a company's ability to build positive employee relations programs. Successful programs are built on the complex interplay between employees and three variables: individual, organizational, and relational. We explore these next.

Individual Behaviors

Many of the individual behaviors that influence the degree of engagement have been described in this chapter and in Chapter 6. Factors such as personality, motivational preferences, and a person's degree of emotional intelligence must be factored into an employer's positive employee relations programs. Doing so, however, may be easier said than done, particularly with a diverse workgroup that has unique needs, desires, and individual goals.

That's not to imply that it cannot be done. It simply means that thoughtful leaders understand that a one-size-fits-all approach will miss the mark as often as it hits the mark. For this reason, understanding what drives individual employees should be the first step in a strategic intervention designed to improve relations with employees.

Engagement surveys are one tool that can help HR assess the individual needs and attitudes of employees. Attitude surveys can be designed to measure job satisfaction, motivation, employee grievances, inclusiveness, pay, safety, and so forth. Senior-level HR professionals must begin with the end in mind when designing feedback surveys, identifying first what it is they are hoping to measure. Surveys that are too broad can dilute the message. Knowing the target audience is also an important factor in successful survey design. Barriers to meaningful feedback may include the length of a survey, surveys that do not take into consideration native languages, and surveys that are reliant on emails in a workforce where all do not have access. Once these barriers have been mitigated and feedback collected, HR can begin to build employee relations strategies that are aligned with employee needs.

Some companies, such as Zappos, have on staff a life coach to help employees build strengths and minimize weaknesses. Other companies use personality profiling such as DISC (discprofile.com) or Myers-Briggs Type Indicator (MBTI) (mbtionline.com) to create development plans and improve team communication. Some countries, such as France, have instituted "email curfews," also known as right-to-disconnect laws, that support employees' right to not answer work-related emails after hours or while on vacation. These and other efforts must be justified by employee feedback and developed, implemented, and evaluated by senior-level HR professionals. HR must also align these programs with organizational needs.

Organizational Behaviors

Organizational behaviors that help create positive employee relations strategies are those that exist in both theory and practice, in policies, and actions. Two examples include culture and the practice of positive discipline.

Culture

Studies are showing that organizational behaviors play a critical role in positive employee relations. Edgar Schein (ocli.org) developed what is perhaps the most well-known model of workplace culture. He defined three factors that build the workplace culture:

- **Artifacts:** Elements of a company culture that are seen, heard, or felt and that help to create a collective identity. One manufacturing company in the Central Valley of

California, for example, has a rather large ladder fondly referred to by employees as Godzilla. This same company reinforces workplace standards of behavior using the acronym CDR (courtesy, dignity, and respect). Managers may address uncivil behavior by simply asking employees if they are acting with CDR. If not, then the behavior goes against culture and is corrected. This same company hosts an annual culture fair (produced by employees, not managers) that is designed around the company values of respect, communication, professional development, and attitude, just to name a few. Other factors such as company dress code and the design of office space fall within Schein's definition of artifacts that serve the development of a company culture.

- **Values:** Fundamental to Schein's model is the presence of company values, more often than not presented along with a company's mission and vision. While this trio is discussed in depth in Chapter 7, "SPHR Exam: Leadership and Strategy," values in the context of culture are more than just the statement. Values are espoused to employees through company behaviors, strategies, goals, and interventions. The company declares these values by what they choose to expend their resources on.

- **Assumed values:** Schein defines organizational culture as being represented by assumed values. These are the assumptions made by employees about what the company actually values, as opposed to what they say they value. Assumed values are often informally communicated by what behaviors a company rewards and what behaviors are disciplined.

An emerging issue that is an interesting reflection of values is that of face time—not the app, but the amount of time a person is seen at work (passive face time); the amount of time a person engages with someone else, such as in meetings (dynamic face time); or the amount of time a person's presence is noticed after hours or off-site (extracurricular face time). If an employee who returns emails after hours is viewed as being more dedicated, this is a reflection of an assumed value. Considered a form of bias, face time is an increasingly important issue that affects many parts of a senior-level HR professional's role.

Geert Hofstede also contributed significant work to the domain of organizational culture. Hofstede pioneered many of the studies on the global factors of culture, some of which translate quite nicely into concepts related to positive employee relations (geerthofstede.com). They include the following:

- **Power distance:** Perhaps the best way to understand Hofstede's dimension of power distance is in the realm of executive pay. For example, a high-profile executive in the United States has a pay ratio of 434:1. This means, that for every dollar in median worker pay, the CEO earns $434. This company would reflect a culture of high power distance in that there is a large gap of power and reward between management and employees.

- **Uncertainty avoidance:** Companies that seek to build creative and innovative work environments should seek to find employees who are flexible and adaptive and have a high tolerance for lack of strict structure. For example, Australian company Atlassian regularly gives their engineers 24 hours to "go work on anything." At the end of the day, a marathon meeting is held where ideas are shared and adopted. This company and others who have used similar strategies report a high degree of successful, innovative solutions that would not have been priority in an otherwise 9-5 tasks-driven routine. Conversely, employees who prefer to avoid uncertainty would be a better fit for the more bureaucratic organizations that have clear reporting structures and routinized tasks.

- **Individualism vs. collectivism:** Often understood through the filter of country of origin, this dimension of culture speaks to the degree of independence and freedom. Highly individualized countries and companies place a high value on factors such as autonomy. This is well reflected in, for example, companies that have a 100 percent virtual workforce, a trend that continues to grow as a tech-enabled, service-driven economy influences organizational competitiveness. Individualistic societies are those in which connections are looser than their counterpart, collectivist societies, in which integrated, cohesive teams are the norm.

- **Long-term vs. short-term orientation:** Self-discipline and sacrifice are the hallmarks of those with an orientation toward the long term. Short term–oriented individuals place a higher value on what is "in the now," making choices that feel good and serve the present moment. On a macro business scale, short term–oriented companies are focused on the quarterly or annual bottom line, whereas long term–oriented businesses sow seeds for future growth and profits.

Ultimately, organizational behaviors reflected through the filter of culture have a significant effect on how employees build their identity at and through the company they work for.

Positive Discipline

Corrective action must also be explored in the context of positive employee relations. Businesses that engage in positive discipline techniques are oriented toward problem-solving rather than punishment. The positive discipline approach has several characteristics, the first of which is the use of counseling. Counseling is focused on making the employee aware of the behaviors that need to change. When approached constructively and with respect, most employees will change undesirable behaviors fairly quickly. Some employers use a performance improvement plan (PIP) that is focused on actionable steps the employee needs to take, along with the type of support and feedback they should expect from their supervisors while they seek to correct their behavior. PIPs are success plans, not termination plans, and thus should be worded as such. Managers must be adequately trained in constructive coaching techniques to help them avoid treating the process as though it is a step in progressive discipline.

Relational Behaviors

The study of leadership has produced reams of paper and Internet "experts" on management; it seems that everyone has an opinion on whether leaders are born or made. This focus is justified, as a primary reason for employee turnover is the relationship with their supervisor.

Leader-member exchange (LMX) theory is different from trait-based or situational theories of leadership that analyze the characteristics of the leader or the follower to assess leadership effectiveness. LMX theory focuses on the reciprocity of relationship factors—specifically, the nature of the interactions between leaders and followers. LMX delivered the concept of "in-groups" and "out-groups"—employees become members of one group or the other based on the relationship they develop with the leader. In-group members will have special access to the leader and expanded roles with increased responsibilities. They may be seen as trusted by the leader as well as having trust in the leader. Members of the out-group usually have less of a leader-member fit and are most likely the employees who fail to fully engage in the work tasks or form deep commitments to the team. On the face of it, it may seem that in-group members are favored by their leader, and in some cases, that perception is true. That does not make it unlawful or an ineffective practice as LMX theory notes that out-group members must still be treated and rewarded fairly.

Early studies found that the quality of the in-group relationships was related to positive outcomes for leaders, followers, groups, and the organization in general. Later studies that analyzed LMX relationships consistently found links between in-group behaviors and job satisfaction, commitment, clarity, and turnover intentions. Those who support LMX theory believe that leaders should actually seek to form in-groups, treat out-group members fairly, and offer all employees the opportunity to become in-group members.

Another relational factor in positive employee relations strategies is the nature and influence of social belonging. There are many external sources that have influence on employee work attitudes and behaviors. They include co-workers, supervisors, family members, customers, and friends. The fundamental premise of *social information processing* is that the attitudes toward an employee's position or company from these sources will influence how the employees themselves view their work (similar to the concept of emotional contagion covered in Chapter 6). For example, if customers call and consistently complain about a product, an employee may be influenced by the volume of complaints and begin to view the product as low quality, often at the expense of creative problem-solving. Or if a spouse regularly complains about an employee's schedule, the employee may begin to view the schedule as unfair, even if the employee was initially fine with it. From an applied perspective, senior leaders must continually survey their workgroups to monitor the social information being shared about the job or organization. Instead of anonymously asking employees about how they feel about the company, the survey could ask questions about what their family, friends, or customers are saying.

Finally, the nature of the relationship between the employer and employee can be explored through the *psychological contract*. The economic challenges of the not-so-distant past created worries about job security for many of the employed and created a very large pool of the qualified unemployed (launching the gig economy; see Chapter 5, "PHR Exam: Total Rewards"). Many millennials who graduated from college were unable to find any work at all, let alone in their fields of study. Technology, globalization, and economic uncertainty destabilized a pillar of the American economy, the labor force population. According to HRCI, the psychological contract is "an unwritten agreement of the mutual beliefs, perceptions, and informal obligations between an employer and an employee, which influence how they interact." For example, employees who see their co-workers lose their jobs due to downsizing could be expected to have lower degrees of loyalty toward the employer. Conversely, it would be expected that employers who adopt a "no layoff" practice or policy would increase loyalty due to the nature of the psychological contract. The psychological contract applies to both tangible and intangible items.

Career Planning and Management

One HR activity combines individual, organizational, and relational positive employee relations strategies: the process of helping employees develop and manage their careers. Many individuals believe that their career happens by accident; perhaps they needed a job right out of school and so accepted the first offer available. Or they chose a college major when they were young that they did not find completely satisfying post-graduation, so they settled into a career or industry that was convenient. Others may lack the self-awareness necessary to analyze and adjust accordingly to their natural strengths and weaknesses. For this reason, employers should begin at the beginning by encouraging employees to take active ownership of their careers.

An *individual development plan (IDP)* is a written career plan that is built to an employee's career goals. For example, Yale University uses a tool that helps connect the individual, organizational, and relational behaviors of career pathing. Yale's IDP begins with an annual meeting between an employee and their supervisor. This brainstorming session results in a plan that includes realistic, tangible steps the employee can take toward their professional development goals. Individually, the employee is encouraged to identify what they want in a career and are evaluated for their talent strengths and weaknesses. These are then aligned with the skills that the organization needs the employee to develop for the current or future role. Relationally, the IDP requires positive interaction and support from an employee's direct supervisor.

Performance Management

Performance management is yet another area where there is a crossover in responsibilities between the PHR and the SPHR exam. While the PHR is focused on processes, procedures, and analysis, the SPHR is geared toward performance management strategies. In fact, the SPHR appears to be designed around performance management strategies that improve employee satisfaction. Since the traditional performance appraisal process is usually viewed as unsatisfactory by both managers and employees, this is an excellent opportunity for senior-level HR professionals to demonstrate their problem-solving skills through the improvement of talent management systems.

 Operationally, HR professionals must be familiar with the different types of performance appraisals. While the operational nature of appraisals is more of a focus of the PHR exam, senior leaders should still be familiar with the basics and so are well advised to review the "Performance Appraisal" section of Chapter 6.

Strategy

One of the most prolific writers on the topic of organizational strategy is Michael Porter (hbs.edu). He noted that the essence of strategy is deciding what *not* to work on. With that in mind, an effective performance management strategy must align to what is most important to the company; strategic alignment runs from the top down. For example, if an organizational strategy is to expand globally, a talent management strategy must be built around that outcome and through all HR processes, including talent acquisition, total rewards, and feedback. Note that this means that a talent management strategy must be fluid, never stagnant. Senior-level HR leaders will perform their best when regularly evaluating performance systems at all stages of the employee life cycle to ensure they stay aligned with organizational goals.

Additionally, top employees will remain satisfied when there is a clear line of sight between their performance and the goals of an organization. Senior leaders will be called upon not only to build the strategic elements, but to clearly and concisely communicate said elements to those who must execute. When there is a lack of clear line of sight, questions should be asked of whether or not the performance initiative is the most critical thing a team should be working on. As Patrick Lencioni said, "If everything is important, then nothing is" (tablegroup.com) It is for HR to lead the way in clearly articulating the priorities of employee performance.

Employee Socialization and Onboarding

An important side note to what you read about in Chapter 8, "SPHR Exam: Talent Planning and Acquisition," regarding employee socialization is that the acclimatizing process occurs *throughout the life cycle of the employee*. Socialization is the process of an employee adapting their style to that which is accepted, tolerated, and rewarded at work through both written and unwritten rules or principles. In fact, there is a strong correlation between organizational socialization and organizational citizenship behaviors (OCB) such as cooperation, altruism, conscientiousness, courtesy, and sportsmanship. These in turn are related to how well or poorly the behavioral expectations are established within the first few months of employment. From this, employees develop a pattern of behavior that either serves or detracts from company culture and thus must be managed as part of the evaluation process. Senior-level HR professionals must review their talent management practices to ensure that it is capturing the non-task-related elements of employee performance, such as OCBs.

Ethics

In the domain of Employee Relations and Engagement, senior-level HR professionals are directed to design and evaluate strategies that improve employee satisfaction. Additionally, knowledge requirement 55 from the exam content outline notes that in order to improve employee engagement and satisfaction, HR must also lead the way in the development of and act in accordance with ethical standards and guidelines.

The relationship between employee satisfaction, engagement, and ethics has been the subject of some research in the last several years. Specifically, it has been noted that companies that have robust, written and communicated measurement systems for ethical behavior experience increased reporting by employees who observe unethical or unlawful behavior. This real-time reporting by employees is one of the most effective tools for managing risk before it escalates beyond an employer's control, such as to external agencies or worse, YouTube or other social media sites.

Additionally, a 2018 Global Business Survey conducted by ECI noted that as with unlawful harassment, retaliation against employees for reporting wrongdoing such as bribing public officials and making improper political contributions continues to be the highest report of misconduct by employees of employers. The report advocated what this chapter has spent so much time on, that building positive employee job attitudes is about much more than a mission, vision, and values statement. The report noted that a company's culture significantly impacts employee behavior. ECI found reinforcing ethical expectations by holding management accountable, setting performance goals for senior leaders that are based on company values, and reinforcing reporting by rewarding employees and prohibiting retaliation are all effective steps employers can take to make ethics and compliance a top priority.

 View and download the 2018 Global Ethics Survey titled "The State of Ethics & Compliance in the Workplace" in its entirety at www.ethics.org.

Diversity and Inclusion

A key component of employee engagement and relations is building a diverse, inclusive workforce. As businesses become global entities employing individuals with diverse cultural, racial, and ethnic backgrounds, understanding diversity in the workplace becomes more critical to organizational success.

For purposes of exam content, HRCI defines diversity as "a combination of various people working together, often with differences in culture, race, generation, gender, or religion." This definition aligns precisely with the I/O psychology term of surface-level diversity, which is thought of as the biological variables that may or may not correlate to job attitudes or overall performance.

A second I/O definition for diversity exists as well, that of deep-level diversity. In terms of employee relations and behavior management, this is a more valuable concept. "Deep-level" refers to individual differences in values or beliefs. When employee values and attitudes are aligned with organizational culture and outcomes, job performance is enhanced.

Organizations implementing programs to increase diversity realize benefits such as improved productivity and bottom-line results for shareholders. There are many other business reasons to make workplace diversity a priority:

A diverse workforce is more creative. Increasing the variety of perspectives available to an organization brings new points of view to decision-making processes, challenging conventional wisdom and creating an atmosphere that encourages the synergy of ideas.

A diverse workforce reflects the population. When businesses increase the diversity of their workforces, they increase their ability to attract customers. Customers are attracted to organizations when they feel comfortable with its representatives, and employees who understand and communicate well with customers help increase the customer base for a company's products or services.

A diverse workforce increases the candidate pool. As the economy continues to slowly recover, the Department of Labor (DOL) predicts an increasing shortage of qualified candidates for available positions throughout the next decade, particularly in the fast-growing industry of healthcare. Conversely, the diversity of the labor force will continue to increase, with the DOL estimating Hispanics, Asians, and "all other racial groups" increasing their presence in the labor force most rapidly; by 2024, Hispanics will experience the most population growth of all race and ethnicity groups. Increasing the candidate pool by including a wide diversity of applicants will continue to be essential in filling open positions.

Workplace diversity presents challenges that organizations look to HR professionals to address, including the difficulty associated with change and the need to do things in new ways. It's challenging for individual employees to work with people who behave and communicate differently than what is recognizable or comfortable. For example, something as seemingly simple as differences in the amount of personal space that are customary in different cultures can create uncomfortable situations, such as one person backing away from another to increase the space between them while the other moves closer seeking to decrease the space.

The following sections will explore some key areas of diversity such as cross-generational relationships, representation of women in leadership, LGBTQ rights, and cultural competence in the workplace.

Generations at Work

While age is a form of surface-level diversity, there has been research that has shown there are underlying beliefs and values that shape generations. Generations such as the baby boomers, generation X, and millennials share important values related to work–life balance, types of benefits, career goals, and workplace etiquette. For these reasons, understanding the generational values that exist can help organizations better manage HR systems in alignment with these groups at work.

Consider how each generation communicates. A significant amount of communication at work now takes place digitally, via instant messaging, texting, or email. The receiver cannot interpret meaning via body language or tone, resulting in a loss of critical tools that help interpret meaning. The millennial generation may resolve this by the use of emoticons, while the baby boomers may find this unprofessional. Additionally, many meeting notes are now transcribed on a laptop or tablet. An older generation may interpret this as a lack of attention, whereas millennials see it as efficiency. Regardless, HR may be called on to train and manage the expectations of this type of behavior at work.

Women in Leadership

According to the Center for Creative Leadership (CCL), factors such as gender bias, discriminatory practices, and inflexible organizational cultures all have resulted in a very low representation of women in executive leadership roles. Additionally, women themselves fail to believe in their own leadership abilities, often thinking that they must have the proven experience to lead, whereas men may be hired based solely on potential (Ryan, J. [March, 2018] "Here's How to Propel More Women into the C-Suite," Center for Creative Leadership, www.ccl.org). This lack of diversity has a negative impact on business decision-making, creativity, innovation, and the diverse representation of nearly half of the workforce. HR must take the lead in identifying existing bias or practices that do not recognize the value of women at all levels of leadership. This may take on the form of several HR interventions, including an audit of hiring practices, demographics at all levels, or coaching and mentoring to develop future female leaders.

Sexual Orientation and Gender Expression/Identity

Statistically, the Lesbian, Gay, Bisexual, Transgender, and Queer (LGBTQ) community is one of the largest populations that experience discrimination in the workplace. Addressing issues that are specific to this community should be an important objective for senior-level HR leaders. A 2011 survey of this demographic by the National Gay and Lesbian Task Force (NGLTF) (thetaskforce.org) found that:

- 50 percent of respondents reported being harassed at work.
- 26 percent said they lost their job because they were transgender or gender nonconforming.
- 20 percent said they were removed from direct contact with a company's clients because they were transgender.

Additionally, NGLTF found that the LGBTQ community had twice the unemployment rate of the general population and noted that they experience workplace discrimination in other areas such as healthcare, promotion, training, pay, and other benefits.

While Title VII of the Civil Rights Act of 1964 originally protected an employee's gender at birth, there has been some progress toward including LGBTQ employees for protection under antidiscrimination laws. Regardless, it is still an emerging issue and guidance for employers is somewhat unclear. In 2014, President Obama signed an executive order allowing for certain protections for these individuals in the workplace. In 2016, an appeals court allowed sexual orientation to be included for protection against workplace discrimination but did not address gender identity. In 2017, another appeals court excluded sexual orientation from protection by Title VII. The Americans with Disabilities Act specifically *excludes* sexual orientation, as the LGBTQ community does not want their identity to be considered a disability.

Harassment laws clearly prohibit offensive conduct that interferes with an employee's right to work, and that includes comments about gender identity or orientation. Hostile workplaces and other bullying behaviors are considered to be "status-blind," meaning offensive behavior that is unwelcome, severe, or pervasive is prohibited for all employees, regardless of a protected status. Regardless of the level of cohesiveness among the major labor laws, HR has a responsibility to protect all workers from harassing behaviors. Practical implications of this responsibility include ensuring that sexual orientation and gender identity and expression are included in company policies that prohibit harassment and abusive conduct against workers. Employers should provide diversity training that includes this group as being protected from harassment and discrimination at work.

HR must also be sensitive to the beliefs of employees who have religious opposition to this protection, being careful to not allow hostile, abusive, or discriminatory behaviors based on characteristics that are not job-related.

Cultural Competence

In addition, HR professionals should be familiar with *cultural competence*: the ability of a diverse group of people to achieve organizational aims, and a measure of a company's ability to work with individuals from multiple walks of life. Cultural competence is a necessary component of a corporate diversity management program and should focus not only on the operational needs of the workgroup but also on the more subjective realities of cross-cultural needs. HR has a broad influence in developing and assessing an organization's cultural competencies. Examples of this influence include addressing cross-cultural conflict, assessing the hiring patterns of managers, sensitivity training efforts, recruitment practices, leave policies, healthcare benefits design, and anti-harassment policy development.

Diversity Concept: Cultural Competence

According to the U.S. Department of Health and Human Services Office of Minority Health: "Culture refers to integrated patterns of human behavior that include the language, thoughts, communications, actions, customs, beliefs, values, and institutions of racial, ethnic, religious, or social groups. Competence implies having the capacity to function effectively as an individual and an organization within the context of the cultural beliefs, behaviors, and needs presented by consumers and their communities."

Based on Cross, T., Bazron, B., Dennis, K., and Isaacs, M., (1989). *Towards a Culturally Competent System of Care, Volume I.* Washington, DC: Georgetown University Child Development Center, CASSP Technical Assistance Center.

Difficulties also arise for employees whose backgrounds are dissimilar to the group. They may feel uncomfortable in situations requiring them to make major adjustments in order to be accepted by a group whose culture or demographic is different from their own, such as when managing a multigenerational workforce, for example. The workforce of today spans more generations than at any other time in history, with an average age-span difference ranging between 20 and 30+ years and many older workers unable or unwilling to retire. Although this is a boon in terms of talent availability based on work and life experiences, the result is a generational division that plays out in the hallways of the corporate landscape. Differing values, expectations, and cultural identities are the hallmarks of the type of factors influencing a company's ability to manage a multigenerational workforce. Examples of the HR factors that must be considered include training design, benefits utilization, and diversity management programs.

The comfort level for all involved can be improved with *diversity training*, which seeks to educate all groups about the cultures, needs, and attitudes of other groups in the workforce to ensure the inclusion of all groups in workplace activities. One example many may remember is the 2018 training by Starbucks in which they closed all of their stores for four hours to address *unconscious bias*. Unconscious bias is a form of stereotyping that is so deeply embedded in a person's psyche that they are unaware of it, even as it influences behaviors. While humans are often unable to recognize bias in their own actions, they seem capable of recognizing it in others. For this reason, companies may wish to train institutionalized practices that encourage employees to "check" behaviors with a co-worker or supervisor before acting. For example, Starbuck's training was prompted by a racial profiling incident where an employee called 911 to report two African-American customers who were then falsely arrested. Had this employee understood the nature of unconscious bias and then, based on company practice, checked her desire to call 911, the profiling may not have occurred.

A *diversity initiative* seeks to increase the diversity of the workforce or to increase the effectiveness of an already diverse workforce. As with any company-wide objective, top management support is essential for success of the initiative, as is a clear picture of the challenges the initiative will address. Communicating the purpose of the initiative and providing feedback mechanisms for employees to ask questions will help ease any fears about the changes taking place in the organization. The initiative may begin with training designed to educate employees about the need for and benefits of diversity for the organization and to explain the benefits of diversity to them as individuals. As with any HR program, an evaluation of its effectiveness should be conducted at an appropriate time.

 Real World Scenario

Pitfalls of Diversity Training

When engaging a diversity trainer or designing an in-house program, some trainers use the approach of identifying stereotypes currently held by employees, but this may not be the best solution. Aside from the fact that it can serve to create division instead of bring employees together, there can be legal consequences as well. In the case of *Stender vs. Lucky Stores*, a diversity trainer asked employees to describe attitudes or comments attendees had heard in the workplace. These were some of the comments expressed:

- "Women won't work late shifts because their husbands won't let them."

- "Women don't have much drive to get ahead."

- "Women are not the breadwinners."

Members of the HR team were present and took notes during the training.

Sometime later, female employees filed a lawsuit, citing gender discrimination claiming they had been denied promotions because they were women. The court used the notes as "evidence of discriminatory attitudes and stereotyping of women," which led to a settlement in the tens of millions of dollars.

Workplace Safety and Security

Chapter 6 describes in detail the many levels of compliance that workplace safety and security systems must align with, particularly in regard to OSHA and the Sarbanes-Oxley Act. This section addresses the SPHR content that is focused on strategic implementation of safety and security initiatives. This includes special issues related to crisis response, such as workplace violence and data breaches. The exam content focuses senior-level HR professionals to create business continuity plans as part of their crisis response plans. And in many employee relations situations, HR must be able to lead the company through impartial and legally defensible internal investigations.

 It is unclear from the exam content outline alone just how much specific labor law will be on the SPHR exam. However, understanding labor law as it relates to effective risk management is fundamental to HR leader competencies. For this reason, we recommend that you rigorously study Appendix C, which covers the major legislation related to the field of Human Resources and specifically, to employee relations, sexual harassment and safety.

Crises in Leadership

Ian I. Mitroff in his compelling booklet "Crisis Leadership" (mitroff.net) provides perhaps the most succinct definition of organizational crises as follows: "In every case, a major crisis results when there is a serious breakdown, or malfunction, between people, organizations and technologies" (p. 3). He notes that (1) individual personalities, capabilities, values, and conflict management styles are highly unique. Similarly, (2) organizations have diverse business strategies, structures, and values; and (3) the nature of possible disasters provides multiple moving targets for which HR must devise detection and prevention plans. The complex interactions between these three crisis elements are fundamental to senior leader responsibilities for educating, managing, and most importantly, preventing workplace crises.

Mitroff's summary is significant, as it shapes the way a senior leader should approach the planning for and response to the types of crises that occur in 21st century workplaces. He advises that all leaders approach crisis response from a holistic viewpoint, considering the complex interaction of the individual/organizational/crisis type dynamic.

For purposes of the SPHR exam, the content outline directs senior leaders to "evaluate employee safety and security strategies (for example: emergency response plan, building access, data security/privacy)." These objectives guide this section.

As with many areas within this domain, OSHA has offered guidance for company emergency response plans. They include requirements for emergency action, fire, hazard communication and other written plans. Although you should be familiar with the operational aspects of an employer's IIPP and other response planning of Chapter 6, for senior leaders, crisis planning goes beyond the operational responses reviewed on the PHR. Several other types of incidents will require more strategic leadership; these are covered in the following sections.

Public Relations Crises

Consider the period of 2017–2018 for United Airlines. Beginning with law enforcement dragging a wailing passenger off an aircraft, and spiraling down from there with the tragic death of a dog aboard their airline in 2018, United had a major PR crisis on their hands. This was not a private, internal matter, but rather a public relations scandal being played out in the news and in viral videos and mocked more than once by the satirical social commentators of *Saturday Night Live*. Strategically, this matters. Stock prices suffered, and one survey showed that millennials specifically will avoid flying United where possible.

HR can and should take steps to be part of the policy and procedure development process, as well as the training of frontline staff. HR may also lead the crisis response through media relations policies and training, while at the same time educating their employers on what employee speech may (and may not be) limited. Consider the case of the Chipotle worker who was awarded reinstatement and back wages after being fired, in part, for complaining about low wages.

Financial Crises

Companies who are fiscally irresponsible or even downright unlawful may find themselves experiencing (or causing) a financial crisis. Perhaps the most infamous of all was Enron. Company leaders were engaged in fraudulent accounting practices that spawned an era of major distrust of large companies and possibly had a hand in the recall election of then California governor Gray Davis. Not only did Enron employees lose their retirement savings, but C-suite executives went to jail, and the SEC updated corporate guidelines as a result.

Additionally, fraud and embezzlement from individuals both within and outside of the organization occur with much more frequency than many may realize. From charging gas on company credit cards to cash receipts fraud and diversion of customer payments, and the more serious fraudulent accounting practices that were the hallmark of Enron, the opportunity for financial losses are evident in nearly every part of a business and across all industries.

HR is an integral business partner working with legal and other departments to ensure that the proper controls are in place to prevent these types of corporate malfeasance. This includes having systems in place for legitimate whistleblowing and the appropriate protections. It also includes writing job descriptions that appropriately segregate responsibilities to ensure that the proper checks, balances, and audits are embedded in responsibilities and practices.

Workplace Disasters

Perhaps the most well-known workplace disaster of this generation were the attacks on the World Trade Center and the Pentagon on September 11, 2001. Many of the close to 3000 fatalities were those who were at work at the time of the attacks, including those at the World Trade Center and the first responders. Being able to control access to physical assets such as buildings and vehicles from both the air and the ground are important considerations. This is especially true for those managing public spaces or high-value targets such as utilities, hospitals, amusement parks, and stadiums, as well as those in the food manufacturing industries and governments. Prevention plans, evacuation training, surveillance systems, and building access limitations are all strategies HR must help shape and manage.

For international business travelers to high-risk areas, HR may choose to partner with external agencies to mitigate risk. These include purchasing kidnap and ransom insurance or coordinating security escorts. A travel risk plan that includes medical and other emergency response techniques is another area where HR may add value.

Workplace Violence

The horrifying headlines of mass shootings such as that which occurred in San Bernardino, California, at a company holiday party is a stark reminder of the intense responsibility HR has to prevent workplace violence events. The active shooting crisis resulted in the deaths or injuries of more than two dozen people, most of whom were co-workers of the shooter.

Although there is no single risk factor that is a predictor of which employee may engage in a violent act at work, there are signs. As with the introductory definition of crises, these signs are often a combination of individual and organizational factors along with the nature of the grievance in general. Individual risk factors may include a fascination with weapons or a past history of violence. Organizational factors include downsizing or unfair treatment by a supervisor. Grievances may be related to personal or political values, or to a relationship gone bad.

Sometimes it is the nature of the work itself that is a risk factor. Working with patients who are volatile or in high-risk jobs such as convenience store clerks on the night shift may require higher degrees of employee protections than other jobs. Additionally, the incidents of sexual assault on night-shift janitorial workers has been described as both violent and pervasive, prompting activism long before the higher-profile "me too" movement.

While mental health issues are not the most common source of violent offenders at work, personal issues or emotional states can contribute to the risk factors. Employers should make sure that the mental health issues of employees are just as important considerations as their physical health by designing employee assistance programs (EAPs) or offering stress management classes. Other practices include response plans that include training for first responders as well as regular evacuation or other response drills.

Appendix B includes a more in-depth review of employer crisis response in a workplace violence situation.

For more on the important issue of workplace mental health, including issues of alcoholism, anxiety, and opioid use, visit http://workplacementalhealth.org.

Data Breaches

What do Equifax, Uber, and Verizon have in common? If you guessed data security breaches by hackers of their customer information, you are correct. Equifax in particular was egregious in that they knew about the breaches to their consumers' data months before they actually disclosed it, thereby limiting their customer's ability to take steps to reduce the risk of identity theft.

Some would say that the voluntary sharing of customer personal data—such as was the Facebook/Cambridge Analytica scandal of 2018—is even worse than the illegal hacking example. Known as surveillance capitalism, companies such as Facebook and Google seek to monetize their free services by gathering macro-scale data and then selling it to advertisers or other users.

The strategic implications of these issues are significant. Equifax made matters worse when they decided to offer free identity protection to the victims, but then were less than forthcoming that acceptance of this service locked victims into mandatory arbitration to settle any losses. Many consumers responded by "freezing" their credit, which ironically reduced the need for Equifax's credit checking services in general. Facebook in particular has been the target of online campaigns such as #deletefacebook. The Financial Post reported that Facebook lost more than $70 billion in just 10 days in the aftermath of the data sharing breach-of-trust. In addition, the Facebook CEO was required to testify before Congress on how the information of more than 50 million users was shared without their explicit knowledge.

HR leaders should anticipate the development of government regulations in the next few years that will govern consumer privacy—and a business's response—should a breach occur. HR should also help company leaders design practices that positively influence all stakeholders regardless of legal requirements to avoid the negative impact of an incident on their customers, the brand, and the bottom line.

Cyberstalking and Cyberbullying

This type of behavior happens both inside and outside of the workplace. In one high-profile case, an acrimonious divorce resulted in two deaths and criminal charges filed against the ex-husband, his sister, and his mother. HR leaders must update their definition of stalking, bullying, and harassment to include online incidents and incidents that may occur outside of the workplace. This is especially true because most events of cyberstalking or bullying are committed by those the victim knows, including those they work with. In terms of practices, employers should take steps to protect sensitive information such as home addresses, phone numbers, and work schedules, and caution employees about social media behaviors that may violate the company harassment policies.

Business Continuity

All of these types of crises could occur at any company and in any industry across all parts of the country. For this reason, senior-level HR professionals must become an integral part of a company's response planning. Part of a company's emergency response planning includes preparing to return to regular operations as soon as is reasonably possible. Often, a business continuity plan addresses the critical functions that must come back online, usually identified in a *contingency plan*. A contingency plan includes the written protocols that employees and responders must follow should a crisis occur. A contingency plan is valuable because it is both descriptive and prescriptive: it both describes what "normal" or benchmark functioning is and prescribes the steps necessary to return to that state.

Priorities that should be addressed through planning include these:

- Employee safety and well-being
- Financial and customer data protection
- Building and other physical asset security
- Company productivity or continuation of services

The Department of Homeland Security (DHS) and the Federal Emergency Management Agency (FEMA) note that there are several activities related to contingency planning:

- **Conducting a business impact analysis:** Consider the types of losses that may occur, the financial loss (sales, expenses, fines), the potential duration of a crisis, and types of business disruptions (physical damage, interruptions to supply chain, etc.).

- **Identifying and documenting the critical business functions:** Consider the core competencies of your business and the services or tasks that must be the least disrupted or most quickly recovered.

- **Coordinating and training a response team:** Identify who should be involved in responding to a crisis, and train them to follow the plan.

- **Evaluating and testing the plan:** Walkthroughs and full-scale drills are recommended by the Department of Homeland Security's website dedicated to emergency response planning, www.ready.gov. This will help identify what elements of an employer's plan may be ineffective or irrelevant, and allow for real-time adjustments before a crisis occurs.

 For a more detailed look at the operational aspect of business continuity planning, you should also review the sections of Chapter 6 that discuss business continuity.

Internal Investigations

Unfortunately, most incidents at work will require some level of investigation. This task usually falls to a senior-level HR professional who is properly trained in conducting an unbiased, legal investigation. While the nature of an investigation may change, the purpose is generally two-fold: (1) to find out the facts of what occurred, and (2) to determine what, if any action, should be taken.

One type of investigation that requires senior-level support are employee complaints filed with a federal or state agency, such as discrimination complaints, or employee complaints that come in litigated, such as wrongful termination. When these occur, there are several factors that HR must remain involved with:

- Engaging the necessary resources for a response, such as an outside investigator, legal representation, or insurance agent
- Addressing the need for confidentiality and discretion
- Providing relevant records in accordance with the demand

- Prohibiting retaliation against the complainant
- Conducting witness interviews where necessary
- Creating and/or finalizing a report

Other types of incidents that will require an internal investigation are those that occur in the domain of employee safety and security. Workplace injuries and accidents, for example, will require an investigation that is focused on preventing the incident from happening again. An angry altercation between two employees would require an investigation to determine if a policy has been violated or unlawful harassment occurred. The process for conducting an investigation would include the following:

- Identifying the what, where, when, why and who was involved in the incident, including any witnesses
- Interviewing those involved, and documenting the facts
- Reviewing the response plans that were engaged, and evaluating the effectiveness of the plans (what parts of the response went well and what needs to be revised)
- Discussing how the incident could be prevented from occurring in the future

Labor Unions

Management of employee relations is not always direct; sometimes it runs through a third party, such as when a labor union is in place at a company. Labor unions are selected to represent a bargaining unit in an election that is overseen by the National Labor Relations Board (NLRB).

While the organization campaign tactics of labor unions is covered in detail in Chapter 6 and the labor laws in Appendix C, this section specifically addresses the collective bargaining process, remaining union free, and a brief review of the cooperative strategies being adopted by many organized companies.

Collective Bargaining

The National Labor Relations Act (NLRA) imposes a duty to bargain in good faith on both employers and unions. Mandatory subjects for the bargaining process include wages, hours, terms and conditions of employment, the agreement itself, and any questions that arise from the agreement. Bad faith in the bargaining process is evidenced by a lack of concessions on issues, refusing to advance proposals to decision makers, stalling tactics, or withholding information that is important to the process. Evidence of bad faith by management in the bargaining process can also be evidenced by attempts to circumvent the union representative by going directly to employees with proposals before they have been presented to the union. Another indicator of bad faith bargaining by management occurs when unilateral changes are made to working conditions. An indication of bad faith by the union would be failing to notify management of the intent to renegotiate the contract within 60–90 days before it expires.

Collective-Bargaining Positions

Before discussing the components of collective bargaining, it's important to understand the different bargaining positions that can be taken and how each position affects the bargaining process. There are three basic approaches to negotiating:

Positional Bargaining   *Positional bargaining* is a strategy represented by demands made by each side. During positional negotiations, each side views the object of the negotiation as something finite that must be shared, stakes out the position they believe is in their own interest, and concentrates on "winning" that position for their side. This makes the process an adversarial, competitive one. Also known as *hard bargaining* or *distributive bargaining*, positional bargaining is a zero-sum game; in order for one side to gain something, the other side must lose something.

Ultra-concession or *concession* bargaining occurs when a union gives back a previous gain or surrenders negotiations in exchange for member job security. This type of bargaining may be necessary when a union recognizes that an employer's position is economically justified, such as in the print news industry beginning in 2009. Concession bargaining is seen by some as eroding the relevance of union representation because it requires the union to give up past gains for its members instead of making new ones. Additionally, union contracts are often negotiated based on the conditions of a previous contract, so any erosion impacts future gains as well. In ultra-concession bargaining, the employer may use threats to the union, dealing in extremes in order to remain competitive. Consider, for example, the aftermath of the September 11, 2001 terrorist attacks. Hijackers took control of three airplanes and flew them into the Twin Towers and the Pentagon. The impact these events had on the airline industry was significant. Travel was down and the cost of jet fuel rose by double digits. One airline's response to the downturn was to demand that mechanics agree to a 24 percent pay cut under threat of the airline declaring bankruptcy. Under similar conditions, the unions at Delta Airlines agreed to a contract that netted more than $1 billion in annual savings for the company.

Principled Bargaining   *Principled bargaining* as a negotiating strategy is characterized by parties who are more interested in solving a problem than they are in winning a position. In doing so, the parties remain open to looking at the problem in new ways, brainstorming for ideas, and often coming up with an agreement that solves the original problem in a way that wasn't originally contemplated by either side. The most common forms of principled bargaining are as follows:

Integrative Bargaining   In *integrative bargaining,* the parties look at all the issues and are able to make mutually agreeable trade-offs between those issues.

Interest-Based Bargaining (IBB)   *Interest-based bargaining* (IBB) is based on the concept that both sides in the negotiation have harmonious interests. In labor-management negotiations, for example, both labor and management have an equal interest in the continuing viability of the business—for management to earn profits and for labor to have continued employment.

Collective-Bargaining Strategies

In addition to collective-bargaining positions, HR professionals should be aware of the four basic negotiating strategies used in union environments:

Single-Unit Bargaining   The most common strategy, *single-unit bargaining*, occurs when one union meets with one employer to bargain.

Parallel Bargaining   In *parallel bargaining*, also known as *pattern bargaining*, *whipsawing*, or *leapfrogging*, the union negotiates with one employer at a time. After a contract has been reached with one employer, the union uses the gains made during the negotiation as a base for negotiating with the next employer.

Multi-Employer Bargaining   In *multi-employer bargaining*, the union negotiates with more than one employer in an industry or region at a time. This situation can occur when temporary workers are part of a client employer's bargaining unit and the union negotiates with both the temp agency and the client employer on employment issues.

Multi-Unit Bargaining   *Multi-unit bargaining*, or *coordinated bargaining*, occurs when several unions represent different bargaining units in the company. An example of this occurs in the airline industry, when the employer negotiates with the unions representing pilots, flight attendants, and mechanics or other employee classes. This allows the employer to coordinate negotiations on mandatory and permissive bargaining subjects while allowing the unions to cooperate on issues that have similar meaning to their various members.

Collective-Bargaining Subjects

The subjects open for negotiation during the collective-bargaining process fall into four areas:

Mandatory Subjects   The NLRA defines the subjects that are mandatory in the collective-bargaining process. These are wages, hours, other terms and conditions of employment, and the negotiation of the agreement and bargaining related to questions that arise from the agreement. Both parties must bargain on mandatory subjects, and unresolved issues on them are the only ones that may be the subject of a strike or lockout.

Illegal Subjects   The NLRA also identifies topics that are unlawful for inclusion in a collective-bargaining agreement, including hot-cargo clauses and closed-shop security agreements.

Voluntary Subjects   Voluntary or permissible subjects for negotiation would be any lawful topic other than those identified as mandatory by the NLRA. These generally include management rights, such as production scheduling, operations, and selecting supervisors.

Reserved-Rights Doctrine   Management generally includes a clause in the contract that states that any rights not covered specifically in the agreement are the sole responsibility of management.

Contract Enforcement

Disagreements that arise during the course of negotiating a collective-bargaining agreement (CBA) may take many forms; some are easily resolved through the grievance process established in the CBA, and others may go to arbitration before they're resolved.

Grievance Procedure

When disagreements occur in a union environment, the grievance process described in the CBA provides the framework for resolving them. The framework describes the steps to be taken and the time frames in which actions must be implemented to either resolve or reply to the grievance. Many grievances can be resolved at the first step in the process with the immediate supervisor, grievant, and union steward working together. If resolution isn't possible at that level, a union official takes the dispute to the next level of company management, where the grievant generally doesn't attend but is represented by the union. If the dispute isn't resolved at the second level, a member of the union grievance committee meets with the next level of management in the company. Grievances that are serious enough to be unsolved at the highest management level in the process then go to a third party for resolution. Depending on the terms of the CBA, this may involve binding arbitration, as is the case in the majority of contracts, or it may use mediation or another form of alternative dispute resolution.

Binding Arbitration

As discussed in Chapter 6 in the section "Tools for Dispute Resolution," arbitration is one method of resolving disputes without litigation. In the union environment, binding arbitration is used to resolve conflicts without resorting to work stoppages. Compulsory arbitration is mandated by legal statute to resolve disputes in the public sector where labor strikes are prohibited.

Mediation

The process used to mediate disputes in a union environment is the same as it is in a non-union environment. With the aid of the mediator, the parties to the disagreement work to develop a solution that is acceptable to both of them.

Court Injunctions

Injunctions are sought when immediate action is needed to temporarily prevent something from occurring. One example of the use of injunctions in the collective-bargaining process is the national emergency strike. The Taft–Hartley Act empowers the president to seek an injunction to stop a strike or lockout for an 80-day cooling-off period.

Duty of Successor Employers

In the event that a company with CBAs is acquired by a new company, the new management may be required to maintain the union contract. Whether the NLRB will consider an acquiring owner to be a successor employer is based on the following factors:

- Substantial continuity in operations
- The number of employees assimilated into the new company
- Similarity of operations and products
- The agreement with the previous employer

Although the terms and conditions may be changed by the new employer, the changes are required to be made through the collective-bargaining process and can't be made unilaterally by the employer.

Remaining Union-Free

To begin with, employers can make truthful statements about the consequences of unionization in response to union claims—as long as the TIPS guideline is followed (do not Threaten, Interrogate, Promise, or Spy). The FOE acronym is also useful to help supervisors respond to organizing activities (supervisors should state only Facts, Opinions, and give specific Examples). Just as union organizers work to convince employees to join the union, management may communicate their reasons for opposing unionization. During any organizing campaign, an experienced labor attorney should review management statements about the union before they're disseminated. All members of the management team should be coached on unfair labor practices (ULPs) and how to avoid them, particularly first-line supervisors because they interact most frequently with rank-and-file employees. First-line supervisors also have more influence with their direct reports than any other member of management, and employers should use this relationship by providing them with the information they will need to effectively represent the management view to employees.

Finally, organizers understand that enthusiasm and support for the union peaks at a certain point and then support begins to dwindle. For that reason, unions like to schedule elections to coincide with the peak of interest, and they gear their organizing activities to that goal. If an employer can delay the election, the chances of prevailing against the union are improved.

Most employers prefer to operate in a union-free environment. An effective ER program and organization culture that treats employees with dignity and respect is more likely to remain union-free because employee needs are being met without a union. Some characteristics of organizations that are less vulnerable to unionization attempts include the following:

- An open, inclusive work environment
- Clear communication about organization goals and successes
- Consistent, equitable application of organization policies, procedures, and work rules
- An established conflict-resolution or complaint process that provides an outlet for solving problems so that employees feel heard and appreciated.
- Disciplinary procedures that include an impartial, complete review of facts prior to taking action, particularly for termination decisions

When employees are treated poorly, are overworked, are stressed about their jobs, and don't have management support, union promises of better pay and working conditions are attractive, and employees often turn to unions with the hope that the union will be able to improve their work situation. Unions also offer leadership opportunities as shop stewards and union officers for members who may otherwise not have those opportunities.

Nonunion Philosophy

A carefully worded statement of an employer's philosophy regarding unions can be a useful strategy to help avoid union-organizing activities. While employees have the right to organize, an employer also has the right to communicate its desire to maintain an environment of close management-employee relations. Many employers fear that if they discuss unions with their employees, the employees will be motivated to begin organizing. However, open communication about the factual limitations of unions serves to educate employees, enabling them to respond favorably to the employer if approached by a union. For example, it's prudent for the employer to remind employees that a union can't provide for them anything the employer doesn't agree to through the collective-bargaining process and that if they need or desire specific working conditions or benefits, the employer is open for discussion with the employees directly. A nonunion philosophy statement can't threaten retaliation or promise benefits, but it may discuss the employer's desire to avoid third-party relationships. A nonunion philosophy statement should be properly vetted by a labor attorney to ensure compliance with the NLRA.

Climate Assessments

The best opportunity to identify and respond to labor/management communication deficiencies is before the relationship deteriorates. Assessing the organizational climate through employee surveys, committees, and third-party facilitation can provide the information necessary to get in front of issues before they grow into large-scale morale problems—a climate ripe for promises by unions of better working conditions. Building trust through open and honest communication and problem-solving will help reduce the likelihood of successful union authorization.

Management Training

Managers need to be trained to recognize union organizing activities such as the following:

- Increased interest in policies and benefits
- Surge of complaints against managers
- Unusual/excessive grouping of employees, such as in the parking lot
- Excessive strangers or visitors on-site with no clear purpose
- Open talk about unions, or the use of union terms when discussing working conditions or policies

These are just some examples of behavioral indications that a union may be attempting to organize. Further training of managers should include enforcement of open-door policies, fair and proper treatment of employees, responsiveness to complaints, and what they can/can't do if they suspect union organizing.

Metrics: Measuring Results

The ultimate measure of success in employee relations is in the realm of job attitudes: engagement, job satisfaction, and organizational commitment. These three major job attitudes can be measured through business impact and tactical accountability.

Business Impact Measures   Two indicators of employee satisfaction that *can* be measured are absenteeism and turnover. Excessive, unplanned absences can be an indication of employee stress, dissatisfaction with job requirements, supervisory conflicts, and a feeling of being undervalued by the employer. Measuring absence rates over time can provide feedback on the success of ER programs, as well as provide indicators of supervisory issues that may be resolved through coaching or training. As discussed in Chapter 4, "PHR Exam: Learning and Development," the turnover rate is the ultimate indicator of dissatisfaction with the supervisor, company, and/or ER programs.

Employee surveys, over time and conducted on an annual or other regular schedule, can also measure more subjective employee-satisfaction metrics. With a baseline established, positive or negative trends can be identified and ER programs adjusted or implemented to reverse negative trends.

Another important measure of employee satisfaction is the level of satisfaction customers have with products or services. An increase in customer service complaints or a survey that indicates a lack of customer satisfaction can indicate that employee performance is affecting business results. These results must, of course, be viewed in context with other factors that may affect customer satisfaction, such as higher prices due to increased transportation costs.

Depending on the nature of the business, another indication of employee satisfaction is the presence or absence of union-organizing activity. If the business is already unionized, the success of ER programs can be measured by the frequency of strikes, slowdowns, boycotts, or lockouts.

Tactical Accountability Measures   One way to measure the effectiveness of ER programs is by tracking legal-compliance issues, such as the number of claims filed with the EEOC, the number of lawsuits filed, the cost of settlements reached, and other consequences of poorly designed or communicated programs.

In the area of performance management, HR can track its effectiveness against the timeliness of performance reviews (measured against an established timeline) and their quality (measured against established criteria, such as comments that provide meaningful feedback or training plans developed) or the number of positions with written goals and objectives.

Summary

Effective management of employee relations and engagement is a critical element of a successful business. Employees who are treated with dignity and respect and given the tools they need to succeed in turn reward employers with increased production, fewer sick days, and a loyal and committed workforce. Organizational culture begins with management attitudes toward employees and ranges from those that are based on an autocratic philosophy characterized by top-down communication and interactions to those of employee empowerment where individuals and work teams make the decisions necessary to get their jobs done.

Effective dispute-resolution programs that solve employment disagreements without the need for legal action are both cost-effective and more successful than lawsuits. HR professionals can add value to their organizations by establishing programs that resolve issues and give employees who feel they have been mistreated an opportunity to be heard before the situation escalates and a lawsuit is filed.

The management of the employment relationship is subject to the laws prohibiting discrimination in all terms and conditions of employment, as well as to common-law doctrines. HR professionals must be aware of the requirements of these statutes and doctrines in order to provide sound advice to management in making employment decisions and to ensure that the programs and policies developed by HR are in compliance with them.

Labor relations are governed by a number of laws designed to protect the rights of employees. The unionization process is strictly regulated by the National Labor Relations Board (NLRB). Unions, whose membership has steadily declined over the past 50 years, are now seeking to expand their organizing efforts by targeting nontraditional union members and developing sophisticated methods for attracting new members. The most effective way for management to avoid unionization of the workplace is to treat employees fairly and give them a voice in decisions that affect their day-to-day work.

Exam Essentials

Be aware of the impact human relations have on positive employee outcomes. Human relations theories are built upon the ideas that people are designed to be part of a social, supportive system that facilitates growth and engagement. Employer practices that fail to meet these social needs will find disengaged employees, leading to low employee morale, reduced productivity, and higher turnover.

Be aware of the different types of job attitudes and how to measure them. Work engagement, job satisfaction, and organizational commitment are three of the most researched topics of 21st century organizational sciences. Gathering feedback from employees about both their realities and perceptions will allow HR to build meaningful responses designed to target real-time concerns.

Be aware of the need to build positive employee relations programs. Individual, organizational, and relational behaviors all influence the design of positive employee relations strategies and programs. Understanding the impact of individual traits such as personality and emotional intelligence can aid HR in designing programs that meet the unique needs of a diverse workgroup. Embedding strategies that build a company culture around shared values will improve multiple outcomes. The social and relational nature of work including the relationship between followers and leaders, and employees and those who influence them should be understood and managed.

Understand the impact of performance and other talent management strategies on employee engagement. While SPHR candidates should have a strong working knowledge of the operational techniques for managing performance, their value is in aligning organizational strategy with performance expectations.

Be able to analyze and evaluate strategies that promote diversity and inclusion. As business becomes more global and talent scarcer, it is important for HR to lead the efforts to build a culture that not only embraces diversity, but also deploys it for the benefit of all stakeholders. Diverse workgroups have been shown to be more creative problem solvers, reflecting the needs of customers. Building programs to address both surface-level and deep-level diversity will increase retention of talent and contribute to building a culture of respect and inclusion.

Be competent in evaluating workplace safety and security strategies beyond legal compliance. As with all functional areas, senior-level HR professionals must not only have a good understanding of labor laws, but also be able to build strategies that are preventive in nature. Crisis planning, emergency response, business continuity, and other written plans must take into account the evolving risks for 21st century employers.

Understand the collective-bargaining process and strategies to remain union-free. The collective-bargaining process is required by the National Labor Relations Act and provides that employers must bargain in good faith with the union representative chosen by the employees. Employers have a duty to bargain in good faith on mandatory subjects, which include wages, hours, and other terms and conditions of employment.

Review Questions

You can find the answers in Appendix A.

1. The study of behavior of people in groups belongs to which field of organizational science?
   A. Organizational behavior
   B. Social science
   C. Human relations
   D. All of the above

2. Which of the following was the main findings of the Hawthorne studies?
   A. That scientific management no longer has a place in the service-oriented economies of the 21st century
   B. That employees are more productive when their human needs are considered
   C. That more companies should be open to action research
   D. That working conditions such as illumination have no effect on worker productivity

3. Which of the factors below does *not* increase a feeling of psychological empowerment in employees?
   A. Recognition
   B. Meaning
   C. Competence
   D. Self-determination

4. Of the three job attitudes, which is the result of employees finding meaning and satisfaction in their job tasks and responsibilities?
   A. Organizational commitment
   B. Job satisfaction
   C. Employee engagement
   D. Psychological empowerment

5. Increasing an employee's optimism and resilience is a hallmark of which of the following organizational interventions described by Dr. Richard?
   A. Job resource building
   B. Job attitude resource building
   C. Leadership training
   D. Personal resource building

6. A company that uses artwork from the movie *Office Space* to decorate their workstations is representing which element of Schein's dimensions of culture?

    A. Autonomy

    B. Values

    C. Artifacts

    D. Attitudes

7. Companies that encourage, support, and build systems for the management of telecommuting programs is likely to be high in which dimension of Hofstede's theories of culture?

    A. Individualism

    B. Uncertainty avoidance

    C. Long-term orientation

    D. Collectivism

8. Which of the following is recognized as a form of positive discipline techniques?

    A. Verbal warnings

    B. Performance improvement plans

    C. Decision-making leaves

    D. Sabbaticals

9. LMX theory is focused on which of the following?

    A. Personality traits of leaders

    B. Situations in which leaders must act

    C. The relationship between leaders and their followers

    D. The environment in which leaders must perform

10. An employee suddenly begins complaining to you about the existing commission structure, believing it to be unfair. He did not seem to have any issues with it before, and when HR last did an employee survey related to wages, commissions were not mentioned as a pain point. As you probe for more information by interviewing the employee, you discover that his significant other started a new job where the commission structure is much more generous. What has occurred?

    A. Emotional contagion

    B. Social comparisons

    C. Peer pressure

    D. Social information processing

11. Which of the following conditions represents the nature of the psychological contract?

    A. Safety

    B. Job security

    C. Fair pay

    D. All of the above

12. Employees who are able to see how their performance is directly tied to organizational performance are said to have a clear _____.

    A. Work strategy

    B. Alignment

    C. Purpose

    D. Line of sight

13. Studies are showing that employers with written ethics policies are most likely to have employees _____.

    A. Report unethical behavior

    B. Require whistleblower protection

    C. Grow within the company

    D. Develop trusting relationships with co-workers

14. In the context of employee engagement, age, gender, and ethnicity are best represented by which description?

    A. Unlawful treatment

    B. Discriminatory criteria

    C. Surface-level diversity

    D. Deep-level diversity

15. Once a union begins an organizing campaign, managers may do all of the following *except*?

    A. A statement of the company's desire to remain union-free

    B. Factual statements about the disadvantages of unions in the labor/management relationship

    C. A description of what a union cannot do for the employees

    D. A promise of extended benefits if the company remains union-free

16. Which of the following is a form of bias that relates to the unintentional application of stereotypes to co-workers or customers?

    A. Face time bias

    B. Unconscious bias

    C. The halo effect

    D. The horn effect

17. OSHA requires which of the following plans to be provided in written form?

    A. Hazard communication

    B. Emergency response

    C. Fire prevention

    D. All of the above

18. Which of the following tools would be the *best* first line of defense against employee embezzlement?

   A. A written policy

   B. Segregated job descriptions

   C. Accounting audits

   D. Computerized financial data

19. Which of the following would be *inadvisable* for an employer to do if they wish to limit comments made by employees on their social media accounts?

   A. Banning the use of personal cell phones on the job

   B. Blocking social media sites from the company servers

   C. Disciplining employees for posting comments about wages on social media websites

   D. Writing an acceptable use of social media policy

20. During negotiations the auto manufacturer for which you work noted that unless employees decreased their wages by 12 percent, the company would have to pursue bankruptcy and begin layoff proceedings. This is an example of what type of bargaining?

   A. Principled

   B. Integrative

   C. Concession

   D. Parallel

Appendix A

Answers to Review Questions

Chapter 2: PHR Exam: Business Management

1. D. While all of the above may become part of actively engaging in the legislative process, the true activity is finding support (pro or against) for labor-related bills.

2. A. Corporate restructuring examines individual business units to eliminate redundancy, reduce costs, and increase production. Employee assimilation (B) is accomplished with new-hire orientation and similar programs. Reengineering looks at the entire organization to improve efficiency and increase customer satisfaction.

3. D. The mission statement describes who the organization is, what it does, where it is going, and how it is different from others. The corporate values statement (A) communicates the executive team's expectations for the way the organization conducts business. Corporate goals (B) describe what the organization plans to achieve in the future. The vision statement (C) is a short, inspirational statement of what the organization will accomplish in the future.

4. C. As an organization becomes more successful during the growth phase, it can afford to provide competitive compensation and benefits for employees. Executive benefit packages (A) are often enhanced during the maturity stage of organizational growth. During the maturity stage, the organization is able to hire new employees with less experience (B) and train them to grow into positions requiring additional experience. Employees work the closest with organization founders (D) during the startup phase.

5. B. The greatest effect of technology is increased worker productivity. Employee morale (A) may be affected positively or negatively by technological improvements but is not the main impact. The cost of living (C) is a function of the cost of consumer goods and is a factor in an environmental scan. Span of control (D) may also be affected by technological improvements, allowing managers to directly supervise a larger number of employees, but it is not the main effect.

6. A. HR audits, including that of hiring practices related to diversity, are designed to help identify potential or real problems. This creates the opportunity for organizations to design preventive measures or correct existing issues prior to the need for attorneys, or in advance of an audit of compliance.

7. C. An HR audit examines HR policies and procedures for compliance and to determine whether the department is successfully meeting the organization's needs. This includes analyzing the employer handbook to ensure it is current with ever-changing labor laws.

8. A. The four p's of marketing are product, price, placement, and promotion, which summarize the responsibilities of the marketing team.

9. A. A SMART goal is specific, measurable, action-oriented, realistic, and time-based.

10. B. Once Congress forwards a bill, the president has 10 days to sign it. A pocket veto occurs when Congress adjourns before the 10 days are up and the president does not sign it. When the president vetoes a bill (A), Congress may try to override it with a two-thirds vote of a quorum in each house. If the bill does not pass, the veto stands. If Congress cannot raise a quorum to override a veto (C), the veto stands. If Congress submits a bill to the president and stays in session (D), the bill becomes law if the president does not sign it within 10 days.

11. C. Mentoring programs are a valuable training tool but do not necessarily reflect a corporate mission, vision, or values when the mentor is outside of the organization. Written policies (A) help an organization mitigate risk by identifying employee rights and responsibilities. Modeling appropriate behavior from the top down (B) shows employees how to act and contributes to the corporate culture. Coaching (D) gives the employee the opportunity to modify and correct behavior in accordance with company guidelines.

12. A. Employee handbooks are one tool used to compile written policies that aid in compliance with various state and federal laws but are not specifically required by any one law or standard.

13. D. An HR audit can serve many strategic and operational purposes. In all three of the other answers, the HR audit allows for a comparison of the current environment to the future desired state.

14. B. Sustainability is behavior that does not deplete the resources used to achieve an outcome. Viable sustainability programs are those that are able to have a regular, systematic impact on resource depletion, thereby reducing waste and increasing efficiencies.

15. D. Corporate responsibility has influence across all HR functions. Examples of CR concepts explored throughout the strategic planning process include worker rights, legal compliance, company culture development, and corporate governance (A, B, C).

16. A. When funding is low due to startup conditions, a decision must be made regarding obtaining the talent necessary to do the work. Because organizations at this stage do not typically have the funds to develop employees from within such as in the growth and maturity stage (B, C), they often must choose which positions are critical to day-to-day operation and outsource the rest.

17. A. An HR budget reflects how many and what types of resources are necessary to accomplish a goal. The addition of employees, costs to train, and the purchase of new equipment are all examples of items that require cash to achieve strategic goals.

18. B. Just-in-time inventory is an inventory-management strategy that purchases smaller amounts of inventory more frequently to reduce inventory and ensure a steady supply of products for distribution.

19. D. A *prima facie* violation of whistle-blower protection must demonstrate that an employee was engaged in a protected activity, that the employer knew or suspected that the employee was engaged in a protected activity, that the employee suffered an unfavorable employment action, and that the unfavorable action was the result of engaging in a protected activity.

20. B. Creating an HR budget takes into account standard expense items associated with having employees. They include salaries, taxes, benefits, training, travel, and equipment costs, to name a few. A compensation strategy defines pay equity both internally and externally (C) and the cost of recruiting is a measurement of HR activities return on investment (D) and can be a measurement of business impact.

Chapter 3: PHR Exam: Talent Planning and Acquisition

1. D. The candidate profile is developed after the job requirements have been determined, beginning with the job description and developing the competencies (broad requirements of the position) and the specifications necessary for successful performance. Job competencies (A) identify skills and qualities beyond tasks and responsibilities specific to the position that help determine how well a candidate will fit into the work group, such as team orientation vs. individual contribution or ability to learn new skills quickly. The job description (B) provides the tasks and responsibilities that must be accomplished. Job specifications (C) define the job-specific KSAs that will be needed for success in the position.

2. C. According to the EEOC, there are no circumstances where race or color are a BFOQ. (A) is incorrect because Title VII specifically allows religious organizations to give preference to members of the religion. (B) and (D) are incorrect because Title VII specifically allows sex as a BFOQ if it is "reasonably necessary" for business operations.

3. A. *Griggs* identified adverse impact to mean that discrimination need not be intentional to exist; *Albemarle Paper* (B) extended the concept to require that tests must be validated in accordance with the EEOC Uniform Guidelines for Employee Selection Procedures. *Washington* (C) determined that employment tests resulting in adverse impact are acceptable if they predict future success on the job. *Taxman* (D) found that employment decisions made on the basis of race are discriminatory.

4. A. A staffing needs analysis begins with an assessment of the KSAs needed to achieve future goals along with those that are currently available within the organization. Although the tasks, duties, and responsibilities (B) are used to determine what the KSAs are, it is possible for individuals with the same or similar KSAs to perform different jobs, so (B) is not used in a needs analysis. KSAs available in the local labor market (C) will be used to develop the recruiting strategy and plan but are not relevant to the staffing needs analysis. The organization's core competencies (D) are factors that make the organization unique but are not generally part of the staffing needs analysis.

5. C. The GM could be influenced by his similar experience working his way through college. Knowledge-of-predictor bias (A) is a factor when the interviewer knows that a candidate scored particularly high or low on an assessment test. The halo effect (B) occurs when interviewers allow one positive characteristic to overshadow other, less positive attributes. The gut feeling bias (D) occurs when interviewers rely on intuition to make hiring decisions.

6. B. To calculate the selection rate, divide the number of applicants hired by the total number of applicants in each group:

Black	23 ÷ 140 = 16%
Asian	21 ÷ 120 = 18%
Hispanic	19 ÷ 145 = 13%
Caucasian	35 ÷ 230 = 15%
Native American	2 ÷ 15=13%

7. C. To determine whether adverse impact has occurred, multiply the highest selection rate, which is Asian, at 18%, by 4/5 or 80%. (18% × .80=14%)

8. D. Government contractors with 50 or more employees and contracts of $50,000 or more each year must complete Affirmative Action Plans. (A) was the original compliance requirement for Title VII and was changed to 15 employees by the EEOA of 1972. The criteria in (B) apply to employers that must comply with the Rehabilitation Act and federal contractors that must take affirmative action for all terms and conditions of employment based on executive orders. (C) is not a compliance requirement.

9. C. ADEA waivers are valid during a reduction in force only if the employee has 45 days to consider the agreement. Once employees sign a RIF-related waiver, the ADEA requires that they have 7 days (A) to revoke it. Terminations that are not part of a RIF require only 21 days (B) for consideration. An employee has 180 days (D) to file a charge with the EEOC in states that do not have their own EEO enforcement agency.

10. D. IRCA allows, but does not require, employers to make copies of documents presented for employment eligibility. The employee section of the I-9 must be completed by the end of the first day of employment (A). The employer section must be completed and documents checked by the end of the third day of employment. Employers who make a good faith effort to comply with IRCA (B) have an affirmative defense to inadvertently hiring an unauthorized alien. IRCA requires that I-9 forms be maintained and available for audit (C) by the USCIS for 3 years from date of hire or 1 year after the date of termination.

11. C. E-Verify is a system-wide approach to helping employers comply with post-hire documentation regulations. Recertifying (B) and requesting updated documents (D) may be appropriate on a case-by-case basis but neither is a long-term solution to the problem.

12. B. Although the decision to store employment records online is influenced by all of these factors, the ability to limit access is a strong element of labor law and privacy compliance.

13. C. Strategic staffing and recruitment involves taking a picture of the company at a 30,000-foot level, rather than from an operational perspective. Identifying recruitment sources such as employee referrals may prove to be valuable once the strategies have been defined. Conducting a labor market analysis allows HR to identify the availability of a qualified workforce for use in the achievement of strategic objectives. Total rewards packages include conducting wage surveys and utilization reviews to understand compensation and benefits trends, designed to compete with internal and external market conditions. Defining the employer brand not only creates an employer identity, but helps to differentiate a company from their competition.

14. B. Any tool used to select employees must be job-related and a valid predictor of success on the job. If a selection tool results in discrimination against an individual who is a member of a protected class (A), the criteria used must be shown to be job-related and valid. For example, a bona fide occupational qualification occurs when religion, sex, or national origin is "reasonably necessary to the normal operation" of the business.

15. D. State employment agencies are required under VEVRAA to give priority to Vietnam-era veterans when providing referrals to job openings. The act further requires that contractors and subcontractors meeting certain criteria list all job openings with these same state agencies. The Rehabilitation Act of 1973 prohibits discrimination against veterans of the US armed services, and the executive orders prohibit discrimination in employment by federal contractors, sub-contractors and the government.

16. B. Negligent hiring occurs when an employer knows or should have known about an applicant's prior history that endangered customers, employees, vendors, or others with whom the employee comes into contact. While this behavior may be classified as a criminal act (D), it is not a violation of employee privacy (A) but rather a function of workplace violence that may have been prevented through proper screening at the time of hire.

17. C. A major life activity under the ADA defines major life activities under two categories: general activities such as caring for oneself and major bodily functions such as breathing. A physical or mental impairment in and of itself does not constitute a disability (A, C) qualified for protection under the ADA. Mitigating factors (B) are considered if they allow an otherwise qualified individual to perform the essential functions of the job.

18. A. The EEO-1 report requires employers to group jobs into job categories based on average skill level, knowledge, and responsibility. Exempt workers are defined by professional, executive, and administrative exemption criteria (B), and these are not examples of the protected class groups under federal law (D).

19. C. Job bidding allows internal candidates to express interest in a job prior to it becoming available. It gives employees the opportunity to develop the skills necessary to successfully compete for the position once it becomes available. A job posting is an internal job announcement (A); RFP's (B) are typically used to allow outside vendors to bid on project work, and the ranking of job applicants is a function of the selection process used to identify the most qualified individual for the job.

20. B. Any inquiries into an applicant's citizen status must be specific to the requirements of the job. In this example, it is not necessary for the employer to know specifically whether the applicant is a U.S. citizen, but rather, whether the applicant is authorized to work in the United States.

Chapter 4: PHR Exam: Learning and Development

1. **C.** Systems thinking refers to the characteristic of a learning organization that uses a variety of information-gathering techniques to acquire knowledge about new technology, determine its value, and convert this knowledge into new and improved practices and procedures. Assessment centers (Option A) are used to determine what kind of training an individual needs. Massed practice (Option B) is a form of practicing job tasks during training in which all tasks are practiced at the same time. Programmed instruction (Option D) is a type of self-instruction that requires trainees to complete each step in the training before moving on to the next step.

2. **A.** Supervisory training programs concentrate on topics related to interactions with employees, such as conflict management. Budgeting skills (Option B) and internal control training (Option D) are included in management development programs. Rotation through various divisions (Option C) is part of a leadership development program.

3. **B.** The learning evaluation method focuses on how well the training resulted in learning new skills. The reaction evaluation method (Option A) focuses on participant reactions. The behavior evaluation method (Option C) measures on-the-job behavior changes as a result of training, and the results evaluation method (Option D) measures organizational results. Of the four methods, the results evaluation method is considered the most valuable for the organization.

4. **B.** A lack of job reinforcement can adversely affect transfer of training. Other adverse impacts are the result of interference from the immediate work environment and a nonsupportive organizational climate. The trainer's expertise (Option A) could affect how well trainees learn information but does not specifically affect transfer of training. The subject of the training (Option C) affects how receptive trainees are to the information but not necessarily how the information transfers to the job.

5. **A.** The positively accelerating learning curve begins with smaller increments but increases in pace and size as learning continues. The negatively accelerating curve (Option B) begins with larger increments that decrease as learning continues. The S-shaped learning curve (Option C) is a combination of the positively and negatively accelerating learning curves, whereas a plateau (Option D) occurs when no learning seems to take place.

6. **D.** The most common reason for the failure of change initiatives is that people were not prepared for the change and given time to assimilate the reasons for the change. Failing to communicate a change in strategic direction (Option A) as the basis for organization changes in and of itself will not lead to failure of a change initiative. Leaders who do not support change (Option B) do have an influence on employees, but that factor alone is not the most common reason for failure. The absence of a training system (Option C) may negatively impact the change process, but it is not the most common reason for failure.

7. B. An Ishikawa diagram is an effective tool for organizing information about a problem when brainstorming with a group. A Pareto chart (Option A) graphically represents the 80/20 rule. A stratification chart (Option C) shows the individual components of a problem in addition to the total or summary. A histogram (Option D) provides a way of looking at random occurrences to find out if there is a pattern.

8. C. The first three choices are all employee growth and assessment programs. Behavioral-based performance assessment (Option A) focuses on behaviors, whereas skills-based performance assessment (Option B) focuses on skills. MBO programs measure the successful attainment of objectives. The continuous-feedback program (Option D) is a performance management program.

9. C. The AGILE model of instructional design is characterized by "chunking" training content (and projects) into smaller, more manageable pieces. AGILE is most likely to result in training content delivered in multiple modules as opposed to ADDIE (Option A), which is more linear than short-cycled. SAM (Option B) is also cyclical, but it's more useful for smaller design projects that do not require complicated technical elements such as video.

10. C. A mentor is someone who takes a personal interest in an employee's career and who guides and sponsors them. Although a supervisor may be a mentor, mentors are usually individuals who are outside the chain of command and may even be from outside the organization. The functions in Options A, B, and D are not generally performed by mentors.

11. D. Formative evaluation is a technique used prior to the commencement and during the design phase of training. It is used to gather data that will be used in training to ensure that the objectives are met and that the training meets the needs of the workgroup. This is different from summative evaluation (Option A), which occurs after the training has taken place. Knowledge banking (Option B) and an attitude assessment (Option C) are not used in the evaluation of training.

12. B. The ADDIE model is a process that begins with an analysis of the specific training needs. In this example, management may believe that the negative reviews are the result of a lack of training, but until a thorough needs analysis is conducted—including the gathering of relevant data—it is not possible to create specific training objectives that will result in the desired outcomes. While training design (Option A), participant identification (Option C), and scheduling (Option D) are components of training, they do not launch the ADDIE model.

13. A. Job design is made up of several factors related to how the work gets done, broken into two categories: job enrichment and job enlargement (Option B). Task identity, task significance, and feedback are examples of job-enrichment activities that can significantly influence job satisfaction through design. KPIs (Option C) can be used as performance appraisal criteria (Option D), but they are not directly related to job-enrichment activities.

14. D. Job crafting is a form of employee ownership over their work that increases employee autonomy by allowing them to contribute to the redesign of their jobs. When properly managed, job crafting can increase job satisfaction and allow employees to build a role suited to their strengths while at the same time aligning with organizational goals and process outcomes.

15. C. Asynchronous training is self-paced training that typically occurs using computer-based tools. Although timelines for completion may be preestablished (such as specifying that all assignments must be submitted no later than 11:59 p.m. Sunday evening), participants typically are able to set their own schedule for when they engage in learning the material. Vestibule training is a form of OJT (Option A), mobile learning (Option B) is a type of e-learning that occurs typically through mobile devices, and the Delphi technique (Option D) is a decision-making or forecasting activity that relies on a group of experts to reach a consensus.

16. B. Formative evaluations are designed to gather information prior to the design of training to measure the needs of the participants. This allows the designer to include content and exercises that will aid in the participant transfer of the training to the job. Summative evaluations (Option C) are used after the training has taken place and often include a measure of participant reactions (Option A) and trainer evaluations (Option D).

17. A. Peer-to-peer coaching is useful when a management work group has shared values or objectives. Assigning a one-on-one peer coach or using a team approach maximizes the diversity of skills available in any particular peer group. A mentor relationship (Option B) implies a hierarchy (the mentor and a subordinate), an executive coach (Option C) is used for more one-on-one upper-level management development, and strategic planning (Option D) is a broad organization-wide string of activities related to planning the direction of the company.

18. B. Training cost per employee is calculated by dividing the total of all associated training costs by the number of full-time equivalent employees. The proper calculation is $4,500 divided by 25 full-time equivalent employees.

19. C. A case study allows participants to review real-world scenarios related to their topic of study. Practical application and transfer of training are typically more successful when participants can see how it's done in the work environment. Vestibule training (Option A) occurs "on the job," facilitation (Option B) uses an individual to create an interactive training experience, and a Socratic seminar (Option D) is a type of training that welcomes opposing viewpoints in a problem-solving setting.

20. C. While all of the options may be used to address production line inefficiencies, Six Sigma in particular is useful because of its systematic and controlled approach; it was originally developed to address process and quality deficiencies on production lines. Process flow mapping (Option A) is a diagram tool that can help with outline workflow and may support Six Sigma efforts. A learning organization (Option B) is characterized by a company culture that relies on employee learning and development to compete. Total quality management (TQM) (Option D) is a long-term intervention strategy that continuously looks at process improvements.

Chapter 5: PHR Exam: Total Rewards

1. B. With the rise of independent contractors creating a "gig" economy, HR must budget for labor differently. The employee burden will be different, and depending on the nature of the contractors, the labor costs may need to be calculated on a project basis. Gig workers do not necessarily have a higher base pay (Option A), and employers may not unlawfully discriminate against any worker (Option C). True independent contractors are not eligible for mandated benefits (such as Social Security) through an employer (Option D).

2. A. Improperly classifying a worker as an independent contractor can be determined by several factors. Behavioral factors include the degree of control an employer has over when and the way a worker performs the work. Financial factors include how the worker is paid, and how expenses are reimbursed (Option B), and the type of relationship may be determined by the presence of written contracts or benefits (Option C). The entire relationship should be reviewed when making a determination of worker classification.

3. B. Intrinsic rewards are those in which esteem is achieved from within oneself. Options A, C, and D are examples of extrinsic rewards that come from external sources.

4. A. A total rewards philosophy helps determine what kind of employees will be attracted to the organization. Developing a philosophy to target employees with the KSAs needed by the organization can help advance the organization's mission. The pecking order for jobs (Option B) is based on the value of those jobs to the organization. The philosophy defines leading the competition as a strategy; positioning the company to do so (Option C) is a result of creating the compensation structure. An entitlement culture is maintained (Option D) by continuing to pay employees for time on the job instead of for performance.

5. A. An entitlement culture rewards longevity in the job. If increased productivity is a function of time on the job, an entitlement culture will encourage employees to stay with the company. Line of sight (Option B) occurs when employees know that their performance impacts their pay. A highly competitive workforce (Option C) is more likely to exist in a pay-for-performance culture. A workforce with a highly desired skill set (Option D) would be better served by a pay-for-performance culture.

6. D. Options A and B are both obviously correct. Although Option C may seem counterintuitive to some because many employers are hesitant to terminate employees for policy violations, those terminated for cause generally aren't eligible for unemployment insurance. Because retaining an employee who is not contributing to the organization is a poor business decision, maintaining adequate records to demonstrate the reasons for termination provides the tools to fight claims that are unjustified.

7. D. From an employer perspective, unlimited time-off plans reduce the administrative burden of tracking accruals. Unlimited time off actually can make it more difficult to schedule workflow, so Option A is incorrect. Managing timecards is irrelevant in this scenario, so Option B is incorrect. Option C is an advantage to the employee, not the employer.

8. C. The correct choice in this situation is to tell the employer that paying less than the state minimum wage is illegal. However, you may back this statement up by creating wage bands to make the argument that paying within range will help him retain employees (Option B). Options A and D are both unlawful.

9. D. Commission-based pay is a form of incentive designed to drive employee behaviors specifically related to selling products. While it does so by making a portion of employee pay at risk, commission plans may not result in an employee making less than minimum wage and is not the primary purpose of this type of incentive (Option A). Commissions are not always a measure of employees who work hard, so Option B is incorrect. In some cases, employees paid on commission are among the highest paid employees in the organization, so Option C is untrue as well.

10. D. Summary plan descriptions are required only for group health plans, and not for defined contribution plans, defined benefit plans, or FSAs.

11. A. Gym memberships are not reimbursable under flexible spending accounts. Psychiatric care (Option D), durable medical equipment (Option B), and acupuncture (Option C) are all allowable expenses.

12. C. Group incentives share common elements including the reward of individuals based on their collective efforts. Employee stock ownership plans, employee stock purchase plans, profit-sharing, and gainsharing (Option B) are all examples of group incentives. Deferred compensation (Option A) refers to tax-deferred retirement plans, and a sales bonus (Option D) is a type of commission paid to workers.

13. B. Call-back pay is a premium paid to employees who are called to work before or after their scheduled hours. On-call pay is provided to employees who are required to be regularly available to respond to work-related issues on short notice and who must be available via pager, telephone, or email (Option A). Reporting pay is given when a worker shows up to their job and there is no work to perform (Option C). Hazard pay is given for dangerous circumstances (Option D). While a worker at a nuclear facility may (or may not) be given hazard pay, in this instance the premium is being given for coming to work early, not for potential hazards.

14. A. Wage compression occurs when employer pay rates do not keep up with external market conditions and the economy as a whole. When the cost of living goes up, pay rates should be adjusted as well. For this reason, employers often tie pay increases to the consumer price index published by the Bureau of Labor Statistics (BLS).

15. B. For fully trained employees with satisfactory performance who have been with the company less than five years, the mid-point of the salary range is reasonable. Placing them below mid-point puts them at risk for leaving (Option A), and paying above mid-point may mean the employer is overpaying for performance (Option C). Paying them somewhere in between mid-point and maximum would require more information to determine (Option D), such as the supply of the skill set in the labor market.

16. C. Prescription medication coverage is an example of an employee health and welfare benefit.

17. A. Medicare is a type of involuntary benefit introduced by the Social Security Act of 1935. Along with retirement (Social Security), these mandated benefits are subsidized by a tax on both the employer and the employee called FICA (Federal Insurance Contribution Act). Vision, retirement, and sick pay (Options B, C, and D) are all examples of voluntary benefits that employers may choose to offer their employees.

18. C. A key component of a gainsharing plan is the shared responsibility of outcomes between management and employees. Productivity is reviewed, new performance is measured, and both workgroups share in the gain. ESPPs, bonuses, and Improshare (Options A, B, and D) all could be used but are not specifically grown around the concept of shared responsibility between management and employees.

19. B. Intrinsic rewards are driven by internal versus external factors. Job fulfillment based on work relationships, the opportunity to use strengths, and career growth are examples of nonmonetary compensation. Extrinsic rewards (Option C) are those rewards that are driven by external factors, usually in the form of monetary (Option A) or benefit rewards (components of a total rewards system [Option D]).

20. A. Gross pay is the amount paid to an employee based on several factors, including the employee's base pay rate, shift differentials, tips, and bonuses; how many hours the employee worked during the pay period; and whether any paid leave was used. It is the amount due to an employee before any mandatory or voluntary deductions are made. Once the deductions are taken out, employees receive their net pay (Option B), often the amount that is referred to as "take-home pay." The burden rate is the amount of indirect costs of employment, such as workers compensation insurance (Option C), and wages, salaries, and tips (Option D) is only one component of calculating gross pay.

Chapter 6: PHR Exam: Employee and Labor Relations

1. C. Weingarten rights give all union members the right to request that a co-worker or shop steward be present during an interview if the employee believes the interview could lead to disciplinary action. The employer may decide to use other facts available without interviewing the employee. The Weingarten ruling does not entitle employees to have an attorney present (Option A). Employers are not required to wait for a lengthy period of time until the co-worker returns (Option B). The interview must be discontinued while waiting for the co-worker (Option D). As of 2004, employers are required to honor Weingarten requests only for union members.

2. A. The company may make truthful statements about a unionized environment during an organizing campaign, such as pointing out that employees will have to pay dues to the union. Although nonunion employees are free to talk about their reasons for not wanting a union (Option B), it is an unfair labor practice for the employer to encourage them to do so. Telling employees that the company will have to move the jobs to another country if the union is elected (Option C) is also a ULP, because it constitutes a threat. Employers may not threaten, interrogate, promise, or spy on (TIPS) employees during an organizing campaign (Option D).

3. A. Job burnout due to emotional labor most often occurs in customer service jobs where employees must suppress how they really feel. Emotional labor may lead to job dissatisfaction (Option B), a negative attitude (Option C), and eventual turnover due to decreased commitment (Option D).

4. A. The NLRB will conduct a decertification election if the employees present a petition signed by 30 percent of the employees in the bargaining unit. Management may not participate in or encourage employees to circulate the petition or provide any support in the process. Doing so is considered an unfair labor practice. A union can be deauthorized (Option B) if employees want to remove a union security clause, such as dues check-off. If there is a valid collective bargaining agreement (CBA) in place (Option C), the NLRB will not direct an election. The NLRA prohibits an election if one took place during the preceding 12 months (Option D).

5. D. Three instances when organizational and recognitional picketing are unlawful include picketing when another union is already the legal bargaining representative, when a petition isn't filed within 30 days of the start of picketing, and when a representation election hasn't been held within 12 months.

6. B. In the forced ranking method, managers use a bell curve, rating small groups of employees at the low and high ends and placing most of the employees in the center of the curve. In the ranking method (Option A), employees are listed in order from the highest to the lowest performer. In the paired comparison method (Option C), all employees in the group are compared to one employee at a time.

7. C. The 360-degree feedback is an employee appraisal using data gathered from various sources such as peers, subordinates, supervisors, customers, and suppliers. Although this form of feedback includes supervisors, it also includes many other sources. For this reason, Option B is not the best answer here.

8. D. Salting occurs when a union hires an individual experienced at organizing tactics to apply for a job with a company that has been targeted for an organizing campaign (Option D). Options A, B, and C are tactics used by unions during organizing campaigns.

9. A. Exit interviews are one method used to gauge employee job satisfaction or lack thereof. Brown bag lunches (Option B), employee committees (Option C), and suggestion boxes (Option D) are all employee communication tools, but they are not necessarily conducive to measuring overall employee job satisfaction in a consistent, measurable way.

10. B. WIA programs provide a range of services to assist with education, skills assessment and training, job-search counseling and support, mentoring, and access to job-search information. All of these further the goals of reducing welfare reliance (Option A), improving workforce quality (Option C), and enhancing productivity and competitive ability (Option D). WIA has nothing to do with reforming Social Security (Option B).

11. A. Unusual activity related to employee meetings (Option B), complaints against supervisors, the sudden use of union terms (Option C), and an increased interest in employee benefits (Option D) are all signs of potential union activity.

12. C. The NLRB was established by the NLRA to enforce provisions of the act related to conducting elections and preventing unfair labor practices. The LMRA, LMRDA, and the Norris-La Guardia Act are all examples of legislation influencing the application of unions in the workplace.

13. C. Weingarten rights were upheld by the NLRB, establishing that union workers have the right to representation in any meeting that may amount to an investigatory interview that could lead to disciplinary action. These rights do not currently apply to nonunion workers (Option D). Any employee has the right to consult with an attorney post-discipline, and employers do not have the right to deny representation to union workers (Options A, B) in a meeting that may result in discipline.

14. B. Wrongful discipline and wrongful termination are two actions that can lead to the need for ADR methods. Mediation (Option A), ad hoc arbitration (Option C), peer-review panels (Option D), constructive confrontation, and the use of an ombudsman are all examples of dispute methods that are an *alternative* to court action. A peer review panel, mediation, and arbitration represent the continuum of elevating through the alternative dispute methods.

15. A. The receptionist is exhibiting symptoms of all three types of stress: physical, emotional, and mental. SARS (Option D) is a type of disease, and while her symptoms could be attributed to job dissatisfaction (Option B), there must still be a root cause.

16. D. Personality theories such as the Big Five continue to evolve and be used in a work setting, in some cases to predict employee performance. The trait of openness is most often characterized by being naturally flexible and open to new ideas and experiences.

17. C. EAPs provide counseling for a variety of employee needs, including substance abuse (Option B), stress (Option D) and sometimes even outplacement counseling (Option A). The plans typically do not cover union organizing.

18. A. OSHA injury and illness prevention plans (IIPP) are designed to protect employees from preventable workplace injuries and illnesses. They include emergency response, fire prevention, and safety and health management plans. Although discrimination is a serious matter, it is not an injury or an illness and is not covered by OSHA.

19. C. OSHA inspections are conducted at the request of an employee based on a safety violation, as a preprogrammed high-hazard inspection, or on a random basis. The four characteristics of a safety and health management plan are senior management support (Option A), ongoing worksite analysis (Option B), active hazard-prevention and -control programs (Option D), and ongoing safety and health training.

20. D. Although a review and analysis of OSHA logs (Option A) or workers' compensation records (Option B) can be used to determine any injury patterns occurring in the workplace, observing the incumbent (Option D) performing the work is necessary to determine whether there is an ergonomic hazard in the job. An SDS (Option C) describes chemical hazards unrelated to ergonomics.

Chapter 7: SPHR Exam: Leadership and Strategy

1. C. HR participates in the strategic planning process by providing expertise on attracting, retaining, and managing a qualified workforce. Organization strategies (Option A) are formulated by the executive team. Each business function participates in the environmental-scanning process (Option B) gathering information about its area of responsibility. Strategic goals (Option D) are identified by the executive team during the strategy formulation phase.

2. D. The mission statement describes who the organization is, what it does, where it is going, and how it is different from others. The corporate values statement (Option A) communicates the executive team's expectations for the way the organization conducts business. Corporate goals (Option B) describe what the organization plans to achieve in the future. The vision statement (Option C) is a short, inspirational statement of what the organization will accomplish in the future.

3. A. An HR budget reflects how many and what types of resources are necessary to accomplish a goal. The addition of employees, costs to train, and the purchase of new equipment are all examples of items that require cash to achieve strategic goals.

4. B. Creating an HR budget takes into account standard expense items associated with having employees. They include salaries, taxes, benefits, training, travel, and equipment costs, to name a few.

5. B. A business case lays out the desired result of an action or program, presents alternative solutions, describes possible risks from both implementing and not implementing the action, and defines the criteria used to measure success. ROI and CBA may be included as part of the business case, and a SWOT analysis may have identified the need for a program or action.

6. C. A human resource information system is generally designed and used to house a virtual employee personnel file. It has two primary purposes: to store information and to aid to the operational efficiencies of an HR department. Expense reports would be more a function of accounting than of HR.

7. A. The ability to interpret and apply information related to internal sources allows HR to respond to specific elements of an organization's strategic plan. For example, understanding how an HRIS system can integrate with an accounting database is one example of cross-functional strategic decisions. Scanning the legal and regulatory environment (Option B), analyzing industry changes (Option C), and staying abreast of technological advances (Option D) are all examples of external forces that impact a strategic plan.

8. A. An income statement, also referred to as a profit and loss statement, provides financial information about revenue and expenses in a set reporting period. The statement of cash flow (Option B) communicates the ways in which monies came in and out of the organization, and the balance sheet (Option C) is a thumbnail sketch of assets, liabilities, and equity at a certain time.

9. B. A product-based structure is useful for an organization with multiple well-defined product lines. The structure and subsequent job responsibilities are divided by product line, rather than shared company-wide. The functional structure (Option A) is the more traditional format where the organization is divided by departments such as production and sales. A divisional structure (Option C) groups the company based on market or industry, useful for decentralized divisions. A flat-line structure (Option D) is a different term for a seamless organization, one in which hierarchies do not exist.

10. B. Paying low wages resulting in high turnover is an internal weakness that affects an organization's ability to compete.

11. D. The economic climate, including cost of living, is an example of an external threat that affects an organization's ability to compete in its relevant market.

12. B. The threat of substitutes or replacements is a threat that obtaining a U.S. patent may mitigate. A design patent grants the inventor the exclusive rights to profit from their unique design.

13. B. What a company believes in and commits to is often found in corporate values' statements. These values serve as a guide for how a company will conduct their business, both internally with employees and externally with other stakeholders.

14. A. A balance sheet reflects the company assets at any given time. This is identified by adding together both equity and liabilities, which must equal the company assets, thus the name "balance sheet."

15. D. The Generally Accepted Accounting Principles (GAAP) are standards developed by the Financial Accounting Standards Board (FASB) to create checks and balances for accounting professionals recording business transactions. This helps to prevent fraudulent recordkeeping and employee hiding theft, among other things.

16. B. A budget built on past spending is called a historic budget.

17. C. The key in this question is not so much the locations but how the financial recordkeeping is held. Because each location has their own profit and loss statements, budgets, and so forth, it is the best example of a decentralized business structure.

18. B. The staff functions of organizations are those that do not generate revenue or otherwise produce the core goods and services. This includes accounting and finance.

19. D. The planning phase of project management will describe the deliverables, budget, and scope of the project.

20. D. A human capital management plan (HCMP) is a critical tool to help develop tactical action plans for the achievement of company goals. An HCMP is most effective when it aligns with the company strategy, properly forecasts the talent necessary to achieve goals, and supports the creation of a competitive advantage through the company's people.

Chapter 8: SPHR Exam: Talent Planning and Acquisition

1. C. The selection ratio for women is calculated 16 / 45, or 35 percent. The selection ratio for men is 27 / 60, or 45 percent. 35 percent divided by 45 percent equals 78 percent, which is less than 80 percent (4/5ths), so there is evidence of adverse impact in this example.

2. A. The job analysis process is used to inform many HR decisions, not the least of which is to help predict candidate success on the job. From job analysis, job descriptions are built, recruiting ads are written, and valid preemployment tests—including face-to-face interviews—are designed.

3. D. Human capital projecting is a planning tool that analyzes inputs such as skill sets and gaps and creates outputs such as workforce plans and budgets.

4. B. Internal and external data is used to make human capital projections. External factors include the labor market data and projections for the area in which workforce plans and budgets are being created.

5. C. Many states have their own departments that track workforce statistics. Companies may access unemployment rates, cost of living, competitive organizations, and much more that may then be used to begin to build a business case to present to the executive team.

6. D. Senior-level HR leaders are responsible for recruiting strategy. This includes applying creative solutions and designing intervention strategies that will influence the selection process. In many cases, the recruiting and selection process starts from within. This includes identifying employees who may be groomed for promotion, building engagement programs that retain key talent, and redesigning jobs for simplification so that there are less qualifications (and thus a larger labor pool) necessary to do the work.

7. D. Although all of the answers may occur as part of the new hire acculturation process, the focus is to help the employee succeed in the early months of their job.

8. B. The job analysis process is fundamental not only to the talent planning and acquisition function, but to all other HR systems as well. Job analysis is fundamental to recruiting, writing interview questions for employee selection, crafting performance feedback, building wage structures, and completing hazard assessments in risk management, just to name a few.

9. C. Anchoring bias occurs in decision-making when a point is established from which other decisions are then made. Higher starting points in salary negotiations are often correlated with higher final wages being paid.

10. C. Having a solid system in place to notify nonselected candidates is an HR best practice. A standard email may be appropriate for some, whereas a personal phone call—particularly for those who received interviews—leaves a positive impression and potential for future sourcing.

11. A. Allowing the employee to proceed through the application process is the best answer in this scenario. Not only does it give her the opportunity to compete, but it allows HR to work with the existing manager to develop a timely replacement plan.

12. D. Job bidding may serve many purposes, including supporting a company that desires to promote from within. It is also helpful for highly competitive jobs in order to give employees the opportunity to notify HR of their interest. This also gives HR an instant applicant pool from which to draw from for future openings.

13. B. Human capital management is a talent planning and acquisition process that is tied to the strategic plan. Designing total rewards—while important—is not a typical part of the HCM planning process.

14. D. During strategic workforce planning, skills inventories are used as part of the gap analysis process. It is a tool that identifies the current skill set of the workforce which is then compared to the skills necessary to execute strategy. Any gaps will need to be planned for accordingly.

15. D. Employee severance packages are given to separating employees for several reasons. It helps to offset lost wages due to company layoffs or reductions in force. A severance package may be used as a risk management tool in which the employee accepts the payment in exchange for the right to sue. And it can serve as a reward for loyalty to exiting employees.

16. A. Relocation services are used by employers when employees are asked to transfer locations. These services may include housing assistance, spousal support in finding jobs, accessing schools in the area, tax and legal support, and other types of assistance as relevant.

17. C. In strategic workforce planning, forecasting is used to anticipate the future hiring needs when items such as natural attrition and growth plans are factored in.

18. D. A talent pool approach identifies more than a single successor for a single role. This allows for greater flexibility and adaptability for employers relying on succession plans for future competitiveness.

19. A. The reuse of land previously used for industry or manufacturing is known as a brownfield operation.

20. B. The best answer is that of a greenfield operation. The key to this answer is that the company is building a new business facility in a new location, which specifically refers to the growth strategy of a greenfield operation.

Chapter 9: SPHR Exam: Learning and Development

1. C. A company's learning and development system must seek to integrate with other human resource outcomes such as Talent Acquisition as well as align with other business outcomes such as workforce planning and goal achievement.

2. A. Ensuring the business continues in an ever-changing competitive landscape is one major outcome of designing effective career progression and coaching activities. This is particularly true when the focus is on aligning employee development goals with business development goals through succession planning.

3. C. The 21st century workforce is much more focused on career development and creating value, both for themselves and their employer. This means that L&D programs that support training, challenging work, and meaningful tasks are much more likely to increase employee loyalty and thus retention.

4. B. With the cost of having employees ever on the rise, the value of any type of investment—training or otherwise—should be effectively measured and clearly communicated. Regularly doing this allows for real-time adjustments, increasing the odds that the program will achieve the desired results.

5. B. Malcolm Knowles introduced the concept that adults and children learn new things very differently. The term *andragogy* refers to the process by which adults learn.

6. D. Self-determination is one of many theories of motivation. Research (and anecdotal evidence) has found that leaders who are self-determined rarely wait for others to drive their best behaviors. As a general rule, they strive to be proactive.

7. A. Some adults require a deeper level understanding of a training session's context and purpose—in short, the "why" behind a training initiative. By providing the sales employee with this information—such as how selling techniques are a reflection of what the company values—the company is more likely to gain his buy-in.

8. C. Being fluid in the generation of ideas is the premise behind idea fluency. Similar to language fluency, ideas build on each other until a coherent concept emerges, rather like words build a sentence.

9. B. Individuals (and cultures) that score high on Geert Hofstede's "uncertainty avoidance" dimension of culture are less likely to embrace change for the sake of innovation. These employees may require higher degrees of support as a company takes on creative or innovative endeavors.

10. D. As with so many HR activities, conducting a job analysis allows for the discovery of how a job may progress for an employee as they gain the required knowledge, skills, and other competencies to move within and outside of job families. Once identified, the skill set and professional goals of incumbents may be reviewed, career goals established, and the replacement needs/timelines identified.

11. C. Part of measuring the effectiveness of any L&D intervention activity is knowing what the "before" conditions are prior to implementation. This allows for periodic checks to ensure that the program is doing what it was intended to do.

12. A. Needs analysis may be done at an individual or an organizational level. Prior to any type of intervention strategy, it is useful for HR to gain a clear understanding of the degree of need. For example, leaders may be required to make more strategic decisions, whereas individual contributors may be required to make more task-level decisions. Some employees may be "better" at making decisions than others. Once collected, this data will help HR make decisions about how to design the program (modes of delivery, timing) and develop content.

13. C. Training as an intervention strategy is typically used by organizations that identify a skills gap. This may be part of an organizational, departmental, or individual needs assessment, or even an outcome of strategic planning.

14. D. Return on investment (ROI) may be measured using both tangible and intangible criteria. Examples may include hard costs, reduced turnover, improved employee retention, and higher customer satisfaction.

15. D. There are several advantages to using technology to evaluate training program outcomes. This example refers to the deep-learning techniques that allow for macro and micro data collection. This is a form of workforce analytics that is used to evaluate program design effectiveness.

16. C. The impact of neuroscience research on organizational and individual employee behavior is just beginning to scratch the surface of workplace breakthroughs. Neuroscience is making significant contributions toward the behavioral sciences in change management, decision-making, and leadership development, just to name a few.

17. A. The self-determination theory of motivation is built on the idea that the quality, depth, and origin of motivation matters just as much as how much motivation an employee has. Intrinsic motivators tend to have a stronger force than external motivators.

18. A. The creative process requires a period of trial and error. Some ideas will simply not work. If a leader or a culture does not inspire trust from employees, employees will fear that these failures will result in a negative professional outcome and so are reluctant to speak up.

19. B. A succession plan may unearth the fact that there is no current employee who is either ready for promotion or ready to be groomed for promotion into a new role. Therefore, the succession planning process may need to connect with the talent acquisition process to ensure a qualified person is in place and ready to go at the time of need.

20. D. Developing adequate resources for a successful career management program requires the inclusion of both hard and soft costs. This includes salaries and the cost of any training program or materials.

Chapter 10: SPHR Exam: Total Rewards

1. C. Total rewards programs and strategies must be developed to align with two main goals: finding and retaining critical talent while also building programs that are affordable. Both factors impact an organization's ability to compete.

2. D. People determined to have a fiduciary responsibility in an organization are held to the highest ethical standards. Breaching this responsibility includes acting in one's own self-interest, putting HR department needs above the integrity of pay systems, and profiting from the decision-making authority inherent in senior-level duties.

3. A. Companies that choose to pay below-market rates for talent are lagging the relevant labor market in pay rates. This is often in response to a skill set that is abundant in a labor market, making it easier to find workers.

4. D. Strong economies are partially reflective of companies that are growing and thriving. This means they need to hire talented workers, resulting in fewer unemployed individuals in the market.

5. A. The Department of Labor (DOL) released a new factors test to help employers justify the use of unpaid internships. Fundamental to all factors is the degree to which the intern—not the employer—is the primary beneficiary of the position.

6. C. As a general rule, companies are able to forecast out their cost of total rewards programs for about two years. Knowing the employer's planning horizon can help HR gather data to inform the strategic allocation of TR programs that are in line with business goals, hiring, and retention.

7. B. Integrative TR practices serve both the employer and the employee. By understanding what employees really want and need, HR can design programs that meet those needs without overdependence on pay rates as the primary motivator.

8. A. Many bureaucratic business structures such as the ones found in government and academia often rely on traditional salary grades. While fair in application, traditional structures often minimize flexibility to attract and keep talented workers.

9. B. The job evaluation and pricing processes are used by employers to determine the relative worth of jobs when compared to internal and external factors.

10. A. It is important for senior HR leaders to ensure they are selecting the right salary survey to meet organizational needs. Having line managers and front-line supervisors involved in comparing job duties and responsibilities helps to validate that survey data is relevant to the business.

11. D. Companies in the early stages of the business life cycle often find themselves having to build systems from scratch. In the highly competitive tech world, job evaluation may actually become necessary earlier than in other industries. With limited resources in the HR department, the priority for Jamie is most likely ease of development and use.

12. C. Two-tiered wage systems are used in collective bargaining to help stabilize the cost of labor over a contract period. With this approach, wages for employees who have not yet been hired are used to bargain for incumbent pay increases or other features of the collective bargaining agreement.

13. B. Forecasting the cost of labor is a strategic activity usually completed by senior-level HR. This information is used to build budgets and strategically allocate Total Rewards funds based on employee needs and wants.

14. A. Accrued expenses are those that have been incurred but not yet paid out.

15. D. The Generally Accepted Accounting Principles (GAAP) are a set of standards established by the Financial Accounting Standards Board. They include best practices related to building in checks and balances in Accounting roles and responsibilities to minimize the opportunity for theft or deceit.

16. D. Companies using the zero-based budget method are able to account for changing or emerging business needs. This is because it is not reliant on historical data as benchmarks for building budgets for a new fiscal year.

17. A. Creating scarcity of rewards is one method used to design incentive and other rewards programs that motivate workers.

18. D. Current research from the social sciences tells us a lot about the effect of wages on employee motivation and individual traits. Some studies are finding that there is a threshold for the impact money has on employee motivation, meaning that once a threshold has been met, other conditions will need to exist in order for it to continue to be a motivator. These other conditions are often based on individual employee needs, values, and characteristics.

19. D. Stock options are a form of equity compensation in which employees gain a financial interest in the organization and its performance on the stock market.

20. D. Executive compensation can be made up of many elements, some of which include base pay, equity options, and perks.

Chapter 11: SPHR Exam: Employee Relations and Engagement

1. C. Human relations studies is focused on the behavior of people in groups. This includes the workplace. The field includes research in applied psychology, industrial-organizational psychology, and organizational behavior, just to name a few.

2. B. The Hawthorne studies contributed to the organizational sciences in significant ways. One way is the discovery that human beings have human needs—including psychological and social needs—that must be included in management and organizational best practices.

3. A. Psychological empowerment is a type of intrinsic motivation. It occurs in the context of the four dimensions of meaning, competence, self-determination, and impact.

4. C. Of the three job attitudes of employee engagement, organizational commitment, and job satisfaction, engagement is occurring when an individual invests their physical, mental, and emotional energies into the work tasks themselves.

5. D. Personal resource building as a type of job attitude intervention requires employers to collect data. This data can then be used to design programs that will increase employee engagement, job satisfaction, and/or organizational commitment. This includes programs that help increase employee feelings of optimism, resilience, and a positive view of their behaviors and capabilities.

6. C. Edgar Schein noted that there are several dimensions that contribute to organizational culture. They include artifacts—items that can be seen, heard, or felt—in order to increase the collective identity of a group and its members.

7. A. Geert Hofstede is a pioneer in the development of theories of culture. One dimension is that of individualism versus collectivism. Companies that place a high value on independence and autonomy—such as what is necessary for a virtual work team—are said to be high on the individualism scale.

8. B. The focus of positive discipline strategies is problem-solving. A performance improvement plan is a tool that managers may use to help the employee understand what behaviors need to change and what resources will be available to support the change.

9. C. The nature of the relationship and exchanges between a leader and a follower is the focus of the leader-member exchange theory. It is constructed from the premise that in-group members establish reciprocal trust with the leader and therefore assume more responsibility, with increased loyalty and productivity as a result.

10. D. Social information processing is the idea that employee job attitudes are influenced by the people around them, including family, friends, co-workers, and customers.

11. B. Job security is the primary element that makes up the nature of the psychological contract. This contract governs the unwritten expectations employees have regarding the commitment from their employer, influencing the commitment they have to their employer.

12. D. Line of sight is the phrase used to refer to how clearly the employee is able to tie individual, team, or organizational performance to their efforts.

13. A. Employees that witness unethical behavior by others are the first line of risk management. Written ethics policies that both encourage reporting and prohibit retaliation have been shown to increase internal reporting, allowing employers to quickly respond and resolve issues before they get out of hand.

14. C. Of the two types of diversity, surface-level refers to the observable traits of a specific demographic such as age, gender, or ethnicity.

15. D. Employers may be accused of an unfair labor practice (ULP) if they threaten, interrogate, promise, or spy on employees (TIPS).

16. B. Unconscious bias occurs when people act on stereotypes that they are unaware that they have. Training employees to be aware that this bias is unconscious can help reduce and eliminate behavior that is built from this bias.

17. D. There are several written plans that are required of employers in order to be compliant with the Occupational Safety and Health Act's standards. These written plans include hazard communication, emergency response, and fire prevention.

18. B. While written policies, audits, and the computerization of financial data for tracking purposes may all help reduce employee embezzlement, eliminating the opportunity by segregating job duties is the most effective as a first line of defense. For example, a single employee should not have the ability to receive, post, and physically deposit customer payments. Being able to do so would make it easier for an employee to alter the books to hide any deceit.

19. C. Employers must take care to not unintentionally violate employee free speech or privacy rights with their social media use policies. This includes their right to engage in concerted protected activity under the National Labor Relations Act. Concerted protected activity includes the right to make statements about wages and working hours, and this extends to the online environment as well.

20. C. Concession and ultra-concession bargaining is a tool used by employers that are having financial difficulties. It requires that unions agree to roll back previous gains in order to help keep the company financially solvent.

Appendix

B

PHR® and SPHR® Case Studies

Case Study 1: Human Resources Role in Preventing Workplace Violence

By Hector Alvarez, CTM

PRESIDENT, ALVAREZ ASSOCIATES, LLC (WWW.WVPEXPERTS.COM)

The threat of workplace violence is a growing concern for organizations of all sizes and has placed a significant burden on human resources professionals to help intervene and prevent incidents from occurring—a significant threat to a productive and harmonious work environment than the fear of being injured. Although there is a growing body of knowledge of the problem, no mandatory standards are in place to direct organizations on how to address this complex, multifaceted issue.

There are, however, two significant documents that every human resources (HR) professional should be familiar with. The General Duty Clause, Section 5(a)(1), of the Occupational Safety and Health Act of 1970 states that employers are required to provide their employees with a place of employment that is "free from recognized hazards that are causing or are likely to cause death or serious harm." The second was released in 2011 in collaboration between the Society for Human Resource Management (SHRM) and the American Society for Industrial Security (ASIS). ASIS/SHRM WVP.1-2011, *Workplace Violence Prevention and Intervention*, provides the framework for identifying and intervening to prevent acts of violence. What is not specifically addressed in either of these two provisions is exactly how an organization—and specifically HR professionals—should approach this challenging issue.

It is helpful to consider a real-world scenario. A high-tech firm in the greater San Francisco Bay area employed a husband and wife who worked in two different parts of the organization. Both people were stellar employees who received high marks from their respective supervisors. On a Monday morning the female employee, "Jane," went to HR and stated that she had been assaulted by her husband over the weekend and that she had the bruises to prove her story. She stated that she was granted a restraining order by the local police, but she did not want it to be an issue at the office. She merely wanted to let HR know "just in case" and didn't want anybody to find out about what had happened over the weekend.

This story highlights the types of challenges that anybody working in HR faces on a regular basis. The issues are complicated and the potential impact to the organization can be considerable. It's important to recognize that many of these issues are too complicated for one person or department to manage on their own. One of the main themes the ASIS/SHRM standard stresses is to take a multidisciplinary approach to evaluating the seriousness and credibility of a threatening situation. The reality is that it's not that simple. Establishing an effective workplace violence prevention program requires building and maintaining a significant level of trust in people who work outside the realm of HR. In the scenario described here, the security staff discovered that the husband was apparently dating a woman who also worked at the company.

The one thing that every HR professional should know is that preventing workplace violence is as much an art as it is a science and requires organization-wide commitment. The OSHA and ASIS/SHRM standards and guidelines provide a framework, but trust and ultimately intuition cannot be overemphasized. The reality is that violence is intimate and personal. It's of the upmost importance to recognize that preventing violence requires involvement and collaboration from teams across the organization. Legal personnel, security staff, individual businesses units, and senior management all have a role to play in identifying and preventing violence, and they certainly will each have an opinion on what the best course of action is. HR professionals often have the role of coordinating and balancing what may be competing goals and agendas.

In the scenario of the married couple who worked at the high-tech firm, the HR employee who Jane spoke to about the assault made the decision to respect her wishes and took no further action. As a result, even though security personnel had pertinent information, the HR employee was not made aware of the extramarital affair until after there was an intense and heated argument in the company breakroom that involved Jane, her husband, and the other woman. After the argument, Jane came to HR and loudly yelled, "Now what are you going to do?"

In the end, Jane filed a hostile work environment complaint with the Equal Employment Opportunity Commission, the husband was arrested and ultimately fired for job abandonment, and the other employee quit her job at the company. The moral of this story: preventing violence is a complicated issue that requires the involvement of multiple parties. Don't try to do it alone. While HR should take a lead role in creating a collaborative environment that brings together the key stakeholders to evaluate the seriousness and credibility of a situation, every employee has a role to play in preventing violence in an organization.

Find the complete text of the ASIS/SHRM *Workplace Violence Prevention and Intervention* guidelines at www.shrm.org. Search for the term "ASIS/SHRM WVPI.1-2011."

Questions

1. How can human resources professionals balance the need for workplace confidentiality with the goal of preventing an act of violence?

2. Who in the organization is ultimately responsible for preventing acts of workplace violence?

3. When should human resources involve other business partners regarding concerns of inappropriate or concerning behavior?

Answers

1. Establishing trusted partnerships with key organizational players in the legal, security, risk management, and similar departments allows for timely communications regarding inappropriate or concerning behavior. Addressing potential issues early decreases the likelihood that they will escalate. Doing so can also help limit the number of people who must be involved; as issues become problems, it's much more difficult to maintain confidentiality.

2. Everybody in an organization has a role in preventing acts of violence. However, HR plays an extremely important role in helping create an organizational culture that encourages and supports employees being able to share their concerns. Not unlike the environment that supported the #MeToo movement, employees must feel that somebody is taking them seriously.

3. Employee relations issues can quickly transition from routine personnel matters to critical threats. Unfortunately, there is no clearly defined line indicating when to reach out for help from business partners. HR professionals should be mindful of the reality that they may not be in a position to see all the issues surrounding a person of concern. Frequent collaboration with key business partners can help close this information gap. Evaluating the seriousness and credibility of concerning behavior is a high-risk activity. Leveraging the collective resources of your organization can help minimize this risk.

Case Study 2: Where the Green Glass Grows

Where the Green Glass Grows (WGGG) is an eco-friendly glass manufacturer located in California. It services the numerous wine producers of the coastal region, manufacturing glass wine bottles in various sizes and colors. Starting with four employees in a small manufacturing facility in 1964, the company went through a major growth initiative 10 years ago. This resulted in a renovation of its manufacturing facility, bringing the company to its current four-line production configuration. Output is approximately 24 million bottles annually, working with a single shift of workers. WGGG's current sales volume peaked 3 years ago at $1.2 million. Now at 42 employees, the company has committed to undergo a series of strategic interventions to respond to the rapid growth of international wine sales. Figure B.1 shows the organizational chart for the company.

FIGURE B.1   WGGG organizational chart

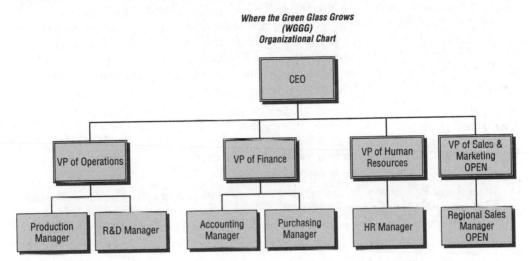

The Company

Sustainability and innovation became corporate objectives for WGGG long before they were considered trendy.

"At WGGG, our mission is all about growth. Growing our talent, growing our resources, and growing our financial stability are at the heart of everything we do," said Emerald Cyan, CEO and granddaughter of the founder, Forrest Gumby.

Furthermore, WGGG has an established business practice of using a minimum of 85 percent recycled glass for all products as evidence of its commitment to sustainable business practices and the environment.

WGGG's competitive advantage is significant: the ability to manufacture glass bottles that weigh 20 percent less than those produced by industry counterparts. WGGG's technology enables the company to melt down an existing glass bottle, remove a portion of the glass, and replace it with an injection of a patented gel solution, re-forming it into a new mold. The result is a lighter-weight bottle that is more durable (and thus shatter-resistant) than what is currently available on the market. Because the weight of the bottle accounts for up to 49 percent of the cost to ship wine, producers took notice.

The Customer

The United States surpassed France as the nation that consumes the most wine in 2014. California wine accounted for a 61 percent volume share of the total U.S. wine market, with sales at 199.6 million cases, up 1 percent from the previous year. Retail value was

$18.5 billion. In addition, since the reversal of an 80 percent import tax to Hong Kong, wine imports into China from across the globe saw a record $491 million in sales, 8 percent of which was from America. It is anticipated that over the next 3 years, American wine imports to the region will reach as much as 138 percent of existing sales. Combine that with the growth of homeland consumption, and American wine producers are near giddy with anticipation. If WGGG wants to service wine producers across the United States, it needs to grow again.

Exercises

1. Using Table B.1, complete a thumbnail SWOT (strength, weakness, opportunity, threat) audit for WGGG using all available data.

2. Using Table B.2, match the internal HR activity to its proper function. Apply the most appropriate letter from the following list to each cell in the first column of Table B.2 (each letter can be used more than once, and not all letters will necessarily be used):

   A. Business Management and Strategy

   B. Workforce Planning and Employment

   C. Human Resource Development

   D. Compensation and Benefits

   E. Employee and Labor Relations

   F. Risk Management

3. Using Table B.3, match WGGG's activity with the correlating driving external force. Apply the most appropriate letter from the following list to each cell in the first column of Table B.3 (each letter can be used more than once, and not all letters will necessarily be used):

   A. The political/legal climate

   B. Geographic limitations or opportunities

   C. The economic climate

   D. The competition

TABLE B.1   SWOT audit

Internal	Strengths	Weaknesses
External	Opportunities	Threats

TABLE B.2   Internal HR activities

Effectively recruit for and select a sales and marketing department.

Conduct a cost–benefit analysis on running a second shift.

Develop the leadership to effectively manage the rapid changes that will occur.

Assess the security levels of trade secret data.

Conduct wage surveys by geographic location where potential new facilities are being considered.

Increase the use of new vs. recycled glass.

Measure the ROI of projected growth due to the increase in staff.

Engage in planning activities to map out strategic short-term and long-term goals.

Design training for sales staff across multiple geographic locations through the use of mixed media.

Plan and prepare for the regulatory compliance required of 50 employees.

TABLE B.3   WGGG's activities

Compliance with the regulation of chemical use in food storage by various governmental agencies

Accounting for the cost of production in the wine coast region

Evaluating the quality of the labor force population

Accounting for the cost of labor in the wine coast region

Establishing the rate of pay required for a second shift

Evaluating the strength of WGGG's trade patent

Procuring and evaluating the availability of additional glass suppliers

Monitoring the status of trade relations with China

Mitigating the threat of new market entrants

Answers and Additional Exercises

1. A SWOT audit allows a company the opportunity to see where it excels and where it's deficient. Although we provide only a snapshot here, you can see how taking a 50,000-foot approach via a SWOT audit will allow the company to create a 5,000-foot operational plan, taking into consideration its internal strengths and weaknesses and external opportunities and threats. See Table B.4.

2. Clearly assessing the need for HR activities in strategic interventions is the first step toward contributing to organizational development. This case study gives you a sampling of the types of activities to consider, ordered by functional HR area. See Table B.5. *Can you identify at least three more examples of HR activities WGGG will need to undertake?*

3. Porter's 5 Forces (Chapter 7, "SPHR Exam: Leadership & Strategy") reflect on the drivers that exist in the external business climate. Being able to anticipate which of those forces will impact strategic initiatives and how they will do so is critical to putting mitigation or risk management measures into place. Table B.6 provides a sampling of the considerations relevant to the case study. *Can you identify at least three more examples of external forces WGGG will need to consider?*

TABLE B.4   SWOT audit: Answers

Internal	Strengths	Weaknesses
	Competitive advantage	Understaffed
	Longevity	Doesn't have the facilities necessary to produce forecasted demand
	Existing customer base	Doesn't have a functioning sales and marketing department

External	Opportunities	Threats
	Cross-functionality of the product, diversifying the product line	Competition and copycat technology
	The global market	Possible limits on glass procurement
	The potential for decreased overhead via a relocation	Cost of capital improvements or relocation
		The rise of alternative sources, such as plastic

TABLE B.5 Internal HR activities: Answers

B	Effectively recruit for and select a sales and marketing department.
A	Conduct a cost–benefit analysis on running a second shift.
C	Develop the leadership to effectively manage the rapid changes that will occur.
F	Assess the security levels of trade secret data.
D	Conduct wage surveys by geographic location where potential new facilities are being considered.
A	Increase the use of new vs. recycled glass.
B	Measure the ROI of projected growth due to the increase in staff.
A	Engage in planning activities to map out strategic short-term and long-term goals.
C	Design training for sales staff across multiple geographic locations through the use of mixed media.
B	Plan and prepare for the regulatory compliance required of 50 employees.

TABLE B.6 WGGG's activities: Answers

A	Compliance with the regulation of chemical use in food storage by various governmental agencies
B	Accounting for the cost of production in the wine coast region
C	Evaluating the quality of the labor force population
B	Accounting for the cost of labor in the wine coast region
C	Establishing the rate of pay required for a second shift
A	Evaluating the strength of WGGG's trade patent
D	Procuring and evaluating the availability of additional glass suppliers
A	Monitoring the status of trade relations with China
D	Mitigating the threat of new market entrants

Appendix C

Federal Employment Legislation and Case Law

The body of federal employment legislation and case law is extensive. This appendix provides a good introduction to this area of knowledge.

Affirmative Action Plans (AAPs)

All federal contractors and subcontractors who have at least 50 employees and designated monetary levels of government contracts or subcontracts must prepare and update annually two or three affirmative action plans (AAPs). Each AAP has specific requirements dictated by regulations. The three potential AAPs are as follows:

Executive Order 11246 AAP Covers women and minorities and is required for each establishment, if a supply or services contractor (or subcontractor) has 50 or more employees and a government contract (or subcontract) of at least $50,000. Federally assisted construction contractors, however, do not prepare traditional EO 11246 but have 16 equal employment opportunity (EEO) and *affirmative action (AA)* specifications that they must meet and document.

Vietnam Era Veterans' Readjustment Assistance Action (VEVRAA) of 1974, as amended, 38 U.S.C. 4212 AAP Covers protected veterans and is required for each establishment, if a government contractor (or subcontractor) has 50 or more employees and has a government contract (or subcontract) of at least $150,000. Federally assisted construction contractors must also prepare the same type of AAP. The categories of protected veterans are disabled veteran, recently separated veteran (three-year period), active duty wartime or campaign badge veteran, or an armed forces service medal veteran.

Section 503 of the Rehabilitation Act of 1973, as amended, 29 U.S.C. 793 AAP Covers individuals with disabilities and is required for each establishment, if a government contractor (or subcontractor) has 50 or more employees and a government contract (or subcontract) of at least $50,000. Federally assisted construction contractors must also prepare the same type of AAP. The government allows the VEVRAA AAP and the Section 503 AAP to be combined into one if both are required.

NOTE Even if an organization does not need to prepare written AAPs, there still are federal affirmative action requirements for government contracts or subcontracts that are greater than $10,000, if aggregated or for a contract or subcontract greater than $15,000.

The Office of Federal Contract Compliance Programs (OFCCP) in the U.S. Department of Labor constructs and enforces the affirmative action regulations. The OFCCP periodically will audit federal contractors and subcontractors on the contents of their AAPs and other regulatory requirements. The OFCCP's mission statement is as follows:

Mission Statement   At the Office of Federal Contract Compliance Programs (OFCCP), we protect workers, promote diversity, and enforce the law. OFCCP holds those who do business with the federal government—contractors and subcontractors—responsible for complying with the legal requirement to take affirmative action and not discriminate on the basis of race, color, sex, sexual orientation, gender identity, religion, national origin, disability, or status as a protected veteran. In addition, contractors and subcontractors are prohibited from discharging or otherwise discriminating against applicants or employees who inquire about, discuss or disclose their compensation or that of others, subject to certain limitations.

Executive Order 11246 AAP

The required components of an Executive Order 11246 AAP appear in Table C.1.

TABLE C.1   Required Components of Executive Order 11246 AAP

AAP component	Description
Organizational profile	Employers choose the format that works best: organizational display (traditional organization chart) or workforce analysis (listing of job titles from lowest to highest paid).
Job group analysis	Places job titles with similar content, wages, and opportunities into job groups for analysis
Placement of incumbents in job groups	Lists percentages of minorities and women employed in each job group
Determining availability	Estimates the number of qualified minorities or women available for employment in a given job group, often within a specific geographic area
Comparison of incumbency to availability	Compares the percentage of minorities and women in each job group with the availability for those job groups within a specific geographic area
Placement goals	When the percentage of minorities or women employed in a particular job group is less than would reasonably be expected given their availability percentage in that particular job group, the contractor must establish a placement goal. Placement goals serve as objectives or targets reasonably attainable by means of applying every good-faith effort. Placement goals are not quotas or preferences.

TABLE C.1   Required Components of Executive Order 11246 AAP *(continued)*

AAP component	Description
Designation of responsibility	Assigns responsibility and accountability for the implementation of EEO and the affirmative action program to an official of the organization
Identification of problem areas	Requires analysis of the total employment processes to determine whether and where impediments to equal opportunity exist
Action-oriented programs	The contractor must develop and execute action-oriented programs designed to correct any problems identified and to attain established goals and objectives.
Internal audit and reporting system	The contractor must develop and implement an auditing system that periodically measures the effectiveness of its total affirmative action program.

VEVRAA AAP

The required components of the VEVRAA AAP include:

Policy Statement   The contractor's (note: when the term *contractor* is used, it also applies to subcontractors) equal opportunity policy statement should be included in the AAP and be posted on the organization's bulletin board.

Review of Personnel Processes   The contractor shall periodically review such processes and make any necessary modifications to ensure that its obligations are carried out. A description of the review and any modifications should be documented.

Physical and Mental Qualifications   Provides for a schedule for the periodic review of all physical and mental job qualification standards to ensure that to the extent that qualification standards tend to screen out qualified disabled veterans, they are job-related for the position in question and are consistent with business necessity

Reasonable Accommodation to Physical and Mental Limitations   Includes a statement that the contractor will make reasonable accommodation to the known physical or mental limitations of an otherwise qualified disabled veteran unless it can demonstrate that the accommodation would impose an undue hardship on the operation of the business

Harassment   Includes a statement about what the contractor has done to develop and implement procedures to ensure that its employees are not harassed because of their status as protected veterans

External Dissemination of Policy, Outreach, and Positive Recruitment   Includes listing the organization's outreach efforts, including sending written notification of the organization's EEO/AA policy to all subcontractors, vendors, and suppliers. Also requires the contractor to review, on an annual basis, the outreach and recruitment efforts it has taken over the previous 12 months to evaluate their effectiveness in identifying and recruiting qualified protected veterans. If not effective, the contractor shall identify and implement alternative efforts. These assessments are to be retained for a three-year period.

Internal Dissemination of Policy   The contractor outlines its efforts to implement and disseminate its EEO/AA policy internally.

Audit and Reporting System   The contractor describes and documents the audit and reporting system that it designed and implemented to measure the effectiveness of its affirmative action program, among other things.

Responsibility for Implementation   The contractor documents which official of the organization has been assigned responsibility for implementation of the contractor's affirmative action program. His or her identity should appear on all internal and external communications regarding the contractor's affirmative action program.

Training   Describes the efforts made to train all personnel involved in the recruitment, screening, selection, promotion, disciplinary actions, and related processes on the contractor's commitments in the affirmative action program

Other VEVRAA requirements not included in the AAP, but required by the regulations, include:

Data Collection Analysis   Annual documentation, maintained for a three-year period, of the number of applicants who self-identified as protected veterans, the total number of job openings and the total number of jobs filled, the total number of applicants for all jobs, the number of applicants hired, and the number of protected veterans hired.

Hiring Benchmark   The contractor shall either establish and document a hiring benchmark for protected veterans, based on specific criteria, or use the OFCCP-dictated hiring benchmark, which is 6.9 percent as of the time of publication. These records shall be retained for a period of three years.

- Contractors must now invite protected veterans to self-identify as such at both the pre- and post-offer stages. However, the protected veteran is not *required* to self-identify at any stage.
- Inclusion of the Equal Opportunity Clause in covered purchase orders and subcontracts
- Annual notice to the State Employment Service Delivery System where the organization's jobs are located
- Listing all external job openings with the State Employment Service Delivery System, except for temporary positions (for three days or less) or executive positions

VEVRAA and Other Posters

- Allowing access to the protected veterans AAP for both applicants and employees
- Annual union notification letter/email
- Annual filing of protected veterans VETS-4212 report (used to be VETS-100A)
- Required job listing, posting, or ad tagline

Section 503, Individuals with Disabilities AAP

The required components of Section 503, Individuals with Disabilities AAP, include:

Policy Statement   The contractor's (always includes subcontractors) equal opportunity policy statement should be included in the AAP and be posted on the organization's bulletin board.

Review of Personnel Processes   The contractor shall periodically review such processes and make any necessary modifications to ensure its obligations are carried out. A description of the review and any modifications should be documented.

Physical and Mental Qualifications   Provides for a schedule of the periodic review of all physical and mental job qualification standards to ensure that to the extent that qualification standards tend to screen out qualified individuals with disabilities, they are job-related for the position in question and are consistent with business necessity.

Reasonable Accommodation to Physical and Mental Limitations   Includes a statement that the contractor will make reasonable accommodation to the known physical or mental limitations of an otherwise qualified individual with a disability unless it can demonstrate that the accommodation would impose an undue hardship on the operation of the business

Harassment   Includes a statement about what the contractor has done to develop and implement procedures to ensure that its employees are not harassed on the basis of disability

External Dissemination of Policy, Outreach, and Positive Recruitment   Includes listing the organization's outreach efforts, including sending written notification of the organization's EEO/AA policy to all subcontractors, vendors, and suppliers. Also requires the contractor to review, on an annual basis, the outreach and recruitment efforts it has taken over the previous 12 months to evaluate their effectiveness in identifying and recruiting qualified protected veterans. If not effective, the contractor shall identify and implement alternative efforts. These assessments are to be retained for a three-year period.

Internal Dissemination of Policy   The contractor outlines its efforts to implement and disseminate its EEO/AA policy internally.

Audit and Reporting System   The contractor describes and documents the audit and reporting system that it designed and implemented to measure the effectiveness of its affirmative action program, among other things.

Responsibility for Implementation   The contractor documents which official of the organization has been assigned responsibility for implementation of the contractor's affirmative action program. His or her identity should appear on all internal and external communications regarding the contractor's affirmative action program.

Training   Describes the efforts made to train all personnel involved in the recruitment, screening, selection, promotion, disciplinary actions, and related processes on the contractor's commitments in the affirmative action program

Other Section 503, Individuals with Disabilities, requirements not included in the AAP, but required by the regulations, include:

Data Collection Analysis   Annual documentation, maintained for a three-year period, of the number of applicants who self-identified as individuals with disabilities, the total number of job openings and the total number of jobs filled, the total number of applicants for all jobs, the number of applicants hired, and the number of individuals with disabilities hired

- Contractors must now invite individuals with disabilities to self-identify as such, at both the pre- and post-offer stages, using the OFCCP's designed form. However, the individual with disability is not *required* to self-identify at any stage.

- Inclusion of the Equal Opportunity Clause in covered purchase orders and subcontracts

- Website accessibility language

- Section 503 and other posters allowing access to the individuals with disabilities AAP for both applicants and employees

- Annual union notification letter/e-mail

- Annual utilization analysis with an OFCCP-determined goal of 7 percent individuals with disabilities per job group

- Required job listing, posting, or ad tagline

- Requirement to track any reasonable accommodation requests by applicants and employees and any resulting action taken

- The contractor shall invite each of its employees to voluntarily inform the contractor whether the employee believes that he or she is an individual with a disability. This invitation shall be extended to employees the first year the contractor becomes subject to these regulations and at five-year intervals thereafter. At least once during the intervening years between these invitations, the contractor must remind its employees that they may voluntarily update their disability status at any time.

Age Discrimination in Employment Act of 1967 (ADEA)

The purpose of the Age Discrimination in Employment Act (ADEA) is to "promote employment of older persons based on their ability rather than age; to prohibit arbitrary age discrimination in employment; to help employers and workers find ways of meeting problems arising from the impact of age on employment."

The ADEA prohibits discrimination against persons 40 years of age or older in employment activities, including hiring, job assignments, training, promotion, compensation, benefits, terminating, or any other privileges, terms, or conditions of employment.

The ADEA applies to private businesses, unions, employment agencies, and state and local governments with more than 20 employees. As with Title VII, the ADEA provides for the following exceptions:

- Bona fide occupational qualifications (BFOQs) that are reasonably necessary to business operations
- The hiring of firefighters or police officers by state or local governments
- Retirement of employees age 65 or older who have been in executive positions for at least two years and are eligible for retirement benefits of at least $44,000 per year
- Retirement of tenured employees of institutions of higher education at age 70
- Discharge or discipline for just cause

Individuals who think they have been subjected to an unlawful employment practice must file charges with the Equal Employment Opportunity Commission (EEOC), which has federal enforcement responsibility for the ADEA, or with the state equal employment agency (if one exists for the location in which the incident occurred). Timely filing of charges is essential for complainants, since the EEOC will not investigate charges that are not made according to the guidelines.

Older Worker Benefit Protection Act Amendment to the ADEA

The Older Worker Benefit Protection Act (OWBPA) amended the ADEA in 1990 to include a prohibition on discrimination against older workers in all employee benefit plans unless any age-based reductions are justified by significant cost considerations. This amendment allows seniority systems as long as they do not require involuntary terminations of employees based on their age and extends ADEA protections to all employee benefits, as well as guidelines for legal severance agreements.

The OWBPA defines the conditions under which employees may waive their rights to make claims under the act. To be acceptable, waivers must include the following components:

- Waiver agreements must be written in a way that can be understood by the average employee.
- Waivers must refer specifically to the rights or claims available under the ADEA.
- Employees may not waive rights or claims for actions that occur subsequent to signing the waiver.
- Employees must receive consideration in exchange for the waiver in addition to anything to which they are already entitled.
- The waiver must advise employees of their right to consult an attorney prior to signing the document.
- In individual cases, employees must be given 21 days to consider the agreement before they are required to sign; when a group of employees is involved, employees age 40 and older must be given 45 days to consider their decision.

- Once the waiver is signed, employees may revoke the agreement within seven days.

- In cases of group terminations (such as a reduction in force or early retirement program), employees must be advised of the eligibility requirements for any exit incentive programs, any time limits for the programs, and a list of the job titles and ages of employees who have been selected or who are eligible for the program.

The federal agency responsible for enforcement of the OWBPA is the EEOC.

Americans with Disabilities Act of 1990 (ADA)

The *Americans with Disabilities Act (ADA)* of 1990 was based in large part on the Rehabilitation Act of 1973 (discussed later in this appendix), and it extended protected class status to qualified persons with disabilities. Employment discrimination is covered by Title I of the Act and identifies covered entities as employment agencies, labor unions, joint labor-management committees, and employers with 15 or more employees (including those who work on a part-time or temporary basis) for each working day in each of 20 weeks in the current or previous calendar year. Excluded from coverage are the federal government and 501(c) private membership clubs. The ADA prohibits discrimination in job application procedures; the hiring, advancement, or discharge of employees; employee compensation; job training; and other terms, conditions, and privileges of employment.

The ADA requires covered entities to make *reasonable accommodation* to develop employment opportunities for qualified persons with disabilities in two areas:

- Facilities should be accessible to persons with disabilities.

- Position requirements may be adjusted to accommodate qualified persons with disabilities.

The ADA allows that accommodations constituting an *undue hardship* to the business are not required and defines undue hardship as an accommodation that places an excessive burden on the employer. The Act identifies the factors to be considered in determining whether an accommodation is an undue hardship by looking at the cost, the financial resources of the organization, the size of the organization, and other similar factors.

In 2008, Congress enacted the ADA Amendments Act of 2008, which took effect on January 1, 2009. According to language in the amendment, Congress took the action to clarify the intention of the original legislation, which was to make the definition of "disability" consistent with the way the courts had defined the term under the Rehabilitation Act of 1973. In fact, court interpretations under the ADA had "narrowed the broad scope of protection" originally intended. The amendment more clearly describes the intent of Congress in the following areas:

Broadly Defines "Disability" A disability is a physical or mental impairment that causes *substantial limitation* to one or more *major life activities* for an individual, a record of impairment for an individual, or an individual who is regarded as being impaired.

Defines "Major Life Activity"   The amendment defines major life activities in two areas: general activities and major bodily functions. Table C.2 lists activities Congress cites in the law as examples but is not meant to be a complete list.

Ignores Mitigating Measures   Congress directs that, except for "ordinary glasses or contact lenses," mitigating measures such as medication, prosthetics, hearing aids, mobility devices, and others may not be used to limit the definition of disability for an individual.

Clarifies the Definition of "Regarded As"   This amendment requires that individuals who are able to demonstrate that they have been the subject of prohibited activities under the ADA, whether or not they actually have some type of impairment, are protected by its requirements.

Explicitly Authorizes the EEOC to Regulate Compliance   The amendment mandates the EEOC to develop and implement regulations and guidance for employers to follow, specifying the inclusion of a definition for "substantially limits" that is consistent with the intent of Congress in the legislation.

Prohibits "Reverse Discrimination" Claims   The amendment clearly states that individuals without disability may not use the ADA to file claims of discrimination when disabled individuals receive favorable employment actions.

A key element of ADA compliance is the requirement to engage in an interactive process with disabled individuals requesting a reasonable accommodation that will enable them to perform essential job functions.

TABLE C.2   Major life activities

General activities	Major bodily functions
Caring for oneself, performing manual tasks, seeing, hearing, eating, sleeping, breathing, learning, reading, concentrating, thinking, communicating, working	Functions of the immune system; normal cell growth; and functions of the digestive, bowel, bladder, neurological, brain, respiratory, circulatory, endocrine, and reproductive systems

Civil Rights Act of 1964 (Title VII)

Title VII of the Civil Rights Act of 1964 introduced the concepts of *protected classes* and *unlawful employment practices* to American businesses. Unlawful employment practices are those that have an adverse impact on members of a protected class, which is a group of people who share common characteristics and are protected from discriminatory practices. Title VII established the basis for two types of unlawful practices: disparate treatment and disparate impact. *Disparate treatment* happens when employers treat some candidates or employees differently, such as requiring women to take a driving test when they apply for a job but not requiring men to take the test when they apply for the same job. Practices that have a *disparate impact* on members of protected classes seem fair on their face but result in adverse impact on members of protected classes, such as requiring all candidates for firefighter positions to be a certain height. Although the requirement applies to all candidates equally, some Asian and female candidates who might otherwise qualify for the position might be eliminated because they are generally shorter than male candidates of other races.

The Act identified five protected classes: race, color, religion, national origin, and sex. It also defined the following unlawful employment practices:

- Discriminatory recruiting, selection, or hiring actions
- Discriminatory compensation or benefit practices
- Discriminatory access to training or apprenticeship programs
- Discriminatory practices in any other terms or conditions of employment

Legitimate seniority, merit, and piece-rate payment systems are allowable under Title VII as long as they do not intentionally discriminate against protected classes.

Title VII allowed for limited exceptions to its requirements, some of which are listed here:

- *Bona fide occupational qualifications (BFOQs)* occur when religion, sex, or national origin is "reasonably necessary to the normal operation" of the business.
- Educational institutions were not originally subject to Title VII.
- Religious organizations may give preference to members of that religion.
- A potential employee who is unable to obtain, or loses, a national security clearance required for the position is not protected.
- Indian reservations may give preference to Indian applicants and employees living on or near the reservation.

Title VII created the Equal Employment Opportunity Commission (EEOC) with a mandate to promote equal employment opportunity, educate employers, provide technical assistance, and study and report on its activities to Congress and the American people. The EEOC is the enforcement agency for Title VII and other discrimination legislation.

Amendments to Title VII

Title VII was amended in 1972, 1978, and 1991 to clarify and expand its coverage.

Equal Employment Opportunity Act of 1972

Created in 1972, the Equal Employment Opportunity Act (EEOA) provides litigation authority to the EEOC in the event that an acceptable conciliation agreement cannot be reached. In those cases, the EEOC is empowered to sue nongovernmental entities, including employers, unions, and employment agencies.

The EEOA extended coverage of Title VII to entities that had been excluded in 1964:

- Educational institutions
- State and local governments
- The federal government

In addition, the EEOA reduced the number of employees needed to subject an employer to coverage by Title VII from 25 to 15 and required employers to keep records of the discovery of any unlawful employment practices and provide those records to the EEOC upon request.

The EEOA also provided administrative guidance for the processing of complaints by providing that employers be notified within 10 days of receipt of a charge by the EEOC and that findings be issued within 120 days of the charge being filed. The EEOC was empowered to sue employers, unions, and employment agencies in the event that an acceptable conciliation agreement could not be reached within 30 days of notice to the employer. The EEOA also provided protection from retaliatory employment actions against whistle-blowers.

Pregnancy Discrimination Act of 1978

Congress amended Title VII with the Pregnancy Discrimination Act of 1978 to clarify that discrimination against women on the basis of pregnancy, childbirth, or any related medical condition is an unlawful employment practice. The Act specified that pregnant employees should receive the same treatment and benefits as employees with any other short-term disability.

Civil Rights Act of 1991

The Civil Rights Act (CRA) of 1991 contained amendments that affected Title VII, the Age Discrimination in Employment Act (ADEA), and the Americans with Disabilities Act (ADA) in response to issues raised by the courts in several cases that were brought by employees based on Title VII.

The purpose of the Civil Rights Act (CRA) of 1991, as described in the Act itself, is fourfold:

1. To provide appropriate remedies for intentional discrimination and unlawful harassment in the workplace
2. To codify the concepts of "business necessity" and "job relatedness" articulated by the Supreme Court in *Griggs vs. Duke Power Co.* and in other Supreme Court decisions
3. To confirm statutory authority and provide statutory guidelines for the adjudication of disparate impact suits under Title VII of the Civil Rights Act of 1964
4. To respond to recent decisions of the Supreme Court by expanding the scope of relevant civil rights statutes in order to provide adequate protection to victims of discrimination

Amendments contained in the CRA affected Title VII, the ADEA, and the ADA. One of the issues addressed is that of disparate impact, first introduced by the *Griggs vs. Duke*

Power Co. case in 1971. Disparate impact occurs when an employment practice, which appears on its face to be fair, unintentionally discriminates against members of a protected class. The CRA places the burden of proof for discrimination complaints on the complainant when there is a job-related business necessity for employment actions. When an individual alleges multiple discriminatory acts, each practice in itself must be discriminatory unless the employer's decision-making process cannot be separated, in which case the individual may challenge the decision-making process itself. The CRA also provides additional relief for victims of intentional discrimination and harassment, codifies the concept of disparate impact, and addresses Supreme Court rulings over the previous few years that had weakened equal employment opportunity laws.

The CRA made the following changes to Title VII:

- Provided punitive damages when employers engage in discriminatory practices "with malice or with reckless indifference"
- Excluded back pay awards from compensatory damages
- Established a sliding scale for compensatory and punitive damages based on company size
- Provided that any party to a civil suit in which punitive or compensatory damages are sought may demand a jury trial
- Expanded Title VII to include congressional employees and some senior political appointees
- Required that the individual alleging that an unlawful employment practice is in use prove that it results in disparate impact to members of a protected class
- Provided that job relatedness and reasonable business necessity are defenses to disparate impact and that if a business can show that the practice does not result in disparate impact, it need not show the practice to be a business necessity
- Provided that business necessity is not a defense against an intentional discriminatory employment practice
- Established that if discrimination was a motivating factor in an employment practice it was unlawful even if other factors contributed to the practice
- Allowed that if the same employment decision would have been made whether or not an impermissible motivating factor was present, no damages would be awarded
- Expanded coverage to include foreign operations of American businesses unless compliance would constitute violation of the laws of the host country

Common Law Doctrines

Common law doctrines are the result of legal decisions made by judges in cases adjudicated over a period of centuries. A number of doctrines have implications for employment relationships, the most common of which is the concept of *employment at will*. Other common law issues that affect employment relationships are *respondeat superior*, constructive discharge, and defamation.

Employment at Will

In *Payne vs. The Western & Atlantic Railroad Company* in 1884, Justice Ingersoll of the Tennessee Supreme Court defined employment at will in this way: "...either party may terminate the service, for any cause, good or bad, or without cause, and the other cannot complain in law." This definition allowed employers to change employment conditions, whether it was to hire, transfer, promote, or terminate an employee, at their sole discretion. It also allowed employees to leave a job at any time, with or without notice. In the absence of a legally enforceable employment contract, this definition was unaltered for more than 70 years.

Although there have always been exceptions to at-will employment based on employment contracts, beginning in 1959 the doctrine began to be eroded by both court decisions and statutes. This erosion resulted in several exceptions to the at-will concept, including public policy exceptions, the application of the doctrine of good faith and fair dealing to employment relationships, and the concepts of promissory estoppel and fraudulent misrepresentation.

Contract Exceptions

Employment at will intentions may be abrogated by contracts, either express or implied. An *express contract* can be a verbal or written agreement in which the parties state exactly what they agree to do. Employers have been known to express their gratitude for a job well done with promises of continued employment, such as "Keep doing that kind of work and you have a job for life" or "You'll have a job as long as we're in business." Statements such as these can invalidate the at-will doctrine.

An *implied contract* can be created by an employer's conduct and need not be specifically stated. For example, an employer's consistent application of a progressive discipline policy can create an implied contract that an employee will not be terminated without first going through the steps set forth by the policy. A disclaimer can offset the effects of an implied contract; however, there is little agreement in the courts as to what and how the disclaimer must be presented in order to maintain at-will status.

Statutory Exceptions

The at-will doctrine has been further eroded by legislation. At-will employment may not be used as a pretext for terminating employees for discriminatory reasons as set forth in equal opportunity legislation or other legislation designed to protect employee rights.

Public Policy Exceptions

Erosion of the doctrine of at-will employment began in 1959 when the California Court of Appeals heard *Petermann vs. International Brotherhood of Teamsters*, in which

Mr. Petermann, a business agent for the union, alleged that he was terminated for refusing to commit perjury on behalf of the union at a legislative hearing. The court held that it is "...obnoxious to the interest of state and contrary to public policy and sound morality to allow an employer to discharge any employee, whether the employment be for a designated or unspecified duration, on the ground that the employee declined to commit perjury, an act specifically enjoined by statute."

The public policy exception to employment at will was initially applied conservatively by the courts, but over time, its application has been expanded. In general, the public policy exception has been applied in four areas. The first is exemplified by the *Petermann* case—an employee who refuses to break the law on behalf of the employer can claim a public policy exception. The second application covers employees who report illegal acts of their employers (whistle-blowers); the third covers employees who participate in activities supported by public policy, such as cooperating in a government investigation of wrongdoing by the employer. Finally, the public policy exception covers employees who are acting in accordance with legal statute, such as attending jury duty or filing a workers' compensation claim.

While the public policy exception to at will employment originated in California, it has been adopted by many, although not all, states.

Duty of Good Faith and Fair Dealing

This tenet of common law provides that parties to a contract have an obligation to act in a fair and honest manner with each other to ensure that benefits of the contract may be realized. The application of this doctrine to at-will employment issues varies widely from state-to-state. The Texas Supreme Court, for example, has determined that there is no duty for good faith and fair dealing in employment contracts. On the other hand, the Alaska Supreme Court has determined that the duty is implied in at-will employment situations.

Promissory Estoppel

Promissory estoppel occurs when an employer entices an employee (or prospective employee) to take an action by promising a reward. The employee takes the action, but the employer does not follow through on the reward. For example, an employer promises a job to a candidate who resigns another position to accept the new one and then finds the offered position has been withdrawn. If a promise is clear, specific, and reasonable, and an employee acts on the promise, the employer may be required to follow through on the promised reward or pay equivalent damages.

Fraudulent Misrepresentation

Similar to promissory estoppel, fraudulent misrepresentation relates to promises or claims made by employers to entice candidates to join the company. An example of this might be a company that decides to close one of its locations in six months but, in the meantime, needs to hire a general manager to run the operation. If, when asked about the future of the company during the recruiting process, the company tells candidates that the plant will be expanded in the future and withholds its intention to close the plant, the company would be fraudulently misrepresenting the facts about the position.

Respondeat Superior

The Latin meaning of *respondeat superior* is "let the master answer." What this means is that an employer can be held liable for actions of its employees that occur within the scope and course of assigned duties or responsibilities in the course of their employment, regardless of whether the act is negligent or reckless. This concept has implications for many employment situations; one is sexual harassment, which will be discussed later in this appendix. Another could be an auto accident where a third party is injured when an employee hits another vehicle while driving an employer's delivery truck. *Respondeat superior* could also come into play if a manager promised additional vacation time to a candidate and the candidate accepted the position based on the promise. Even if the promise was not in writing and was outside the employer's normal vacation policy, and the manager made the promise without prior approval, the employer could be required to provide the benefit based on this doctrine.

Constructive Discharge

Constructive discharge occurs when an employer makes the workplace so hostile and inhospitable that an employee resigns. In many states, this gives the employee a cause of action against the employer. The legal standard that must be met varies widely between the states, with some requiring the employee to show that the employer intended to force the resignation, and others requiring the employee to show only that the conditions were sufficiently intolerable that a reasonable person would feel compelled to resign.

Defamation

Accusations of defamation in employment relationships most often occur during or after termination. Defamation is a communication that damages an individual's reputation in the community, preventing the person from obtaining employment or other benefits. When an employer, out of spite or with a vengeful intent, sets out to deliberately damage a former employee, the result is malicious defamation.

Concerns about defamation have caused many employers to stop giving meaningful references for former employees, in many cases responding to reference requests only with dates of employment and the individual's last title. Employers are generally protected by the concept of "qualified privilege" if the information provided is job-related, truthful, clear, and unequivocal. Obtaining written authorization prior to providing references and limiting responses to the information being requested without volunteering additional information can reduce the risks of being accused of defamation.

Copyright Act of 1976

The use of musical, literary, and other original works without permission of the owner of the copyright is prohibited under most circumstances. The copyright owner is the author of the work with two exceptions. The first is that an employer who hires employees to create original works as part of their normal job duties is the owner of the copyright because the employer paid for the work to be done. The second exception is that the copyright for work created by a freelance author, artist, or musician who has been commissioned to create the work by someone else is owned by the person who commissioned the work. These exceptions are known as *work-for-hire* exceptions.

For trainers who want to use the work of others during training sessions, two circumstances do not require permission. The first is related to works that are in the *public domain*. Copyrights protect original works for the life of the author plus 70 years; after that, the works may be used without permission. Works-for-hire are protected for the shorter of 95 years from the first year of publication or 120 years from the year of creation.

Other works in the public domain include those produced as part of the job duties of federal officials and those for which copyright protection has expired. Some works published without notice of copyright before January 1, 1978, or those published between then and March 1, 1989, are also considered to be in the public domain.

The second circumstance for use of published works without permission is known as the *fair use doctrine*. The Act specifies that use of a work for the purposes of criticism, commentary, news reporting, or teaching (including multiple copies for classroom use, scholarship, or research) is not an infringement, depending on four factors:

- **The purpose and character of the use:** Is it to be used for a profit or for a nonprofit educational purpose?
- **The nature of the work itself:** Is it a work of fiction? Or is it based on facts? How much creativity did it require?
- **The amount of work:** How much of the work (one copy or 50?) or what portion (a paragraph or an entire chapter?) will be used?
- **The effect:** What effect will the use of the material have on the potential market value of the copyrighted work?

Permission for the use of copyright-protected material that is outside the fair use exceptions can generally be obtained by contacting the author or publisher of the work.

Davis-Bacon Act of 1931

The Davis-Bacon Act was the first federal legislation to regulate minimum wages. It requires that construction contractors and their subcontractors pay at least the prevailing wage for the local area in which they are operating if they receive federal funds. Employers with federal construction contracts of $2,000 or more must adhere to the Davis-Bacon Act.

Drug-Free Workplace Act of 1988

The Drug-Free Workplace Act of 1988 applies to businesses with federal contracts of $100,000 or more each year. Contractors subject to the Act must take the following steps to be in compliance:

Develop and publish a written policy.   Contractors must develop a written policy clearly stating that they provide a drug-free workplace and that illegal substance abuse isn't an acceptable practice in the workplace. The policy must clearly state what substances are covered and the consequences for violating the policy.

Establish an awareness program.   The employer must develop a program to educate employees about the policy, communicate the dangers of drug abuse in the workplace, discuss the employer's policy, inform employees of the availability of counseling or other programs to reduce drug use, and notify employees of the penalties for violating the policy. The program can be delivered through a variety of media—seminars, brochures, videos, web-based training—whatever methods will most effectively communicate the information in the specific environment.

Notify employees about contract conditions.   Employees must be made aware that a condition of their employment on a federal contract project is that they abide by the policy and inform the employer within five days if they're convicted of a criminal drug offense in the workplace.

Notify the contracting agency of violations.   If an employee is convicted of a criminal drug offense in the workplace, the employer must notify the contracting agency within 10 days of being informed of the conviction by the employee.

Establish penalties for illegal drug convictions.   The employer must have an established penalty for any employees convicted of relevant drug offenses. Within 30 days of notice by an employee of a conviction, the employer must take appropriate disciplinary action against the employee or require participation in an appropriate drug-rehabilitation program. Any penalties must be in accordance with requirements of the Rehabilitation Act of 1973.

Maintain a drug-free workplace.   Contractors must make a good-faith effort to maintain a drug-free workplace in accordance with the Act, or they're subject to penalties, including suspension of payments under the contract, suspension or termination of the contract, or exclusion from consideration from future contracts for a period of up to five years.

EEO Survey

Working together, the Equal Employment Opportunity Commission (EEOC) and the Office of Federal Contract Compliance Programs developed a reporting format designed to meet statistical reporting requirements for both agencies. This form, known as the EEO-1 survey or report, must be filed on or before September 30 of each year using employment data from one pay period in July, August, or September of the current survey year. All employers who meet the following criteria must complete the report:

- All federal contractors who are private employers and (a) are not exempt as provided by 41 CFR Section 60-1.5; (b) have 50 or more employees; *and* (i) are prime contractors or first-tier subcontractors, and have a contract, subcontract, or purchase order amounting to $50,000 or more, or (ii) serve as a depository of government funds in any amount, or (iii) are a financial institution that is an issuing and paying agent for U.S. Savings Bonds. Only those establishments located in the District of Columbia and the 50 states are required to submit. No reports should be filed for establishments in Puerto Rico, the Virgin Islands, or other American protectorates.

- All private employers who are subject to Title VII of the Civil Rights Act of 1964, as amended, with 100 or more employees.

Exceptions to the EEO-1 reporting requirements include:

- State and local governments
- Primary and secondary school systems
- Institutions of higher education
- Indian tribes
- Tax-exempt private membership clubs (other than labor organizations)

The preferred method for filing the EEO-1 survey is through the online filing application. Refer to the EEOC website at www.eeoc.gov for information on how to file the EEO-1 survey.

- Starting with the EEO-1 report of 2017 data, the "workforce snapshot period" will be October 1 to December 31, 2017. In other words, each employer may choose any pay period during this three-month "workforce snapshot period" to count its full-time and part-time employees for the EEO-1 report. To give employers more time to make the transition and to allow for alignment with the W-2 reporting cycle, the EEO-1 deadline for the 2017 report will be March 31, 2018. Employers will have a total of 18 months from October 1, 2016, to March 31, 2018 (2017 report deadline) to make the change.

Report Types

Employers with operations at a single location or establishment complete a single form, whereas those who operate at more than one location or establishment must file employment data on multiple forms.

Headquarters Report   All multiple-establishment employers must file a Headquarters Report, which is a report covering the principal or headquarters office.

Establishment Report   Locations with 50 or more employees file a separate Establishment Report for each location employing 50 or more persons.

Locations with fewer than 50 employees may be reported on an Establishment Report or on an Establishment List. The Establishment List provides the name, address, and total number of employees for each location with fewer than 50 employees along with an employment data grid combining this data by race, sex, and job category.

Consolidated Report   Data from all the individual location reports and the headquarters report are combined on the Consolidated Report. The total number of employees on this report must be equal to data submitted on all the individual reports.

Parent corporations that own a majority interest in another corporation report data for employees at all locations, including those of the subsidiary establishments.

Race and Ethnicity Categories

Employers are required to report on seven categories of employees:

- Hispanic or Latino
- White
- Black or African American
- Native Hawaiian or Other Pacific Islander
- Asian
- American Indian or Alaska Native
- Two or More Races (not Hispanic or Latino)

Job Categories

The EEO-1 report requires employers to group jobs into job categories based on the average skill level, knowledge, and responsibility of positions within their organizations:

- Executive/senior-level officials and managers
- Midlevel officials and managers
- Professionals
- Technicians
- Sales workers
- Administrative support workers
- Craft workers
- Operatives
- Laborers and helpers
- Service workers

Data Reporting

Beginning with the 2017 reporting period (October 1, 2017 to March 31, 2018), for private employers and federal contractors with 100 or more employees, the EEO-1 report will require additional reporting components of employment data. These reports include:

Employee Report   Total employees in the workforce snapshot for each job category and pay band

Pay Report   W-2 Box 1 earnings for all employees identified in the workforce snapshot

Hours Worked Report   Hours worked for all employees in the snapshot in their job category and pay band

The 12 pay bands are:

- $19,239 and under
- $19,240–$24,439
- $24,440–$30,679
- $30,680–$38,999
- $39,000–$49,919
- $49,920–$62,919
- $62,920–$80,079
- $80,080–$101,919
- $101,920–$128,959
- $128,960–$163,799
- $163,800–$207,999
- $208,000 and over

Employment Retirement Income Security Act of 1974 (ERISA)

The Employment Retirement Income Security Act (ERISA) was created by Congress to set standards for private pensions and some group welfare programs such as medical and life insurance. In July 2016, the Department of Labor, Internal Revenue Service, and Pension Benefit Guaranty Corporation proposed changes that, if accepted, will require plan sponsors and providers to comply with updated reporting requirements in 2019. While not accepted as of this writing, it will be important to watch for changes.

ERISA requires organizations to file three types of reports: a summary plan description, an annual report, and reports to individual participants of their benefit rights.

Summary Plan Description (SPD)

A *summary plan description (SPD)* provides plan participants with information about the provisions, policies, and rules established by the plan and advises them on actions they can take in utilizing the plan. ERISA requires that the SPD include the name and other identifying information about plan sponsors, administrators, and trustees, along with any information related to collective bargaining agreements for the plan participants. The SPD must describe what eligibility requirements must be met for participating in the plan and for receiving benefits, as well as the circumstances under which participants would be disqualified or ineligible for participation or be denied benefits.

The SPD must also describe the financing source for the plan and the name of the organization providing benefits. Information on the end of the plan year and whether records are maintained on a calendar, plan, or fiscal year basis must be included in the description.

For health and welfare plans, the SPD must describe claim procedures, along with the name of the U.S. Department of Labor (DOL) office that will assist participants and beneficiaries with Health Insurance Portability and Accountability Act (HIPAA) claims. The SPD must also describe what remedies are available when claims are denied.

A new SPD reflecting all changes made must be prepared and distributed every five years unless no changes have occurred. Every 10 years, a new SPD must be distributed to participants whether or not changes have occurred.

Annual Reports

ERISA requires annual reports to be filed for all employee benefit plans. The reports must include financial statements, the number of employees in the plan, and the names and addresses of the plan fiduciaries. ERISA mandates that any persons compensated by the plan (such as an accountant) during the preceding year be disclosed, along with the amount of compensation paid to each, the nature of the services rendered, and any relationship that exists between these parties and any party in interest to the plan. Information that is provided with regard to plan assets must be certified by the organization that holds the assets, whether it is the plan sponsor, an insurance company, or a bank.

The annual reports must be audited by a CPA or other qualified public accountant, and any actuarial reports must be prepared by an enrolled actuary who has been licensed jointly by the Department of the Treasury and the Department of Labor to provide actuarial services for U.S. pension plans.

The DOL is given authority to simplify filing and reporting requirements for plans with less than 100 participants.

Once submitted, annual reports and other documents become public record and are made available in the DOL public document room. The DOL may also use this information to conduct research and analyze data.

Participant Benefit Rights Reports

Participants may request a report of the total benefits accrued on their behalf along with the amount of the benefit that is nonforfeitable. If there are no nonforfeitable amounts accrued at the time the report is requested, the earliest date that benefits will become non-forfeitable must be provided. Participants are entitled to receive the report no more than once per year.

ERISA records must be maintained for six years from the date they were due to be filed with the DOL. In addition to requiring the preparation of these reports, ERISA regulations stipulate that annual reports are to be filed with the DOL within 210 days of the end of the plan year. The DOL may reject reports that are incomplete or that contain qualified opinions from the CPA or actuary. Rejected plans must be resubmitted within 45 days, or the DOL can retain a CPA to audit the report on behalf of the participants. ERISA authorizes the DOL to bring civil actions on behalf of plan participants if necessary to resolve any issues.

In addition to the reporting requirements, ERISA sets minimum standards for employee participation or eligibility requirements, as well as vesting requirements for qualified pension plans.

Employee Participation

A participant is an employee who has met the eligibility requirements for the plan. The law sets minimum participation requirements as follows:

- When one year of service has been completed or the employee has reached the age of 21, whichever is later, unless the plan provides for 100 percent vesting after two years of service. In that case, the requirement changes to completion of two years of service or reaching age 21, whichever is later.

- Employees may not be excluded from the plan on the basis of age; that is, they may not be excluded because they have reached a specified age.

- When employees have met the minimum service and age requirements, they must become participants no later than the first day of the plan year after they meet the requirement, or six months after the requirements are met, whichever is earlier.

Vesting

Qualified plans must also meet minimum vesting standards. Vesting refers to the point at which employees own the contributions their employer has made to the pension plan whether or not they remain employed with the company. The vesting requirements established by ERISA refer only to funds that are contributed by the employer; any funds contributed by plan participants are owned by the employee. Employees are always 100 percent vested in their own money but must earn the right to be vested in the employer's contribution.

Vesting may be immediate or delayed. Immediate vesting occurs when employees are 100 percent, or fully, vested as soon as they meet the eligibility requirements of the plan. Delayed vesting occurs when participants must wait for a defined period of time prior to becoming fully vested. There are two types of delayed vesting: cliff vesting and graded vesting:

- With cliff vesting, participants become 100 percent vested after a specified period of time. ERISA sets the maximum period at five years for qualified plans, which means that participants are zero percent vested until they have completed the five years of service, after which they are fully vested.

- Graded vesting, which is also referred to as graduated or gradual vesting, establishes a vesting schedule that provides for partial vesting each year for a specified number of years. A graded vesting schedule in a qualified plan must allow for at least 20 percent vesting after three years and 20 percent per year after that, with participants achieving full vesting after seven years of service. See Table C.3 for a graded vesting schedule that complies with ERISA requirements.

TABLE C.3   ERISA graded vesting schedule

Years of service	Percent vested
3	20 percent
4	40 percent
5	60 percent
6	80 percent
7	100 percent

Benefit Accrual Requirements

ERISA sets specific requirements for determining how much of an accrued benefit participants are entitled to receive if they leave the company prior to retirement. Plans must account for employee contributions to the plan separately from the funds contributed by the employer since the employees are entitled to all the funds contributed by them to the plan when they leave the company.

Form and Payment of Benefits

ERISA sets forth specific requirements for the payment of funds when participants either reach retirement age or leave the company. The act also provides guidance for employers to deal with qualified domestic relations orders (QDROs), which are legal orders issued by state courts or other state agencies to require pension payments to alternate payees. An alternate payee must be a spouse, former spouse, child, or other dependent of a plan participant.

ERISA also defines funding requirements for pension plans and sets standards for those who are responsible for safeguarding the funds until they are paid to employees. Finally, ERISA provides civil and criminal penalties for organizations that violate its provisions.

Funding

An enrolled actuary determines how much money is required to fund the accrued obligations of the plan, and ERISA requires that these funds be maintained in trust accounts separate from business's operating funds. These amounts must be deposited on a quarterly basis; the final contribution must be made no later than eight and a half months after the end of the plan year.

Fiduciary Responsibility

For purposes of ERISA, a fiduciary is a person, corporation, or other legal entity that holds property or assets on behalf of, or in trust for, the pension fund. ERISA requires fiduciaries to operate pension funds in the best interests of the participants and their beneficiaries and at the lowest possible expense to them. All actions taken with regard to the plan assets must be in accord with the prudent person standard of care, a common law concept that requires all actions be undertaken with "the care, skill, prudence, and diligence...that a prudent man acting in like capacity" would use, as defined in ERISA itself.

Fiduciaries may be held personally liable for losses to the plan resulting from any breach of fiduciary responsibility that they commit and may be required to make restitution for the losses and be subject to legal action. They are not held liable for breaches of fiduciary responsibility that occur prior to the time they became fiduciaries.

ERISA specifically prohibits transactions between pension plans and parties in interest.

Administration and Enforcement

Criminal penalties for willful violations of ERISA include fines of between $5,000 and $100,000 and imprisonment for up to one year. Civil actions may be brought by plan participants or their beneficiaries, by fiduciaries, or by the DOL to recover benefits or damages or to force compliance with the law.

Amendments to ERISA

Amendments to ERISA include COBRA and HIPAA.

Consolidated Omnibus Budget Reconciliation Act of 1986 (COBRA)

Prior to 1986, employees who were laid off or resigned from their jobs lost any health-care benefits that were provided as part of those jobs. ERISA was amended in 1986 by the Consolidated Omnibus Budget Reconciliation Act (COBRA), which requires businesses with 20 or more employees to provide health plan continuation coverage under certain circumstances. Employers who meet this requirement must continue benefits for those who leave the company or for their dependents when certain qualifying events occur.

Employers must notify employees of the availability of COBRA coverage when they enter the plan and again within 30 days of the occurrence of a qualifying event. Table C.4 shows the qualifying events that trigger COBRA, as well as the length of time coverage must be continued for each event.

TABLE C.4   COBRA qualifying events and coverage requirements

Qualifying event	Length of coverage
Employee death	36 months
Divorce or legal separation	36 months
Dependent child no longer covered	36 months
Reduction in hours	18 months
Reduction in hours when disabled*	29 months
Employee termination	18 months
Employee termination when disabled*	29 months
Eligibility for SSA benefits	18 months
Termination for gross misconduct	0 months

*An employee who is disabled within 60 days of a reduction in hours or a termination becomes eligible for an additional 11 months of COBRA coverage.

Employers may charge COBRA participants a maximum of 102 percent of the group premium for coverage and must include them in any open enrollment periods or other changes to the plans. Employers may discontinue COBRA coverage if payments are not received within 30 days of the time they are due.

Employees must notify the employer within 60 days of a divorce, a separation, or the loss of a child's dependent status. Employees who fail to provide this notice risk the loss of continued coverage.

Health Insurance Portability and Accountability Act of 1996 (HIPAA)

The Health Insurance Portability and Accountability Act (HIPAA) was another amendment to ERISA and prohibits discrimination on the basis of health status as evidenced by an individual's medical condition or history, claims experience, utilization of healthcare services, disability, or evidence of insurability. It also places limits on health insurance restrictions for preexisting conditions, which are defined as conditions for which treatment was given within six months of enrollment in the plan. Insurers may exclude those conditions from coverage for 12 months or, in the case of a late enrollment, for 18 months.

Insurers may discontinue an employer's group coverage only if the employer neglects to pay the premiums, obtained the policy through fraudulent or intentional misrepresentation, or does not comply with material provisions of the plan. Group coverage may also be discontinued if the insurer is no longer offering coverage in the employer's geographic area, if none of the plan participants reside in the plan's network area, or if the employer fails to renew a collective bargaining agreement or to comply with its provisions.

In April 2001, the Department of Health and Human Services (HHS) issued privacy regulations that were required by HIPAA. The regulations defined protected health information (PHI), patient information that must be kept private, including physical or mental conditions, information about healthcare given, and payments that have been made. Although these regulations were directed at covered entities that conduct business electronically, such as health plans, healthcare providers, and clearinghouses, they have had a significant impact on the way employers handle information related to employee health benefits. Many employers had to redesign forms for open enrollment periods and new hires, and update plan documents and company benefit policies to reflect the changes. The regulations have an impact on employers in other ways as well.

Although flexible spending accounts (FSAs) are exempt from other HIPAA requirements, they are considered group health plans for privacy reasons, so employers who sponsor FSAs must comply with the privacy requirements for them.

Employers who are self-insured or who have fully insured group health plans and receive protected health information are required to develop privacy policies that comply with the regulations, appoint a privacy official, and train employees to handle information appropriately.

Although the HIPAA regulations do not prevent employees from seeking assistance from HR for claim problems or other issues with the group health plan, they do require employees to provide the insurance provider or third-party administrator with an authorization to release information about the claim to the HR department.

The new regulations include stiff civil and criminal sanctions for violations; civil penalties of $100 per violation and up to $25,000 per person each year can be assessed. There are three levels of criminal penalties:

- A conviction for obtaining or disclosing PHI can result in a fine of up to $50,000 and one year in prison.

- Obtaining PHI under false pretenses can result in fines of up to $100,000 and five years in prison.

- Obtaining or disclosing PHI with the intent of selling, transferring, or using it to obtain commercial advantage or personal gain can be punished with a fine of up to $250,000 and 10 years in prison.

Executive Orders

Executive orders (EOs) are presidential proclamations that, when published in the Federal Register, become law after 30 days. EOs have been used to ensure that equal employment opportunities are afforded by federal agencies and private businesses that contract or sub-contract with those agencies. Certain executive orders relating to equal employment issues are enforced by the OFCCP.

Executive Order 11246, amended by 11375, 13279, and 13672   Executive Order 11246, established in 1965, prohibits employment discrimination on the basis of race, color, religion, sex, sexual orientation, gender identity, or national origin and requires affirmative steps be taken in advertising jobs, recruiting, employing, training, promotion, compensating, and terminating employees. Executive Order 13279 limits the impact of this executive order on religious corporations, associations, educational institutions, or societies in certain situations. Executive Order 11246 applies to federal contractors and federally assisted construction contractors and subcontractors who meet certain thresholds. See the section on affirmative action plans (AAPs) for additional information on the requirements for this executive order.

Executive Order 11478, Amended by 13087, 13152, and 13672   This order, written in 1969, prohibits discrimination against federal government employees on the basis of race, color, religion, sex, sexual orientation, gender identity, status as a parent, national origin, handicap, or age.

Executive Order 12138   In 1979, with the implementation of EO 12138, the National Women's Business Enterprise policy was created. This EO also required federal contractors and subcontractors to take affirmative steps to promote and support women's business enterprises.

Executive Order 12989, Amended by 13286 and 13465   This order requires contractors with qualifying federal contracts to electronically verify employment authorization of: (1) all employees hired during the contract term, and (2) all employees performing work in the

United States on contracts with a Federal Acquisition Regulation (FAR) E-Verify clause. A federal contractor may be exempt from these clauses if any of the following apply:

- The contract is for fewer than 120 days.
- It is valued at less than $150,000, the simplified acquisition threshold.
- All work is performed outside the United States.
- It includes only commercially available off-the-shelf (COTS) items and related services.

The E-Verify rule does not extend beyond the United States, applying only to employees working in the United States, which includes the 50 states, the District of Columbia, Guam, Puerto Rico, the U.S. Virgin Islands, and the Commonwealth of the Northern Mariana Islands (CNMI).

Fair Credit Reporting Act of 1970 (FCRA)

The FCRA was first enacted in 1970 and has been amended several times since then, most recently with the Fair and Accurate Credit Transactions (FACT) Act in 2003. Enforced by the Federal Trade Commission (FTC), the FCRA requires employers to take certain actions prior to the use of a consumer report or an investigative consumer report obtained through a consumer reporting agency (CRA) for use in making employment decisions.

Familiarity with three terms is valuable for understanding why these consumer protection laws are important for HR practitioners:

- A consumer reporting agency (CRA) is an individual, business, or nonprofit association that gathers information about individuals with the intent of supplying that information to a third party.
- A consumer report is a written document produced by a CRA containing information about an individual's character, reputation, lifestyle, or credit history for use by an employer in determining that person's suitability for employment.
- An investigative consumer report is a written document produced by a CRA for the same purpose as a consumer report but is based on information gathered through personal interviews with friends, coworkers, employers, and others who are acquainted with the individual.

The FCRA established the following four-step process for employers to follow when using CRAs to perform background investigations:

1. A clear and conspicuous disclosure that a consumer report may be obtained for employment purposes must be made in writing to the candidate before the report is acquired.
2. The candidate must provide written authorization for the employer to obtain the report.
3. Before taking an adverse action based in whole or in part on the credit report, either the employer must provide the candidate with a copy of the report and a copy of the

FTC notice, "A Summary of Your Rights Under the Fair Credit Reporting Act," or, if the application was made by mail, telephone, computer, or similar means, the employer must notify the candidate within three business days that adverse action is being taken based in whole or in part on the credit report. This notice must provide the name, address, and telephone number of the CRA and indicate that the CRA did not take the adverse action and cannot provide the reasons for the action to the candidate. If a candidate requests a copy of the report, the employer must provide it within three days, along with a copy of the FTC notice just described.

4. Candidates must be advised of their right to dispute the accuracy of information contained in the report.

When employers request investigative consumer reports on candidates, they must comply with these additional steps:

- Provide written disclosure of its intent to the candidate within three days of requesting the report from a CRA.

- Include a summary of the candidate's FCRA rights with the written notice.

- Advise the candidate that he or she has a right to request information about the type and extent of the investigation.

- If requested, provide complete disclosure of the type and extent of the report within the later of five days of the request or receipt of the report.

The FCRA was amended in 2003 by the Fair and Accurate Credit Transactions (FACT) Act of 2003. Designed to improve the accuracy of consumer credit information, it gives consumers one free credit report per year. The Act also requires disclosure to consumers who are subject to risk-based pricing (less favorable credit offers) or who are denied credit altogether because of a credit-related record.

FACT describes "reasonable measures" for destroying credit reports, depending on the medium:

- Paper documents must be shredded, pulverized, or burned in a way that prevents them from being reassembled.

- Electronic files or media must be erased in a way that prevents them from being reconstructed.

- Either type may be destroyed by an outside vendor once the employer has conducted due diligence research to ensure the vendor's methods are reliable.

Fair Labor Standards Act of 1938 (FLSA)

Enacted in 1938, the Fair Labor Standards Act (FLSA) today remains a major influence on basic compensation issues for businesses in the United States. FLSA regulations apply to workers who are not already covered by another law. For example, railroad and airline employers are subject to wage and hour requirements of the Railway Labor Act, so the FLSA does not apply to their employees.

There are two categories of employers subject to the requirements of the FLSA: enterprise and individual. Enterprise coverage applies to businesses employing at least two employees with at least $500,000 in annual sales and to hospitals, schools, and government agencies. Individual coverage applies to organizations whose daily work involves interstate commerce. The FLSA defines interstate commerce so broadly that it includes those who have regular contact by telephone with out-of-state customers, vendors, or suppliers; on that basis, it covers virtually all employers in the United States.

The FLSA established requirements in five key areas to HRM:

- It introduced a minimum wage for all covered employees.

- It identified the circumstances in which overtime payments are required and set the overtime rate at one and one half times the regular hourly wage.

- It identified the criteria for determining what jobs are exempt from FLSA requirements.

- It placed limitations on working conditions for children to protect them from exploitation.

- It identified the information employers must keep about employees and related payroll transactions.

Minimum Wage

The FLSA regulates the federal minimum wage, which is set at $7.25 per hour as of the most recent 2009 update. Some states, such as Alaska, California, and New York, have set the minimum wage at a higher rate than the federal government; when this is the case, the state requirement supersedes the federal minimum wage. In other states the minimum is lower than the federal rate. In those states, the federal minimum wage supersedes state requirements. The DOL provides a useful map showing current minimum wage requirements by state at www.dol.gov/whd/minwage/america.htm.

Nonexempt employees must be paid at least the minimum wage for all compensable time. The FLSA defines compensable time as the time an employee works that is "suffered or permitted" by the employer. For example, a nonexempt employee who continues to work on an assignment after the end of the business day to finish a project or make corrections must be paid for that time.

Maximum Hours and Overtime

The FLSA defined the maximum workweek for nonexempt employees as 40 hours per week and required overtime to be paid for any compensable time that exceeds that maximum. The FLSA defined overtime for nonexempt workers as one and one half times the regular hourly wage rate for all compensable time worked that exceeds 40 hours in a workweek (also commonly known as time and a half).

Although double-time, or two times regular pay, is not required by the FLSA, it may be required by some states or may be part of a labor agreement.

While the FLSA does not require payment of overtime for exempt employees, it also does not prohibit overtime payments for them. Employers who choose to compensate exempt employees for hours worked exceeding the regular workweek are free to do so without risking the loss of exemption status. As long as overtime payments are in addition to the regular salary, exemption status is not affected. Exempt overtime can be paid at straight time, at time and a half, or as a bonus.

State or local government agencies may compensate employees with what is known as compensatory time off, or comp time, instead of cash payment for overtime worked. For example, a road maintenance worker employed by a city government may work 20 hours of overtime during a snowstorm. Instead of being paid time and a half for the overtime hours, the employee may receive 30 hours of additional paid time off (1.5 times 20 hours) to be used just as paid vacation or sick leave. From time to time, initiatives to expand comp time to private employers are presented in Congress, but at this time, the FLSA does not permit private employers to use comp time.

Overtime calculations are based on time actually worked during the week. For example, in a week with a paid holiday, full-time nonexempt employees will actually work 32 hours even though they are paid for 40 hours. If some employees then work 6 hours on Saturday, for a total of 38 actual hours worked during the week, those hours are paid at straight time, not time and a half (unless, of course, a state law or union contract requires otherwise). This requirement also applies when employees use paid vacation or sick leave or some other form of paid time off (PTO).

To accurately calculate overtime payments, it is necessary to understand the difference between compensable time—hours that must be paid to nonexempt employees—and noncompensable time. The FLSA defines several situations for which nonexempt employees must be paid, such as the time spent in preparing for or cleaning up after a shift by dressing in or removing protective clothing. Other types of compensable time include the following.

Waiting Time

Time spent by nonexempt employees waiting for work is compensable if it meets the FLSA definition of engaged to wait, which means that employees have been asked to wait for an assignment. For example, a marketing director may ask an assistant to wait for the conclusion of a meeting in order to prepare a Microsoft PowerPoint presentation needed for a client meeting early the next morning. If the assistant reads a book while waiting for the meeting to end, that time is still compensable.

Time that is spent by an employee who is waiting to be engaged is not compensable. For example, time spent by an employee who arrives at work 15 minutes early and reads the newspaper until the beginning of a shift is not considered to be compensable.

On-Call Time

The FLSA does not require employees who are on call away from the work site and are able to effectively use the time for their own purposes to be paid for time they spend waiting to be called. These employees may be required to provide the employer with contact information. If, however, the employer places other constraints on the employee's activities, the time could be considered compensable.

Employees who are required to remain at or close to the work site while waiting for an assignment are entitled to on-call pay. For example, medical interns required to remain at the hospital are entitled to payment for all hours spent at the hospital waiting for patients to arrive.

Rest and Meal Periods

Although rest and meal periods are not required by the FLSA, if they are provided, that time is subject to its requirements. Commonly referred to as breaks, short periods of rest lasting less than 20 minutes are considered compensable time. Meal periods lasting 30 minutes or longer are not compensable time unless the employee is required to continue working while eating. For example, a receptionist who is required to remain at the desk during lunch to answer the telephone must be paid for that time.

Lectures, Meetings, and Training Programs

Nonexempt employees are not required to be paid to attend training events when all four of the following conditions are met:

- The event takes place outside normal work hours.
- It is voluntary.
- It is not job-related.
- No other work is performed during the event.

Travel Time

Regular commute time (the time normally spent commuting from home to the regular work site) is not compensable. There are, however, some situations in which the FLSA requires that nonexempt employees receive payment for travel time.

Emergency Travel from Home to Work

Any time an employee is required to return to work for an emergency after working a full day, the employee must be compensated for travel time.

One-Day Off-site Assignments

When nonexempt employees are given a one-day assignment at a different location than their regular work site, the travel time may be considered compensable in certain circumstances. For example, if an employee drives to the off-site assignment, the travel time is compensable, but if he or she is a passenger in the car, the travel time is not compensable.

Travel between Job Sites

Nonexempt employees (such as plumbers or electricians) who are required to drive to different work sites to perform their regular duties must also be paid for the driving time between work sites.

Travel Away from Home

Travel away from home is defined as travel that keeps employees away from their homes overnight. When nonexempt employees must travel overnight, the FLSA considers the travel time during regular work hours as compensable time. This includes time traveled on non-workdays (weekends, for example) when it occurs during the employee's regular work hours. The DOL excludes the time spent outside of working hours as a passenger on an airplane, train, boat, bus, or automobile from compensable time calculations. If the employee is driving or working while traveling, the time is compensable.

Exemption Status

The FLSA covers all employees except those identified in the law as exempt from the regulations. All other employees are considered nonexempt and must be paid in accordance with FLSA requirements.

Certain positions may be exempt from one or all of the FLSA requirements (minimum wage, overtime, or child labor). For example, police officers and firefighters employed by small departments of fewer than five employees are exempt from overtime requirements but not exempt from the minimum wage requirement. On the other hand, newspaper delivery jobs are exempt from the minimum wage, overtime, and child labor requirements.

The determination of exemption status is often misunderstood by both employers and employees. Employers often think that they will save money by designating jobs as exempt and paying incumbent employees a salary. Employees often see the designation of a job as exempt as a measure of status within the company. Neither of these perceptions is accurate, and jobs that do not meet the legal exemption requirements can have costly consequences for employers.

To assist employers in properly classifying positions, the DOL regulations include exemption tests to determine whether a job meets those requirements and is therefore exempt from FLSA regulations.

Salary Basis Requirement

The DOL defines a salary as a regular, predetermined rate of pay for a weekly or less frequent basis (for example, biweekly, semimonthly, monthly, and so on). Employees must be paid a minimum salary of $455 per week, or $23,660 per year, as well as meet certain tests outlined next regarding their job duties in order to qualify as exempt. Job titles alone do not determine an employee's exempt status.

Executive Exemption

Employees who meet the salary basis requirement may be exempt as executives if they meet all of the following requirements:

- They have as their primary duty managing the enterprise, or managing a customarily recognized department or subdivision of the enterprise.

- They customarily and regularly direct the work of at least two other full-time employees.

- They have the authority to hire, fire, promote, and evaluate employees or to provide input regarding those actions that carries particular weight.

- Employees who own at least a 20 percent equity interest in the organization and who are actively engaged in management duties are also considered bona fide exempt executives.

Administrative Exemption

Employees who meet the salary basis requirement may qualify for the administrative exemption if they meet all of the following requirements:

- The primary duty is to perform office or non-manual work directly related to management or general business operations.

- The primary duty requires discretion and independent judgment on significant matters.

Professional Exemption

The DOL identifies two types of professionals who may qualify for exemption:

- **Learned professional exemption:** Employees who meet the salary basis requirement may qualify for exemption as learned professionals if they also meet both of the following criteria:

    - The primary duty requires the use of this advanced knowledge for work that requires the consistent use of discretion and judgment.

    - They have advanced knowledge in a field of science or learning acquired through a prolonged course of intellectual instruction.

- **Creative professional exemption:** Employees who meet the salary basis requirement may qualify for exemption as creative professionals if they also meet this criterion:

    - The primary duty requires invention, imagination, originality, or talent in a recognized field of artistic or creative endeavor.

Highly Compensated Employee Exemption

Highly compensated employees (HCEs, paid $100,000 or more) may also be considered exempt. To meet this exemption requirement, employees must perform office or nonmanual work and, on a customary and regular basis, at least one of the duties listed earlier for the executive, administrative, or professional exemptions.

Computer Employee Exemption

Employees who meet the weekly salary requirement or who are paid at least $27.63 per hour may qualify for the computer employee exemption if they perform one of the following jobs:

- Computer systems analyst
- Computer programmer
- Software engineer
- Other similarly skilled jobs in the computer field

and if they perform one or more of the following primary duties as part of the job:

- Apply systems analysis techniques and procedures, including consulting with users, to determine hardware, software, or system functional specifications.

- Design, develop, document, analyze, create, test, or modify computer systems or programs, including prototypes, based on and related to user or system design specifications.

- Design, document, test, create, or modify computer programs related to machine operating systems.

- Perform a combination of the previously described duties, at a level requiring the same skill.

Specifically excluded from this exemption are employees engaged in manufacturing or repairing computer hardware or related equipment and those such as engineers, drafters, or computer-aided designers who rely on computers and software programs to perform their work.

Outside Sales Exemption

Unlike the other exemptions, there is no salary requirement for outside sales personnel. To qualify for this exemption, employees must meet both of the following requirements:

- The primary duty of the position must be making sales or obtaining orders or contracts for services or for the use of facilities for which a consideration will be paid by the client or customer.

- The employee must be customarily and regularly engaged away from the employer's place of business.

Salary Deductions

There are certain circumstances where an employer may make deductions from the pay of an exempt employee. The DOL defines permissible salary deductions as the following:

- Absence for one or more full days for personal reasons other than sickness or disability

- Absence for one or more full days because of sickness or disability if the deduction is made in accordance with a bona fide plan, policy, or practice of providing compensation for salary lost due to illness

- To offset amounts employees receive for jury or witness fees or military pay

- For good-faith penalties imposed for safety rule infractions of major significance

- Good-faith, unpaid disciplinary suspensions of one or more full days for infractions of workplace conduct rules

- During the initial or terminal weeks of employment when employees work less than a full week

- Unpaid leave under the Family and Medical Leave Act

Employers who have an "actual practice" of improper deductions risk the loss of exemption status for all employees in the same job classification, not just for the affected employee. The loss of exemption status will be effective for the time during which the improper deductions were made.

Actual Practice

The DOL looks at a variety of factors to determine whether employers have an actual practice of improper deductions from exempt pay. These factors include the following:

- The number of improper deductions compared to the number of employee infractions warranting deductions
- The time period during which the improper deductions were made
- The number of employees affected
- The geographic location of the affected employees and managers responsible for the deductions

Safe Harbor

The DOL provides a safe harbor provision for payroll errors that could affect exemption status. The safe harbor applies if all of the following are met:

- There is a clearly communicated policy prohibiting improper deductions that includes a complaint mechanism for employees to use.
- The employer reimburses employees for improper deductions.
- The employer makes a good-faith commitment to comply in the future.

Employers who meet these criteria will not lose exemption status for the affected employees unless they willfully violate the policy by continuing to make improper deductions after receiving employee complaints.

2016 Overtime Final Rule

In 2016, then President Obama updated the salary basis for executive, administrative, and professional workers. However, on November 22, 2016, a U.S. District Court judge in Texas granted an injunction that prevents the Department of Justice from implementing and enforcing the updated Final Rule. The injunction is on appeal as of December 1, 2016. If the injunction is lifted, then the following changes will be made to the FLSA.

Employees must be paid a minimum salary of $913 per week, or $47,476 per year, to be classified as exempt. Highly compensated employees (HCEs) are subject to a minimal duties test and must have an annual salary of at least $134,000. Employers are able to use nondiscretionary bonuses and incentive payments (including commissions) to satisfy up to 10 percent of the standard salary level. Such payments may include, for example, nondiscretionary incentive bonuses tied to productivity and profitability. The 2016 ruling also establishes an automatic update to salary thresholds every three years beginning in January 2020.

Child Labor

The FLSA regulates the employment of workers under the age of 18. Children 16 years of age and up may work for an unlimited amount of hours. Children of any age may work for businesses owned entirely by their parents, unless they would be employed in mining, manufacturing, or other hazardous occupations. There are no restrictions on a youth 18 years of age or older.

Children 14 and 15 years of age can work in nonmanufacturing, non-mining, and non-hazardous jobs outside of school hours if they work the following hours:

- No more than 3 hours a day or 18 hours in a workweek

- No more than 8 hours on a non-school day or 40 hours in a non-school workweek

During the school year, youths between the ages of 14 and 15 can work between 7 a.m. and 7 p.m. During the summer months, June 1 through Labor Day, the workday can be extended to 9 p.m.

Record Keeping

There are two common methods for reporting time worked: positive time reporting, in which employees record the actual hours they are at work along with vacation, sick, or other time off, and exception reporting, in which only changes to the regular work schedule are recorded, such as vacation, sick, or personal time. Although the DOL regulations accept either method, in general the positive time method is best for nonexempt employees because it leaves no doubt as to actual hours worked by the employee and protects both the employee and the employer if there is ever a question about overtime payments due. Exception reporting is more appropriate for exempt employees because their pay is not based on hours worked.

The FLSA does not prevent employers from tracking the work time of exempt employees. These records may be used for billing customers, for reviewing performance, or for other administrative purposes, but they may not be used to reduce pay based on the quality or quantity of work produced. Reducing the salary invalidates the exemption status and subjects the employee to all requirements of the FLSA.

The FLSA requires the maintenance of accurate records by all employers. The information that must be maintained includes the following:

- Personal information, including full name, Social Security number (SSN), home address, occupation, sex, and date of birth if younger than 19 years old

- The hour and day when the workweek begins

- The total hours worked each workday and each workweek

- The basis on which employee's wages are paid (e.g., "$9 per hour" or "$440 per week")

- The total daily or weekly straight-time earnings

- The regular hourly pay rate for any week, including overtime

- Total overtime pay for the workweek
- Deductions and additions to wages
- Total wages paid each pay period
- The pay period dates and payment date

These FLSA records are usually maintained by the payroll department. Records must be preserved for at least three years. They must include payroll records, collective bargaining agreements, and sales and purchase records.

Penalties and Recovery of Back Wages

It is not uncommon for an employer to make an inadvertent error in calculating employee pay. In most cases when that happens, the employer corrects the error as soon as the employee points it out or the employer catches the error in some other way. Although distressing for employees, employers who make a good-faith effort to rectify the error in a timely manner remain within FLSA requirements.

In other cases, employers intentionally violate FLSA regulations by either paying employees less than the minimum wage, not paying overtime, or misclassifying employees as exempt to avoid overtime costs. These and other employee complaints about wage payments are investigated by state or federal agencies. If the complaints are justified, the employers are required to pay retroactive overtime pay and penalties to the affected employees. The investigation of a complaint by a single employee at an organization can trigger a government audit of the employer's general pay practices and exemption classification of its other employees and may result in additional overtime payments or penalties to other employees if they are found to be misclassified.

Employees whose complaints are verified can recover back wages using one of the following four methods the FLSA provides. The least expensive cost to the employer requires payment of the back wages.

- The Wage and Hour Division of the DOL can supervise the payment of back wages.
- The DOL can file a lawsuit for the amount of back wages and liquidated damages equal to the back wages.
- Employees can file private lawsuits to recover the wages plus an equal amount of liquidated damages, attorney fees, and court costs.
- The DOL can file an injunction preventing an employer from unlawfully withholding minimum wage and overtime payments.

There is a two-year statute of limitations for back pay recovery unless the employer willfully violated the FLSA. In those cases, the statute extends to three years. Employers may not terminate or retaliate against employees who file FLSA complaints. Willful violators of the FLSA may face criminal prosecution and be fined up to $10,000; if convicted a second time, the violator may face imprisonment. A civil penalty of up to $1,100 per violation may be assessed against willful or repeat violators.

FLSA Amendments

The FLSA has been amended numerous times since 1938, most often to raise the minimum wage to a level consistent with changes in economic conditions.

Two significant federal amendments have been added to the FLSA since 1938: the Portal to Portal Act and the Equal Pay Act. Additionally, the Patient Protection and Affordable Care Act, commonly referred to as Obamacare, affected the FLSA requirements.

Portal to Portal Act (1947)

The Portal to Portal Act clarified what was considered to be compensable work time and established that employers are not required to pay for employee commute time. This Act requires employers to pay nonexempt employees who perform regular work duties before or after their regular hours or for working during their lunch period.

Equal Pay Act (EPA) (1963)

The Equal Pay Act, the first antidiscrimination act to protect women, prohibits discrimination on the basis of sex. Equal pay for equal work applies to jobs with similar working conditions, skill, effort, and responsibilities. The Equal Pay Act applies to employers and employees covered by FLSA and is administered and enforced by the Equal Employment Opportunity Commission (EEOC). The EPA allows differences in pay when they are based on a bona fide seniority system, a merit system, a system that measures quantity or quality of production, or any other system that fairly measures factors other than sex. Prior to the EPA, the comparable worth standard was used by the U.S. government to make compensation decisions. When Congress passed the EPA, it deliberately rejected the comparable worth standard in favor of the equal pay standard.

Patient Protection and Affordable Care Act (PPACA) (2010)

In March 2010, President Barack Obama signed into law the Patient Protection and Affordable Care Act (PPACA). Largely intended as substantial healthcare reform, it included provisions for lactation accommodation in the workplace. The amendment requires that employers provide a reasonable break time for an employee to express breast milk for her nursing child for one year after the child's birth each time such employee has need to express the milk, and an appropriate place (other than a bathroom) that provides privacy. There is some dispute as to whether this time must be paid, however. While the amendment states that the time need not be compensated, current FLSA language reads otherwise: "Rest periods of short duration, generally running from 5 minutes to about 20 minutes, are common in industry. They promote the efficiency of the employee and are customarily paid for as work time. It is immaterial with respect to compensability of such breaks whether the employee drinks coffee, smokes, goes to the rest room, etc." This is an excellent example of when existing employment practices must be considered when applying the law. For example, if an employer allows additional paid break time for employees who smoke (unprotected activity), it may be prudent for said employer to count lactation accommodation (protected activity) as paid time as well.

Family and Medical Leave Act of 1993 (FMLA)

In 1993, President Bill Clinton signed the Family and Medical Leave Act (FMLA), which was created to assist employees in balancing the needs of their families with the demands of their jobs. In creating the FMLA, Congress intended that employees not have to choose between keeping their jobs and attending to seriously ill family members.

In addition to protecting employees from adverse employment actions and retaliation when they request leave under the FMLA, the Act provides three benefits for eligible employees in covered organizations:

- Twelve weeks of unpaid leave within a 12-month period (26 months for military caregiver leave)
- Continuation of health benefits
- Reinstatement to the same position or an equivalent position at the end of the leave

Designation of FMLA Leave

Employers are responsible to designate leave requests as FMLA-qualified based on information received from employees or someone designated by employees to speak on their behalf. When the employee does not provide enough information for the employer to determine if the leave is for a reason protected by the FMLA, it is up to the employer to request additional information. The FMLA regulations do not require employees to specifically request FMLA leave, but they must provide enough information to allow the employer to determine if the request is protected by the FMLA. If leave is denied based on a lack of information, it is up to the employee to provide enough additional information for the employer to ascertain that the leave is protected by the FMLA.

The regulations allow employers to retroactively designate leave as FMLA-qualified, as long as sufficient notice is given to the employee and the retroactive designation does not cause harm or injury to the employee. The retroactive designation can be made by mutual agreement between the employee and employer. When an employer fails to appropriately designate that a leave is FMLA-qualified at the time of the employee's request, the employee may be entitled to any loss of compensation and benefits caused by the employer's failure. This can include monetary damages, reinstatement, promotion, or other suitable relief.

Failure to Designate in a Timely Manner

In 2008, the FMLA was amended by the National Defense Authorization Act (NDAA). One of the changes incorporated the Supreme Court ruling in *Ragsdale vs. Wolverine Worldwide, Inc.*, a case that addressed what happens when an employer fails to designate a leave as FMLA-qualified in a timely manner. Prior to the *Ragsdale* case, some employees interpreted the regulations in a way that required employers to provide more than the 12 weeks of unpaid leave required by the FMLA. The regulations now state that, if an employer neglects to designate leave as FMLA, employees who are harmed may be entitled to restitution for their losses.

Waiver of Rights

Prior to the 2008 changes, the DOL required any settlement of past claims, even those mutually agreeable to both parties, to be approved by either the DOL or a court. The 2008 final rules amend this, allowing employers and employees who mutually agree on a resolution to settle past claims between them, avoiding costly and unnecessary litigation. However, the regulations do not permit employees to waive their future FMLA rights.

Substitution of Paid Leave

DOL regulations permit employees to request, or employers to require, the use of all accrued paid vacation, personal, family, medical, or sick leave concurrently with the FMLA leave. Eligible employees who do not qualify to take paid leave according to policies established by their employers are still entitled to the unpaid FMLA leave.

Perfect Attendance Awards

Employers may now deny perfect attendance awards to employees whose FMLA leave disqualifies them as long as employees who take non-FMLA leave are treated the same way.

Light Duty Assignments

Some courts interpreted light duty assignments following an FMLA leave as a continuation of the leave. The 2008 final rules stipulate that light duty work assignments are not counted against an employee's FMLA entitlement. In addition, the employee's job restoration rights continue until the employee is released to full duty or until the end of the 12-month FMLA leave year.

Record-Keeping Requirements

FMLA leave records must be kept in accordance with record-keeping standards established by the Fair Labor Standards Act (FLSA) and may be maintained in employee personnel files. The FMLA does not require submission of FMLA leave records unless requested by the DOL, but they must be maintained and available for inspection, copying, or transcription by DOL representatives for no less than three years. The DOL may not require submission more than once during any 12-month period without a reasonable belief that a violation has occurred.

Employers Covered

The FMLA applies to all public agencies and schools, regardless of their size, and to private employers with 50 or more employees working within a 75-mile radius. The law provides detailed descriptions on how employers determine whether these requirements apply to them.

Fifty or More Employees

Employers must comply with the FMLA when they employ 50 or more employees for each working day during each of 20 or more calendar workweeks in the current or preceding year. The statute does not require the workweeks to be consecutive. Guidelines in the FMLA count the number of employees at a work site as being determined by the number of employees on the payroll for that site.

Employers remain subject to FMLA rules until the number of employees on the payroll is less than 50 for 20 nonconsecutive weeks in the current and preceding calendar year. This means that if employers with 50 employees on the payroll for the first 20 weeks in 2016 reduce the number of employees for the rest of 2016 and remain at the reduced level throughout 2017, they must continue to comply with FMLA through the end of 2017.

Work Sites within a 75-Mile Radius

The number of employees at each work site is based on the employees who report to work at that site or, in the case of outside sales representatives or employees who telecommute, the location from which their work is assigned.

This can be either a single place of business or a group of adjacent locations, such as a business park or campus.

A work site may also consist of facilities that are not directly connected if they are in reasonable geographic proximity, are used for the same purpose, and share the same staff and equipment.

Employees such as construction workers or truck drivers who regularly work at sites away from the main business office are counted as employees in one of the three following ways:

- At the business site to which they report
- At the work site that is their home base
- At the site from which their work is assigned

However, these employees may not be counted at a work site where they may be temporarily deployed for the duration of a project.

Notice Obligations

Employers have two notice obligations for the FMLA: the first obligation is to inform employees of their FMLA rights and the second requires specific information to be provided in response to an FMLA leave request.

Informational Notice

Upon hire, employers must provide employees with a general informational notice in two formats. The DOL provides a poster (WH Publication 1420) explaining FMLA rights and responsibilities. Employers must post this information in an area frequented by employees.

Employers must also provide information about employee rights and responsibilities in the employee handbook, collective bargaining agreement (CBA), or other written documents. When an employer does not have a handbook or CBA, DOL provides Fact Sheet #28, a four-page summary of the FMLA that the employer may distribute to employees.

Notice in Response to Leave Request

Once an employee requests an FMLA leave, the final rules require employers to respond within five business days. At this time, employers must inform employees of their eligibility, rights, and responsibilities for an FMLA leave, and designate the leave as FMLA. The DOL provides two forms for this purpose: WH-381 and WH-382.

The eligibility, rights, and responsibilities notice (Form WH-381) informs employees of the following:

- The date of leave request, and beginning and ending dates of the leave
- The reason for the leave (birth or adoption of a child or serious health condition of employee or family member)
- Employee rights and responsibilities under the FMLA
- That employee contributions toward health insurance premiums continue and whether or not the employee will be required to reimburse the employer for premiums paid if the employee does not return to work after the leave
- Whether or not the employer will continue other benefits
- Whether or not the employee is eligible for an FMLA leave
- Whether or not the employee is designated as a *key employee* and therefore may not be restored to employment upon the end of the leave
- Whether or not the employer requires periodic reports on the employee's status and intention to return to work

The designation notice (Form WH-382) informs employees of the following:

- Whether or not the requested leave will be counted against their FMLA leave entitlement
- Whether or not a medical certification is required
- Whether or not the employer requires them to use their accrued paid leave for the unpaid FMLA leave; if not required, whether or not the employee chooses to substitute accrued paid leave for all or part of the FMLA leave
- Whether or not the employer requires a fitness-for-duty certificate prior to the employee's return to work

Employers are not required to use the DOL forms, but if a substitute form is used, it must include all information required by the regulations.

Employers may not revoke an employee's eligibility, once confirmed. Similarly, if an employer neglects to inform an employee that he or she is ineligible for FMLA leave prior to the date the leave begins, the employee is considered eligible to take the leave, and the employer may not deny it at that point.

Employees Eligible for FMLA

The FMLA also provides guidelines for determining which employees are eligible for leave. This includes employees who:

- Work for an employer that is subject to FMLA as described previously.

- Have been employed by the employer for at least 12 months, which need not be consecutive, but time worked prior to a break in service of seven or more years does not need to be counted unless the service break was to fulfill a military service obligation. Employees who received benefits or other compensation during any part of a week are counted as having been employed for that week.

- Worked at least 1,250 hours during the 12 months immediately preceding the leave, based on the FLSA standards for determining compensable hours of work. If accurate time records are not maintained, it is up to the employer to prove that the employee did not meet the requirement; if this is not possible, the law provides that the employee will be presumed to have met the requirement. The determination of whether an employee meets the requirement for 1,250 hours of work within the past 12 months is counted from the date the leave begins.

Key Employee Exception

An FMLA leave is available to all employees of covered organizations who meet the FMLA eligibility requirements. FMLA includes a provision that key employees may be denied reinstatement to the position they held or an equivalent position if the employer demonstrates that the reinstatement would cause "substantial and grievous economic injury" to its operations. A key employee is defined by FMLA as a salaried employee among the highest-paid 10 percent of employees at the work site as defined previously. The law requires that the determination of which employees are the highest paid is calculated by taking the employee's year-to-date earnings (base salary, premium pay, incentive pay, and bonuses) and dividing the total earnings by the number of weeks worked. Whether an employee meets the definition of a key employee is to be determined at the time leave is requested. The employee must be advised of this status, either in person or by certified mail, as soon as possible. The employer must also explain why restoring the employee's job will cause substantial and grievous economic injury.

If the employee decides to take the leave after being informed of the implications of key employee status, the employee may still request reinstatement upon return to work. The employer must review the circumstances again and, if substantial and grievous economic injury would still occur under the circumstances at that time, notify the employee in writing, in person, or by certified mail that restoration is denied.

Key employees continue to be protected by the FMLA unless they notify their employer that they will not return to work, or until the employer denies reinstatement at the end of the leave.

Employee Notice Requirement

One FMLA requirement that caused difficulty for employers was an interpretation of previous rules that employees had up to two full days after an FMLA-qualifying event occurred to notify their employers of the need for FMLA leave. This made it difficult for employers to meet production schedules and ensure necessary coverage of critical work needs.

The 2008 final rules eliminated this language and clarified the timing of employee notices for two situations: foreseeable and unforeseeable leaves. In either case, employees must provide verbal notice so that the employer is aware of the need for FMLA-qualified leave, the expected timing and length of the leave, and information about the medical condition described in the upcoming section, "Reasons for FMLA Leave." Employees are not required to specifically request FMLA leave or mention FMLA for the first occurrence of a qualified event, but they are required to answer reasonable questions about the need for leave so that employers can determine whether the leave is qualified under the FMLA.

Foreseeable Leave

When the need for leave is foreseeable, FMLA rules require employees to notify their employers at least 30 days prior to the anticipated start date of leaves such as for the birth of a child, adoption, placement of a foster child, or planned medical treatment for a serious health condition. If the circumstances surrounding the planned leave change (such as a child is born earlier than expected), notice must be given as soon as practicable. This means as soon as both practical and possible, on the same day or the next business day. In these circumstances, a family member or someone else representing the employee may provide notice.

If the leave is foreseeable more than 30 days in advance and an employee fails to provide notice at least 30 days in advance without a reasonable excuse for delaying, the employer may delay FMLA coverage until 30 days after the date the employee provided notice.

If the need for FMLA leave is foreseeable less than 30 days in advance and the employee fails to notify the employer as soon as practicable, the employer may delay FMLA coverage of the leave. The amount of delay depends on the circumstances of each leave request and is evaluated on a case-by-case basis. Generally, the employer may delay the start of FMLA leave by the amount of delay in notice by the employee.

Unforeseeable Leave

At times, employees may be unable to notify their employers of the need for FMLA leave in advance. In these circumstances, the 2008 change to FMLA rules requires employees to provide notice in accordance with the usual and customary practice for calling in an absence unless unusual circumstances prevent the employee from doing so. An employee's representative, such as a spouse or another responsible person, may provide the notice if the employee is unable to do so. In emergencies when employees are unable to contact employers, they are permitted to supply the notice when they are able to use a telephone.

In order for employees to provide notice in accordance with the regulations, they must be aware of their responsibility to do so. The FMLA provides that proper posting of FMLA notice requirements by employers satisfies this requirement. Employers may waive FMLA notice requirements or their own rules on notice for employee leaves of absence at their discretion. In the absence of unusual circumstances, employers may choose not to waive their internal notice rules for employees who fail to follow those rules when requesting FMLA leaves, as long as those actions are consistent with practices regarding other leave requests. This is acceptable under the regulations as long as the actions do not discriminate against employees taking FMLA leave or violate the FMLA requirements described earlier.

Reasons for FMLA Leave

FMLA presents covered employers with a list of circumstances under which FMLA leave must be provided if requested by an eligible employee. Passage of the 2008 NDAA added care for military personnel and their families in some circumstances to existing circumstances that qualify for leave:

- **The birth of a child and caring for the infant:** FMLA leave is available to both fathers and mothers; however, if both parents work for the same employer, the combined total of the leave may not exceed the 12-week total. In addition, the leave must be completed within 12 months of the child's birth.

- **Placement of an adopted or foster child with the employee:** The same conditions that apply to the birth of a child apply here as well; in this case, the leave must be completed within 12 months of the child's placement.

- **To provide care for the employee's spouse, son, daughter, or parent with a serious health condition:** For purposes of FMLA leave, a spouse must be recognized as such by the state in which the employee resides.

A parent can be the biological parent of the employee or one who has legal standing *in loco parentis*, a Latin term that means "in place of the parent" and applies to those who care for a child on a daily basis. In loco parentis does not require either a biological or a legal relationship.

A son or daughter may be a biological child, adopted or foster child, stepchild, legal ward, or the child of someone acting *in loco parentis*. A child must also be younger than 18 years of age or, if older than 18, unable to care for him- or herself because of a physical or mental disability. Under the FMLA, persons who are *in loco parentis* include those with day-to-day responsibilities to care for or financially support a child. Courts have indicated some factors to be considered in determining *in loco parentis* status:

- The age of the child
- The degree to which the child is dependent on the person
- The amount of financial support, if any, provided
- The extent to which duties commonly associated with parenthood are exercised

In a 2015 amendment to the definition of spouse, eligible employees in legal same-sex marriages are able to take FMLA leave to care for their spouse or family member, regardless of where they live. The 2015 change means that eligible employees, regardless of where they live, will be able to take:

- FMLA leave to care for their lawfully married same-sex spouse with a serious health condition

- Qualifying exigency leave due to their lawfully married same-sex spouse's covered military service, or

- Military caregiver leave for their lawfully married same-sex spouse

- FMLA leave to care for their stepchild (child of employee's same-sex spouse) regardless of whether the *in loco parentis* requirement of providing day-to-day care or financial support for the child is met

- FMLA leave to care for a stepparent who is a same-sex spouse of the employee's parent, regardless of whether the stepparent ever stood *in loco parentis* to the employee

Employers may require those employees requesting FMLA leave to provide reasonable documentation to support the family relationship with the person for whom they will be providing care.

Employees may qualify for FMLA leave for their own serious health condition, defined as an illness, injury, impairment, or a physical or mental condition that requires the following:

- Inpatient care or subsequent treatment related to inpatient care

- Continuing treatment by a healthcare provider because of a period of incapacity of more than three consecutive calendar days *Incapacity* refers to an inability to work, attend school, or perform other daily activities as a result of the condition.

- Incapacity because of pregnancy or prenatal care

- Treatment for a serious, chronic health condition

FMLA time is available to employees who need to provide care for a covered service member with a serious injury or illness sustained while on active duty. In this situation, family members are eligible to take up to 26 weeks of leave in a 12-month period.

Additionally, FMLA-protected time is available to eligible employees for qualifying exigencies for families of members of the National Guard and Reserves. Qualifying exigencies include the following:

- Short-notice deployments

- Military events and related activities

- Child care and school activities

- Financial and legal arrangements

- Counseling

- Rest and recuperation

- Post-deployment activities

- Leave for other related purposes when agreed to by the employee and employer

Medical Certification Process

FMLA regulations allow employers to require medical certifications to verify requests for any qualified leave as long as the employee is notified of the requirements. The DOL provides the following forms for this purpose:

- WH-380-E (for employee's serious health condition)
- WH-380-F (for family member's serious health condition)
- WH-384 (for exigency leave for military families)
- WH-385 (for serious injury or illness to covered service member)

Employers should request initial certification within five business days of the employee's leave request. Additional certifications may be required at a later date to verify that the leave continues to be appropriate. Employers must provide at least 15 calendar days for the employee to submit the certification but may allow more time.

FMLA regulations require employees to provide "complete and sufficient" certification for the employer. If the certification does not meet the complete and sufficient standard, employers may request, in writing, the additional information needed to comply. A certification is not considered complete and sufficient if one or more of the entries on the form are not completed or if the information is vague, ambiguous, or nonresponsive. Employees must be allowed a minimum of seven days to return the form with the additional information. When employers request the certification or additional information, they must advise employees of the consequences for failing to provide adequate certification of the serious illness or injury. If employees do not return the certification or they fail to provide a complete and sufficient certification upon notice of deficiencies in what was submitted, FMLA regulations allow employers to deny the FMLA leave.

Employers are not required to use the DOL forms but may only request information that is directly related to the serious health condition necessitating the leave, including the following:

- Contact information for the healthcare provider
- Approximate date the serious health condition began and an estimate of how long it will last
- A description of the medical facts about the health condition, such as symptoms, diagnosis, hospitalization, doctor visits, prescribed medication, treatment referrals, or continuing treatments
- For employees with serious health conditions, the certification must establish the inability to perform essential job functions, describe work restrictions, and indicate the length of the inability to perform job functions.
- For family members with serious health conditions, the certification must establish that the patient requires care, how often, and how long care will be necessary.
- Information that confirms the medical necessity for reduced or intermittent leave with estimated dates and length of treatment

FMLA leave certifications may be complicated when workers' compensation, ADA, or employer-provided paid leave programs are used concurrently. FMLA regulations address certifications under these circumstances as follows:

- When FMLA runs concurrently with a workers' compensation leave, employers are prohibited from collecting information for workers' compensation purposes that exceeds what is allowed for FMLA purposes.

- Employers may require additional information in accordance with a paid leave or disability program but must advise employees that the additional information is required in conjunction with the paid-leave plan, not with the FMLA leave. Whatever information is collected may be used to evaluate continuation of the FMLA leave. Failure to provide the additional information does not affect continuation of the FMLA leave.

- When FMLA leave runs concurrently with ADA, employers may follow ADA procedures for collecting information. This information may be used to evaluate the claim for FMLA-protected leave.

Employees are responsible for providing their own medical certifications. If they choose to do so, they may provide employers with an authorization or release to obtain information directly from their healthcare providers, but employers may not require them to do so.

Types of FMLA Leave

FMLA provides for three types of leave: continuous, reduced leave, and intermittent. A *continuous FMLA leave* is one in which the employee is absent from work for an extended period of time. A reduced *FMLA leave schedule* is one in which the employee's regular work schedule is reduced for a period of time. This can mean a reduction in the hours worked each day or in the number of days worked during the week. An *intermittent FMLA leave* is one in which the employee is absent from work for multiple periods of time because of a single illness or injury. When utilizing intermittent leave, employees must make an effort to schedule the leave to avoid disruption of regular business operations. In addition, the employer may assign an employee requesting intermittent leave to a different position with equivalent pay and benefits in order to meet the employee's needs.

Calculating the FMLA Year

FMLA provides four possible methods for employers to use in calculating the FMLA year, the 12-month period during which employees may use the 12 weeks of leave. An FMLA year can be calculated as any of the following:

- The calendar year

- Any fixed 12-month period (such as the fiscal year or anniversary date)

- The 12-month period beginning when an FMLA leave begins

- A rolling 12-month period that is measured back from the date FMLA is used by an employee

Although the most difficult to administer, for many employers the rolling 12-month period is best. Other methods are more open to abuse of FMLA by some employees, resulting in the use of 24 weeks of leave by bridging two 12-month periods, allowing an employee to be on continuous FMLA leave for 24 weeks.

If an employer does not have a stated policy, the FMLA year must be calculated in the way that provides the most benefit to employees. Whichever method is selected, it must be used to calculate FMLA for all employees. Employers that decide to change the way they calculate the FMLA year must provide written notice to employees 60 days in advance of the change and obtain written acknowledgment of the change.

Tracking Reduced and Intermittent FMLA Leave

Although keeping track of the amount of FMLA used for a continuous leave is fairly straightforward, ensuring that accurate records of reduced and intermittent FMLA records are maintained can be a bit more difficult. In either case, only the amount of leave used may be deducted from the 12 weeks available to the employee. For example, an employee whose regular work schedule of 40 hours per week is reduced to 20 hours per week would be charged one-half week FMLA leave for each week that the employee works the reduced schedule.

For intermittent leave, employers may charge for leave in increments of not less than one hour. Employees should provide at least two days' notice of the need to utilize the intermittent leave whenever possible.

Ending FMLA Leave

FMLA leave ends when the employee has used the full 12 weeks of leave, the serious illness of the employee or family member ends, or, in some cases, when the family member or the employee dies. When one of these three circumstances occurs (other than the employee's own death), the employee may return to the same or an equivalent position with no loss of benefits. If the employee wants to continue the leave at that point, the company is under no obligation to grant it, unless there is a company policy in place to provide a longer leave.

Employers may require employees returning from FMLA leaves to provide a fitness-for-duty certification from their healthcare providers, attesting to their ability to return to work. If they choose to do so, employers may require the fitness-for-duty report to specify the employee's ability to perform the essential functions of the job. Employers that choose this type of certification must provide a job description or list of the employee's essential job functions with the designation notice provided to the employee. Similarly to medical certifications, employers may contact healthcare providers to clarify and authenticate information contained in the fitness-for-duty certificate, but they may not request information unrelated to the serious health condition that is the reason for the FMLA leave. Employees may be required to provide the fitness-for-duty certification prior to returning to work. Employees who neither provide the certificate nor request an extension of the leave are no longer entitled to reinstatement.

FMLA Implications for Employers

HR professionals need to ensure that supervisors and managers throughout their organizations are aware of the requirements for FMLA leaves and the consequences for non-compliance. FMLA requirements are complex and confusing, particularly when used in conjunction with workers' compensation or the ADA, and managers of other functional areas may not be aware of their obligations for FMLA requests.

There are some things employers can do to ensure that they comply with FMLA requirements. To start, review current leave practices to ensure that they comply with FMLA requirements and any state laws with more stringent requirements. FMLA leave policies should be included in the employee handbook; new hires must be advised of their rights to take leave under the Act. It is important for HR professionals to work with supervisors and managers throughout the organization to ensure that they understand the implications for situations that may be subject to FMLA regulations and encourage them to talk to HR about potential FMLA leave situations. HR needs to take an active role in educating the management team about the interaction of FMLA, ADA, and workers' compensation requirements. Before an FMLA situation occurs, a documentation procedure and policy should be developed, and HR should take an active role in ensuring that all leaves comply with established procedures to avoid possible claims of discriminatory practices. When workers' compensation and FMLA leaves occur simultaneously, make sure to advise the employee that the leaves run concurrently.

Foreign Corrupt Practices Act of 1977

The Foreign Corrupt Practices Act (FCPA) of 1977 made it unlawful for certain classes of people and entities to make payments to foreign government officials to assist in obtaining or retaining business. Made up of antibribery provisions, the FCPA prohibits people and entities from making any:

> offer, payment, promise to pay, or authorization of the payment of money or anything of value to any person, while knowing that all or a portion of such money or thing of value will be offered, given or promised, directly or indirectly, to a foreign official to influence the foreign official in his or her official capacity, induce the foreign official to do or omit to do an act in violation of his or her lawful duty, or to secure any improper advantage in order to assist in obtaining or retaining business for or with, or directing business to, any person.

In 1988, amendments applied the antibribery provisions to foreign persons, prohibiting them from engaging in any of these activities within the United States.

The FCPA requires companies whose securities are listed in the United States to keep accurate records and maintain accounting controls to ensure that the records accurately and fairly represent corporate financial transactions.

Genetic Information Nondiscrimination Act of 2008 (GINA)

When research into the use of human genomic information made it possible to identify genetic predisposition to particular diseases, many people became uncomfortable with the idea of information so personal being made available to insurance companies or employers that could use it for discriminatory purposes. For more than 10 years, Congress worked on legislation that would prevent that from happening. President George W. Bush signed the resulting legislation, the Genetic Information Nondiscrimination Act (GINA), into law in May 2008.

GINA prohibits employers from unlawfully discriminating against employees or their family members in any of the terms or conditions of employment included in Title VII. The Act defines genetic information as the results of genetic tests for employees and their family members or as information about genetic diseases or disorders revealed through genetic testing.

The Act makes it unlawful for employers to request, require, or purchase genetic information but does not penalize them for inadvertently obtaining the information. GINA allows employers to obtain the information for wellness or health programs they offer when the employee authorizes access to the information in writing. In those cases, the information obtained through genetic testing may be provided only to healthcare professionals or board-certified genetic counselors providing services to employees. This information may be provided to employers only in aggregate form that does not identify specific employees.

Employers may request the information as required by the Family and Medical Leave Act (FMLA) or similar state laws but may use it only as required by those laws. Employers can also use genetic information if federal or state laws require genetic monitoring of biological effects from toxic substances in the workplace, but only if the employee receives written notice and provides informed, written consent to the monitoring and the monitoring complies with federal and state laws. Any test results may be provided to employers only in aggregate form without identifying individual information.

The DOL issued a request for comments on the implementation of GINA prior to beginning the rule-making process. The submission period ended in December 2008, and the DOL began evaluating regulatory needs with the Department of Health and Human Services and the Treasury Department since aspects of the law impact agencies in those departments as well.

Glass Ceiling Act of 1991

In 1991, Senator Robert Dole introduced legislation known as the Glass Ceiling Act, which was eventually signed into law as an amendment to Title II of the Civil Rights Act of 1991. An article in the *Wall Street Journal* in 1986 had coined the term *glass ceiling* to describe the limitations faced by women and minorities when it came to advancing into the senior ranks of corporate management. The Act established a commission whose purpose was to determine whether a glass ceiling existed and, if it did, to identify the barriers to placing more women and minorities in senior management positions. The commission found that although CEOs understood the need to include women and minorities in the ranks of senior management, this belief was not shared at all levels in the organization. The study went on to identify three barriers that prevented women and minorities from advancing to senior levels: societal, internal structural, and government barriers.

Societal Barriers

Societal barriers result from limited access to educational opportunities and biases related to gender, race, and ethnicity.

Internal Structural Barriers

Internal structural barriers encompass a wide range of corporate practices and shortcomings over which management has some control, including outreach and recruiting programs that do not try to find qualified women and minorities, as well as organizational cultures that exclude women and minorities from participation in activities that will lead to advancement, such as mentoring, management training, or career development assignments.

Governmental Barriers

Governmental barriers are related to inconsistent enforcement of equal opportunity legislation and poor collection and dissemination of statistics that illustrate the problem.

The commission also studied organizations that have successfully integrated glass ceiling initiatives into their operations and found some common traits that can be adopted by other organizations. Successful initiatives begin with full support of the CEO, who ensures that the initiative becomes part of strategic planning in the organization and holds management accountable for achieving goals by tracking and reporting on progress. These comprehensive programs do not exclude white men but do include a diverse workforce population. Organizations implementing programs to increase diversity benefit from improved productivity and bottom-line results for shareholders.

As a result of the study, the EEOC conducts glass ceiling audits to monitor the progress that organizations make toward including women and minorities at all levels.

Illegal Immigration Reform and Immigrant Responsibility Act of 1996 (IIRIRA)

The Illegal Immigration Reform and Immigrant Responsibility Act of 1996 reduced the number and types of documents allowable to prove identity, employment eligibility, or both in the hiring process and established pilot programs for verification of employment eligibility. It also allowed for sanctions against employers who failed to comply with the hiring requirements.

Immigration Reform and Control Act of 1986 (IRCA)

The Immigration Reform and Control Act (IRCA) was enacted in 1986 to address illegal immigration into the United States. The law applied to businesses with four or more employees and made it illegal to knowingly hire or continue to employ individuals who were not legally authorized to work in the United States. Unfair immigration-related employment practices were defined as discrimination on the basis of national origin or citizenship status.

Employers were required to complete Form I-9 for all new hires within the first three days of employment and to review documents provided by the employee that establish identity or employment authorization or both from lists of acceptable documents on the Form I-9. IRCA requires employers to maintain I-9 files for three years from the date of hire or one year after the date of termination, whichever is later, and allows, but does not require, employers to copy documents presented for employment eligibility for purposes of complying with these requirements. The Act also provides that employers complying in good faith with these requirements have an affirmative defense to inadvertently hiring an unauthorized alien. Substantial fines for violations of both the hiring and record-keeping requirements were provided in the law. Failure to maintain acceptable Form I-9 records is subject to fines of not less than $110 (per United States Citizenship and Immigration Services [USCIS]) or more than $1,100 for each employee without a completed form available upon request to an authorized agent of the USCIS. In addition for penalties assessed for missing or incomplete I-9 forms, IRCA established fines for unauthorized employees. Table C.5 outlines the fines for hiring violations under IRCA.

TABLE C.5   IRCA fines

Violation	Amount of fine
First	Not less than $375 or more than $3,200 for each unauthorized employee
Second	Not less than $3,200 or more than $6,500 for each unauthorized employee
Third	Not less than $4,300 or more than $16,000 for each unauthorized employee

In addition to the fines listed, employers that knowingly hire unauthorized workers are subject to fines of $3,200 per employee and/or six months' imprisonment.

Employers are required to store I-9 forms on paper, on microfilm or microfiche, or on PDF files or other electronic formats, provided they meet the obligations for security and access upon demand.

E-Verify

E-Verify is a free service offered through the USCIS. It is a tool that helps employers comply with IRCA's requirement that employers must verify the identity and employment eligibility of new employees. Accessed through the Internet, the employer inputs basic information gleaned from the Form I-9 and receives a nearly instant "employment authorized" or "tentative non-confirmation" (TNC) reply from the website. The employer then prints the results. A TNC result will give the employee more information about the mismatch and a statement of his or her rights and responsibilities under the law. It is important to note that an employer may not terminate an employee for the initial TNC; it is only when a final non-confirmation is received that an employer may terminate under E-Verify.

To get started in the program, an employer must first enroll the company, distribute a memorandum of understanding (MOU), and commit to using E-Verify for every new employee at the affected hiring site. Under federal law, the use of E-Verify may be designated to certain locations, although this may be restricted under some state laws.

Amendments to IRCA: Immigration Act of 1990

The Immigration Act of 1990 made several changes to IRCA, including adding the requirement that a prevailing wage be paid to H-1B immigrants to ensure that U.S. citizens did not lose jobs to lower-paid immigrant workers. The Act also restricted to 65,000 annually the number of immigrants allowed under the H-1B category and created additional categories for employment visas, as shown in Table C.6.

TABLE C.6   Employment visas

Visa	Classification
	Visas for temporary workers
H-1B	Specialty occupations, DOD workers, fashion models
H-1C	Nurses going to work for up to three years in health professional shortage areas
H-2A	Temporary agricultural workers
H-2B	Temporary workers: skilled and unskilled, nonagricultural
H-3	Trainees
J-1	Visas for exchange visitors
	Visas for intracompany transfers
L-1A	Executive, managerial
L-1B	Specialized knowledge
L-2	Spouse or child of L-1
	Visas for workers with extraordinary abilities
O-1	Extraordinary ability in sciences, arts, education, business, or athletics
	Visas for athletes and entertainers
P-1	Individual or team athletes
P-1	Entertainment groups
P-2	Artists and entertainers in reciprocal exchange programs
P-3	Artists and entertainers in culturally unique programs
	Visas for religious workers
R-1	Religious workers
	Visas for NAFTA workers
TN	Trade visas for Canadians and Mexicans

In 2016, several changes related to employees on work visas were made. Effective January 2017, they allowed certain high-skilled individuals in the United States with E-3, H-1B, H-1B1, L-1, or O-1 nonimmigrant status, including any applicable grace period, to apply for employment authorization for a limited period if:

- They are the principal beneficiaries of an approved Form I-140 petition.

- An immigrant visa is not authorized for issuance for their priority date, and

- They can demonstrate that compelling circumstances exist that justify DHS issuing an employment authorization document in its discretion. Such employment authorization may be renewed in only limited circumstances and only in one-year increments.

Additionally:

- Clarified various policies and procedures related to the adjudication of H-1B petitions, including, among other things, providing H-1B status beyond the six-year authorized period of admission, determining cap exemptions and counting workers under the H-1B cap, H-1B portability, licensure requirements, and protections for whistleblowers.

- Established two grace periods of up to 10 days for individuals in the E-1, E-2, E-3, L-1, and TN nonimmigrant classifications to provide a reasonable amount of time for these individuals to prepare to begin employment in the country, to depart the United States, or to take other actions to extend, change, or otherwise maintain lawful status.

- Established a grace period of up to 60 consecutive days during each authorized validity period for certain highly skilled nonimmigrant workers when their employment ends before the end of their authorized validity period, so they may more readily pursue new employment and an extension of their nonimmigrant status.

- Automatically extend the employment authorization and validity of Employment Authorization Documents (EADs or Form I-766s) for certain individuals who apply on time to renew their EADs.

For more information, visit the "Working in the US page" found at www.uscis.gov/ working-united-states/working-us.

International Labour Organization (ILO)

The International Labour Organization (*ILO*) was established in 1919 by the Treaty of Versailles to address working conditions and living standards in all countries. It has a tripartite structure comprised of member states' government, employers, and workers. The ILO currently has 185 member countries that agree to the labor standard development outcomes of *ILO conventions* and recommendations. Conventions are legally binding directives, whereas recommendations are nonbinding guidelines.

In 2000, the ILO adopted the Declaration of Fundamental Principles and Rights at Work, which includes the commitment by businesses to support, respect, and protect international human rights; the recognition of worker rights to organize and collectively bargain; to abolish child labor; and to eliminate unlawful discrimination.

International Trade Organizations

For many reasons, some countries have found it to be mutually beneficial to enter into trade agreements. These agreements clarify expectations and establish rules that impact tariffs, employment visas, and employee rights between blocs of trading countries. Though not without controversy, the most prominent of these agreements are reviewed next.

European Union (EU)

The European Union is the world's largest international trading bloc, formed of a common market around which tariffs are reduced and free trade is established. It is designed to clarify the rules of trade, people movement (immigration), and social rights between member countries. Examples include standardized taxes and the rights of most service providers to practice in all member countries. Nineteen of the member countries use the euro as their form of currency.

The EU has both social and political influence over HR practices. The Social Charter of the EU was first adopted in 1989, establishing the 12 fundamental rights of workers. Since their passage, the EU has been working to translate the rights into specific directives to be observed by member countries. Various treaties have been adopted to reinforce the fundamental rights, including employee rights to data protection, the rights of asylum, equality under the law, nondiscriminatory treatment, protection against unfair dismissal, and access to social security. These directives in some form or another apply to all organizations, both local and foreign owned.

The EU currently has 28 member states: Austria, Belgium, Bulgaria, Croatia, Cyprus, Czech Republic, Denmark, Estonia, Finland, France, Germany, Greece, Hungary, Ireland, Italy, Latvia, Lithuania, Luxembourg, Malta, Netherlands, Poland, Portugal, Romania, Slovakia, Slovenia, Spain, Sweden, and the United Kingdom.

The Schengen area is the geographic locations where legal residents may move freely between member countries without special visas. Ireland and the United Kingdom have declined to participate.

In 2016, the United Kingdom voted to leave the European Union. Commonly referred to as Brexit, the separation is headed by the Department for Exiting the European Union (DExEU), the agency responsible for (potentially) completing the exit (as of this writing) sometime in 2019. Depending on the final terms of the separation, there may be an impact on work visas and permits for employees on assignment in neighboring countries.

Mercosur

Mercosur is a Southern trading bloc made up of four countries: Argentina, Brazil, Paraguay, and Uruguay. Venezuela was suspended in 2016 for failing to incorporate trade and human rights elements into its laws; also in 2016, Bolivia was in the final stages of becoming a member. Chile, Colombia, Ecuador, Guyana, Peru, and Suriname are considered associate members. Founded in 1991, Mercosur aims to form a common market, allowing for a common external tariff and free movement of goods, services, and people across member nations. A Common Market Council makes decisions, and a Trade Commission deals with tariffs and foreign affairs. The Economic and Social Consultative Forum was established in 1994 to serve in an advisory role to the Trade Commission about labor and social issues. One major goal of Mercosur is to establish a trade agreement with the European Union.

North American Free Trade Agreement (NAFTA)

Formed in 1994 as a trade agreement between the United States, Canada, and Mexico, the North American Free Trade Agreement (NAFTA) is aimed at promoting free trade and closer economic ties between the three participating members. In response to worries from labor unions, the North American Agreement on Labor Cooperation (NAALC) was included to provide problem-solving mechanisms to address the living and working conditions of workers. The NAALC agreement established national administrative offices (NAOs) in each of the countries to implement the agreement and to serve as points of contact between national governments focused on improved working conditions and standards of living in each member country.

Additionally, the Free Trade Area of the Americas is an agreement that has been in the process of negotiation for more than 18 years as of 2019. If completed, it would expand NAFTA to include countries in South America, the Caribbean, and Central America, binding them together into a trading bloc similar to that of the European Union. While not off the table per se, the negotiations are considered to be at an impasse.

Mine Safety and Health Act of 1977 (MSHA)

The Mine Safety and Health Act of 1977 established the *Mine Safety and Health Administration (MSHA)* to ensure the safety of workers in coal and other mines. The act establishes mandatory safety and health standards for mine operators and monitors operations throughout the United States. MSHA has developed a comprehensive website (www.msha.gov) that is a resource for miners and mine operators, providing access to information on prevention of accidents, information on year-to-date fatalities, and guidance on specific mine hazards. The site also contains a link to the complete text of the Act.

Occupational Safety and Health Act of 1970 (OSHA)

For more than 100 years beginning in 1867, sporadic legislation was enacted by different states and the federal government to address specific safety concerns, usually in regard to mine safety or factory conditions, but there was no comprehensive legislation requiring employers to protect workers from injury or illness. That changed with the Occupational Safety and Health Act of 1970 (the OSH Act), a comprehensive piece of federal legislation that continues to have an impact on employers in virtually every company in America.

Although normally this law is referred to as OSHA, this appendix talks at length about both the Act and the agency that is known by the same initials. For the sake of clarity, the law is referred to as the OSH Act throughout the discussion.

In the years prior to passage of the OSH Act, there was a growing recognition that employers were largely unwilling to take preventive steps to reduce the occurrence of injuries, illnesses, and fatalities in the workplace. On December 6, 1907, a total of 362 miners died in an explosion at the Monongah coal mine in West Virginia—the worst mining disaster in American history. In that year alone, a total of 3,242 coal miners lost their lives. As a result, in 1910 Congress established the Bureau of Mines to investigate mining accidents.

There was a long period of time in the United States when it was cheaper for employers to fight lawsuits filed on behalf of workers killed or injured on the job than it was to implement safety programs. Because the courts rarely held employers accountable for worker injuries, many chose this approach. Employer attitudes in this regard didn't change until the shortage of skilled workers during World War II gave employees plentiful options for places to work—and they opted to work for employers that provided safe environments over those that didn't.

The tragic nature of large accidents in the railroad and mining industries captured public attention and created pressure on the federal government to take action. This led Congress to enact legislation requiring safety improvements in the coal mining and railroad industries, but these measures were specifically targeted to those industries. Little attention was paid to equally dangerous workplace safety and illness issues that didn't produce the spectacular accidents prevalent in mines or on railroads. In the late 1960s, some 14,000 American workers lost their lives each year due to injuries or illnesses suffered while on the job. The federal government had been working on solutions but was mired in bureaucratic turf battles over which agency should have control of the process. The Department of Health, Education, and Welfare wanted legislation that applied only to federal contractors, and the DOL, spurred by Secretary W. Willard Wirtz's personal interest in the subject, wanted to protect *all* American workers. After several years of this infighting, the proposal by the DOL was sent to the Congress and enacted as the Occupational Safety and Health Act of 1970. A key component of this legislation was the creation of the *Occupational Safety and Health Administration (OSHA)*, which now sets safety standards for all industries. OSHA enforces those standards with the use of fines and, in the case of criminal actions, can call on the Department of Justice to file charges against offenders.

The intent of Congress, as stated in the preamble to the OSH Act, is to ensure safe and healthful working conditions for American workers. To accomplish this purpose, the Act establishes three simple duties:

- Employers must provide every employee with a place to work that is "free from recognized hazards that are causing or are likely to cause death or serious physical harm."

- Employers must comply with all safety and health standards disseminated in accordance with the OSH Act.

- Employees are required to comply with occupational safety and health standards, rules, and regulations that have an impact on their individual actions and behavior.

As mentioned previously, the OSH Act created OSHA and gave it the authority to develop and enforce mandatory standards applicable to all businesses engaged in interstate commerce. The definition of interstate commerce is sufficiently broad to cover most businesses, except only those sole proprietors without employees, family farms employing only family members, and mining operations, which are covered by the Mine Safety and Health Act (discussed earlier in this appendix). The Act encouraged OSHA to work with industry associations and safety committees to build upon standards already developed by specific industries, and it authorized enforcement action to ensure that employers comply with the standards. OSHA was charged with developing reporting procedures to track trends in workplace safety and health so that the development of preventive measures would be an ongoing process that changed with the development of new processes and technologies.

The OSH Act also created the *National Institute of Occupational Safety and Health (NIOSH)* as part of the Department of Health and Human Services. NIOSH is charged with researching and evaluating workplace hazards and recommending ways to reduce the effect of those hazards on workers. NIOSH also supports education and training in the field of occupational safety and health by developing and providing educational materials and training aids and sponsoring conferences on workplace safety and health issues.

In 2011, OSHA celebrated 40 years in the business of protecting American workers. Its focus in the coming years includes increasing enforcement of the standards through additional hiring, and making sure vulnerable workers, such as those who speak English as a second language, are heard. How this translates into the workforce remains to be seen, but we can infer from the statements several key points, discussed next.

More Inspections

With OSHA pushing for an increased budget, it stands to reason that the hiring of additional enforcement officers means more inspections and fines.

Emphasis on Safety Communication

The 2010 National Action Summit for Latino Worker Health and Safety helped to launch OSHA's Diverse Workforce Limited Proficiency Outreach program, designed to "enhance (vulnerable) workers' knowledge of their workplace rights and improve their ability to exercise those rights." Conducting training and providing material in a language all workers can understand is a logical outcome from this focus.

Reporting of Injuries

In 2016, OSHA issued a new rule prohibiting employers from discouraging workers from reporting an injury or illness, including through safety-incentive programs rewarding employees for no injuries being reported. This rule requires employers to inform employees of their right to report work-related injuries and illnesses free from retaliation, which can be satisfied by posting the already required OSHA workplace poster. The rule also clarifies the existing implicit requirement that an employer's procedure for reporting work-related injuries and illnesses must be reasonable and not deter or discourage employees from reporting, and it incorporates the existing statutory prohibition on retaliating against employees for reporting work-related injuries or illnesses. These provisions became effective.

Finally, the OSH Act encourages the states to take the lead in developing and enforcing safety and health programs for businesses within their jurisdictions by providing grants to help states identify specific issues and develop programs for enforcement and prevention.

Employer Responsibilities

The OSH Act has three requirements, two of which pertain to employers. Not only must employers provide a workplace that is safe and healthful for employees, but they must also comply with established standards. OSHA has established other requirements for employers as required by the law:

- Employers are expected to take steps to minimize or reduce hazards, and ensure that employees have and use safe tools, equipment, and personal protective equipment (PPE) that are properly maintained.

- Employers are responsible for informing all employees about OSHA, posting the OSHA poster in a prominent location, and making employees aware of the standards that apply in the work site. If employees request a copy of a standard, the employer must provide it to them.

- Appropriate warning signs that conform to the OSHA standards for color coding, posting, or labels must be posted where needed to make employees aware of potential hazards.

- Compliance with OSHA standards also means employers must educate employees about safe operating procedures and train them to follow the procedures.

- Businesses with 11 or more employees must maintain records of all workplace injuries and illnesses and post them on Form 300A from February 1 through April 30 each year.

- Within eight hours of a fatal accident or one resulting in hospitalization for three or more employees, a report must be filed with the nearest OSHA office.

- An accident report log must be made available to employees, former employees, or employee representatives when reasonably requested.

- When employees report unsafe conditions to OSHA, the employer may not retaliate or discriminate against them.

Under an OSHA rule effective January 1, 2017, certain employers must electronically submit injury and illness data that they are already required to record on their on-site OSHA Injury and Illness forms. Analysis of this data will be a factor used by OSHA to determine how to allocate its enforcement and compliance resources. Some of the data will also be posted to the OSHA website.

The reporting requirements were phased in over two years:

- Establishments with 250 or more employees in industries covered by the record-keeping regulation had to submit information from their 2016 Form 300A by July 1, 2017. These same employers were required to submit information from all 2017 forms (300, 300A, and 301) by July 1, 2018. Beginning in 2019 and every year there-after, the information must be submitted by March 2. These employers are required to submit OSHA Form 301, where prior to this new rule, they could submit either an OSHA Form 301 or other equivalent documentation such as workers' compensation records.

- Establishments with 20 to 249 employees in certain high-risk industries had to submit information from their 2016 Form 300A by July 1, 2017 and their 2017 Form 300A by July 1, 2018. Beginning in 2019 and every year thereafter, the information must be submitted by March 2. A list of industries covered by this provision can be found at www.osha.gov/recordkeeping/NAICScodesforelectronicsubmission.html.

OSHA State Plan states must adopt requirements that are substantially identical to the requirements in this final rule within six months after publication of this final rule.

Employer Rights

Employers have some rights as well, including the right to seek advice and consultation from OSHA and to be active in industry activities involved in health and safety issues. Employers may also participate in the OSHA Standard Advisory Committee process in writing or by giving testimony at hearings. Finally, employers may contact NIOSH for information about substances used in work processes to determine whether they are toxic.

At times, employers may be unable to comply with OSHA standards because of the nature of specific operations. When this happens, they may apply to OSHA for temporary or permanent waivers to the standards along with proof that the protections developed by the organization meet or exceed those of the OSHA standards.

Employee Rights and Responsibilities

When the OSH Act was passed in 1970, employees were granted the basic right to a workplace with safe and healthful working conditions. The act intended to encourage employers and employees to collaborate in reducing workplace hazards. Employees have the responsibility to comply with all OSHA standards and with the safety and health procedures implemented by their employers. The Act gave employees the specific rights to do the following:

- Seek safety and health on the job without fear of punishment.

- Know what hazards exist on the job by reviewing the OSHA standards, rules, and regulations that the employer has available at the workplace.

- Be provided with the hazard-communication plan containing information about hazards in the workplace and preventive measures employees should take to avoid illness or injury, and to be trained in those measures.

- Access the exposure and medical records employers are required to keep relative to safety and health issues.

- Request an OSHA inspection, speak privately with the inspector, accompany the inspector during the inspection, and respond to the inspector's questions during the inspection.

- Observe steps taken by the employer to monitor and measure hazardous materials in the workplace, and access records resulting from those steps.

- Request information from NIOSH regarding the potential toxic effects of substances used in the workplace.

- File a complaint about workplace safety or health hazards with OSHA and remain anonymous to the employer.

OSHA Enforcement

OSHA's success is the result of strong enforcement of the standards it has developed. As demonstrated in the nineteenth and twentieth centuries, without the threat of financial penalty, some business owners would choose to ignore injury- and illness-prevention requirements. Construction and general industry continue to be the sources of the most frequently cited OSHA standards violations through 2018. That being the case, OSHA established fines and penalties that can be assessed against businesses when violations occur. Table C.7 describes the violation levels and associated penalties for noncompliance that are in effect as of January 2019. Students should note that OSHA plans to update these penalties every January to adjust for inflation.

TABLE C.7   Categories of penalties for OSHA violations

Violation	Description	Fine
Willful or repeated	Evidence exists of an intentional violation of the OSH Act or "plain indifference" to its requirements; OSHA previously issued citations for substantially similar conditions.	Up to $132,598 per violation
Serious	Hazards with substantial probability of death or serious physical harm exist.	Up to $13,260 per violation
Other than serious and posting requirements	An existing hazard could have a direct and immediate effect on the safety and health of employees.	Up to $13,260 per violation
Failure to abate	The employer failed to abate a prior violation.	Up to $13,260 per day beyond the abatement date

Source: https://www.osha.gov/penalties/

OSHA Record-Keeping Requirements

OSHA requires employers to record health and safety incidents that occur each year and to document steps they take to comply with regulations. Records of specific injuries and illnesses are compiled, allowing OSHA and NIOSH to identify emerging hazards for research and, if warranted, create new standards designed to reduce the possibility of similar injury or illness in the future. These records include up-to-date files for exposures to hazardous substances and related medical records, records of safety training meetings, and OSHA logs that record work-related injuries and illnesses.

As of January 1, 2002, OSHA revised the requirements for maintaining records of workplace injuries and illnesses in order to collect better information for use in prevention activities, simplify the information collection process, and make use of advances in technology. Three new forms were developed:

- OSHA Form 300, Log of Work-Related Injuries and Illnesses
- OSHA Form 300A, Summary of Work-Related Injuries and Illnesses
- OSHA Form 301, Injury and Illness Incident Report

Completion of the forms doesn't constitute proof of fault on the part of either the employer or the employee and doesn't indicate that any OSHA violations have occurred. Recording an injury or illness on the OSHA forms also doesn't mean that an employee is eligible for workers' compensation benefits.

The following paragraphs cover the basic requirements for OSHA record keeping, including who should file OSHA reports, which employers are exempt from filing, and what injuries are considered work-related.

Who Must Complete and File OSHA Forms?

All employers with 11 or more employees are required to complete and file the OSHA forms just discussed.

Are There Any Exemptions?

Employers with 10 or fewer employees aren't required to file the forms. In addition, OSHA has identified industries with low injury and illness rates and exempted them from filing reports. These include the retail, service, finance, insurance, and real estate industries. Unless OSHA has notified a business in writing that reports must be filed, the business is exempt from the requirement.

What Must Be Recorded?

OSHA regulations specify which employees are covered for reporting purposes. Injury or illness to any employee on the employer's payroll must be recorded, regardless of how the employee is classified: full-time or part-time, regular or temporary, hourly or salary, seasonal, and so on. Injuries to employees of temp agencies, if under the employer's direct supervision on a daily basis, must also be recorded. The owners and partners in sole proprietorships and partnerships aren't considered employees for OSHA reporting purposes.

Privacy concern cases are new protections developed by OSHA to protect employee privacy by substituting a case number for the employee name on the OSHA Form 300 log. Cases where this is appropriate include injury or illness that involved an intimate body part or resulted from a sexual assault; HIV infection, hepatitis, or tuberculosis; needle-stick injuries involving contaminated needles; and other illnesses when employees request that their names not be included on the log.

An injury or illness is generally considered to be work-related if it occurred in the workplace or while performing work-related duties off-site. The basic OSHA requirement records any work-related injury or illness that causes death, days away from work, restricted or limited duty, medical treatment beyond first aid, or loss of consciousness. Diagnosis of an injury or illness by a physician or other healthcare professional, even if it doesn't result in one of the circumstances listed, must also be reported.

Once the employer has determined that the injury or illness is work-related, the employer must determine whether this is a new case or a continuation of a previously recorded case. To a certain extent, this decision is left to the employer's common sense and best judgment. OSHA considers a new case to have occurred when an employee hasn't had a previous injury or illness that is the same as the current occurrence or when the employee has recovered completely from a previous injury or illness of the same type.

Annual Summary

At the end of each year, employers must review the OSHA Form 300 log and summarize the entries on Form 300A, which must then be certified by a company executive as correct and complete and posted, as previously mentioned, in February of the following year.

Retention

The OSHA Form 300 log and annual summary, privacy case list, and Form 301 Incident Report forms must be retained for five years following the end of the calendar year they cover.

Employee Involvement

Employers are required to provide employees and employee representatives, former employees, or a personal representative of an employee with information on how to properly report an injury or illness, and they're also required to allow employees or their representatives limited access to the records of injury and illness.

The OSHA Form 300 log must be provided to these requestors by the end of the following business day.

The OSHA Form 301 Incident Report must be provided by the end of the next business day when the employee who is the subject of the report requests a copy. When an employee representative requests copies, they must be provided within seven calendar days, and all information except that contained in the "Tell Us about the Case" section must be removed.

OSHA Assistance

OSHA provides many sources for employers and employees to obtain information about workplace health and safety issues. Chief among these is an extensive website (www.osha.gov) that provides access to the laws, regulations, and standards enforced by OSHA as well as general information on prevention. In addition to the website, OSHA publishes a number of pamphlets, brochures, and training materials that are available to employers. While OSHA exists to protect workers' safety rights, there are services such as consultation and voluntary participation programs that exist specifically to aid employers in complying with the standards.

OSHA Consultants

Educating employers and employees about workplace health and safety issues is key to preventing injuries and illnesses in the workplace. OSHA provides training programs for consultants who work with business owners in establishing effective health and safety programs. These free consultation services give employers an opportunity to learn which of the standards apply in their work site, involve employees in the safety process, and correct possible violations without a citation and penalty. Once the consultant becomes involved, the employer must abate any violations, or the consultant will refer the violation to an OSHA inspector.

The *Safety and Health Achievement Recognition Program* (*SHARP*) recognizes small, high-hazard employers that have requested a comprehensive OSHA consultation, corrected any violations, and developed an ongoing safety management program. To participate in the program, the business must agree to ask for additional consultations if work processes change.

Partnerships and Voluntary Programs

The *Strategic Partnership Program* is a means for businesses and employees to participate in solving health and safety problems with OSHA. Partnerships currently exist in 15 industries, including construction, food processing, logging, and healthcare, to develop solutions specific to their businesses.

The *OSHA Alliance Program* provides a vehicle for collaboration with employer organizations interested in promoting workplace health and safety issues. The program is open to trade and professional organizations, businesses, labor organizations, educational institutions, and government agencies, among others.

The *Voluntary Protection Program* (VPP) is open to employers with tough, well-established safety programs. VPP participants must meet OSHA criteria for the program and, having done so, are removed from routine scheduled inspection lists. The program serves to motivate employees to work more safely, reducing workers' compensation costs, and to encourage employers to make further improvements to safety programs. Acceptance into the VPP is an official recognition of exemplary occupational safety and health practices.

Health and Safety Inspections

The OSH Act authorizes both OSHA and NIOSH to investigate health or safety hazards in the workplace. The majority of OSHA inspections are focused on industries with higher hazard risks based on injury and illness rates. Some inspections occur at the request of an employer or employee in a specific organization. Less than 1 percent of OSHA inspections occur as part of the agency's Enhanced Enforcement Program that monitors employers with a history of repeat or willful violations.

NIOSH inspections, known as *health hazard evaluations*, always occur in response to the request of an employer, an employee, or a government agency.

No matter which agency conducts an investigation, employees who request or participate in them are protected by the OSH Act from retaliation or adverse employment actions.

OSHA Inspections

Most OSHA inspections are conducted without notice by a compliance safety and health officer (CSHO) who has been trained on OSHA standards and how to recognize safety and health hazards in the workplace. OSHA has established a hierarchy of situations to give priority to inspection of the most dangerous workplace environments.

During an inspection, OSHA follows a distinct procedure. In advance of the inspection, the CSHO prepares by reviewing records related to any previous incidents, inspections, or employee complaints. The inspector also determines what, if any, special testing equipment will be necessary for the inspection. Upon the inspector's arrival at the work site, the inspection commences with an opening conference, proceeds to a workplace tour, and ends with a closing conference:

1. The CSHO arrives at the work site and presents credentials. If the credentials aren't presented, the employer should insist on seeing them before the inspection begins. It's critical that any employee who may be the first person approached at the work site be

instructed as to who should be contacted when a CSHO arrives. Employers have the right to require the inspector to have a security clearance before entering secure areas. Any observation of trade secrets during the inspection remains confidential; CSHOs who breach this confidentiality are subject to fines and imprisonment.

2. The CSHO holds an *opening conference* during which the inspector explains why the site was selected, the purpose of the visit, and the scope of the inspection, and discusses the standards that apply to the work site. The CSHO requests an employee representative to accompany the CSHO on the inspection along with the management representative. If no employee accompanies the inspector on the tour, the CSHO will talk to as many employees as necessary to understand the safety and health issues in the workplace.

3. The next step is a tour of the facilities. During the tour, the inspector determines what route to take, where to look, and which employees to talk to. During this part of the inspection, the CSHO may talk privately to employees, taking care to minimize disruptions to work processes. Activities that can occur during an inspection include the following:

    ▪ Reviewing the safety and health program

    ▪ Examining records, including OSHA logs, records of employee exposure to toxic substances, and medical records

    ▪ Ensuring that the OSHA workplace poster is prominently displayed

    ▪ Evaluating compliance with OSHA standards specific to the work site

    ▪ Pointing out unsafe working conditions to the employer and suggesting possible remedial actions

4. The inspector holds a *closing conference* where the inspector, the employer, and, if requested, the employee representative discuss the observations made and corrective actions that must be taken. At this time the employer may produce records to assist in resolving any corrective actions to be taken. The CSHO discusses any possible citations or penalties that may be issued, and the OSHA area director makes the final determination based on the inspector's report.

Should the OSHA area director determine that citations are necessary to ensure employer compliance with OSHA, the director will issue the citations and determine the penalties to be assessed according to established guidelines that consider various factors, including the size of the company. The OSHA area director also determines the seriousness of the danger(s), how many employees would be impacted, and good-faith efforts on the part of the employer to comply with the standards, among others.

During the course of an OSHA inspection, an employer may raise an affirmative defense to any violations observed by the inspector. Possible affirmative defenses include the following:

▪ It is an isolated case caused by unpreventable employee misconduct. This defense may apply when the employer has established, communicated, and enforced adequate work rules that were ignored by the employee.

- Compliance is impossible based on the nature of the employer's work, and there are no viable alternative means of protection.

- Compliance with the standard would cause a greater hazard to employees, and there are no alternative means of protection.

The employer has the burden to prove that an affirmative defense exists. If it is successfully proven, the OSHA area director may decide that a citation and penalty aren't warranted. Employers have specific responsibilities and rights during and after the inspection:

- Employers are required to cooperate with the CSHO by providing records and documents requested during the inspection and by allowing employees or their representatives to accompany the inspector on the work site tour.

- Should a citation be issued during the inspection, the employer must post it at or near the work site involved, where it must remain for three working days or until the violation has been abated, whichever is longer. It goes without saying, of course, that the employer is required to abate the violation within the time frame indicated by the citation.

- Employers may file a *Notice of Contest* within 15 days of a citation and proposed penalty. If there will be an unavoidable delay in abating a violation because the materials, equipment, or personnel won't be available, the employer may request a temporary variance until the violation can be corrected.

Within 15 days of receipt of a citation by an employer, employees have the right to object in writing to the abatement period set by OSHA for correcting violations. Employees who have requested an inspection also have the right to be advised by OSHA of the results of the inspection.

NIOSH Evaluations

The NIOSH mandate contained in the OSH Act is to identify and evaluate potential workplace hazards and recommend actions to reduce or eliminate the effects of chemicals, biological agents, work stress, excessive noise, radiation, poor ergonomics, and other risks found in the workplace. NIOSH established the *Health Hazard Evaluation* (HHE) program to respond to concerns about these and other risks expressed by employers, employees, unions, and government agencies.

NIOSH has an established process for responding to requests for assistance:

- A written response acknowledging the request is provided within a few weeks.

- NIOSH reviews the request and, depending on the nature and severity of the hazard being described, responds in one of three ways:

  - NIOSH may have written materials that address the concern or may refer the request to another government agency better equipped to respond. If written materials aren't available, a project officer is assigned to assess the need for further assistance.

  - The project officer telephones the requestor to discuss the request. In some cases, the request is resolved during the call.

  - The project office may determine that the appropriate response is a site visit.

If an on-site visit is required, NIOSH will conduct an investigation, gathering information by touring the site, meeting with management and employees, and reviewing relevant records maintained by the employer. The project office may also use other investigative procedures such as sampling devices or medical tests to gather information. During an on-site visit, employees, employee representatives, and NIOSH project officers have seven legal rights considered nonnegotiable by NIOSH:

▪ NIOSH has the right to enter the workplace to conduct an HHE.

▪ NIOSH has the right to access relevant information and records maintained by the employer.

▪ NIOSH has the right to meet privately with management and employees for confidential interviews.

▪ An employee requestor or other employee representative has the right to accompany NIOSH during the evaluation inspection. NIOSH may also request participation from other employees if necessary to complete the evaluation.

▪ Employee representatives have the right to attend opening and closing conferences.

▪ Employees and managers have the right to participate in the investigation by wearing sampling devices and to take part in medical tests or in the use of sampling devices.

▪ The interim and final HHE reports must be made available to employees; the employer must either post the final report in the workplace for 30 days or provide NIOSH with employee names and addresses so that the report can be mailed to them.

Once the information-gathering phase is complete, NIOSH analyzes the data collected during the HHE and compiles a written report that is provided to the employer, employee, and union representatives.

Many activities that occur during either an OSHA consultation or NIOSH HHE seem similar and may cause confusion about which type of assistance is appropriate for any given situation. Table C.8 provides guidelines for determining which agency should be involved.

TABLE C.8   OSHA consultation versus NIOSH HHE

OSHA consultation	NIOSH HHE
Identify workplace hazards.	Identify the cause of employee illness.
Suggest ways to correct hazards.	Evaluate the potential for hazard from exposure to unregulated chemicals or working conditions.
Assist in creating an effective safety and health program.	Investigate adverse health effects from permissible exposures to regulated chemicals or working conditions.
Assist in reducing workers' compensation costs.	Conduct medical or epidemiologic hazard investigations.

OSHA consultation	NIOSH HHE
Assist in improving employee morale.	Investigate higher-than-expected occurrences of injury or illness.
	Evaluate newly identified hazards.
	Investigate the possible hazard of exposure to a combination of agents.
	Evaluate the potential for hazard from exposure to unregulated chemicals or working conditions.

Organisation for Economic Co-operation and Development (OECD): Guidelines for Multinational Enterprises (MNEs)

The mission of the Organisation for Economic Co-operation and Development (OECD) is to promote policies that will improve the economic and social well-being of people around the world. This group works with government agencies and makes recommendations to address social, economic, and corruption/fairness issues in business dealings across boundaries (geographic, social, and political), all with a focus on the well-being of global citizens. The Guidelines for Multinational Enterprises lists responsible business conduct. They provide voluntary principles and standards in the areas of employment and industrial relations, human rights, environment, information disclosure, combating bribery, consumer interests, science and technology, competition, and taxation. First adopted in 1976, the guidelines have been reviewed and updated five times since then to reflect changing conditions. The most recent update in 2011 included a human rights addition, adapted from the United Nations' Guiding Principles on Business and Human Rights. Additionally, issues such as due diligence, sustainable supply chain management practices, and provisions on Internet freedom were reinforced.

The governments committed to adhering to the principles are responsible for establishing a National Contact Point (NCP). The NCPs establish relationships with other participants, the business community, labor unions, and any other group needing implementation support of the Guidelines. Governments must commit to the following through their NCP: visibility, accessibility, transparency, and accountability. The NCPs facilitate grievances, called "specific instances," although they are not judicial bodies. The NCPs facilitate problem-solving through methods of conciliation and mediation.

Additionally, OECD Watch supports nongovernmental organizations (NGOs), helping them identify and hold businesses accountable for sustainable development and the eradication of poverty through policy development, education, and interactions with businesses and unions.

Patient Protection and Affordable Care Act of 2010 (PPACA, ACA, Obamacare)

On March 23, 2010, President Barack Obama signed into law a healthcare reform bill that had several employer implications. It established criteria to ensure that Americans had access to affordable healthcare.

It is important to note that the PPACA does not require that employers provide healthcare insurance. It does, however, impose penalties on large employers who fail to provide access to affordable "minimal essential coverage" beginning in the year 2014. A large employer is defined as those who employed an average of at least 50 full-time equivalent employees during the preceding calendar year, with an employee working 30 hours a week counted as one full-time worker, and the others prorated. In 2011, the following elements became active:

- Prohibition of lifetime limits for essential health services such as ambulatory care, emergency care, and maternity/newborn care

- Prohibition of denial of coverage for preexisting conditions for dependents under the age of 19

- The provision of healthcare for those otherwise qualified under the age of 26

- Reimbursement under Flexible Spending Accounts, Health Savings Accounts, Medical Savings Accounts, and Health Reimbursement Arrangements for over-the-counter drugs is no longer allowed; reimbursement is now limited to prescription drugs or insulin.

- The value of employee health benefits must be communicated on the employee's W-2.

In 2014, the state exchanges went live and individual responsibilities, employer obligations, and Medicaid expansions took effect. It is unclear how the results of subsequent American elections may impact all or part of the PPACA, so HR will need to stay updated to ensure ongoing compliance.

On his 2017 inauguration day, President Donald Trump signed an executive order designed to "minimize the economic burden" of key provisions of the PPACA. While still unclear on how the order will affect the status and requirements of the current law, HR practitioners will need to keep a close eye on any changes as they occur as the result of this and any further orders, amendments, and interpretations.

Pension Protection Act of 2006 (PPA)

The main focus of the Pension Protection Act of 2006 was to require employers to fully fund their pension plans to avoid future cash shortfalls in the plans as employees retire. Beginning in 2008, companies had seven years to bring their plans into compliance; for those that didn't comply, the Act provided a penalty in the form of a 10 percent excise tax. The Act also specified funding notices that must be provided by defined benefit plans.

One of the biggest changes to pension rules made by the PPA was to allow employers to automatically enroll employees in 401(k) plans. Employees who do not want to participate must now opt out of the plan. Another change was that plan advisers may now provide investment advice to plan participants and their beneficiaries under certain conditions.

Largely as a result of the Enron scandal, the PPA included a requirement for defined contribution plans that include employer stock to provide at least three alternative investment options and allow employees to divest themselves of the employer's stock.

When the Economic Growth and Tax Relief Reconciliation Act of 2001 (EGTRRA) was enacted, Congress increased contribution limits for 401(k) plans and individual retirement accounts (IRAs) and allowed catch-up contributions for taxpayers older than 50 years of age. These changes were set to expire in 2010, but the PPA made them permanent. Employees older than age 50 will be able to make 401(k) catch-up contributions to retirement funds. For 2009, the maximum contribution is $5,500; this amount may be adjusted for inflation in multiples of $500 each year.

Privacy Act of 1974

The Privacy Act of 1974 was an attempt by Congress to regulate the amount and type of information collected by federal agencies and the methods by which it was stored in an effort to protect the personal privacy of individuals about whom the information had been collected. The Act requires written authorization from an individual prior to releasing information to another person. The Act does not currently apply to private employers.

First, the Act provides individuals with the right to know what kind of information is being collected about them, how it is used and maintained, and whether it is disseminated. The Act prevents this information from being used for purposes other than that for which it was collected, and it allows individuals to obtain copies of the information, review it, and request amendments to inaccurate information. The Act requires the government to ensure that information collected is not misused. Except under specific circumstances covered by the Privacy Act, such as law enforcement or national security needs, the information collected by one agency must not be shared with another. Damages for violation of these requirements may be sought in federal district court and, if found by the judge to be warranted, are subject to reimbursement of attorney's fees and litigation costs, as well as a fine for actual damages incurred by the individual of up to $1,000 paid by the federal government.

Rehabilitation Act of 1973, Sections 501, 503, and 505

The Rehabilitation Act of 1973 was enacted to expand the opportunities available for persons with physical or mental disabilities. The employment clauses of the Act apply to agencies of the federal government and federal contractors with contracts of $10,000 or more during a 12-month period. Section 501 addresses employment discrimination, while Section 505 details the remedies available for those who have been subjected to unlawful employment practices. The EEOC has enforcement responsibility for Section 501. Under Section 503, individuals with disabilities who think a federal contractor has violated the requirements of the Rehabilitation Act may also file complaints with the Department of Labor through the Office of Federal Contract Compliance Programs (OFCCP).

Sarbanes-Oxley Act of 2002 (SOX)

Although the main focus of *Sarbanes-Oxley Act (SOX)* compliance is the reporting of financial transactions and activities, HR professionals may be called on to participate in SOX reporting requirements. SOX requires information that materially affects an organization's financial status to be reported to the Securities and Exchange Commission (SEC), in some cases immediately, when the organization becomes aware of the information. Some instances where this would apply to HR management are the following:

- Ensuring that material liabilities from pending lawsuits or settlements of employment practices claims are reported in the financial statements

- Participating in the review and testing of internal controls for hiring, compensation, and termination practices

- Reporting immediately any material changes to the organization's financial condition. Although in most cases this wouldn't be an HR responsibility, the settlement of a large class action lawsuit could potentially reach the threshold of a material change.

Failure to provide this information within the time frames required by SOX can result in criminal penalties, including incarceration, for employees who obstruct legal investigations into financial reporting issues. SOX also prohibits employers from retaliating against whistle-blowers who report financial conduct that they reasonably believe violates federal laws designed to protect shareholders from fraudulent activity.

Service Contract Act of 1965 (SCA)

The McNamara-O'Hara Service Contract Act of 1965 requires any federal service contractor with a contract exceeding $2,500 to pay its employees the prevailing wage and fringe benefits for the geographic area in which it operates, provide safe and sanitary working conditions, and notify employees of the minimum allowable wage for each job classification, as well as the equivalent federal employee classification and wage rate for similar jobs.

The SCA expands the requirements of the Davis-Bacon and Walsh-Healey Acts to contractors providing services to the federal government, such as garbage removal, custodial services, food and lodging, and the maintenance and operation of electronic equipment. Federal contractors already subject to the requirements of Davis-Bacon, Walsh-Healey, or laws covering other federal contracts, such as public utility services or transportation of people or freight, are exempt from the SCA.

Sexual Harassment

Title VII of the Civil Rights Act of 1964 and its subsequent amendments require employers to furnish a workplace that is free from *sexual harassment*. There are two forms of sexual harassment that must be prevented: quid pro quo and hostile work environment.

Quid pro quo is a legal term that means, in Latin, "this for that." Quid pro quo harassment, therefore, occurs when a supervisor or manager asks for sexual favors in return for some type of favorable employment action. "Sexual favors" is a broad term that covers actions ranging from unwanted touching to more explicit requests.

A *hostile work environment* has been defined by the EEOC as one in which an individual or individuals are subjected to unwelcome verbal or physical conduct "when submission to or rejection of this conduct explicitly or implicitly affects an individual's employment, unreasonably interferes with an individual's work performance, or creates an intimidating, hostile, or offensive work environment." When investigating these charges, the EEOC looks at many factors. In most cases, a single incident of inappropriate and unwelcome behavior does not rise to the level of a hostile work environment, but in some cases when the actions or behaviors are particularly offensive or intimidating, the EEOC may find that harassment has occurred. A hostile work environment can also be found to exist for victims who have been affected by unwelcome offensive conduct toward someone other than themselves.

Hostile Work Environment Harassment

Courts have held employers responsible for the harassing actions of their employees, whether or not the employer was aware of the harassment. Beginning in 1986, the Supreme Court issued a number of rulings to clarify employer responsibilities in the prevention of sexual harassment. The most commonly cited of these for HR purposes are *Meritor Savings Bank vs. Vinson* (1986), *Harris vs. Forklift Systems* (1993), and two cases decided at the same time in 1998, *Faragher vs. City of Boca Raton* and *Burlington Industries vs. Ellerth*.

Meritor Savings Bank vs. Vinson (1986)

Mechelle Vinson applied for a job at a branch of Meritor Savings Bank in 1974 when Sidney Taylor was a vice president and manager of the branch. Taylor hired Vinson, who worked at the branch for four years, starting as a teller trainee and working her way up to assistant branch manager, based on her performance in the jobs she held. Once she passed her probationary period as a trainee, Vinson claims that Taylor began to harass her, requesting that they go to a motel to have sexual relations. Although Vinson refused Taylor's advances initially, she gave in eventually because she believed she would lose her job if she did not. Vinson claims that Taylor's harassment escalated to the point that she was fondled in front of other employees and expected to engage in sexual relations at the branch both during and after work. In September 1978, Vinson took an indefinite medical leave, and the bank terminated her in November 1978.

The Supreme Court issued its opinion in June 1986, finding that a claim of "hostile environment" sex discrimination is actionable under Title VII. The Court rejected the idea that the "mere existence of a grievance procedure and a policy against discrimination" is enough to protect an employer from the acts of its supervisors. The opinion indicated that a policy designed to encourage victims of harassment to come forward would provide greater protection.

Harris vs. Forklift Systems (1993)

In April 1985, Teresa Harris was employed by Forklift Systems, Inc., as a manager, reporting to the company president, Charles Hardy. Hardy insulted Harris frequently in front of customers and other employees and made sexually suggestive remarks. When Harris complained in August 1987, Hardy apologized and said he would stop the conduct. But in September of that year, Hardy once again began the verbal harassment, and Harris quit on October 1.

Harris then filed a lawsuit against Forklift, claiming that Hardy had created a hostile work environment on the basis of her gender. The District Court found that although Hardy's conduct was offensive, it did not meet the required standard of severity to seriously affect her psychological well-being.

The Supreme Court agreed to hear the case in order to resolve conflicts in the lower courts on what conduct was actionable for a hostile work environment. The Court found that the appropriate standard is one that falls between that which is merely offensive and that which results in tangible psychological injury. Although this is not a precise guideline, it does allow courts to take into consideration a number of factors about the work environment, the frequency and severity of the conduct, the level of threat or humiliation that the victim is subjected to, and whether the conduct interferes unreasonably with performance of the employee's job.

Faragher vs. City of Boca Raton (1998)

Beth Faragher and Nancy Ewanchew were two of six females out of more than 40 lifeguards for the City of Boca Raton in Florida from 1985 to 1989. During their tenure, they were verbally and physically harassed by two supervisors, Bill Terry and David Silverman. They both complained to a third supervisor, Robert Gordon, about the harassment but did not file a formal complaint, and no corrective action was taken. Ewanchew resigned in 1989 and wrote to the city manager in 1990 to complain about the harassment. The city investigated and (when it found that both Terry and Silverman had acted inappropriately) reprimanded and disciplined both supervisors.

The Supreme Court found that employers are responsible for actions of those they employ and have a responsibility to control them. Going further, the Court determined that a supervisor need not make an explicit threat of an adverse tangible employment action (TEA), which the Court defined as "a significant change in employment status, such as hiring, firing, failing to promote, reassignment with significantly different responsibilities, or a decision causing a significant change in benefits" in order for harassment to be actionable. The Court determined that subordinates know that the possibility of adverse supervisory actions exists whenever requests are made, even if the adverse actions are not stated.

Burlington Industries vs. Ellerth (1998)

Kimberly Ellerth worked for Burlington Industries in Chicago as a salesperson from March 1993 to May 1994. During that time, Ellerth claims that she was subjected to ongoing sexual harassment by Ted Slowick, who was not her direct supervisor but did have the power to approve or deny a TEA with regard to her employment. Although Ellerth was aware of Burlington's policy prohibiting sexual harassment during her employment, she did not complain about the harassment until after she resigned. After resigning, she filed a complaint with the EEOC and, when she received a right-to-sue letter in October 1994, filed suit against Burlington.

A key issue in this case was that of *vicarious liability* (an element of the legal concept of *respondeat superior*) that, in this context, means an employer may be held accountable for the harmful actions of its employees, whether or not the employer is aware of those actions. The Supreme Court decided in part that "An employer is subject to vicarious liability to a victimized employee for an actionable hostile environment created by a supervisor with immediate (or successively higher) authority over the employee."

In 1997, the first case of same-sex harassment reached the U.S. Supreme Court. In the majority opinion issued for *Oncale vs. Sundowner Offshore Services, Inc.*, Justice Antonin Scalia observed that "...male on male sexual harassment was assuredly not the principal evil Congress was concerned with when it enacted Title VII. But statutory prohibitions often go beyond the principal evil to cover reasonably comparable evils...." A number of cases following *Oncale* resulted in substantial awards or settlements in cases of same-sex harassment. In 1998, President Bill Clinton amended an executive order to include sexual orientation as a protected class.

EEOC Guidelines for the Prevention of Sexual Harassment

The EEOC has developed detailed guidelines entitled "Enforcement Guidance: Vicarious Employer Liability for Unlawful Harassment by Supervisors" to assist employers in developing policies that clearly express the employer's prohibition against harassment and conducting investigations that meet EEOC standards.

To summarize the guidelines, employers are encouraged to develop antiharassment policies, along with complaint procedures for those who believe they have been harassed. The policy should clearly explain unacceptable conduct and reassure employees who complain that they will be protected against retaliation. The complaint process should describe multiple avenues for reporting harassment and provide assurances of confidentiality to the extent it is possible. Investigations of allegations should be prompt and impartial, and if the investigation finds that harassment did indeed occur, the policy should provide for immediate corrective action.

Uniformed Services Employment and Reemployment Rights Act of 1994 (USERRA)

Congress enacted the Uniformed Services Employment and Reemployment Rights Act (USERRA) in 1994 to protect the rights of reservists called to active duty in the armed forces. The Act provides reemployment and benefits rights and is administered through the Veterans Employment and Training Service (VETS) of the Department of Labor. USERRA applies to all public and private employers in the United States, including the federal government. The DOL issued revised rules for employers that became effective on January 18, 2006. These revisions clarified some of the requirements previously issued. Some of its stipulations are the following:

Coverage

- All employers, regardless of size, are required to comply with USERRA regulations.
- Members of all uniformed services are protected by USERRA.
- USERRA prohibits discrimination due to past, current, or future military obligations.
- In addition to service during times of war or national emergency, USERRA protects any voluntary or involuntary service such as active duty, training, boot camp, reserve weekend duty, National Guard mobilizations, and absence due to required fitness for duty examinations.

Notice Requirements

- In most circumstances, employees must give verbal or written notice to the employer that they have been called to active service. If an employee is unable to give notice, a military representative may provide the notice.
- If military necessity prevents advance notice, or if giving notice is impossible or unreasonable, employees are still protected by USERRA.

- To be eligible for reemployment rights, service members must report back to work within time frames that vary according to the length of service. Table C.9 shows the reporting time requirements established by USERRA for returning to work based on varying lengths of service.

Duration

- The employer must grant a leave of absence for up to five years, although there are several exceptions that extend coverage beyond five years.
- Types of leave protected without limits include the following:
    - Boot camp
    - Initial service period
    - Waiting for orders
    - Annual two-week mandatory training
- Employees are permitted to moonlight during off-duty hours without losing reinstatement rights.
- Employees do not lose reinstatement rights if they leave their jobs to prepare for mobilization but the mobilization is canceled.

Compensation

- USERRA does not require employers to pay employees during military absences, unless the employer has an established policy of doing so.
- Employers may not require employees to apply accrued vacation pay to their military leaves, but employees may choose to do so.

Benefit Protection

- Employees on military leave are entitled to the same benefits employers provide for others on a leave of absence.
- Employees continue to accrue seniority and other benefits as though they were continuously employed.
- For leave greater than 30 days but less than 240 days in duration, the employer must offer COBRA-like health coverage upon request of the employee; for service less than 31 days, and at the employee's request, the employer must continue health coverage at the regular employee cost.
- Returning service members are entitled to participate in any rights and benefits provided to employees returning from nonmilitary leaves of absence.

Pension Protection

- Employee pension rights are protected by USERRA.
- Vesting and accrual for returning service members are treated as though there was no break in employment.

- Employer pension contributions must be the same as though the military leave did not occur.

- For defined contribution plans, service members must be given three times the period of the military leave absence (not to exceed five years) to make up contributions that were missed during the leave. Plans with an employer matching component are required to match the makeup funds.

Reinstatement

- The employer must "promptly" reinstate regular employees to positions that the employees would have earned had they remained on the job, referred to as an *escalator position*. The Act does not specify a definition of "promptly," since the timing will depend on the length of the leave. For example, an employee on leave for annual two-week training would be expected to be reemployed on the first workday following the end of leave. On the other hand, someone who has been serving on active duty for five years may be promptly reemployed after notice to vacate the position is given to the incumbent.

- Temporary employees do not have reinstatement rights.

- Seasonal or fixed-term contract employees are not entitled to reinstatement.

- Reemployment rights are forfeited if the employee has been discharged dishonorably or other than honorably from the service, has been expelled as a result of a court martial, or has been absent without leave (AWOL) for 90 days.

Continued Employment

- Employees returning to work from leaves of more than 30 but less than 181 days may not be discharged without cause for six months after the date of reemployment.

- Employees returning to work from leaves of 181 days or more may not be discharged without cause for one year from the date of reemployment.

Disabled Veterans

The employer must make reasonable accommodation to provide training or retraining to reemploy a returning service member disabled as a result of service; if reasonable accommodation creates an undue hardship, reemployment can be made to a position "nearest approximate" in terms of status and pay and with full seniority to which the person is entitled.

TABLE C.9   USERRA reemployment reporting times

Length of service	Reporting time
1 to 30 days *or* absence for "fitness for service" exam	The first regularly scheduled full workday that begins eight hours after the end of the service completion

Length of service	Reporting time
31 to 180 days	Submit application for reemployment no later than 14 days after the end of service or on the next business day after that.
181 or more days	Submit application for reemployment no later than 90 days after the end of service or on the next business day after that.
Disability incurred or aggravated	Reporting or application deadline is extended for up to two years.

United States Patent Act of 1790

A *patent* allows inventors exclusive rights to the benefits of an invention for a defined period of time. Generally, the term of a new patent is 20 years from the date on which the application for the patent was filed in the United States or, in special cases, from the date an earlier related application was filed, subject to the payment of maintenance fees. U.S. patent grants are effective only within the United States, U.S. territories, and U.S. possessions. Patents protect an inventor's "right to exclude others from making, using, offering for sale, or selling" the invention in the United States or "importing" the invention into the United States. Patent laws in the United States define three types of patents:

- *Design patents* protect new, original, and ornamental designs of manufactured items. Design patents are limited to 14 years.

- *Utility patents* protect the invention of new and useful processes, machines, manufacture or composition of matter, and new and useful improvements to the same. Utility patents are limited to 20 years.

- *Plant patents* protect the invention or discovery of asexually reproduced varieties of plants for 20 years.

Wage Garnishment Law, Federal

The Federal Wage Garnishment Law is found in Title III of the Consumer Credit Protection Act (CCPA) of 1968 and applies to all employers and employees. Employers are required to withhold funds from an employee's paycheck and send the money to an entity designated in the court order or levy document.

Title III of the CCPA protects employees in three ways:

- Prohibits employers from terminating employees whose wages are garnished for any one debt, even if the employer receives multiple garnishment orders for the same debt

- Sets limits on the amount that can be garnished in any single week. Currently, the weekly amount may not exceed the lesser of two figures: 25 percent of the employee's disposable earnings, or the amount by which an employee's disposable earnings are greater than 30 times the federal minimum wage (currently $7.25 an hour).

- Defines how disposable earnings are to be calculated for garnishment withholdings

Earnings that may be garnished include wages, salaries, bonuses, and commissions. Other income from pension plans or employer-paid disability may be subject to garnishment as well. The law does not protect employees from termination if the employer receives garnishments for more than one debt.

Walsh-Healey Public Contracts Act of 1936

The Walsh-Healey Public Contracts Act requires government contractors with contracts exceeding $10,000 (for other than construction work) to pay their employees the prevailing wage for their local area as established by the Secretary of Labor.

Worker Adjustment Retraining and Notification Act of 1988 (WARN)

The WARN Act was passed by Congress in 1988 to provide some protection for workers in the event of mass layoffs or plant closings. The Act requires that 60 days' advance notice be given to either the individual workers or their union representatives. The intent of Congress was to provide time for workers to obtain new employment or training before the loss of their jobs occurred. The WARN Act is administered by the Department of Labor and enforced through the federal courts.

Employers with 100 or more full-time employees or those with 100 or more full- and part-time employees who work in the aggregate 4,000 hours or more per week are subject to the provisions of the WARN Act. The employee count includes those who are on temporary leave or layoff with a reasonable expectation of recall.

The WARN Act established that a mass layoff occurs when either 500 employees are laid off or at least 50 employees making up 33 percent of the workforce and are laid off. A plant closing occurs when 50 or more full-time employees lose their jobs because a single facility shuts down, either permanently or temporarily. In cases where the employer staggers the workforce reduction over a period of time, care must be taken that appropriate notice is given if the total reductions within a 90-day period trigger the notice requirement.

The WARN Act also established rules on notice. For instance, notice is required to be given to all affected employees or their representatives, the chief elected official of the local government, and the state dislocated worker unit. Notice requirements vary according to which group the notices are being sent to, but they must contain specific information about the reasons for the closure, whether the action is permanent or temporary, the address of the affected business unit, the name of a company official to contact for further information, the expected date of closure or layoff, and whether bumping rights exist.

The WARN Act provides for three situations in which the 60-day notice is not required, but the burden is on the employer to show that the reasons are legitimate and not an attempt to thwart the intent of the Act:

- The faltering company exception applies only to plant closures in situations where the company is actively seeking additional funding and has a reasonable expectation that it will be forthcoming in an amount sufficient to preclude the layoff or closure and that giving the notice would negatively affect the ability of the company to obtain the funding.

- The unforeseeable business circumstance exception applies to plant closings and mass layoffs and occurs when circumstances take a sudden and unexpected negative turn that could not have reasonably been predicted, such as the cancellation of a major contract without previous warning.

- The natural disaster exception applies to both plant closings and mass layoffs occurring as the result of a natural disaster, such as a flood, earthquake, or fire.

Workers' Compensation

Workers' compensation laws require employers to assume responsibility for all employee injuries, illnesses, and deaths related to employment. These laws are enacted and enforced by the individual states, and provide benefits for employees that cover medical and rehabilitation expenses, provide income replacement during periods of disability when employees are unable to work, and pay benefits to their survivors in the event of an employee's death.

The amount of compensation paid is based on actuarial tables that take into account the seriousness of the injury, whether the disability is permanent or temporary, whether it is a full or partial disability (such as the loss of an eye or hand), and the amount of income lost because of the injury. In most cases, employers fund workers' compensation obligations by purchasing coverage through private insurance companies or state-sponsored insurance funds. The premiums for workers' compensation coverage are based on a percentage of the employer's payroll in various job categories. The percentages are different and depend on previous claim activity in each category. The rate charged for a roofer, for example, is much higher than that for an office worker because of the inherent danger of the job and the number and severity of claims that result.

In some states, companies may self-fund workers' compensation programs, meaning that they pay the total costs of any injuries or illnesses when they occur instead of paying insurance premiums. These are known as *nonsubscriber plans* and are rare; generally, self-funded insurance plans make economic sense only for very large organizations with the financial base to support the payment of large claims when they occur.

Although increased emphasis on safety programs and training has led to a reduction in the number of nationwide workers' compensation claims filed each year, the insurance rates are increasing largely because of increased medical costs. This is most evident in California, where employers saw costs double between 2000 and 2003, but it has also led to state reform of workers' compensation programs in Florida, West Virginia, Washington, and Texas.

Implementing programs aimed at reducing the cost of workers' compensation coverage for their organizations is one way HR professionals can show a positive impact on the bottom line. Implementing safety training and injury prevention programs, as discussed in Chapter 6, "Employee and Labor Relations" is one way to reduce job-related injury and illness and to prevent claims. The costs of individual claims can be reduced by ensuring the availability of jobs that meet "light duty" medical requirements so that employees are able to return to work earlier, shortening the length of their leave.

Quick Reference Guide: Agencies, Court Cases, Terms, and Laws; General Record-Keeping Guidelines

Table C.10 presents information on agencies, court cases, terms, and laws, and Table C.11 provides general record-keeping guidelines.

TABLE C.10 Agencies, court cases, terms, and laws

Name	Description
Adverse impact	According to the Uniform Guidelines on Employee Selection Procedures, adverse impact is a substantially different rate of selection in hiring, promotion, or other employment decision, which works to the disadvantage of members of a race, sex, or ethnic group. Occurs when the selection rate (hiring, training, promotion, etc.) for protected class groups is less than four-fifths, or 80 percent, of the selection rate for the group with the highest selection rate.
Albemarle Paper vs. Moody	Required that employment tests be validated; subjective supervisor rankings aren't sufficient validation; criteria must be tied to job requirements.

Name	Description
Automobile Workers vs. Johnson Controls, Inc.	In response to a sex-based discrimination suit filed by women "capable of bearing children," the U.S. Supreme Court found that "decisions about the welfare of the next generation must be left to the parents who conceive, bear, support and raise them, rather than to the employers who hire those parents."
Bates vs. United Parcel	Established that when employers apply an unlawful standard that bars employees protected by the ADA from an application process, the employees don't need to prove they were otherwise qualified to perform essential job functions. The employer must prove the standard is necessary to business operations.
Black Lung Benefits Act (BLBA)	Provided benefits for coal miners suffering from pneumoconiosis due to mine work
Bureau of Labor Statistics (BLS)	An agency within the DOL that was established to study and publish statistical economic and industrial accidents data
Burlington Northern Santa Fe Railway Co. vs. White	Established that all retaliation against employees who file discrimination claims is unlawful under Title VII, even if no economic damage results
Circuit City Stores vs. Adams	Arbitration clauses in employment agreements are enforceable for employers engaged in interstate commerce except for transportation workers.
Citizen and Immigration Services, United States (USCIS)	A component of the Department of Homeland Security charged with overseeing lawful immigration to the United States. Individuals wishing to live or work in the United States must submit applications through the USCIS; employers must comply with Form I-9 and/or E-Verify for new hires.
Civil law	Regulations set by countries or legislative groups about the rights of people (different from common laws, which are set by judges)
Clause	A part of a document, agreement, proposal, or contract that gives more detail
Clayton Act	Limited the use of injunctions to break strikes; exempted unions from the Sherman Antitrust Act
Commercial diplomacy	The effort by multinational corporations to influence foreign government policy on issues such as tariffs, banking, and other financial regulations; antitrust/competition laws; workplace standards such as safety; data privacy; and corporate conduct in areas such as corruption, governance, and social responsibility

TABLE C.10   Agencies, court cases, terms, and laws *(continued)*

Name	Description
Congressional Accountability Act (CAA)	Required all federal employment legislation passed by Congress to apply to congressional employees
Davis vs. O'Melveny & Myers	Established that arbitration clauses in employment agreements won't be enforced if they're significantly favorable to the employer and the employee doesn't have a meaningful opportunity to reject the agreement
Department of Labor (DOL)	Charged with the administration and enforcement of U.S. labor laws
Disability	A physical or mental condition that limits, but does not prevent, the performance of certain tasks
Disparate impact	Occurs when protected class groups are treated differently than other groups in employment-related decisions; includes practices that are neutral on the surface but have a negative effect on protected groups (such as requiring a high school diploma in areas where minority groups have a lower graduation rate than nonminority groups)
Due process	The way a government enforces laws; in the United States, the way a government enforces its laws to protect its citizens (e.g., guaranteeing a person a fair trial)
Energy Employees Occupational Illness Compensation Program Act (EEOICPA)	Provided compensation for employees and contractors subjected to excessive radiation during production and testing of nuclear weapons
Energy Policy Act of 1992	Allowed employers to provide a nontaxable fringe benefit to employees engaged in qualified commuter activities such as bicycling and mass transit
Equal employment opportunity (EEO)	U.S. laws that guarantee equal treatment and respect for all employees
Equal Employment Opportunity Act (EEOA)	Established that complainants have the burden of proof for disparate impact; provided litigation authority for the EEOC; extended the time to file complaints
Equal Employment Opportunity Commission (EEOC)	U.S. agency charged with investigating complaints of job discrimination based on race, color, religion, sex (including pregnancy, gender identity, and sexual orientation), national origin, disability, age (40 or older), or genetic information, and with taking action to stop the discriminatory behavior when found

Name	Description
Extraterritorial laws	Laws from a multinational enterprise's home country that have application in other countries. U.S. laws with extraterritorial application include Sarbanes-Oxley, Foreign Corrupt Practices Act, Americans with Disabilities Act, Age Discrimination in Employment Act, and Title VII of the Civil Rights Act of 1964. These laws give American workers the right to sue in the United States for unlawful acts that occurred outside of the country.
Federal Employees Compensation Act (FECA)	Provided benefits similar to workers' compensation for federal employees injured on the job
Federal Insurance Contributions Act (FICA)/ Social Security Act	Required employers and employees to pay Social Security taxes
Federal regulations	In the United States, laws that apply in every state (as opposed to laws unique to every state)
Federal Unemployment Tax Act (FUTA)	Required employers to contribute a percentage of payroll to an unemployment insurance fund
Forum shopping	Looking for a legal venue most likely to result in a favorable outcome; the practice of trying to get a trial held in a location that is most likely to produce a favorable result
Griggs vs. Duke Power	Required employers to show that job requirements are related to the job; established that lack of intention to discriminate isn't a defense against claims of discrimination
Immigration and Nationality Act (INA)	Eliminated national origin, race, and ancestry as bars to immigration; set immigration goals for reunifying families and preference for specialized skills
Intellectual property	Creations or inventions protected by law; an original invention or something created by the mind, which is usually protected by patents, trademarks, or copyrights
Internal Revenue Service (IRS)	The U.S. government agency responsible for collecting taxes and enforcing tax laws
Jespersen vs. Harrah's Operating Co.	Established that a dress code requiring women to wear makeup doesn't constitute unlawful sex discrimination under Title VII
Jurisdiction	The right and power to interpret and apply the law, often within a certain geographical region

TABLE C.10   Agencies, court cases, terms, and laws *(continued)*

Name	Description
Labor-Management Relations Act (LMRA; Taft-Hartley)	Prohibited closed shops; restricted union shops; allowed states to pass "right to work" laws; prohibited jurisdictional strikes and secondary boycotts; allowed employers to permanently replace economic strikers; established the Federal Mediation and Conciliation Service; allowed an 80-day cooling-off period for national emergency strikes
Labor-Management Reporting and Disclosure Act (LMRDA; Landrum-Griffin)	Controlled internal union operations; provided a bill of rights for union members; required a majority vote of members to increase dues; allowed members to sue the union; set term limits for union leaders
Licensing	Giving permission to use, produce, or sell; a written contract in which the owner of a trademark or intellectual property gives rights to a licensee to use, produce, or sell a product or service
Lobbying	The act of monitoring and seeking to influence new labor laws and regulations by contacting local, state, and national representatives of the U.S. government
Longshore and Harbor Workers' Compensation Act	Provided workers' compensation benefits for maritime workers injured on navigable waters of the United States or on piers, docks, and terminals
Mental Health Parity Act (MHPA)	Required insurers to provide the same limits for mental health benefits that are provided for other types of health benefits
National Labor Relations Act (NLRA; Wagner Act)	Protected the right of workers to organize and bargain collectively; identified unfair labor practices; established the National Labor Relations Board (NLRB)
Needlestick Safety and Prevention Act	Mandated record keeping for all needle-stick and sharps injuries; required employee involvement in developing safer devices
Epilepsy Foundation of Northeast Ohio vs. NLRB	Extended *Weingarten* rights to nonunion employees by allowing employees to request a coworker be present during an investigatory interview that could result in disciplinary action
NLRB: *IBM Corp.*	NLRB reversed its 2000 decision in *Epilepsy*, withdrawing *Weingarten* rights from nonunion employees.
NLRB: *M. B. Sturgis, Inc.*	Established that temporary employees may be included in the client company's bargaining unit and that consent of the employer and temp agency aren't required to bargain jointly

Name	Description
NLRB vs. J. Weingarten, Inc.	U.S. Supreme Court: Established that union employees have the right to request union representation during any investigatory interview that could result in disciplinary action
Norris–La Guardia Act	Protected the right to organize; outlawed yellow-dog contracts
Omnibus Budget Reconciliation Act (OBRA)	Revised rules for employee benefits; set the maximum deduction for executive pay at $1,000,000; mandated some benefits for medical plans
Payne vs. The Western & Atlantic Railroad Company	Defined employment at will
Personal Responsibility and Work Opportunity Reconciliation Act	Required employers to provide information about all new or rehired employees to state agencies to enforce child support orders
Pharakhone vs. Nissan North America, Inc.	Established that employees who violate company rules while on FMLA leave may be terminated
Phason vs. Meridian Rail Corp.	Established that when an employer is close to closing a deal to sell a company, WARN Act notice requirements are triggered by the number of employees actually employed and the number laid off on the date of the layoff, even if the purchasing company hires some of the employees shortly after the layoff
Proprietary	Relating to an owner or ownership; rights of property ownership relating to key information, materials, or methods developed by an organization
Public Contracts Act (PCA; Walsh-Healey Act)	Required contractors to pay prevailing wage rates
Railway Labor Act	Protected unionization rights; allowed for a 90-day cooling-off period to prevent strikes in national emergencies. Covers railroads and unions
Repa vs. Roadway Express, Inc.	Established that when an employee on FMLA leave is receiving employer-provided disability payments, the employee may not be required to use accrued sick or vacation leave during the FMLA absence
Retirement Equity Act	Lowered the age limits on participation and vesting in pension benefits; required written spousal consent to not provide survivor benefits; restricted conditions placed on survivor benefits

TABLE C.10 Agencies, court cases, terms, and laws *(continued)*

Name	Description
Rule of law	A political system in which the law is supreme; all citizens are subject to the laws of their country, no individual is above the law, and everyone must obey it.
Service Contract Act	Required government contractors to pay prevailing wages and benefits
Sherman Antitrust Act	Controlled business monopolies; allowed court injunctions to prevent restraint of trade. Used to restrict unionization efforts
Sista vs. CDC Ixis North America, Inc.	Established that employees on FMLA may be legally terminated for legitimate, nondiscriminatory reasons, including violations of company policy if the reason is unrelated to the exercise of FMLA rights
Small Business Job Protection Act	Redefined highly compensated individuals; detailed minimum participation requirements; simplified 401(k) tests; corrected qualified plan and disclosure requirements
Small Business Regulatory Enforcement Fairness Act (SBREFA)	Provided that a Small Business Administration (SBA) ombudsman act as an advocate for small business owners in the regulatory process
Smith vs. City of Jackson, Mississippi	Established that ADEA permits disparate impact claims for age discrimination comparable to those permitted for discrimination based on sex and race
Supra-national laws	Agreements, standards, and laws that transcend national boundaries or governments. Examples include directives and regulations from the EU to its member countries.
Taxman vs. Board of Education of Piscataway	Found that in the absence of past discrimination or underrepresentation of protected classes, preference may not be given to protected classes in making layoff decisions
Taylor vs. Progress Energy, Inc.	Established that the waiver of FMLA rights in a severance agreement is invalid. FMLA clearly states that "employees cannot waive, nor may employers induce employees to waive, any rights under the FMLA."
Uniform Guidelines on Employee Selection Procedures (UGESP)	Established guidelines to ensure that selection procedures are both job-related and valid predictors of job success

Name	Description
Velazquez-Garcia vs. Horizon Lines of Puerto Rico, Inc.	Established that the burden of proof that a termination wasn't related to military service is on an employer when an employee protected by USERRA is laid off
Visas and work permits	Documents used by various countries to control immigration and job placement of foreign workers. Most countries require a work permit whenever a foreign individual is transferred or takes a job in the country for a period of six months or more.
Washington vs. Davis	Established that employment selection tools that adversely impact protected classes are lawful if they have been validated to show future success on the job
World Trade Organization (WTO)	An international body in which members negotiate tariffs and trade barriers, and trade disputes are reviewed and adjudicated
Works council	Groups that represent employees; organizations that function like trade unions and represent the rights of workers. Work councils are most common in Europe and the United Kingdom.

TABLE C.11   General record-keeping guidelines

Record type	Length of retention	Requirements
Affirmative action plan/data	Two years	Applications and other personnel records that support employment decisions (e.g., hires, promotions, terminations) are considered "support data" and must be maintained for the present AAP and the prior AAP. Records required by 41CFR60-300.44(f)(4), 60-300.44(k), and 60-300.45(c) must be kept for a period of three years from the date of making the record. This also applies to records required by 41CFR60-741.44(f)(4) and (k).
Applications for employment	One year from making the record or making the hiring decision, whichever is later; two years if a federal contractor or subcontractor has 150 or more employees and a government contract of at least $150,000	If a charge or lawsuit is filed, the records must be kept until the charge is disposed.

TABLE C.11 General record-keeping guidelines *(continued)*

Record type	Length of retention	Requirements
Drug test records	One year for non-DOT employers	Department of Transportation records for commercial drivers:
		1 year: Negative drug test results. Alcohol test results less than 0.02
		2 years: Records related to the alcohol and drug collection process
		3 years: Previous employer records
		5 years: Annual MIS reports. Employee evaluation and referrals to SAPs
		Follow-up tests and follow-up schedules. Refusals to test
		Alcohol test results 0.02 or greater. Verified positive drug test results
		EBT calibration documentation
Employment benefits	Until no longer relevant to determine benefits due to employees	Except for specific exemptions, ERISA's reporting and disclosure requirements apply to all pension and welfare plans, including summary plan descriptions, annual reports, and plan termination.
		Pension and insurance plans for the full period the plan is in place
EEO-1	Annually, unless a federal contractor or subcontractor	The current EEO-1 report must be kept on file. Federal contractors and subcontractors must produce three years' worth of EEO-1 reports, if audited by the OFCCP.
Family Medical Leave records	Three years	Basic employee data, including name, address, occupation, rate of pay, terms of compensation, daily and weekly hours worked per pay period, additions to/deductions from wages, and total compensation. Dates of leave taken by eligible employees. Leave must be designated as the FMLA leave. For intermittent leave taken, the hours of leave. Copies of employee notices and documents describing employee benefits or policies and practices regarding paid and unpaid leave. Records of premium payments of employee benefits. Records of any dispute regarding the designation of leave

Record type	Length of retention	Requirements
Form I-9	Three years after date of hire or one year after date of termination, whichever is later	See retention formula in Chapter 3, Talent Planning and Acquisition and Chapter 3: "PHR Exam: Talent Planning and Acquisition"
Merit and seniority pay systems	Two years	Includes wage rates, job evaluations, seniority and merit systems, and collective bargaining agreements or any other document that explains the basis for paying different wages to employees of opposite sexes in the same establishment
Payroll records, etc.	Three years (EEOC, FLSA, ADEA): Payroll records, collective bargaining agreements, sales and purchase records Two years: Time cards and piecework tickets, wage rate tables, work and time schedules, and records of additions to or deductions from wages	If a charge is filed, all related records must be kept until the charge is settled. Basic payroll records that must be kept according to the FLSA are: • Employee's full name and Social Security number • Address, including zip code • Birth date, if younger than 19 • Sex and occupation • Time and day of week when employee's workweek begins • Hours worked each day • Total hours worked each workweek • Basis on which employee's wages are paid (e.g., "$9 per hour," "$440 a week," "piecework") • Regular hourly pay rate • Total daily or weekly straight-time earnings • Total overtime earnings for the workweek • All additions to or deductions from the employee's wages • Total wages paid each pay period • Date of payment and the pay period covered by the payment

TABLE C.11   General record-keeping guidelines *(continued)*

Record type	Length of retention	Requirements
Personnel records	One year from making the record or taking the action, whichever is greater (EEOC) Three years if applicable under the Davis-Bacon Act Two years if a federal contractor or subcontractor with 150 or more employees, or government contract of $150,000 or more	Records related to promotions, demotions, transfers, performance appraisals, terminations, requests for reasonable accommodations
Polygraph test records	Three years	Polygraph test result(s) and the reason for administering
Selection and hiring records	One year after creation of the document or the action is taken, whichever is later Two years if a federal contractor or subcontractor with 150 or more employees, or government contract of $150,000 or more	Job ads, assessment tools, credit reports, interview records, and other documents related to hiring decisions
Tax records	Four years from date tax is due or paid	Amounts of wages subject to withholding. Agreements with employee to withhold additional tax Actual taxes withheld and dates withheld. Reason for any difference between total tax payments and actual tax payments. Withholding forms
Work permits	No retention requirements	Employers must keep current work permits for minors.

Appendix D

Resources

Thousands of references are available for every aspect of human resources, so it's just not possible to include every great resource here. The resources included in this appendix are those that add dimension or different perspectives to the information presented in this book. Although the best preparation for both the PHR and SPHR exams is diverse generalist experience, these resources will provide a more in-depth refresher than is possible in this book.

A Word About the Internet   A wealth of information is available on the Internet that is current and easily accessible. The best way to access this information is through a search engine such as Google (www.google.com). If you haven't used a search engine before, you can get instructions on how to search by clicking the Help button on each search page. When you type in the phrase you want to research, you will get a list of websites to check out.

Information About the Test   For information about eligibility requirements and test dates, the best source is the Human Resource Certification Institute (HRCI). There are two sources for information from HRCI. The first is the *PHR/SPHR/GPHR Certification Handbook* (described in the introduction of this book), which is free of charge and published annually. The handbook provides all the information necessary to apply for the exams and includes pricing, deadlines, and general information. The second source is the HRCI website (www.hrci.org). The website contains a great deal of information about the exams and also allows you to view the handbook online, download a copy, or request that a hard copy be mailed to you. Another helpful information source is HRCI's *A Guide to the Human Resource Body of Knowledge (HRBoK™)*. This guide serves as a general resource for all HR professionals and can be purchased from several national online booksellers.

Professional Associations   Professional associations are often a great source of information about current trends in a particular practice area. Some of them are member-only sites, but even those often have useful information available to nonmembers.

As mentioned earlier, many sources of HR information are available. The inclusion of these resources is not an endorsement of the information contained in them. They are provided only as suggestions for further reading should you feel the need for more detail in one of these areas. For ease of use, the list is combined and organized according to functional area.

At the time of publication, the URLs included in this appendix were operational; given the changing nature of the Internet, though, some of them may have been changed or no longer exist.

Business Management, Leadership, and Strategy

Resources included with Business Management, Leadership, and Strategy cover general human resource books and resources for other business disciplines with which HR professionals interact on a daily basis.

Books

Beugre, Constant. *The Neuroscience of Organizational Behavior.* Northampton: Edward Elgar Publishing Limited, 2018.

Calder, Alan, and Steve Watkins. *IT Governance: An International Guide to Data Security and ISO27001/ISO27002 6th ed.* Philadelphia: Kogan Page, 2015.

Chase, Richard B., F. Robert Jacobs, and Nicholas J. Aquilano. *Operations Management for Competitive Advantage, 11th ed.* Boston: McGraw-Hill/Irwin, 2006.

Friedman, Thomas. *The World Is Flat 3.0: A Brief History of the Twenty-First Century, 3rd ed.* New York: Picador, 2007.

Kaplan, Robert S., and David P. Norton. *The Balanced Scorecard: Translating Strategy into Action.* Boston: Harvard Business School Press, 1996.

Losey, Mike, Dave Ulrich, and Sue Meisinger. *The Future of Human Resource Management: 64 Thought Leaders Explore the Critical HR Issues of Today and Tomorrow.* Hoboken, NJ: John Wiley & Sons, Inc., 2005.

Mathis, Robert L., and John H. Jackson. *Human Resource Management, 13th ed.* Mason, OH: Thomas South-Western, 2010.

Mitchell, Barbara, and Cornelia Gamlem. *The Big Book of HR, 2nd ed.* Newburyport, MA: Career Press, 2017.

Phillips, Jack, Ron Stone, and Patricia Phillips. *The Human Resources Scorecard: Measuring the Return on Investment (Improving Human Performance).* Boston: Butterworth-Heinemann, 2001.

Schein, Edgar H., and Schein, Peter. *Organizational Culture and Leadership (The Jossey-Bass Business & Management Series) 5th ed.* Hoboken, NJ Wiley, 2016.

Tracy, John A. *How to Read a Financial Report: Wringing Vital Signs Out of the Numbers, 8th ed.* Hoboken, NJ: John Wiley & Sons, Inc., 2014.

Ulrich, Dave, David Kryscynski, Mike Ulrich, and Wayne Brockbank. *Victory Through Organization: Why the War for Talent Is Failing Your Company and What You Can Do About It.* New York: McGraw Hill, 2017.

Professional Associations

American Institute of Certified Public Accountants, www.aicpa.org

American Management Association, www.amanet.org

American Marketing Association, www.ama.org

HR People & Strategy, www.hrps.org

ROI Institute, https://roiinstitute.net

Society for Human Resource Management, www.shrm.org

Talent Planning and Acquisition

These resources are some of the many related to workforce planning needs, including talent acquisition and deployment.

Books

Ahlrichs, Nancy S. *Competing for Talent: Key Recruitment and Retention Strategies for Becoming an Employer of Choice.* Palo Alto, CA: Davies-Black Publishing, 2000.

Bechet, Thomas P. *Strategic Staffing: A Comprehensive System for Effective Workforce Planning*, 2nd ed. New York: AMACOM, 2008.

Bradt, George B., and Mary Vonnegut. *Onboarding: How to Get Your New Employees Up to Speed in Half the Time.* Hoboken, NJ: John Wiley & Sons, Inc., 2009.

Manning, Paula, and Jennifer Brugh. *Recruiting and Retaining Employees for Dummies.* New York: Hungry Minds, 2001.

Phillips, Jack J., and Adele O. Connell. *Managing Employee Retention: A Strategic Accountability Approach.* Boston: Butterworth-Heinemann, 2003.

Steingold, Fred S. *The Employer's Legal Handbook: Manage Your Employees and Workplace Effectively*, 10th ed. Berkeley, CA: Nolo Press, 2011.

Truesdell, William H. *Secrets of Affirmative Action Compliance*, 9th ed. Walnut Creek, CA: Management Advantage, 2010.

Walsh, David. *Employment Law for Human Resource Practice*, 5th ed. Nashville, TN: South-western College, 2015.

Professional Associations

American Staffing Association, www.staffingtoday.net

Association for Talent Acquisition Professionals, https://atapglobal.org

International Public Management Association for Human Resources, www.ipma-hr.org

National Association of Personnel Services, www.naps360.org

Learning and Development

These resources provide additional information about developing talent within organizations.

Books

Becker, Brian E., Mark A. Huselid, and Dave Ulrich. *The HR Scorecard: Linking People, Strategy, and Performance.* Boston: Harvard Business School Press, 2001.

Dirksen, Julie. *Design for How People Learn, 2nd ed.* San Francisco, CA: New Riders, 2015.

Hodell, Chuck. *ISD from the Ground Up: A No-Nonsense Approach to Instructional Design, 4th ed.* Alexandria, VA: ASTD Press, 2016.

Knowles, Malcolm S., Elwood F. Holton, and Richard A. Swanson. *The Adult Learner: The Definitive Classic in Adult Education and Human Resource Development, 6th ed.* Boston: Butterworth-Heinemann, 2005.

Marquardt, Michael J. *Building the Learning Organization: Achieving Strategic Advantage Through a Commitment to Learning, 3rd ed.* Boston: Nicholas Brealey, 2011.

Philips, Jack, and Ron D. Stone. *How to Measure Training Results: A Practical Guide to Tracking the Six Key Indicators.* New York: McGraw-Hill, 2002.

Senge, Peter M. *The Fifth Discipline: The Art and Practice of the Learning Organization, rev. and updated ed.* New York: Doubleday/Currency, 2006.

Wilcox, M. *Effective Talent Management: Aligning Strategy, People and Performance.* New York: Routledge, 2016.

Professional Associations

American Society for Talent Development, www.astd.org

Association for Educational Communications & Technology, www.aect.org

The Elearning Guild, www.elearningguild.com

Total Rewards

Additional information about compensation and benefit issues and processes is available in the following resources.

Books

Beam, Burton T., Jr., and John J. McFadden. *Employee Benefits, 9th ed.* Chicago: Real Estate Education, 2012.

Berger, Lance A., and Dorothy R. Berger, eds. *The Compensation Handbook: A State-of-the-Art Guide to Compensation Strategy and Design, 6th ed.* New York: McGraw-Hill, 2015.

Choy, Samuel, Sarah Downie, Brian D. Hector, Arthur H. Kohn, Doreen E, Lilienfeld, and Henrik P. Patel. *Recent Changes in Employee Benefits and Executive Compensation, 2016 ed.: Leading Lawyers on Understanding ERISA Changes, Navigating Disclosure … Compliance Strategies (Inside the Minds).* Eagan, MN: Thomson Reuters, 2016.

Professional Associations

American Payroll Association, www.americanpayroll.org

Employee Benefit Research Institute, www.ebri.org

International Foundation of Employee Benefit Plans, www.ifebp.org

International Society of Certified Employee Benefit Specialists, www.iscebs.org

WorldatWork (formerly American Compensation Association), www.worldatwork.org

Employee and Labor Relations and Engagement

These resources provide additional information on labor and employee relations as well as work engagement and the field of industrial-organizational psychology.

Books

Berger, Lance A., and Dorothy R. Berger, eds. *The Talent Management Handbook, 2nd ed.* New York: McGraw-Hill, 2011.

Cassel, Robert M., and Charles S. Loughran. *Negotiating a Labor Contract: A Management Handbook, 4th ed.* Washington, DC: BNA Books, 2010.

DelPo, Amy, and Lisa Guerin. *Dealing with Problem Employees: A Legal Guide, 6th ed.* Berkeley, CA: Nolo Press, 2011.

Fay, John J. *Contemporary Security Management, 3rd ed.* Burlington, MA: Butterworth-Heinemann, 2011.

Holley, William H., Kenneth M. Jennings, and Roger S. Wolters. *The Labor Relations Process, 11th ed*. Mason, OH: South-Western, 2016.

Kaye, Beverly, and Sharon Jordan-Evans. *Love 'Em or Lose 'Em: Getting Good People to Stay, 5th ed*. San Francisco: Berrett-Koehler Publishers, 2014.

Levy, Barry S., David H. Wegman, Sherry L. Baron, and Rosemary K. Sokas. *Occupational and Environmental Health: Recognizing and Preventing Disease and Injury, 6th ed*. New York: Oxford University Press, 2011.

Levy, Paul E. *Industrial Organizational Psychology, 4th ed*. New York: Worth Publishers, 2013.

Mitroff, Ian I. *Crisis Leadership: Planning for the Unthinkable*. Hoboken, NJ: John Wiley & Sons, Inc., 2003.

Newport, Cal. *Deep Work: Rules for Focused Success in a Distracted World*. New York. Grand Central Publishing, 2016.

Pedneault, Stephen. *Preventing and Detecting Employee Theft and Embezzlement: A Practical Guide*. Hoboken, NJ: John Wiley & Sons, Inc., 2010.

Scandura, Terri A. *Essentials of Organizational Behavior*. Thousand Oaks, CA: Sage Publications, 2016.

Sheridan, Kevin. *Building a Magnetic Culture: How to Attract and Retain Top Talent to Create an Engaged, Productive Workforce*. New York: McGraw-Hill, 2012.

Professional Associations

National Public Employer Labor Relations Association, www.npelra.org

American Society of Safety Professionals, www.asse.org

International Labour Organization, www.ilo.org

National Association of Safety Professionals, www.naspweb.com

National Diversity Council, www.nationaldiversitycouncil.org

National Safety Council, www.nsc.org

Society for Industrial and Organizational Psychology (SIOP), www.siop.org

Appendix E

Summarizing the Summaries: What Meta-Analyses Tell Us About Work Engagement

Dr. Erin M. Richard, PhD.

ASSISTANT PROFESSOR OF LEADERSHIP AND HUMAN RESOURCE DEVELOPMENT, LOUISIANA STATE UNIVERSITY

Work engagement (also referred to as employee engagement) is somewhat of a buzzword in organizations today, but many organizational scientists remain skeptical about the construct and its overlap with other job attitudes. It's common for management fads to gain popularity so quickly that the practices or interventions associated with the topic start to outrun the science. For some time, engagement was in danger of becoming one of those fads, but fortunately, the science has begun to catch up with the practice. In fact, work engagement is now one of the most researched topics in organizational science (Carasco-Saul, Kim, and Kim, 2015). Because it can be difficult to digest the results of such a large number of studies, some researchers have attempted to statistically summarize this research using meta-analyses. In a meta-analysis, the results of multiple studies are combined in order to obtain the best possible estimate of the true relationship between variables. In this appendix, I summarize three meta-analyses on work engagement that I believe offer some key, take-home messages on the topic.

Christian, Garza, and Slaughter, 2011

Is work engagement really just "old wine in a new barrel"? A key criticism of engagement is that we've simply taken older constructs such as job satisfaction and involvement and repackaged them as something new. Christian, Garza, and Slaughter (2011) addressed this criticism in their meta-analysis published in *Personnel Psychology*.

One of the most common definitions of engagement is *a psychological state consisting of vigor, dedication, and absorption* (Schaufeli, Salanova, Gonzalez-Roma, & Baker, 2002). However, engagement has been defined in many different ways, and the lack of consensus on a definition has been one of the criticisms of the construct. Christian and colleagues reviewed the research on work engagement in order to come up with an agreed-upon definition that (a) summarized the key components of most definitions and (b) distinguished it from other concepts. The result was the following definition of work engagement:

> A relatively enduring state of mind referring to the simultaneous investment of personal energies in the experience or performance of work. (Christian et al., 2011, p. 95)

Christian and colleagues emphasized two key components of this definition, which can be traced back to work by Kahn (1990):

- Work engagement refers to a psychological connection with the performance of *work tasks* (rather than an attitude toward the organization or job situation).

- Work engagement involves the investment of *multiple* resources (i.e., physical, emotional, and cognitive energy) into one's work.

These components of the definition help distinguish engagement from other job attitudes. First, the target of engagement is the work itself; it refers to how one feels when performing work tasks. This focus distinguishes it from job satisfaction, which is an evaluation of the overall job situation, and it distinguishes it from job involvement, which refers to psychological identification with the overall job situation. When we consider that the focus of engagement is on work tasks themselves, it also helps distinguish engagement from organizational commitment, which is an attachment to the organization (or members of an organization). Second, because engagement refers to the simultaneous investment of multiple resources (e.g., physical, emotional, and mental energies) into one's work, Christian and colleagues argue that attitudes like job involvement, which is mainly cognitive, or affective commitment, which is mainly emotional, may be better represented as components of engagement rather than equivalent to engagement.

Christian and colleagues' meta-analysis statistically combined the results of 91 different studies that had examined potential causes and consequences of engagement. They found that engagement was related to job performance across studies, and more importantly, it predicted variation in job performance above and beyond the other three job attitudes. Christian and colleagues' work also offers clues as to how we might increase employees' work engagement. Predictors of engagement included task variety (getting to do many different things at work) and task significance (perceived importance of those tasks). Employees who were more conscientious and higher in trait positive mood also showed higher levels of engagement.

The implications of these findings are that having engaged employees gives companies a competitive advantage and that engagement might be increased through employee selection and job redesign. However, the way in which companies measure engagement varies greatly. To ensure that an organization is measuring something distinct that will be uniquely linked to performance, Christian and colleagues suggest using measures that conceptualize engagement in line with their definition.

Depending on how it's defined and measured, employee engagement can represent a construct that is distinct from other job attitudes and that represents an important predictor of productivity. Work engagement is higher in employees who perceive variety and significance in their tasks and in employees who are high on trait conscientiousness and positive mood.

Maricutoiu, Sulea, and Iancu, 2017

One common but somewhat controversial view of engagement is that it is the opposite of burnout (e.g., Maslach and Leiter, 1997). Burnout refers to a psychological state characterized by three dimensions: exhaustion (a feeling of being emotionally and physically drained), depersonalization (cynicism or a detached attitude), and inefficacy (a reduced sense of personal accomplishment). Although there is evidence to suggest that engagement and burnout are different things (e.g., Schaufeli, Taris, & van Rhenen, 2008; Langelaan, Bakker, Van Doornnen, & Schaufeli, 2006; Schaufeli & Salanova, 2014), the fact remains that the two are highly correlated, and most researchers believe that one likely influences the other. The question is: *Which comes first? Low work engagement or burnout?*

To answer this question, Maricutoiu and colleagues (2017) meta-analyzed 25 studies that measured engagement and burnout at two different time periods. They found evidence for reciprocal causation (i.e., the two variables likely influence each other). However, the negative effect of burnout (particularly exhaustion) on engagement appears to be stronger than the negative effect of engagement on burnout. The effects also might take some time to show up. They found that significant relationships only appeared when the lag between measurements was 12 months.

There is evidence that burnout may reduce work engagement over time, and vice versa: low levels of work engagement may lead to higher burnout. However, detecting these effects seems to require at least a year between measurement occasions, suggesting that the effects might take some time to develop.

Knight, Patterson, and Dawson, 2017

According to a meta-analysis by Knight et al. (2017), four different types of organizational interventions are targeted at increasing work engagement:

- **Personal resource building interventions:** Focuses on increasing employees' optimism, resilience, or positive views of themselves (e.g., self-efficacy)

- **Job resource building interventions:** Focuses on increasing work resources, such as autonomy, social support, or feedback

- **Leadership training interventions:** Attempts to build job resources and motivate employees indirectly by increasing the knowledge and skill of their leaders

- **Health-promoting interventions:** Attempts to increase engagement by promoting healthier lifestyles aimed at building and sustaining personal resources

The purpose of Knight and colleagues' meta-analysis was to estimate the average effectiveness of these interventions and determine which kinds of interventions are most effective. Unfortunately, they found only 20 studies that used controlled designs to examine intervention effectiveness. This limited their statistical ability to detect differences in effectiveness between different types of engagement interventions. However, they were able to draw a few preliminary conclusions.

First, they found that engagement interventions have a small but reliable positive effect. Specifically, work engagement for employees receiving an intervention was an average of 0.29 standard deviations higher than the engagement of the control groups. Second, interventions seem to have stronger effects on the individual dimensions of engagement (i.e., vigor, dedication, and absorption) compared to overall engagement. On average, the intervention groups scored 0.95 standard deviations higher on vigor, 0.75 standard deviations higher on dedication, and 0.78 standard deviations higher absorption compared to the control groups. Third, there was a great deal of variability in the effectiveness of engagement interventions across studies, and Knight and colleagues (2017) point out that more research is needed to determine what makes some interventions more effective than others.

For example, the four types of interventions identified here did not differ significantly in their effectiveness; however, there was some preliminary evidence that group-based interventions (which had medium to large effects on engagement) may be more effective than individual-based interventions.

More research needs to be conducted on the effectiveness of organizational interventions for increasing work engagement. However, the preliminary evidence suggests that such interventions are indeed effective, particularly those that are group-based.

References

Carasco-Saul, M., W. Kim, and T. Kim. 2015. "Leadership and Employee Engagement: Proposing Research Agendas through a Review of Literature." *Human Resource Development Review* 14: 38–63.

Christian, M., A. Garza, and J. Slaughter. 2011. "Work Engagement: A Quantitative Review and Test of Its Relations with Task and Contextual Performance." *Personnel Psychology* 64: 89–136.

Kahn, W. A. 1990. "Psychological Conditions of Personal Engagement and Disengagement at Work." *The Academy of Management Journal* 33 (4): 692–724.

Knight, C., M. Patterson, and J. Dawson. 2017. "Building Work Engagement: A Systematic Review and Meta-Analysis Investigating the Effectiveness of Work Engagement Interventions." *Journal of Organizational Behavior* 38: 798–812.

Langelaan, S., A. B. Bakker, L. J. Van Doornnen, and W. B. Schaufeli. 2006. "Burnout and Work Engagement: Do Individual Differences Make a Difference?" *Personality and Individual Differences* 40: 521–532.

Maricutoiu, L., C. Sulea, and A. Iancu. 2017. "Work Engagement or Burnout: Which Comes First? A Meta-Analysis of Longitudinal Evidence." *Burnout Research* 5: 35–43.

Maslach, C., and M. Leiter. 1997. *The Truth about Burnout.* San Francisco, CA: Jossey-Bass.

Schaufeli, W. B., and M. Salanova. 2014. "Burnout, Boredom and Engagement in the Workplace." In M. C. Peeters, J. de Jonge, & T. W. Taris (Eds.), *An Introduction to Contemporary Work Psychology.* Chichester UK: Wiley Blackwell, 293–320.

Schaufeli, W. B., M. Salanova, V. Gonzalez-Roma, and A. B. Baker. 2002. "The Measurement of Engagement and Burnout: A Two Sample Confirmatory Factor Analytic Approach." *Journal of Happiness Studies* 3: 71–92.

Schaufeli, W. B., T. W. Taris, and W. van Rhenen. 2008. "Workaholism, Burnout and Engagement: Three of a Kind or Three Different Kinds of Employee Well-Being." *Applied Psychology: An International Review* 57: 173–203.

Appendix F

Neuroscience Principles and Applications for HR Leaders

Reut Schwartz-Hebron
FOUNDER OF THE KEY CHANGE INSTITUTE

Introduction

The design of human resource and organizational development systems involves access to a diverse knowledge base in which HR competencies may develop and thrive. In fact, successfully facilitating coaching, developing leaders, building teams, and providing training all rely on studies from numerous fields, particularly those that seek to understand effective change management. One of the more recent contributions to these processes comes from studying neuroscience.

Unlike other cells in the body, brain cells, or neurons, have the ability to directly communicate with each other. Understanding how behaviors, responses, preferences, and choices are represented in neural pathways in the brain has immediate and highly practical applications to change facilitation at every level.

Neuroscience findings clarify why it is difficult for some employees to change or let go of previous ways of doing things. They explain why some change processes can get difficult, complicated, confusing, or frustrating and how to get past change obstacles. The research provides us with specific principles so that we can guide and support the rewiring of new responses and behaviors at the individual level.

The result of combining neuroscience with transformation-related methodologies are true "inside-out" science-based models. For the first time, we have access to models that tie adoption of new ways of doing things on an individual level with leadership development, training in general, and wide-scope organizational change. We can bring the missing link of change acquisition to the organizations, teams, and individuals we support. Neuroscience principles shed light on questions like how to gain buy-in when people don't see the need for change, how to bridge the knowing-doing gap to get from awareness to adoption, and how to correctly identify and effectively overcome different types of resistance.

These and many others are questions that neuroscience can now answer, and they are particularly relevant for HR leaders. Mastering how to apply key neuroscience principles allows HR leaders to provide unique value by enhancing organizational well-being and retention, diminishing undesired behaviors, establishing acquisition and usage of new processes and systems, ensuring skill acquisition and improved performance, and increasing overall growth. Learning to apply neuroscience principles has been redefining the role of HR leaders as internal change guides and partners who provide direction, focus, and clear steps for their clients to achieve desired outcomes. Out of the emerging studies related to neuroscience research and change management, the following three principles are perhaps the most important.

The Principles

Of the different neuroscience principles that apply to change facilitation, perhaps the most critical ones to be aware of are:

1. Understanding the unlearning-relearning process and how to successfully manage it
2. Redefining resistance, how to identify its different types, and how to effectively overcome it
3. Engaging the right system in the brain to facilitate change acquisition and behavioral change

Principle 1: The Unlearning-Relearning Process

Up until about 15 years ago it was not uncommon to find research indicating that our development and ability to change is dramatically reduced after the age of five. Although we do learn and develop most dramatically early in life, new science and, particularly the study of "plasticity," countered the belief that our abilities to learn new skills or change is reduced in later years. Both the science and application of how adults unlearn and then relearn is covered next.

The Science

According to neuroscience, concepts, beliefs, thoughts, and, as a result behaviors, responses and habits are represented in "neural pathways." Although the formation of new neurons is limited late in life, the neural pathway—the sequence of communication between neurons that represents a specific response—can form and be adjusted at *any time*, no matter how old we are. The main difference is that later in life, new neural pathways and hence new responses, habits, and behaviors typically don't simply form; they need to re-form or change. When you were little and someone yelled at you, a neural pathway was created in your brain to represent your response. If you withdrew, one pathway was formed. If you got defensive, a different pathway formed. If you got angry and responded aggressively, yet a different pathway formed. Furthermore, if you continued to withdraw every time someone yelled at you as the years went by, this initial pathway was reinforced much like a riverbed gets deeper and wider as more water flows through it. The difference between the early formation of neural pathways, and hence responses and behaviors early in life and adopting new skills, responses, and thinking patterns later in life, is that as an adult you need to simultaneously form new neural pathways while letting go of previously reinforced relevant neural pathways. Early enough in life you only need to learn, but later in life you often need to unlearn and relearn.

Although most of us are somewhat fluent when it comes to learning, we recognize that unlearning is more difficult, and we typically try to navigate it with awareness and motivation. Unfortunately, understanding unlearning is one of those aspects of change that can sometimes catch us off guard. Most of us weren't taught to effectively manage our unlearning processes, so we developed common-sense solutions like trying to will ourselves to achieve desired outcomes, which unfortunately does not align with scientific findings as being effective.

Neuroscience teaches us that *unlearning is a specific process.* It has steps and obstacles between steps. Using the science allows us to navigate change successfully and guide others to adopt new skills, behaviors, and responses that allow for unlearning more quickly and seamlessly than we were able to do before.

Application

To more intuitively understand the difference between learning and the unlearning-relearning process, try to think of a time you needed to learn something brand-new such as adopting effective time management skills. Take a moment and try to identify the steps you took in order to initially learn how to effectively manage your workload. Perhaps you studied time management techniques online. You may have broken the new learning down into smaller, more manageable chunks, and used trial and error to learn through practice. Whatever approach you took, since there is currently a lot of emphasis on active learning as we grow up, most people know how to learn and are proficient at taking those steps. Now, however, take a moment and think of a time you needed to *unlearn* something. Continuing with our effective time management example to simplify things, imagine someone else didn't have the foresight of learning the topic early on. Instead, this individual developed less-than-ideal habits, behaviors, and thinking patterns around time management. Maybe this individual agrees to take on more than capacity permits and then procrastinates. In this second example, unlearning is required to successfully adopt new effective time management skills; this individual will need to go through the steps of letting go of previous ways of doing things.

Understanding how to facilitate transformation and change when people need to let go of previous ways of doing things is of great importance in numerous avenues of organizational growth. Two particularly interesting such applications are leadership development and organization-wide cultural change.

Traditionally, leadership development uses a variety of models and methodologies to manage the acquisition of effective leadership practices. Prior to learning about the need to facilitate the unlearning-relearning process, leadership development focused almost solely on teaching effective leadership skills. Although learning from what highly effective leaders do and trying to adopt new, more desirable ways of behaving, thinking, and responding is valuable and important, neuroscience findings indicate we also need to manage the process of letting go of previous practices. If a leader is overly controlling and micromanages her team, it is important to provide her with highly effective team management skills. However, without guiding her to successfully complete the unlearning-relearning process, whatever new behaviors this manager can sustain through awareness and motivation will most often be shortly lost. We now know that the habits and patterns associated with previous patterns such as being controlling and micromanaging don't get "unwired" or "overwritten" when we focus on acquiring new skills. If we are highly motivated, we can typically sustain the new desired state for a few weeks, but soon enough the presence of previous response patterns will make it very difficult to sustain this success. If a leader doesn't listen to his team's opinions and perspectives and is defensive whenever anyone asks to provide him with feedback, it is important to provide him with effective listening skills. However, it is not unusual for leaders in this position to have strong, preexisting, less-than-ideal response patterns. If those are sufficiently reinforced as previous neural pathways, they will most likely be stronger than any new skills. Without guiding this leader to let go of these previous responses, it is highly unlikely he will adopt new needed behaviors in a lasting way.

Cultural change is another great example for the importance of managing the unlearning-relearning process. Traditionally, the main focus for adopting new desired culture is to define and clarify the new cultural environment. Workshops and training will then be conducted to facilitate understanding, engagement, and practice of specific behaviors, processes, structures, and other aspects that are aligned with the new culture. Although these are important, neuroscience helps us recognize that cultural change is often preceded by an existing culture. Omitting the focus on facilitating unlearning will leave the effort more vulnerable to failure. An organization hoping to adopt a new culture of diversity and inclusion may focus on new behaviors and responses such as collaboration, open debate, honest communication, effective accountability, personal integrity, empowering independent thinking, innovation, and shared decision-making. Every organization is different, but if, for example, the culture prior to this initiative is of the thinking that there is always only one "right" answer, overly critical negative thinking, focusing on what isn't working, and argumentativeness, some response patterns will need to be unlearned before the desired culture could be acquired in a lasting way. Furthermore, though the scope of cultural change initiatives is typically organization-wide, neuroscience principles can be designed to reach transformation on the individual level.

The benefit of having access to these scientific findings means understanding why there is a need to manage unlearning and how to guide people through it. It's easy to see why, without adding this new knowledge, obstacles of some change efforts may be unnoticed or unclear. Understanding unlearning is one of the great examples of how neuroscience findings demystify change challenges, contributing the long-term acquisition and making change facilitation more predictable and successful.

Principle 2: Redefining Resistance

Successfully managing resistance to change is an extremely vital (but, the most misunderstood) aspect of change facilitation. Understanding resistance in the context of neuroscience research sheds new light on the very definition of resistance and how to effectively overcome it.

The Science

Resistance to change is defined as a phenomenon that delays or slows change adoption or implementation. It is often described as a set of behaviors such as denial, inaction, avoidance, cynicism, and refusal to cooperate. Prior to recent developments in neuroscience, the causes for resistance focused on perceived threats such as disagreement, sense of losing control, loss of influence or perceived value, and insufficient understanding of why the change is needed. As a result of how resistance was defined in the past, change models were designed to resolve or prevent these aspects of it.

Neuroscience provides us with a new way of looking at resistance to change. We now know that whenever we need to unlearn something, we will experience a natural degree of discomfort as part of the process of forming new neural pathways. This discomfort is inherent, and most will respond to it in one of two ways: Avoid it or work through it. If avoided, new pathways will not form. However, it is important to recognize that working through and fully experiencing the discomfort will actually help re-form the neural pathways and work to reinforce the change. This new finding diverts us from the assumption that we need to avoid or prevent resistance. It also directs senior HR professionals to build change systems that help employees recognize this resistance and accept that it is part of the process of forming new behaviors.

Most traditional references to resistance define it as a reaction to an external perceived threat. Although it is important to maintain an effective *external* environment for change, neuroscience directs us to look at the way people respond to that *internal* resistance, regardless of environmental conditions.

Unfortunately, unlike external resistance, which is observable, internal resistance is invisible and people are often unaware of it. Those who successfully overcome their internal resistance adopt new ways of doing things by continuously experiencing the "pull" to do things the old way but continue to move in the new direction despite of that pull. For example, if they want to adopt better presentation skills and are uncomfortable speaking in public, they embrace the discomfort and practice the very thing they are uncomfortable with. If someone is uncomfortable with conflict and wants to adopt a more assertive communication style when needed, their internal resistance and the discomfort associated with it show up as they are trying to adopt new responses, but they practice new responses despite it.

Whereas external resistance is a hindrance to change facilitation, internal resistance from a neuroscience perspective is not a blocking element. In fact, internal resistance provides us with an important deep transformative opportunity. The experience of the discomfort combined with the choice to move forward despite the discomfort is an extremely powerful rewiring mechanism. Internal resistance is not a phenomenon that should be prevented. Instead, it is a powerful change mechanism at the heart of accelerated transformation efforts that form lasting change.

Application

Just like unlearning, understanding how to effectively overcome internal and external resistance is of great importance in most if not all behavioral OD intervention strategies. Two good examples of such interventions are coaching and team building.

Traditionally, coaching models focus on building understanding, acceptance, and motivation as a foundation for achieving a successful transformation process. If the individual is highly motivated and positive toward the need for change, we may assume he is not resisting change. However, with the new knowledge we draw from neuroscience, this conclusion needs to be somewhat revisited. A highly motivated individual will still experience internal resistance. He may be very clear about the importance of the change and may very much want to adopt the new way of doing things yet, due to the experience of the internal resistance, still fail to acquire desired behaviors, thinking habits, or responses. Think about people who truly want to adopt a healthier diet but despite their motivation and acceptance of the need for change struggle to adopt new habits in a lasting way. The same struggle applies when we want to adopt more effective communication strategies, think more strategically, give and accept feedback more effectively, and acquire a wide range of other highly effective skills. Motivation to improve is important, but if it comes as an initial drive and grows thinner with time, it is often not enough to overcome the long haul of day-to-day continuous effort to re-form neural pathways. New science-based models recognize the presence of internal resistance even if people are highly motivated, providing individuals with effective accountability structures to support transformation as needed. This is why mentoring can be such a powerful tool to support change.

Similarly, if the individual is frustrated, avoidant, stubborn, angry, or passive, we often assume she is resisting in response to less-than-ideal external factors. As a result, we attempt to minimize the resistance to change by building trust, explaining how the change will affect the individual, engaging individuals in the change process, and focusing on benefits the change will have. However, though all these practices are valuable and important, because we may not take external resistance into account, we may not manage the response patterns individuals bring to the party. Knowing that people often respond ineffectively to their internal discomfort allows us to incorporate more evolved skills into coaching practices. Thanks to neuroscience, new coaching models combine creating the right environment and providing people with "change-readiness skills." By getting people to adopt effective ways to respond to their internal discomfort, we allow even particularly resistant-seeming individuals to become highly cooperative with the coaching process.

Team building is another great example of how a new understanding of resistance to change can be extremely valuable. Although this can apply to a wide variety of scenarios, imagine two small teams from two different cultures being merged into one team. Team 1 comes from a centralized culture. They bring clear structures, are able to follow directives, and have the ability to quickly align with new procedures. Team 2 comes from a decentralized culture. They enjoy the freedom of making independent, flexible decisions on a case-by-case basis and the ability to quickly offer creative solutions. Bringing these diverse teams together creates friction as the team is required to redefine the way it operates. Traditional team development models would rightfully focus on clarifying what the new way of operating will be and how it will affect different team members, including and engaging team members in the process, and focus on building transparency and trust. However, with all of this important work, individuals on the team may still not respond in the desired way. Team members may understand the need for change but be so accustomed to the nuances of the old way of doing things that they will fail to make the transition. Others may try to continue doing things the way they've always done, just now under the radar. Some may become argumentative. Subgroups may form, leading to a variety of secondary team dynamics issues. Despite the best effort to minimize the external factors that could lead to resistance, resistance is often very much brewing under the surface. When accompanied by neuroscience-based knowledge, managing team building is designed to support overcoming internal resistance. Doing so by providing effective accountability structures supports the individuals who are positively struggling to adopt all the nuances of the transition. It is also designed to preemptively or continuously provide team members with skills to respond effectively to their internal resistance to minimize ineffective external resistance responses.

This new understanding of resistance to change means we can answer questions around why some change efforts fail despite the fact we do everything "by the book." It enables us to accelerate change efforts at every level and guide people through change in a way that will make early motivation turn into lasting results. It means we can effectively support the transformation of difficult individuals and effectively resolve the challenges that are at the very heart of a variety of difficult change efforts.

Principle 3: Engaging Behavioral Change

When it comes to change acquisition, perhaps the most wonderful benefit of recent neuroscience developments is the removal of what once were invisible obstacles. This third principle removes much of the mystery when, for some unseen reason, people who are part of a change process just seem to go back to their desk and adopt old routines as if nothing much changed. It clarifies why individuals and teams who accept the need for change and are supported through it still don't adopt the new culture or don't follow new processes.

The Science

This third principle has to do with two different systems in the brain: the *explicit* system, which is linked to awareness, and the *implicit* system, which is linked to experience. Simply put, if we engage both systems, people will adopt new habits. Engaging only the explicit system is not enough. People will leave with new understanding, knowledge, and even acceptance but will, for the most part, not put the new behaviors into practice. A good analogy to make intuitive sense of the difference between the two systems is to think about learning how to swim. Imagine you are standing by a pool and given verbal instructions on how to float, move your limbs, and breathe. If you are focused, you will probably be able to repeat the instructions, indicating that you acquired the information and know-how to swim. However, if you were asked to jump and swim right away, you would most likely find it difficult. This is because when you were taught to swim outside the pool, only your explicit system was engaged. To move from awareness to application, the implicit system needs to be engaged as well. The same thing happens when we try to teach new managers how to effectively lead their teams.

To adopt a new skill in a way that will translate into applying it, you'll need to engage your brain through *both* knowledge and experience. The pitfall is that experience in neuroscience terms has very specific requirements and is somewhat different than the everyday definition of the word. Experience in neuroscience terms is a specific event, framed in a specific time and location, initiated by the acquiring individual, and with some sense of emotional importance. Also, unlike the everyday use of the term, because of the way the implicit system operates, it doesn't have to be something the acquiring individual has done and it doesn't have to be taking place in the present. If you watch someone else being treated with disrespect, it can be just as much your experience as it is theirs, as long as you had an emotional response to the situation. Furthermore, recalling or remembering an event in which you or someone else was treated unfairly is just as much an experience for the implicit system as being treated unfairly in the here and now—that is, as long as you initiated the memory rather than responded to encouragement from someone else to retrieve that particular event. This means that as long as we follow the brain's rules, recalling examples and remembering case studies is the equivalent of going through experiences in "real life."

Furthermore, to establish behavioral change, relevant experiences need to be tied to new interpretations or conclusions. For example, if you want to adopt more assertive behaviors but at some point in your life linked being dismissed or ignored with the conclusion that you are less valuable, having new experiences won't be enough. You'll need to change the interpretation you assign to experiences of being dismissed in order to adopt more assertive behaviors in the future. Unfortunately, these conclusions or interpretations are often hidden and invisible, but they don't have to be. Changing the meaning people assign to experience can be facilitated and can be as easy as asking for it. You just need to know that it is something you need to focus on for behavioral change to occur.

Engaging the implicit system through examples that follow neuroscience requirements and linking those experiences to new, more effective interpretations is a powerful behavioral change combination. We may be accustomed to navigating change through logical discussion, which ignores the implicit system. We may be used to facilitating change by trying to motivate and support others and, by so doing, eliminate the need for much initiative on their part. We've simply never had access to the specific do's and don'ts of how to engage behavioral change before and so may not realize how big those small missteps are in terms of blocking change acquisition. However, when done right, engaging the implicit system means bypassing the "awareness trap," shortening long change processes, and being in awe of how versatile we can be if we match the models we use with what our brain needs in order to change.

Application

Although behavioral change requires engaging both the explicit and the implicit systems, organizations tend to be very good at using the first and insufficiently applying the other. Knowing how to effectively engage both systems at every level of learning, transformation, and change in organizations leads to accelerated transfer of new knowledge into practice in a lasting way. Examples for the importance of this third principle are numerous; training is a particularly important example and is worth a deeper dive.

Traditionally, training models focus on providing participants with new knowledge, processing that knowledge, and practice. In that context, if we were to train customer care representatives how to better respond to complaints, we would typically tell them what the right approach is, illustrate it by showing them examples of effective and ineffective responses, practice, and then discuss and review the specific practiced examples.

It is easy to see that traditional models engage the explicit system. They do so first by providing knowledge and illustrating best practices. Interestingly, although it may seem like getting participants to practice is equivalent to engaging the implicit system and discussion is equivalent to creating the important link between experience and interpretation, the small nuances in design prevent the engagement of the implicit system. For example, it is not uncommon for the practice to be using examples provided by the facilitator. While using examples of specific events that are properly framed in the context of time and location, this practice removes the need for the experience to be initiated by participants and usually is not associated with any emotional importance for participants. By so doing, these minor aspects make the practice under traditional training models highly valuable for understanding but not an experience that can form new behaviors.

Furthermore, though not in all cases, it is not unusual for traditional training models to provide the desired conclusions for an experience without asking participants for their interpretation. Going back to our customer care training example, imagine that some of the participants link the distress and anger in the customer's voice to being threatened. This subconscious interpretation may lead some of them to respond unpleasantly. To replace this link with a new interpretation, it is not enough to explain to these participants logically that the client isn't attacking them and that the right approach is to combine empathy with healthy boundaries and practical guidance to resolve the issue. These participants need to sufficiently practice linking new examples in which the same client behavior is actively linked to a new interpretation.

Conclusion

We can think of the most impactful neuroscience contributions to change facilitation in recent years as forming a triangle. Understanding the unlearning-relearning process is one strategy, redefining resistance is another, and understanding how to engage the right system in the brain to achieve behavioral change completes the trio. There are, of course, many other valuable findings and principles, but even just this taste, combining these three principles, makes a powerful recipe for increasing change acquisition success rates.

Suggested Reading

Begley S. 2007. *Train Your Mind Change Your Brain: How a New Science Reveals Our Extraordinary Potential to Transform Ourselves.* New York: Ballantine Books.

Bi, G., and M. Poo. 1998. "Synaptic Modification in Cultured Hippocampal Neurons: Dependence on Spike Timing, Synaptic Strength, and Postsynaptic Cell Type." *Journal of Neuroscience* 18 (24).

Blakeslee, S. 2000. "A Decade of Discovery Yields a Shock About the Brain." *New York Times*, Jan. 4.

Bloom, F. E., and A. Larsen. 1985. *Brain, Mind, and Behavior.* New York: Freeman.

Boyke, J., J. Driemeyer, C. Gaser, C. Buchel, and A. May. 2008. "Training-Induced Brain Structure Changes in the Elderly." *Journal of Neuroscience*, 28 (28).

Bruer, J. 1999. *The Myth of the First Three Years: A New Understanding of Early Brain Development and Lifelong Learning.* New York: Free Press.

Buonomano, D., and M. M. Merzenich. 1998. "Cortical Plasticity: From Synapses to Maps." *Annual Review of Neuroscience* 21 (1).

DiSalvo, D. 2011. *What Makes Your Brain Happy and Why Should You Do the Opposite.* New York: Prometheus Books.

Hebb, D. O. 1949. *The Organization of Behavior.* New York: John Wiley & Sons.

Jacobs, C. S. 2010. *Management Rewired: Why Feedback Doesn't Work and Other Surprising Lessons from the Latest Brain Science.* New York: Portfolio.

LeDoux, J. 2002. *Synaptic Self: How Our Brains Become Who We Are.* New York: Penguin.

Medina, J. 2008. *Brain Rules: 12 Principles for Surviving and Thriving at Work, Home, and School.* Seattle, WA: Pear Press.

Schacter, D. 1996. *Searching for Memory: The Brain, the Mind, and the Past.* New York: Basic Books.

Schwartz, J. M., and S. Begley. 2002. *The Mind and the Brain: Neuroplasticity and the Power of Mental Force.* New York: HarperCollins.

Seung, S. 2012. *Connectome: How the Brain's Wiring Makes Us Who We Are.* New York: Houghton Mifflin Harcourt.

Siegel, D. J., and M. Hartzell. 2004. *Parenting from the Inside Out: How Deeper Self-Understanding Can Help Raise Children Who Thrive.* New York: Penguin.

Siegel, D. J. 2010. *Mindsight: The New Science of Personal Transformation.* New York: Bantam.

Index

I

N

O

S

W-X-Y-Z

Comprehensive
Learning Enviro

Register to gain one year of FREE access to the online interact
and test bank to help you study for your PHR and SPHR
included with your purchase of this bo

The online test bank includes the following:

- **Assessment Test** to help you focus your study to specific ol
- **Chapter Tests** to reinforce what you've learned
- **Practice Exams** to test your knowledge of the material
- **Digital Flashcards** to reinforce your learning and provide l
  the exam
- **Searchable Glossary** to define the key terms you'll need to

Register and Access the Online Te

To register your book and get access to the online test bank, fo

1. Go to `bit.ly/SybexTest`.
2. Select your book from the list.
3. Complete the required registration information, including
   verification to prove book ownership. You will be emailed
4. Follow the directions in the email or go to `https://www.wiley`
5. Enter the PIN code you received and click the "Activate PI
6. On the Create an Account or Login page, enter your userna
   click Login. A "Thank you for activating your PIN!" messa
   don't have an account already, create a new account.
7. Click the "Go to My Account" button to add your new boo